The Libyan Economy

Waniss Otman · Erling Karlberg

The Libyan Economy

Economic Diversification and International Repositioning

With 30 Figures and 89 Tables

Springer

Waniss A. Otman
University of Aberdeen
Fraser Noble Building
King's College
Old Aberdeen
Aberdeen AB24 3UE
Scotland
United Kingdom
w.a.otman@abdn.ac.uk
o_waniss@hotmail.com

Erling Karlberg
80 Fernhill Drive
Aberdeen AB16 6QX
United Kingdom
admin@malindoconsulting.com

Library of Congress Control Number: 2007920898

ISBN 978-3-540-46460-0 Springer Berlin Heidelberg New York

Springer is a part of Springer Science+Business Media
springer.com

Typesetting: Integra Software Services Pvt. Ltd., Pondicherry, India
Cover design: WMX-Design, Heidelberg

Printed on acid-free paper SPIN: 11893158 42/Integra 5 4 3 2 1 0

Foreword

I hereby have the pleasure to introduce an important and excellent work about the economic history and modern diversification of the Libyan economy, in which the information has been presented and analysed in a way that answers many questions about the unique Libyan community and its economic system. It also examines important economic and legal changes currently taking place in Libya as the country engages in a new stage of its economic development, after the lifting of the US sanctions in late 2004.

I believe that this work will become necessary reading for foreign investors in Libya, regional and international organizations, and educational, academic and political institutions.

This important book will also assist in bridging the existing knowledge gap about present day Libya, and enable readers to understand an international destination that is very little known, either geographically, sociologically, economically, or politically. This is because, for those interested in Libya, most information about conditions in the country, until very recently, has been acquired through the international media, which continues, even up to the present, to be very negative about the country and its leader and people.

This gap of knowledge and poor knowledge of Libya's recent history has affected the ability of international investors to make a competitive diagnosis about the advantages of investing their capital in Libya in comparison with other countries. This work thanks to the detailed analysis of the current policy of extending the property base in Libya (i.e. Privatization), the recent reforms in the financial and banking fields as well as laws related to Foreign Direct Investment since the issuance of the Foreign Capital Encouragement Law No. 5 of 1997 have assisted in effectively bridging that knowledge gap. This will now enable investors to evaluate comprehensively the immense advantages of investment in Libya.

We also believe that the kind reader, through reading this work, will quickly comprehend the very real social, health, and educational gains, particularly those related to women's rights, which the Libyan people have gained since 1969. These have positioned Libya in international, Arabic, and African perspectives as one of the leading countries in which its citizens are proud of holding a strong national identity and being part of a unique and socially consolidated society.

We are also convinced that Libya today is ready and prepared for success through the ongoing modernization and expansion of its historically important hydrocarbon sector, and the development of its highly promising tourism sector, due to its enviable location at the crossroads of the Mediterranean world and the African Continent. It is therefore with confidence that a promising future for future and present generations of Libyans can be predicted, through maintaining the momentum of the present economic and financial changes and through consolidation in all economic sectors in every municipality of the Great Jamahiriya.

Dr. Baghdadi Ali Mahmoudi
The Libyan Prime Minister

I commend the writers, and in particular the leading Libyan author Waniss Otman, on this important new book on Libya's economic development, for their initiative in creating this timely addition to knowledge on Libya. The sweeping economic changes currently impacting the Libyan economy and society mean that the country is presently embarking on a new type of economic development, aimed at relaxing most of the government-owned economic controls engineered in the early 1970s.

At this watershed in Libya's history the necessity for careful policies for systematic development, to guarantee a secure and rewarding lifestyle for future generations of Libyans, has never been more important. These policies must account not only for demographic forces but also major issues and trends identified in this book, such as privatization, public sector reform, globalization, and the economic diversification processes. They must also address fundamental issues related to education, regional and international trade alignments, institutional capacity building as part of the domestic decentralization process, and the development of Libya's human capital in the digital age.

Based on their detailed analysis of Libya's privatization plans and their understanding of important contemporary issues in Libya such as food and fuel subsidies, I believe that this book will provide significant insights for the future direction of Libya's economic development. This includes not only industrial diversification away from the country's overdependence on the petroleum industry, but also the tremendous potential for success in Libya's tourism, agriculture, and fishing industries, all of which are comprehensively discussed and analysed in the book. The importance of increased environmental awareness and long-term sustainability are also discussed in an important section of the book, and are key components in the future attainment of Libya's ambitious socio-economic goals. I therefore recommend that all of those who are interested in Libya's economic transition and Libyans should read this thought provoking work.

Dr. Shukri M. Ghanem
Former Libyan Prime Minister

Libya has realized within the last decade of the previous millennium that the world has been quickly changing. There is no longer a First World or Third World or Developed countries or Developing countries. Rather, there is a rapidly changing world in which the international economy has moved from a geographical framework to a framework of virtual space. Here there are no political limits that can stand against the dynamic economic changes witnessed in today's global community.

This has largely come about through the unanimous adoption in the late 1980s and early 1990s, of the necessity to build globalization and liberate commerce and the flows of Foreign Direct Investment and other capital flows, which are the essential building blocks of economic success in the developing countries. Perhaps, the most obvious economic miracle of the latest twenty years resulting from such an approach has been China, whose "Open Door" Policy has played a fundamental role in the encouragement of its rapid economic development, which has today achieved an annual growth rate of more than 8 per cent.

This impetus towards globalization has demonstrated that closed and self-dependent economies are no longer feasible, since they are now completely out of step with the realities of the international economy. In order, therefore, to move faster, any economy wishing to succeed in economic growth has to get engaged with the international economy. This is in fact what is happening at the moment in the Jamahiriya, where serious steps have been taken by giving the highest priority to restructuring the Libyan economy through privatization and property-based extension. Through this process the property of companies and factories affiliated to the public sector are being privatized, thereby increasing their productivity, efficiency, and ability to compete.

In addition, the Jamahiriya is also positively promoting local products in diversifying economic activities, in order to help and accelerate the process of Libya's joining the World Trade Organization. Towards this goal, Libya has recently approved a series of important laws dealing with foreign investors and companies, in particular Law No. 5 and its subsequent modifications regarding Foreign Investment, as well as a series of resolutions taken by the General People's Committee, in particular its recent Resolution No. 134 regarding the establishment of the Libyan Stock Exchange.

Another important step which has led to improvement in the Libyan national economy has been the unification of exchange rate of the Libyan Dinar with foreign currencies, a key move necessary to correct the many distortions facing the Libyan economy in previous years. As well as this the establishment of a Free Zone in Misuratah has also been an important move forward to make Libya internationally competitive. In this respect Libya is presently seeking a foreign investor to operate Misuratah Free Zone as well as the ports of Tripoli and Benghazi.

It is therefore our hope that this new work will provide an accurate picture of all these crucial changes currently taking place in Libya, whether economic, social or legal, with regard to investment activity in all sectors.

Al-Tayib al-Safi al-Tayib
The Libyan Minister of Economy, Trade & Investment

Preface

In late 2004, when we first mooted the idea for this book, the sequence of events leading to Libya's rapprochement with the United Nations and the United States was reaching its final stages. On 19 December 2003, Libya's publicly announced renunciation of WMD was the final act which led to Libya's diplomatic rehabilitation, consummated on 20 September 2004 when President George W. Bush officially lifted the US sanctions against Libya. These international events were paralleled by sweeping domestic changes, which commenced in 2000, when the Libyan leader initiated a drastic makeover of Libya's political and administrative system, which was failing to deliver social and economic goals. In June 2003, a programme to liberalize, privatize, and diversify the Libyan economy started in earnest.

A watershed in Libya's history had been reached which inspired us to write this book. During its preparation it became only too apparent that there was a huge gap in knowledge about Libya, not only among the general public but also among academics, foreign governments, and global investors. This gap spanned not only recent developments, but also basic information about the country itself, its geography, history, economy, and political system. Most recent knowledge of the country has been acquired through the international media, which has been almost uniformly hostile to Libya. One of the primary objectives of us, the authors, therefore, was to set the record straight.

We were fortunate in having official access to a huge range of primary documents and Libyan legislation, a large selection of which have been translated from Arabic and analysed in the relevant chapters. Throughout the course of the writing in 2005–2006, we have been in constant touch with the most senior Libyan policymakers, who have welcomed the critical, objective, and analytical approach which has been adopted. The perceptive reader will also rapidly comprehend the very real social, health, and educational benefits which have, despite the sanctions, been attained by the Libyan people, making the country, in an Arab as well as in a global context, a nation with a strong identity and exceptional potential.

In engineering and implementing the reform process there will undoubtedly be political and economic casualties along the way, as the changing of the Libyan Cabinet in March 2006 clearly demonstrated. Yet, in this exciting new era in Libya's unique and often controversial history, we believe that genuine diversification, based on free competition and market forces, will energize the Libyan economy, as the economic and fiscal reform processes are consolidated.

Waniss Otman and Erling Karlberg
November 2006

Table of Contents

1 An Introduction to Libya

1.1 The Geography of Libya

Libya or, to give its official name, the Great Socialist People's Libyan Arab Jamahiriya has an area of approximately 1,775,500 km^2, making it the fourth largest country in Africa. It is greatly under-populated and most of its people live in the narrow coastal strip next to the Mediterranean Sea, with more than half of the population living in the two major cities of Tripoli in the far west of the country, and Benghazi in the east.

It lies between latitudes of 22°N and 32°N of the Equator and longitudes of 10°E and 25°E of Greenwich. From east to west it covers roughly 1,100 km, and from north to south 8–9 km, and the country stretches along the north-east coast of Africa between Tunisia and Algeria in the west and Egypt in the east. It shares common borders with Algeria (982 km), Chad (1,055 km), Egypt (1,115 km), Niger (354 km), the Sudan (383 km), and Tunisia (459 km). The Libyan coastline measures 1970 km from the Tunisian border to Egypt, but as the crow flies the coast it is much shorter, since it follows the deep indentation of the Gulf of Sirte. In geological terms the Sirte Embayment extends onshore in a line south-easterly for at least 300 km, and this projection comprises the Sirte Basin which has historically been the centre of Libya's oil production.

Its massive size, being one-sixth larger than Alaska, displays unique and often surprising characteristics. Although conventionally regarded as Saharan, the terrain is extremely mixed. The shape of the landscape runs from the coastal plain through plateaux to the high mountain ranges in the south.

Broadly speaking, the country has been divided into three separate regions: Tripolitania in the north-west, Cyrenaica in the east and the Fezzan in the south-west. Running from west to east is the coastal region, which is interrupted by two hilly, sometimes mountainous areas at the western and eastern extremities of the country, gradually ascending as it moves towards the south. An excellent highway traverses the coastline and links the country with Tunisia and Egypt. Branching inland from this highway are roads striking inland, a main one being the highway to Sebha. Most of the desert close to the coastal area is accessible although some sabkhas (marshes) are found which cannot be traversed by motor vehicles.

To the north-east of the country the Cyrenaica Platform rises and within it the Gebel Akhdar, or Green Mountain, an area of outstanding beauty, is situated. South of the Gebel Akhdar towards the Egyptian border is the Great Calanscio Sand Sea. After losing height and tapering off, the dunes of Calanscio gain strength once more and form the Rebiana Sand Sea that occupies the western edge of the Libyan Desert.

Libya climbs slowly from the Mediterranean coast to its desert hinterland, which although mainly flat contains many rocky outcrops and prominences. These are located in the central-western part of the country, and to the far south, where the country borders on Algeria and Chad. Whilst the Libyan terrain is mostly flat, many of the plateau areas are elevated, considerably dissected by sub-aerial erosion even in the most arid desert parts.

The desert can be traversed by suitable four-wheel-drive vehicles, but occupying almost a quarter of the country are the great sand seas. These are fields of shifting dunes that migrate according to the prevailing winds and act as a major barrier to land travel. Some of the dunes are of the so-called *seif*-type, which are sword-shaped and wander across the desert pushed in a moving line by the wind. Others are vast piles of unconsolidated sands heaped into irregular mounds which are often impassable. Wind-blown sand is a great hazard in the Sahara desert and means that the driver must be constantly attentive, since even the metal roads can be covered after sandstorms.

Further to the south are the massifs of Arkenu, Uweinat, and Kissu. These granite mountains are very ancient, having formed much before the sandstones surrounding them. Arkenu and Western Uweinat are ring complexes very similar to those in the Air Mountains. Eastern Uweinat (the highest point in the Libyan desert) is a raised sandstone plateau adjacent to the granite part further west. The plain to the north of Uweinat is dotted with eroded volcanic features, and Gebel Umainat reaches 1893 m above sea level, representing a memorable landmark in the far south-eastern corner of the country where the political borders of Libya, Chad, the Sudan and Egypt meet virtually at one point.

In the far south is the important oasis of Kufra, which supports a substantial population and was an important centre of resistance to the Italian occupation of the country. The Kufra Basin contains great quantities of water in reservoirs of the Cretaceous Nubia sandstone and these reserves have been developed as part of the Great Man-Made River Project. This visionary scheme is designed to bring water by pipeline from Kufra to the arid coastal regions of Mediterranean Libya for irrigation for agricultural expansion. Some scientists claim that reserves are “fossil-water” and therefore non-sustainable, while others claim that these reserves might be recharged by aquifers far to the south in contact with the seasonal rains that affect the Sahel.

Moving west south-westwards from Kufra for about 400 km the Tibesti is reached. This mountain chain strikes north-west to south-east right along the Libyan–Chad border and is one of the remotest corners of the earth. The highest parts of the Tibesti are to be found at the peaks in Chad, Emi Koussi at 3,415 m, Tarso Emissou at 3,376 m, and Tarso Tarro at 3,325 m. Among the Tertiary crater lakes in the area is the famous and almost perfect volcanic Wau Namus, the Lake of the Mosquitoes.

The Wau Namus caldera ranks among the greatest natural wonders of the world. This ancient caldera broke through the aquifer layer beneath the desert, and a number of shallow lakes formed at its centre. More recently a fresh eruption built a small central cone and produced the fine black ejecta that covers all the caldera and the surrounding desert in a radius of 10–20 km. The vista is spectacular for the first-time visitor, as from the outside nothing is revealed. Driving through featureless desert for hundreds of kilometres, the landscape suddenly turns dark, leading to the huge depression.

Running north and west of the Tibesti is the Murzuq Sand Sea, on the southernmost edge of the Murzuq Basin which runs into Niger and Algeria. The Acacus Mountains mark the extension of the Algerian Hoggar into Libyan territory, in fact an extension of the line which runs from the Hoggar in Algeria to the Tibesti and then on to Gebel Marra in the Sudan. Running northwards along the Algerian–Libyan border from Murzuq the Hamada el Hamra is reached. This very large and elevated plateau lies around 500 m above sea level. Five hundered kilometres to the east and a little south of the Hamada el Hamra is the Gebel Haruj or Haruj al Aswad, the Black Mountain, a Tertiary volcanic moonscape also lying above 500 m and apparently devoid of life. Finally, proceeding north-westwards from the Gebel Haruj the traveller crosses the high hills of the Gebel Nefusa, south of the city of Tripoli (Otman and Bunter 2005).

In terms of numbers Libya is one of the most sparsely populated countries of the world. Population distribution by Municipality/Capital is presented in Chap. 4.

1.2 Independent Libya

The form and existence of Libya as a nation can be traced to a statement made in the British parliament by Sir Anthony Eden, the British Foreign Secretary, on 8 January 1942, when he asserted that the Sanusi tribesmen of Cyrenaica, who had actively collaborated with the British forces in the North African Campaign of the Second World War, would in no circumstances be again ruled by Italy (Louis 1984). This was the initial step in Britain's policy of securing what eventually became Libya as a client state strategically sited in the centre of the North African littoral. Before the age of intercontinental ballistic missiles, this key location was perceived by both Britain and its Second World War ally, the United States, as an important staging post and airbase for long-distance bombers. The Anglo-American role in the creation of Libya has been described as "an unblushing venture of military and economic imperialism" (Blackwell 2003).

From 1945, a series of political and diplomatic manoeuvres in which the United Nation, Britain, the United States, Italy, France, the Soviet Union and Egypt played key roles eventually led to Libya's independence in 1951. Given legitimization through Islam, his pre-colonial political, social, and economic influence, and his critical role in resisting Italian colonialism, as well as British promises made in 1942, it was not surprising that Idris al-Sanusi became King of Libya in 1951.

Like so many post-colonial nations of the Middle East and Africa, Libya was in fact an artificial creation, similar to those created in an earlier era by the Sykes–Picot Agreement of 1916, where Britain and France defined spheres of influence over independent Arab nations emerging from the dismemberment of the Ottoman Empire. It welded together the three distinct regions of Cyrenaica, Tripolitania, and Fezzan, which had developed separately since the beginnings of recorded history in the Phoenician, Ptolemaic, Roman, Meccan, and Ottoman eras. It can be said that it emerged by default in its definitive form at the time of

Libyan independence, with political elements in two of its three regional components (Cyrenaica and Tripolitania) pressing for recognition as individual independent territories.

1.3 Problems of Historical Perspective

Western readers and intellectuals, when examining Arab culture or institutions, are burdened by a vast amount of intellectual baggage. Descriptive terms such as "Fertile Crescent", "Middle East", and "Orient" represent mental maps for navigation of specific regions constructed in an era in which imperialist ambition, military technology and the availability of printed modern maps had made inventing new and larger descriptive geographical "spaces" a fashionable trade among politicians, geographers, and journalists (Scheffler 2003).

Similarly, during the Second World War, the dynamics of emergent nationalisms could only be held in check by the overwhelming presence of Allied forces, which imposed, for the first time in history, a "Middle Eastern" regime on the region. In order to coordinate military operations against the Axis powers in the Mediterranean, Africa, and South-west Asia, a large military province, the "Middle East Command", was established by the British Army in 1939. With its boundaries in permanent flux, but endowed with a resident Minister of State, a military Commander-in-Chief and an economic infrastructure, the Middle East Supply Centre, the Middle East Command had authority over a vast area, including Malta, Greece, Crete, Cyprus, Tripolitania, Cyrenaica, Egypt, the Sudan, the three Somalilands, Ethiopia, Eritrea, Palestine, Trans-Jordan, Syria, Iraq, the Arabian Peninsula, and Iran.

These spatial mental maps of Western readers and authors are usually associated with similar ideas of socio-political norms and concepts of Western democracy against which Arab countries are measured in a sort of sliding scale of approval. In this context, the current stereotyped view of Libya, and of North Africa in general, is a desert land of nomads and sedentaries, a somewhat marginalized Arab "Maghreb" from the mainstream Arab "Mashreq" (Scheffler 2003). In this view, for example, the vibrant economic life of the major cities of Cyrenaica and Tripolitania and their historical wealth as thriving trading entrepots in the Roman era between the whole of Africa and the rest of the Roman Empire is conveniently forgotten.

In the conventional view, the process of "desertification", a concept invented by the French to provide moral justification for their appropriation of Morocco, Algeria, and Tunisia in the nineteenth century, is the result of human intervention. In this version of history, based largely on French readings of classical sources such as Herodotus, Pliny, Strabo, and Ptolemy, North Africa was seen as once being "the most fertile region in the world" (Davis 2004). The 39-volume "Exploration Scientifique de l'Algerie", published in the 1840s, categorically stated "this land, once the object of intensive cultivation, was neither deforested nor depopulated as today . . . it was the abundant granary of Rome" (Lavauden 1927).

The corollary of this image of the successful exploitation of the natural fertility of North Africa by the Romans was of course the subsequent destruction, deforestation, and desertification of the North African environment by hordes of Arab nomads and their rapacious herds of goats and camels. The so-called "devastation" wreaked by the Arabs led to the conclusion that the Arabs must be "immobilized and civilized", as expressed in the French historian Verne's brutal assessment of Algerian nomads and the "civilising" effects of French colonial civilization.

> Thus will civilization advance ... it follows that the establishment of individual (private) property and the extension of colonization are indispensable where the Arabs are concerned; that military authority must maintain the indigene in a state of immobility which will permanently (fatally) lead to their extinction. A barbaric people cannot find themselves faced with an advanced civilization without engaging in a duel to the death. Civilization must conquer barbarism or perish itself. Let us work therefore to transform this race: there lies our interest, there also lies their salvation. (Verne 1869)

Fortunately, scholars and historians are now aware of the dangers and damage caused by such traditional approaches to misunderstanding the North African nations and their development. The relatively new multi-disciplinary science of historical ecology, using detailed analyses of the palaeoecological records, has shown, for example, that "desertification", far from being due to human intervention, took place because of large-scale climatic changes affecting the Mediterranean and North Africa since the last Ice Age (Crumley 1996).

Across North Africa and the Sahara, the physical evidence points to a more humid climate prevailing around 4000–3000 BC, which lasted with a few variations until approximately 1000 BC, when a much more arid and stochastic climate became the norm (Claussen et al. 1999). This humid period produced a much wetter environment in what is now known as the pre-Saharan regions, supporting such tropical animals as elephants and rhinoceros. Evidence from north-eastern Algeria shows signs of this wetter phase, with forest vegetation dominating the local landscape until approximately 2000 BC, when it began to decrease and steppe vegetation began to increase (Ritchie 1984). In the majority of North African pollen cores taken by scientists, the levels of grass pollen has remained remarkably constant, with some fluctuations, from well into the Pleistocene until the present (Lamb et al. 1989). The available evidence of climate change and vegetation history of the region have led to the conclusion that it is difficult to distinguish between manmade degradation and the natural trend towards aridification at lower elevations over the last 2000–3000 years (Rognon 1987).

It is therefore important to be constantly aware of the stereotyped historical and geographical perceptions of non-indigenous writers when trying to understand the history, and come to terms with the current status, of countries such as Libya. In, for example, the "Fourth Shore" (Segrè 1975), the author, using impeccable primary historical research derived from the archives of the Comitato per la Documentazione delle Attivita Italiane in Africa, and the Instituto Agronomico per l'Oltremare, Florence, examines the Italian colonization of Libya which commenced with the Italo-Turkish war of 1911 and effectively ended in 1943 with the expulsion of the Axis forces from Tripoli.

His thesis is to determine whether Italy's conquest and subsequent appropriation of Libya was uniquely different from other imperialist expansion in Africa and Asia in the nineteenth century – "Can a nation conquer and administer huge blocks of overseas territory, call itself an empire, and still not be 'imperialist?' " is the initial question that is posed in his work. Apologists have argued that Italian colonization of Libya was different from British colonization of Malaya or Dutch colonization of the East Indies, in which a thin layer of Europeans presided over a plantation economy supported by the labour of native peoples. Libyan colonization was to be a "collonizzazione demografica" or proletarian colonization, in which Italians, forming the backbone of the colony, were to form a dense network of small independent farmers who laboured in the fields alongside Libyans. Sergè eventually concludes that "it is difficult to see that the Italians were any less imperialist than the other colonial powers". By criminalizing many traditional uses of the land – their policy of forced land acquisition (sometimes but usually not compensated when viewed as "rebel land") and the racial laws of 1938 and the Special Citizenship of 1939, relegating the indigenous Libyans to second-class citizens in their own land – the Italian colonial regime demonstrated that it had no intention of granting social or economic equality to indigenous Libyans.

Other commentators have been less hospitable in their assessment, stating that more than half of the native Libyan population perished during the entire period of Italian colonization. Little is said in Segrè's book about the profound effect of the colonization on the Libyan people themselves, which lead to the alienation of most Libyans from their land, and the pauperization of all but a small number of elites. It is small wonder that, combined with the devastation wreaked on the Libyan people and landscape by the Second World War, Libya, when it achieved independence in 1951, was one of the poorest countries in the world.

Today, in Libya Omar el-Muktar, who successfully opposed Italy's colonization for over 10 years, is revered as a national hero, with a major thoroughfare in Tripoli, Omar el-Muktar Street, named after him. Yet in the whole of Segrè's book, he is only mentioned in one sentence. He states, "With the occupation of Cufra (Al Kufrah) in 1931 and the capture and execution of Omar el-Muktar, the Italians were finally victorious" (p. 79). Can there be any more damning critique of the eurocentric approach to North African history?

1.4 Early Libyan History

As part of the shoreline of the Mediterranean and the continent of Africa, Libya has been host to a succession of cultures, identified by written records as well as the vast number of artefacts and structures still standing or uncovered, known as the archaeological record. But new archaeological evidence, now available because of the increasingly interdisciplinary nature of archaeology, as well as advances in technology where such disciplines as geoarchaeology, aided for example by satellite remote sensing and archaeobotany, are becoming commonplace, have contributed to a more complete understanding of the earth's conditions, climate shifts, and how people have adapted to change over large regions.

Earlier we stated that Libya was a synthetic political creation. However, the archaeological record has recently provided data which suggests that the Mediterranean coast and the interior, the Fezzan (after *Phaisania*, the Roman name), have always been very closely related – so much so that a question arises "Should the main interpretive context for Libyan history be a Mediterranean-oriented one, or an African one?" Seen in this light the present impetus of Libyan foreign policy, with its recent marked diplomatic successes in the African Union (AU) spearheaded by Colonel Qadhafi's visionary concept of a "United States of Africa", appears to be a rewriting of African history.

The Italian archaeologist Graziosi has declared that the vast area of Tassili–Acacus–Hammada of the Murzuq region of the far south of Libya and Algeria is certainly one of the richest in prehistoric remains in North Africa (Graziosi 1969). More than a century after the first reports of prehistoric carvings by the German traveller Heinrich Barth (Barth 1857), the rock art of the Fezzan is now universally recognized as part of humanity's cultural heritage. In 1985 the Tadrart Acacus mountains were included on the World Heritage List by UNESCO, thus conferring upon them special status, limiting their usage and management and guaranteeing their conservation and protection.

The findings in 2002 of the Italian–Libyan Archaeological Mission in the Acacus and Messak areas close to Murzuq in the south-west of Libya have uncovered astonishing evidence of human activity there. The Tadrart Acacus and the Messak Settafet are punctuated by thousands of rock carvings and images created by the first Early Holocene communities of hunter-gatherers, dated to around 10,000 years ago. At the beginning of the Holocene these regions were richer in vegetation, and were populated by animals which have since disappeared.

The art of these ancient hunters has as its subject large animals, probably considered more prestigious, such as *Bubalus antiquus*, an enormous wild buffalo, already extinct in ancient times. This animal, which is strikingly depicted in the wadis of the Messak Settafet, marks the stylistic phase known as the "Bubalus" period.

It is apparent that from as early as around 8,500 years ago, the central Sahara was the scene of a flourishing painting tradition, spectacular in both themes and execution, characterized by the presence of anthropomorphic figures with rounded heads or discs completely lacking in facial features. It was this characteristic, widespread throughout the Sahara, which led a prominent archaeologist to coin the term "Round Head" style (Lhote 1958). This artistic trend seems to have been confined to part of the Sahara massifs – Tassili-n-Ajjer, Acacus, Ennedi – and spanned a considerable period, probably more than two millennia. These "Round Head" paintings are fairly diverse, varying from simplified monochrome anthropomorphic figures to very large multi-coloured compositions, usually enriched by the representation of wild animals, mainly antelope and Barbary sheep within ritual scenes and enigmatic elements which are difficult to interpret.

Around 7,000 years ago, the Sahara was swept by an incredible cultural movement, of amazing richness and artistic power. This is the Pastoral phase, also known as the "Bovidian" period. Thousands of paintings and carvings decorate blocks of stone, rock walls, and isolated stone slabs. The human and archaeological landscape is in a state of constant flux, and the central Sahara in this period probably represents the world's largest concentration of prehistoric art. To walk along the wadis of the Messak Settafet is genuinely like strolling around an open-air art gallery, with extraordinary scenes from everyday life, such as the building of camps, the milking of animals and exchanges of objects (Anag et al. 2002).

In this naturalistic and narrative art, the centre of the universe has become livestock: herds of large spotted cattle move along the rock walls of Uan Tabu, Tagg-n-Tort and Teshuinat. These animals are portrayed with enormous accuracy with the horns taking on enormous figurative and symbolic importance, and scenes of both work and social activities are shown. From these paintings we can deduce that the Sahara was thickly populated, the country fertile with large herds of cattle grazing on good pasture with abundant water for cultivation (Liverani et al. 2000).

The paintings of the Horse phase, so-called after the introduction of this animal from the east and thus giving a precise chronological reference point (around 1000 BCE), have recently been re-evaluated within the context of research on the birth of the archaic state in the Fezzan, that of the Garamantes. Recent research has demonstrated that the Garamantian civilization had a complex social structure, based on the political, and perhaps military, control of trade routes between the Mediterranean coasts and sub-Saharan Africa (Liverani et al. 2000). Goods, people, and animals travelled along the caravan routes, and this art provides us with elements to confirm and enrich the historical and archaeological context. It is during this phase that organized irrigation systems and the cultivation of date palms were introduced, with the latter frequently appearing in the Acacus paintings. Defence infrastructures, taxation and the use of writing also characterized Garamantian civilization, with mountain passes and aqbas, outposts and check points marked by deliberately placed fortifications or settlements, such as Aghram Nadharif, where the rocks are literally covered in ancient Libyan inscriptions.

Turning now to historical developments on the Mediterranean coastline, from at least the eighth millennium BCE the coastal plain of Libya was inhabited by settled peoples who herded cattle and cultivated crops and who later traded with other regions of the Mediterranean. In fact, between the eighth century BCE and the eighth century CE the North African coast harboured nascent African kingdoms, a series of Phoenician colonies, including the metropolis of Carthage, the Greek colony of Cyrenaica and later several provinces of the Roman empire. The Phoenician settlements in what is now Tunisia were made by those distinct Mediterranean peoples, nowadays almost forgotten with their language surviving as Maltese. Carthage was their greatest achievement, threatening the power of Rome itself.

Cyrenaica itself was an early objective of Greek colonization and it eventually emerged as a local centre of Hellenistic culture. Its first colonial language was Greek, but in time it developed its own peculiar dialect of Greek, and its cultural orbit was with Crete and eastern Mediterranean rather than with Tripolitania to the west, which was part of a different Mediterranean world. Detailed study of the most numerous diagnostic artefacts of trade in the Hellenistic, Roman and Byzantine periods – fine ceramic wares and transport amphorae – has revealed in the most striking fashion possible the almost total separation of these two worlds. The fine ceramics and amphorae connected with the agricultural exports of Tripolitania, at the easternmost extension of the Maghrib, circulated wholly within a western Mediterranean world of exchange, whereas those of Cyrenaica were limited almost wholly to eastern circuits of trade, with Greece and the Levant coast (Fulford 1989). Whereas Cyrenaica looked to the Aegean and north-east Mediterranean, Tripolitania looked to Tunisia, Western Italy, and Sicily (Shaw 2003). These cultural and geographical distinctions reflect the difficulties faced in the post-Second World War era by the great powers in "welding together" these regions, together with the Fezzan, into one country.

The Romans had always had an interest in North Africa particularly as their great rival was the North African city-state, Carthage. Roman settlement into North Africa was encouraged under the reign of the emperor Augustus during the first century BCE and important cities were established near the coast (Haynes 1965). The best known of these are Sabratha and Leptis Magna close to Tripoli, which have been wonderfully preserved in almost their original form by the pure desert air. These two cities are famed as some of the finest examples of the Roman architectural expression to be found anywhere.

The Romans used the word "Libya" in a general sense to describe the whole of North Africa and in an administrative sense as an official name for the region between Alexandria and Cyrenaica (Reynolds 1976). But, as we have seen, the Romans were by no means the first Mediterranean colonists to establish a presence in North Africa although the name Tripoli (*Tri-polis*, three cities) was given by them to the three cities of Oea (Tripoli itself), Sabratha, and Leptis Magna. The importance of North Africa within the Roman empire cannot be in doubt. As one of the Roman provinces, the proconsular province of Africa was one of the two elite senatorial gubernatorial postings of the Roman imperial state. At the height of its development, this single North African province was ranked amongst the wealthiest parts of the Roman Empire (Shaw 2003).

Subsequently, North Africa was the seat of a Vandal kingdom, and then a prefecture and an exarchate of the Byzantine state, for by the fifth century AD the centre of gravity of the Roman empire had shifted from Italian Rome to Greek Byzantium, Constantinople, although its peoples still called themselves Roman and were regarded as such by other nations. The eastern Roman Empire, *Rum*, was a Christian polity, although becoming increasingly distant from the Christianity of Rome. Its domains stretched along the North African coast from Egypt to as far west as Tunisia. However, the Byzantines were undoubtedly despotic and cruel rulers who lost the adherence of many of their subject peoples. Eventually the dominance of Christianity in Byzantine Libya was challenged by the rise of Islam.

This unforeseen and unforeseeable event in the middle of the seventh century CE was destined to have a permanent influence on Libya and the whole of North Africa. Islam swept through the entire region spreading west from Egypt when the Arab general Amr ibn al-As under Caliph Umar ibn al Khattab led the invasion of Egypt in 640, besieging Misrah (Memphis) for 7 months. Its capital Alexandria was subsequently besieged for 14 months and succumbed in 642 CE. In the same year Amr conquered Cyrenaica, establishing his headquarters at Barce. In 643 CE he had siege to Oea, Arab Tripoli, and the city fell to him in November 643. By the end of the decade, the isolated Byzantine garrisons on the coast were overrun and the Arabs control of the region consolidated. Uqba inb Nafea, another Arab general, invaded the Fezzan in 663, forcing the capitulation of Germa (Christides 2000).

Contrary to popular belief, the Muslim conquest of North Africa was the work of decades and its effective Islamicization the work of centuries. At first it was spread into the cities through conquest, but it was only in the fifteenth and sixteenth centuries CE that Islamicization of the interior Berber tribes was consolidated through the Sufi movement, who, concerned about Spanish and Portuguese military gains on the North African Mediterranean coast, successfully disseminated Islam into the interior of the Sahara in a way that the urban-based orthodoxy had never achieved (Holt et al. 1997).

In the last quarter of the eleventh century, Islam dominated the Mediterranean world, with the Muslim conquests in North Africa and South Europe virtually defining the Mediterranean as an Arab lake. However, the expulsion in the eleventh century of the Saracens from Sicily and Southern Italy by the Normans was followed by attacks on Tunisia and Tripoli. Somewhat later a busy trade with the African coastlands, and especially with Egypt, was developed by Venice, Pisa, Genoa, and other cities of North Italy. By the end of the fifteenth century, Spain had succeeded in expelling the Muslims, but Portugal, another European maritime nation, was strong enough to carry the war into North Africa and in 1415 a Portuguese force captured the citadel of Ceuta on the African coast.

Throughout the sixteenth century, Spain and the Ottomans were pitted in a struggle for supremacy in the Mediterranean. Spanish forces had already occupied a number of other North African ports when in 1510 they captured Tripoli, destroyed the city and constructed a fortified base from the rubble. Tripoli was of only marginal importance to Spain, however, and in 1524 the king-emperor Charles V entrusted its defence to the Knights of St. John of Malta.

Khair ad Din, also known as Barbarossa, seized Algiers in 1510 on the pretext of defending it from the Spaniards. Barbarossa subsequently recognized the sovereignty of the Ottoman sultan over the territory that he controlled and was in turn appointed the Sultan's regent in the Maghreb. Using Algiers as a base, Barbarossa and his successors consolidated Ottoman authority in the central Maghreb, and extended it to Tunisia and Tripolitania.

In 1711, Ahmed Karamanli, a Turkish cavalry officer, seized Tripoli and then purchased his confirmaton by the sultan as Pasha with the property confiscated from Turkish officials he had massacred during the coup. Intelligent and resourceful, as well as ruthless, he increased his revenues from piracy, pursued an active foreign policy with the European powers and used a loyal military establishment to win the allegiance of the interior tribes, later extending his authority into Cyrenaica.

However, the Karamanlis in 1835 were forced to surrender to Ottoman rule again, when it became progressively clear that Yusuf Pasha was faced with problems that he could no longer solve. These were largely brought about by the new relationship and obligations that the European powers had imposed on him during the Napoleonic wars, which culminated in steps taken by the European powers in 1819 to force the Barbary states to give up entirely the attacks on Mediterranean shipping on which they, and particularly Tripoli, depended for their revenues (Hume 1980).

It was mainly out of fear of a European takeover of Tripoli, encouraged by France's seizure of Algiers in 1830, that the Ottoman Sultan Muhammad II sent Turkish troops to Tripoli, ostensibly to put down the numerous rebellions against the Pasha and to restore order, but in fact to reinstate Ottoman rule in Tripoli.

The administrative system imposed by the Turks was typical of that found elsewhere in the Ottoman Empire. Tripolitania, as all three historic regions were collectively designated, became a Turkish Vilayet (province) under a Wali (Governor-General) appointed by the Sultan. The province was composed of four Sanjaks (sub-provinces), each administered by a Mutasarrif (Lieutenant Governor) responsible to the Wali. These sub-provinces were each divided into about 15 districts, with executive officers from the governor-general downwards being Turks. The Mutasarrif was in some cases assisted by an advisory council and, at the lower levels, Turkish officials relied on aid and counsel from the tribal chiefs. Administrative districts within each Sanjak corresponded to the areas that remained the territorial focus of each tribe.

Although the system was logical and appeared efficient, it was never consistently applied throughout the country. Although the Turks encountered strong local opposition through the 1850s, they established southward posts in Ghadames in 1862, in Murzuk in 1865 and in Ghat in 1875. These strategic oases lay along the main trade routes from Tripoli, and at the time a European traveller into the interior had to first obtain a laissez-passer from the Wali of Tripoli. There was a constant north/south flow of commerce along these routes and the Wali was in frequent communication with his fellow Islamic tribal chiefs and the Sudanic Sultanates.

In 1879, Cyrenaica was separated from Tripolitania, its Mutasarrif reporting thereafter directly to Constantinople. After the 1908 reforms of the Ottoman government, both were entitled to send representatives to the Turkish parliament. In an effort to provide the country with a tax base, the Turks attempted unsuccessfully to stimulate agriculture. However, in general, nineteenth-century Ottoman rule in Libya was characterized by corruption, revolt, and repression. The region was perceived as a backwater province in a decaying empire that had been dubbed the "sick man of Europe". Nonetheless, the Ottoman administrative structure established in 1835 lasted until the Treaty of Ouchy of 15 October 1912, which required the Ottoman Empire to withdraw from Tripolitania and its hinterland, which the Ottomans had been attempting to secure from a three-pronged French aggression from West Africa, the French Congo, and Algiers, which eventually led to France's convergence on Lake Chad in 1900 (International Court of Justice 1993).

Italy's somewhat belated seizure of Tripoli in 1911 was the final stage of "the scramble for Africa", which dominated the foreign policy of the major European nations throughout the nineteenth century. Anglo-French rivalry, which led to the General Act emerging from the 1885 Berlin Conference, also gave new impetus to the colonial scramble for Africa. As Jules Ferry, Prime Minister of France, stated in 1885, "a policy of withdrawal or abstention is simply the high road to decadence! In our time nations are great only through the activity they deploy; it is not by spreading the peaceable light of their institutions...that they are great, in the present day" (Robiquet 1897). Anglo-French rivalry continued throughout the ninteenth century and culminated in 1898 in the Fashoda crisis, which almost led to war between Great Britain and France.

In 1830 the French occupied Algiers, but subsequently came up against the Berber jihad launched by the Qadariyya brotherhood under the leadership of Abd al-Kadir. Persistent and tireless in his opposition to the French, Abd al-Kadir was not defeated until 1847 when he was exiled. Shortly after Louis Philippe's constitutional monarchy was overthrown in the revolution of 1848, the new government of the Second Republic ended Algeria's status as a colony and declared the occupied lands an integral part of France which it remained until 1954.

At the beginning of the nineteenth century, Tunisia had a prosperous economy and cosmopolitan culture. Under Ahmed Bey there was a modest programme of modernization. But foreign debts mounted giving France an excuse to establish a Finance Commission, leading to Tunisia in 1881 becoming a French Protectorate.

In Egypt a nationalist movement began to take root by the late 1870s which alarmed the British. Riots and military rebellion prompted the British to send in an army of occupation in 1882, which provoked a further rift between the British and the French.

Morocco remained independent in the nineteenth century when European-style modernization was instituted under Hasan I (1873–1894), but plans for secular education and the levying of taxes met with resistance from Muslim clerics. Morocco finally lost its territorial integrity in 1912 and was partitioned between France and Spain.

Italy, as earlier noted, was one of the last European powers to engage in imperial expansion. This was primarily because the Italian city-states were not unified until the second half of the nineteenth century. Consequently, the Italian government was unable to exploit effectively the early colonial opportunities that Africa offered to France, Britain, and the other European states. On 1 January 1890 the Italian king Umberto I proclaimed the Colony of Eritrea, and his army secretly began plans for the invasion of Ethiopia. The invasion plans were implemented in November 1895. After losing a few skirmishes near Makalle, the Italians attacked Adowa. In one of the only major battles in which an African power has defeated a European one, Menelik's armies outfought the Italians in the 3-day battle and drove them back across the Mareb river. It was a great victory for Menelik and a humiliating defeat for Italy, who lost 12,000 soldiers as well as international prestige, although Eritrea was retained by Italy and a protectorate established over much of Somaliland.

1.4.1 Key Developments in Recent Libyan History

It was in part the humiliation of Adowa that led to Italy's seizure of Tripoli in 1911. In December 1902, France and Italy created spheres of interest in North Africa, when they concluded a secret treaty that recognized the "special interests" of France in Morocco and Italy in Libya. Many Italians believed it was their historic right and obligation to seek Italian sovereignty in Libya, once ruled by the Roman Empire.

Italy declared war on Turkey on 29 September 1911, because the latter had failed to accept the Italian 24-hour ultimatum to allow Italy to occupy Tripoli and Cyrenaica. By formal royal decree on 5 November 1911, confirmed by an act of parliament, 25 February 1912, these two provinces were declared to be under the full and complete sovereignty of the Italian Kingdom.

However, the Italian colonization of the Ottoman provinces of Tripolitania and Cyrenaica was never wholly successful. In September 1911 the Italian army invading the two provinces expected to carry out a quick, overwhelming occupation of these long-coveted North African states. Instead the ensuing war presented the spectacle of a massive Italian army stalemated in Libya for a year by a few thousand Turks and their indigenous allies (Herrmann 1989). One reason for the stiff resistance was the attitude of the Young Turks after the reforms of 1908. One fundamental concern of the Committee of Union and Progress (CUP) was to "save" the state from separatist movements and European penetration that had eroded the Ottoman empire under the old regime (Lewis 1968).

Several major reorganizations of the colonial authority were necessary in the face of the armed Libyan opposition. From 1917 to 1923, known as the period of accords, the Italian government attempted to negotiate with a variety of Libyan factions in an effort to consolidate peacefully its occupation of the country. But after the Fascist takeover in October 1922, the Italian government of Benito Mussolini implemented a much more rigid colonial policy. In early 1923 the Italian armed forces embarked on a brutal reconquest of Libya. Enjoying an overwhelming superiority in men and equipment, the Italian army had some 20,000 men in the field, while Libyan guerrilla forces seldom numbered more than 1,000. Even Graziani, later the Governor of Libya, reluctantly conceded that the resistance was largely due to "our irreducible enemy, the faithful and able servant of Idris, the indomitable Omar Al Muktar, the heart and soul of the Cyrenian rebellion" (Herrmann 1989).

Administratively, in the period 1919–1929 the Italian government maintained the two traditional provinces, with separate colonial administrations. A system of controlled local assembies with limited local authority was set up, but it was revoked on 9 March 1927. In 1929, Tripoli and Cyrenaica were united as one colonial province, then in 1934, as Italy struggled to retain colonial power, the classical name "Libya" was revived as the official name of the colony, which was split into four provinces: Tripoli, Misuratah, Bengasi, and Derna.

The Libyan population by the mid-1930s had been cut in half due to emigration, famine, and war casualties. The loss of much of the educated elite and middle class, in the face of a severe disruption of coastal agriculture and domestic trade, was especially significant. When assessing the full impact of Italian colonial practices, it is telling to note that the Libyan population in 1950 was at the same level as in 1911, approximately 1.5 million in 1911 (St. John 1998).

On 9 January 1939, the colony of Libya was incorporated into metropolitan Italy and thereafter considered an integral part of the Italian state, until the North African campaigns of the Second World War left Libya in British and French hands.

On 9 August 1940, some time after the Italians had declared war on the Allies, the Libyan freedom fighters offered their military cooperation to the British. Five battalions of the new Libyan Arab Force were recruited from amongst the exiled community and from Libyan prisoners-of-war. After the collapse of France the British and the empire troops fought alone unaided against the Fascist powers of Germany and Italy. For the Germans the conquest of North Africa was a necessity since it provided a direct route to the Suez Canal and to the oilfields of Iraq and Iran.

After some initial reverses the British forces under General Sir Bernard Law Montgomery smashed Rommel at the Battle of El Alamein in 1942 and advanced into Cyrenaica (Crump 1974). Meantime the Free French had fought their way up from Chad and had occupied Kufra, defeating the Italian garrison there (Rodger 1944). The British fought their way throughout Libya defeating the Afrika Korps rapidly proceeding to Tunis, where the Germans finally surrendered (Douglas 1966).

At the Potsdam Conference in 1945 the Allies had decreed that the Italian colonies liberated during the war – Ethiopia, Eritrea, and Libya – would not be returned to Italian control. After the war and under the authority of the United Nations the British established a mandate over Tripolitania and Cyrenaica whilst the French retained the Fezzan. In 1949 the United Nations voted to confer complete independence on Libya which it attained on 24 December 1951 as the Kingdom of Libya. Initially, the kingdom was federated with three provinces of equal weight and with their own regional centres of government. Later on, in 1963 the Federal Constitution of the country was amended by Law No. 1 of that year and a unitary government established itself in Tripoli (Wright 1969).

As we stated in the beginning of this brief survey of Libyan history, its somewhat artificial creation was primarily due to British and American strategic requirements emerging from the remnants of the Italian colonial era. The Libyan king, backed by a constitution that created an authoritarian federalist monarchy, pursued an external policy after 1952 that displayed an accommodating attitude to the Western powers. Among the first initiatives of his foreign policy was signing the Anglo-Libyan treaty in 1953, and in the following year an agreement with the Eisenhower administration confirmed American military base rights in return for economic aid. In fact, in 1956, the British were also considering establishing their own regional nuclear deterrent at their El Adem base in Cyrenaica (Public Records Office 1956).

In the context of overall British strategy in the Middle East, Britain was correct in its evaluation of the strategic location of Libya, since by the late 1950s Libya was the focus of an intense conflict for influence between Nasser, the Soviet Union, and the Western powers. This increasingly revealed the weakness of the post-war Anglo-American reliance on conservative rulers, besieged by popular radical Arab nationalism promoted by President Nasser in Cairo, aimed at subverting pro-Western Arab regimes. When Anglo-Egyptian antagonism eventually resulted in the Suez crisis, London was unable to use its forces in Libya against Nasser due to political objections from the Libyan government, whose explicit view was that wider considerations of Arab nationalist opinion ruled out any use of troops based in Libya against Egypt. As a consequence the new British government under Harold Macmillan considered abandoning Libya in 1957 before it relented under pressure from Washington. The British subsequently concentrated on keeping the Libyan monarch alive and in power, a policy that led to direct military intervention in July 1958.

In 1958 the overthrow and murder of the Hashemite royal family in Baghdad on 14 July significantly heightened the possible consequences of the subversive threat to the Libyan regime. The suddenness of the revolution and the collapse of the Arab Union of Iraq and Jordan were seen in Libya as the harbinger of a general regional uprising. The King and his ministers were "seriously alarmed" by news of the Baghdad coup, and London's immediate response was to order the destroyer HMS Bermuda with a company of Royal Marines to Tobruk. Plans were also made to reinforce the British units in Libya and move troops already stationed in Tripolitania to Cyrenaica in order to safeguard the government (British Foreign Office 1958).

The July intervention had effectively forestalled a coup in Libya, but the survival of the Libyan monarchy remained a problematic issue for Britain and the United States. The close call he experienced in 1958 induced the king to cling more tightly to British protection, alienated from the most of the people and especially from the younger generation of Libyans (Blackwell 2003). The fragility of the regime raised further doubts in London and Washington over long-term policy towards the country. The State Department in particular increasingly felt that the "Anglo-American military presence in the country was untenable and that due to the awakening of Arab nationalism in Libya, the situation could not continue indefinitely."

Somehow the Libyan monarchy managed to remain in power until the Libyan revolution in 1969. The upheavals experienced in the late 1950s nevertheless indicated that the King's legitimacy was seriously curtailed and depended on external powers to guarantee his survival. In addition to this, the political consequences of the massive oil strikes of the 1960s could not be so easily contained. The Standard Oil Company began exporting oil from the country in 1961, and by 1970 Libya had become the fourth largest oil producer in the world.

The awareness of the potential wealth of the country, combined with the perception that the oil revenues actually benefited only a small minority of the population, further polarized Libyan politics. More importantly, the young officers of the armed forces became increasingly influenced by Nasser's nationalist ideology. In the early 1960s, London tacitly acknowledged the bankruptcy of the policy of using troops to prop up the monarchy. A tentative rapprochement with Cairo also increased British embarrassment over the presence of armored forces in Libya. The result was a quiet and gradual disengagement with the majority of the British troops being withdrawn by 1966. The eventual success of the revolution of 1969 had been anticipated by the crisis of 1958, and the outcome of the military coup itself was accepted with muted resignation by the Labour government in London (Healey 1989).

With the success of this bloodless coup, a new Libya was to embark on a complex social experiment, the effects of which are being experienced until the present. This was initiated in April 1973 in a "popular revolution" undertaken to destroy the old government bureaucracy and to give the people themselves the power to hire and fire public officials. At the same time, the idealistic and visionary policies of Colonel Qadhafi were to have a significant impact on the world stage, far out of proportion to Libya's size, as his regional policies eastwards towards the Arab heartland, and southwards into Africa demonstrated the problems faced by small but potentially influential states seeking security as well as a meaningful regional role, which we shall examine in greater depth in the following pages. Eventually, these controversial policies and their implementation would increasingly isolate Libya, especially in the years following 1986 when the US Sanctions took effect.

1.5 Libya's Political System

The prevailing lack of knowledge or understanding of the Libyan system of government among foreign observers leads to much confusion. Many, caught in a Western straightjacket of looking for "democracy" in every country, cannot understand why there are no Libyan "elections" in the conventional Western sense, to periodically shape the government. In short, in trying to compare Libya's system of government to prevailing Western, or even other existing Arab political systems, they miss the point, which is that Libya's political system is a one-off and singular creation, and must be understood as such.

As we have noted, the system which the Libyan revolution replaced in 1969 was a federal monarchy. Regarding its constitutional form, John Wright, a leading historian on Libya, remarked, "Britain, in effect, unilaterally decreed that if there was to be an independent Libyan state at all...it would take only the form that Idris, Britain and Britain's Western allies wanted: a federal monarchy under the Sanusi crown (Wright 1969)."

According to the Libyan electoral law, which was written by the appointed National Assembly, strongly influenced by the king and his supporters, suffrage was initially restricted to sane and solvent males, 21 years old and above. The law further provided that the secret ballot was to be used only in urban districts (Khadduri 1963), which meant that the government would be able to control the votes of the rural population. Although the National Congress (opposition) party appealed to the United Nations for supervision of the balloting, this was rejected (Wright 1969). When the first elections took place on 19 February 1952, the pattern for the rest of the reign was laid down. The opposition Congress party easily won the elections in Tripoli, but government candidates were declared the winners everywhere else. Congress supporters suspected government manipulation of the results and rioting broke out. The government brutally repressed the disorders, exiled the Congress party's leader, and banned political parties (Sicker 1987).

For the duration of the monarchy, parliamentary elections were tampered with to ensure results favourable to the government in power. For example in 1964, opposition spokesmen were arrested to facilitate the electoral triumphs of pro-government candidates. In response, the opposition reconstituted itself from elected members of the Lower House. In response to this challenge, the king took the dramatic step of dissolving parliament. In the subsequent election of 1965 the ballot boxes were broken into by the police in order to ensure the victory of pro government candidates (Sicker 1987).

Although the monarchy was undoubtedly pro-British and American, the waves of nationalism sweeping the Arab world in the 1950s and 1960s were beginning to exercise a strong effect on Libyan public opinion. The Suez war in 1956 severely undermined Western prestige in the region, and by 1957 the US Embassy in Libya was reporting that the most popular person in the country was the Egyptian leader Gamal Abdel Nasser (US Dept of State 1967). The possibility of a Nasserite coup could not be discounted, and in 1959 US policy makers recommended that in such an eventuality "Tunisia ... appropriately beefed up by the United States ... should seize Tripolitania" (Wright 1981). In 1964, Nasser called upon all Arab nations to expel foreign military bases from their soil. After the 1967 Arab–Israeli war, the demand within Libya to break military ties with the United States and Britain became even more insistent. Nationalist agitation led Libyan oil workers to temporarily cut off petroleum exports to the West in the aftermath of the June war (Wright 1969).

Another crucial factor emerged in 1959 when oil was discovered, with Libya becoming in the next few years one of the world's leading petroleum producers. The new-found wealth served to undermine the British and US positions in Libya, and consequently the monarchy, because of three factors. First, Libya was no longer desperately dependent on foreign financial support. In 1957, the US Ambassador could be confident that "dollar diplomacy" would buy time for the continued operation of US bases (US Dept of State 1967), but after the oil discoveries the days of US financial leverage were limited. Secondly, the new oil money brought in its wake massive corruption on the part of Libyan officials. "Despite prospects of huge oil revenues", a secret US government report informed President Kennedy in 1962, "Libyans have gone in for so much uncontrolled spending (and grafting) that a cash shortage has arisen" (Blundy and Lycett 1987). As a former CIA official noted, the oil companies got their concessions in Libya by allying themselves in fact and in the public mind with the most corrupt elements in the society (Cooley 1982).

The third way in which the new oil wealth served to undermine the US position was by raising popular expectations for a better life, which the monarchy had failed to deliver. Despite a huge growth in gross national product, the trickle-down effect did not happen. A 1967 study found that "the levels of nutrition are still what they have been for centuries – very low" (Wright 1969). A volume sponsored by the US government reported that "the beneficial effects of a rapidly rising national income...initially were slow in providing relief to the poverty-stricken common people...the new oil wealth only reinforced a class structure that clearly benefited the elite and other favoured elements of a weak loyal minority" (Nelson 1979).

Against these domestic and foreign problems it was clear that the days of the Libyan monarchy were numbered. In 1969 the king was 79 years old and seemed increasingly remote from his royal responsibilities. Public support for the dynasty had never matched that for the king himself (US Senate Sub-Committee 1970), and he had no heir. Coup-plotters seemed to be everywhere and there were widespread reports that the king was considering abdicating or, on the other hand, launching a coup of his own (Haley 1984).

It therefore came as no surprise when on 1 September 1969, while the king was taking one of his extended vacations outside the country, a group of young military officers under the lead of Colonel Qadhafi launched an almost bloodless coup. The new government promised to introduce new policy to extend the benefits of the oil wealth to all.

We have discussed at some length above some of the unique characteristics of Libyan society, because it is important to understand how difficult it was going to be for the new government to graft a set of new ideologies onto an old and very deeply rooted society. It was the religious and patriotic credentials of Ahmed Sharif, the founder of the Libyan resistance to Italian occupation, and his crucial nationalist role against Italian aggression which bestowed legitimacy on the Libyan monarchy, no matter how corrupt and ineffectual it had been. From this we can observe that the relationship between Islam and politics was extremely close, as most forms of political activity had earlier been authenticated through Islamic appeal. The prolonged Italian occupation during which many Libyans were forced to flee and retreat into the interior of the country in fact served to buttress the traditional sectors, as the Italians with their "collonizzazione demografica", hoping to resettle Libya in massive numbers, did not develop a strong local elite. Consequently, the judicial and educational spheres remained the domain of religious leaders. As we have seen above, despite the post-independence development of a constitution and parliament, the monarchy did not encourage strong political parties or national institutions. In many ways it was Islam that kept the otherwise fragmented tribal society intact.

Initially it appeared that in early 1970s the new Libyan government was seeking to construct a socioeconomic and political system rooted firmly in Sharia (Islamic law). Far from propagating a new vision of Islam, he conformed to that defined by the orthodox Muslim establishment, and sought to legitimize the revolution by associating it with traditional Libyan values (Takeyh 2001).

But from 1973, having consolidated its position, the revolutionary government embarked on a series of measures for the reconstruction of Libyan society. Using the opportunity of the Prophet Muhammad's birthday anniversary on 15 April 1973, the Libyan government declared certain key measures to preserve the revolution. These radical actions by the government included the abrogation of all reactionary laws, the prosecution and elimination of political groups which represented counter-revolutionary forces (communists, capitalists, and the Muslim Brotherhood), the distribution of weapons to the revolutionary masses, a bureaucratic and administrative revolution and the declaration of a cultural revolution. Following the speech of Colonel Qadhafi in June 1973, 450 People's Committees were formed, taking control over the national administration of universities, hospitals, schools, factories, and farms. In essence, a form of direct democracy had emerged.

On 6 April 1974 it was reported that Colonel Qadhafi had been relieved of his traditional administrative and traditional duties (*NY Times*, 6 April 1974). For the Western media, this initially caused great confusion, signalling, as they thought, a regime change. However, it simply meant his assumption of a new role. By 1976, in this role as theoretician of the revolution, Colonel Qadhafi had published Part I of the Green Book and was ready to launch the new era of the Libyan Jamarihiya.

It was at the concluding meeting of the emergency session of the General People's Congress held in Sebha (28 February–2 March 1977) that he declared,

> From the same place, from Sebha, in the heart of the desert, where the idea of the revolution emanated, the declaration of the establishment of the people's power was proclaimed. All corners of the world will respond to this Jamahiriya. From the desert a new era dawns on humanity ... the era of the masses. From the desert our people announce, at the end of the twentieth century, the end of traditional republics just as the French people announced in the eighteenth century the end of the era of the monarchies and the beginning of the era of the republics. Today, in a part of the desert called the Great Sahara, the homeland of the Arabs ... in that place the foundation is laid for the era of the masses, the era of Jamahiriya.

The concept of Jamahiriya and its precise political expression was in fact what Qadhafi termed in his Green Book as the "Third Universal Theory", which he defined as an alternative to both capitalist and communist ideologies. Libya, renamed the Socialist's People's Libyan Arab Jamahiriya, was to be the first nation to adopt this doctrine. In essence, the Third Universal Theory in its political expression represented the organizational framework within which the Jamahiriya, that is direct democracy, was to be exercised.

1.5.1 How the Libyan Political System Functions

The March 1977 Session of the General People's Congress, based on the Third Universal Theory, adopted measures to abolish the Revolutionary Command Council, which, since the constitutional declaration of 11 December 1969, had been the highest political authority in the country. Political power was transferred to the basic People's Congresses, their Committees and the General People's Congress. As well as this, traditional forms of government along with the institutions and offices of the Cabinet, Ministers, Directors and so on were abolished in favour of a General Secretariat of the People's Congress, comprising a Secretary General and a number of other Secretaries, each responsible for a particular state activity – for example, Agriculture, Foreign Affairs, and Labour – and to People's Committees at the local level. Finally, the session adopted a decision to elect Colonel Qadhafi as Secretary General of the People's General Congress (El-Shahat 1978). However, he relinquished this position on 1 March 1979, together with all other titles, to be known thereafter as only "Leader of the Revolution".

From this point onwards the system of government was firmly based on Basic People's Congresses and People's Committees, the building units of "direct democracy", or the "authority of the people", although their numbers could vary from time to time. At its most basic level, all Libyan citizens in whatever category – labourers, farmers, fishermen, workers, businessmen, students or employees – are part, geographically, of Basic People's Congresses, with membership being the right of all citizens. As a simple example, for the city or sha'abiyat of Sebha with 126,600 inhabitants, there are currently six Basic People's Congresses.

Through interaction and direct vote, each Basic People's Congress democratically elects a working committee which selects its own Secretary and Assistant

Secretary. The working committee is responsible for the administrative affairs of that particular basic congress such as matters relating to health, infrastructure, education, security, finance, tourism, agriculture, even foreign policy, and so on. It arranges for meetings, follows up the daily activities of the People's Committees, and drafts a comprehensive report to be submitted to the congress during its regular session. It is in accordance with this report that the People's Committees within the area of that Popular Congress are called to account.

The Basic People's Congresses directly choose the People's Committees which replace government administration at various levels. They are responsible for carrying out the decisions of the Basic People's Congresses.

In addition to being, as citizens, members of the basic people's congresses, each Libyan, whether they be industrial or commercial workers, peasants, merchants, craftsmen, officials or professionals, establish their own unions, syndiccates, or professional organizations.

The Basic People's Congresses, the People's Committees, the unions, syndiccates, and professional associations gather annually in the General People's Congress, the national legislative authority, to give final shape to the people's decisions and recommendations.

The General People's Congresses also appoints *Al-Lajna al-Sha'biya al-A'mma*, the General Popular Committee, a body that corresponds roughly to the Cabinet in other countries. It represents the highest executive authority in the country and conventionally, up to the year 2000, consisted of 20 Secretariats (Obeidi 2001).

The decisions and recommendations approved by the General People's Congress will in turn be transferred back to the Basic People's Congresses for execution by the People's Committees.

In March 2000, in decisive and sweeping changes enacted during the General People's Congress, the General Peoples' Committees were reduced to seven Secretariats: Services Affairs; Production Affairs; Justice and Public Security; Foreign Affairs and International Co-operation; Finance; Information, Culture and Tourism; and African Unity. The functions of the remaining 13 were transferred to 32 Sha'abiyat (in March 2006, subsequently reduced to 20 Sha'abiyat) or provincial governments. The idea behind this was to encourage decentralization and give more responsibility and autonomy to the regions at the local levels (Official Gazzette, Tripoli 2000), as well as to correct imbalances, which has stressed the development of the big cities. Since then, additional Secretariats have again been instituted, and at the end of 2005, they stood at 12 Secretariats and four Sectoral Executive Representatives, that is Industry, Health, Housing and Infrastructure, and Agriculture and Animal Resources.

In addition to the above political framework and structures there are two other key components of the political system in Libya which, although in strict terms are not "officially" part of the political system, play a very significant role in shaping Libyan politics, especially at the domestic level. These are the Revolutionary Committees Movement and the Popular Social Leadership. The Revolutionary Committees Movement started in the late 1970s and were devoted to revolutionary activities. They formed committees all over the country, for example in every educational institution, in offices, in the armed forces and in the Basic People's Congresses in order to "help the masses take a firm grasp of the reins of power and all sources of power within society" (Al Qadhafi 1984).

Their membership was open to anyone and is not based on election. Members of the Revolutionary Committees operate outside the framework of the People's Congresses. They were regarded as a temporary movement, performing duties which are necessary and immediate, and would in fact theoretically disappear when the "state of masses" came into existence.

With regard to the Revolutionary Committees and their role in Libyan society, there are a number of comments that can be made. First, they rapidly dominated the political life of Libya. Secondly, they have developed a broad power-base within the society, determined to eliminate any opposition. Thirdly, at specific times during the 1980s and 1990s they became one of the sources of recruitment to the People's Committees at the Basic People's Congress level, and the General People's Committees at the local and national levels.

Another "unofficial" force in Libyan politics is the Popular Social Leadership. For the first time since the revolution in 1969, the regime in Libya created a role for the traditional elite in managing and interacting with the population by establishing a new institution within the framework of the political system, *al-Qiyadat al-Sha'biya al-Ijtima'iya*, the Popular Social Leadership, announced in September 1993.

This was defined as the leading national umbrella under which all forces within Libya were grouped. With the emphasis, in practice, placed on regional leadership, a popular social leadership was brought into being, covering the area socially and geographically. Its members were the "respected natural leaders" of the local communities, which in turn choose a group of "Coordinators" for 3 years. A General Co-ordinator is chosen to represent the area in the popular social leadership at the Sha'biyat or province/municipality level. A General Co-ordinator at the national level is chosen for a period of 6 months from the 20 Co-ordinators at the provincial level. The main duties of the popular social leadership involved the resolution of local conflicts, liaising with the People's Congresses and Committees, and finally observing the implementation of socio-economic development plans for their areas.

In concluding this brief survey of Libya's political system it should be observed, therefore, that the original ideological framework of the Libyan political system has had to be refined by practical considerations imposed by the reality, as we stated earlier, of the traditional nature of Libyan society which has, to a certain extent, resisted the creation of a new type of society and structure.

1.6 Macroeconomic Framework

Having recently successfully achieved diplomatic rehabilitation as a result of the Lockerbie settlement and its renunciation of Weapons of Mass Destruction (WMD), Libya is now seriously examining its economic options. It has been labelled as a classic "rentier/distributive state", a term used to describe Iran (Mahdavi 1970) and Libya, Saudi Arabia, Kuwait and Qatar (Vandervalle 1998). In this context a rentier/distributive state is one which, through the considerable revenues or economic rent derived from the production and foreign sale of, usually, oil, enables its rulers to act as domestic distributors of this rent in the form of social, health, housing, and education services, allowing them to demand political compliance in return. More recently, others have postulated a link between rent-rich regimes and economic reforms (or lack of these) in Middle East countries (Glasser 2001); again, in a recent analysis of the post-oil Norwegian experience of economic diversification, the author has also pointed out how historical differences affect economic diversification, comparing Norway with other, mainly Gulf, oil producers (Noreng 2004).

Successive attempts by both the pre-revolutionary and the revolutionary governments to lessen Libya's reliance on income from petroleum have not succeeded, although impressive progress has undoubtedly been made since 1970 in the fields of infrastructure development, agriculture, education, housing, health, gender issues as well as in banking and corporate reforms. However, the Libyan economy still remains largely state controlled and heavily dependent on the oil sector. Since the lifting of the UN and US Libya-specific trade sanctions in September 2003 and 2004, respectively, the pace of economic and structural reforms has picked up, and a series of measures have been taken to enhance the role of the private sector in the economy. Despite expectations from potential foreign investors, many of these reforms appear to be implemented in an ad hoc and non-transparent manner.

Because of its chronic inability to diversify the economy away from the oil and gas sectors, Libyan fiscal policy continues to be dominated by the amount of oil revenues generated to the government and the need to support the huge burden of SOE and civil service employment, and maintain the extensive subsidy system. Still, as at mid-2006, Libya's macroeconomic position remained strong and is projected to remain as such over the medium term, largely of course because of the high international price for Libya's crude oil. This averaged around US $38 for the year 2004 (Central Bank of Libya, CBL), US $50.64 for 2005, and US $63.05 for 2006 up to mid-September (OPEC September, 2005). As well as this, Libya's transformation and diversification programmes will continue to attract overseas investors, particularly in the tourist and hydrocarbon sectors, with foreign investment increasingly becoming an important driver of growth. Even so, projected growth rates under existing policy will not be enough to generate employment opportunities for the new entrants to the labour force, as well create new jobs for the workers made redundant by the current privatization programme.

Based on data from the International Monetary Fund (IMF), real GDP in 2003 grew by an estimated 9.1 per cent, reflecting a 28 per cent rise in oil production and a modest 2.2 per cent increase in non-hydrocarbon activities. Deflation, as measured by the official Consumer Price Index, decelerated to 2.1 per cent from 9.9 per cent in 2002. The favourable developments in the oil market contributed to a significant improvement in the external current account surplus, which reached 15.4 per cent of GDP. Gross international reserves increased to about US $19 billion, equivalent to 22 months of 2004 imports.

The fiscal stance continued to be expansionary, with a non-oil fiscal deficit widening to 36 per cent of GDP. However, reflecting higher hydrocarbon revenues, the overall consolidated surplus remained stable at about 10.5 per cent of

GDP. Non-oil revenue declined by 3 percentage points of GDP as a result of widespread tax evasion and low efficiency in tax collection. While capital expenditures were compressed to make room for the payment of one instalment (US $1.1 billion) of the Lockerbie settlement, current expenditure, excluding the Lockerbie payment, remained high at 30 per cent of GDP.

Broad money increased by 9.4 per cent. As a result of the improved fiscal situation, net banks' claims on the government declined sharply, whereas credit to the economy increased by about 13 per cent of beginning-of-the-year money stock, reflecting mainly credit to public enterprises. Reform measures in the money and banking area included a further strengthening of banking supervision. Also, the authorities have lowered interest rates across the board in an effort to encourage private sector demand for credit, and developed a strategy to modernize the payment system.

In 2004, macroeconomic and financial conditions continued to be favourable. Based on figures from the IMF, real GDP growth was 4.6 per cent, while consumer prices declined by 2.2 per cent. Sustained increases in crude oil prices led to a major improvement in the external current account surplus, which reached some 24 per cent of GDP. Gross international reserves rose to about 24 months of projected 2005 imports.

The fiscal stance was expansionary, with a large non-oil fiscal deficit of 33.5 per cent of GDP. Due to high oil prices, the overall fiscal surplus reached 17.5 per cent of GDP, while non-oil revenue increased by about 1 percentage point of GDP, based on stronger collections by customs because of increased imports and improvements in the revenue collection system. Total expenditure and net lending declined by 0.5 per cent of GDP, as the large increment in capital expenditure (8 per cent of GDP) on account of expenditure on several major public projects was more than offset by a sharp drop in extra-budgetary current expenditure.

The IMF data also showed broad money growing by 9.2 per cent. As a result of the improved government financial situation, the government's net creditor position with the banking system was about 50 per cent of GDP. Overall credit to the economy declined by 1 per cent largely because of government buy-back of public enterprise bank debt and a limited increase in credit to the private sector.

In macroeconomic terms, therefore the Libyan economy has performed extremely well in the period 2003–2004, reflecting the favourable developments in the world oil market, where oil and gas prices have strengthened significantly. Fiscal and external current account balances registered large surpluses, and international reserves rose sharply.

In 2005, macroeconomic performance remained relatively strong. Real GDP growth was about 3.5 per cent, and inflation remained low (2.5 per cent). Unlike precious years, economic growth is estimated to have been generated mainly in the non-oil economy (4.5 per cent). While activity in the oil sector grew only 1.5 per cent, due to output capacity constraints, the pick-up in activity in the non-oil sector was due to significant increases in government spending. Sectors showing strong growth were trade, hotels and transportation (7 per cent), and construction and services (5 per cent). While gains in agriculture remained modest, at 2.5 per cent, the manufacturing sector picked up and registered positive growth of 1.8 per cent for the first time in 5 years.

Based on preliminary data from the IMF, the overall fiscal surplus reached 32.5 per cent of GDP, reflecting strong oil revenues (68 per cent of GDP) and reduced expenditure (in terms of GDP). Non-oil revenue is estimated to have declined by about 15 per cent, due largely to the non-transfer of interest on the Oil Reserve Fund balances by the CBL, and also to lower collections by customs and the local governments, in part due to the downside effects of the new tax law and customs tariff. Overall, the non-oil fiscal deficit widened to 35 per cent of GDP.

Monetary developments were characterized by strong broad money growth of 29 per cent. Both money and quasi-money grew significantly, by 33 per cent and 20 per cent, respectively. These developments also reflect a remonetization of the economy consistent with improved domestic economic conditions and increased public confidence following the lifting of sanctions, and the sharp increase in bank credit to public enterprises, at 23 per cent. With the sustained improvement in the government's financial situation, the government's net creditor position with the banking system increased to 70 per cent of the GDP. While bank credit to the private sector grew only modestly (about 3 per cent), most of the private sector credit needs were met by the government through specialized banks.

In external terms, the current account surplus widened to 41 per cent of GDP largely because of a 48 per cent increase hydrocarbon exports to about US $29 billion. Imports grew 24 per cent to some US $11 billion, boosted by increased domestic demand. Gross international reserves rose to about 32 months of projected 2006 imports (IMF 2006).

It is also worth noting that there appeared to be no indication of pressure on the present exchange rate of the Libyan Dinar, which was valued at US $0.76 as on 27 July 2006. Nontheless, in future it is important that the government prepares itself to adjust the peg if necessary in response to market developments, particularly fluctuations in the crude oil price, and keep exchange rate policy under constant review as the reform process continues apace, to assist competitiveness in the non-oil sector, ensuring that economic reforms and diversification keep Libyan products internationally competitive. Regarding the fixed-term interest rates on LD deposits, this went down in 2005 from 5.5 per cent, where they had stood for the last 10 years, to 4.5 per cent as announced by the CBL for deposits of 1–4 years. Since there is no organized Western-type capital market reflecting scarcity or abundance of lendable funds, interest rates are not determined by market forces but by the CBL.

To date, the government's preparations since 1997 to reform the regulatory and institutional framework to support the transition to a market economy have been considerable, and, given time, Libya's efforts to re-connect itself with the global economy should undoubtedly be successfully achieved. But clearly such key issues as the initial primitive level of economic development as well as the present magnitude of long-term economic distortions in industrial structure and trade patterns need to be analysed and overcome.

In this connection, both for international credibility and for self-assessment of the efficacy of economic reforms, it is crucial that a system such as the IMF's General Data Dissemination System (GDDS) is adopted and practised in Libya. This is a structured process through which countries regularly upgrade and improve the quality of the data compiled and disseminated by their national statistical systems over the long term, to meet the needs of macroeconomic analysis. In this way Libya can gauge its progress in making major economic reforms in comparison with other countries, as well countering present international criticism of the current lack of transparency within the Libyan Government.

In Appendix 1, a series of tables of Macroeconomic Indicators for Libya for the period 2000–2006 is presented, derived from IMF, Libyan Ministry of Finance and CBL data.

1.7 Reappraising Libya

When, on 19 December 2003, the Libyan Foreign Minister, Abdel Rahman Shalgam announced his government's decision to discontinue its production of WMD, a final and crucial stage had been reached in the reintegration of Libya into the international community. Libya's rehabilitation, after decades of isolation, had not come about by chance – Tripoli had invested heavily both financially and diplomatically, in fact since the time of the Clinton administration, in re-establishing international respectability (*The Financial Times* 2004). US/Libyan rapprochement reached its zenith in May, 2006, when US Secretary of State Secretary Condoleezza Rice announced the restoration of full diplomatic relations with Libya, and the opening of an embassy in Tripoli. In the same announcement, she stated that the United States intended to remove Libya from the list of designated state sponsors of terrorism, and omitted it from the annual certification of countries not cooperating fully with United States anti-terrorism efforts (US Department of State 15 May 2006). This was followed on May 31 by an exchange of diplomatic notes between the two countries confirming the upgrade of the US Liaison Office in Tripoli to a US Embassy.

Since its renunciation of WMD, there has been continuing international debate as to exactly why Libya has decided to reposition itself internationally. The more hawkish elements of the Bush administration have been quick to claim full credit by suggesting that this reversal in Libyan policy was a by-product of the war in Iraq. However, this claim not only discounts long-standing Libyan diplomatic efforts, rebuffed by the United States, to seek rapprochement, but is belied by the fact that as early as March 2003, before the beginning of the US-led Operation Iraqi Freedom, Libya had been in contact with the British government to resolve US WMD concerns.

As well as this, there had also been considerable pressure from individual Western governments, primarily Italy, for rapprochement with Libya. Their motive is not that dissimilar to that of Tripoli – primarily economic. Libya is keen to attract foreign investment to invigorate its long isolated economy. Western companies, meanwhile, had been applying pressure on their governments to end the ban on trade with Libya that was depriving them of considerable business. The oil lobbies in individual countries, including the United States, have been particularly aggressive, since Libya with its advantageous location vis-a-vis Europe and its considerable proven and potential oil and gas reserves, offers a potentially rich area for long-term investment in this sector.

Benefits to Libya from its radical shift in policy towards the international community mainly stem from its new status as a country others can now visit freely and with which they can interact and deal. In March 2003, for example, British Prime Minister Tony Blair visited Libya, paving the way for the return of British business. British companies were soon competing to invest in the country, primarily in the oil and tourism sectors.

The progress continued when, in April 2004, Colonel Qadhafi visited Belgium, after which the European Commissioner for Transport and Energy visited Libya, and approval was obtained for the establishment of a Euro-Mediterranean transport and energy network in which Libya would cooperate.

On 1 October 2004, Italian Prime Minister Silvio Berlusconi visited Libya for the third time in a year. Italy is Libya's primary trade partner and obtains much of its oil requirements from that country. The high point of the visit was the inauguration of a 540-km-long gas pipeline, the Greenstream, with a total investment of $5.6 billion, between the Libyan town of Mellita and Gela in Sicily, which now supplies Italy with much of its gas requirements.

Gerhard Schroeder's mid-October visit to Libya, the first by a German Chancellor, saw him praise Tripoli's stance and the reforms carried out by the Libyan government. Germany is Libya's second most important trade partner, after Italy, while Libya is the fourth largest exporter of oil to Germany. Schroeder affirmed during the trip that Germany would back Libya's attempt to join the WTO, as well as support its membership of the Barcelona process, which aims to link the European Union and the southern and eastern Mediterranean states in a free trade zone. The Chancellor expressed that it was important for Libya to enhance its relations with the European Union and that it could play an important role linking Africa, the Arab world and Europe – a pivotal role which Libyan policy makers understand only too well.

Jacques Chirac's trip in late November, which is, very significantly, the first official French visit to Libya since the North African state attained independence in 1951, came within the framework of the normalization of the two countries' economic relations following Libya's decision to compensate the victims of the UTA plane bombing. Accompanying Chirac was a 23-strong delegation of leading French trade representatives, and agreements were signed covering transport, industry, education, and tourism. The volume of trade between the two countries, however, is notably small. Libya's annual exports to France account for around $1 billion while its imports from France are approximately $0.5 billion.

Before Chirac's visit, Libya's Finance Minister had gone to settle a number of bilateral financial issues in Paris, where he signed agreements with French officials on double taxation and his country's payment of some $44 million owed to France as well as other outstanding interest payments.

One remaining issue, though, is that of Libya's unpaid contributions to the budget of the Institut du Monde Arabe, located in the French capital, which now stand at 14 million euros. Tripoli refuses to pay the full amount on the grounds that the institute has not held events related to Libya for many years. From a Libyan perspective, France's military presence in Africa – and its intervention in Côte d'Ivoire in 2004 – also remains something an issue of contention between the two sides.

Libya, however, does not seem to have benefited from its reconciliatory efforts as much as it had expected. During talks with Chirac in Tripoli with senior Libyan officials, they expressed disappointment at the lack of rewards and the inadequate security guarantees offered by the United States, Europe, and Japan in return for his country's surrender of nuclear, chemical, and biological weapons. They noted that if these issues were not addressed, others – presumably referring to North Korea and Iran – would be unlikely to follow Libya's example.

What Libya had in mind in terms of rewards and guarantees was international support to turn its military capabilities into civilian ones, and the state-of-the-art technology needed to do so. Europe, however, responded coldly to what it considered Libya's premature demands. Chirac declared that Libya's aspirations concerning a civil nuclear programme were not up for consideration and that France and its fellow nuclear states were bound by the rules of the International Atomic Energy Agency (IAEA), which sets the conditions for the transfer of technology for the development of civil nuclear activities.

In fact the Libyan–European rapprochement does not yet mean full normalization of relations. One of the main impediments is Libya's status in the Barcelona process, in which it is the only Mediterranean Arab country without full membership, although it has joined as an observer. However, by 2005, the 10th anniversary of the Barcelona process, the process had still a long way to go, with many south and east Mediterranean members, including Libya, suspicious about its real agenda, perceiving it as a peaceful European recolonization of North Africa. In any case, in pragmatic terms, Libya presently achieves most of what it wants and needs from Europe, without commitment to the Barcelona *acquis*, since in effect it enjoys all the advantages of a free trade area with the European Union, because its primary export, hydrocarbons as either crude oil or gas, is not subject to tariffs.

Though there may remain certain issues to be resolved between Libya and the countries of Europe, Tripoli's recent efforts to enhance its relations with its northern neighbours have put an end to its international isolation, and effectively rule out any pretext for aggression against it. As stated above, what lies behind Libya's change of policy is a sincere desire to revitalize an economy devastated by years of international sanctions and isolation, and to reconnect itself to the global economy.

Ensuring sustained and rapid growth in the Libyan economy in the years ahead, as we will discuss comprehensively in the chapters to come, will call for a business environment conducive to greater private investment, consolidation of human capital assets and further strengthening the macroeconomic fundamentals. Libya currently suffers from a structural private investment gap, since most economic growth has relied more on public investment, and less on private investment and human capital. In the years ahead it is investment in the key energy, agriculture, tourism and aviation sectors that will successfully power the Libyan economy as the country repositions itself for dramatic growth.

2 Libya's Foreign Policy and External Relations

2.1 Libya's Regional Identity

Because of its location, in the centre of the southern Mediterranean coastline and on the northern coast of the North African continent, the analysis of Libya's foreign relations initially poses some crucial questions. Libya can be seen as a part, both culturally and geographically, of four larger regions – Mediterranean, Islamic, Arab or African. A Maghreb historian has summed up this situation succinctly by posing these questions – "Should the main interpretive context for North African history be a Mediterranean-oriented one or a more African one? Or should the larger unit of historical analysis be a grand east–west perspective that would envisage North African lands as part of a continuum stretching from the Iranian plateau to the shores of the Atlantic?" (Shaw 2003).

While the first question is reinforced by the common membership of the North African Arab nations of Mauritania, Morocco, Algeria, Tunisia, Libya, Egypt, Sudan, Somalia, Djibouti, and Comoros in the Arab League (founded in 1946), and in the African Union, reconstructed from the old OAU by the Libyan leader's Sirte speech of 1999, the idea of an Arab continuum stretching from Mauretania to Iran is belied by the conventional approach to Arab affairs and history which perceives a Maghreb/Mashreq dichotomy, while the North African and Middle Eastern Arab nations face distinct regional problems.

To this historical approach we have to add the political dimension – the position of Libya and the other North African nations in a post-colonial context, as newly independent nations seeking identity and security. In the Libyan case, its relatively small population, huge geographical area and desirable hydrocarbon assets made it, in security terms, particularly vulnerable. We can therefore interpret Libyan foreign relations as the legitimate quest for external security – through unification with its Arab neighbours, such as with Egypt and Syria in 1971–1973, with Tunisia in 1972 and 1974, or with its African neighbours to the south, as with Chad in 1981.

To understand the complex objectives and motives that have directed Libya's foreign policy, we will analyse Libya's relations with key parties and regions, and conclude that, despite the US/UN sanctions and American efforts to destroy the country and its system, Libya in 2005 has emerged geographically, economically and politically intact. The Libyan leader himself, who can now be characterized as a grizzly veteran of international politics, has emerged as a realist determined to bequeath to Libya, as his political legacy, a new set of external paradigms, enabling the country to deal with the complex problems it faces it in an increasingly globalized world.

2.2 Libya's Relations with Arab States

Although Libya, as we have said, is conventionally considered to be part of the Maghreb, in fact only its western region of Tripolitania can be said to share a similar history and culture with the other Maghreb countries, while its eastern region, Cyrenaica, has historically and culturally been more aligned with its Egyptian neighbour and the Mashreq. While, for example, the ideal of Maghreb unity was firmly embedded in the constitutions of Tunisia (1959), Morocco (1962–1972) and Algeria (1962), no such concept existed in the Libyan constitution of 1951 (Aghrout and Sutton 1990). It was not, in fact, until after the Libyan revolution of 1969 that Libya's position in the Maghreb regional dynamics began to assume any importance. Prior to that, its role was peripheral, and as one researcher has commented, it functioned only as a kind of hinge between the Maghreb and the Mashreq (Zartman, in Hudson (ed.) 1999).

However, all this changed with the discovery and export of oil in the 1960s, and rise to power in 1969, and later consolidation throughout the 1970s, of the new Libyan government. In this initial post-revolutionary period Libya adopted a more assertive regional posture which changed Maghreb regional dynamics (Deeb 1991). For example, Libya in 1969 withdrew from the Maghreb Permanent Consultative Committee and its adjunct, the Committee for Industrial Cooperation, founded in 1964. Reasons for this were its somewhat subservient position vis-a-vis the more dominant Maghreb states of Morocco and Algeria, as well as its politically divergent political development. The youthful ideology of Colonel Qadhafi himself, the political disciple and perceived heir (by some at least) of Nasser, and his early espousal of pan-Arabism and anti-Israeli stance, inevitably drew his focus towards the Arab heartland.

This is not to say that Libya did not possess a foreign policy towards its Maghreb neighbours. In the new post-1969 regional dynamics, the first major thrust of Libyan policy was to seek a union with Tunisia, to bolster its security in regional terms against the other larger Maghreb states. In a series of diplomatic initiatives starting in 1972 the Libyan government called for a merger with Tunisia, but this request was rejected by the Tunisian President Habib Bourguiba. Again in early 1974 a new unification plan was pursued by Libya at a meeting with Bourguiba at Djerba, the formation of an Arab Islamic Republic, this time initially accepted but then again rejected by Bourguiba. Throughout the 1980s relations between the two countries continued to fluctuate and in 1980 diplomatic relations between the two countries were in fact suspended.

However, the key issue which dominated Libyan foreign relations with its Maghreb neighbours was the outbreak of the Western Sahara conflict in 1975. Algeria and Libya signed an agreement at Hassi Messaoud to support the Polisario Front, the Western Saharan independence movement, against Morocco. The escalation in the conflict almost erupted on several occasions into open war between Algeria and Morocco. In 1983, however, in a dramatic policy reversal, Algeria established a friendship treaty with Tunisia and Mauretania, explicitly refusing membership to Morocco and Libya (Meliani 1985; Ibrahimi 1988). This was followed by a similar treaty between Libya and Morocco in 1984 which disintegrated 2 years later (Deeb 1989).

However, it was an external threat, this time economic rather than military, which served to draw the Maghreb nations together again. This was the enlargement of the EU countries and their retreat behind harmonized tariff walls excluding their competitors (Aghrout and Sutton 1990). The admission of the Iberian countries to the EC and the passage of the Single Europe Act (SEA), both in 1986, posed a very real economic challenge to North Africa, motivating the Maghreb countries to seek a united front and build trade and industry through an integrated region. The closing of Europe to North African immigrants, rising racial animosity against those already established in Europe, and the shift of European suppliers to the more developed product and labour markets of the Far East such as Malaysia and Thailand all alarmed the Maghreb nations.

As well as this, the prolonged stalemate in the Western Saharan war by 1981 also required some type of closure. This stimulated the parties involved to attempt to resolve regional antagonisms, at the same time countering the European threat. Morocco–Algerian summits at Akid Lotfi and Zouj Bghal in May 1987, their joint declaration of May 1988, and the five-state Maghreb summit during the larger Arab summit in Zeralda in June 1988 all led to a broader reconciliation. This finally led to an all Maghreb summit on 17 February 1989, at Marrakech, where the Maghreb Arab Union, better known by its French name and acronym Union du Maghreb Arabe (UMA), was formed during the meeting of the Heads of State of Algeria, Libya, Mauretania, Morocco and Tunisia. Article 2 of the Union de Maghreb Arab Treaty stated as one of its main objectives, "To work progressively towards the free movement of persons, services, goods and capital within its constituent borders."

But its progress has not been smooth. In 1994, Libya, then suffering both US (since 1986) and UN (since 1991) sanctions, threatened to leave the UMA unless Member States ceased to comply with the UN sanctions imposed on Libya, and by 1995 Libya refused to assume the chairmanship of the organization, owing to their continuing compliance to the UN sanctions. As well as this major disagreements between Rabat and Algiers over the Western Sahara conflict persisted. It was not until two events occurred in 1999 which led to interest in its revival. One was the election of the new Algerian President Abdul Aziz Bouteflika, which was favourably received in Rabat and other Arab Maghreb states. The other was the settlement of Libya's Lockerbie issue through the successful intervention of Nelson Mandela. Combined, these events led to a realistic expectation that it could be meaningfully revived again.

Yet another problem undermining the Arab Maghreb Union (AMU) is related to Mauretania's establishment of full diplomatic relations with Israel in 1999, while none of the other UMA states have done so. However, it was the continuation of the persistent problems between Algeria and Morocco over the Western Sahara which led Libya again, in 2004, to threaten to leave the Union if these could not be resolved. Morocco maintains that the Western Sahara is an integral part of its national territory while Algeria, backed by the United Nations, labels the Western Sahara as a territory occupied by Morocco. Throughout this dispute, Algeria's support for an independent Sahrawi carved out of the Western Sahara has been consistent. As one commentator has noted, "undoubtedly, real stability of the Maghreb region hinges upon good Algerian–Moroccan relations and, whatever other factors, conflict in Western Sahara is the main impediment to Maghreb integration" (Zoubir 2000). In 2005, on account of this, the Morocco–Algerian border was closed.

To all intents and purposes, then, by 2005 the AMU, in so far as it ever seriously attempted to become a meaningful socio-economic union, was dead, and its members had never achieved either developmental or meaningful economic unity, but at the most, at certain periods in its existence, close diplomatic relations.

2.3 Libya and the Middle East Conflict

In May 1949, prior to Libyan independence in 1951, the British foreign minister Bevin and his Italian counterpart Sforza proposed a trusteeship arrangement for Libya in the United Nations, in which the British should hold the trusteeship over Cyrenaica, France over the Fezzan, and Italy over Tripolitania, with Britain administering the entire territory until 1951. Thereafter the tripartite trusteeship arrangements would be put in place, ending in 1959 when Libya would become independent. A subcommittee of the General Assembly duly approved this arrangement, with the United States supporting the majority against the objections of the Soviet bloc and the Arab–Asian nations.

However, the recommendation of the General Assembly subcommittee still had to be approved by the UN body as a whole. In the middle of May, the resolution fell one vote short of the necessary two-thirds majority (UN 1949). It was the crucial Israeli abstention which scuttled the Bevin–Sforza proposal, ensuring Libya's independence 8 years before its envisaged timeframe. Israel's Ambassador to the United Nations, Abba Eban, admitted that Israel's decision was partially caused by anti-British sentiments, adding, however, that it would have looked ridiculous if Israel had chosen to recommend a trusteeship in Libya after fighting against British rule (Eban 1977).

Had the Israelis known in 1949 of the direction that future Libyan–Israeli relations were to take, it is unlikely that they would have voted as they did. As an Israeli Foreign Ministry official commented, "When Israel's abstention helped frustrate the trusteeship plan, it did not expect to gain Libya's friendship, but neither did it anticipate its rabid hostility" (Rafael 1981).

During the monarchy period, 1951–1969, Libya, because of its absolute reliance on Western aid and advice, as well as Western investment in its nascent oil sector, maintained cordial if not close relations with Western countries. In the early 1950s, Libya established close ties with Britain and the United States, allowing them to operate military bases in the country in exchange for economic aid. It could hardly have been otherwise, in view of Libya's dire economic circumstances immediately post independence and before the discovery of oil later in the decade. The British view was that Libya, in view of its strategic location, should be a British client state (Louis 1984). In this early post-independence period, its pro-Western policy encouraged Israel to think that Libya would maintain a benign or at least a neutral attitude towards the Arab–Israeli conflict.

In fact history had witnessed Libyan solidarity with the Arab states long before independence. Demonstrations had occurred in the urban areas of the former Italian colony during the Palestinian rebellion of 1936. Support for the Palestinian cause in the Libyan regions was shown regularly after the Second World War, reaching a climax during Israel's War of Independence in 1948. The Voice of Cairo radio broadcasts ensured that Libyans knew of the problems of the Palestinians. For example, when the Cyrenaican Assembly discussed the issue of boycotting Israel in 1951, Israel's opponents called for a strict embargo on the Jewish State, dominating the moderates who favoured neutrality on that issue. This particular dispute ended in the suspension of that session by the Libyan Prime Minister (De Candole 1990). Later, in 1953, Libya joined the Arab League, originally founded in 1945.

When Nasser nationalized the Suez Canal in 1956, Libya decisively demonstrated pro-Arab solidarity. Although Libya attempted to maintain a more moderate posture towards Egypt's conflict with the Western powers, pan-Arab pressures were too strong to ignore. After attacks by the Western media on Nasser, the Libyan government declared that Nasser's decision to nationalize the Suez Canal was legal and justified (*Tarablus al Gharb* 29 July 1956). Pan-Arab pressure also ensured Libyan solidarity with Arab states in their efforts to isolate and boycott Israel. In 1957 Libya passed a law prohibiting individuals and companies from trading with Israelis and Jews. Contravening the law involved a punishment of 3–10 years' imprisonment.

Apart from enforcing sanctions against the Jewish State, the Libyan government also felt compelled in the early period to demonstrate sympathy for the Palestinian cause. Its official position on the Palestinian question became clear in the spring of 1965, when Libya stated in a radio broadcast that the creation of Israel constituted a gross injustice and a flagrant violation of human rights, and that the Palestinians were entitled to return to their land and decide their own destiny. Moreover, Libya insisted that any solution to the Palestinian problem must be based on resolutions made by the Arab states in their summit meeting, which was held during that year.

But Libya's policy was not uniformly hostile towards Israel, and pragmatism also prevailed. When West Germany announced its decision to recognize Israel, the Arab states held a meeting in which they agreed to recall their ambassadors in Bonn; sever diplomatic ties with West Germany if it decided to establish diplomatic relations with Israel; consider effective means for an economic boycott of West Germany; and to reassess relations between the Arab countries and any country that decided to recognize Israel. In the vote on the resolution, Libya joined Morocco and Tunisia in expressing reservations about the first two points. Libya did not in fact sever its ties with Bonn, nor did it recall its ambassador. Although this policy led to a wave of demonstrations and attacks on the West German embassy in Benghazi, the Libyan government continued with its moderate policy towards West Germany, apologizing for the incident and placing guards around the building, promising to find and punish the perpetrators (*Maghreb Digest* 1965).

Although Libyans were not directly involved, sympathy for the Arab states after the decisive and humiliating Israeli victory in the 6-Day War in June 1967 led Libyans to demonstrate greater sympathy for the Arab states. In Tripoli and other cities Libya's trade unions and students attacked Jews and ravaged their property.

It was only the intervention of the Libyan monarch immediately after the war that enabled a Jewish mass evacuation to Rome, thus forestalling greater bloodshed (De Felice 1985). In the aftermath of the war, on 29 August 1967, a summit conference of the Arab League met in Sudan. There they laid down the "Three No's" policy: no to recognition of Israel, no negotiations with Israel, and no peace with Israel. In the fund-raising for another war, Saudi Arabia agreed to provide an annual contribution of £50 million and Kuwait £55 million, while Libya pledged to contribute £30 million (Raviv and Melman 1990).

Despite its anti-Israeli stance, the Israeli government had endeavoured to keep the monarchy in power as the lesser of two evils, fearing an escalation in hostility to Israel should he be deposed. According to Mossad chief Zvi Zamir, Israeli intelligence had in early 1969 warned the monarchy that a coup d'etat in Libya was imminent. By that time, however, both the British and the Americans were either unable or unwilling to forestall the events which led to the Libyan revolution.

For the British, the logic of bolstering the monarchy in a post-Suez context had become questionable. As one observer noted, "economic constraints on Britain's military posture in the Middle East. . . . (and) changing strategic priorities and military rationalization ensured that Libya was subjected to intense scrutiny after Harold Macmillan replaced Eden as Prime Minister in 1957" (Blackwell 2003). For the United States, foreign policy concerns about the conduct of the Vietnam War as well as major domestic problems related to civil uprisings demanded most attention, while the strategic importance of Libya and the Wheelus airbase in the age of ballistic intercontinental missiles was much reduced.

Accordingly, it was no surprise that after the Libyan revolution there was a dramatic deterioration in Libyan–Israeli relations. The new Libyan government refused to follow Egypt's lead in accepting UN Resolution 242, which demanded Israeli withdrawal from the occupied territories, but recognized its right to exist within secure boundaries (Heikal 1975). Essentially, Libya's stance was the denial of Israel's right to exist.

With the death of Nasser in 1970, a new period of tension in Israeli–Libyan relations was set in motion. Recognizing its military inability to challenge Israel directly, Libya initiated a campaign aimed at indirectly utilizing Libya's financial resources to cut Israel's ties with all its friends and allies. The main efforts were directed towards small and poverty-stricken Third World states, which could benefit most from Libya's financial assistance.

Therefore, during the late 1960s and 1970s, Libya joined other Arab oil-producing countries in providing monetary aid to African countries willing to terminate their diplomatic relations and commercial dealings with Israel (Klieman 1990). When Libya established diplomatic relations with Chad on 23 December 1972, one of her conditions was that its diplomatic relations with Israel should be severed immediately. Consequently, Chad cut all links with Israel and expelled all its military advisors (Raviv and Melman 1990). Libya also claimed responsibility for Niger, Congo, and Mali's diplomatic breaks with Israel (Arnold 1996). Libya's diplomatic success became evident after the Yom Kippur War, when most African countries decided to sever their diplomatic relations with Israel.

In Tripoli's vision of a new Middle East, there was no place for a Jewish state, which had recently emerged as unwelcome and relatively recent growth in the heart of the Arab nation. In this view Israel had been established by the imperialist powers, as a result of clever lobbying by the Zionist leader Chaim Weitzman towards the end of the First World War, which resulted in the British government's Balfour Declaration of 1917, which stated, "His Majesty's Government views with favour the establishment in Palestine of a national home for the Jewish people." By supporting the Zionist movement, the imperialist powers sought to create a Jewish state whose purpose was seen by Palestinians and Arabs alike as disinheriting the indigenous Palestinian inhabitants and exploiting the Arab masses.

As Libya saw it, the only solution to the Arab–Israeli conflict was the elimination of the state of Israel, since the existence of two entities in Palestine on the same territory was contradictory to the law of nature, which dictated that one must survive, while the other should be annihilated. In the Libyan diplomatic view, it was largely due to Arab complacency that the Zionists were capable of establishing a state in the region with the collaboration of the imperialist powers. Therefore the elimination of Israel, which was regarded as an expression of US imperialism, could be achieved only through Arab unity (Lemarchand 1988). Libya held the Arab leaders responsible for failing to maintain a sense of unity, which could have prevented the imperialists from inflicting injustice on the Arab inhabitants. Instead of concentrating on the need to liberate Palestine, the Arab leaders became involved in petty squabbles and useless arguments, which dissipated the energy of the Arab nation and weakened its ability to resist Zionism and imperialism.

Libya consequently had strong objection to all the efforts made by Israel and the Jewish communities throughout the world to encourage Jews to immigrate to Israel. Its objection to the immigration of the Falashas to Israel intensified its diplomatic hostility to Sudan's government during President Nimeiri's administration, whose cooperation with Israel made the rescue operation possible. When news about the Israeli operation aimed at rescuing the Falasha Jews of Ethiopia leaked out in the beginning of 1985, Libya requested a special meeting of the Arab League to discuss the issue. Similarly, Libya did not approve of the Soviet Union's improved attitude towards Israel and criticized President Michael Gorbachev for allowing Jews to immigrate to Israel (Sicker 1987). Libya's anti-Israeli stance was also impacted by its increasingly strained relationship with Nasser's successor as Egyptian president, Anuar Sadat.

Consequently, Egypt's marginalization of Libya and its perceived central role in the Middle East and Sadat's willingness to accept the Camp David accords reinforced Libya's refusal to soften its position towards Israel. Since the struggle for hegemony in the Arab world centred on the Arab–Israeli conflict, Libya could not hope to challenge Egyptian hegemony in the Arab world, unless it was willing to reverse the conciliatory trend adopted by Sadat. Hostility towards Israel provided justification for its unique role in the Middle East, and this became abundantly clear after the Camp David accords. Consequently, Libya welcomed Syria's President Hafez al Assad, who visited Libya in September 1979, in order to revive the "Steadfastness Front", established by the radical Arab states.

2.3.1 Libya and Palestine

As we have noted, Libyans had identified with the Palestinian cause even before independence, by listening to the distant broadcasts of Radio Cairo. After 1969 Libya's concern for the Palestinians began to manifest itself not only in the Libyan leader's rhetoric, but also in the form of financial contribution. A special committee was nominated by the regime shortly before the revolution to raise funds for the Palestinian cause, and almost immediately it managed to collect 50,000 Libyan pounds (Al Hayat, Beruit January 1969). Shortly afterwards, PLO leader Yasser Arafat came to Tripoli to express his gratitude for Libya's generosity. In one of his interviews in March 1970, the Libyan leader stated that his greatest ambition was to witness the liberation of Palestine (Africasia 1970).

However, Libya also had disagreements with the Palestinians, particularly with the members of the Popular Front for the Liberation in Palestine-General Command (PFLP-GC). By March 1971, the conflict between Libya and the Palestinian groups culminated in the arrest and the deportation of more than a hundred Palestinian workers. But this incident did little to seriously damage Libya's enthusiasm for the Palestinian cause. Domestically, however, support for the Palestinian cause was not as popular among the Libyan populace as was anticipated. By the summer of 1971, several offices were opened in Libya in order to recruit volunteers to fight for the Palestinian cause, but the number of the volunteers remained so low that the Libyan leader was compelled to state that it was the example not the numbers that mattered (Al Haqiqa, Tripoli 15 July 1971).

Still, by the end of the 1980s, Libya had become displeased with Arafat who had appeared to moderate his stand towards Israel. Later, however, the Libyan government seemed willing to reconcile with Arafat in order to bring unity in the Palestinian camp, and to neutralize the members of the PFLP-GC. Libya's relations with the Palestinians were characterized by periods of instability followed by reconciliation. It is worth noting that, for example, between 1994 and his death, Arafat did not once visit Libya. In 1995 the Libyan government expelled a large number of Palestinians, stating, somewhat emotionally, that since the peace process was complete, they should go back to their homeland after many decades of Libyan hospitality. This decision was in fact part of Libya's protest against the Oslo Middle East Peace Process, in which Libya was not consulted. Since no Arab country, including the Palestinian Authority, agreed to accept them, they remained in tents on the Libyan–Egyptian border and in boats in Cyprus harbour. Eventually, some were allowed to return to Libya and some found refuge in Syria. In the beginning of 1997, some Palestinians still remained in the Libyan border area (Farsoun and Zacharia 1997).

2.3.2 Libyan–Israeli Tension

Israeli–Libyan relations became particularly tense in 1973, when on 21 February a Libyan Airlines plane en route to Cairo lost its bearings and headed towards the Sinai Peninsula, where it was shot down by an Israeli aircraft, killing 108 Libyan passengers. Despite Israel's explanation that the airliner was mistakenly shot down by pilots who believed it to be a military aircraft on its way to destroy Israel's nuclear reactor in Dimona, the incident greatly antagonized Tripoli.

Libya was also unhappy about being sidelined prior to the Yom Kippur War, but although Libya criticized the direction and the objectives of the war, it still supported it (Deeb 1991), with Libyan forces being stationed in Egypt before the war began. But the limited successes of the war provided Tripoli with an opportunity to criticize Syria and Egypt for their restricted objectives and Jordan for not even daring to challenge Israel. In Libya's view it was a far cry from being the total war of liberation it had hoped for. When the ceasefire negotiations began, Colonel Qadhafi was infuriated. In a message alluding to Sadat's ceasefire agreement with Israel, he said that what happened at Kilometer 101 was "a terrible and peculiar nightmare" to him, and that the Arabs should have maintained their honour by continuing the struggle against Israel at all costs.

In an interview to Le Monde shortly after the war, Colonel Qadhafi exploited the opportunity to vent his anger against Sadat and Assad, who did not consult him before going to war. He dismissed their plan as worthless saying, "I can't take part in a war which I regard as a comedy." According to Qadhafi, the Arabs' main objective should not be to recover the territories conquered by Israel, but to liberate Palestine. He explained that participating in such a war was beneath his dignity and went on to say, "I will not participate in any war unless its objective is the expulsion of the usurpers and the return of the Jews of Europe to the countries whence they came" (Tremlett 1993).

The Israeli viewpoint was that militarily Libya's attitude did not constitute a serious threat. However, Libyan aid to the Palestinian radicals enraged many Israelis and caused friction between Israel and its Western allies. Thus, for example, in the autumn of 1973, Arab commandos were reported to have had a scheme to launch a surface-to-air missile at an EL AL jet, which was about to take off from Leonardo Da Vinci airport in Rome. When the Italian authorities released the suspects and flew them to Tripoli on the grounds that there was no sufficient evidence to convict them, Israeli Prime Minister Golda Meir said that Italy needed to be warned not to collaborate with Tripoli.

The tension in Libyan–Israeli relations increased further in the summer of 1976, when Israel carried out its spectacular raid on Entebbe's Airport in Uganda, in an attempt to free the Israeli passengers held hostage by Palestinian commandos. This event greatly outraged Tripoli. As a result of this, Libya's campaign in the United Nations became acrimonious. Its representative joined Benin and Tanzania in sponsoring a resolution demanding that Israel compensate Uganda for all losses that occurred during the raid. While Tunisia and Morocco responded to the raid in a moderate fashion, Tripoli lashed out at the United States and threatened to cut off all oil exports unless it stopped supporting Israel.

Libya's policy towards Israel continued the same pattern of hostility during the 1980s. On 1 September 1980, Libya proposed a union with Syria. The Syrian government agreed and both sides decided to establish a democratic union against Zionism, imperialism and reaction. However, the plan never got off the ground as the past hostility between Libya and Egypt lessened following Sadat's assassination on 6 October 1981. But Libyan–Israeli antagonism continued, and on 13 July 1982, Tripoli announced that it had discovered a joint Egyptian–Israeli plot to attack Libya

(Sicker 1987). Moreover, Colonel Qadhafi himself blamed Israel for terrorizing the Arabs with its nuclear programme, calling the Israeli nuclear plan "real terrorism" (*Newsweek* 20 July 1981).

Libya continued to be suspicious of Israeli–Egyptian accommodation, and in a speech commemorating Syria's 21st anniversary of the revolution, he blamed Egypt for signing the Camp David peace accord with Israel, saying that Egypt allowed the Israeli Chief of Staff to inspect the Libyan border. He asked his audience, "Who can guarantee that the Israeli forces would not be capable of passing through Egypt and thus threaten Libya?"

What increased the bilateral tension even further were the reports that Israel had provided full support to the United States during its bombing of Libya on 17 April 1986 during the US Operation El Dorado Canyon (Black and Morris 1991). The Israelis responded to this by saying that Libya could be contained only with force. On 27 April 1986, Israel's Foreign Minister Yitzhak Shamir met Norway's Deputy Foreign Minister, who informed him that his government had increased its security measures against terrorism; Shamir responded by saying, "Security measures are not enough." When his guest asked how was it possible to convince countries such as Syria and Libya to desist from supporting terrorism, Shamir said, "Israel believes that the only way is a military strike similar to the one carried out by the Americans in Libya."

After the American bombings of Tripoli and Benghazi of 1986, and the US/UN sanctions of the middle and late 1980s, Libya began to experience serious economic problems, exacerbated by a falling oil price. Although Libyan anti-Israeli rhetoric continued throughout the 1990s, the end of the Cold War and the onset of the Israeli–Palestinian dialogue created a new reality, which Tripoli was forced to recognize. The decision made by Morocco and Tunisia to normalize relations with Israel had greatly irritated Libya. When a Moroccan economic delegation visited Israel in the autumn of 1993, Tripoli criticized the visit, saying that it constituted a violation of the Arab League's embargo on the Zionist enemy. All the same, beneath the rhetoric there began a thaw in Libyan–Israeli relations as it became increasingly obvious to the Libyan leader that his revisionist plan for a Middle East dominated by Libya could not materialize, leading to Libya's reluctant acceptance of the Arab–Israeli peace process. At a Middle East economic conference held in Casablanca in early November 1994, the Libyan leader asked Turkey's Prime Minister Tansu Ciller to visit Libya on her way back to Turkey. At that meeting he asked her to convey to Washington his willingness to accept the peace process and to turn over the two Libyans accused of planting the bomb on the Pan American jet. In return, the Libyan government asked that the United States lift its economic sanctions, and allow the two suspects to be tried in a neutral country.

Throughout the entire Palestine–Israeli conflict Libya has, among all the Arab nations, historically taken the most extreme anti-Israeli stance, and has repeatedly proposed that the only solution to the Arab–Israeli conflict would be a combined Arab attack on Israel to liberate all occupied Arab territories. Tripoli has consistently advocated a hawkish Egyptian–Arab policy against Israel aimed at its total elimination. The cumulative effects of its extreme anti-Israeli stance have been to marginalize the Libyan leader in the eyes of the Arab World.

The Israeli–Palestine struggle has continued for 30 years, and after the end of the Oslo peace process and the start of the Second Intifada in September 2000, it seemed that peace between Israel and Palestine has reached a stalemate, with neither side willing to compromise and attacks and retaliations endlessly repeated. But what also became clear was that violence which had been tried on numerous occasions to eliminate Israel did not produce the desired result. In 1948, 1967 and 1973 Arab countries tried to crush the state of Israel and failed dismally. In each case, Israel became stronger, and in fact further expanded its borders. It appears also that the results of the Intifada had not served to secure the interests of the Palestinians. There have been far more Palestinians than Israelis killed, and the Intifada appeared to have strengthened right-wing extremists whilst undermining the more moderate forces in Israeli politics.

In a more recent context, the "road map" for a solution to the Israel–Palestinian conflict was presented to Israel and the Palestinians by President George Bush on 30 April 2003. Later this was followed by a Middle East summit meeting, hosted by Jordanian King Abdullah II and attended by US President Bush, Prime Minister Sharon, and Palestinian Prime Minister Abbas in Aqaba on 4 June 2003.

However, the "Hudna" (cease-fire) announced by the Fatah and Hamas on 29 June 2003 ended violently on 19 August 2003 with the suicide bombing of a bus in Jerusalem, in which 22 people were killed and over 130 wounded. This led to a further escalation in the Israeli war against Hamas and the freezing by Israel of diplomatic relations with the Palestinian Authority.

On 6 June 2004, Israel's cabinet approved the plan for disengagement from the Palestinians in the Gaza Strip and northern Samaria. The Knesset endorsed the plan on 25 October 2004. This was followed by a summit meeting held on 8 February 2005, attended by Prime Minister Ariel Sharon, Palestinian Authority Chairman Mahmoud Abbas, Egyptian President Hosni Mubarak, and King Abdullah of Jordan, when it was agreed that all Palestinians would terminate acts of violence against the Israelis, and Israel would cease all its military activity against the Palestinians. On 15 August 2005, Israel's disengagement from the Gaza Strip and four northern Samaria communities commenced. Disengagement from the Gaza Strip was completed on 22 August, and from northern Samaria on 23 August 2005. By 12 September 2005 all Israeli forces had left the Gaza strip, with the Israelis signing a declaration confirming the end of military rule there after 38 years.

Now in a post-sanctions world, with Libya's rapprochement with the West firmly in place, Tripoli's approach to the Arab–Israeli conflict appears quite different, and its vision for the settlement of the crisis is embodied in "The White Book", a 12-page document written by the Libyan leader which analyses the history of the Israeli–Palestine crisis. The establishment of a new state, "Israteen", in which Palestinians and Israelis would live in peace is proposed as a workable solution, replacing both the existing ones. The rationale is that their present combined territory "is too narrow to accommodate two states, and that fighting between them is inevitable, because the land of one of them is the land of the other according to their beliefs" (Al Qadhafi 2002, p. 11). Other more pragmatic reasons for one state are that "the source of working force for Israeli factories is mainly Palestinians, and…there is interdependence between the two sides…let us say integration, in goods and services".

Israteen would have free elections, supervised by the United Nations, and would be free of WMD. Regarding several of the more thorny issues, Tripoli supports the right of return for Palestinian refugees who fled in 1948 and later, and proposes the internationalization of Jerusalem, as a special city for many religions, as well as Israteen's membership of the Arab League. In fact the proposed one-state solution, although discounted by many observers as unrealistic and impractical in view of the last 50 years of history, contains many merits, and is based firmly on historical and religious grounds, when, since the historical emergence of the Muslim religion, Jews and Muslims, as "People of the Book", have traditionally respected each other's religions.

This initiative is based on the legitimacy of various international resolutions and agreements. The right of return of refugees, for example, was stipulated in Security Council Resolution 191, while the internationalization of Jerusalem was recommended by the United Nations' famous resolution on the division of Palestine. This major shift in Libya's policy towards Israel was perhaps no more apparent than during the first 5+5 Euro-Mediterranean dialogue summit, held in Tunisia in December 2003 between five countries from Arab North Africa and five from Europe. Here, Col Qadhafi told a reporter from the Israeli daily *Yediot Ahronot*, "There is no place for weapons in the world of today" and "I take no stances against the United States or the Jews."

2.4 Relations with the European Union

As touched on in the introduction to this chapter, the proximity of Libya and the North African nations to Europe is not only geographical, with the town of Marsala on the far western tip of Sicily being only 150 km from the northern tip of Tunisia, and the Italian islands of Pantellaria closer to Tunisia than to Sicily, but also, in terms of history, political, where their fates have been inextricably bound together. Before the Arab invasion of 642, North Africa was home to a series of Phoenician, Greek, and Varangian colonies, and contained several important provinces of the Roman Empire.

In more recent times the relations of the North African nations with the European Union have been profoundly influenced by the colonial legacy of European powers such as France, Italy, Spain, and the United Kingdom. For example, Tunisia achieved independence from France in 1956 while, until 1962, Algeria, the most populous country of the Maghreb, was an integral part of France. Italy invaded the Ottoman provinces of Tripolitania and Cyrenaica in 1911, incorporating Libya into Metropolitan Italy in 1939, as Italy's "Fourth Shore" (Segrè 1975).

Today Italy is still Libya's most important trading partner, accounting for 39.6 per cent and 39.3 per cent, and 18.4 per cent and 18.3 per cent of Libya's exports and imports in 2003 and 2004 respectively (IMF 2006). In fact, even during the UN sanctions period, Italy pursued a pragmatic policy towards Libya, attempting to build good relations and benefit from Libya's vast hydrocarbon potential. By 1996, before the suspension of the sanctions, Italy had recommenced a diplomatic dialogue with Libya, which led directly to the signature of an Italo-Libyan declaration in July

1998, which attempted to resolve outstanding issues dating from the colonial period, as well as instituting regular consultations on issues such as terrorism, immigration, and religious differences, at the same time establishing an Italo-Libyan Commission to develop economic cooperation between the two nations.

But while Italy has achieved significant diplomatic success with Libya, the efforts of the European Union to engage Libya through the Barcelona process have yet to produce results. Libya has perceived its formation and objectives as eurocentric, essentially another phase of Western interventionism in North Africa. Its eurocentricity can be seen in the events which led to its creation. The 1995 Euro-Mediterranean Conference that launched the Barcelona Process was a deliberate act of the European Union to establish much closer relations between its Member States and 12 "partners" of the southern Mediterranean (Algeria, Cyprus, Egypt, Israel, Jordan, Lebanon, Malta, Morocco, the Palestinian Authority, Syria, Tunisia and Turkey). It attempted, in fact, to create a new security concept to replace the Cold War paradigm that previously underpinned Mediterranean policy.

With the dissolution of the Soviet Union, EU Member States no longer saw a nuclear threat or the potential for North–South conflict. Rather, they saw south–south struggles and a range of new transnational risks such as terrorism, illegal arms, drugs, and person trafficking as potential new threats to European security. Underlying these perceived threats is the huge differential in wealth that characterizes the two sides of the Mediterranean, seen as posing significant threats to Europe's long-term stability and prosperity.

But from the point of view of the southern component members, the European Mediterranean Partnership (EMP) is a very one-sided affair. From an economic point of view, the Arab countries see themselves as having little choice but to integrate into the European economic sphere in an increasingly globalized world. Again, the European concept of a "common destiny" for the Mediterranean region sits uneasily with the Arab members. There is also, with Libya and other Arab members, a feeling that the European members demonstrate a profound lack of understanding about what Arabic civilization and Arabs really are. In dividing the Arab countries into different areas of cooperation such as the Barcelona Process members, the Gulf States, and the balance of the members of the Arab League, the EMP is regarded with grave suspicion as a "divide and rule" type approach to the Arabs.

For these reasons, Libya has kept its distance for the EMP, with its traditional posture towards Israel as a co-member being perhaps a deciding factor in its policy towards this body. Currently, although based on the consensus among the 27 Euro-Med partners reached at the third Euro-Med Conference in April 1999 in Stuttgart, Libya can become a full partner of the Barcelona Process if it accepts the full Barcelona *acquis*; Libya remains a passive observer, attending Foreign Affairs Ministerial meetings, high level political dialogue meetings, and the Euro-Med Committee meetings. More importantly, Libya has also attended, as an observer, two high level sectoral Euro-Med meetings on Energy in 2003. However, in view of its new outward looking policy in a post-sanctions scenario, it is likely that this will change.

2.5 US/UN Sanctions and Their Impact on Libyan Foreign Policy

On 5 April 1999, after 13 years of US sanctions and 7 years of UN sanctions, the Libyan government turned over to British authorities two suspects in the terrorist bombing of Pan Am flight 103. Four years later, in December 2003, Libyan Foreign Minister Abdel Rahman ShalGam announced his government's decision to discontinue its production of WMD (White House 19 December 2003). What happened in those years to cause a change in Libyan policy with respect to terrorism and WMD? What were the main factors and considerations that contributed to Libya's foreign policy reversal? We believe that some answers to these questions can be found by examining the influence of US policy towards Libya through four successive US presidential administrations: the Reagan, George H.W. Bush, Clinton, and George W. Bush. US policy will also be examined in the light of UN sanctions and other relevant events to determine what, if any, and how the US strategy towards Libya was applied, and how it contributed to Libyan foreign policy change. This analysis will in general demonstrate that while US influenced strategy did not succeed in the short term, it was ultimately successful in forcing Libyan policy changes in the long haul.

To fully understand the Reagan Administration's dealings with Libya, it is important to briefly examine US relations with Libya up to 1980. At the time of the revolution in 1969, US foreign policy towards the new Libyan government was conciliatory. The Revolutionary Command Council (RCC) had declared itself anti-Soviet, anti-communist, and non-aligned, and therefore initially appeared to support Washington's concerns about the potential spread of communism in the Middle East.

Prior to 1973, Washington's dealings with Libya can be considered to be cordial if not exactly friendly, with Washington adopting a wait-and-see attitude towards the new Libyan regime. However, a series of events in 1973 led the US government to alter its conciliatory policy in favour of an opposition stance to the new Libyan government (Davis 1990). The first event was the US discovery of the apparent Libyan involvement in the PLO embassy seizure in Sudan, resulting in the deaths of two US diplomats. Thereafter, two Libyan Mirage jets fired on US RC-130 reconnaissance aircraft operating near Libya in international waters, a situation repeated several times in the 1980s. The United States applied an arms embargo against Libya, blocking the delivery of eight C-130 aircraft that the government assessed would increase Libya's military capabilities (Davis 1990). US–Libyan friction intensified during the Ford Administration, resulting in the deaths of more US citizens abroad. In 1981 Libya further alarmed the United States when it declared the entire Gulf of Sidra a closed bay and threatened death to any violators of her "red line". This declaration, which was perceived by the United States as a clear violation of international law, was challenged on multiple occasions by the United States, often ending in direct military engagement. Over the course of the next 5 years, these confrontations resulted in the downing of several Libyan fighter planes and the loss of Libyan coastal patrol boats (Atlantic Council 2001).

The Carter Administration policy towards Libya was more engagement-oriented in the hope of improving relations, but though Carter was more conciliatory, Libya was not. The Libyan leader's anti-American sentiment and rhetoric increased due to the US efforts to facilitate the Middle East peace process and his own anti-imperialist stance. Finally, in 1979, the US embassy in Libya was shut down, and in the same year the US government officially designated Libya as a state sponsor of terrorism.

The period 1981–1985 saw a spate of attacks against US targets and interests throughout the world. The Reagan Administration in its rhetoric demonstrated an increasing concern over state sponsorship of terrorism, with the most likely suspects being Syria, Iran, Libya, and North Korea. Concurrently, Reagan expressed a growing concern, specifically with Libya's terrorism-based foreign policy. This period saw several "tit-for-tat" exchanges of military force between the United States and Libya. These exchanges were often the result of US military deployments into areas considered territorial waters by Libya and international waters by the United States. As a result of these direct confrontations between the two militaries and concern over Libyan foreign policy, the Reagan Administration took a series of diplomatic steps signalling their disapproval with the actions of the Libyan government. These steps included closing the Libyan People's Bureau (i.e. the Libyan Embassy) in Washington and placing restrictions on the movement of Libyan diplomats assigned to the United Nations in New York. The Reagan Administration also took economic steps to signal their disapproval, such as the denial of export licences for sale of technology that had military applications and any other exports with potential to be used against the United States (in conventional or non-conventional use of force). Finally, with Executive Order 12538 in the November of 1985, the Reagan Administration placed an embargo on Libyan oil imports to the United States.

On 7 January 1986, President Reagan issued Executive Orders 12543 and 12544. These Orders declared a national state of emergency with Libya and imposed broad economic sanctions against Tripoli, including the freezing of Libyan assets in US territories. Further, these Executive Orders banned travel to Libya by US citizens and resident aliens. US–Libyan relations thus deteriorated significantly during the Reagan Administration. After numerous terrorist attacks against US targets and interests overseas, the Reagan Administration, being convinced of Libyan complicity, applied an aggressive strategy to punish Tripoli for their support of the Palestinian movement. To deter Libya, the Reagan Administration went so far as to conduct air strikes against Libyan targets in Benghazi and Tripoli.

In the end, however, the policy failed to effect any substantial change in Libyan policy and its support of global radical movements. Libyan analyst Ronald Bruce St. John argues convincingly that despite the efforts of the Reagan Administration, Libya's foreign policy did not change during the 1980s in "content or direction" (St. John 2002). Commenting on the failure of the 1986 air strikes to achieve the desired change in Libyan policy, St. John wrote:

> While there were significant shifts in the foreign and domestic policies of the Libyan government in the coming twelve months. . . . few of them supported the objectives articulated by the Reagan administration when it launched the attack. After a period of seclusion, Col Qadhafi returned to the world stage with the major tenets of his

> policies intact. His support for state-sponsored terrorism might now be more circumspect, but he remained adamantly opposed to the international status quo and determined to employ all of Libya's resources to overthrow it. (St. John 2002)

It can also be maintained that the 1986 air strikes actually increased support for Colonel Qadhafi, and strengthened him in his agenda struggle against US imperialism. The April 1986 bombing raid, designed by the United States, in fact, to assassinate Qadhafi using state-of-the-art precision bombing, and overthrow the Libyan government, had the opposite effect as it actually strengthened resistance against US foreign policy. Furthermore, the continued diplomatic and economic involvement by Libya's primary trade partners in Europe such as Italy, Germany, Spain and the United Kingdom weakened US punitive measures, by providing petroleum markets and developmental support to fill the void left by the United States.

During the first Bush Administration (1989–1993) US–Libyan relations were initially characterized by rhetoric and diplomatic exchanges over WMD. Later, after 14 November 1991, the indictment of two Libyans for the Pan Am 103 bombing became the prime focus of US policy. US actions against Libya in this period included continued support for the national state of emergency and economic sanctions established with Executive Orders 12543 and 12544, increased flight restrictions on aircraft going to or coming from Libya in April 1992 (*Bush Public Papers* 1993), and the freezing of an additional $260 million in Libyan assets for a total of $950 million (St. John 1998).

There were no exchanges of force between Libya and the United States during the first Bush Administration, though, notably, the United States did conduct their largest and most successful military operation since Vietnam, Operation Desert Storm in Iraq. However, the Bush Administration went to great lengths to generate international support for sanctions against Libya. Although these efforts initially met with limited success, the level of international support changed dramatically when two Libyan citizens were suspected of involvement in Lockerbie crisis. On 14 November 1991, Scottish and American officials indicted two Libyan agents for the bombing of Pan Am 103. Following this indictment, two Joint Declarations were published demanding first that Libya support the ongoing bombing investigations and subsequent judicial proceedings, and second that Libya cease support to and involvement in international terrorism. Specifically, the US–UK Joint Declaration demanded the surrender of the suspects indicted for the Pan Am bombing, disclosure of any information about the bombing, and the payment of compensation to victims (*US Presidential Public Papers* 1992).

An additional US–UK–France Joint Declaration condemned terrorism and the states involved in it and defined indirect state involvement in terrorism as "harbouring, training, providing facilities, arming, or providing financial support or any form of protection" to terrorists. This declaration also urged Libyan compliance with the Pan Am and UTA investigations and demanded a Libyan commitment to ceasing support for foreign movements. Following the November indictment, the United States and the United Kingdom also pressed for a UN resolution condemning Libyan support to international terrorism and demanding their full participation in the Lockerbie and UTA investigations (St. John 2002). Their efforts were met with the successful passage of UN Resolution 731. However, UN demands on Libya were not met and as a result the United Nations passed Security Council

Resolution 748, determining that Libyan intransigence was a threat to international peace and security and imposing UN sanctions. This resolution demanded immediate Libyan compliance with the aircraft bombing investigations and the prompt, demonstrable, renunciation of terrorism. Additionally, UN Resolution 748 adopted the following measures, effective from 15 April 1992:

- Denial of the ability of any aircraft to take off from, land in, or overfly other UN states if the same aircraft had taken off from or was to land in Libya.
- Prohibition of the supply of any aircraft or aircraft components, aircraft engineering or maintenance, certification of airworthiness, payment of aviation-related insurance claims, or the issuance of new direct insurance for Libyan aircraft.
- Prohibition of the provision of arms or related material of all types and the technical advice or training relating to those arms and items.
- Reduction of Libyan personnel manning Libyan diplomatic missions and consular posts and restriction of the movement of those officials who remained in Member State's territories.
- Expulsion of and denial of entry to all Libyan personnel denied entry to or expelled from other States due to their involvement in terrorism.

These prohibitions, as will be seen later, began a process of international marginalization of Libya which was to have a severe effect on Libyan economic and diversification plans as the 1990s proceeded.

On its first internal review of UN Resolution 748 in August 1992, the United Nations determined that Libya had not yet complied with the requirements of UN Resolution 731 and threatened tighter sanctions with continued non-compliance.

Although, as stated earlier, there were no actual exchanges of force between Libya and the United States, it is worth remembering that Bush was part of the Reagan Administration's decision to use force against Libya in 1986. But Bush's successful use of force in Operation Desert Storm against Iraq in 1991, in every sense a significantly larger operation than the El Dorado Canyon operation against Libya in 1986, unequivocally demonstrated the technical prowess of US forces. It bolstered US military credibility, and showed the willingness of Bush to use force as an instrument of policy to secure the US international interests.

It is worth noting that Tripoli provided little appreciable support for terrorism during this period, indicating that the aggressive US military policy was having an impact on Libya. The UTA 772 bombing in 1989 was, arguably, Libya's last major act of international terrorism. Also, there are indications that Tripoli's support to terrorism actually decreased, involving the closure of Palestinian bases in Libya. Undoubtedly, also, the initial effects of the combination of the US/UN sanctions on Libya and ordinary Libyans, especially on its largely American-designed and American-installed hydrocarbon industry, began to be seriously felt throughout the 1990s, effectively crippling its oil and gas sector.

The Clinton Administration (1993–2000) made it clear at the outset that resolution of the Pan Am 103 bombing was the primary issue to improving relations with Libya. In an interview with Egypt's President Mubarak, Clinton articulated US policy towards Libya.

> The question was about our policies with regard to Libya. Well, as you know, we have one huge barrier that overrides everything else right now, and that is the determination of the United States to see that the people who have been charged with the Pan Am 103 disaster are released from Libya and subject to a legitimate trial....It is an enormous issue in the United States, and nothing else really can be resolved with regard to Libya until that issue is resolved. (US Presidential Documents 1993)

In the same interview, Clinton threatened tougher sanctions in the absence of Libyan compliance. "The President Mubarak and I discussed this today. I think that it is inevitable that we will press for tougher sanctions if the Government of Libya does not release the people that have been charged." The international community answered the call for tighter sanctions against Libya in the passage of UN Resolution 883 in November 1993. Citing 20 months of non-compliance with previous UN resolutions (731 and 748), this resolution ordered the freezing of all funds and financial resources owned or controlled by the Government of Libya, with the exception of petroleum-related funds, and expanded the list of equipment that Member States were prohibited from selling to Libya, primarily petroleum infrastructure-related equipment UN Resolution 883, November 1993. Unlike its predecessors, UN Resolution 883 provided explicit assurances that sanctions would be suspended with both the handover of the Lockerbie suspects and the compliance with the UTA investigation, and lifted entirely after full compliance with UN Resolutions 731 and 748. Following UN Resolution 883, the Clinton Administration subsequently reinforced the US trade embargo by prohibiting the re-export of US-originated goods from third-party countries to Libya, including equipment used in the refining and transportation of oil. Furthermore, Clinton called for even stronger measures against Libya, including a worldwide oil embargo:

> The United States continues to believe that still stronger international measures than those mandated by UNSC Resolution 883, including a worldwide oil embargo, should be enacted if Libya continues to defy the international community. We remain determined to ensure the perpetrators of the terrorist acts against Pan Am 103 and UTA 772 are brought to justice. (US Presidential Documents 1994)

Clinton's determination to increase pressure on states which supported regional terrorism would reach its peak in late 1996. During the first few years of his administration, the United States had suffered a series of minor attacks on persons overseas and at least two major attacks: the 1993 World Trade Centre car bombing and the 1996 Al Khobar Towers truck bombing. Additionally, the world witnessed the first use of chemical weapons in a terrorist attack in 1995, when the Aum Shinri-kyu cult used Sarin gas against passengers in two different Tokyo subway stations. In mid-1995 Clinton began speaking about the nexus of rogue states, international terrorism, and WMD and the need to contain states involved in these activities, namely Iran, Iraq, and Libya (US Presidential Documents 1995). The outcome of this discussion was a three-pronged strategy aimed at eliminating terrorism, step one being the containment of state sponsors. To that end, Clinton signed the 5-year Iran–Libya Sanctions Act (ILSA) on 5 August 1996. This controversial legislation placed sanctions on non-US companies investing money in Iran or Libya. The intent of this measure was to target foreign investment in Iranian and Libyan petroleum sectors; in so doing, the United States hoped to limit Iranian and Libyan capabilities to finance terrorist operations and WMD programmes (US Presidential Documents 1996).

The ILSA was not well received by US allies, particularly European countries who felt that US laws were being applied extraterritorially to their citizens. To avoid a major trade dispute between the United States and the Europen Union, its largest trade and investment partner, Clinton waived ILSA sanctions against the first European-based sanctions violator in the May of 1998. This waiver and the US promise of future waivers for similar violators were accompanied by assurances from the European Union of increased cooperation on non-proliferation and counter-terrorism issues (US Presidential Documents 1998).

Although during the Clinton Administration terrorism was the primary focal point in the US–Libyan relationship, Libya's continued pursuit of a chemical weapons capability became an issue again in 1996. Concerns emerged around this time that Libya was nearing completion of a large, secure chemical weapons complex at Tarhuna, which when complete would be the largest underground chemical weapons plant in the world (Shenon 1996).

Subsequently, Secretary of Defence William Perry clarified in an interview that the United States had no intention of allowing the plant to become fully operational, hinting at a willingness to use force, even nuclear weapons, as needed. The Libyan response was to claim that the Tarhuna complex was part of the Great Man-Made River Project to provide better irrigation to northern Libya and not a chemical weapons plant. Despite the threatened use of force, Assistant Secretary of Defence Kenneth Bacon followed up the Perry statements with assurances that the United States was pursuing diplomatic and economic tools as a "first line of defence" against the completion of Tarhuna: "Our first line of preventive defence is diplomacy. Diplomacy has worked in this connection before. We believe it will work again. We're not trying to saber-rattle in this. We want to be very clear. We are not talking about using nuclear weapons against the Tarhuna Plant" (Bacon 1996). True to form, the Clinton Administration did pursue this issue further via diplomatic means. This was through its ratification of the Chemical Weapons Convention (CWC). The CWC was created to ensure the disarmament of chemical weapons under precise international controls. Signatories pledged to destroy their existing chemical weapons and production facilities. The convention punishes non-signatories by denying them access to treaty-controlled chemicals. Initially there was disagreement between the executive and the legislative branches on details of the convention, but the United States did eventually ratify the CWC on 24 April 1997.

It is clear that Clinton believed in the fundamental building blocks of the US influence policy towards Libya, namely the denial of resources needed to fund international movements and produce WMD. He strengthened the previously established US policy by continuing the national emergency and sanctions regime throughout his administration; he called repeatedly for tighter international sanctions against Libya in response to its non-compliance with international demands, including a worldwide oil embargo; and at the risk of damaging relations with US allies in Europe, he signed the ILSA in an attempt to limit Libya's options. What is unique about Clinton's approach to Libya, however, is that after having strengthened the American posture towards Libya with no apparent change in

Libya's stance, his administration changed tactics and pursued a policy of limited conditional engagement, a policy which eventually resulted in the handover of the two Lockerbie suspects. In a small but highly significant change of policy towards Libya, the Clinton Administration acceded to Libyan demands that the Pan Am 103 trial take place in a neutral third-party country, the Netherlands. The announcement of this concession by the then Secretary of State Albright in the August of 1998 was accompanied by an admission that the United States felt that sanctions were not working to bring the Lockerbie case to trial and a new approach was needed. Though this was a non-punitive move, a first in US policy towards Libya, the offer was accompanied by very clear boundaries:

> Today, I'm announcing another effort to bring terrorists to justice. It has been a decade since Pan Am flight 103 exploded over Lockerbie, Scotland. . . . Unfortunately, year after year has passed without resolution. The sanctions have not altered Libyan intransigence. . . . The cause of justice was not being served. . . . We now challenge Libya to turn promises into deeds…the plan the US and UK are putting forward is a "take-it-or-leave-it" proposition. It is not subject to negotiation or change, nor should it be subject to additional foot dragging. (Lippman 2000)

The United Nations welcomed this concession and shortly thereafter passed a new resolution reaffirming previous resolutions, assuring the immediate suspension of sanctions with the handover of the suspects, and threatening additional punitive action should Libya delay further (United Nations Security Council, Resolution 1192 27 August 1998). Four months later, after having received mixed signals from Libya, President Clinton made reference to the Netherlands offer and threatened additional punitive action should the trial be delayed further: "Since then the Libyan government leader has given us mixed signals. We believe there is still some possibility he will accept our offer… This is a take-it-or-leave-it offer. We will not negotiate its terms...if the suspects are not turned over by the time of the next sanctions review, we will work at the United Nations with our allies and friends to seek yet stronger measures against Libya" (US Presidential Documents 1998).

Demonstrably, Clinton's pursuit of limited conditional engagement had provided the breakthrough for a series of small but positive steps by both states. In addition to handing over the Lockerbie suspects, Libya closed the Libyan training camps of the Palestinians and expelled them from Libya. The Clinton Administration perceived this move as a concrete step towards Libya's renunciation of terrorism. A State Department spokesperson concluded, "As far as we can tell, the Libyan government's actions are not window-dressing, but a serious, credible step to reduce its involvement with that terrorist organization" (Neumann 1999). In response, the Clinton Administration modified sanctions by not objecting to the suspension of UN sanctions, and also allowed four US oil companies to travel to Libya to assess the status of their holdings. Though these were small steps, they were steps which can be seen as the first crucial moves towards achieving the US objectives of securing major policy changes by Libya which would eventually reap results for both sides.

Shortly after George W. Bush assumed the US presidency in January 2001, the Lockerbie trial concluded with conviction of one of the two indicted Libyans, Abdel Basset Ali Megrahi. Tripoli's reaction to the verdict was to claim that the

Government of Libya had no connection with the Lockerbie bombing and to refuse the idea of compensating victim's families (BBC News 5 February 2001) In the same interview, however, the Libyan government signalled that Libya was willing to seek peaceful relations with the United States, should the United States choose to seek peaceful resolution of past conflicts. It declared, "If the US wants peace, we also want peace and we have no interest in war and confrontation." When asked whether the conviction would result in a change in US policy towards Libya, namely the lifting of US sanctions, Bush indicated that his intention was to continue sanctions until the Libyan government admitted to their complicity in the Lockerbie bombing and paid restitution to families (US Presidential Documents 2001). Accordingly, Bush renewed the national emergency and economic sanctions against Libya at each 6-month renewal point. Additionally, despite his uncertainty over the effectiveness of sanctions, he ultimately approved a 5-year extension of the controversial ILSA, arguing that the Libyan government had yet to meet all of the UN resolution demands.

It was, however, the audacious attacks of 11 September 2001 which brought about a decisive new era in the US policy towards foreign terrorism. In their aftermath, the people and government of the United States found a new resoluteness in the fight against terrorism; a swift and determined momentum to seek out terrorists and bring them to justice. This new paradigm guiding US foreign policy was articulated in Presidential speeches and also in foundational documents such as The National Security Strategy of the United States (September 2002), the National Strategy to combat WMD (December 2002), and the National Strategy for Combating Terrorism (February 2003).

The demonstration in practice of the Bush Doctrine was the 2001 Operation Enduring Freedom, a swift and effective attack on the Taliban regime and Al-Qaeda elements in Afghanistan. The second, more controversial demonstration was the 2003 Operation Iraqi Freedom, the hunt for WMD, removal of the Iraqi government, and establishment of democratic governance in Iraq. With the whole world's media aware of these dramatic US foreign policy moves, it is hard to imagine that Tripoli was uninfluenced.

In fact for Libya the entire Lockerbie saga had, from a Libyan foreign policy perspective, also been part of a well-orchestrated if subtle operation to secure Libya's re-admittance into the international community. Throughout this complex affair Libya had yielded gradually, securing at the same time tangible results for her concessions. Even the support and strength of the Bush Doctrine and the momentum following 9/11 did not bring Libya back into the international fold, since Libya also had her own foreign agenda.

In conjunction with Libya's gradual and conditional re-engagement, British diplomacy had also worked in tandem with the Bush Administration's hard-line policy to facilitate Libyan policy change. The United Kingdom had severed diplomatic ties with Libya in 1984 after policewoman Yvonne Fletcher was allegedly shot near the Libyan embassy in London. As with the 1988 Lockerbie bombing, Tripoli initially refused to accept responsibility for the act; but in 1999 Libya agreed to pay compensation to Fletcher's family. Britain then restored diplomatic relations and subsequently took a leading role in mediating the resolution of, first, the Lockerbie settlement and, later, US WMD concerns. In the latter case, Libyan intelligence officials contacted British MI6 officials proposing an exchange of data on suspected terrorists as well as to seek their support in resolving US WMD concerns as early as March 2003, before, in fact, the beginning of Operation Iraqi Freedom (Tyler 2004). Between March and December 2003, British and US diplomats worked with their Libyan counterparts to hammer out the details of what would be Libya's December 19 renunciation of WMD. British diplomatic efforts served as a balance to US punitive rhetoric and actions and provided a means to positive reconciliation of the Libyan leadership with the international community and the United States.

From the US standpoint, their long international diplomatic and economic-sanctions-based approach which had commenced 17 years earlier was still in place right up until the final moment of Libya's renunciation of WMD. For example, the Director of Central Intelligence reported to Congress in both 2002 and 2003 that Libya was continuing to pursue offensive nuclear, chemical, and biological weapons capability and since the lifting of UN sanctions had renewed contacts necessary to do so (CIA 2003). Similarly, in testimony before the House International Relations Committee, Under Secretary of State for Arms Control and International Security John Bolton articulated Bush's larger strategy to stop WMD proliferation:

> We aim ultimately not just to prevent the spread of WMD, but also to eliminate or "roll back" such weapons from rogue states and terrorist groups that already possess them or are close to doing so. . . . While we pursue diplomatic dialogue wherever possible, the United States and its allies must be willing to deploy more robust techniques, such as (1) economic sanctions; (2) interdiction and seizure...and (3) as the case of Iraq demonstrates, pre-emptive military force where required. . . . Proliferators, and especially states still deliberating whether to seek WMD, must understand that they will pay a high price for their efforts.

In October 2003, again demonstrating resolve behind their rhetoric and the sanctions, an American-led Proliferation Security Initiative (PSI) team intercepted a German-flagged ship, *BBC China*, bound for Libya with 1,000 fully assembled gas centrifuges and related components.

But not everyone is convinced, however, that Bush Administration policies, particularly the war in Iraq, were the key to Libyan policy changes. Many argued after Libya's December 2003 announcement that international diplomacy and the willingness of first Clinton then Bush to engage in conditional engagement were the critical factors in Libya's return to the international community. In his assessment of Libyan foreign policy change, Flynt Leverett, Senior Director for Middle Eastern affairs at the National Security Council (2002–2003), argued for the application of both sticks and carrots: "The lesson from Libya's policy changes is incontrovertible: to persuade a rogue regime to get out of the terrorism business and give up its weapons of mass destruction, we must not only apply pressure but also make clear the potential benefits of cooperation."

To conclude, we can state that in the case of Libya, US and UN sanctions worked together to isolate Libya from the world both economically and diplomatically. Combined, sanctions targeted Libya's petroleum industry, as its primary revenue generator. This was done to punish Libya for suspected involvement in terrorism and WMD and also to limit the funds available to the Libyan government for its ambitious foreign policy. The Libyan government estimates their economy suffered $33 billion in losses due to UN sanctions alone. The World Bank estimates this figure at $18 billion (Takeyh 2001). But because the US and UN sanctions were largely concurrent, it is difficult to determine in the long term if one was more effective than the other.

The second factor influencing Tripoli's change of heart was the Libyan government realization that virtually the entire world had changed ideologically and left Libya behind. Between the imposition of US sanctions in 1986 and Libya's renunciation of WMD in late 2003, the international system had changed dramatically. At the outset of the US–Libyan battle for influence the world was bi-polar and Libya enjoyed a relationship with the Soviet Union, the primary ideological counterweight to the United States. The end of the Cold War effectively resulted in the world forced to accept US economic and political hegemony. With the spread of the process of globalization, anti-imperialism, Pan-Arabism, and other secular revolutionary ideals have largely dissipated in the face of global economic liberalization. With multilateral sanctions in place, and a poorly managed and performing economy, it had become increasingly clear to Libya's leaders that Libya was falling further and further behind the rest of the world economically.

2.5.1 Reassessing Lockerbie

Two key initiatives from the Libyan side secured the ending of the country's international pariah status. The first was the surrender of the two Libyan suspects in the Lockerbie bombing to Dutch custody, after flying them from Tripoli to an airbase near the Hague, on 5 April 1999. The second was Libya's letter to the UN Security Council of 15 August 2003 in which it stated, "out of respect for international law and pursuant to the Security Council resolutions, Libya as a sovereign state has facilitated the bringing to justice of the two suspects charged with the bombing of Pan Am 103, and accepts responsibility for the actions of its officials". This led to the immediate lifting of the UN Sanctions against Libya on the same day. A compensation payment of US $2.7 billion from the Libyan government to the families of the victims, deposited with the Bank for International Settlements in Basel shortly afterwards, sealed the deal.

But commencing from the earliest days of the official investigations into the Lockerbie bombing, the entire case has been shrouded in controversy. Even before the start of the trial in The Hague in 2000, strong doubts from many sources had been raised about the guilt of the two accused Libyans, Al-Amin Khalifa Fhimah and Abdel Basset Ali al-Megrahi.

Immediately after the crash in 1989 the hypothesis which dominated the investigation by the Scottish police and the FBI was that the bombing had been carried out by the Syrian-based Popular Front for the Liberation of Palestine-General Command (PFLP-GC), acting on behalf of Iran. Ayatollah Khomeini had vowed to retaliate for the US Navy's July 1988 downing of an Iranian airliner over the Persian Gulf, saying that the skies would "rain blood" and offering a $10 million reward to anyone who "obtained justice" for Iran. Ayatollah Ali Akbar Mohtashemi, Teheran's envoy in Damascus in 1988, was believed to have recruited the Syrian group for the task (Middle East Intelligence Bulletin June 2000). When Syria joined the US–led coalition against Iraq in 1991, the investigation unexpectedly changed course and in November US investigators issued indictments against the two alleged Libyan intelligence agents.

Two months before the disaster, German police had arrested PFLP-GC leader Hafez Dalkamoni and the group's chief bomb-maker, Marwan Khreesat, in Germany in possession of three explosive devices consisting of Semtex hidden inside Toshiba cassette recorders, almost identical to the one used in the Lockerbie bombing. In fact the only difference was that these devices had barometric triggers instead of electronic timers of the type that investigators claim detonated the explosives on board Pan Am flight 103. It was also reported that the US officials had received advance warnings that a flight to New York would be targeted around the time of the Lockerbie bombing. Stephen Green, a senior Drug Enforcement Agency (DEA) administrator, John McCarthy, the US Ambassador to Beirut, and several other US officials were originally scheduled to fly on the ill-fated airliner on 21 December, but they rescheduled their flight at the last minute.

Much more recently, many key personalities connected with the trial have expressed extreme dissatisfaction at the conviction of al-Megrahi. One of these is Dr Hans Köchler, the international observer of the International Progress Organization, nominated by the Secretary General of the United Nations Kofi Annan at the Lockerbie trial in the Netherlands (2000–2002), who severely criticized the trial in his official report to the United Nations on it. Köchler observed that the trial had been politically influenced and was in breach of legal traditions and principles. By abandoning legal principles and politicizing it, the trial became a "show trial" of the type that many Western liberals condemn in non-Western societies. In a statement in August 2003 he said, "It is to be recalled that neither in the trial nor the appeal proceedings at the Scottish Court in the Netherlands was any material evidence presented linking the sentenced Libyan national to the crime. The verdict was entirely based on inferences and circumstantial evidence. Many of the statements of the Prosecution's witnesses were contradictory – or even proven wrong in the course of the trial. The co-accused Libyan national, Mr. Fhimah, was acquitted by the Court – not because of lack of evidence ("not proven"), but because it was proven, in the opinion of the Court, that he had nothing to do with the crime (although the entire strategy of the prosecution was based on the assumption that the two accused had prepared the crime together)" (Köchler 2003).

More recently, Lord Fraser of Carmyllie, the former Scottish Lord Advocate who issued the arrest warrant for al-Magrehi, has also cast doubt on the reliability of the main witness in the trial, a Maltese shopkeeper whose testimony was central in securing a conviction against al-Megrahi, as "not quite the full shilling" and "an apple short of a picnic" (*Scottish Sunday Times* 23 October 2005). In the same article Fraser advised that Megrahi should be free to return to his native Libya to serve the remainder of his sentence.

Professor Robert Black, another key participant in the trial – Emeritus Professor of Scots Law at Edinburgh University, who was the proponent of the non-jury scheme whereby al-Megrahi and co-accused Al-Amin Khalifa Fhima could be brought to trial under Scots law at Camp Zeist in the Netherlands in 2000 – not only believes that the convicted Lockerbie bomber Al-Megrahi is innocent, but that his murder conviction "was the worst miscarriage of justice in Scots Law" (*The Scotsman* 1 November 2005).

More telling is the record in Hansard of 19 January 2005, in which the M.P. for North-West Norfolk, Mr. Henry Bellingham, asked, in a debate entitled "Lockerbie", in reply to a series of statements questioning the outcome of the Lockerbie by Mr. Tam Dalyell:

> Is he (Dalyell) aware of my constituents, Martin and Rita Cadman, who are the parents of one of the victims on the aircraft? Above all else, they want closure. They want the truth; for them that is very important. They want to get on with their lives. Is the Hon. Gentleman also aware that most of the relatives feel that the Libyan leader was forced into making his offer to them, for purely political reasons? They are not impressed by it; they want the truth more than anything else.

The pressure for a retrial has meant that an independent legal watchdog, the Scottish Criminal Cases Review Commission (SCCRC), will probably, after an enquiry into the case sometime in 2006, refer the case back to the Scottish High Court. For the time being the final words rest with Professor Black:

> I am convinced they (the SCCRC) will refer the case back and there will be a second appeal. This time, the right questions, I hope, will be argued. I think the conviction of Megrahi, on the evidence that was led at Camp Zeist, is the most disgraceful miscarriage of justice in Scotland for 100 years – it's as bad as that. It's not just that I think there was a minor mistake, and that these things happen in the best regulated legal systems – it is just unbelievably bad. Scotland's reputation throughout the world in the criminal justice sphere will be gravely damaged unless and until this is rectified.

2.6 Libya and the African Continent

2.6.1 Libya and Sub-Saharan Africa

Libya's policy in Sub-Saharan Africa has displayed a consistency in which, in line with the Libyan government's anti-imperialist and anti-colonial stance, it has supported governments and movements perceived to be in sympathy with it. From earliest history, North Africa and the Sahel have been interconnected through commerce and, latterly, the Muslim religion. European colonization of Africa in the eighteenth and nineteenth centuries disrupted these historic links, as overland caravan routes to the Sahel countries and Nigeria were made economically redundant by more competitive European shipping routes.

Two distinct phases of Libyan policy towards Africa can be perceived – the extreme phase of the 1970s and 1980s, which ended with Libya's pullout from Chad in 1981, later reinforced in 1994 by the International Court of Justice's decision in favour of Chadian sovereignty over the disputed Aouzou strip. In this phase Libya supported many African independence movements, in Angola, Guinea-Bissau, Mozambique, Namimbia, and Zimbwabe, as well as funding a wide range of African liberal and anti-colonial movements. The Libyan leader's ideology and his policy of trying to negate Western influence also ensured his long-term support for Nelson Mandela, Patrice Lumumba as well as John Garang in neighbouring Sudan.

However, in the 1990s a new phase took shape, in which there was a definite impetus towards the promotion of regional groupings, together with Libyan government involvement in resolving disputes between African nations, through its mediation and conflict resolution, both aimed at regional stability. The decline of the oil price during this period and severe domestic problems in Libya itself also began to place restraints on Libya's direct influence in Africa, exacerbated by the growing economic impact of the US sanctions.

This phase was also accompanied by a major shift in Libya's foreign policy, away from the Arab heartland of the Middle East, towards Africa. Appropriately in 1998 the Libyan leader declared that the Libyan state-owned radio "Voice of the Arab World" was to be renamed "Voice of Africa", and a number of African leaders breached the UN embargo on Libya. This second phase of Libyan–black-African involvement was also underpinned by Tripoli's disappointment with the negative stance of most of the Arab countries towards Libya in upholding of the international sanctions imposed on Libya after the explosion of Pan Am flight in 1988. In fact the Organization of African Unity (OAU) was the first regional organization to defy the sanctions, while South African President Nelson Mandela took the lead in helping to resolve the Lockerbie crisis, which eventually led to the lifting of the UN and US sanctions against Libya. These two phases were succinctly defined by Colonel Qadhafi himself:

> During the great wave of national liberation, I fought side by side with Angola, Zimbabwe, South Africa, Namibia, Guinea-Bissau, Cap Verde, Algeria and Palestine. But today, we can put our guns away and work instead to build peace and develop our countries. That is my role. War is now a thing of the past. Do you see South Africa or Namibia coming to me asking for weapons? Once, they did. But now, those countries are seeking economic, cultural, technological, agricultural and industrial development.

This second stage was consolidated by Colonel Gadhafi's speech at the extraordinary summit of the OAU held in the Libyan city of Sirte in September 1999, when he proposed the formation of a "United States of Africa", detailing an ambitious development plan designed to end war and underdevelopment throughout the African continent. The United States of Africa would emerge as a solid political and economic bloc which, although intrinsically rich in population and natural resources, has been undermined by "a capitalist veto". "In my view", he elaborated at Sirte, "Africa isn't a poor continent at all. It may not have any money to spend, but it has resources in the shape of raw materials." The main problem was that "capitalist countries don't want our continent to develop. They intend to keep Africa as it is, in order to extract its raw materials."

The post-Lockerbie period has witnessed a continuation of Libya's pragmatic diplomacy, with Libya's diplomatic approach enabling it to emerge as one of the leading mediators of African crises. It brokered the accord leading to departure of Chadian forces from Congo and an apparent reconciliation between Kinshasa and Kampala. It was also instrumental in convincing the many internal factions in Congo to resume discussions with an eye towards some type of reconciliation. In May 2005, Tripoli hosted an African mini-summit on Sudan's war-torn region of Darfur, in which the Libyan leader, emphasizing his role in helping to resolve African conflicts, stated, "The meeting will take place in Tripoli at the request of many of you", in front of representatives of two Darfur rebel groups (*Sudan Tribune* 11 May 2005).

The first explanation for Libya's diplomatic activism in Africa is that, as discussed above, when rebuffed by the Arab world, the country sought an international role through visible mediation efforts and significantly high levels of aid to African states. On the other hand, this is not to say that Libya is without friends in the Arab world. Libya has used its relationship with Egypt to escape isolation in the Middle East, while it also has close relations with Syria, Iran, Iraq, and Sudan, although relations with Saudi Arabia have tended to fluctuate. Even the moderate regime of Jordan and the Gulf sheikhdoms, especially Dubai in the post-sanctions period, have embarked on a rapprochement with Libya. Thus, the notion that Libya is seeking a role in Africa because it is denied a position at the Arab negotiating is only part of the truth.

The second rationale of Libya's involvement in Africa has been to gain strategic and regional advantage. Certainly, in Central Africa, the coalition of the states of Angola, Zimbabwe, and Sudan, which have attempted to maintain Laurent Kabila's regime in Congo, have close relations with Tripoli. For Libya, Kabila is a more acceptable ruler than the alternatives, as the personal relationship between the Libyan leader and Kabila goes back to the 1980s when Libya was one of the few states to support the latter's rebellion. Moreover, Kabila's ideas seem compatible with Libyan diplomacy, as he desires regional solidarity and is very suspicious of the United States, which supported Mobutu's dictatorship for decades. Thus, a negotiated settlement that keeps Kabila in power is likely to be in Libya's interests. A nexus of Libya, Sudan, Zimbabwe, Angola, and the Congo is consistent with Libya's ideological and strategic objectives. Such an alignment can provide Libya with a base of operations in the heart of Africa as well as an important bloc of support in the African Union (AU) .

2.6.2 Libya and CEN-SAD

The Community of Sahel–Saharan States (CEN-SAD) was established on 4 February 1998 at a conference of leaders and Heads of States held in Tripoli. The original signatories were Libya, Burkina Faso, Mali, Niger, Chad, and Sudan, joined by the Central African Republic and Eritrea during its First Summit Conference in Sirte in Libya in April 1999, and then by Senegal, Djibouti, and Gambia during the N'djamena Summit Conference held in February 2000. It currently has 18 Member States. In economic terms its main objectives are to achieve the following objectives within the CEN-SAD bloc:

- Free movement of persons, capital, and interests of nationals of Member States.
- Right of establishment, ownership, and exercise of economic activity.
- Free trade, movement of goods, commodities and services originating from the signatory countries.

Libya, as the driving force behind CEN-SAD, meant to position it as an African Regional Economic Community (REC), one of the basic building blocks of African unity and integration, in line with the concept of RECs laid down in the OAU Abuja Treaty for Establishing the African Economic Community of 1991. Originally five RECs were designated – the Southern Africa Development Community (SADC); the Economic Community of Central African States (ECCAS); the Economic Community of West African States (ECOWAS); Common Market for Eastern and Southern Africa (COMESA); and the Arab Maghreb Union (AMU). It is worth noting that in the long-term time frame of 40 years for achieving its economic objectives envisaged by the Abuja treaty of 1991, the coordination and harmonization of tariff and non-tariff barriers among various RECs with a view to establishing an African Common market is a major goal.

Because the AMU, as we have seen, was virtually from its foundation a "dead duck" because of internal Algerian–Moroccan tensions over the Western Sahara, the Libyan leader, in frustration, decided to establish and consolidate CEN-SAD as a regional replacement for the AMU, at the same time stamping his authority and patronage over this body as another platform for his African policy. It is worth noting that Tunisia and Morocco are members, while recently the Libyan leader has been trying to get Algeria to join. Presently, CEN-SAD has 23 members after Ghana and Sierra Leone joined during its Seventh Ordinary Session in Burkina Faso in early June 2005. Unsurprisingly, the Secretariat of CEN-SAD is located in Libya.

Overlapping membership of some members of CEN-SAD with other RECs such as COMESA and ECOWAS currently represents a peculiar but not insurmountable feature of CEN-SAD. Full credit must be given to the Libyan leader in forging a potentially formidable socio-economic bloc as a powerful driver for his visionary African policy, aimed at the eventual establishment of a United States of Africa. The significant presence and acquiescence by key African politicians such as such as Hosni Mubarak of Egypt and Olusegun Obasanjo of Nigeria to be part of this 400 million population bloc means that CEN-SAD must in the future emerge as a very significant force in Africa.

2.6.3 Libya and COMESA

The treaty which established COMESA was ratified in 1994. Its aims and objectives, as defined in Article 3 of its Treaty of Establishment entitled "Aims and Objectives of the Common Market", are as follows:

- To attain sustainable growth and development of the Member States by promoting a more balanced and harmonious development of its production and marketing structures.

- To promote joint development in all fields of economic activity and the joint adoption of macro-economic policies and programmes to raise the standard of living of its peoples and to foster closer relations among its Member States.
- To cooperate in the creation of an enabling environment for foreign, cross-border, and domestic investment including the joint promotion of research and adaptation of science and technology for development.
- To cooperate in the promotion of peace, security, and stability among the Member States in order to enhance economic development in the region.
- To cooperate in strengthening the relations between the Common Market and the rest of the world, and the adoption of common positions in international fora.
- To contribute towards the establishment, progress, and the realization of the objectives of the African Economic Community.

From its beginnings COMESA has been primarily focused on economic concerns, and in many ways its establishment was a conscious and deliberate plan to deal with the effects of globalization, and in its website it identifies "the last decade of the 1990s as the globalization decade". Recognizing that globalization has many winners and losers, it goes on to state, "The challenge for COMESA is to ensure that, through its regional integration arrangement, domestic growth and competitiveness of small economies are strengthened, powers of domestically entrenched special-interest groups and rent-seekers weakened, and policy stability and credibility enhanced thus making it easier to attract investment."

The COMESA's initial goal of establishing a Free Trade Area (FTA) was achieved on 31 October 2000, when 9 member countries – Djibouti, Egypt, Kenya, Madagascar, Malawi, Mauritius, Sudan, Zambia, and Zimbabwe – eliminated all tariffs on products from fellow COMESA countries, while Rwanda and Burundi joined the FTA in 2004, bringing the total number of countries to 11.

Clearly COMESA, with a combined population of its 20 members of 374 million and its immediate neighbours Egypt and Sudan as members, was an organization that Libya could not afford to be left out of, despite concerns of overlapping membership with CEN-SAD. Accordingly, in March 2003 Libya submitted an official request to join COMESA at its eighth Heads of State Summit held in Khartoum, Sudan. At the time of its submission Libya's African Unity Minister Ali Abdel Salam Triki said his country supported "any African action that advances the development of the African continent" (Economist Intelligence Unit, Country profile Libya 2004). On 6 June 2005, Libya was officially admitted as a member, later ratified when Libya deposited the instrument of ratification in August 2006.

The rationale for Libya joining this regional grouping can be analysed on several levels. First, in economic terms, it seems that COMESA had achieved, in practice, with its initial FTA of 11 countries in 2004, many of the economic objectives that many of the regional groupings such as AFTA and UMA had been unable to achieve over a much longer period. In pragmatic terms, the attractions of membership of a functioning regional Free Trade Area also fits in well with the economic reforms and privatization programme which Libya embarked on in

2003. Secondly, as we will discuss later, Libya, in the context of its current diplomatic thrust to seek international recognition and respectability, would like to be a member of the WTO. There were obvious attractions in joining COMESA in this regard, since COMESA as a regional trading bloc was notified to the WTO under its Enabling Clause on 29 June 1995, and was the only African regional trade arrangement in this position, while 16 COMESA members were also members of WTO. Thirdly, the Libyan leader, seen by himself and by many as the legitimate heir of Nelson Mandela as senior African statesman, could also not afford not to be a member of COMESA. Although Libya was the driving force behind CEN-SAD, in terms of realpolitik it was highly desirable for Libya to have a presence in COMESA.

2.6.4 Libya and the African Union

Although in its earlier years the relationship between Libya and the OAU could be described as rocky, especially after 1977 when Libya occupied Northern Chad, Libya's interventions and support for many African governments had by the mid-1990s rehabilitated the Libyan leader in African eyes. For example, in the OAU Summit in Youande of 1996 the African countries adopted a resolution calling for the immediate lifting of UN sanctions against Libya. The African leaders further suggested that, should the Security Council fail to remove the sanctions, the OAU countries may find themselves compelled to act on their own to restore normal air links and trade with Libya in order to spare the Libyan people further suffering. Subsequently, resolutions calling for sanctions against Libya to be lifted were passed at every OAU Summit from 1997 onwards.

It was in fact in the Sirte declaration of September 1999 that the Libyan leader made his ambitious bid to become Africa's elder statesman. His objective was in fact a United States of Africa with a single army, currency, and powerful leadership, held by many to be akin to dreaming. It is, however, worth noting how far, in terms of a visionary plan for Africa, as well as deference to the Libyan leader, that the Declaration went. For example, Article 7 stated,

> In our deliberations, we have been inspired by the important proposals submitted by Colonel Muammar Ghaddafi, Leader of the Great Al Fatah Libyan Revolution and particularly, by his vision for a strong and united Africa, capable of meeting global challenges and shouldering its responsibility to harness the human and natural resources of the continent in order to improve the living conditions of its peoples.

In practical terms, Clause 8 (1) called for "the establishment of an African Union, in conformity with the ultimate objectives of the Charter of our Continental Organisation and the provisions of the Treaty establishing the African Economic Community" and called for "the shortening of the implementation periods of the Abuja Treaty".

The revamping of the OAU into an "African Union", with a new Constitutive Act to strengthen and update the organization's scope and mandate, was in fact scheduled to be launched at another extraordinary summit in Libya in 2001; however, the Lusaka Summit of 2001 decided that South Africa would host the

AU inauguration at the ordinary session of July 2002. At this assembly there were clear signs of dissension at the top, especially between Colonel Qadhafi and President Mbeki of South Africa. Libya proposed a range of amendments to the Constitutive Act, including a single army for Africa, an AU Chairman with presidential status and greater powers of intervention in Member States, again institutions in line with the Libyan leader's proposals at that came closer to a "United States of Africa". Qadhafi argued that since the Assembly was the supreme organ of the AU it could simply adopt these amendments and refer them to individual parliaments for subsequent approval. In his position as Chairman, President Mbeki made the procedural argument that according to Rule 8 of the Rules of Procedure of the Assembly, items proposed by a member state must be submitted 60 days before the session and supporting documents and draft decisions communicated to the Chairperson of the Commission 30 days before the session (Sturman and Baimu 2003). Again, for the time being at least, Col. Qadhafi's ambitious plans for a United States of Africa were temporarily suspended.

Clearly Africa, as demonstrated by Libya's key roles in CEN-SAD, COMESA, and the new AU, is now a focal point for Libyan foreign policy. In some ways African Unity is proceeding too slowly from the Libyan standpoint, which has led some observers to claim that "CEN-SAD has long gone beyond being a community of Sahelian states. Its members have adopted ambitious plans, including entering into obligations of a political, security and military nature. To many, CENSAD looks like a 'fast track AU' strongly influenced by Libya" (National Intelligence Council 2004).

2.6.5 Libya, South Africa and NEPAD

Africa's claim that the twenty-first century belongs to the continent has already been realized. The African Union (AU) and the New Partnership for Africa's Development (NEPAD) have become cornerstones of this realization since both initiatives are at the heart of the continent's political, economic, and social rejuvenation in a global setting. While NEPAD has been bruited as the blueprint for putting people first, within certain political circles there are doubts over whether such initiatives can reach their expected outcomes. At one level the initiatives appear ambitious, especially on the issue of good governance where it is expected that the practice of self-policing/appraisal should be carried out by Member States (through the peer review mechanism) on their performance. At a substantive level, however, two interrelated questions stand out: does Africa have the capacity to execute such plans, and if so, who will be the main drivers of them?

So far South Africa has been identified as the principal country to lead both initiatives. This was demonstrated in the way South Africa has eclipsed other countries to play a leading role in the AU and NEPAD. On the one hand, South Africa hosts the NEPAD Secretariat, headed by Prof. Wiseman Nhkulu (President Mbeki's economic adviser) and housed in Midrand (Johannesburg). On the other hand, South Africa is the first chair of the newly constituted AU, which formally replaced the OAU at an inaugural summit, hosted by the South African authorities in July 2002. Such responsibility places an onerous task on the shoulders of the South African government towards harmonizing political relations and fostering unity across the continent, especially if one considers that Africa has another major player in Libya.

Conversely, Libya's African momentum and ambitions for the continent may hold serious long-term implications for Pretoria and more importantly for President Mbeki's NEPAD vision. This becomes increasingly apparent when the role of these respective states on the continent are analysed. South Africa's role as intermediate between Africa and the resource-rich North openly clashes with Libya's originally perceived African role of expelling Western imperialism from the continent and establishing a United States of Africa. However, in a post-sanctions era in which Libya, after its renunciation of WMD, will become increasingly aligned to the United States and Southern Europe through the Barcelona process, it is conceivable that their aims for Africa might eventually coalesce.

2.7 The Post-sanctions Period and Globalization

The speed of Libya's rapprochement with the United States has taken many observers by surprise, but as discussed it has been achieved through a systematic process initiated by the Libyans which started as early, at least, as the Clinton administration. In the later part, its eventual success was actively aided by the United Kingdom, for the unilateral nature of the ILSA of 1996 had offended many European countries with strong historic commercial ties to Libya, as well as major US interests in Libya's hydrocarbon industry.

It came about through the implementation of "a performance-based roadmap (which) requires that clear, concrete steps – not simply commitments or promises – on one side be rewarded by agreed-upon, reciprocal steps on the other" (St. John 2003), essentially starting with the handover of the Lockerbie bombing suspects and concluding with the agreed settlement to the families of the Lockerbie victims.

From the US standpoint, it was seen as a major victory, and the icing on the cake, Libya's denunciation of WMD in December 2003, was hailed as such by the US president in his State of the Union Address in January, 2004:

> Last month, the leader of Libya voluntarily pledged to disclose and dismantle all of his regime's weapons of mass destruction programs, including a uranium enrichment project for nuclear weapons. Colonel Qadhafi correctly judged that his country would be better off and far more secure without weapons of mass murder. Nine months of intense negotiations involving the United States and Great Britain succeeded with Libya, while 12 years of diplomacy with Iraq did not. And one reason is clear: For diplomacy to be effective, words must be credible, and no one can now doubt the word of America. (George W. Bush 20 January 2004)

In diplomatic terms, the United States hoped that the rapid elevation of Libya's status would encourage other governments to cooperate with the United States and international arms control regimes, showing, for example, to Damascus that a similar framework for the improvement of US–Syrian relations could be worked out.

From a Libyan standpoint, common interests in the war against terrorism, the devastating effects of the sanctions, as well as a frank admission of the United States's overwhelming power, in terms of both intelligence capacity and military might, all played their part. Tangible benefits to Libya were immediate and dramatic, among the main ones being the return to Libya of the Occidental and Oasis Group (Conoco, Marathon and Amerada Hess) in 2005, as well as two highly publicized and successful Exploration and Production Rounds (EPSA IV) in January and November 2005, while Shell and BP signed major contracts in the petrochemical and gas sectors in the same year.

Libya's readmission into the global mainstream has also significantly enhanced the potential for the successful implementation of its current domestic privatization and diversification programme, although undoubtedly for a transition period, as will be discussed in subsequent chapters, economic dislocation and negative impacts on the country's still fairly primitive manufacturing sector will undoubtedly be felt. Few doubt, however, that over the next 20 years Libya will undergo fundamental social and economic changes as a new generation of Libyans discards the subsidy mentality and the country embarks on a major economic overhaul.

For the future, Libyan foreign relations will undoubtedly be much more restrained and less activist, aimed at preserving Libya's economic and political security, both regionally and in global terms. Despite the sanctions, or perhaps because of them, Libya has emerged in 2005 with many options. Relations and initiatives towards its North African neighbours have frequently been frustrating for Libya, but clearly the dynamics of the Morocco–Algerian confrontation has, for the moment at least, limited greater North African integration.

Regarding the Arab world, Libya's sense of disillusionment with its marginalization by many Middle East countries will mean that any major thrust or entanglements in this direction may be unlikely, although there appear to be signs of some sort of rapprochement with Israel, as witnessed by Seif Al Islam's comments at a World Economic Forum meeting in Jordan in May 2005. Here he stated that he had "no problem dealing and speaking with Israelis", although Libyan Foreign Ministry officials distanced themselves from Al Islam's statements, restating the official Libyan support for a "Single State of Israteen" solution to the Israeli–Palestinian conflict as outlined in Colonel Qadhafi's "White Book". Obviously, Libyan policy in the Middle East and its future relations with Israel will be strongly affected by any breakthrough in the Israeli–Palestinian deadlock.

Whether the country will continue to successfully play the African card, or re-engage with Europe in the light of its clear advantages of market proximity of the European Union is yet to be seen. Undoubtedly, Libyan standing in Africa is high, and investments through a special US $10 billion African Investment Fund will continue to grow, as synergies in the hydrocarbon, transport, aviation, and tourist sectors will lead to significant commercial opportunities for Libya there.

As for re-engagement with Europe, this is a positive direction that Libyan future relations might well take, in view of the imperatives of dealing with the huge EU market literally "across the pond". The strategic location of Libya cannot be denied, with its potential for becoming a major tourist destination and a prosperous entrepot between Africa and Europe both representing intriguing and desirable prospects for the Libyan policy makers.

3 The Libyan Legal System and Key Recent Legislation

3.1 Foundations of the Libyan Legal System

Because of European colonial influence, most Arab nations of North Africa and the Middle East assimilated, in the nineteenth and early twentieth centuries, legal systems and laws moulded on Western models, with only a few exceptions, in particular Saudi Arabia, North Yemen, and Oman, which maintained traditional legal systems utilizing only Islamic and customary law. This trend towards Europeanization was accentuated in 1830, when the Ottoman Empire, which still held a strong influence on its Middle East and North African provinces, adopted the French commercial code of 1804, replacing the Islamic code of Civil Law, "*Majallat al-ah Kam al-ad Liyat*".

Later, an influential piece of legislation was the 1948 Egyptian Civil Code, which again sought its inspiration in the French Civil Code; and the Egyptian Code subsequently influenced the Civil Codes of Iraq, Syria, and Libya. Of primary concern in its composition, of course, were the inherent tensions between the principles of Islamic Law and the Western commercial ideas and practices, summed up in the Qur'anic prohibitions of *riba* (interest), *gharar* (uncertainty), and *akl al-mal bil-batil* (unjust enrichment), the morality of which provides the source of much of the Sharia's systematic nature and many of its unique rulings.

This inherent conflict led the drafter of the Egyptian Civil Code, Abd-al Razzaq al-Sanhuri, to assert, "I can assure you that during the elaboration of this law we have abandoned none of the essential principles of Sharia. We have taken from the Sharia everything that was possible to take, bearing in mind the essential principles of modern legislation."

In Libya, these historical influences, together with Italy's seizure of its coastal provinces of Tripolitania and Cyrenaica as well as the Fezzan from 1911 to 1943, meant that the Commercial Code of 1953 and the Civil Code and Civil Code of Procedure of 1954 were based on French and Italian Civil Law, which functioned alongside Islamic legal principles known as the Sharia. As laid down in the first article of the Libyan Civil Code, the formal sources of the law therefore included legislative provisions, Islamic principles, custom, and principles of natural law and the rules of equity. In addition, judicial decisions and the thoughts and doctrines of eminent Islamic jurists also serve as informal sources of law guiding judicial decision-making.

In the Libyan Constitutional Declaration (Proclamation) issued on the 11 December 1969, several months after the revolution of 1 September, legal continuity was expressed by Article 34, "Regarding Old Law" which stated, "All existing provisions of laws, decrees, and regulations which are not in conflict with the provisions set forth in this constitutional proclamation remain in effect. References to the King and Parliament in these laws shall be regarded as references to the Revolutionary Command Council, and reference to the Kingdom shall be regarded as reference to the Republic."

3.1.1 The Constitutional Base

The 1969 Constitutional Declaration vested sovereignty in the people. The aim of the state was to realize socialism and to liberate the national economy from foreign dependency. Self-sufficiency in production, equity in distribution, work as right and honour are among the socialist principles specifically spelled out in the constitution. The 1969 Declaration guarantees freedom of opinion "within the limits of public interest and the principles of the revolution". It precludes discrimination based on race, sex, religion, disability, language, or social status. It also grants equal rights to women. Constitutionally, public ownership is seen as the basis of development, but private ownership is protected if it is "non-exploitative". Education, housing, and health are rights guaranteed by the state.

Many of the provisions of the Constitutional Declaration of 1969 remain intact, and complement the Declaration on the Establishment of the Authority of the People in 1977, the stipulations of which outline the general constitutional framework in Libya. The 1977 Declaration changed the official name of the country from the Libyan Arab Republic to the Socialist People's Libyan Arab Jamahiriya, identifying its ideological stance based on a form of Islamic socialism. Regarding the status of Islam as the official state religion stipulated in Article 2 of the Constitutional Declaration of 1969, the 1977 Declaration goes much further and states that the Qur'an is the constitution of the Jamahiriya, though in practice it is not generally invoked as such. According to the 1977 Declaration, only the people control leadership, authority, wealth, and arms so as to realize the "society of freedom".

As explained in detail in Chap. 1, the basis of the political system in Libya is the people themselves, who exercise their authority directly through the Basic People's Congresses, People's Committees, Trade Unions, Vocational Syndicates, and the General People's Congress (GPC), which is in effect the Libyan parliament. The GPC elects the Head of State and the General People's Committee, consisting of a Secretary General and a number of secretaries, each of which supervises one of the sectors of state activities. The General People's Committee supersedes the executive power in Libya that used to be exercised by the Council of Ministers defined by the Constitution of 1969. The Secretary General of the General People's Committee at the time of writing (Prime Minister) was Dr. Baghdedi Mahmudi. Technically, the Head of State at the time of writing, also Secretary of the GPC, was Muhammad al-Zinati.

It should be noted that the Constitutional Declaration of 1969 and the Declaration on the Establishment of the Authority of the People of 1977 do not form a constitution in the modern sense, and can be superseded by laws issued by the GPC. For this reason, the organizational structure of the Libya is in many ways an amalgam of often contradictory laws, with the most recent law taking precedence in cases of conflict. The general principle of organization, and the primacy of the GPC, has remained unaltered since the 1977 Declaration, but the internal structure of the GPC has been altered numerous times since its founding. In 2000 the membership of the General People's Committee, the effective government of the country, was reduced with many of its functions devolving to 32 Sha'abiyat or provincial governorships. Another law, Act 1 of 2001, reorganized the structure of the People's Congresses, who in turn choose the members of the GPC.

It is interesting to note that Article 37 (1) of the Constitutional Declaration of 1969 stated, "The present constitutional proclamation shall be in effect until a permanent constitution is issued. It will be amended by the Revolutionary Command Council only in case of necessity and in the interest of the Revolution." However, since 1969 there have been several key legislative enactments; among these are the 1977 Declaration on the Establishment of the Authority of the People, the Human Rights Act of 1988, the Human Rights Law of 1991, as well as important legislation regarding the position of women, among them the Law No. 176 of 1972 on Women's Rights in Marriage and Divorce, Law No. 10 of 1984 on Family Law, and Law No. 22 of 1991 and Law No. 9 of 1994, both amending the law relating to polygamy. Together these represent, from 1969 to date, a considerable body of new law relating to the basic rights of all Libyans.

In general terms we can state that in many countries the constitution is the main pillar on which effective government rests. The question which comes to mind is that in order to consolidate this significant amount of major new legislation covering the fundamental rights of Libyans, might this not be the ideal time for all of this to be unified into one Libyan Constitution, as proposed by Saif al-Islam Al Qadhafi at the the first forum of the National Organization of Libyan Youth at Sirte in August 2006.

This is because Libya, after more than 50 years as an independent nation, has now reached a turning point in her history. The protracted process of the lifting of the UN and US sanctions was successfully accomplished in 2004, and a reformist government is now in place, with a mandate for economic reconstruction and transformation. Will there ever be a better time to draft and issue a "permanent constitution" as provided for in the 1969 Declaration?

3.1.2 The Legislative System

The unicameral GPC, or *Mu'tamar al-Sha'ab al-'Aam*, established in 1977, exercises the legislative power in Libya. The GPC is made up of 760 members, who are elected for a 3-year term of office from a complex and changing network of around 2000 Basic Popular Congresses that theoretically involve all Libyan nationals over 18 years of age.

At the top of the political hierarchy, the GPC is composed of the officials of the congresses and committees lower down in the chain. The GPC has the power to issue decrees with the force of law. It chooses a Secretary (Head of Parliament) to preside over its sessions, to sign the laws by order of the Congress, and to accept the credentials of the representatives of foreign countries.

The GPC elects a five-member General Secretariat to make policy and serve as its permanent body. This General Secretariat prepares the sessions of the GPC and draws up its agenda. The Secretariat consists of a Secretary General and a number of Secretaries. These include the Secretariat for Women's Affairs, the Secretariat for Affairs of the People's Congresses, the Secretariat for Affairs of the Trade Unions, Syndicates and Professional Associations, and the Secretariat for Foreign Affairs. It meets for only 2 weeks each year. For the remainder of the year, the functions of government are carried out by the General People's Committee.

The GPC appoints the General People's Committee, which functions as a Cabinet. At the time of writing (September, 2006) the Secretary General of the General People's Committee (i.e. the Prime Minister) was Dr. Mahmoudi Al Baghdadi. Other Secretariats (Ministries) are Agriculture & Animal & Water Resources; Culture & Information; Economy, Trade, & Investment; General Education; Finance; Foreign Liaison & International Cooperation; Health & Environment; Higher Education; Industry, Electricity & Mines; Justice; Planning; Public Security; Social Affairs; Telecommunications & Transport; Tourism; Workforce, Training & Employment; and Youth & Sports.

The agenda for meetings of the GPC is jointly determined by the General People's Committee as well as the Basic People's Congresses and also issues raised by the GPC, while Laws are ultimately approved by the GPC. These laws are then issued as Executive Resolutions, the implementing regulations, by the General People's Committee, signed by either the Prime Minister or the Secretary (Minister) of the sector concerned.

In an international context the GPC is a member of both the Inter-Parliamentary Union (IPU) and the Arab Inter-Parliamentary Union (AIPU).

3.1.3 The Judicial System

In Libya the Maliki school is the predominant madhab, and as well as being fundamental in the Constitution, Islamic law remains influential in several ways. First, as everywhere in the Arab world, Islamic law is the law of the family, covering marriage, divorce, child custody, and inheritance though subjected to modernizing reforms such as Libya's Law on Women's Rights in Marriage and Divorce in 1972, superseded by Law No. 10 of 1984 which was in turn reformed by Law No. 22 of 1991. Secondly, as was noted in the case of the drafting of the Egyptian Civil Code, Islamic law has had a significant influence in the drafting of codes adopted after independence. Thirdly, Muslim judges in their use of Western legal language and concepts are undoubtedly influenced, whether consciously or not, by traditional Islamic doctrine.

At the time of the revolution in 1969 the judicial system inherited from the monarchy comprised of separate Sharia and secular courts. In 1973, Law No. 87 was passed, replacing the two-court system by a single-court system which sought to integrate Islamic and secular principles. Concurrently, the major legal codifications discussed above underwent significant amendments aimed at bringing them in line with the ideals of the revolution. It is from this period that many of what might now be perceived as obstacles to Libya's modernization and integration into the global community might be said to have emerged.

The Supreme Council for Judicial Authority is the administrative authority of the judiciary, handling matters of appointment, transfer, and discipline. The judicial system is composed of a four-tiered hierarchy. At the base are the summary Courts, located in small towns, which hear cases involving misdemeanours of lesser value. The decisions of this court may be appealed to the Courts of First Instance, located in each of Libya's three former governorates. These courts are composed of chambers of three judges and have the authority to adjudicate in all civil, criminal, and commercial cases. In addition, the jurors apply the Sharia principles in cases involving personal status. Cases from the Courts of First Instance may be appealed to the Courts of Appeal. There are three such courts, located in Tripoli, Benghazi, and Sebha. The Court sits in panels of three judges to hear cases. The Sharia judges who once would have constituted the personnel of the Sharia Court of Appeals now sit in the regular courts of appeal, specializing in Sharia appellate cases. The Supreme Court has five chambers: civil and commercial, criminal, administrative, constitutional, and Sharia.

The Libyan Civil Code of 1954 remains the primary law for civil transactions covering real and personal rights and obligations such as contracts, unlawful acts, and unilateral undertakings. It deals with specific performance, evidence, assessment of damages, and the contractual relationships surrounding sale, exchange, partnership, and agency. In the Civil Code a contract is created from the moment two parties exchange concordant intentions, and can be verbal, written or implied, when neither the law nor the parties require its expression. A contract cannot be revoked or amended without mutual consent by both parties.

Commercial and business activities are regulated by the 1953 Commercial Code. Here, a transaction is deemed to be commercial if it satisfies three conditions – it is listed in the Commercial Code, it is carried out by a commercial entity, and is based on the concepts of "speculation, circulation and enterprise". It also deals with sale, supply, lease, transportation and shipment, bank transactions and credit instruments such as Letters of Credit and promissory notes, as well as bankruptcy.

A new Criminal Code was adopted in 1973, and it criminalized certain acts against the security of the state and introduced the death penalty for "offences against the principles of the revolution", such as high treason, attempt to forcibly change the form of government, and premeditated murder. After the attempted coup in 1975, the Libyan GPC amended the Criminal Code, criminalizing a conspiracy with foreigners against the state, divulgence of military or state secrets, and possession of devices to engage in espionage.

It should be noted that traditional Sharia punishments like limb amputation and flogging are seen as inhuman in Libya. Without formally rejecting Sharia punishment, Libyan criminal justice extensively uses modern forms of punishment such as varying terms of imprisonment. While the death penalty is still applicable in Libya, its lifting is presently under review and highly likely.

3.2 Key Legislation Regarding Foreign Investment

As part of its reform policy, Libya began enacting various laws in the late 1990s, and this process has continued steadily since that time. However, it is important to note that, despite these major legislative reforms creating a more attractive environment for Foreign Direct Investment (FDI), the sanctions effectively meant that foreign companies were either unable or unwilling to invest in Libya, despite such major reforms. In the following section we have selected and analysed what we believe to be key enactments dealing with economic reform and diversification as these relate to FDI.

3.2.1 Law No. 5 for the Year 1997 Concerning Encouragement of Foreign Capital Investment

The above law together with its amendments and implementing regulations is undoubtedly the most important law dealing with foreign capital investment in Libya, creating the most liberal legal framework for attracting FDI ever adopted by the Libyan government. Many informed observers might pose the interesting question, "Why was this law passed at the height of the US/UN sanctions, when the Libyan government knew that foreign investors, even if they wished to invest in the country, were denied doing so by the tight conditions of the sanctions?" One reason perhaps was the signals sent out to the Libyan government by the international community after the introduction of the "second US sanctions", the ILSA, or the D'Amato Act of 1996. This unilateral piece of US legislation aimed at penalizing non-US companies investing more than US $40 million in Libya's oil and gas sector in any 1 year. The extra-territorial nature of legislation incensed European oil firms, many of which had a long history of involvement in Libya, and some even threatened to take their case to the World Trade Organization (WTO) (Otman 2004). Not only this, but Libya had successfully concluded several EPSA III deals with European companies such as Agip, Repsol, and Total for developing discoveries such as El-Sharara, Mabruk, and Al-Wafa in the period 1995–1997. The Libyan policymakers were clearly aware of the very high level of foreign investor interest in the country, and decided to build on this by constructing a more encouraging FDI framework (Otman and Bunter 2005).

The Foreign Investment Law attempts to cover not only purely foreign investment, but also Libyan private capital abroad. It opened up many sectors that were previously closed to the private sector and to foreign investment. Although it took a conservative approach and adopted a list of permissible investment sectors, rather than simply opening up investment to all sectors, the list of investment sectors is in fact continuously growing and will be discussed extensively in the FDI section of Chap. 7. The current list in the main covers Industry, Health, Tourism, Services and Agriculture, as well as any other sectors specified by the Ministry of Economy and Trade, and oil-related services not covering the upstream sector, which is covered by the Libyan Petroleum Law No. 25 as amended, as well as the Exploration and Production Agreements (EPSA IV) introduced in September 2004.

The 1997 Law provided the opportunity for 100 per cent foreign equity ownership of companies licensed under the law. It provided for various preferential treatments for licensed projects such as an exemption from corporate income tax for 5 years with a possible extension of 3 years provided net profits were reinvested in the project. It provided for an exemption from customs duties on imports of machinery, tools, and equipment needed for the execution of the project to continue for a period of 5 years during the operation of the project. It also provided for an exemption from excise taxes on exported goods.

Investors were permitted to open an account in convertible currency, to repatriate profits, to employ expatriates when there was no qualified local labour and to own and lease property for the purposes of the investment. They were protected against expropriation and permitted access to arbitration.

Yet, despite these incentives and the great opportunities in Libya, FDI has remained low. More importantly, statistics show that relatively few projects have been licensed, and of those licensed, fewer still are yet to be operational.

This is because, for the foreign investor, the problems associated with FDI are still perceived to be complex and time-consuming. Under the Foreign Investment Law, the licensing process is actually a lengthy procedure rather than one in which the Foreign Investment Board verifies compliance of applicants with a list of requirements. It includes an in-depth analysis based on criteria that are unclear to the investor. The minimum capital needed is left to the discretion of the Libyan Foreign Investment Board (LFIB) and is not specified in the law. The Board often requires a minimum investment of 600,000 euros.

In support of this process, the foreign investor must submit an application to the LFIB with a detailed feasibility study and a 5-year financial plan which will be reviewed by the Board. The Board, in turn, will make recommendations to the Secretary on the application and the minimum capital required for the company to be formed. This process is uncertain and the investors are given no guidance as to the requirements they are expected to meet to ensure approval.

The sectors that remain closed under the law are the very ones that are attractive to foreign investors. Telecommunications and the financial sector, for example, remain government monopolies. Retail and wholesale operations are restricted to Libyan nationals.

The Law does not afford "national treatment" to Foreign Investment projects. This has a significant impact when these projects have to compete with state enterprises and may have serious implications in the context of dispute resolution in the courts. Furthermore, Libyan courts would not concede jurisdiction to foreign courts and Libya is not a member of the New York Convention on Enforcement of Foreign Arbitral Awards, although local courts may defer to arbitral proceedings if there is proof that these will proceed in a timely fashion.

The real problems and obstacle are those that arise from the former policies. These policies go to the root of the difficulties surrounding foreign business establishment and operation in Libya. As a result of abolishing real property ownership for investment purposes, the commercial real estate market has been completely distorted. There exists now a private land market and a public land market with a price gap that creates considerable uncertainty for both foreign and local investors. Compounding the problem, the Foreign Investment Law is not clear as to whether real property can be used as collateral or even can be freely transferred without government approval. The Libyan government has, however, addressed many of these issues in Law No. 3 of 2004, dealing with the resolution of many rules relating to real estate ownership, in particular clarifying rental of houses to non-Libyans as well as the ownership of second homes by Libyans themselves.

3.2.2 Decision No. 21 of 2002 Regarding Encouragement of Foreign Capital Investment

Executive Decision No. 21 of 2002 Regarding Law No. 5 for the Year 1997 Concerning Encouragement of Foreign Capital Investment details the regulations covering the application of Law No. 5, and lays out in detail and clarifies many areas discussed above which were felt to be uncertain or ambiguous. Law No. 5 can be said to provide Libya with an investment climate for FDI described as one of the most liberal in the world, reinforced by the World Bank in July 2006 which described it, with certain reservations, as "rather liberal" (World Bank Country Economic Report 2006).

Part 1, Article 1, "Areas of Investment and Conditions Thereof", states that it is permissible to invest foreign capital owned by Libyan Arab nationals and subjects of Arab and non-Arab States in the areas of Industry, Agriculture, Tourism, Health, and Services of all kinds as well as other such areas as may be added by the General People's Committee. The law stated that it is also permissible for the national capital of natural and juristic persons to participate with the foreign capital in the investments. It also stated that the People's Committee of the Investment Board should determine the percentage of participation and the conditions to be satisfied for each project separately.

Duty-free importation of machinery and equipment for the approved project is dealt with in Article 13, stating that every Investor permitted to invest shall be entitled to import all the needs and requirements of the project from abroad whether in the form of machinery, instruments, or equipment required for the execution of the Project, or in the form of spare parts or raw materials required for the operation of the project.

Imported items shall be exempted, within the limits stated in Article 10 of Law No. 5 of 1997, from all custom fees and duties and taxes of similar effect imposed on the imports, in accordance with the following conditions:

- The items are imported in the name and for the benefit of the project.
- The imported items shall be commensurate, quantitatively and qualitatively, with the area of the permitted investment.
- The permit of investment is valid at the time of import.
- An undertaking to use such items in the Project and not to dispose of them in any way to any other entity without the written consent of the Investment Board.

In the event of approval of the sale of such machinery, instruments, or equipment to a person who does not enjoy a similar custom exemption, the Investor will have to pay the custom duties required thereon, which he had been exempted from.

Regarding exemption from Stamp Duties, Article 16 states that the investment project established according to the Law shall be exempted from the stamp duties imposed on the commercial papers and documents it uses.

The employment of foreign nationals is defined in a straightforward and unequivocal way in Article 17, and states that the investor is entitled to employ and import foreign manpower and technical foreign expertise needed for establishing and operating the project, according to the following rules and conditions:

- The investor has a valid permit issued in accordance with the provisions of the Law.
- The manpower imported should be qualified, technically specialized, and not available in the local market.
- The investor has obtained the approval of the authority.
- The investor should sign written contracts with the imported manpower specifying the duration of employment, terms, and wages.

Requests for the import of foreign manpower shall be presented to the Investment Board on the forms and according to the procedures set forth by the competent authority in charge of foreign labour. The Investment Board will follow up such requests with the competent authority and provide the Investor with the approvals as soon as they are issued.

Long-standing complaints by potential foreign investors on the ownership and renting of real estate are addressed in Article 22. Prior to this, foreign ownership of property in Libya had been prohibited, but Article 22 clears the way for ownership of property in Libya by foreigners, stating that the Investor shall be entitled to own land for use, rent or construct buildings onto them, and shall be entitled as well to own or rent buildings under the following conditions:

- That it is necessary for the establishment or operation of the Project, or for the accommodation of its employees.
- That the real estate is suitable for the purpose for which it is to be owned or rented.
- The investor obtains the approval of the authority to buy or lease.
- The land is suitable for the purpose of establishing the project thereon or its operation, and its use does not contradict the approved urban zoning nor does it cause any harm to the environment or the natural, tourist, or agricultural resources.

Finally Article 32, on The Transfer of the Investment Project Ownership, deals with a situation which is increasingly normal in a globalized world where transboundary mergers and acquisitions and asset swaps are happening every day, and states that the ownership of the Project may be transferred from one owner to another in part or in whole by way of sale or assignment. The person seeking the disposal of the Project shall submit an application to the Secretary of the People's Committee of the Investment Board containing comprehensive information on the Project along with the date and the number of the permit decision, name and nationality of the acquiring person, data on his financial and technical capabilities and reasons for the transaction. The transaction will become effective only after the following conditions are satisfied:

- Approval of the People's Committee of the Investment Board.
- The consent of all owners where there are more than one owner for the project; if the project is owned by a juristic entity the consent shall be granted by the corporate body designated in the articles of association of the entity.

As for the transfer of ownership by way of inheritance, the new owner or his representative shall present a certificate establishing that he or his representative is the legitimate heir, issued by the appropriate authorities in his country of origin authenticated by the Libyan Embassy in that country or by any Arab Embassy if Libya has no political or consular representation there provided there is

- A written undertaking to the effect that the project will continue in the same field of activity.
- An undertaking to the effect that the new owner will subrogate the former one in the rights, duties, and obligations arising from the Law and other legislation in force.

The new owner shall satisfy the same conditions as the former owner in so far as technical and administrative expertise and other qualifications decreed in this Regulation.

Taken together, it can be said that the 2002 Regulations, if fully understood by foreign investors, appear to make the investment environment in Libya very promising whether for real estate, tourism, manufacturing, agriculture, or a wide range of investment sectors.

3.2.3 Approved Activities for FDI: Decision No. 13, 2005

The Libyan Government has specified the list of activities permitted by foreign companies in Libya in the Decision of the Secretariat of the General People's Committee No. 13 for the Year 2005, and these are detailed as follows.

Contracting and Civil Works

- Roads paving and bridges and dam construction.
- Marine construction such as marine quays, barriers, and shipyards and seaport dredging.
- Airport and airstrip construction.
- Railway laying and station erection.

Electricity Sector

- Establishment and maintenance of power-generating stations and voltage increase/decrease stations of all types.
- Establishment and maintenance of cable networks to transfer electric power.
- Establishment of water desalination plants relying on the thermic and membrane methods.

Oil Field Sector

- Exploration for oil including the geological survey work for oil using different geological, geophysical, and geochemical means and other techniques.
- Inspection, analysis, and presentation of geological studies.
- Oil well drilling and maintenance, including the installation and provision of maintenance services of oil well drilling equipment, and submersible pumps.
- Cementing works and clay and mud services.
- Construction of oil and gas pipelines, tanks and pumping stations and their maintenance and the required cathodic protection.
- Construction of oil and gas exploration floating offshore platforms.
- Installation and maintenance of oil refineries and petrochemical factories.
- Marine transport services for the products and materials related to offshore drilling works.
- Mine removal from oilfields.
- Inspection and consultation of oil shipments.

This activity is granted temporarily to foreign companies' branches until the foundation of national companies with sufficient numbers to perform it, provided that such companies employ national (technical) manpower with a percentage not less than 60 per cent of the total technical personnel employed in the branch and its projects in Libya.

Communications Sector

- Wireless and cable communications systems and stations, installation and maintenance.
- Erection of stations, towers, and antennae related to the wireless communications and aerial navigation stations and their maintenance.

Industry Sector

- Electrical, mechanical, and electromechanical works necessary for factory machinery installation and maintenance.
- Metallurgical and metal exploration and extraction works except oil products.

- Thermal oven construction, building, and maintenance necessary for different types of factories.
- Installation and maintenance of industrial safety and security systems.

Surveying and Planning Sector

- Surveying, aerial photography, and mapping using different means and for different purposes.
- Engineering consultancy for urban planning.

Environment Protection Sector

- Erection of environment protection stations.
- Treatment and transformation of wastes and the creation of waste treatment and recycling stations.
- Treating environment pollution, and installation and maintenance of equipment designed for that purpose.
- Treating the interference of seawater with groundwater and the maintenance of water transfer and drainage networks and the elevated stations.

Computer/IT Sector

- Automatic control systems installation, and manufacturing and preparation of software, and their maintenance.

Consultancy and Technical Studies Field

- Preparing studies in the field of information and wireless communications and automatic control technologies and the presentation of consultation required for that purpose.
- Conducting technical and financial evaluation of major projects in order to determine their share value in the financial market.
- Design of major projects using advanced techniques in terms of installation and performance.

Health Sector

- Medical machinery and equipment installation, maintenance, and calibration.

3.2.4 New Libyan Taxation Law: Income and Corporate Tax

Libya's taxation framework dates from pre-independence when the Income Tax Act (Act No. LIV of 1948) was passed. This has now been completely reformed by Law No. 11, which was enacted in April 2004. It provides that all income arising from economic activity in Libya (and elsewhere) is taxable for residents. This new legislation provides an overall taxation framework and a mechanism for the imposition of taxes according to the economic activity carried out, and tax assessment and collection can now be carried out effectively.

There is a sliding scale of taxes on corporate profits and these are subdivided into trading profits (maximum rate 35 per cent) and industrial and handicraft profits (maximum rate 30 per cent). The law lists the schedules of taxes payable but not capital allowances. It also provides for a series of steps to be taken to resolve disputes between the Libyan tax authorities and the corporate bodies. Personal taxes are assessed on a sliding scale of between 8 and 35 per cent based on income. Exemptions are permitted for religious and other charities, certain income arising from bank deposits although there are other interest payments which are taxable, as well as income arising from books and from scientific and cultural research, export-oriented industrial operations, and certain agricultural activities.

The detailed tax provisions of Law No. 11 are summarized in the following section. First, the General Income Tax is cancelled, while there are reductions of the tax on wages and salaries as follows:

- Exemption of LD 100.00 per month for a single person from LD 45.00 in the previous law.
- Exemption of LD 150.00 per month for a married person with no children up from LD 60.00 in the previous law.
- Exemption of LD 200.00 per month for a married person with children up from LD 75.00 in the previous law. The new tax rates for an employee are shown in Table 3.1.

The new corporate tax rates effective from the year 2005 are shown in Table 3.2.

Table 3.1. Libyan income tax, 2005

Income	LD	New rate	Percentage
First	4,800	Per annum	8
Next	4,800	Per annum	10
Over	9,600	Per annum	15

Table 3.2. Libyan corporate tax, 2005

Income	LD	New rate	Percentage
First	200,000	Per annum	15
Next	300,000	Per annum	20
Next	500,000	Per annum	25
Next	500,000	Per annum	30
Next	500,000	Per annum	35
Over	2,000,000	Per annum	40

Other important changes are that the deposit for submitting a claim request against the tax assessment has been reduced from 40 to 20 per cent of the disputed amount, and penalties for delay in settling the amount of tax due is 1 per cent per month until a ceiling of 12 per cent is reached (under the old law, there was no ceiling).

As well as the above, there is also a Contract Registration Tax of 2 per cent for a main contract and 1 per cent for a sub-contract.

3.2.5 Company Law and Incorporation

The requirements for foreign companies which wish to perform work or services in Libya are, despite the progress made in recent years, still considered by foreign investors to be time-consuming and very expensive, and in practical terms these are counterproductive rather than conducive to investment in Libya. In general terms the legal background for establishing a foreign company for business in Libya is covered by the Libyan Commercial Code of 1953, the establishment of Joint Ventures (JVs) as provided for in Law No. 65 of 1970 and Law No. 21 of 2000, Regarding the Practice of Economic Activities, and Law No. 5 of 1997 and its subsequent regulations and amendments. In practical terms there presently exist four options for foreign companies entering the Libyan market, which are to establish a Branch office, set up a JV, register a Representative Office, or obtain project approval through the LFIB as provided in Law No. 5 of 1997 and its subsequent amendments discussed earlier.

Branch Office

To register a branch office, applicant companies must currently submit the following to the Secretariat of Economy and Trade for Foreign Company Registration:

- A 25,000-euro registration fee.
- A completed application Form No. 7, including the name and address of the branch in Libya, its activities, and the branch's capital.
- An original authenticated copy of the Company's Articles of Association.
- Validated extract by Chamber of Commerce or other official body proving registration of the company in the Commercial Registry where its main office abroad is located, including registration number and date.
- Certificates and attestations confirming the experience of the company in the fields of desired activity in Libya, issued by the organizations for which the company carried out work in other countries or in the home country, validated by the Chamber of Commerce in those countries where such works have been executed, issued by the company's clients and confirming the executed work.
- A certificate which confirms the transfer of 150,000 LD into the company's local bank account.
- A copy of the manager's passport.

- A board resolution covering the following:
  - The decision to establish the Libyan branch of the Company.
  - The objectives of the Libyan branch.
  - The name, surname and nationality of the branch manager.
  - An undertaking by the Board of Directors of the parent company not to interfere in the political affairs of the country.
  - An undertaking by the Board of Directors of the parent company confirming that they will prepare the Libyan Branch's Annual Budget/Balance Sheet and Profit and Loss Account indicating the financial position.

JV with Libyan Companies/Individuals

- Memorandum of Incorporation.
- Board Resolutions.
- Articles of Incorporation.
- Certificate of Deposit from Libyan Bank confirming the receipt in transferable currency of not less than 3/10 of subscribed capital of the company, including the share of foreign partner.

Representative Office

With effect from January 2005, foreign companies may open a representative office, but this does not automatically give them any right to sell goods or services in the domestic market, although in certain cases such a representative office may meet rules proving a local presence when bidding for government contracts. An application to open such an office should be addressed to the Secretariat of Registration within the Ministry of Economy and Trade, providing details of the name of the designated agent, profession, and mailing address.

Entering the Libyan Market Through Law No. 5 of 1997 and Later Amendments

In the section above, this law and the categories currently approved for FDI were discussed extensively. Because of its many generous incentives to foreign investors, as well as the very broad spectrum of sectors and activities now covered by this law, foreigners interested in investing in Libya should seriously consider approval through the LFIB under this law, which, as discussed, as well as containing a huge range of tax breaks and incentives also allows a foreign company to own up to 100 per cent of the Libyan entity.

Subsequent Requirements

Once a foreign entity has been approved by the relevant authorities, it must also register with the relevant municipality or Sha'abiyat commercial registry in which the business is situated. In general the documents supplied for formal registration and approval as discussed earlier will be sufficient for this. Additionally, a foreign company or branch must register with the Libyan Chamber of Commerce. For this the necessary original and certified documents in Arabic translation, including the Memorandum and Articles of Incorporation, a Power of Attorney or Letter of Authority to the local manager, and proof of registration with the Libyan Secretariat of Economy and Trade and the appropriate Sha'abiyat are required.

It should be noted that for all of the above registration/submission procedures the required documents must be submitted in the original and endorsed by commercial authorities in the country issuing the documents, such as a Chamber of Commerce or relevant Ministry, and all documents must be provided in Arabic translation. Translations from outside Libya must be notarized and stamped by the respective Libyan Embassy or Liaison Office.

3.2.6 Law No. 7, 2004, and the Future of the Libyan Tourist Sector

The promotion of tourism in Libya is one of the priority diversification areas for the Libyan Government, but clearly it recognizes that it needs to be handled carefully and sensitively, in order to maintain the unique culture, geography, ecology, and history of the country. Although aware of its potential as a hard currency income earner, as witnessed by the successful tourist industries of its neighbours Tunisia and Egypt, Libyans do not want their beautiful and unique country to be ruined by a low-cost, high-volume tourism strategy. It is with this development in mind that an ongoing tourist and investment document is currently being prepared for the sector under the guidance of World Tourism Organization. The Tourist Law No. 7 in fact goes a long way in defining these objectives, at the same time outlining a regulatory framework within which the industry can operate.

The objectives of tourism are laid out in Article 2 which lists the intended achievements of Libyan tourism, which are to

- Create employment opportunities for nationals.
- Contribute to economic and social development.
- Highlight the civilization and history of the Libyan people, and display its material and moral achievements and transitions.
- To show, individually and collectively, the modern lifestyle and social achievements of Libyans.
- Contribute to and elevate the national heritage.
- Enable Libyan individuals to relate to and cooperate with other nationals.
- Maintain tourist sites and utilities, and develop, promote, and cherish them, as well as providing entertainment for citizens and tourists.
- Exchange know-how in the different tourist fields and activities, through establishing conferences, symposiums, meetings, festivals, exhibitions, and tourist weeks, in Libya and abroad, and participating in these.
- Encourage Libyan and foreign investors to invest in tourist projects aimed at providing resources to increase national income.

Issues related to overt bureaucracy and the present recognized difficulty in obtaining Libyan visas are dealt with in Article 3, which states that the relevant bodies undertake, each within their own competencies, to provide suitable conditions to encourage tourism in Libya, especially with respect to visa granting, simplifying procedures in entry ports, welcoming the reception of tourists, managing their movements and lodgings, offering them assistance, providing security and safety requirements, enhancing the supervision and control on bodies offering services to tourists, in line with the executive regulation of the law.

Areas in which tourist development can take place are determined in Article 4, which states that the General People's Committee for Tourism undertakes to determine areas of tourist development and tourist attraction, to prepare detailed and general plans for such areas, and to give them a tourist character and to manage and supervise them according to approved plans, in coordination with the relevant bodies.

Major incentives for tourist projects are listed in Article 8, which states that, without prejudice to the exemptions in Law No. 5 of 1997, tourist projects are exempted from the following taxes and levies:

- Customs duties on construction materials, tools and equipment, furniture, tourist transport, and different types of equipment necessary to construct and operate tourist utilities and projects. The General People's Committee for Tourism undertakes to determine such needs and to approve their quantities.
- Income, buildings, and entertainment levies for a period of five years starting from the actual date of the start of the project, which may be extended for a further five years, by virtue of a decision issued by the General People's Committee, upon a proposal to be submitted by the General People's Committee for Tourism.
- Any other exemptions and incentives to be proposed by the General People's Committee for Tourism, with a decision shall be issued with respect thereto by the General People's Committee.

The establishment of the "National Council for Tourism" is covered in Articles 11 and 12, and its areas of competence are defined as follows:

- Proposing policies to ensure tourism development and promotion.
- Proposing and studying drafts of laws and regulations related to tourism.
- Proposing financial allocations necessary for the tourism sector.
- Handling cases related to tourism, which require cooperation among different sectors and resolving problems related to these.
- Coordination between public and private bodies having connections with the execution of the tourist development plans and programmes, and proposing the role conferred on each.
- Dealing with other matters determined by the Secretary of the Council.

Important issues related to the usage of non-Arab languages which have previously been prohibited in Libya are dealt with in Article 13, which now allows tourist companies and partnerships, travel and tourism offices, and tourist public areas, licensed to practise the activity, to use foreign languages in performing their activities and in publishing tourist advertising material in different languages.

Tourist Public Areas are defined in Section Two, Articles 14–17, as hotels, motels, tourist cities and villages, entertainments, camps, resorts, amusement locations, tourist restaurants and cafeterias, traditional industries and souvenir sale shops, and the like, and provides for their licensing and rates to be charged, in consultation with the Secretary of the General People's Committee for Tourism.

The tourist profession as such is defined in Articles 18, 19, and 20 as well as the roles of tourist companies, travel offices and guides, shipping and aviation companies, as well as land transport companies, and provide for their regulation and the procedure for obtaining licences and permits from the General People's Committee for Tourism to practise these professions. Article 21 stipulates the need for tourist operations to pay a cash deposit or insurance to safeguard their professional conduct and performance, with the amount to be determined by a decision issued by the General People's Committee for Tourism.

Articles 22 and 23 define the situation in which a tourist organization or guide is deemed to violate his professional obligations, or conditions in which the operation of a tourist facility or service will be terminated or a licence not renewed, citing "a crime or a felony violating the public morals and etiquette or the public order".

A detailed definition of a tourist guide is given in Article 24, being "any person practicing tourist guidance works and providing explanations for the historical, scientific and artistic landmarks and the likes, against a compensation, undertaking to accompany tourists in their movements in the different tourist areas".

Fines and punishments for violation of the law or for setting up or managing tourist facilities without a licence, or any breaches in the conditions, are comprehensively covered in Articles 25 and 26.

In the last and Sixth Section, "Final Rules", it is stated that tourist companies and partnerships and offices of travel and tourism, as well as tourist guides and owners of tourist public areas, shall settle their situations according to the rules of this law within 6 months as of date of its coming into force; otherwise, they will be considered as practising the profession without a licence.

To conclude, this important piece of legislation has attempted to provide a comprehensive framework within which the tourist industry in Libya can move forward in a professional and responsible way, addressing issues related to the institutional structure underlying the tourism sector; the training of tourist personnel within the public and private sectors; the personal security of tourists; the definition of organizations involved in tourism-related activities; the improvement and establishment of infrastructure and specially designated tourist areas. All of these legal changes are aimed at improving and enhancing the image of Libya and its tourist industry both domestically and abroad.

3.2.7 Administrative Contracts Regulations 2000

This is an important piece of comprehensive legislation governing administrative contracts entered into by a second party, which might be a foreign company, with

Libyan administrative units defined in Part 1, Article 1 of the regulations as Libyan government Secretariats (Ministries), Public Corporations, Public Authorities, and Public Organizations. An Administrative Contract is defined in Article 2 as "every contract concluded by any of the bodies mentioned in the previous article, intending to execute a project approved in the development plan and the budget...whenever such a contract includes exceptional terms, not usual in the civil works, intending to achieve the general welfare".

The following contracts are considered as administrative contracts, whenever the above-mentioned conditions apply:

- Public works contracts.
- Supply contracts and supply and installation contracts.
- Maintenance and operation contracts for projects and public utilities.
- Management contracts of all types related to industrial or tourist corporations and others.
- Sale contracts of items decided to be dispensed with.
- Contracts for employment of consultants and procurement of engineering services.

A foreign contracting party needs to be initially aware of the significance of Article 90, "Language of the Contract", where it is stated that the administrative contracts and their annexes shall be written in Arabic Language while "in cases of contracting with foreign companies or establishments the contract may be written in a foreign language, in addition to the one written in Arabic language, provided that the Arabic version is the original and the relied upon contract in the interpretation and the reference in any dispute".

Again, from a foreign contractor's viewpoint, it is important to have a thorough understanding of the meaning of such "exceptional terms not usual in the civil works" since these could well have a major impact on the profitability of the contract, or in any future legal wrangles surrounding non-compliance or cessation of contract works for whatever reason. The following are some examples of "exceptional terms" which should be particularly noted by foreign contractors.

"The contractor bears the taxes and customs fees and other fees, revenues and all amounts due on him by virtue of the customs law, regulation and decisions, on account of goods imported into Libya" (Article 30). This, it must be noted, is very different from contracts with LNOC under the Petroleum Law No. 25, where equipment is imported duty-free.

Regarding the competence of the Libyan Courts in contract disputes, Article 91 states that in the administrative contracts, it is particularly essential to set forth the competence of the Libyan Courts in examining any disputes that may arise from these contracts, that is all contract disputes will be decided in Libyan courts. Regarding payment for goods, work, or services performed the foreign contractor should also be aware that "all payments due to the contractor have first to be approved by the General Popular People's Committee for the Financial Control Board" (Article 99).

The use of national products is also specified in Article 103, which states that the foreign contractor undertakes with the administration body to use the national products and materials having local origin including construction materials such as bricks, sand, marble, and similar materials available locally as well the domestic manufactured and semi-manufactured products. Regarding subcontracting, Article 107 states that in the case of subcontracting, where in fact this is permitted (in general it is not permitted) priority will be given to Libyan nationals.

Particular attention must also be given by any foreign contractor to Article 109, which deals with amendments to the agreed contract price, either upwards or downwards, in which it is stated, "With no prejudice of the provisions of Article (20) of the present regulation, the contractual body has the right to amend the contract subject, by increase or decrease, within the limits of the proportion agreed upon in the contract, provided that this proportion does not exceed 15 per cent of the contract value, and the contractor shall not have the right to claim for any amendment in prices."

As stated earlier, it is essential that foreign companies undertaking contracts with Libyan government bodies and public institutions fully understand in detail all the provisions of the Administrative Contracts Regulations. Currently, in fact, these regulations apply to virtually every Libyan publicly owned company, apart from the Libyan National Oil Corporation, which is governed by the Petroleum Law No. 25. Failure by a foreign company to understand in full these regulations, such as Article 109 for example, could prove to be a very costly mistake.

3.2.8 Practice of Economic Activities: Recent Executive Regulations

The Executive Regulations of Law No. 21 of the Year 2001, regarding the Practice of Economic Activities, and their amendment by Law No. 1 for the Year 2004 are key pieces of legislation covering a wide range of economic activities in Libya and the nature of the business entities which can perform them. Article 1 defines the economic activities as those practised "in the different field of industrial, agricultural, animal and marine wealth, metallurgical, quarrying, construction and erection, communications and transport production, as well as handicraft and vocational works, such as education, medicine, engineering, counting, consultations, brokerage, trading agencies and contracting, in addition to import, export and distribution of goods and merchandise and other economic activities, according to the rules of the present regulation".

The forms or business structures permitted to carry out these economic activities are defined in Article 2 as follows:

- Individual activity.
- Family activity.
- Partnership.
- JV companies including holding companies and trading companies.
- Public corporations and companies.
- Companies stipulated in the Commercial Law.

It adds that "the General People's Committee may add any type of other companies and corporations to practice economic activities".

The rules of individual employment as opposed to partnership in a business are defined in Article 4, which states that the employment shall be effected by virtue of a written contract concluded according to the rules of the labour law, and consistent with the guiding form of the employment contract, which is a two-page document that is an intrinsic part of the regulation.

With regard to "Joint Venture Companies", Section Five in Articles 22–30 defines the various types of private sector JV companies. Article 22 defines a JV company as "the company established by physical or moral persons by virtue of a memorandum of association, with their shares as nominal or in the name of their holder". Regarding share values Article 23 states, "The value of each share in the joint-venture company and the percentage of individual shareholders therein shall be according to the rules of the Commercial Law."

Significantly, bringing Libyan law in line with international financial practices, Article 24 permits the issuing of nominal shares.

> The shares may be nominal or for their holder, according to what is determined by the company's establishing assembly. No share shall be issued for its holder until its value has been paid in full. The general assembly of the company may transfer the shares from nominal to their holders or vice-versa, according to the rules of commercial law, while the company's capital shall be appropriate to its objectives determined in the memorandum of association. (Article 24)

It then defines in Articles 25–28 a holding company as

> a joint-venture company which owns, solely, the entire capital of another or other companies, having moral personality and independent financial liability, or owns a percentage of shares in one or more companies, to practice several different economic objectives and activities. The holding company will have, over the owned companies, the power of the general assembly, in the limits of capital owned thereby. The holding company's capital shall not be less than one million Libyan Dinars. (Articles 25–28)

Regarding the formation of JV companies, Article 27 states, "The holding company undertakes, through the companies belonging thereto, the investment of its funds as well as it may, and when necessary, perform the investment by itself." It has the right, in order to achieve its objectives, to

- Establish JV companies, individually or partnering with public and private moral persons.
- Purchase shares of JV companies, individually or partnering with public and private moral persons, or sell the same in the financial papers market.
- Establish funds to manage the financial papers of the company, including the shares, checks, securities, and other financial papers.

The regulations then define supporting companies and rental companies, both of which represent new forms of organizations in Libyan law bringing it in line with international forms and practices.

Public Companies are dealt with in Section Six, which defines these in Article 36 as “a company of which the State owns all the capital, established by virtue of a decision issued by the General People’s Committee”. The public bodies allowed to practise economic activities are defined in Article 37 as Public Corporations, Public Companies, and General Boards, which are subject to the normal procedures for obtaining the licence necessary to practise the activity from the competent body.

The nature of these public entities are defined in Articles 38–41 with Article 40 reinforcing an important principle laid down in the Libyan revolution, where workers in the public companies are “Partners not Wageworkers”, in terms of the dividends payable to workers in the Public Companies. It would appear that these articles are in fact part of the groundwork process for privatization and its effects and advantages to the employees of privatized companies, a current issue of burning concern in Libya.

“Prices and Channels of Import, Export and Distribution” are defined in Section Seven, in which Articles 42–52 elaborate a series of rules covering pricing, price controls, price tags, licensing, hoarding, speculation, and rules for the orderly import, export, and distribution of goods. While attempting, again, to bring Libya more in line with international import, export, and distribution practices, it is important to note that the Libyan government, in the transition period from a public, centrally controlled economy to a market economy accompanied by economic liberalization, still assumes responsibility for fair prices as well as limiting inflationary tendencies and excess profit-making. This is intended to control and avoid the excess of economic misery suffered, for example, by the Russian people in the post-Perestroika period of the 1990s.

The unique position of non-Libyan Africans and Arabs is covered in Section Eight and confirms their rights and status, consolidating the basic tenets of Libya’s liberal foreign and immigration policy towards its African and Arab neighbours. This is again, currently, a very controversial topic in Libya.

Section Nine deals briefly but comprehensively with the support facilities and assistance that Libyans can expect from domestic State and Trade banks to ensure business success, such as loans and credit, Letters of Credit for imported manufacturing equipment, as well as assistance in securing land for their projects. It also reinforces the government’s commitment to ensure the success of Libyan export-oriented projects, which in the future will be crucial to sustain Libya’s economic diversification. These include strong financial support in the early years of the project, precedence in obtaining loans from Libyan domestic banks, support from Libyan technical centres as well as “facilitating their participation (i.e. the export companies) in local and international exhibitions in a manner enabling the projects to market their products”.

While the provisions of the Regulations discussed so far are primarily of interest to Libyans and Libyan enterprises, it is Section Ten, “Financial Papers Market”, which is of most interest to foreign investors and for the attraction of FDI to Libya. In this regard the lack of a stock market in Libya has been cited by economists, investors, and foreign multinationals as one of the main obstacles preventing large-scale FDI into Libya. The importance of this section warrants the quotation in full of the relevant sections covering the regulations for the establishment of a private Libyan Stock Exchange.

"The bodies, on which the establishment of a financial papers market is conferred, are determined by virtue of a decision to be issued by the Secretariat of the General People's Committee, provided that those bodies shall be among those practicing financial, banking or investment works." The Central Bank of Libya is charged to proceed to deal with the financial papers until the establishment of an integrated financial papers market (Article 57), while The Articles of Association of the financial papers market shall include the determination of the following (Article 58):

- Market type, head-office, objectives, and the extent of its work.
- Market capital and the sharing percentage of each body establishing it.
- Type of financial papers to be circulating in the market.
- Market management structuring, and statement of its financial resources, financial system, control and auditing body.
- Rights and duties of members and intermediates, and the condition of their work performance.
- The mechanism of dealing with the financial papers in the market, ownership transfer processes, clearance and settlement, and others.
- Ways of reviewing data and information related to the financial papers circulating in the market, and manner of spreading them.
- Partnership percentage of foreigners, and the matters organizing the same.
- Guarantees necessary for the safety of dealing in the market, and non-disclosure of data and information related to the market.

Finally, Article 59 concludes in the normal manner that the rules related to the organization of the financial papers market, determination of its competencies and body undertaking the supervision of its works, and other relevant rules will be issued by virtue of a decision to be taken by the Secretariat of the General People's Committee.

3.3 Present Needs and Future Direction of Libyan FDI Legislation

From the above analysis of recent FDI legislation in Libya it is clear that the country is moving methodically towards the creation of a business environment and legal framework in which FDI can be successfully attracted to the country. As we have discussed, the legal basis for setting up a Libyan Stock Exchange has now been established, positioning the country alongside its North African neighbours such as Tunisia and Egypt as well as the Gulf Arab states such as Dubai, Abu Dhabi, Kuwait, and Saudi Arabia. As the country continues to privatize its inefficient State-Owned Enterprises (SOEs) and moves towards economic diversification, the need for an active Libyan Stock Exchange becomes increasingly vital as an engine to attract major foreign funds and investments, as well as a competitive source of capital for the growth and expansion of Libyan domestic companies. Obvious examples of the effective role that a Libyan stock exchange might have are the privatization of the major Libyan industrial enterprises such as cement factories and steel plants, as well as petrochemical plants and the marketing arms of the LNOC, should the government decide to do this. Another matter of the utmost importance which currently requires urgent attention by the Libyan policy makers is the New Draft Petroleum Law. In the following section the authors will propose a series of key initiatives and economic changes which might be addressed by this law. These, if implemented, have the potential to bring about major and lasting changes in Libya's ambitious plans for economic diversification.

3.3.1 Protection of Intellectual Property Rights

Libya does not have a comprehensive law on intellectual property rights, similar, for example, to Egypt's Law No. 82 of 2002 pertaining to the Protection of Intellectual Property Rights. Nor is it a Member State of the World Intellectual Property Organization (WIPO). Similarly, it is not a member of WTO, although it applied formally to join this organization and in July 2004, when WTO members agreed to allow Libya to start negotiations on terms for joining. But in view of existing legal and governance issues, it is probable that the approval process will take several years. This therefore means that Libya is not a party to the WTO's TRIPS (agreement on Trade-related Aspects of Intellectual Property Rights). Although domestic laws exist to protect copyright, trademarks, and patents, foreign companies and investors should be aware that trademark violations involving pirate copies of known brands are a common feature in Libya's retail shops and markets.

4 Social Policy and Trends

4.1 Libyan Demographic Trends

4.1.1 Population Growth

Libya has one of the highest rates of population growth in Africa, averaging more than 3 per cent annually for most of the second half of the twentieth century. The major influx of foreign workers into the country from neighbouring states such as Egypt and Tunisia as well as the African nations to its south in the 1960s and later accounts for part of this rapid growth, but Libya's annual rate of natural increase (birth rate minus death rate) has also been one of the highest averages in Africa. In this respect, Libya is one of the 26 countries in the developing world whose population could conceivably double in the next 25 years.

Population between 1954 (the first national census) and 2006 increased from 1.041 million to approximately 5.67 million. For every 1,000 population, crude birth rate declined from 48.0 to 36.0 and crude death rates from 22.7 to 7.0. The natural increase rate was 2.5 per cent in 1954, reached a peak of 3.8 per cent in 1973 and thereafter declined to 1.83 per cent in 2006. Between 1949 and 2002, infant mortality rates per 1000 live births had fallen from 300 to a bare minimum of 24.4, while at the same time life expectancy had risen from 42.4 to 69.5 years.

Based on the 2006 census, issued on 14 September 2006, the breakdown of the Libyan population by region, including non-Libyans, is given in Table 4.1.

4.1.2 Trends in Population Growth, 1954–1995

The population growth rate generally increased throughout this period. However, it decreased unexpectedly and significantly to reach 2.5 per cent for the period 1984–1995. Reasons for this decline in the rate of population growth can be ascribed to the following main factors:

- Increase in the average age of first marriage within the period 1973–1984 from 25 to 32 years for males, and from 19 to 23 for females.
- Decrease of fertility level as indicated by average children per single Libyan women of child-bearing age (15–49 years).
- Increase of the rate of females joining school aged between 15 and 24 years and also advances in education for the population in general.
- Increase of the rate of Libyan woman participating in economic and social activities.

Table 4.1. Distribution of population, 2006

	Number of families	Total inhabitants	Libyans			Non-Libyans		
			Male	Female	Total	Male	Female	Total
Albitnan	22798	159536	76225	74830	151055	4700	3781	8481
Derna	26573	163351	78347	78259	156606	3987	2758	6745
Aljabel Alakhder	31120	203156	95405	96191	191596	7816	3744	11560
Almerj	25550	185848	88343	88585	176928	6519	2401	8920
Benghazi	119257	670797	320699	302148	622847	29192	18758	47950
Alwahat	26281	177047	81774	80530	162304	11279	3464	14743
Alkofra	8052	50104	21265	21623	42888	5023	2193	7216
Sirte	29355	193720	88959	88892	177851	11934	3935	15869
Musrata	91234	550938	261720	255758	517478	25783	7677	33460
Almirqeb	71148	432202	208593	206711	415304	13911	2987	16898
Tripoli	192447	106540,5	513167	491239	1004406	41711	19288	60999
Aljfara	80003	453198	216376	209482	425858	21520	5820	27340
Al-Zawia	53085	290,993	137349	134594	271943	14022	5028	19050
Alnnikat Alghames	54227	287662	135567	135132	270699	12550	4413	16963
Aljabel AlGharbi	51254	304159	146649	143686	290335	11368	2456	13824
Nalut	15633	93224	43778	43351	87129	4878	1217	6095
Sebha	35954	212694	98369	95540	193909	13095	5690	18785
Wadi Al-haya	12867	76858	35988	35086	71074	4692	1092	5784
Murzuq	13409	78621	35725	36657	72382	4561	1678	6239
Ghat	3652	23518	10847	10552	21399	1532	587	2119
Total	963899	5673031	2695145	2628846	5323991	250073	98967	349040

Source: Libyan Higher Committee for Statistics and Census, 2006.

In the earlier periods, population growth was strongly affected by increases in non-Libyan nationals in the population; although increasing only 0.3 per cent through the period 1954–1963, this increased to 16.7 per cent through the period 1964–1973 and 6.7 per cent, for the period 1974–1983. However, for the period extending from 1984 to 1995, the non-Libyan population realized a negative growth of 0.05 per cent.

The main reason for these significant increases in non-Libyan nationals was predominantly the discovery and export of oil in the early 1970s, accompanied by the launching of a vast programme of economic and social development, which meant there was a severe labour deficiency which was met by the recruitment of foreign manpower. This is shown by the fact that the percentage of non-Libyan population increased from 5 per cent in the beginning of the 1970s to about 20 per cent in 1993.

However, in 1995, as a result of the opening of Libyan borders to Arabs and Africans, and the cancellation of the requirement for entry visas, the number of non-Libyan population doubled again, with immigrants searching for work in

Libya in unregulated activities such as agriculture, animal breeding, repair and maintenance works, selling in open markets, and building and construction works.

The enumeration process itself, however, may be called into doubt since enumeration was based on a fixed place of residence. Many immigrants, on the other hand, resided in groups in old houses or buildings under construction, or people's markets, leaving their sleeping places in the morning and returning to these only in the night. Because of this, it is believed that the total of non-Libyan population included in the 2006 census, at 349,040 people, is considerably less than the actual total.

4.1.3 Population Distribution

Libya, in terms of population, can be considered as one of the most sparsely populated countries in the world, at 1,775,060 km^2 with a population of approximately 5.67 million; this works out at around three persons per square km.

It is usual in discussing population distribution to define the terms "urban" and "rural". In a Libyan context, the definition of urban areas has varied from one census to another, depending on socio-economic development in the country. In the 1954–1963 and 1964–1973 censuses, against the background of a backward and fairly primitive socio-economic situation, Bedouin life prevailed and social position depended largely on agricultural and pastoral activity, with a large number of the Libyan population outside the coastal cities, and many settlements comprising of either migrating and semi-migrating populations. Mainly, because of this, no data appeared on population distribution separately delineating urban and rural areas in the 1954 and 1964 censuses.

However, in the 1974 census, a distinction between urban and rural localities was used. Urban localities were defined as those located in the centre of municipalities or, if not located in the centre of a municipality, with a population of 5,000 or more. In the 1984–1995 census, this definition was extended to localities identified in city plans.

Referring to the available data from the results of the census for the years 1973, 1984, and 1995 concerning population distribution using this definition of urban populations, urbanization rates in Libya developed very rapidly. Urban population increased from 1.344 million in 1973 to 4.812 million inhabitants in 1995, an annual growth rate of 6.0 per cent over this period. As a result of this, the percentage of urbanization increased from 59.8 per cent in 1973 to 85.6 per cent in 1995, and correspondingly, the percentage of the rural population decreased from 40.2 per cent to 14.4 per cent within the same period.

The highest urbanization rates in 1973 were in the Tripoli and Benghazi areas with percentages reaching 95.7 per cent and 84.9 per cent respectively. Other areas had smaller urbanization percentages, not exceeding 58.0 per cent in most cases. In 1973, urbanization rates in Misuratah was 14 per cent, Ghryan 17.2 per cent, and Al Khums 23.5 per cent. However, by 1995, all areas assumed very high urbanization rates, more than 73 per cent, except Ghryan with a rate of 62.4 per cent, while Misuratah had the second highest urbanization rate in Libya after Tripoli, with a rate of 92.5 per cent. Reasons for this rapid development in urbanization in Libya in only two decades are attributable to the following main reasons:

- There were major achievements in the establishment of infrastructure in the national economy throughout this period, including the construction of municipal utilities such as lighting, drainage, water networks, roads and pavements, modern houses, as well as the establishment of local and regional units in the education, health, public security, and municipality administration sectors. These were achieved in both large cities and small villages, resulting in a great similarity in lifestyle between those living in cities and those living in what previously might have been described as rural areas.
- Planning for the extensions of cities which led to the inclusion of villages and rural areas. Consequently, these areas became urban gatherings according to the approved definition in the census in 1995.
- Increase of population growth rate which meant that many localities met the condition of 5,000 people which defined an urban population community.

However, it is worth noting that in the context of the Arab world the high rate of urbanization of Libya cannot be considered to be unique. Urbanization in Kuwait (98 per cent), Qatar (93 per cent), Bahrain (92 per cent), Saudi Arabia (86 per cent), and Oman (84 per cent) bring home this point.

4.1.4 Trends in Population Growth, 1995–2006

The results of the latest Libyan 2006 Census, illustrated earlier in Table 4.1, for the period 1995–2006 illustrate that the number of families in the country was 963,899. Compared to the number of families at 721,358 in the 1995 census, this is an increase of 242,541 families. However, the average number of inhabitants per family has decreased from 6.65 in 1995 to 5.89 in 2006. This decrease can be attributed to several factors. First, even though forms of birth control have been available in Libya for over two decades, in the last decade its cultural acceptance and usage became more prevalent. Secondly, marriages are taking place at a greater age for both men and women. Thirdly, as will be seen below, the increasing role of women in the workplace has meant that smaller families are more manageable.

Of the total Libyan population of 5,323,991, 67.60 per cent or 3,599,278 are aged above 15 years, with the balance of 1,724,713 or 32.40 per cent aged less than 15 years. Comparing these figures with the 1995 census, it can be observed that in the 1995 census Libyans aged less than 15 years accounted for 1,714,263 or approximately 39.05 per cent of the total, which shows a decline in this age group of the total population by 6.64 per cent (Table 4.2).

Table 4.2. Distribution of Libyan population, 1995 and 2006

Population	Ages	Number in population			Percentage of total population		
		Male	Female	Total	Male	Female	Total
1995	Below 15	870342	843921	1714263	39.01	39.09	39.05
	Above 15	1360737	1314739	2675476	60.99	60.91	60.95
	Total	2231079	2158660	4389739	100.0	100.0	100.0
2006	Below 15	847098	877615	1724713	31.43	33.38	32.40
	Above 15	1848047	1751231	3599278	68.57	66.62	67.60
	Total	2695145	2628846	5323991	100.00	100.00	100.00

Source: Libyan Higher Committee for Statistics and Census, 2006.

The 2006 census also illustrates some important data regarding participation/non-participation in economic activities for those aged above 15 years, by number and gender. In 1995, of a total of 1,100,956 engaged in some form of economic activity, males represented 895,187 and females 205,769, or 65.79 per cent and 15.65 per cent respectively. But by 2006 the total figure for those engaged in such activities had increased to 1,574,520, of which males represented 60.48 per cent and females 29.59 per cent, demonstrating that female participation in the workforce had almost doubled in this period and confirming that, in line with a series of laws enacted since 1969 regarding women's role in Libyan society, women's participation was beginning to have a significant effect (Table 4.3).

4.1.5 Age Structure of Population

The high population growth rates that prevailed in the period under review led to important changes in the age structure of the Libyan population. One certainty in demographic studies is that high rates of population growth result in an increase in

Table 4.3. Comparison of 1995 and 2006 census: Libyan population above 15 years working/non-working

Population	Category	Number of population			Percentage of total population		
		Male	Female	Total	Male	Female	Total
1995	Economic working	895187	205769	1100956	65.79	15.65	41.15
	Non-economic working	465550	1108970	1574520	34.21	84.35	58.85
	Total	1360737	1314739	2675476	100.0	100.0	100.0
2006	Economic working	1117612	518171	1635783	60.48	29.59	45.45
	Non-economic working	730435	1233060	1963495	39.52	70.41	54.55
	Total	1848047	1751231	3599278	100.0	100.00	100.00

Source: Libyan Higher Committee for Statistics and Census, 2006.

the percentage of young population groups. This, in turn, leads to a heavier burden of expenditure on non-productive services such as education, health, housing, utilities, and social security, essentially signifying that there are more consumers than producers. Income from work is normally spent in this situation on consumption and social services. This, in turn, weakens saving capabilities and capital formation.

But against this there is another viewpoint that the economic and social burden imposed on a country due to this youthful category of population is a temporary one, and the day when this category will be available for employment will definitely come. The important point, therefore, is for planners and development policy makers to optimize resources, prioritizing development expenditure in programmes and projects for education and human resource development to provide the basis for long-term prosperity.

This fact is reinforced by the experience of several countries that do not possess major mineral or agricultural resources, and basically rely on human resources for prosperity. Singapore under Lee Kwan Yew and administrations succeeding him springs to mind as a good example of a country which has achieved great progress both socially and economically, based largely on its human capital.

Although, therefore, due to reasons discussed earlier such as later ages for marriage and enhanced educational opportunities the proportion of Libyan population of less than 25 years slowed down in proportion to the total of population up to 1984, it recorded the highest growth rate within the period 1984–1995, constituting the highest percentage of the total population, at 64 per cent, although by 2005 this had declined to slightly more than 58 per cent.

This change in age structure of the Libyan population is already having important implications in all socio-economic fields, and will continue to do so in future years.

4.1.6 Ratio of the Sexes

Another fact emerging from census comparisons over this period shows that the sex ratio began to change with effect from 1964, in favour of females. It decreased from 108.5 per cent in favour of males in 1964 to 103.2 per cent in 1995 and to 102.6 per cent in 2000, that is a decrease of about 6 per cent between 1964 and 2000. By 2006 there were 2,695,145 and 2,628.846 females, that is, the sex ratio in favour of males had further declined to 102.5 per cent. If this trend continues at the same rate as in the period surveyed, the number of females shall be equal to or more than the number of males by the middle of the third decade in the twenty-first century.

This trend of the sex ratio in favour of females requires an accompanying development and refinement of national policies and strategies towards Libyan women. Current and future policies should progressively include and integrate women into public life and reinforce their standing in Libyan society, as well as providing them with more employment opportunities as the diversification of the national economy proceeds apace.

To provide the reader with an overall picture, we present in Tables 4.4 and 4.5 general demographic, health, gender, human development, and socio-economic indicators, in which the Libyan demographic experience can be directly compared to the countries of the Middle East and North Africa (MENA) taken as a unit, and the world. Later in this chapter we will discuss these sectors in detail.

Table 4.4. General demographic and health indicators, 1950–2025 (projected)

Demographic and health indicators	Libya	MENA	World
Total population (in thousands of people)			
- 1950	1029	111647	2519495
- 2002	5529	423296	6211082
- 2025 (projected)	7972	631320	7936741
Population density (people per square km), 2000	3.0	31.3	45.1
Average annual population growth rate, 1980–2000			
- Total	3.1%	2.5%	1.6%
- In rural areas	−1.5%	1.0%	0.9%
- In urban areas	4.2%	3.9%	2.4%
Percentage of population			
- Under age 15 as on 2002	33%	35%	29%
- Over age 65 as on 2002	4%	4%	7%
- Living in urban areas, 2000	88%	61%	47%
Average fertility rate (a)			
- 1975–1980	7.4	5.9	3.9
- 2000–2005	3.3	3.5	2.7
- Infant mortality rate (b), 2000–2005	25	52	55
- Under-five mortality rate (b), 2000	20	64	83
Life expectancy at birth (Year), 2000–2005			
- Female	73.3	69.9	68.1
- Male	69.2	66.5	63.9
Birth attended by trained personal, 1994–2000©	94%	67%	57%
Adults and children infected with HIV or AIDS, 2001	7000	500000	40 million
Percent of the adults age 15–49 Infected with HIV or AIDS, 2001	0.2%	×	1.2%
Number of children orphaned By AIDS since the beginning of epidemic, 2001	×	65000	14 million
Safe water and sanitation©, Access to improved sanitation, 2000			
Urban	97%	91%	85%
Rural	96%	70%	40%
Safe water and sanitation©, Access to improved water source, 2000			
Urban	72%	89%	95%
Rural	68%	74%	71%

Table 4.4. (Cont.)

Demographic and health indicators	Libya	MENA	World
School enrollment and literacy©			
Net primary school enrollment, both sexes			
- 1980	×	×	×
- 1997–1999©	100%	×	×
Net secondary schools enrollment, 1997–1999©			
- Female	76%	×	×
- Male	67%	×	×
Gross tertiary school enrollment, 1996–1999©	57%	×	×
Adults literacy rate 2002			
Female	71%	67%	8%
Male	92%	80%	86%
Adults literacy rate (ages 15–24), both sexes			
1980	79	67	87
2002	97	86	87

Source: Earth Trends, 2003.

4.1.7 Trends in Illegal Immigration

Libya's official population as shown in Table 4.1 amounted to 5,673,031 for the year 2006. Figures for both official (legal) and illegal immigration, as well as emigration, are difficult to estimate. This is because of the permeable nature of Libya's borders – it has a coastline of approximately 1,970 km on the Mediterranean, and shares 4,400 km of porous land borders with six countries: Tunisia, Algeria, Niger, Chad, Egypt, and Sudan. In practical terms, patrolling and monitoring these borders is virtually impossible, based on Libya's existing manpower and technical resources.

The situation is exacerbated by the lack of an effective online computer-based database in Libya which could monitor, online and in real time, by using a dedicated and linked Libyan immigration LAN system, the entry and exit of everyone, Libyans and foreigners alike, through Libya's official entry/exit points from/to international destinations where official government immigration facilities exist. These currently are, for example, at Tripoli International Airport as well as other airports offering direct international flights such as Benghazi and Sebha, with currently Misuratah under preparation, Libyan seaports, and the terrestrial border checkpoints of Libya with Tunisia at Ra's Ajdir, Algeria at Ghat, Niger at Al Quatrun, Chad and the southern region at Al Kofra, Sudan also at Al Kofra and with Egypt at Tobruk. This at least would provide a resource based on which Libyan demographers, economists, and officials could acquire accurate data on the movement of Libyan individuals and foreign nationals in and out of Libya at any given time or period, empowering Libyan policy makers to identify trends and effect key decisions affecting national priorities, at the same time justifying such decisions with factual data.

In this very unsatisfactory current situation, it is difficult if not impossible to estimate not only the number of foreigners working even legally in Libya, but

Table 4.5. Comparable population and Human Development Index for MENA countries, 2003

HDI Rank		Human Development Index [HDI] Value 2003	Life expectancy at birth (years) [HDI] 2003[a]	GDP per capita [US $] 2003	GDP per capita, highest value [PPP US $] 1975-2003
		High human development			
40	Qatar	0.849	72.8	–[b]	–
41	UAE	0.849	78	–[b]	49432[c,d]
43	Bahrain	0.846	74.3	–[b]	17479[c]
44	Kuwait	0.844	76.9	17421	29760[c,d]
58	Libya	0.799	73.6	–	–
71	Oman	0.781	74.1	–	13965[c]
77	Saudi Arabia	0.772	71.8	9532	24461[d]
81	Lebanon	0.759	72	4224	5074[c]
89	Tunisia	0.753	73.3	2530	7161
99	Iran	0.736	70.4	2066	8443
103	Algeria	0.722	71.1	2090	6319[d]
106	Syria	0.721	73.3	1237	3696
119	Egypt	0.659	69.8	1220	3950
141	Sudan	0.512	56.4	530	1910[d]
152	Mauritania	0.477	52.7	348	1827
170	Ethiopia	0.367	47.6	97	752[c,d]
–	Iraq	–	58.9	–	–
–	Somalia	–	46.5	–	–

Aggregates for Education Index are based on aggregates of gross enrolment data calculated by the UNESCO Institute for Statistics and literacy data as used to calculate the HDI.
[a] The HDI rank is detemined using HDI values to the fifth decimal point.
[b] Data refer to 2002.
[c] Data refer to a period shorter than that specified.
[d] Estimates are based on regression.
Source:
Column 1: Calculated on the basis of data in columns 6-8 of table 1 (HDR 2005); see technical note 1 for details.
Column 2: UN (United Nations). 2005. Correspondence on life expectancy at birth. Department of Economic and Social Affairs, Population Division, New York, unless otherwise noted.
Column 3: Calculated on the basis of GDP and population data from World Bank, 2005. World Development Indicators, 2005. CD-ROM. Washington, DC.; aggregates calculated for the Human Development Report Office by the World Bank.
Column 4: Based on GDP per capita PPP US $ time series from World Bank, 2005. World Development Indicators, 2005. CD-ROM, Washington, DC.
Column 5: Determined on the basis of GEM values in column 2 of Table 25 (HDR 2005).
Source: UNDP, 2005; World Bank World Development Indicators, 2005.

more importantly the number of illegal immigrants. In, for example, a report published by an EU fact-finding delegation to Libya comprising 21 members who were experts in the field of illegal immigration and demography, figures for legal immigrants in Libya were quoted at 600,000, while the total number of illegal immigrants could only be guesstimated at between 750,000 and 1.2 million (EU, Technical Mission to Libya on Illegal Immigration 2004). The figure of 600,000 given by the EU Delegation, which they stated was based on estimates given to them by the Libyan authorities, is more than three times the figure of 187,900 for the year 2000, which we have provided in our analysis of Libyan/foreign labour components in the Libyan workforce from 1962 to 2000 later in this chapter. Clearly and regrettably in Libya today there is no authoritative source for such data, because there is no effective data collection system in place.

There can be no doubt that Libya is now paying the price, in social terms, of a virtually unrestricted immigration policy promoted in the 1990s, which favoured the entry of all Arabs and sub-Saharan Africans to Libya without visas. Illegal immigration, in particular originating from sub-Saharan Africa, is now clearly perceived by the Libyan authorities as a growing threat, which could turn into a national crisis, with a wide range of potentially serious consequences and impacts on the Libyan health, education, housing, and social security sectors. Concerns about organized crime, over-utilization of the Libyan health facilities by foreigners, the very real possibility of the spread of HIV/AIDS and hepatitis, and cultural misunderstandings resulting in tension between Libyan and foreign communities, as well as the infiltration of foreign terrorists, are now being openly expressed by the Libyan public and government officials alike.

It is unquestionable that, in immigration terms, Libya is a destination country. Migration towards Libya is the result of a combination of factors. First, geographic, in view of Libya's strategic location in the middle of the southern Mediterranean coastline, where at some points it is very close to Sicily, as well as its permeable borders. Economic factors are also strong, with the Libyan hydrocarbon industry acting as a magnet for job seekers, as well as providing many job opportunities offered to professionals in the health and education fields. Political factors have also played a crucial role, as the Libyan leader in the late 1990s refocused Libyan foreign policy on Africa and away from the Arab heartland, aiming at a United States of Africa, with a virtually unrestricted immigration policy towards sub-Saharan Africans. Finally, in purely pragmatic terms, the lack of a valid global Libyan immigration strategy and poor border management have meant that Libya was an easy target for illegal immigrants.

However, Libya has also traditionally been a major transit country for a wide range of African economic immigrants wishing to migrate to Europe and then, in many cases, to the United States. According to recent reports, a sharp rise in illegal immigration through the Sicily Channel is currently being experienced, as the Libyan transit route becomes more heavily utilized. Media reports of illegal immigrants attempting to reach Europe from Libya, mainly via the Italian island of Lampedusa and Malta in the Sicily Channel, have become commonplace.

Although the objectives of the EU Technical Mission on illegal immigration discussed above are of course not entirely altruistic, the time has clearly arrived for the Libyan authorities themselves to deal, and to be seen to be dealing, with problems and issues related to illegal immigrants, who see Libya as both a target as well as a transit point for illegal immigration. If not, Libya's attempt to reintegrate itself into the international mainstream will not be taken seriously, and will negatively impact Libya's recent applications to join world bodies such as the WTO, as well as its possible enhanced engagement in the Barcelona Process by upgrading its current status as a passive observer.

In this regard the Libyan decision to create a dedicated Coast Guard Department to police Libya's northern border and crack down on transit immigration to Europe is clearly a step in the right direction towards managing illegal movements of third-party nationals through Libya to Europe. Priorities for Libya such as the reinforcement of terrestrial border staff numbers of around 3,500 personnel, mainly military, as well as to enhance training and equipment, must also be addressed, since the existing number of personnel is clearly insufficient to effectively police over 4,000 km of porous borders. Within Libya itself a special task force could be established, with a remit to understand the present dimensions of the illegal immigration problem, and propose new policies for dealing with these. Similarly, a media campaign to show the Libyan people the downsides of illegal immigration might also reinforce the government's will and ability to deal with this serious problem.

Also of the utmost importance is the establishment and operation of a national immigration database, with online and real-time capability and computer stations at every Libyan frontier point, whether land, sea, or air. Although it will take time to train Libyan operatives for the installation, operation, and maintenance of such a system, this is an important key for the successful understanding of trends in Libyan immigration, both legal and illegal, and for the determination of Libyan future immigration policy and an understanding of immigration's present impacts on Libyan demographics and the economy as a whole.

4.2 The Evolution of the Libyan Education System

Three years after Libyan independence in 1951, the official census figures of 1954 showed that 81.1 per cent of the Libyan population was illiterate. In Table 4.6, education statistics for the first decade of Libyan independence demonstrate how limited basic educational opportunities were for Libyans.

At that time Adrian Pelt, the UN Commissioner for Libya, estimated in his first Annual Report after Libyan independence in 1951 that "the number of students for whom education would have to be provided would considerably exceed 100,000". Two years later, in 1953, it was estimated that in the Libyan province of Tripolitania around 40 per cent of children attended school. However, there were only 800 teachers in the entire province, and only 200 of these had received any formal teacher training, with the rest having received 1- or 2-year education. By 1961, the elementary school population had risen to a figure of 131,000, very close to the target proposed by Pelt 10 years earlier (Wright 1969).

In this early post-independence period, the Education Ordinance of 1952 put the responsibility for education on the provinces. But although, as might be expected, Arabic and Muslim studies were compulsory, one interesting feature is

Table 4.6. Schools and students at three levels, 1951–1961

Period	Kindergarten & elementary		Preparatory & secondary		Professional		Total	
	Schools	Students	Schools	Students	Schools	Students	Schools	Students
1950–1951	194	32115	4	300	10	326	208	32741
1951–1952	202	36949	4	402	10	568	216	37919
1952–1953	228	42500	5	558	13	776	246	43834
1953–1954	266	48278	7	712	13	1093	286	50083
1954–1955	319	57001	11	957	13	1339	344	59297
1955–1956	382	65831	18	3755	13	1659	413	71245
1956–1957	425	78724	28	4293	13	2076	466	85093
1957–1958	446	91632	43	5682	16	2175	505	99489
1958–1959	487	99388	61	6639	19	2389	567	108416
1959–1960	559	113694	75	9186	20	2737	654	125615
1960–1961	632	130077	95	12320	24	4328	751	146725

Source: Kubbah, 1964.

worth noting. Under the Free Schooling Ordinance of 1958, both foreign and private schools could operate under the supervision of the Ministry of Education. But the size of the education task in the 1960s was really formidable. As the Public School Survey for Tripoli in 1965 demonstrated, for example, overcrowding in elementary schools was as high as 97 pupils per class for girls in Grade 1 and 66 for boys in Grade 6 (Kingdom of Libya, Public School Study for Tripoli 1965). In view of this the Study recommended that for Tripoli alone between 1969/1970 and 1975/1975, 62 new schools containing 1,740 classrooms would need to be constructed.

Higher education faced a similarly desperate situation. One report cited that at the time of Libyan independence, there were only 14 Libyans with university degrees (Standard Oil Company, undated). In 1955 the University of Libya was established, and in 1957 two additional higher learning institutes were added: the College of Commerce and Economy in Benghazi and the College of Science in Tripoli. In 1961 the College of Advanced Technology was built with the support of the UN/UNESCO. In 1962, in Benghazi, the College of Laws was established, and in the same year the Muslim University was established, built on the earliest Libyan seat of learning, Jaghboub University at Beida (Farley 1971). Despite these developments, satisfying the early demand for tertiary education was a truly daunting undertaking. In a survey for the projected requirements for professional, technical, and skilled manpower for the period 1964–1969, as Libya expanded into an oil-based economy, it was stated that Libya lacked 21,998 graduates in these fields, including both the public and the private sectors, with the Libyan government alone requiring 1,760 university-trained professionals. Of the 322 physicians and surgeons in Libya in 1965, 316 were foreigners.

Similarly, for the period 1964–1969, it was estimated that 4,484 and 291 teachers were required at the primary and secondary school levels respectively, whereas the teacher training schools could only turn out 1,844, only 39 per cent of the requirement. Nonetheless, progress since the period of the early 1950s was slowly taking place. Statistics reveal that 53 per cent of children between the ages of 6 and 14 were at school in 1962–1963, that is 144,511 out of 268,086. But of these, annual repetition rates for pupils were high while dropouts were a serious problem, with dropout rates for girls, as would be expected in this earlier period, much higher than those for boys.

In the late 1960s and 1970s, oil revenues based on an export volume of over three million barrels per day meant that, in purely financial terms, Libya was now more than capable of financing her educational needs. For example, in the Libyan budget of 1967/1968 a total amount of 20,812,000 Libya pounds or 20.6 per cent of the annual expenditure of 101 million Libyan pounds was allocated for education. The school population had doubled since 1960, and by 1968 over 250,000 pupils were enrolled in more than 1,000 Libyan public and private schools (Wright 1969). But Libya still had a long way to go. In 1964, for example, the census showed that only 0.13 per cent of Libyans had been educated to graduate level. It also revealed that while the male illiteracy rate had dropped from 72 per cent in 1954 to 59.6 per cent in 1964, female illiteracy still stood at around 95 per cent.

In "Economic and Social Achievements", an official handbook issued by the Libyan Secretariat of Planning covering the government's objectives in the initial post-revolutionary years of 1970–1977, its education and vocational training policies are well summarized.

"The education and training policies are directed towards the objectives of raising a generation which is able to shoulder the burden of responsibility and assume leadership of a dynamic society dedicated to continual social change." These policies are translated into various programmes of quantitative and qualitative nature, which embody the following elements:

- The achievement of full compulsory education up to the preparatory or junior high level.
- Correcting the educational structure.
- Diversifying and promoting technical education so as to meet the needs of the economic and social development plans for manpower.
- Promoting higher education in such a way as to cope with scientific and technological progress.

Neither is this policy oblivious to the legacy of illiteracy, as its elimination is seriously contemplated. In fact by 2004, the figure for illiteracy was 12.6 per cent, as shown in Table 4.7, and this percentage, comprising mainly old people, is set to decrease considerably.

As seen in Table 4.7, the government successfully achieved very high levels of literacy among the younger age groups. Not only is literacy high, but, as discussed earlier, there is now little differentiation between gender in the Libyan education system. In fact, Libya's educational attainments place the country among the top achievers in the developing world, and have only been achieved through Libya's intense preoccupation with ensuring educational excellence since Libyan independence up to the present.

Table 4.7. Number and percentage distribution of the population by education status for students of age 10 years and above, 2004

Education status	Number of population			Percentage of the total		
	Male	Female	Total	Male	Female	Total
Illiterate	146179	385959	532138	6.78	18.67	12.6
Less then primary education	254150	244237	498387	11.78	11.81	11.8
Primary education	436459	375008	811467	20.23	18.14	19.21
Secondary education	449830	375843	825673	20.85	18.18	19.54
Intermediate (colleges or A level)	648604	542038	1190642	30.07	26.22	28.18
University and above level	221914	144423	366337	10.29	6.98	8.67
Total	2157136	2067508	4224644	100.00	100.00	100.00

Source: Libyan Authority for Information and Documentation, 2005.

4.2.1 Libyan Educational Philosophy – "Education for All"

In Libya, school is mandatory for completion of basic education, which lasts up to the age of 15. Education is the State's responsibility and is financed by the Libyan government all the way up to completion of university. However, the increasing number of school-aged children and the desire of a large number of them to pursue college education have led to a huge increase in the government's expenditure on education. In the subsequent section we will discuss comprehensively all levels of Libyan education, from pre-school to tertiary education.

Libyan Education Levels

1. Preschool level: Duration 2 years, for Children Aged 4–5

Preschool classes care for children's physical, mental, and social development before they start formal education. They ensure that children adapt to their environment with the help and cooperation of the child's family.

The goals of preschool classes are to

- Provide an adequate environment for developing the child's personality, and for his/her emancipation, and prepare the necessary groundwork to encourage creativity, independence, and the aptitude for self-dependence in order to meet social needs and in having correct relations with individuals and groups.
- Orientate the child's instinctive behaviour and to turn it into something regular.
- Give the child good habits and to develop these through positive encouragement.
- Encourage the child's curiosity and his/her cravings for learning, and help the child to discover natural and social phenomena suitable for his/her intellectual level.
- Stir the child's intelligence and develop his/her learning capabilities.

- Develop the child's language, facilitate communication with others, reinforce good expression, and sharpen his/her sense of beauty.
- Try to develop the child on the linguistic, social, and behavioural levels in order to prepare him/her for formal education.
- Try to develop the child's spiritual and religious side.

2. The Basic Education Level

The first part is primary or basic education, which extends to 6 years for children aged 6–11. The second part is secondary education, which extends 3 years for children aged from 12 to 14. The third part, although not mandatory, leads on to intermediate or specialized colleges (A Level) extending from 3 to 4 years for teenagers aged 15–19.

Basic education is described as "the fundamental basis for the education of the young generation aged 6 to 15. It aims at providing the pupil with necessary principles, behaviour, knowledge, expertise and practical skills. It deals with theoretical and practical issues, creates a link between youths and their different environments, and strengthens the relationship between the knowledge acquired in the school and the pupil's environment. This environment comprises knowledge, research, studies, and activities in all educational subjects. Basic education contributes also to integrate the school in its environment and provide the pupil with the chance of knowing his abilities and capacities and choosing his/her futhure path."

The Objectives of Basic Education in more detail are as follows:

- To ensure the necessary minimum of knowledge and concepts and prepare a suitable environment for acquiring the skills necessary for true citizenship in order for the pupil to be able to assume all their responsibilities when mature.
- To define desired principles and tendencies and develop them into personal manners which constitute a part of the individual's personality.
- To encourage the pupils' creative competencies by investing their tendencies in specific activities according to the development of their intellectual and physical capacities.
- To develop the pupils' muscle-flexibility and mechanical and motor function, encourage them to use their hands and senses, and help them to acquire practical skills to solve their everyday problems.
- To facilitate the pupils' integration in public life, and familiarize them with contemporary technical developments.
- To consolidate the respect for handwork and consider it as one of the essential bases for a decent and productive life.
- To strengthen the pupils' belief in doctrine and cultural and religious values.

Table 4.8 provides a comprehensive picture of Libyan educational institutions, teachers, and students as of 2003.

3. Higher Education, comprising universities, higher institutes, and technical centres. Study at these extends from 3 years for institutes and technical centres

and 4–6 years for some university faculties. While technical centres such as, or for example, The Specific Training Centre of the Petroleum Industry, Al Zawia, and the Petroleum Training and Qualifying Institute, Tripoli, award professional diplomas, universities and higher institutes award a Baccalaureate, Master, or Doctorate depending on the level and the particular university/higher institute.

In Table 4.9, statistics are provided which show the student/teacher ratio in Libya, a key ratio which has implications not only for the cost of education, but also for the quality. As can be seen the ratio has been reduced over the period from 1969

Table 4.8. Municipalities/educational institutes in Libya for the academic year 2002–2003

Municipality	Number of institutions	Number of teachers	Reserve teachers	Students	Classrooms
Tripoli	310	31249	9837	177679	8000
Benghazi	221	14216	2790	122660	3774
Misuratah	181	7028	760	75947	2942
Sebha	64	4765	669	35631	1550
Alnnikat Alghames	212	15986	2723	49189	3032
Baniwaled	66	3900	1110	19328	859
Surman & Sabratha	146	13717	5950	36753	2832
Albitnan	109	7134	1493	40512	1861
Aljabel Alakhder	152	9734	2272	52357	2200
Alwahat	46	925	91	7998	347
Almirqeb	269	11977	1566	85931	3358
Derna	51	4793	1182	22164	1434
Aljofra	43	2563	350	11941	746
Alkofra	29	1191	243	13497	522
Wadi Alhaya	67	2257	187	20204	1364
Turhona & Misllatah	376	12376	1937	76216	4747
Gfara	231	19296	6672	68233	3250
Murzuq	68	3009	358	17935	1277
Sirte	99	3893	726	37549	1979
Algobba	78	3342	385	21217	1277
Wadi Alshate	104	5106	1341	22016	1107
Yfren	159	5181	1079	27233	2208
Al Zawia	163	12485	4555	48433	3921
Almerj	92	4579	747	31852	1267
Nalut	96	3469	385	17589	1484
Ghryan	198	8269	1504	35785	2727
Alhizam Alakhder	109	3943	681	26870	1949
Ghadames	22	788	66	4699	252
Ejdabia	67	5169	1358	37771	2389
Mizda	45	1221	57	11095	515
Ghat	21	541	13	5872	208
Tagoura and Alnohee Alarbaa	211	8422	1275	71666	4527
Total	4105	232623	54253	1337840	69797

Source: Libyan Authority for Information and Documentation, 2005.

to 2001 from 25 and 9.2 to 10.2 and 5.9 for basic and intermediate education respectively. These levels of student/teacher ratios can be considered to be excellent not only regionally but globally, placing Libya at the very top not only in a MENA context but internationally, as shown in Table 4.10.

Libya's record at higher level is also commendable, with many Libyan students also achieving tertiary education at institutes abroad, despite the difficulties

Table 4.9. Basic and intermediate education: student/teacher ratio

Period	Basic education			Intermediate education		
	No of pupils	No. of teachers	Pupil/teacher ratio	No. of pupils	No. of teachers	Pupil/teacher ratio
1969/70	347100	13884	25	15300	1663	9.2
1975/76	679500	32357	21	43300	4330	10.0
1979/80	875000	54688	16	89500	7458	12.0
1985/86	1045200	69680	15	148700	9294	16.0
1994/95	1364900	74995	18.2	441300	35589	12.4
2000/2001	1202900	117931	10.2	380200	64441	5.9

Source: Libyan National Authority of Information and Documentation, 2005.

Table 4.10. MENA pupil/teacher ratios, 2002–2003

	Pupil/teacher ratio, primary: 2002/2003	Pupil/teacher ratio, secondary: 2002/2003
World[a]	22	17
Developing countries	28	20
Arab States	21	18
Algeria	28	21[b]
Bahrain	16[b,z]	12[b]
Djibouti	34[b,z]	28[b,z]
Egypt	22[b]	17[b]
Iraq	19	18
Jordan	20[b]	–
Kuwait	13	10[b,z]
Lebanon	17	8
Mauritania	41	26
Morocco	28	18[b]
Oman	21[b]	16[b]
Qatar	12	10
Saudi Arabia	12	12
Sudan	29[b]	26[b]
Syria	24[b,z]	18[b,y]
Tunisia	22	20[b,z]
UAE	15	14

[a] All values shown are medians;
[b] UIS estimation;
[y] Data are for 1999/2000
[z] Data are for 2000/2001
Source: UNESCO, EFA Global Monitoring Report, 2005.

imposed by the sanctions period. Tables 4.11–4.14 provide useful data on Libyans studying both in Libya and abroad.

The increase in the number of Libyans with advanced education, that is Master's or Ph.D., is shown in Table 4.12 as follows.

Again, in Table 4.13, Lecturer/Student Ratios are shown at tertiary level.

Table 4.11. Number of students in Libyan higher education institutions, 2005

	Number of students
Universities	246,000
Higher institutions	3,286
Higher medical institutes	5,260
Total	254,546

Source: Libyan Ministry of Higher Education, 2006.

Table 4.12. Development of domestic higher education, 1972–2005

Students with master/ PhD qualifications	Number of students
1972–1973	Less than 80
1994–1995	2350
1998–1999	5627
2004–2005	20000

Source: Libyan Ministry of Higher Education, 2006.

Table 4.13. Student: Lecturer ratios within Libyan higher education institutions, 2005

Universities	
Libyans	4143
Non-Libyans	2731
Part-time	3918
Total	10792
Ratio of student to lecturer	35:1
Higher institutions	
Libyans	86
Non-Libyans	58
Part-time	112
Total	256
Ratio of student to lecturer	20:1
Higher medical institutes	
Libyans	30
Non-Libyans	118
Part-time	737
Total	880
Ratio of student to lecturer	30:1

Source: Libyan Ministry of Higher Education, 2006.

Table 4.14. Development of the Libyan higher education students overseas, 1970–2005

Period	Total number of students
1970–1980	5000
1981–2004	7287
2005	645
Total	12932

Table 4.14 highlights how many Libyans have received tertiary education abroad, in total for the years 1970–1980 and 1981–2004, and those studying abroad as on 2005.

Teacher Training

It is a truism that the quality of the students is only as good as that of the teachers, and in Libya teacher training is accorded a high priority.

Due to the increase in entrants to education and in accordance with the legislation pertaining to compulsory education and the need to follow scientific and technological progress, teacher training programmes witnessed tangible progress in the beginning of the 1990s after an appraisal of teachers schools and education faculties led to the establishment of Institutes for Teacher Training in 1995, with the following aims:

- Develop the teacher's personality, on a scientific, educational, social, and professional level.
- Respond to the needs of basic education teachers in all majors.
- Adopt a selective method to accept teacher students in these institutes.
- Provide the teachers with the adequate specialized, educational, professional, and cultural training.
- Underline the importance of pre- and post-training by organizing training sessions for teachers during their work.

In the light of this, Libya expanded the number of Institutes for Teacher Training to 44 in 1998/1999, admitting 25,518 students specializing in applied sciences in addition to preschool and special education.

Libyan Education and the Arab World

As can be seen from the Table 4.15, the educational achievement in Libya compares very favourably most countries both globally and in the Arab World.
A general definition of literacy rate is the percentage of population aged 15 years and over who can both read and write a short simple statement on his/her everyday life. Adult literacy rates show the accumulated achievement of primary education and literacy programmes in imparting basic literacy skills to the population. Literacy in basic terms represents a potential for further intellectual growth and contribution to economic-socio-cultural development of society.

Table 4.15. Literacy rate, ages 15–24, selected Arab countries, 2001–2004

Region	Youth literacy rate (5–24) (%); 2000–2004[1]	Region	Youth literacy rate (15–24) (%), Male; 2000–2004[1]
World[a]	90.5	Mauritania	67.7
Developing countries	88.7	Morocco	77.4
Arab States	84.7	Oman	99.6
Algeria	94.1	Saudi Arabia	98.1
Bahrain	99.2	Sudan[2]	81.6
Egypt	79	Syria	97.1
Jordan	99.3	Tunisia	96.4
Kuwait	92.2	UAE	88.2
Libya	99.8	Yemen	84.3

[1]Data refer to the most recent year available during the period specified. See introduction to the statistical annex for broader explanation of national literacy definitions, assessment methods, sources, and years of data.
[2]Literacy data for the most recent year do not include some geographic regions.
[a]Weighted average.
Source: UNESCO, EFA Global Monitoring Report, 2006.

As can be seen, Libya is ranked first ahead of Oman, Jordan and Bahrein, with 99.8 per cent of the population aged between 15 and 24 years classified as literate. However, although Libya as well as other Arab countries such as Oman and Bahrein have made significant progress in education, particularly since the last quarter of the twentieth century, educational achievement in the Arab countries as a whole, judged even by traditional criteria, is still poor when compared to other parts of the world, even in developing countries. In this respect, it is fair to say that Libya has bucked this trend, especially in gender and attendance, where educational opportunities and enrolment for males and females show little difference. As we will discuss later, however, the quantity of educated students is not the same as the quality of the education received, and in this respect Libya still needs to make progress in the new century.

4.2.2 Trends in Expenditure on Education

Figure 4.1 provides a comprehensive picture of two key national indicators for education for the period 1970–2006: first, the annual expenditure on education and, secondly, the percentage of the State Development Budget spent on education. Starting in 1970, when an amount of 7.6 million LD was spent, this more than doubled to 17.9 million in 1971 and doubled again to 35.1 million in 1972, thereafter rising steadily throughout the 1970s and early 1980s, reaching a peak of 194.3 million in 1982, reflecting high levels of all Libyan sectoral expenditure due

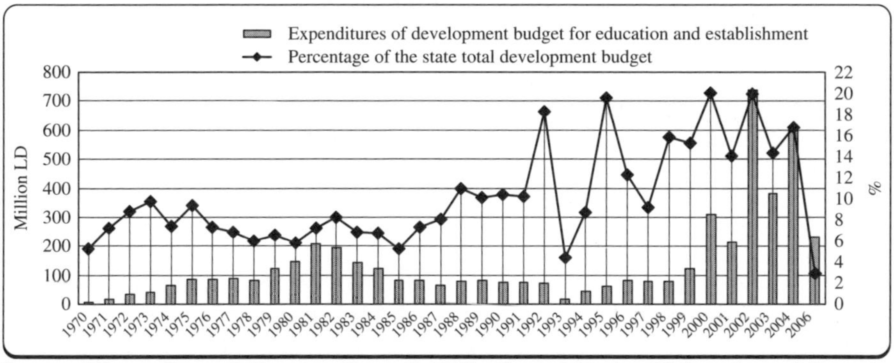

Source: Libyan General Planning Council, 2001; Central Bank of Libya Annual Reports; IMF, 2006

Fig. 4.1. Development budget expenditure on education 1970–2006

to an oil price of over US $40 per barrel occasioned by the Iranian revolution and the Iraqi-Iranian War. From 1986 to 1999, annual expenditure on education was significantly reduced, averaging 72 million LD, reflecting a lower oil price in the mid-1980s of less than US $9 per barrel, as well as the significantly reduced production from Libyan oilfields due to the departure of the US oil companies. It fell to a low of 17.8 million in 1993, the same level as 20 years earlier, before rising significantly again to 72.5, 62.5, 308.1, and 216.1 million LD for the years 1992, 1995, 2000, and 2002 respectively. In 2004 it increased to LD603 million, before falling again to a budgeted LD230 million in 2006.

The percentage of annual government expenditure for education reflects the priority afforded to education in a given country. Analysing Fig. 4.1, the percentage of the State Development Budget spent on education averaged more than 10 per cent throughout the entire period. Despite the sanctions which commenced in 1986, expenditure on education increased steadily and averaged 11.47 per cent between 1986 and 1999, during the sanctions period, falling to a low of 4 per cent in 1993, caused mainly by a collapse in oil prices. For the 4 years 2000–2003 inclusive, due to the lifting of the UN sanctions in 1999 on a considerably improved oil price, it shot up to an average of 17.07 per cent, reaching peaks of almost 20 per cent in the years 2000 and 2002, before falling back to 16.8 per cent in 2004.

4.2.3 Libyan Education and the Future

The Libyan government announced in 2004 that an estimated US $35 billion has been set aside to improve Libya's infrastructure, and in line with Libya's historical emphasis on the importance of education, improvements in this field in a post-sanctions world are vitally necessary. Failure to address these issues will mean that the present and future generations of Libyans will be globally disadvantaged.

In numerous studies the so-called "digital divide" has been proven to exist between various parts of the world, measured through a range of statistical indices, including the number of stationary telephone lines, Personal Computers (PCs), websites, and Internet users and their ratio to the total population. The Arab world in general, including Libya, ranks low on some of these indicators. For example, Arabs represent 5 per cent of the world population but only 0.5 per cent of Internet users.

Again, Arab countries have some of the lowest levels of research funding in the world. Research and Development (R&D) expenditure as a percentage of GDP was a mere 0.4 for the Arab world in 1996, compared to 1.26 in 1995 for Cuba, 2.35 in 1994 for Israel, and 2.9 for Japan. Science and technology output is quantifiable and measurable in terms of the number of scientific papers per unit of population. The average output of the Arab world per million inhabitants is roughly 2 per cent of that of an industrialized country. While Arab scientific output more than doubled from 11 papers per million in 1985 to 26 papers per million in 1995, China's output increased elevenfold from one paper per million inhabitants in 1981 to 11 papers per million in 1995. The Republic of Korea increased its output from 6 to 144 papers per million inhabitants over the same period (UNDP, Arab Human Development Report 2002).

Again, in spite of significant internal variability and compared to world leaders, Arab countries in general clearly lag behind in technology creation (measured by patents granted to residents) and diffusion of recent innovations (measured by the share of high- and medium-technology exports in total goods exports). On the other hand, Arab countries fared relatively better on diffusion of old innovations (measured by telephone lines relative to population).

During the past 20 years, there has been a massive transformation of industrial firms in OECD countries; outsourcing and subcontracting have contributed to breaking down the vertically integrated firm. Integration has instead taken the form of joining a global web of technological expertise; meanwhile, outsourcing has promoted the transfer of technology to Asian and Latin American subcontractors along with the transfer of employment from high-cost to low-cost countries. A number of Asian countries such as Malaysia, Thailand, and Indonesia have successfully secured a considerable share of subcontracting from major transnational corporations, but Arab countries have hardly benefited from the globalization of outsourcing.

Again in terms of industrial productivity, although figures for Libya alone are not available, the World Bank estimates of total factor productivity in the MENA region showed a steady decline (–0.2 per cent a year) from 1960 to 1990, compared to rapid acceleration in other parts of the world. Data from the 1998/1999 World Development Report permit comparisons of GDP per worker in nine Arab countries with those in faster-growing developing countries during the periods 1980–1990 and 1990–1997. On this basis, annual productivity is estimated to have risen by 15 per cent in China, 8 per cent in the Republic of Korea, and 6 per cent in India, but only 4 percent in the Arab countries.

It is therefore clear that, however commendable Libyan educational achievements have been over the last 30 years, Libya must still invest heavily in education, which is the key to the country's future development success. As the end of the sanctions period offers global choices for Libyan education policy makers, a major rethinking for the overhaul of Libyan education is required, addressing what is now known as "borderless education". This should seriously examine reducing barriers to allow foreign universities to have branch campuses in Libya. As early as 1996, for example, Malaysia, through the Private Higher Education Act of that year, encouraged international and private education providers to set up branch campuses in Malaysia, but set out very detailed and stringent requirements for approval, in order to guarantee quality. One of the first to do so was Monash University of Australia, later followed by the University of Nottingham, United Kingdom, Malaysia Campus, and Curtin University in Sarawak, Malaysia.

This allowed Malaysian students to get an internationally recognized and technologically and scientifically up-to-date educational qualification, at the same time saving Malaysia valuable foreign exchange, previously spent on expensive courses in European and US universities. Several Arab countries in fact have already successfully used this approach. Examples are the University of Wollongong, Australia, in the United Arab Emirates, and Cornell University Medical School as well as the University of Texas School of Petroleum Engineering in Qatar.

Perhaps it is now the right time for Libya to examine strategies for attracting international experts and talents in the academic and technological fields to live and teach in Libya, as well as considering a change in legislation to facilitate the establishment of branch foreign campuses to be set up in Libya, similar to the Malaysian Private Higher Education Act of 1996. In this respect it is interesting to note the way in which the Monash Malaysian campus was set up and evolved into its current five schools – Arts and Sciences, Business, Information Technology, Medicine and Health Sciences, and Engineering with almost 3,000 students. In 1997, Monash University of Australia partnered with the Sungei Way Group, a Malaysian business conglomerate, with interests in construction, manufacturing, leisure, and tourism. The Sungei Way Group initially funded the construction of a purpose-built campus close to Kuala Lumpur, the Malaysian capital, and then leased it back over a long-term period to Monash in a win–win business partnership.

In this regard, in a seminar in the United States, in May 2005, the first author of this book was advised that several universities located in Texas with strong faculties in Law, Business, Medicine, and Engineering were seriously interested in contributing their expertise to set up branch campuses in Libya.

It is also important that Libya, in view of its vast and yet untapped tourist potential, and the government's recent announcements regarding massive expansion and diversification of this sector, should start thinking about how to secure tertiary education and qualifications for Libyans who wish to make a career in the hotel, tourist, and hospitality industry. Again, valuable foreign exchange could be saved if such a branch campus were to be set up in Libya, at the same time providing significant career and employment potential for the large number of Libyans under 25 currently unemployed. Similarly, as environmental issues begin to progressively impact legislation and policies globally, Libya needs to ensure that its younger generation does not miss out on the vast opportunities in this field, again by looking at cooperation with international educational institutions recognized in this area.

4.2.4 The Importance of English

Underlying all of these future goals in education, the Libyan government must move back quickly to an acceptance and recognition of the international importance of the English language. Until the mid-1980s English was still a part of the school curriculum in Libya; yet in a change of policy in 1980, to reduce the preponderance of foreign teachers in Libya, the government enacted the "New Educational Structure". School curriculae were restructured in favour of technical subjects and, in the humanities, Arabic language and Koranic education were particularly emphasized, at the expense of English. For Libya this has proved to be a fundamental and disastrous mistake, as witnessed by the first author of this book, made in the name of a misplaced nationalist policy which has set back Libya, in terms of educational quality, by two generations. To cite the Malaysian educational experience again, the policy of "Malay language first" was implemented between 1969 and 1983, and effectively resulted in the replacement of English by Bahasa Malaysia (Malay language) as the medium of instruction in the entire education system. As a consequence, competence in Standard English (SE) declined considerably, leading to falling standards in Malaysia's schools, undermining Malaysia's competitiveness in international trade and technology. In a complete reversal, the Malaysian government under Dr. Mahathir Mohamed radically changed the language policy, leading to a sustained reintroduction of English as the medium of instruction, first, in 1996, in tertiary education and in the sciences, and, subsequently, since 2002, from the beginning of schooling, in sciences and maths. In a statement Dr. Mahathir, although no longer Malaysian Prime Minister, reinforced the position of English even more strongly.

> There is a need for English to be completely mastered because the instructions are no longer going to be simple. It is unfortunate perhaps for the language nationalists but that is the reality today. They must not blight future generations by objecting to the mastery and usage of the English language. They must not obstruct Malaysia's progress and development. (Mahathir Mohamed October, 2005)

The world in the age of globalization faces a new set of rules and competencies. As quoted in a recent BBC series

> Governments across the world, from Chile to China, from Malta to Malaysia, have in the last few years embarked on ambitious educational reforms which will integrate English more deeply into the curriculum. English will cease to be a foreign language for many, perhaps most, of the world's citizens as it becomes repositioned as a "basic skill", to be learned by primary school children alongside other 21st century skills in Information Technology. (Literacy Trust, 2005)

4.2.5 Accelerating Technical Education and IT

The last 20 years have witnessed a revolution in technology brought about by a lowering in prices of both computer hardware and software, effectively revolutionizing every industrial process and commercial sector such as international trade instruments, banking, and finance. The countries which stress lifelong learning and a knowledge-based society, such as, for example, Singapore, are the ones which will survive and expand in this new world where IT skills and knowledge of technological processes count for more than the old inputs of land, labour, and capital in ensuring economic success.

This leads the first author of this book to seriously question the decision, in 2000, by the Libyan Ministry of Education, to close down the Bright Star University of Technology at El Brega, which with its five faculties of Petroleum – Mechanical, Chemical, Electronic and Basic Engineering – was able to produce high quality technical graduates who now hold high level positions throughout the Libyan and MENA hydrocarbon industry. He contends that this was an educational institution, with its massive campus and dormitory facilities, set up at a significant cost, which was ideally suited to propel Libya into the technological age, using state-of-the-art facilities, with the potential to make Libya self-sufficient in oilfield manpower, ranging from the technologist and managerial levels to hands-on operatives in the field. He feels it was a fundamental error in educational policy to close down this very promising institution.

In the aftermath of the lifting of the US sanctions, it is now the right time for initial steps to be taken to plan the re-establishment and re-equipment of this university, in cooperation with international educational institutions, most probably as a branch campus of one or several US universities. With the high level of interest generated among US companies in the EPSA IV rounds of January and September 2005, and the return to Libya of Occidental, Shell, and BP, we believe that Libyan/US/European cooperation in reviving the Bright Star University of Technology would be a very attractive proposition, most definitely in everyone's interest.

4.3 Housing in Libya

As noted from a previous section on demographic trends, Libya experienced an average annual population growth rate of 3 per cent for most of the second half of the twentieth century, at the same time experiencing one of the most rapid rates of urbanization among the Arab countries. Combined, these factors have exerted tremendous pressure on demand for housing in Libya, and an awareness of their impact can help to explain many of the anomalies regarding the current housing situation in Libya. In any country, the knock-on effects of housing policy on the labour market, on saving trends and patterns, as well as on the quality of life and economic growth, are very significant.

In order to fully understand the present status of the Libyan housing sector, we need to look back to the ideological basis of the revolution, embedded in the Libyan Constitution issued at the end of 1969, where Article 6 states, "The aim of the state is the realization of socialism through the application of social justice which forbids any form of exploitation." Social justice, with regard to the right to shelter for every Libyan citizen, was defined in Colonel Qadhafi's Green Book: Part 2, The Solution of the Economic Problem, p. 15, as follows:

> Housing is an essential need for both the individual and the family and should not be owned by others. Living in another's house, whether paying rent or not, compromises freedom. Attempts made by various countries to solve the housing problem did not provide a definite solution because such attempts did not target the ultimate solution – the necessity that people own their dwellings – but rather offered the reduction, increase, or standardization of rent, whether it went to privately or publicly-owned enterprise. In a socialist society, no one, including society itself, has the right to control people's needs. No one has the right to acquire a house additional to his or her own dwelling and that of his or her heirs for the purpose of renting it because this additional house is, in fact, a need of someone else. Acquiring it for such a purpose is the beginning of controlling the needs of others and in need, freedom is latent.

In essence, the ownership of a house was one of the basic rights of every Libyan citizen.

A survey undertaken immediately after the revolution found that 150,000 families lacked decent shelter, the actual housing shortfall being placed upwards of 180,000 dwellings. In order to correct the situation, and to bring this basic right to reality, the new government spent massively on housing in the First (1976–1980) and the Second (1981–1985) Development Plans, with both state-owned housing companies and the private sector actively constructing houses throughout Libya, which were at that period simply given to Libyan citizens.

By the late 1970s and early 1980s, the slum tenements and unsanitary dwellings surrounding Benghazi and Tripoli gave way to modern apartment blocks with electricity and running water, which now characterizes the skylines of these cities. Typical of these developments were entire new cities constructed with houses of generous proportions and futuristic design, such as El Brega Citizens City (3,000 units) and Ras Lanuf (1,500 units). In 1991, in Libya's main seaport of Benghazi, 7,000 modern units of unique Libya design, were constructed, while a similar development in the Angila region of Tripoli was undertaken. Again, all of these units were allocated free of charge to Libyan citizens. Table 4.16 illustrates the number of housing units constructed in the period from 1970 to 1996, when all the major housing initiatives were undertaken, totalling an impressive 382,450 units. After this period, because of the sanctions and low oil prices, no major housing projects were undertaken until 2005, when as discussed below the 50,000-unit Tajoura new city project commenced.

4.3.1 Trends in Development Expenditure on Housing

In the late 1980s and early 1990s, as a more stringent economic atmosphere prevailed because of a sharp decline in international oil prices, the government introduced a system of loans to individual Libyan citizens based on monthly deductions at affordable levels from state employees' salaries for the construction of houses.

Table 4.17 provides a useful overview of loans made to both Libyan individuals and construction projects for the entire period 1966–2005. The rapid rate of expansion from 2001 onwards can be attributed to the government's attempts to deal with a pent-up housing demand due to demographic pressure.

Table 4.16. Number of housing units completed during the major construction period 1970–1996

Housing type	Number of housing units prepared	%
Public housing	95567	25.0
Agricultural housing	13827	3.6
Houses of public projects	3521	0.9
New cities and towns	6319	1.6
El Brega New City	3056	0.8
Ras Lanuf New City	1510	0.4
Housing of Central Secretariats (Sirte & Al Jofra)	4198	1.4
Housing of Farmers of Central Region of Libya	531	0.1
Housing of Saving and Real Estate Investment Bank Loans	2737	0.7
Housing of National Investment Council of Real Estate	8500	2.2
Housing of Social Security	8980	2.3
Housing of Libyan Insurance Company	1335	0.3
Housing of National Investments Company	7776	2.0
Housing loans provided by saving and real estate investment bank loans	63250	16.5
Housing loans by commercial banks and cooperative associations	81194	21.2
Housing by self-sponsoring	80329	21.0
Total	382450	100

Source: Libya: Ministry of Planning, Economics and Trade: Achievements of the National Economy for 27 Years, 1996.

Table 4.17. Savings and real estate investment bank loans, 1966–2005

Year	Loans for housing	Construction projects	Total	Year	Loans for housing	Construction projects	Total
1966	6.0	–	6.0	1986	7.9	0.7	8.6
1967	5.0	–	5.0	1987	11.8	0.5	12.3
1968	3.5	–	3.5	1988	20.3	0.4	20.7
1969	4.8	–	4.8	1989	13.6	3.2	16.8
1970	10.1	–	10.1	1990	26.4	3.3	29.7
1971	16.4	–	16.4	1991	30.0	2.5	32.5
1972	22.3	–	22.3	1992	8.6	1.3	9.9
1973	15.5	15.4	30.9	1993	12.4	1.3	13.7
1974	36.6	15.0	51.6	1994	19.0	1.4	20.4
1975	13.6	1.4	15.0	1995	18.0	1.8	19.8
1976	3.7	0.8	4.5	1996	18.6	2.4	21.0
1977	55.3	0.2	55.5	1997	31.6	4.7	36.3
1978	35.9	–	35.9	1998	17.2	20.2	37.4
1979	8.3	–	8.3	1999	9.9	25.4	35.3
1980	40.4	–	40.4	2000	37.7	17.0	54.7
1981	61.9	–	61.9	2001	75.5	18.7	94.2
1982	78.7	4.2	82.9	2002	302.9	12.6	315.5
1983	39.6	0.6	40.2	2003	511.6	198.6	710.2
1984	53.6	1.4	55.0	2004	886.0	83.8	969.8
1985	7.2	0.2	7.4	2005	1554.0	84.0	1638.0

*In Million LD
Source: Saving and Real Estate Investment Bank, 2005; IMF, 2006.

In Fig. 4.2, loans to the real estate sector by Libyan banks from 1990 to 2005 are shown, generally exhibiting an upward trend.

Figure 4.3 provides a comprehensive picture of two key national indicators for housing for the period 1969–2006: first, the annual expenditure on housing and, secondly, the percentage of the State Development Budget spent on housing. Starting in the year 1968/1969, when an amount of 18.2 million LD was spent, it almost tripled to 52.8 million for the year 1970/1971. However, for the year 1974, in line with the determination of the new government to honour its constitutional pledge of "housing for all", it almost quadrupled to 202.6 million, almost doubling again to 399 million for the year 1979. In fact for the 10 years from 1971 to 1980 an average of 220.73 million was spent on housing. In 1981 a massive 639.7 million was spent on housing, while throughout the 1980s it averaged 367 million. Throughout the 1990s it dropped, however, to around half of the average of the previous decade, to 153 million per year as the

In Million LD

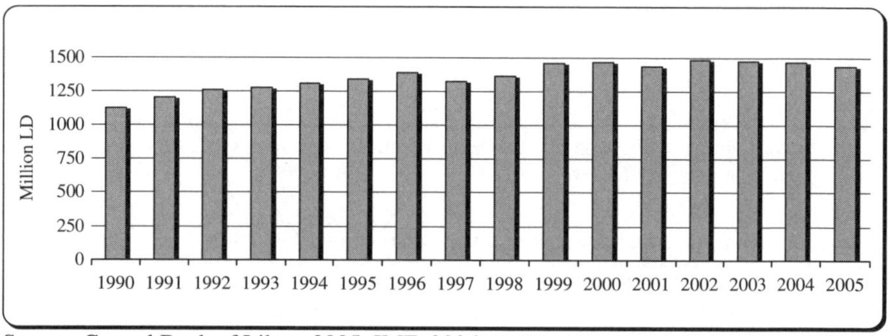

Source: Central Bank of Libya, 2005; IMF, 2006

Fig. 4.2. Commercial banks credit to real estate sector, 1990–2005

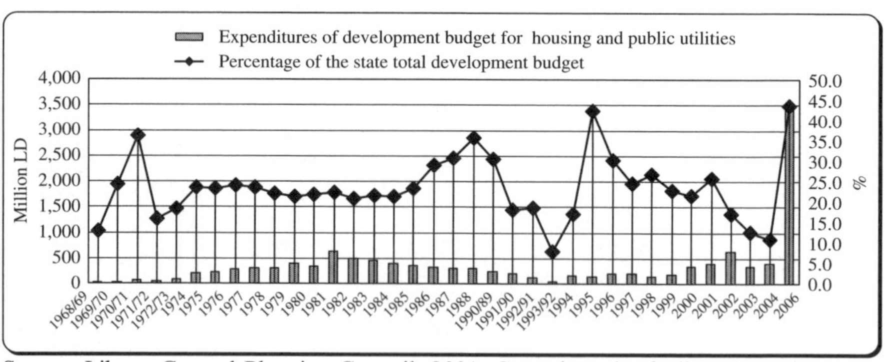

Source: Libyan General Planning Council, 2001; Central Bank of Libya Annual Reports; IMF, 2006

Fig. 4.3. Housing expenditure, 1969–2006

sanctions took their toll on the Libyan population. However, for the 4 years 2000–2003 the average shot up dramatically to 423 million per year, reaching 631 million in 2002 alone. Although it declined to 388 million in 2004, it was budgeted to increase massively to 3.4 billion LD in 2006. This clearly showed the efforts of the Libyan government to cope with a significant housing backlog brought about by the overall lower expenditure, especially throughout the 1990s due, as we have noted, to the impact of the sanctions on the Libyan economy, as well as population growth factors.

In terms of the percentage of government expenditure on housing, the figure reached 36 per cent in 1971, 35 per cent in 1988, 42 per cent in 1995, and a massive 43.5 per cent in 2006 of total government expenditure. In terms of the commitment and success of the government's pledges of home-ownership for all, there is no country in the world which has come anywhere near to the Libyan achievement.

Although, as analysed above, due mainly to fluctuations in the crude oil price, expenditure on housing varied in total from year to year both in amount and as a percentage of annual budget spending, Figs. 4.4 and 4.5 illustrate the success of the Libyan government in its drive towards personal home-ownership for all. Figure 4.4 shows that, by 2003, there were a total number of 829,723 houses for a total Libyan population of 5,678,484, giving an average of 6.84 occupants per house. In this context, it must be remembered that we are talking about well-constructed units with comprehensive infrastructure including roads, water, toilets, and power supplied. As can be seen, of the total, 500,673 houses or 60.34 per cent are described as Arabic Houses, which are single-storey units constructed within separate plots with a garden, while Large Villas, comprising 15.74 per cent, amount to 130,635 units, and are double-storey in design. Family apartments, amounting to 168,194 units, make up most of the balance of 20.27 per cent. These are generally situated in four-storey apartment blocks, although also situated in high-rise apartments, which are a recognized feature of the Tripoli and Benghazi landcapes.

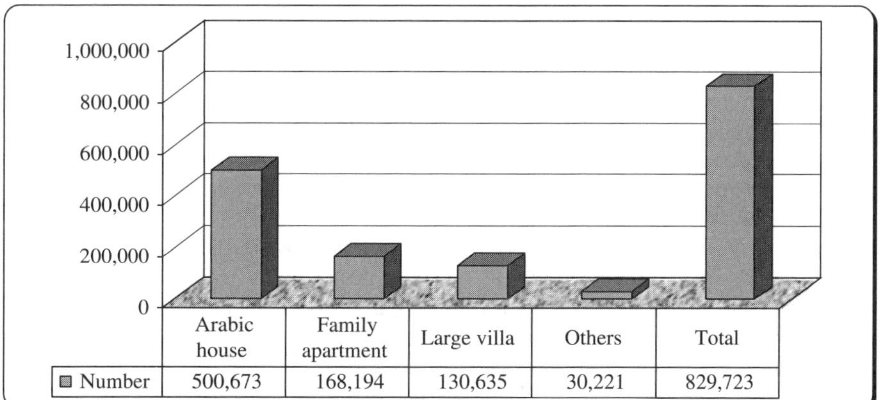

Source: Libyan Information and Documentation Authority, 2005

Fig. 4.4. Breakdown of housing by type, 2003

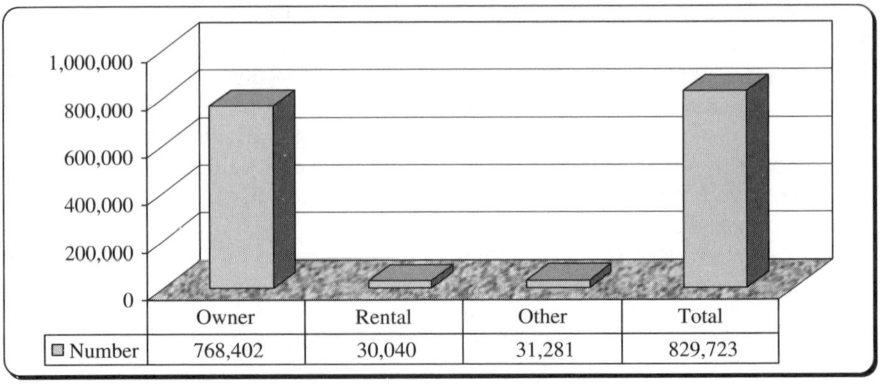

Source: Libyan Information and Documentation Authority, 2005

Fig. 4.5. Breakdown of housing by ownership/rental, 2003

In terms of estimating the success of the Libyan government's policy of home-ownership for all, Fig. 4.5 shows that 92.61 per cent of all houses in Libya are privately owned, with rental and other categories at 3.62 per cent and 3.77 per cent respectively. This undoubtedly places Libya at the top of the home-ownership league globally. In the United States, for example, where citizen home-ownership is also a cornerstone of public policy, home-ownership in the second quarter of 2005 peaked in the US Midwest region, where the highest incidence of home-ownership occurs, at 74.2 per cent of the population (US Bureau of the Census September, 2005). In Norway, the most advanced European country in terms of home-ownership, the figure is 80 per cent. In Asia, Singapore has the highest home-ownership rate at 85 per cent (The National Centre for Policy Analysis 2005). In a North African context, in Tunisia, another Arab nation with a very progressive housing policy, the official figure stands at 80 per cent (Tunisie, Institut National de la Statistique 2005)

Despite the success of the Libyan government's housing policy, it should be noted that there are still, in a regional context, areas where the government's policy of home-ownership for all have not entirely succeeded. Tobruk, Aljabel Alakhder, Albitnan, Algobba, and Sebha are cases in point. However, in most of these areas it must be recognized that constraints on the provision of housing for all exist because of their sparsely populated nature and the correspondingly high cost of infrastructure necessary for the construction of modern serviced housing per head of population.

Similarly, the Libyan government needs to address the severe health and social problems resulting from the creation of unsanitary shanty towns constructed by African immigrants in the Al Zawia municipality, 40 km from Tripoli, as well as several other camps of this type in Sebha, the main entry point to Libya for Africans from the south.

4.3.2 Libyan Housing in the Future

Demographic factors will mean that increasing demand for housing will be a constant and continuous factor in the Libyan economy, with the current trend in population growth effectively meaning that Libyan population could double by 2025. Not only this, but the planned diversification and overhaul of the Libyan economy, as well as its opening up to foreign investment, will also bring about pressure in the housing market, as more foreigners and workers will inevitably require accommodation. Also, when higher expectations and human factors for betterment are also considered, demand for upgrading and second homes by Libyans is certain to increase, since Article 2 of Law No. 3 of 2004 now officially allows Libyan citizens to own more than one house in specific cases, including real estate investment.

In fact, the trend underlying an apparent insatiable demand for housing is already happening in Tripoli, where massive housing projects are now being developed in land officially zoned in the Green Belt, with the Libyan government turning a blind eye. This is a tacit admission by the government that it can no longer deal with demand for housing.

This does not mean, however, that the government has abandoned its housing policy. For example, the foundation stone for a new residential city of 50,000 housing units developed by the government was laid in early September 2005, at a 750-ha site at Tajoura, on the outskirts of Tripoli. In his speech at this ceremony the Libyan Prime Minister Dr. Shukri Ghanem stated that there currently existed a shortage of 95,000 proper sanitary housing units in Tripoli alone, a figure which was set to increase to 300,000 by 2010 if not successfully dealt with by the government. In a similar vein, the Chairman of the Bank of Savings and Investment Bashir Mahdi announced in September 2005 that the bank had recently signed a contract with 226 national construction companies to construct 20,000 housing units in all major cities of Libya, a project worth close to LD1 billion. The Libyan Prime Minister laid the foundation stones for major new housing projects in Sebha, Tripoli itself, and Benghazi in September, 2006.

In general terms, it must also be recognized that, largely due to its overall inefficiency, the public housing approach, which has been abandoned throughout the former Soviet Union and the reforming countries of Eastern Europe, has severe limitations in its ability to deal with Libya's future housing needs for both Libyans and foreign investors alike. As the country modernizes and pressure for housing increases, policy makers must now devise and structure a forward-looking housing policy which will inevitably mean that a greater share of housing and real estate development will be taken up by the private sector.

At the same time, as a consequence of demographic increases, Libya is experiencing a rapid growth in its labour force, especially in the age group of 20–29. This demand from the young married group will again put pressure on the supply of first homes, which the government alone may not be able to satisfy. Again, with a more dynamic approach to housing involving more private sector development, the housing sector has the potential to play a critical role in generating employment among young Libyans looking for work.

Another way of meeting future housing demand would be by the Libyan government encouraging Public Private Partnerships (PPPs) for land development and housing provision. In Libya, where public ownership of land is the cornerstone of housing policy, land serviced with infrastructure is in short supply and, as time passes, this shortage will increase. Land management reforms focusing on land development and public private partnerships and, for example, the provision of basic infrastructure services to identified plots, for later development by the private sector to meet increasing demand, are policies that might be considered by the Libyan government.

Another factor inhibiting housing development and improvement, at both an individual and a commercial level, is the inability of Libyan Banks to provide mortgages to private individuals or entities. For future housing demand to be satisfied, the government must now look into this serious deficiency; otherwise not only privates home-ownership, but also inward investment will suffer. As we saw in Fig. 4.5, rental of housing stood at 3.62 per cent in 2003. But in reality, demand in Libya for rental accommodation is massive not only for foreign investors and immigrants, but also for Libyans themselves, as the process of urbanization continues and attitudes towards social mobility within the country change. Although the Libyan government has succeeded all too well in meeting its social objectives in housing, the full value of housing as an economic asset has now got to be realized and incorporated into the legal system. This should lead to the general availability of mortgages to Libyans who wish to invest in real estate as a productive asset. The position of foreigners who wish to invest, own, and develop properties in Libya also needs to be addressed. Although, as provided in the 1997 Investment Law, foreign companies can now own premises required for the pursuit of their business, the government could consider extending this to allow foreigners to buy or construct houses and become involved in housing development in Libya.

It is only by effecting drastic legal changes in this regard that Libya will truly emerge as a modern nation in the twenty-first century. In this connection, looking back at the Constitutional Declaration of 1969, it is now abundantly clear that although the "housing for all" policy achieved its social objectives, it did so at the expense of breaking down the trust between private investors and the public, leading to a commercially depressed housing sector, as unattractive for Libyans themselves as for foreign investors. This meant that investment in the commercial property sector and in second homes was perceived to be high risk and uncertain, which has led to the present imbalances and shortages, especially in the Libyan rental sector.

Although legislation such as Article 2 of Law No. 3 of 2004 touched on above now provides for second-home-ownership, the Libyan policy makers need to go much further in order to reinvigorate the property sector. In this connection, we have only to look at the recent experience of the UAE, which, with an area of 83,600 km^2, has been very successful in attracting real estate investment from all over the world, especially in the tiny enclave of Dubai. Libya, with a land area of 1,776,000 km^2, is certainly not short of land.

4.4 The Libyan Healthcare System

4.4.1 Evolution of the Libyan Healthcare System

A basic healthcare system existed in Libya at independence in 1951 with very limited resources, comprising 14 hospitals with a total 1,600-bed capacity and several small health centres. After the 1969 revolution, constitutional rights to healthcare for every Libyan citizen were guaranteed by Article 15 of the Libyan Constitutional Declaration which states, "Health care is a right guaranteed by the State to all Libyan citizens through the creation of hospitals and health establishments in accordance with the law."

Healthcare started in earnest in 1969 when the major objective was for basic individual patient care. Between 1970 and 1979 there were massive investments in the health sector, with emphasis on the construction and provision of community health centres and hospitals, services, and associated facilities. Since 1980 the national health policy has been determined by the General People's Committee for Health and Social Security, which has laid down a framework for the health strategy. In broad terms, this strategy determines health programmes aimed at delivering a comprehensive medical care service to all citizens, regardless of locality, with the current motto for health policy being "health for all by all". The strategy is designed to create a society in which every member can play an active role, both socially and economically, and in which health services are equally distributed among the whole population, involving both the provision of public health facilities as well as preventive health.

Until the mid-1980s, all health services were provided by the state. However, in 1987–1988 the Libyan government embarked on a set of reform initiatives based on the concept of "tashrukkiya", or self-management and collective ownership, moving away from the purely public sector model towards private ownership. Although in general terms the reform agenda of this period was not successful, it proved to be a useful model for the health sector. In practice, a group of doctors would combine to establish a medical tashrukkiya which would offer their services to both the Libyan public and the foreigners alike, with treatment paid for by the patients themselves, unlike the public health facilities which were free. These medical tashrukkiya have succeeded largely because of their superior equipment and service, and are now a prominent feature of the Libyan healthcare system. This effectively means that in Libya there is presently a mixed system of public and private health care, rather than a purely state-run model, although most people use the public healthcare facilities for economic reasons.

4.4.2 Structure of the Libyan Healthcare System

In terms of organization of resources, the public health system operates on three levels:

- The first comprises the basic health care units, designed to provide curative and preventive services for 5,000–10,000 patients.
- The second level comprises the basic health care centres, which cater for between 10,000 and 26,000 patients.
- The third level consists of the polyclinics, which perform a key role in maintaining health in Libya's main cities. These are staffed by medical specialists and equipped with laboratories, radiological services, and pharmacies, with the capability of handling approximately 50,000–60,000 patients.

The country's two major hospitals are located in the most important Libyan cities, Tripoli and Benghazi. They are affiliated with medical schools and specialized institutes that train nurses and medical technicians. A wide range of medical services is found at these hospitals. Smaller towns and villages have medical clinics or small hospitals. Mobile health units also travel to rural areas to provide health care. All the major Libyan Universities such as the Al-Fateh University in Tripoli and the Gar-Younis University of Benghazi offer full and internationally well-regarded medical degrees. There is no doubt that in terms of training and providing human resources for the health sector, Libya has done an excellent job, as is witnessed by the very large number of Libyan doctors working in the United Kingdom and Canada for example.

Table 4.18 illustrates key trends in the development of Libyan healthcare system from 1970 to 2004.

Table 4.18. Trends in the development of Libyan healthcare system, 1970–2004

Indicators	Number		Increase
	1970	2004	%
No. of beds	7589	19499	156
No. of clinic complexes	1	39	3800
No. of basic health care centres	12	306	2450
No. of basic health care units	439	886	101
No. of tubercular centres	9	22	144
No. of physicians	783	9234	1079
No. of population per physician	2507	800	319
No. of staff nurses	3073	30085	879
No. of population per nurse	639	207	308
No. of technicians	385	13387	3377
No. of population per technician	5098	443	1150
No. of adminstrative staff	–	24071	–

Source: 1970 figures from Libyan General Council of Planning, 2001; 2004 figures from the Libyan Ministry of Health and Enivironment, 2006.

As can be seen, improvements both in terms of physical healthcare infrastructure such as clinics and healthcare centres, as well as in the general population/healthcare professional ratio have been major.

4.4.3 Primary Health Care

In terms of primary health care, including family planning, clean water supply, sanitation, immunization, and nutrition education, there were substantial increases between 1978 and 1997. For example, the percentage of the population with access to a safe water supply rose from 90 to 95 per cent, adequate excreta disposal facilities from 70 to 86 per cent, immunization coverage of infants from 55 to 92–99 per cent, local health care from 76 to 100 per cent, prenatal care by trained health personnel from 76 to 81 per cent, delivery by trained health personnel from 76 to 99 per cent, infant care by trained personnel from 95 to 100 per cent, and contraceptive use by pregnant women from 5 to 45 per cent. Regarding adequacy of nutritional status, the percentage of neonates weighing at least 2,500 g increased marginally between 1978 and 1997 from 95 to 96 per cent, and acceptable weight-for-age among under-5s increased to 85.5 per cent.

4.4.4 Libyan Healthcare in a Regional Perspective

Per capita health expenditure is a useful indicator which shows the amount per citizen a government spends on the health sector. Although the data are not sensitive to differences in allocations within sectors, for example primary health care in relation to other levels within the health sector, it provides a good basis for a general comparison between countries. In regional terms, Fig. 4.6 provides an insight into Libya's position in North Africa, placing it second with US $327 per head of population.

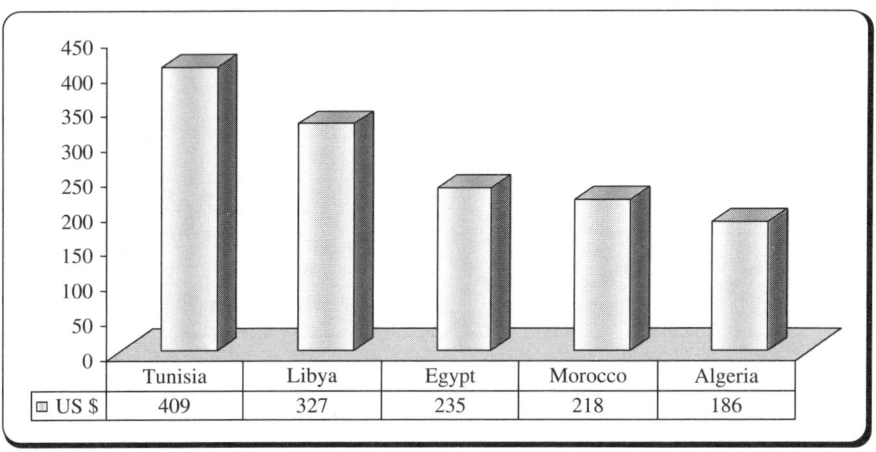

Source: World Health Organization, 2006

Fig. 4.6. Per capita health expenditure in North Africa region, 2004

In comparison to other states in the North Africa and the Middle East, the health status of the Libyan population can be regarded as acceptable. Another useful indicator, the government's expenditure on health as a percentage of GDP, shows that Libya occupies an intermediate position between Qatar at the lower extreme and Lebanon at the top, as illustrated in the Fig. 4.7.

4.4.5 Trends in Health and Social Security Expenditure

Figure 4.8 provides a comprehensive picture of two key national indicators for health for the period 1970–2006: first, the annual expenditure in the State Development

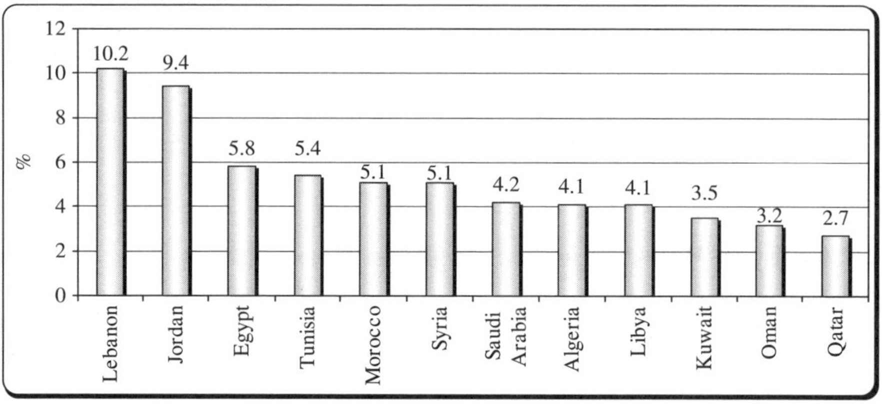

Source: World Health Organization, 2006

Fig. 4.7. Selected MENA countries: health expenditure as a percentage of GDP, 2004

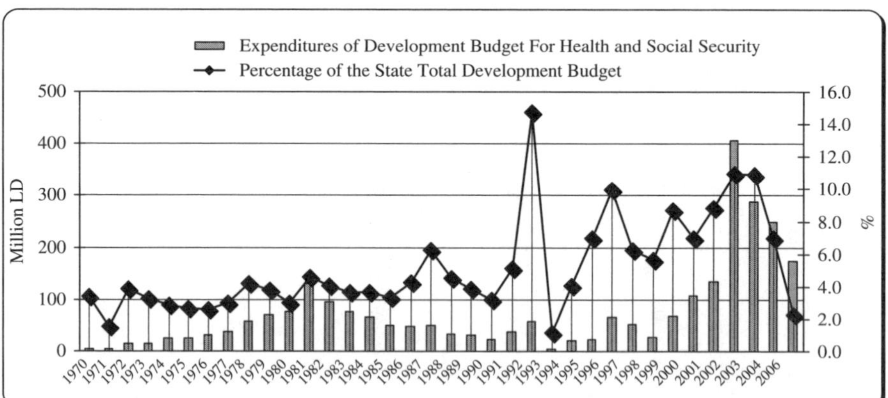

Source: Libyan General Planning Council, 2001; Central Bank of Libya Annual Reports; IMF 2006

Fig. 4.8. Libya: Health and Social Security Indicators 1970–2006

Budget on health and social security, and, secondly, an annual percentage of the State Development Budget. Starting in 1970, when an amount of 4.9 million LD was spent, it more than tripled to 15.4 million by 1972, and by 1976 this figure had doubled to 30.8 million. It continued to rise steadily throughout the 1980s, reaching a figure of 131.7 million by 1981, reflecting the prevailing rising trend in crude oil prices. For the 10 years from 1981 to 1990 it averaged 60.3 million per year, dropping to a low of 4.6 million in 1993 due to the collapse in state revenue from the hydrocarbon sector. For the 10 years from 1991 to 2000 the average annual expenditure had dropped to 46.58 million, although for the 2 years from 2000 to 2001 the annual average increased by a factor of more than five to 277 million, having reached a high of 406.2 million in 2002. Thereafter it declined to 249 million in 2004 and 175 million in 2006.

In terms of the percentage of government expenditure on health and social security, the figure averaged 3.11 per cent, 4.10 per cent, and 6.58 per cent respectively for the 1970s, 1980s, and 1990s. In the period 2000–2003 the average expenditure on health stood at 9.4 per cent of the total development budget expenditure, a significantly higher figure than in previous decades. This rise was because much needed medical equipment and medicines, effectively denied to Libya throughout the sanctions period, could now be imported into Libya in this period.

To conclude, it is fair to say that Libya has, overall, made a very good job of providing comprehensive healthcare to all Libyan citizens whatever their regional domicile in the country, despite the sanctions and the fluctuations in oil price which meant that cuts had to be made in all sectors, including health, from 1985 as a result of the impact of falling oil prices. The development of private clinics and pharmacies has also meant that costs of treatment and medication, in a competitive situation, have actually gone down for Libyan citizens, who opt to pay for these in Libya. But as we have noted above, there is no room for complacency – several other countries in a regional context such as Lebanon, Jordan, Morocco, and Egypt expend higher percentages of GDP on health, while in countries such as Norway, with a similar population size to Libya, as well as being an oil producer, per capita expenditure on health in 2002 was $3409, and health expenditure as a percentage of GDP is 9.6 per cent (WHO 2005) while in Libya's case these figures were 4.1 per cent and US $327 respectively in 2004.

4.4.6 The Future Direction of Libyan Healthcare

In operational terms it can be noted that several practices need to be addressed before the Libyan system can be comparable to those of most healthcare systems in the developed world. These are the lack of a proper referral system and reliable health care information centres both locally and nationally. Also, although as we have noted previously there is a hierarchy of health care delivery systems throughout Libya, these need to be more precisely defined with particular functions and a better coordination between individual health care facilities as is done routinely in most of the developed world.

Some sources also claim that there are major problems with corruption in the health service, and that much of the Libyan population has little confidence in health personnel, especially in view of the low quality of service in the state public health sector. Because of this, those who can afford prefer to travel abroad for medical treatment, especially to Tunisia, Malta, or even Germany (Norwegian Directorate of Immigration 2004).

As yet, no doubt because of the impact of the sanctions, very few internationally recognized health specialist centres operate in Libya, which could attract regional treatment seekers and add significantly to Libya's income. Inevitably, with Libya's economic restructuring as well as the massive expansion planned for the hydrocarbon sector, there will be a flood of European and US personnel who will need medical treatment. As we noted earlier, the very large number of highly educated and experienced Libyan medical doctors operating in the Untied Kingdom and Canada would probably mean that the economic and manpower viability for such a specialist centre presently exists.

It is also important to comment on the very free access to the relatively high quality Libyan healthcare system to non-Libyans, mainly immigrants from neighbouring African countries. The huge numbers of these users of the Libyan healthcare system, who are not Libyan taxpayers and who bring many types of diseases to Libya, including HIV, should be causing alarm bells to ring for Libyan healthcare policy makers. Not only are they placing an intolerable strain on Libya's health facilities, to the expense of Libyan nationals, but they are putting the Libyan population at large at risk. A policy change in this regard is long overdue.

As well as this, the question of salaries for Libyan doctors is another area that requires attention, otherwise the departure of Libyan doctors overseas will continue. This is a short-sighted policy, especially when the vast amount spent by the Libyan government over a 7-year period to educate and train a Libyan doctor at a Libyan university may be wasted, with the benefit going to another country. Not only this, but they have to be replaced by foreign doctors at significantly higher salaries.

4.5 The Growing Role of Women in Libyan Society

One of the well-known labour market phenomena of the period from 1955 to 2005 in Western countries has been the increase in the labour force participation of women, particularly married women with children (Brusentsev 2006). Undoubtedly, in Libya, as we have noted in the earlier section on Libyan education, the results of gender equality in this field will have long-term impacts on females in the labour sector and participation in Libyan society.

In the context of the MENA, discussion of the role and position of women tends to be heavily loaded with a huge amount of religious and historical baggage, which confuses and blurs the issues involved. Historically, Western observers see gender oppression against women in such societies such as Saudi Arabia and North Africa as the social, economic, and political norm governing women's cultural roles and identities, their functions in the state and in the formulation of laws.

In this regard even the United Nation's annual "Arab Human Development Report", in 2002, identified "women empowerment" as one of the three main "deficits" in the Arab region. With regard to Libya, there can be no doubt that there has been an impressive amount of legislation dealing with women's equality, commencing with the Constitutional Declaration of 1969, which asserted the equality of all citizens before the law, and the Declaration of the Establishment of the Authority of the People (1977), which asserted, "Woman and man are equal as human beings. Discrimination between man and woman is a flagrant act of oppression without any justification."

As one prominent Libyan political scientist, a woman herself, expressed it, "The policies introduced by the regime during the 1970s sought to enable women to play a crucial role in society, participating in the building of the country as well as men" (Obeidi 1999). Towards this objective, the legal position of women was reinforced by a series of important enactments throughout the 1980s and 1990s, leading to a situation where women increasingly played an important role in Libyan society – for example, they been judges since 1991 (after the passing of Law No. 8 of 1989 regarding Women's Rights to hold the position of Judge in the Legal system), while many work as doctors and engineers in the oil industry. There are also women lawyers and pilots, and women have a significant presence in the police and military, as for example in Article 2 in Law No. 3 of 1984, People's Army, which stated that every Libyan, male or female, was to undertake and have continuous military training if he/she was medically able (Obeidi 1999). In the People's Congresses, women participate equally in taking political decisions.

Libyan nationality is regulated by Act No. 17 of 1954 and Act No. 18 of 1980 and their implementing regulations. It is noteworthy that women enjoy the same rights as men in regard to the right to acquire, change, or retain their nationality or replace it with another nationality. Their exercise of this right is not affected by any other factors. A woman's nationality is not affected if she marries a non-Libyan or if her husband changes his nationality, since she forfeits her nationality only if she wishes to adopt her husband's nationality.

Act No. 10 of 1984, which replaced Law No. 176 of 1972 and regulates marriage and divorce, provided Libyan women with security and guarantees which effectively enabled their economic freedom, allowing for their greater participation in work and society outside the confines of the family home, her traditionally regarded role and also outlawed forced marriages. It stipulated, among other things, that "A guardian cannot force a young man or woman to marry against his or her will, nor can a guardian prevent his ward from marrying a spouse of his or her choice." Article 9 of the same Act further stipulated that "If a lawful guardian prevents his ward from marrying the spouse of his or her choice, the ward may request a court to authorize the marriage if it deems such to be appropriate", while according to Article 13, a man is not allowed to take a second wife without permission by his first wife or through the issue of a court permit.

Regarding divorce, Article 28 safeguards the women's position, stating, "in all cases divorce shall not be established except by a decree by the relevant court" whether by talaq, mutual consent, or judicial divorce; talaq uttered by a minor, insane, demented, or coerced husband or without deliberate intent is invalid, as is suspended or conditional talaq; talaq to which a number is attached is considered single revocable (except the third of three); a wife may also obtain khul (compensation) from husband for appropriate amount, which may include a deferred dowry or custody over children; if the husband retracts offer of khul "due to obstinacy" the court is empowered to decide on khul in return for appropriate compensation.

Divorce is available to a Libyan woman on the following grounds: a husband's failure or inability to maintain without cause; absence without justification; grounds of defect preventing fulfilment of aims of marriage or other grave defect; *il* or *hajr*, after an appropriate grace period. If the parties do not agree to *talaq* by mutual agreement, the court will appoint arbitrators; if reconciliation efforts fail and harm is established, the judge will issue a decree of divorce with financial effects proportionate to relative fault. With regard to post-divorce maintenance/financial arrangements, the wife may be awarded compensation by the court if the husband is considered to bear responsibility for the causes of *talaq*.

At the GPC meeting at Al Beida, in June 1988, The Great Green Charter of Human Rights was declared. In this highly idealistic document, Article 21 states, "The members of the Jamahiriyan society, men or women, are equal in everything which is human. The distinction of rights between men and women is a flagrant injustice which nothing justifies. They proclaim that marriage is a fair association between two equal partners. Nobody can conclude a marriage contract by constraint, nor divorce in any other way than by mutual consent or by a fair judgement. It is unfair to dispossess the children of their mother, and the mother of her home."

In a similar vein, Article 1 of the Promotion of Freedom Act No. 20 of 1991 stipulates that all male and female citizens of the Jamahiriya are free and equal in regard to their rights, which are inviolable. The law was designed to protect women's rights and, in particular, to ensure their participation in political life.

Article 2 guarantees the right of every Libyan citizen, male or female, to exercise his/her political rights on an equal footing, stipulating that "Every citizen has the right to exercise authority and self-determination in the people's congresses and the people's committees. No citizen may be denied the right to be a member thereof or to elect their secretariats, provided that he or she meets the requisite conditions."

Under Article 30 "Everyone has the right to apply to the courts, in accordance with the law. The court must provide the person concerned with all the requisite safeguards, including a lawyer, and such person has the right to avail himself/herself of the services of a lawyer not chosen by the court provided that he/she bears the costs of the said lawyer's fees."

Another significant piece of legislation relating to women's status is the Charter on the Rights and Duties of Women in Libyan Arab Society. Drafted in 1997 by the government, the charter asserts that women could and should participate in the General People's Congresses and Committees (the Libyan parliament and associated bodies), defend their country, enjoy independent financial status, and assume leadership positions.

In an international context, the Libyan government acceded to the UN Convention on the Elimination of all Forms of Discrimination Against Women (CEDAW) in 1989. However, it maintains reservations as to Articles 2 and 16(c) and (d) on the grounds that they are incompatible with Islamic Sharia law, especially Libya's personal status code.

The government has also established the Department of Women's Affairs as part of the secretariat of the GPC, the national legislative body. Overseen by an Assistant Secretary of the General People's Committee, the Department collects data and oversees the integration of women into all spheres of public life. The government has also established the General Union of Women's Associations as a network of non-governmental organizations that addresses women's employment needs.

4.5.1 Women's Education and Its Impact on Libyan Society

Despite the wealth of legislation concerning women's rights in Libya since the revolution of 1969, the single most important article of any piece of legislation is probably Article 14 of the 1969 Libyan Constitutional Declaration which states, "Education is a right and a duty for all Libyans. It is compulsory until the end of the primary school", – that is for a period of 9 years.

In the conservative Libyan society of the late 1960s, parents and religious authorities, in both urban and rural areas, remained suspicious of this, often condemning compulsory education for girls. Because of this, during this period, the percentage of females in elementary education was between 11 and 19 per cent. But by the early 1970s it had, in line with the law citing compulsory education, shot up to 37 per cent, and by 1990 it had escalated to 48 per cent. It is also worth noting that female education eventually reached parity with males at all levels, primary, secondary, and tertiary, and in all disciplines.

For example, the percentage of women at university level developed from a low 3 per cent in 1961 to 8 per cent in 1966 then to 20 per cent in 1981 and again to 43 per cent by the year 1996. Thus even though female education, at the beginning, moved very slowly, the situation changed dramatically during the 1970s. By the mid-1980s female education was moving at full speed. By the early 1990s the number of females at all levels of education became equal to the number of males. There can be little doubt that one of the significant successes of the revolutionary government was its policy towards women's education.

4.5.2 Is There a Glass Ceiling for Women in Libya?

From the above it is clear that the large body of Libyan legislation directed solely at redefining and protecting the rights and privileges of women in Libya has had a considerable impact on the concept of the traditional role of Libyan women, enabling them to play an increasing part in basic decision-making both within and without the family circle. In many ways, apart from the legislation redefining women's rights and duties and protecting their marriage and divorce rights, as well as outlawing polygamy without the consent of the first wife, these changes were largely attributable to educational advances in all social sectors, urban and rural.

But there remains many inconsistencies in the law despite all the legislation guaranteeing equality for Libyan women. In Libya a child acquires the nationality of his father; in view of the right of all persons to a nationality, Libyan law endeavoured in that way to eliminate cases of statelessness. However, Libyan women do not have the same rights as Libyan men to transfer their nationality to their foreign-born spouses or children. While children of a Libyan father and non-Libyan mother are given Libyan nationality, children of a Libyan mother and a non-Libyan father are not and require visas to enter the country

Critics of the Libyan system also state that, due to the authoritarian nature of the government, there are no genuinely independent women's organizations, and anyone permitted to work on behalf of women's rights must do so within the framework of the state and of what it terms "advancing the revolution". As a result, women's groups are tightly linked to the state and are permitted to cooperate only with international women's organizations that have been sanctioned by the government (Freedom House 2005). A number of women's groups do operate in Libya, such as the Libyan Midwife Association for Mother and Childhood Care and the Al Wafa Association for Human Services. However, little information is available about what these groups are engaged in and the extent of their activities. Moreover, as everything in Libya is done through the state, there are no genuinely independent groups or civil society actors.

4.5.3 Women in Libyan Politics

Over the last 10 years, in a global context, women have continued to be least represented in the parliaments of the Arab States (Inter Parliamentary Union 2005). While regional averages have fluctuated in this period, overall, in Arab States there has been an encouraging increase in the percentage of women in parliament. Currently, the regional average is at its highest, at 6.5 per cent, in Morocco when the electoral law was amended to reserve 30 seats for women in parliament prior to the 2002 elections. Thereafter, 35 women were elected to the Moroccan parliament. Djibouti and Jordan have followed suit. In Djibouti, a quota law was adopted in December 2002 stipulating that among the candidates presented by each party, at least 10 per cent must be of either sex. The results of the 2003 elections saw an unprecedented seven women in parliament, accounting for more than 10 per cent of the newly elected parliamentarians. In Jordan, the electoral law was amended prior to the 2003 elections to reserve six seats for women in the Lower House of the Majlis. With 22.8 per cent, Libya's neighbour Tunisia is the Arab State with the highest percentage of women parliamentarians. Elections held in 2004 saw an increase of more than 10 percentage points of women in the Tunisian parliament, partly due to the introduction of a party quota system in political parties. Since the approval of a referendum held in 2001 in Bahrain, women can vote and stand for office in that country. After a good deal of effort, in May 2005 the National Assembly of Kuwait finally granted women the right to vote and stand for election. In terms of voting numbers, more women than men will be eligible to vote in the next Kuwaiti legislative elections, scheduled for 2007.

As can be seen in Table 4.19, the percentage of women in National Parliaments by ranking as of September 2005 is presented. It shows parliaments

Table 4.19. Women in national parliaments, selected countries, by rank, 2005

Rank	Country	Lower or single house				Upper house or senate			
		Elections	Seats*	Women	% W	Elections	Seats*	Women	% W
1	Rwanda	09 2003	80	39	48.8	09 2003	26	9	34.6
3	Norway	09 2005	169	64	37.9	–	–	–	–
7	Cuba	01 2003	609	219	36.0	–	–	–	–
13	South Africa	04 2004	400	131	32.8	04 2004	54	18	33.3
34	Tunisia	10 2004	189	43	22.8	07 2005	112	15	13.4
41	Pakistan	10 2002	342	73	21.3	03 2003	100	18	18.0
51	United Kingdom	05 2005	646	127	19.7	N.A.	707	126	17.8
64	Turkmenistan	12 2004	50	8	16.0	–	–	–	–
66	Philippines	05 2004	236	36	15.3	05 2004	24	4	16.7
67	USA	11 2004	435	66	15.2	11 2004	100	14	14.0
68	Angola	09 1992	220	33	15.0	–	–	–	–
68	South Korea	04 2004	299	39	13.0	–	–	–	–
80	France	06 2002	574	70	12.2	09 2004	331	56	16.9
80	Syria	03 2003	250	30	12.0	–	–	–	–
85	Indonesia	04 2004	550	62	11.3	–	–	–	–
89	Morocco	09 2002	325	35	10.8	10 2003	270	3	1.1
91	Thailand	02 2005	500	53	10.6	03 2000	200	21	10.5
93	Russian Federation	12 2003	447	44	9.8	N.A.	178	6	3.4
97	Sudan	12 2000	360	35	9.7	–	–	–	–
97	Venezuela	07 2000	165	16	9.7	–	–	–	–
97	Malaysia	03 2004	219	20	9.1	03 2004	70	18	25.7
101	Japan	09 2005	480	43	9.0	07 2004	242	33	13.6
104	Brazil	10 2002	513	44	8.6	10 2002	81	10	12.3
106	India	04 2004	543	45	8.3	06 2004	242	28	11.6
115	Chad	04 2002	155	10	6.5	–	–	–	–
116	Nigeria	04 2003	360	23	6.4	04 2003	109	4	3.7
117	Algeria	05 2002	389	24	6.2	12 2003	144	4	2.8
117	Jordan	06 2003	110	6	5.5	11 2003	55	7	12.7
124	Lebanon	05 2005	128	6	4.7	–	–	–	–
124	Libya	03 1997	760	36	4.7	–	–	–	–
125	Turkey	11 2002	550	24	4.4	–	–	–	–
126	Iran	02 2004	290	12	4.1	–	–	–	–
132	Egypt	11 2000	454	13	2.9	05 2004	264	18	6.8
133	Oman	10 2003	83	2	2.4	2004	58	9	15.5
134	Kuwait	07 2003	65	1	1.5	–	–	–	–
137	Bahrain	10 2002	40	0	0.0	11 2002	40	6	15.0
–	Saudi Arabia	04 2005	150	0	0.0	–	–	–	–

Source: IPU, 2005.
*Figures correspond to the number of seats currently filled in Parliament.
Note: South Africa: The figures on the distribution of seats do not include the 36 special rotating delegates appointed on an ad hoc basis, and all percentages given are therefore calculated on the basis of the 54 permanent seats.

from all parts of the world, although limited to those shown because of considerations of space.

Although the year of the data for Libya, 1997, is not current, it ranks Libya at No. 124, with women parliamentarians (i.e. Members of Basic People's Congresses) amounting to 36 out of 760, representing only 4.7 per cent of total parliamentarians.

Despite constitutional guarantees and the Promotion of Freedom Act No. 20 of 1991, and the encouragements given in the Charter on the Rights and the Duties of Women in Libyan Arab Society drafted in 1997 for women's participation in politics, the fact remains that only one of the Municipal Secretary Generals of the Sha'abiyat was a woman, Mrs Huda Bin Amir of Behghazi. Significantly, also, in 2006, two women were appointed to the most senior levels of Libyan government, Bakhitah Abd-al-Alim al-Shalwi as Secretary of Social Affairs in the General People's Committee, while Amal Nuri Abdullah al-Safar became Secretary of Women Affairs in the GPC, which shows progress in this direction.

While it is accepted that in the 1970s and 1980s Libyan society may have remained profoundly conservative and resistant to the revolutionary impulses for change that emanated from its leaders, why after two generations have Libyan women yet to play their rightful role in Libyan politics? Obviously it cannot be attributed to education, as discussed above. In regional terms Table 4.20 clearly shows how advanced Libya is in terms of female literacy compared to its neighbours, MENA countries, and even globally.

Can it therefore be due to cultural traditional or Islamic values which perceive that politics is the preserve of men? This is unlikely, since in both Pakistan and Indonesia, one an Islamic Republic and the other a Parliamentary democracy in a country with the biggest Muslim population in the world, there have been women Presidents – Benazir Bhutto in Pakistan in 1988 and Megawati Sukarnoputri in Indonesia from 2001–2005. If adherence to traditional values is the cause of women's poor representation in Libyan politics, why have these values not also prevented Libyan women from assuming important roles in most areas of Libyan society, from pilots to doctors to judges to teachers?

Can it be because policy on women's rights came "from above", with post-revolutionary women's and family law being formulated by a political leadership, which, although choosing reform, has also maintained Islamic law, often causing confusion to the Libyan people? Or is it because Libyan women themselves have not seized the opportunities which, on paper at least, the Libyan government has made great efforts to provide them with? Certainly, as the country currently embarks on its ambitious privatization and economic diversification plans, the demand for qualified Libyans of both sexes will accelerate. The current situation, for example, where

Table 4.20. Female literacy rates, 2001–2004

Country		Country		Country	
World	76.8	Jordan	84.7	Saudi Arabia	69.3
Developing countries	69.5	Kuwait	81	Sudan	49.9
Arab States	51.1	Libya	70.7	Syria	74.2
Algeria	60.1	Mauritania	31.3	Tunisia	65.3
Bahrain	83	Morocco	38.3	UAE	80.7
Egypt	43.6	Oman	65.4	Yemen	28.5

Source: UNESCO, EFA Global Monitoring Report, 2006

qualified women often do not work after marriage for social and traditional family reasons will undoubtedly have to change, as Libya moves into the ranks of the developed countries. This is because the very low levels of female participation in the labour force, which means that the country is not capturing a large part of the return on its investment in female health and education, as discussed earlier.

To conclude, perhaps the present position of women in Libyan society it best described by the same woman political scientist quoted earlier, who states,

> Gender differences show that the regime's ideology of gender equality has been taken up in different ways by men and women. Although a minority of men agree with practical implementation, the majority subscribe to equality in principle only. For women there is a stronger commitment to genuine implementation. It has to be said that the reality in Libyan society corresponds to the male position. Women lack authority and participate less, so have less capacity for forcing these issues. However these gender differences, which do not change for those with a religious identity, could have profound significance in the future, especially given the strong commitment of the regime to gender equality (Obeidi 1999).

4.6 Social Security, Health and Safety and Employment Issues

4.6.1 Employment Law and Social Security

Imbued by revolutionary fervour and a strong sense of social justice for all, it is inevitable that the Constitutional Declaration issued on 11 December 1969 would enunciate key principles governing the labour rights of Libyan workers and issues relating to social security. In fact several Articles in the Declaration touch on these matters directly or indirectly, as in Articles 4, 6, and 9.

> Article 4 "Work": Work in the Libyan Arab Republic is a right, a duty, and an honour for every able-bodied citizen. Public functions are the duty of those who are put in charge of them. The goal of the state employees in discharging their duties is to serve the people.

> Article 6 "Socialism": The aim of the state is the realization of socialism through the application of social justice, which forbids any form of exploitation. The state endeavours, through the edification of a socialist community, to achieve self-sufficiency in production and equity in distribution. Its aim is to eliminate peacefully the disparities between social classes and to attain a society of prosperity. Its inspiration is its Arabic and Islamic heritage, humanitarian values, and the specific conditions of the Libyan society.

> Article 9 "Planning": The state will institute a system of national planning covering economic, social, and cultural aspects. Cooperation between the private and the public sectors will be necessary for the achievement of the goals of economic development.

Soon after the Constitutional Declaration, the Libyan Labour Code, Law No. 58 of 1970 was passed. The provisions of this comprehensive piece of legislation are applicable to all employees, whether of the state, or state-owned or private sector companies. This law was amended by Act No. 7 of 1997 which requires child-care facilities to be provided for women workers at factories employing more than 50 persons, and set limits on arduous or dangerous work for women employees, and Act No. 72 of 5 June 1972, which amended Sects. 86 and 87 of the Labour Code relating to hours of work.

The amended Code covers most employment-related issues, including employment of both nationals and foreigners, employment contracts, working hours, dispute resolution procedures, and grounds for termination of employment contracts. It lays down minimum requirements for salaries and benefits, although employers are free to offer more favourable conditions unless subject to Law No. 15 of 1981 discussed below.

4.6.2 Law No. 15 of 1981, Covering Wages and Salaries in the State Sector

Salaries of civil servants and employees of state-owned companies are subject to a special set of conditions under this law. Its provisions also apply to Libyan companies in which there is Libyan public ownership of any part of the share capital. Under this law, salaries have been substantively frozen, with very minimal salary increases and no merit increases since 1981, and in fact this law is currently causing a lot of dissatisfaction among Libyan public sector employees, a topic which we will discuss at length later in this chapter in view of its crucial importance.

In theory, branches of foreign companies are free to offer any salary they wish to their Libyan employees. However, in the oil and gas sector, foreign companies and operators should exercise care, since the application of Law No. 15 can cause problems in the context of provisions relating to an Exploration and Production Sharing Agreement (EPSA) at the point it reaches the development stage, since the policy of the Libyan National Oil Corporation (LNOC) is to require the salary scale of Law No. 15 to be applied to all operations where LNOC co-funds, regardless of the NOC percentage share or whether or not the operating company is wholly foreign owned. However, for companies still operating under the classical concession terms, this does not apply.

4.6.3 Key Provisions of Labour Law No. 58 of 1970

In practical terms, Labour Law No. 58 of 1970 is the basic piece of legislation which regulates working hours, leave, termination, dismissal, and related matters and we discuss these in the section below.

Working Hours

- An employee cannot be engaged in actual work for more than 8 hours per day, not including breaks for meals or rest. Should the daily hours of work be more than six there must be a break of at least 1 hour in total and the employee must not work continuously for more than 6 hours.

- Article 92 specifies 15 years as the age at which children may be employed and 18 years in the case of hazardous occupations, unless a permit for the employment of a child in certain industries and activities is issued by the competent authorities.
- Article 93 specifies 15 years as the age at which juveniles may engage in part-time employment. Only persons who are not juveniles, or who, in other words, have attained 18 years of age, may engage in full-time employment.
- Juveniles are not permitted to work for more than six hours per day, and must have a break or breaks not less than one hour.
- Juveniles are not permitted to work between 8 p.m. and 7 a.m.

Leave

- Each employee is entitled to one day off per week, while an employee working for one year is entitled to fully paid annual leave of 16 days. Juveniles and employees who have worked for 5 years are entitled to fully paid annual leave of 24 days.
- An employee who has worked 3 consecutive years with the same employer is entitled to a fully paid special vacation not exceeding 25 days in order to perform his/her duty of pilgrimage, and this is only allowed once in anyone's lifetime.
- In cases of normal sickness an employee is entitled to 60 per cent of his or her normal income for up to one year. If the illness is caused by a work-related injury, he/she is entitled to 70 per cent of income for the same period.

Female Employees

- Women are not allowed to work between 8 p.m. and 7 a.m. or for more than 48 hours each week.
- In the 18 months after childbirth women are entitled to two rest intervals a day each of not less than half an hour. These form part of the working hours and do not result in any pay reduction.

Termination

- An employment contract may be for a fixed/unfixed term or it may be for a particular project or assignment. If the parties to a fixed-term employment contract continue to use the same contract after the expiry of the initially agreed term, it will be considered as a renewal for an unfixed term. If the term of the contract is not fixed, at least one month's notice must be given before the termination of the contract.
- An employment contract for a fixed term may not exceed 5 years, after which the term of the contract is said to be unfixed. An employment contract is for a fixed term if the duration is stated in the contract or if a fixed-term contract is typical for that particular assignment.
- An employer may terminate the contract where work is entirely or partially suspended for a period of 2 consecutive months, or if the work is temporary by

nature. An employer may also terminate the contract where an employee's disability or illness prevents him/her from performing his/her duties for a continuous period of not less than 120 days or a total number of 200 days in any one year.

- Employers are required to pay a dismissal benefit of 100 per cent of earnings for up to 6 months in the case of unfair dismissal.

Dismissal

An employer can only dismiss an employee without notice and without indemnity or compensation in the following circumstances:

- The employee lied about his/her identification or submitted false certificates or references or other supporting documents.
- The employee was appointed on probation.
- The employee made a mistake which led to grave material loss to the employer, provided the event was reported by the employer to the Labour Office within three days of it coming to his/her attention.
- The employee failed to comply with safety instructions in spite of personal warnings in writing, as long as the instructions were written and posted in a prominent place and a copy of the personal warning letter was sent to the relevant Labour Office.
- The employee was absent without legitimate reason for more than 20 days in total over 1 year, or more than 10 consecutive days provided written warnings were sent after 10 days and 5 days respectively, with copies sent to the relevant Labour Office.
- The employee fails to perform his/her basic obligations under the employment contract.
- The employee discloses secrets relating to his/her work.
- The employee is found guilty of a criminal act or misdemeanour relating to honour integrity or public morality.
- The employee is found drunk or under the influence of drugs during working hours.
- The employee assaults a colleague or manager.

4.6.4 Social Security Concerns

In general terms, the Libyan social security system provides a wide range of protection superior to that available in many or even most developing countries, and equal to that of some developed countries. It is also supplemented by subsidized food, free education and health treatment, housing facilities, utility services such as electricity, water transportation, and fuel at low prices.

Under the provisions of Law No. 13 of 1980 the state provides a wide social security umbrella utilizing a comprehensive social security scheme. Social security is guaranteed to all citizens and is extended to foreigners living in Libya.

It includes provisions for old age, disability, sickness, employment, accident or occupational disease, disaster, death, funeral expenses, pregnancy, and childbirth.

The following persons/entities are entitled to receive benefits under the Libyan social security system in return for payment of their monthly contributions:

- Businesses where the partnership system is applied.
- Civil servants working in the various secretariats, public authorities and agencies, including the police and customs officials.
- Persons working under contracts of employment.
- Self-employed persons engaged in the liberal professions, arts and crafts, and agriculture.
- Industrial operations and similar activities.
- Surviving dependents of persons covered in the above categories.

Key Provisions of Law No. 13 of 1980, which replaced the Social Insurance Law No. 53 of 1957 and the Pension Law of the same year, are quoted in full.

Article 1: Social Security

Social security shall be a right warranted, in conformity with state Law, to all citizens in Libya and a protection extended to non-Libyan residents.

Social Security shall include all schemes or procedures enacted in connection herewith for the purpose of providing protection and care to the individual in case of old age, disability, sickness, work injury, or occupational disease, as well as in cases of loss of the breadwinner, means of subsistence, and in cases of pregnancy and childbirth, or for the purpose of assisting one in bearing one's family's burden and in the events of calamities, disasters, and death.

Social Security shall include also social care to persons deprived of any sustainer, such as children, both males and females, the handicapped, disabled and persons of old age; care and guidance to minors, case of juvenile aberration and/or delinquency.

Social Security shall also comprise arrangements and measures relating to occupational safety, care in cases of work injuries occupational disease, rehabilitation of sick, injured, and disabled persons.

The Social Security Fund

Article 6 states that "there shall be established at the Secretariat for Social Security a Fund, which shall have the status of a public juridical person, an autonomous budget, distinct from the State General budget as well as independent accounts. Fund Affairs shall be run by a Committee presided over by the Secretary of General People's Committee for Social Security and including, as members, the Fund Director and representatives of both the secured persons and the Employers. Setting up of such a Committee, determination of its powers and terms of reference, rules of procedures as to how Committee shall carry out its affairs, shall be in conformity with Regulations to be issued for such purposes."

The Secretary to General People's Committee for Social Security shall act on behalf of the Fund in matters relating to contracts and before Courts of Law, and shall represent the Committee in dealing with third parties.

The appointment of Fund Director and determination of his/her salary shall be set out in a Decision to be issued under the authority of General People's Committee, on submission by the Secretary of General People's Committee for Social Security.

Article Seven: Financial Resources of the Fund

Financial resources of Social Security Fund, these shall consist of the following:

- Social Security Contributions, as shared between contributions, employers, production plants, or enterprises, and public treasury.
- Revenues of any additional taxes and fees as may be imposed to the benefit of Social Security by General People's Committee.
- Annual allocation in the State Public Budget in order to cover balance of Social Security benefit costs and Fund deficits.
- Allocations in the Development Budget, for the purpose of financing Fund Projects.
- Investment revenue of the Fund.
- Zakat revenues.
- Amounts accruing from donations, legacies and proceeds from "Wakaf".
- Any other financial resources.

All assets, rights, credits and properties, as reverted to the Fund from public social security institutions, shall pass in full ownership to the Fund. In the meantime all funds, assets, credits and reserves at present appertaining to pension schemes and the Social Insurance System shall be transferred to the Fund.

Military Personnel Pension Schemes shall have an independent Account, separate from those of the Fund.

4.6.5 Financial Resources and Expenditure of the Social Security Fund

Article 8 states that "The Social Security Fund's financial resources shall be destined exclusively to meet expenses for providing social security benefits in cash and in kind and for purposes related to investment of Social Security funds and reserves. It shall not be permitted to use any such financial resources in administrative and general expenditures of the Secretariat for Social Security. Regulations shall determine types of administrative and general expenditure connected with benefits and investments to be borne by the Fund."

The above articles demonstrate the extremely wide application of the Social Security Law of 1980, the sources of its financial resources, its independent legal status, and its separate character within the Secretariat of Social Security. These provisions ensure that the financial meltdowns and pension erosion which has been typical of many Western pension funds cannot happen in Libya.

Currently, in practical and financial terms, non-Libyan employers are required to pay 75 per cent of each employee's social security contributions. Employees' contributions are withheld from their salary by the employer who is responsible for payment. The total contributions correspond to 15 per cent of an employee's gross salary and are payable monthly. The employer must declare and pay his/her contributions by the tenth day of the month following the month to which they relate. Late payments carry a penalty of 5 per cent per year. In return for this, employees receive benefits in kind and in cash such as a retirement pension and compensation in case of injury.

Old-Age Pensions

This is payable for men aged 65 or women aged 60, and at age 62 for civil service employees and 60 for workers in hazardous or unhealthy occupations, with 20 years of contributions giving a full pension. The minimum pension is 96 dinars per month. The maximum is 80 per cent of average earnings over the 20 years qualifying period. There is also a dependent supplement of 4 dinars a month for a wife and 2 dinars a month for each child under age of 18, with no age limit for an unmarried daughter. The pension is not payable abroad.

4.6.6 Health and Safety Legislation

The Industrial Security and Labour Safety Law dates from 1976 and places upon the employer the general obligation to take all necessary precautions to protect all employees from work-related danger, harm, and disease. In particular the employer is obliged to take all necessary steps to ensure his/her employees' safety when using instruments and machines and when handling harmful materials and to provide necessary medical and first-aid facilities.

When the number of employees in any workplace exceeds 200, the employer must appoint a specialized employee who holds responsibility for the safety of employees in the establishment and for the enforcement of the provisions of the law.

Vocational Training

Starting in 1973, as the government began to appreciate the technological demands placed on the Libyan population because of the petroleum industry and planned diversification, the 1973 Order on Accelerated Vocational Training was issued. This provided for accelerated training programmes to be implemented in the following areas: the construction industry, agriculture, fisheries industry, oil sector, metal and mechanical trades, and the electrical trades, setting forth criteria for participation by Libyan youths in such programmes.

The People's General Committee Order No. 95 of 1989 concerning Vocational Institutions laid down the organization of vocational centres, defined their tasks, and listed the requirements for admission to such centres, while the People's General Committee Order No. 96 of 1989 Concerning Vocational Training regulated the conditions upon which individuals were authorized to join vocational training programmes, including a list of the professions covered by vocational training schemes.

In the 1980s and 1990s many higher technical and vocational institutions were established in science, technology, and engineering. These include higher teacher training institutes; higher institutes to train trainers and instructors for higher technical institutes; higher vocational centres (polytechnics); and specialized higher institutes for technical, industrial, and agricultural sciences. Higher institutes offered programmes in fields such as electricity, mechanical engineering, finance, computer studies, industrial technology, social work, medical technology, and civil aviation. The qualification awarded after 3 years at vocational institutes and centres is the Higher Technician Diploma; otherwise, after 4–5 years, the Bachelor's degree is awarded.

4.6.7 Libyan and Foreign Employees/Work Permits

Certain jobs are reserved for Libyan nationals, such as accountants, typists, drivers and guards. Foreign companies must employ a certain number of Libyan trainees corresponding to at least 20 per cent of the total personnel of the company. If a company fails to do this an equivalent amount is payable to the Vocational Training Fund.

Under the Foreign Investment Law of 1997, the investor is entitled to employ and import foreign staff and technical expertise necessary for the establishment and operation of the project although "the import of normal labour is to be avoided as much as possible". In a very recent piece of legislation, an amendment to the Foreign Investment Law of 2005, Article 14(d) states the following:

> The investor has the right to employ foreigners whenever the national substitute is not available. The foreign employees who come from abroad have the right to transfer abroad a percentage of their salaries and wages and any other benefits or rewards given to them within the framework of the project. Conditions and terms regarding the implementation of this Article shall be set by the Executive Regulation.

In general terms, foreign employees are subject to the same employment laws as nationals as already outlined. Regarding the employment of foreigners, the ruling legislation is contained in People's General Committee Order No. 238 of 1989, which regulates the employment of foreigners and prohibits the employment of any foreigner unless prior approval of the Central Employment Bureau is obtained. It also establishes the procedures and conditions for the employment of foreigners

This is supplemented by People's General Committee Order No. 260 of 1989 concerning Employment Conditions, which states that "employment priority is given to Libyans and Arabs ... employment of foreigners is conditional upon approval by the Central Employment Bureau".

The process for obtaining work permits for foreigners may be somewhat difficult and changes from time to time. Sometimes applicants are required to produce original documents giving evidence of their qualifications, education, and experience. In the oil sector, the process is normally facilitated by a letter of support from the LNOC, and generally speaking it is easier for executives to obtain permits than it is for technical personnel.

4.6.8 Non-nationals in the Libyan Work Force/Legal and Illegal Immigration

A combination of factors meant that Libya, virtually since the discovery and export of oil in the early 1960s, has depended to varying extents on foreign labour. In the early stages of oil exploitation, lack of qualified Libyan personnel meant that in the 1960s and 1970s a considerable proportion of operatives and technologists in the oil sector were foreign. Again, as the drive for comprehensive health and education entered into high gear in the 1970s and 1980s, large numbers of Egyptians and Palestinians, and in the 1990s, Iraqis, entered and worked in Libya as health and education professionals. The very generous social security, health, and education benefit system in itself also attracted a huge number of immigrants, both legal and illegal. In this regard the extent of illegal immigration is difficult to estimate precisely, especially in view of Law No. 6/1987 relating to the entry, residence, and exit of foreign nationals in Libya, which provided for the entry of all nationals from Arab States, as well as the later policy of the Libyan government in the which allowed unrestricted entry without visas for Africans. Because of this policy and the porous nature of Libya's borders with its southern neighbours, it is difficult to get any reliable information on an ongoing basis from official government sources on statistics for illegal immigrants.

For example, in an official report released by the Libyan General People's Committee (the Libyan Cabinet) at the end of 2004, to address certain key issues raised by the Libyan People's Basic Congresses, it was discovered – in an intensive investigation by Libyan officials for only 1 month commencing 8 August 2004, covering 470 public companies, 282 foreign companies, 1568 Tashrukkiyas, 45 Commercial Agencies, and 218 public bodies/boards – that 3,500 persons apparently legally employed were in fact illegal immigrants with no official papers. It is also worth noting that throughout the 1990s and indeed up to the present, Libya, because of its liberal immigration policy, is a recognized transit point for very many of the Africans who finish up as part of the workforces of both the European nations and the United States.

4.6.9 Average Income Trends

In Fig. 4.9 detailed information on the average income of Libyans is provided for the period 1962–2005, derived from the average number of Libyan citizens for

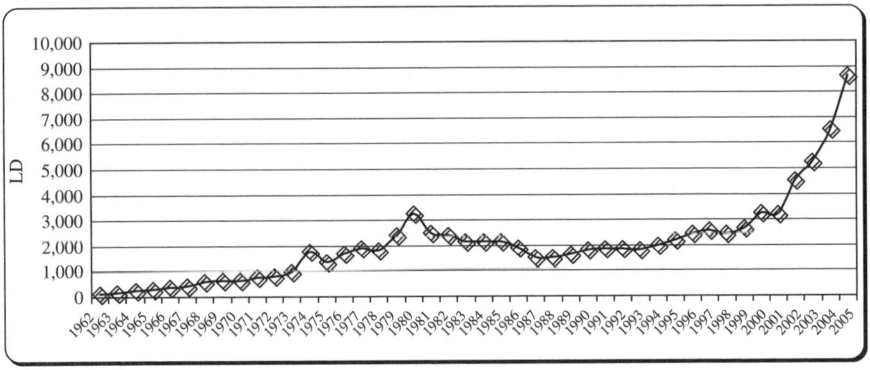

Source: Figures from 1962 to 2000 from Libyan General Planning Council, 2001; Figures from 2001 to 2005 from OPEC Annual Statistical Bulletins, using Libyan Central Bank average annual US $/LD coversion rates

Fig. 4.9. Average income of individuals based on total population and Gross national income for the period 1962–2005

the target years and the GDP for those years. It rose from LD107 in 1962 to LD 654 by 1969. In the first 5 post-revolutionary years from 1970 it rose by 268 per cent from LD656 to LD1763 in 1974, continuing to rise throughout the 1970s to LD 2431 by 1979. Peaking at LD3251 in 1980, it averaged LD2497 in the first 5 years of the 1980s, declining to LD1666 in 1989, a drop in a decade to half of the 1980 figure. Throughout both the US and UN sanction periods in the 1990s it fluctuated from LD2169 in 1990 to a low of LD1526 in 1992 and to a high of LD2169 in 1995, before finishing at LD1666 at the end of the 1990s. In 2000 it virtually doubled to LD3247, signalling the end of the UN sanctions and an improved crude oil price. By 2003 it had risen to LD5255, and by 2004 had more than doubled the 2001 figure, to LD6542, rising significantly again to LD8656 in 2005.

4.6.10 Sectoral Employment

In the following section, sectoral employment trends in Libya over the period 1962–2000 will be analysed based on Appendix 4.1. The expansion of employee numbers in the Funds, Insurance, and Business Sector has been very gradual, rising from a base of 3,400 in 1962 to around 12,000 in the mid-1980s, and then to a high of 33,000 in 2000. It is worth noting that in the last 5 years of the millennium from 1995 to 1999 employees in this sector rose by 50 per cent from 20,000 to 30,000, signalling the end of the UN sanctions in 1999 and Libya's gradual opening up to the outside world. The Energy, Mining, Quarrying, and Water Sector, starting from a base figure of 19,900 in 1962, rose strongly until the mid-1980s, in line mainly with the expansion of the Libyan hydrocarbon industry, settling around 50,000 and staying there for the remainder of the 1980s because of the decline of the oil industry after the departure of the Americans in 1986. Throughout the early 1990s, it increased sharply from around 54,000 in 1990 to 68,400 in 1997, throughout which period there were heavy manpower demands made by the

Water component of this sector by the Great Man-Made River Project, a multi-billion engineering undertaking aimed at revolutionizing access to water for the Libyan people, agriculture, and industry, reaching a total of 93,400 employees in 2000.

The Wholesale, Retail, Restaurant, and Hotel Sector has again risen very gradually, from a base of 27,400 in 1962 to 69,500 in 2000. Its gradual rise is shown by the decade-average figures for this sector – 28,275 in the 1960s, 42,710 in the 1970s, 48,760 in the 1980s, and 64,300 in the 1990s. The trend of the Transport, Storage, and Communications sector is also noteworthy. Having started from a base of 22,400 in 1962, it rose dramatically as demands for these services escalated during the 1970s and 1980s as Libya embarked on massive investment in infrastructure, rising to 92,000 in 1983. After a sharp plunge to 70,000 in the following year, it again rose very steadily, doubling to the 2000 figure of 143,000 as the pace of infrastructure development all over Libya continued apace.

In the Agriculture, Forestry, and Fishing Sector employment has remained relatively stable over the period reviewed, averaging 168,000 employees, with 145,700 in 1962 and 239,000 in 2000. The Health Sector, starting from a low base of 5,000 in 1962, has increased massively to 86,100 employees, as the demands for full health care for Libyans rose gradually throughout the period. Similarly, the Education Sector, again starting from a low base of 13,500 in 1962, has increased very substantially, to a total of 198,200 in 2000, as the comprehensive Libyan Education system embraced all learning age groups to provide a virtual 100 per cent coverage of the Libyan population. The Construction Sector, starting from a base of 32,400 in 1962 rose dramatically to 371,000 in the early 1980s, as Libyan oil wealth was utilized to considerably expand infrastructure, including housing, schools, hospitals, and clinics. After this burst of feverish activity it declined to 179,000 in 1984, and after reaching a trough of 123,000 in 1992, a very bad year for the Libyan economy, it grew again gradually to a total of 222,000 in 2000.

The Public Service sector started from a considerable base of 49,100 employees in 1962, and increased gradually to 76,800 in the 16 years to 1978, in line with demographic trends. Thereafter, it dropped to 61,000 by 1983 rising dramatically by 66 per cent in 1 year alone, to 101,000 in 1984 as the Libyan government reconstructed its public service sector as well as several state companies. It stabilized between 101,000 and 105,000 in the period 1984–1994, rising gradually thereafter to 118,000 in the 6 years leading up to 2000. The Manufacturing sector has also risen very significantly throughout the period, from a base of 23,800 in 1962 to a high of 169,600 in 2000, as Libya gradually acquired a manufacturing base. But the growth of this sector has been erratic. In fact it contracted in the early period, from 23,800 in 1962 to 19,400 in 1969. From 1970 to 1977, it doubled to 41,500. From 1977 to 1983, it doubled again to 80,500 workers, but had only increased to 92,200 by the end of the 1980s. Throughout the 1990s it grew very strongly and steadily, from 99,400 in 1990 to 163,700 by 1999, finishing at 169,600 in 2000.

4.6.11 Unemployment Issues

It is difficult to get precise unemployment figures for Libya, largely because of the poor quality and lack of timeliness of reporting. For example, the IMF 2006

Medium-Term Economic Reform Strategy, Libya, published in April, 2006, is silent on the issue, probably because it is one which is made highly confusing by the nebulous status and large number of African and Arab immigrants, both legal and illegal, and reporting systems for these. However, our source, the Libyan National Authority for Information and Documentation, gives Table 4.21 for the period 1995–2001.

This official Libyan government source shows unemployment rising from a low of 1.4 per cent in 1995 to 7.7 per cent in 2001 – a very dramatic increase over this 7-year period mainly caused by new job seekers from school and college coming into the labour market in line with demographic trends, with a large proportion of them finding no employment. This figure had, according to Libyan official sources, almost doubled to 13 per cent in 2005 (BBC 2005), again largely because of the failure of many recently qualified Libyan students to find jobs, as well as a certain amount of laxity in enforcing mandatory quotas for Libyan employees which have been violated by many foreign companies. Other sources such as the World Bank in its Country Economic Report on Libya of July 2006 put unemployment as high as 25 per cent, while many other less reliable sources place it even higher, at 30 per cent.

It is therefore apparent that as the Libyan administration currently wrestles with the challenges of diversification, globalization, and regional and international integration, national development strategies need to be based on a proper policy mix to ensure that the employment and career expectations of Libya's citizens are satisfied. Not only this, but as imports, as part of this process, are progressively liberalized by Libya, the rapidly changing global trading architecture will have a serious impact on its domestic economy. If this is not handled sensitively, unemployment, especially among young people (those aged under 20 constitute 60 per cent of Libya's population) and recently estimated at 16 per cent of the workforce according to the General Secretary of GPC for Workforce, Training and Employment, July, 2004, could grow significantly (Otman and Karlberg 2005).

4.6.12 The Great Debate in Libya: Public Sector Wage Increases vs. Subsidies

There is currently much debate in Libya concerning the level of wages in the Public sector, effectively frozen since 1981, as we noted earlier, by Law No. 15, which determined wages and salaries in the State Sector. What are termed as

Table 4.21 Manpower, job seekers, and unemployment 1995–2001

Year	Manpower	Registered as job seekers	Numbers successfully placed in jobs	Numbers still unemployed	Percentage of unemployment
1995	917589	26408	13636	12772	1.4
1996	1054000	47994	25851	22143	2.1
1997	1092100	47106	32509	14597	1.3
1998	1006856	54527	23428	31099	3.1
1999	1045566	95153	38500	56653	5.4
2000	1079768	85537	20256	65281	6.0
2001	1110002	115475	29593	85882	7.7

Source: Libyan National Authority for Information and Documentation, 2003.

"basic commodities" are heavily subsidized in Libya. Table 4.22 illustrates the range and quantities of goods annually subsidized for each Libyan citizen.

Table 4.23 shows the price which Libyan citizens pay for the range of subsidized goods. These are imported and distributed by the National Supply Corporation (Nasco), a nationwide organization founded by law No. 68/71 in 1971 with four branches and 22 representative offices throughout Libya, with the remit to implement the consumer subsidy policy and protect consumers from international prices fluctuation and to minimize the burden of inflation.

The first price, from Nasco to the Libyan Consumers Associations all over Libya, is the subsidized price sold to these authorized bodies, while the second is the actual price paid by a Libyan citizen for subsidized items.

Table 4.22. Libyan citizens: subsidized commodities/monthly quantities, 2004

Commodity	Monthly allowance for every Libyan citizen
*Flour (*Algamaita Alastahlakia* or Consumers associations)	3.0 kg
Flour (Bakers)	12.0 kg
Rice	3.0 kg
Cooking oil	2.0 cans Items
Sugar	2.5 kg
Red tea	250 g
Green tea	50 g
Semolina	1.250 kg
Pasta	1.500 kg
Condensed milk	6.0 cans

Source: *Ofuk Magazine*, Tripoli Chamber of Commerce, 2004.
*This is flour for individual consumption distributed by *Algamaita Alastahlakia*: Libyan Consumers Associations.

Table 4.23. Subsidized prices to Libyan citizens, 2004

Item	Gov. subsidised price from Nasco to consumer associations	Subsidised price from consumer associations to libyan citizen [LD]
Imported flour 50 kg (Bag)	2.350	2.600
Imported flours 10 kg (Bag)	1.140	1.250
Rice 25 kg (Bag)	2.950	3.250
Sugar 50 kg (Bag)	5.850	6.500
Domestic olives oil 20 kg (Box)	19.00	20.00
Corn oil 20 kg (Box)	11.300	11.900
Tomato 20 kg (Box)	11.040	12.00
Red tea 20 kg (Box)	23.00	25.00
Green tea 20 kg (Box)	23.00	25.00
Milk, 96 cans (Box)	17.00	18.00
Milk, 48 cans (Box)	17.00	18.00
Semolina 25 kg (Box)	8.500	9.240
Pasta 20 kg (Box)	1.350	2 240

Source: *Ofuk Magazine*, Tripoli Chamber of Commerce, 2004.

Table 4.24 provides details of the quantities of each commodity supplied to each citizen as subsidized items for a period of a year. As can be seen from the final column the total value of subsidies works out at around LD153.537 per Libyan citizen per year.

In terms of annual cost of food subsidies to Libya, Table 4.25 illustrates this for the years 2001–2006.

Table 4.24. Subsidized items, breakdown of annual government subsidies, 2004

Item	Quantity per individual per year	Price after economic liberalisation [Dinar]	Cost of buying specifying quantity [Dinar]	Amount of government subsidy [Dinar]	Cost to Libyan citizen [Dinar]
Flour	144 kg	0.540	77.760	70.992	6.768
Cooking Oil	18 Cans or Items	1.500	27.00	16.830	10.170
Rice	30 kg	0.604	18.120	14.580	3.540
Paste	15 kg	0.805	12.075	9.525	2.550
Semolina	15 kg	0.584	8.760	7.950	0.810
Sugar	24 kg	0.446	10.704	7.896	2.808
Tea	24 kg	2.885	6.924	4.164	2.760
Milk	473 Cans	0.461	21.805	13.433	8.372
Tomato	18 Cans	0.636	11.448	7.308	4.140
Yeast	0 622 kg	2.740	1.704	0.895	0.809
Total	–	–	196.300	153.537	42.727

Source: *Ofuk Magazine*, Tripoli Chamber of Commerce, 2004.

Table 4.25. Annual costs of food subsidies, 2001–2005

	2000	2001	2002	2003	2004	2005
Wheat	23.3	11.6	99.2	–31.0	77.4	0.0
Flour	97.2	123.9	150.7	338.0	526.5	490.5
Sugar	–5.4	11.1	21.8	39.3	44.1	55.3
Rice	15.2	8.0	51.9	45.9	104.3	100.7
Olive and other vegetable Oils	11.7	–6.2	4.6	98.7	164.3	120.4
Tea	7.8	17.8	11.2	15.0	30.5	17.4
Coffee	–1.9	0.0	0.0	0.0	0.0	0.0
Tomato paste	6.7	8.6	8.8	15.7	0.0	0.0
Dry yeast	–1.0	–0.3	0.8	4.2	11.4	10.4
Dry legumes	–0.8	0.0	0.0	0.0	0.0	0.0
Evaporated milk	–1.9	–6.5	3.0	56.1	147.0	0.0
Semolina	0.0	0.0	3.8	36.9	47.0	37.1
Miscellaneous	1.5	4.0	1.5	6.3	6.3	7.0
Pasta	0.0	0.0	0.0	0.0	42.3	0.0
Total	152.4	172.0	357.3	625.1	1,202.2	838.8

*In Million of LD

Source: IMF, 2006.

In an article published in Arabic by the Tripoli Chamber of Commerce, Trade, and Agriculture (Ofuk Magazine November, 2004) Nasco itself it has come up with a proposed solution to deal with current demands for salary rises from the Public Sector, currently a very hot topic in Libya. This is based on scrapping food subsidies and returning these in the form of salary increases, with each grade of Civil Servant receiving a salary increase, based on the monetary value of the scrapped subsidies. This is to be based on subsidies received by the average size of a Libyan family, which has seven members according to the Libyan 2002–2003 Socio-Economic Survey, added to the 13 salary grades in the Public Sector, using a sliding scale. Nasco's proposal is outlined in Table 4.26.

In our view there are many people in Libya who support such a scheme, since both the subsidy system and the subsidy mentality are no longer appropriate for the Libyan people as they prepare for privatization and economic diversification. In this new economic reality subsidies can no longer be an effective policy, for four main reasons. First, by transferring subsidies into cash, this gives the Libyan consumer a wider choice regarding what he/she wants to spend the salary increases on, rather than being limited to the subsidy items. Secondly, from an economic viewpoint, the food subsidy system is very wasteful, with consumers using and cooking larger quantities of the subsidized items than they really need. Thirdly, the system is grossly abused by both the distributors and the consumers, with much of Libya's heavily subsidized food items ending up in neighbouring countries. Fourthly, by ending Nasco's monopoly and state financial support for it, a significant number of new Libyan entrepreneurs will emerge, in turn stimulating and diversifying the Libyan economy.

Table 4.26. Proposed salary increases after abolishing subsidies, 2004

Employment grade	Monthly salary based on law No. 15 of 1981	Value of modification per month	Basic monthly salary after modification	Difference among the grades before modification	Difference among the grades after modification
13	390	87	477	0	0
12	340	88	428	50	49
11	310	89	399	30	29
10	270	90	360	40	39
9	230	92	322	40	38
8	195	93	288	35	34
7	170	95	265	25	23
6	145	96	241	25	24
5	130	97	227	15	14
4	120	99	219	10	8
3	105	101	206	15	13
2	95	103	198	10	8
1	85	105	190	10	8

Source: *Ofuk Magazine*, Tripoli Chamber of Commerce, 2004.

4.7 Impact of Social Trends on Economic Reform

In our survey of Libyan demographic trends, we presented Table 4.4, which detailed key demographic indicators for Libya from 1950 to 2002 and then to 2025 (projected). This showed population growth rising rapidly from 1,029,000 in 1950 to 5,529,000 in 2002, with a projected Libyan population of 7,972,000 by 2025. While, therefore, Libyan population had increased by 537 per cent in the 53 years from 1950 to 2002, it is projected to increase by only 44 per cent in the next 23 years, from 2003 to 2025.

In the same table we provided key indicators relating to health and education for Libya over the later part of the period. It is clear that demographic trends and trends in health and education are inseparable. While, obviously, major improvements in health facilities lead to lower infant mortality rates and a longer life, it is the interplay between female education and female fertility, which declined from 7.4 per cent for the period 1975–1980 to 3.3 per cent in the period 2000–2005, which largely explains Libya's demographic changes. We emphasized, in our survey of the evolution of the Libyan education system, the significance of Article 14 of the Libyan Constitutional Declaration of 1969, which provided for compulsory education for all children, male and female. Here we will emphasize again the crucial importance of this far-sighted and fundamental component of Libyan education policy.

Its long-term impact is clearly shown by the fact that while in 1954–1955 males represented 82 per cent and females 18 per cent of students educated at all levels in Libya, by 2006 there were in fact more females in the education system than males. In practical terms in Libya today this means that virtually all females of optimum reproductive age, that is below 30 years, are educated, either to basic, intermediate, or university level.

Why is this so significant? It is because, in the field of demography, female education has long been identified as the single most important determinant in lowering fertility in countries, such as Libya, that are in the process of demographic transition. No other variable can explain fertility differentials at the individual level, across countries, and over time better than female education (Lutz et al. 1996). In general terms it is obvious that education provides every woman with the opportunities, knowledge, ability, and potential to manipulate and control her immediate environment, especially with regard to marriage, work, fertility, family planning, and so on. Additionally, more girls in school mean fewer or, at least, later marriages, and therefore less children, while school attendance raises aspirations regarding a marriage partner, making women more selective. Educated women also marry later, and are likely to expect less help from their children at home because they themselves have been educated; they would rather see their children attend school than stay at home. Therefore, children are not relied on to secure the future, resulting in fewer births.

In empirical terms many studies have also shown this. For example, the Democratic and Health Survey (DHS) for Egypt (El-Zinaty 1993) conclusively showed the correlation between low fertility and high levels of education, with Total Fertility Rate (TFR) equating 5.03 for women with no education, 3.98 for those with some primary education, 3.03 for those who completed primary or some secondary education, and 2.91 for women who completed secondary or higher education.

In the section on the growing role of women in Libyan society we showed an increasing trend in all sectors, especially in the public sector in the fields of education and health. As Libya diversifies economically, the demand for qualified female professionals, many of whom presently elect to stay at home after marriage because of traditional family values, will also increase, ensuring that their involvement in this diversification process must rise, as skills shortages will dictate that they play a much more active role in work and business. The role of Libyan women in society and economic activity is therefore set to increase substantially. In politics also we feel it is only a matter of time before women make their presence felt more strongly, since in terms of education and knowledge, they are well prepared to take on their responsibilities in this field.

In terms of health services, Libyans have access, despite the sanctions, to a comprehensive health system which literally takes care of them from the cradle to the grave, reaching every part of Libya's vast area with an admirable national doctor/patient ratio. Yet, liberal Libyan immigration and health policies, as we have seen, are placing an almost unbearable burden on this sector, with clinics and facilities constructed for 10,000 people having to cope, in some areas of Tripoli and elsewhere such as Sebha, with double or triple that number because of the vast number of immigrants, legal and illegal, seeking medical treatment.

In terms of housing, we showed how the Libyan government, from 1970 to 2000, lived up to its promise of 1969 of "housing for all", so that by 1997, as Fig. 4.5 illustrated, virtually every Libyan owned his home. However, this key socio-political achievement also came at a price – an inefficient construction sector, a financial system which did not provide for mortgages to enable Libyans to leverage their main economic asset, their home, an inflexible property market, ill prepared for the massive demands for house rental which will accompany Libya's economic diversification, as well as the new domestic mobility of the younger components of the Libyan work force.

In the field of employment law and social security, the Libyan worker can be said to be one of the most protected in terms of job security in the world, with a social security, food subsidy, and pension system which ensure that all his basic food and living expenses are provided for life. But this has led to a type of "subsidy" mentality and a "job for life" outlook which has ill prepared Libyans for the more aggressive and cut-throat world of competition which the planned economic diversification and privatization of the Libyan economy will inevitably bring about.

In terms of achieving social justice and equality, Libya in the period 1965–2005 can be said to have succeeded only too well, at the same time building an infrastructure and quality of life which places the country well ahead of any in Africa and among the leaders of the Arab world. But the winds of change are blowing. The centralized and nationalized system put in place in the 1970s can no longer deliver the aspirations and desires of the Libyan people as the country struggles to come to terms with the realities of globalization. A new mindset is required for the Libyan younger generation as well as for the Libyan policy makers, in which the nanny state must give way to a tougher and more competitive and individualistic approach to life.

In this regard, the former Libyan Prime Minister in August 2005, in an interview with the Libyan newspaper *Libya Today*, stated that Libya could no longer afford to maintain a bloated public sector estimated at over 800,000 employees in a country with a population of around 5.68 million, comparing Libya to neighbouring Tunisia whose population is over 10 million, but whose public sector has levelled off at 350,000 employees. The annual cost to Libya of US $4 billion in salaries alone for maintaining this public sector could, in the long term, cripple the country, making it vulnerable to any downward trends in oil prices and production.

In the section entitled "The Great Debate" we discussed one way in which salary increases now demanded by this sector could be achieved, by abolishing subsidies, but clearly this is an emotive issue which will have to be debated and resolved at all levels in the democratic process, from the grassroots Basic People's Congress level right up to the GPC, because of its crucial importance for Libya's future. In Indonesia in 1997, for example, it was the issue of fuel and food subsidies which brought down the government of President Suharto, a military strongman who had ruled the country for 30 years; the same issue dogged his immediate successor Habibie and led to his downfall after only 100 days in office, and while the Abdulrachman Wahid and Megawati administrations managed to keep the issue at bay as we write, it is this same fuel and food subsidy issue which could make or break the present Indonesian government headed by Bambang Susilo Yudhyono.

For the moment, there appears to be plenty of oil, both as reserves under Libyan land and sea, and as oil flowing through the export pipelines, while the oil price has never been higher. This in fact is exactly what the Indonesian government thought in the period from the 1970s to the 1980s when receipts from oil exports boosted economic growth and enabled the government to generously subsidize fuel prices as well as a wide range of basic commodities. But by the new millennium, Indonesia had become a net importer of oil, with disastrous consequences for the then Indonesian leadership and the welfare of the Indonesian people.

As we have noted elsewhere in this book, over-dependence on this commodity has caused severe dislocation in the Libyan economy before, as its price plummeted at crucial points in the 1980s and 1990s, severely affecting and delaying Libya's ambitious socio-economic development plans. The new Libyan mindset must focus on ways and means of drastically reducing the country's dangerous reliance on only one commodity, at the same time dropping the subsidy mentality. It must ensure that an effective strategy for reducing the inefficient and overstaffed public sector is drawn up and implemented, at the same time gradually achieving genuine economic diversification.

This can, in part, be successfully accomplished by privatizing a wide range of inefficient government-owned companies, as the Libyan government is currently doing, albeit slowly. Another way of achieving rapid diversification could be by taking a long hard look at the petroleum sector itself. So far the Libyan government has not publicly announced any plans for its privatization, either in whole or in part, as is currently happening, for example, in neighbouring Algeria. But clearly certain LNOC wholly owned subsidiaries such as the inefficient and loss-making downstream distribution Brega Oil Marketing Corporation (BOMC) should be prime targets for privatization at some point in the near future, with a wide range of economic and commercial benefits to many Libyan entrepreneurs an private sector businesses virtually guaranteed by this action.

Similarly, the newly drafted Libyan Petroleum Law could legislate for incremental levels of Libyan content in personnel, contractors, services, and equipment, such as Iran's requirement for 50 per cent of total project expenditure to be expended within Iran. By ensuring that any violations and leakages by foreign partners and contractors in this regard are dealt with promptly and severely, the Libyan government would ensure that a successful Libyan oil service and equipment sector is nurtured and successfully grown. This will lead to massive economic spin-offs such as new job creation for technologists and engineers, construction and fabrication activities, equipment manufacturing and maintenance, similar to the successful economic experience of Norway and Scotland, the centre of the UK oil and gas industry, over the last 20 years (Otman and Karlberg 2005).

By successfully and promptly dealing with these critical public sector and diversification issues, the Libyan government can ensure that future generations of Libyans can be guaranteed the comforts of the present generation. The reformist agenda initiated in 2003 must continue to implement and execute the strategies and policies of economic diversification and public sector reform vital for Libya's economic transformation.

5 Infrastructure in Libya

5.1 Historical Background

In September 1911 Italy engineered a crisis with the Ottoman Empire, leading to a declaration of war and the landing of Italian troops and capture of Tripoli on October 1911. Thus began a long-drawn-out colonial war in Libya which ended with the summary execution by the Italian governor of Libya, Rudolfo Graziani, of Umar Al Mukhtar, the leader of the Libyan resistance, in Benghazi in 1931, after which Italian rule could finally be consolidated. By 1934 Tripolitania and Cyrenaica were divided into four provinces – Tripoli, Misuratah, Benghazi, and Derna – which were formally linked as a single colony known as Libya. In 1939 Libya was incorporated into Metropolitan Italy.

The costs of the Italian military pacification of Libya had been enormous, as elaborated in some detail in a landmark work on the Italian colonization of Libya, "The Fourth Shore" (Segrè 1975). Not only this, but a massive capital outlay was also required for the country's economic and transportation infrastructure. Italy invested vast amounts of capital and technology in public works projects, the extension and modernization of cities, highway and railroad construction, port facilities, and large-scale agriculture and irrigation, so much, in fact, that Libyan expenditure was a factor in Italy's effective financial bankruptcy by 1941.

Although these measures had been introduced for the benefit of Italians and an Italian-controlled agricultural estate sector, this was in fact the period in which Libya's 1,822 km long coastal highway was constructed, as well as much urban construction and planning, because in this period before the Second World War, Italian plans envisioned an Italian colony of 500,000 settlers by the 1960s in Libya. Indirectly, despite the ruthlessness of the Italian conquest, this was to provide a lasting legacy to independent Libya in the years after 1951, when a very good basic road and rail infrastructure existed throughout much of the heavily populated coastal strip.

5.2 The Development of the Libyan Communications Sector

In its early 5-year plans the fledgling Libyan government, aided by foreign aid and planners, clearly recognized that communications were going to be vital for the development of agriculture, industry, and commerce (Kingdom of Libya, Ministry of Planning and Development 1963). However, Libya faced two basic difficulties in the field of communications. The first was the huge size of the country and the second was the widely scattered nature of the population. Before the advent of oil, it was practically impossible to reconcile these socio-economic aims with the lack of resources to pay for them.

Although, as we have seen above, a good basic road and rail infrastructure had been in place since the late 1930s, this had undoubtedly suffered from severe war damage. In a post-war context, harbours, roads, bridges, and railways had all also suffered from years of neglect. However, by 1960, according to the World Bank Mission, the Libyan transport system adequately served the needs of the country (International Bank for Reconstruction and Development 1960). At that time roads, air travel, and privately owned and government-owned motor vehicles constituted the main means of internal transport between the three provincial capitals. The railways, run at a loss, were insignificant economically. Coastal shipping was negligible, and the main roads carried very little traffic. Tripoli harbour handled the bulk of Libya's foreign trade, with Benghazi playing a secondary role. Smaller coastal ports were being steadily abandoned, and Tobruk, the only natural harbour in Libya, served a hinterland of little importance. Tripoli, the main international airport, together with Benghazi's Benina Airport, and a number of scattered airports and foreign military airfields, met the needs of the area (Farley 1971).

It was also around this time that, in view of new oil-based economic prospects for Libya, the Government commissioned an international consultancy report aimed at identifying current deficiencies and future transport needs in relation to expectations under a planned development (Dioxidis Associates 1964). For this study a number of economic variables were taken into account. On an assumed population growth of 2.5 per cent, the Libyan population was expected to reach a total of 1,838,300 in 1972 and 2,355,400 by 1982 (Dioxidis Associates 1964, Volume II) with future growth being concentrated in the towns, but with other areas at the same time reaching a certain minimum size. Agricultural production by 2000 was expected to be double the 1963 level in Tripolitania, two and a half times this level in Cyrenaica and three times the level in the Fezzan. Despite this, however, the Libyan agricultural output was still expected to fall far short of Libyan consumption needs thus necessitating imports to fill the gap.

Other assumptions were the persistence of heavy concentration of industrial activity in Tripoli and to a lesser extent in Benghazi, occasioned by government intentions to develop industries. The study predicted that by 1987, for instance, the number of private passenger cars was expected to be 16 times greater than in 1963. The implications for planning were clear in every sector of the transportation complex. Existing roads had to be improved and new roads provided, the telecommunications network modernized, and harbours, airports, and meteorological stations rehabilitated, expanded, or constructed. It was estimated that Tripoli port would need at least 5,000 m of additional quays of a depth of 10 and 12 m together with an extra berth for dangerous cargoes to meet increased traffic needs within the next 4 years. Even allowing for this, the port was expected to be congested by 1987 (Farley 1971).

The estimation cost of meeting the new transport needs of Libya within 25 years was put by Doxiadis Associates in 1963 at 116.5 million Libyan pounds, breaking down as follows: Roads 70 Million, Railways 120,000, Ports 38.35 million, and Airports and Aviation 8.06 million.

This meant an average annual investment over the period 1963–1987 of 4.7 million Libyan pounds. Transportation and public works were so important that together they were allocated 42.8 per cent of Libya's first development budget: 27.5 million Libyan pounds were allocated to transportation, or 16.2 per cent of the total development budget (1963–1968 Five-Year Plan).

In reality, since the early 1970s, Libyan infrastructure demands, represented mainly by the transportation and telecommunications sector, absorbed a large share of the annual development budgets. This expenditure was designed to access every geographically remote area in the country, with the Libyan government demonstrating, as in the housing, education, and health sectors, a high level of commitment to the principal that every Libyan had the right to equal treatment in terms of amenities. Very significant expenditure was therefore allocated to ensure that even the most remote settlement in this vast country was provided with road access and the basic necessities of a healthy life, such as clean drinking water and efficient waste disposal and sewerage systems. Figure 5.1 shows annual expenditure in Libya on Transport and Communications as a percentage of the Development Budgets for the period 1962–2004.

From Fig. 5.1 we can note that throughout the period, an average of 13.37 per cent of the annual development budget has been spent on transport and communications, including new roads, road maintenance, railroads, airports, air services, and posts and communications. In 1982 and 1993 it reached peaks of 21.62 and 16.3 per cent before plunging to only 2.48 per cent in 1994 as a result of crude oil price erosion. It then levelled off at around the average of 13 per centfrom 1998 to 2001, maintaining a level of 8.18 per cent in 2004.

However, as we can note from Fig. 5.2, the annual expenditure on Communications and Transport in absolute terms from 1962 to 1969, although large in percentage terms when it averaged 22.6 per cent, was only LD11.95 million per year. This compares with average figures of LD103.95 per year, or almost 10 times this amount, from 1970 to 1979 and LD370 per year for 1980–1985. From

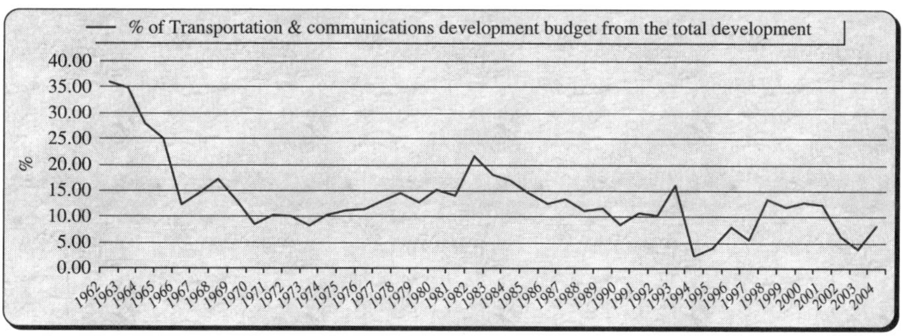

Source: Libyan General Planning Council and Central Bank of Libya Annual Reports

Fig. 5.1. Percentage of expenditure on transport and communications in total development Budget, 1962–2004

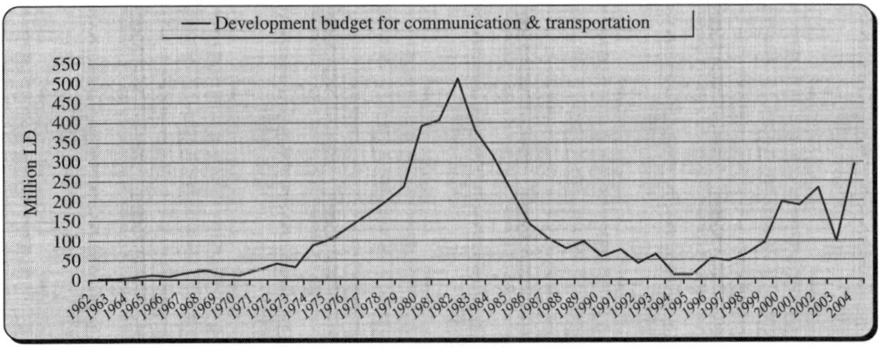

Source: Libyan General Planning Council and Central Bank of Libya Annual Reports

Fig. 5.2. Development budget for the communication and transportation, 1962–2004

1986 to 1990 it fell dramatically to an average of LD96.8 million per year, and then from 1991 to 1999 to LD94 million per year because of oil price collapse and the sanctions, before rising again in the period 2000–2004 to an average of LD202 million per year.

In absolute terms the amounts in LD spent on transport and communications for selected 5-year plan periods are also detailed in Table 5.1.

This figure illustrates the massive amounts spent on infrastructure in Libya, amounting to many billions of LD per year, especially in the periods 1976–1980 and 1981–1985. As we will discuss later, much of this infrastructure, which is now over 20 years old, has deteriorated significantly, contributing to Libya's currently vast infrastructure deficit which we will discuss below.

In a more recent context, Table 5.2 shows the total budget of LD1.181 billion allocated to the Transportation and Communication in the Government Plan, 2002–2006, broken into sectors.

In terms of the present, there are two factors which must be understood in attempting to gauge the overall situation with regard to Libyan infrastructure, and the huge infrastructure deficit which undoubtedly currently exists in the country. The first is the vast amount of capital expended on providing Libya's present inventory of infrastructure in the 1970s and 1980s, which was detailed in Fig. 5.2. This means that much of Libyan infrastructure is now 20–30 years old.

Table 5.1. Expenditure on transport and communications for selected development plan periods

Year	Total amount allocated to development plans, million LD	Total amount allocated to transportation and communication sector, million LD
1970/1972	112.9	969
1973/1975	284.5	2585.9
1976/1980	132.2	8813.2
1981/1985	1868.5	11780
1986/1989	552.8	5405

Table 5.2. Government 5-year plan, 2002–2006: total expenditure in the transportation and communications sector

Sector	Million LD	%
Ongoing projects	100	8.5
Projects of maintenances roads and bridges	251	21.3
Air service	10	0.8
Airports	100	8.5
Air transportation	220	18.6
Postage and communication	100	8.5
Railway project	400	33.8
Total	1181	100

Because of the centralized nature of the Libyan government, this means that the government alone has the sole responsibility of maintaining infrastructure. In fact the Libyan government virtually owns every business, public building, road, port, airport, university, school, and hospital community and social service, library, and park and recreational facility – in fact everything in Libya. This also encompasses a further range of infrastructural facilities, including water distribution and supply, sewage treatment, desalinization plants, sanitary and combined sewerage systems, storm sewers, solid waste and hazardous waste disposal.

The other major factor impacting the infrastructure deficit was the existence of the US and UN sanctions, under which Libya suffered, until 2004, for almost 20 years. These effectively denied access to spare parts and technology to service much of the infrastructure which was installed prior to 1986 when the US sanctions took effect. It means that even if the Libyan government wanted and had the money to buy, for example, the much-needed hospital equipment or supply spare parts to generators or desalinization plants or aircraft, it could not do so. We will see later what one estimate of the costs of this to the Libyan economy revealed.

Combined, these two factors mean that Libya's current infrastructure deficit is undoubtedly massive. Just how big is impossible even to guesstimate. To try to get some perspective the 1995 McGill University–Federation of Canadian Municipalities (FCM) survey of Canada's municipal infrastructure estimated that it would require $44 billion to bring it up to an acceptable level. When the cost of rehabilitation of the infrastructure under the provincial and federal jurisdictions and the private sector are added, the total infrastructure deficit for Canada would far exceed $100 billion. Similarly in 1998 the estimate of the infrastructure renewal needs in the United States by the American Society of Civil Engineers (ASCE) came up with a figure of US $1.3 trillion (Mirza and Haider 2003). Of course Libya is smaller than either the United States or Canada in terms of both size and population, but the scale of the Libyan deficit, which can only be assessed by an infrastructure baseline survey such as was conducted by McGill University in 1998, must be comparatively massive in view of the pent-up demand occasioned by the sanctions and the ageing of most of Libya's current infrastructure.

5.3 Libya's Physical Infrastructure

5.3.1 Roads

Libya's road network has been considerably expanded since the early 1970s. At the end of that decade, for example, Libya had only about 8,800 km of roads, of which 50 per cent were paved. However, by 1985 Libya had between 23,000 and 25,600 km of paved roads. Surfaced roads were also built between the north and the southern oases of Al Kufrah, Murzuq, and Sebha. By 1999 Libya had an estimated total road network of 83,200 km, of which 47,590 km were paved. These roads have meant that virtually every remote settlement in Libya is accessible by road. In particular, the agricultural projects underway in the desert oases have benefited from the more efficient crop marketing made possible by these roads.

The National General Company for Roads oversees all new construction and road maintenance. The key road in Libya is the 1,822-kilometer national coastal highway. It runs from the Tunisian border to the Egyptian border, passing through Tripoli and Benghazi. The number of vehicles in Libya increased steadily in the 1970s and early 1980s. By 1985, 313,000 automobiles and trucks and about 70,000 buses were registered in the country. The ratio of automobile ownership to population was on a par with that of many West European countries.

Currently under planning consideration is the construction of a 1,400 km road linking the country with Chad and Niger as well as a projected $375 million to be spent on developing the road transportation fleet for goods and passengers on this route. Other plans include the construction of an east–west trans-Libyan motorway, 50 km from the coast linking Libya to Tunisia and Egypt. In the long term this is tied up to the Libyan government's present liberalization of trade, freeing all imported goods from customs duties. These economic reforms are linked to a long-term plan to re-build its entire transportation sector with modern facilities. This is targeted at making Libya a transport hub in the African trade zone, carrying passengers and products along the North African coast and through a vertical channel extending from the Mediterranean region to the Gulf of Guinea through neighbouring Chad. However, in view of domestic needs in the post-sanctions period, the authors believe that these long-term and visionary plans need to be put in perspective.

5.3.2 The Aviation Sector

In Libya the aviation sector is regulated by the Libyan Civil Aviation Authority, a 100 per cent state-owned organization. In view of the vast size of the country, air travel is a convenient if heavily used method of transport, with seats sold out long in advance to tour companies, businessmen, and government officials. However, air transport is very cheap, with the journey from Tripoli to Sebha or Benghazi only LD28 one-way.

The country has 142 airports and airfields, with 42 per cent or approximately 59 with paved runways (Libyan Civil Aviation Authority 2004). Table 5.3

Table 5.3. Airports, 2005

Libyan airports ("I" signifies International)		
Airport	Airport code	Location: city
Tripoli international (I)	TIP	Tripoli
Sebha(I)	MRA	Sebha
Benina (I)	BEN	Benghazi
Sert(I)	SRX	Sert
Ghat	GHT	Ghat
Ghadames	LTD	Ghadames
Misuratah	MRA	Misuratah
Ubari	QUB	Ubari
Kufrah	AKF	Kufrah
Martuba	DNF	Derna
Labraq	LAQ	Beida
El Brega	LMQ	Marsa El Brega
Houn	HUQ	Houn
Tobruq	TOB	Tobruq

Note: There are several other airports used by oil companies and other non-commercial services not listed here.

provides details of the principal national and international civilian airports. The leading airport in the country, the Tripoli International Airport, has a current handling capacity of 3.5 million passengers per year, and will be soon upgraded to handle significant projected increases in tourist volume. The second Tripoli airport is Mithiga Airport, formerly the US Wheelus military airbase, which is currently being used by Libyan private air companies for domestic flights. In fact this airport, with an excellent location several hundred meters from the Mediterranean coast and a huge land bank, has great future potential, and the government plans its rebuilding as one of Libya's major airports for international flights.

There is no doubt that the sanctions had an enormous impact on the Libyan road and aviation sectors. The international UN and US embargos resulted in virtually no international flights to Libya, resulting in the suspension of the activities of all Libyan airline companies, as well lack of spare parts. To get a perspective on the massive losses brought about by the sanctions, Table 5.4 provides estimates of losses to these sectors.

However, in the post-sanctions period the government has ambitious plans to upgrade the aviation sector. One indicator of Libya's future policy in this regard took place in April 2001, when the Libyan government and the Italian airline Blue Panorama set up a new carrier, Afriqiyah Airways, of which the Libyan state owns 51 per cent, with the remaining equity held by Libyan, African, and foreign shareholders, while Blue Panorama supplies the planes and staff. The new service, which commenced on 1 December 2001, targets links between the African continent and the regional and long-haul routes, designed specifically to connect Africa to Europe, the Middle East, and Asia. The carrier flies from Tripoli to Benghazi (Libya), Khartoum (Sudan), Niamey (Niger), Accra (Ghana), Bamako (Mali), Ndjamena (Chad), Bangui (Central African Republic), and Ouagadougou

Table 5.4. Estimated losses to Libyan communication and transport sector as result of sanctions, 15th April 1992–5th April 1999

By sector	Value in million US $
General civil aviation authority	126.31
Losses due to dissolution of airports Co.	72.56
Libyan arab airlines	2.86
Light air transport company dissolution losses	197.22
Libyan air-cargo company dissolution losses	197.22
General national maritime transport company	146.09
Sea port company	23.50
General post and telecommunications company	204.71
Road network	35.61
Total	1006.08

Source: First National Report on the Environment, 2002.

(Burkina Faso). Other routes include Dubai, Tunis, and Cairo, Paris, London, Geneva, Belgium, and other European cities. In July 2006, Airbus announced the sale to Afriqiyah of nine jets from the single-aisle A320 family and three larger A330 widebody airliners in a deal worth about $1.7 billion at list price.

As part of their plan for Libyan airport improvements the government has allocated a budget of approximately US $1 billion which calls for the upgrading of infrastructure and the developing of navigation and air control systems, and the training of Libyan national staff. The air transportation fleet has also obtained a large share of future government expenditure with approximately US $3 billion allocated for use before the end of this decade, mainly targeted at purchasing an additional 25 modern passenger aircraft to be operated by the state-owned Libyan Arab Airlines Company (LAAC).

Recently, however, the Libyan government announced its intention to privatize the entire state aviation sector, and LAAC was the first major state organization to be targeted by the reform policy. Presently the company operates and owns 727s and Fokker F-28s as well as two Airbus A-300s. Towards realizing this, on 30 August 2005 the Libyan Prime Minister issued Law No. 54, in which a high level privatization committee was formed, consisting of representatives from all state sectors led by the Ministry of Finance, two members from the Libyan Cabinet, representatives from the General Board of Ownership Transfer (GBOT) (or the Libyan Privatization Board) and four members from the Libyan Civil Aviation Authority. This committee is tasked with evaluating all the LAAC assets, financial data, and properties belonging to the company in Libya or abroad, the first step, presumably, in its partial or total privatization.

Libya also has another private airline company, Al-Buraq Air, which has in 2005 finalized a deal with Boeing to buy six civil aircraft, with the first contract already signed for three 737-800s and the contract for remaining three still under negotiation.

5.3.3 Seaports and Harbours

As listed in Table 5.5, Libya has several commercial seaports but the country has no inland waterways capable of handling vessels. Many of these are long-established, including Benghazi, Al Khums, Marsa El Brega, Marsa El Hariqah Tobruk, Misuratah, Ras Lanuf, El Sider, Al-Zawia, Tripoli, and Zuetina, and certain ports, such as Ras Lanuf and Marsa El Brega, which also serve as oil terminals. Together they are estimated to have a warehouse holding capacity of approximately 14 million tonnes. Tripoli Seaport was created in 1999 as a free port and presently work is continuing on it to significantly expand its capacity.

However, like the aviation sector, the shipping industry was also very severely affected by the sanctions, with its huge losses noted earlier, and the condition of Libya's merchant marine requires extensive upgrading (Table 5.6). A German port study, conducted in 2001, found the Libyan fleet to have more faults than any other merchant fleet surveyed. In 2002 a Libyan cargo ship sank, with a loss of its crew of 25. Again, however, the Libyan government has ambitious plan for the refurbishment and purchase/replacement of an additional 36 vessels at an estimated cost of around US $1.5 billion over the next decade.

5.3.4 Proposed New High Speed Railway System

The original Libyan railway system has been out of operation since early 1965 when the Benghazi–Al-Marj line was abandoned, followed by the 60 km Tripoli light railway, due basically to technical and maintenance problems. As well as these, there were other problems related to profitability of the Libyan railways during this period. As one economist wrote at the time, "Railways have been operating at a loss due to their inability to compete with vehicular traffic in spite of low fares offered" (Kubbah 1964). However, in the mid-1990s the government established an ambitious plan for re-building a comprehensive new high speed railway system for Libya, which resulted in the creation of the Railway Executive

Table 5.5. Principal seaports

Name of seaports	Location or city
Tripoli	Tripoli
Al Khums	Al Khums
Misuratah	Misuratah
Ras Lanuf	Ras Lanuf
El Sidra	Ras Lanuf
El Brega	El Brega
Benghazi	Benghazi
Derna	Derna
Zuwarah	Zuwarah
Marsa El-Hariga	Tobruq
Al-Zawia	Al-Zawia
Zuetina	Zuetina
Sirte	Sirte

Table 5.6. Merchant marine fleet 2005

Quantity	Usage
9	Cargo vessels
1	Chemical tanker
3	Liquefied gas tankers
6	Petroleum tankers
4	Roll-on/roll-off vessels
4	Short-sea passenger vessels

Board, employing about 750 staff, responsible for handling all rail projects. The government plan proposed a budget of US $10 billion (Table 5.7) for the construction of approximately 3,170 km of new railway line of 1.435 m standard gauge. Initially the track was to be laid along the Libyan littoral, linking Tunisia with Tripoli and then to the Misuratah Free Zone to the city of Sirte. Eventually the proposed network will reach the inland city of Sebha, the capital of the southern region while another line will link Egypt from Sollum with Tobruk in Libya.

Although the plan of linking Egypt with Libya should have been completed by 1994, delays impacted by the sanctions and government budget constraints during periods of low oil prices could not support this proposed infrastructure. However, by 1998 the Railways Executive Board (REB) had signed a deal with Bahne of Egypt and Jez Sistmas Ferroviarios of Spain for the supply of crossings and point work for the Egyptian branch. A US $477 contract for the railroad link between Libya and Tunisia was awarded in 2000 to the China Civil Engineering Construction Corporation, which began the first phase of the plan to build a national rail system in Libya. This initial contract was to construct a 163 km line with 16 stations from Ra's Ajdir, the land frontier point between Tunisia and north-west Libya, to Tripoli. Site preparation and some construction were completed in 2001.

Currently the REB is seeking Build Operate Transfer (BOT) ventures with specialized companies, and its plan is based on separate 5-year construction periods, as shown in Table 5.8, with massive budgets for each phase. However, the government is still analysing the feasibility of the entire project, with a study currently being undertaken by a French group of companies.

Table 5.7. Targeted investment for the Libyan railway network project

Description	Value million US$	%
Track works	2280	22.8
Road and bridges	1860	18.6
Earthworks	1640	16.4
Rolling stock and workshops	1500	15
Stations and buildings	1200	12
Signaling and telecommunications	1120	11.2
Feasibility study (design & technical)	400	4
Total	10,000	100

Source: Libyan Railway Executive Board, 2005.

Table 5.8. LREB: railway investment schedule

Project	Year 1	Year 2	Year 3	Year 4	Year 5
Studies, design/tech assistance	100	75	75	75	75
Earthworks	500	380	380	380	0
Bridges works	558	434	434	434	0
Building works	144	264	264	264	264
Track works	684	399	399	399	399
Signalling & telecommunications	336	196	196	196	196
Rolling stock	225	105	390	390	390
Total	2547	1853	2138	2138	1324

*In million US$
Source: Railway Executive Board, 2005.

Some idea of the massive scale of the proposed undertaking is provided in Table 5.9, which lists the main project components.

5.3.5 The Rapidly Emerging Telecommunications Sector

Until recently this sector was regulated in Libya by the state-owned General Post and Telecommunications Company (GPTC) which was established under Law No. 16 of 1984. However, aware of the rising importance of the IT and communications sector in the new world order, the Government in 2005 initiated important legislation aimed at the reconstruction of the state telecommunications sector. On 11 January 2005, Law No. 7 was issued by the Libyan Cabinet establishing the Public Board of Information, Documentation and Telecommunications (PBIDT), as the national authority for this sector. This was followed by Law No. 63 of 14 April 2005

Table 5.9. Proposed Libyan railway network/ main components

No.	Component	Amount
1	Stations	96
2	Bridges	554
3	Crossers	1205
4	Earthworks	115 million m^3
5	Concrete works	2 500 000 m^3
6	Steel for concrete	261 000 tons
7	Steel bars	370 000 tons
8	Concrete rafters	6 800 000
9	Fastenings	27 200 000 pcs
10	Rock fragments	11 600 000 m^3
11	Flint for concrete	2 500 000 m^3
12	Cement	800 000 tons
13	Locomotives	244 units
14	Coaches	8 642
15	Job opportunities	10 000
16	Network length	3170 km

in which Article (1) provided for the establishment of a new commercial body called the Libyan Post, Telecommunications and Information Technology Company (PTITC). Article (5) of Law No. 63 stated that all the four state-owned telecommunications companies, namely GPTC, Al-Madar, Libyana, and Libyan Company for Telecommunications and Technology would henceforth be part of PTITC, which was to be under the management and general supervision of the PBIDT.

Currently telecommunications density in Libya is more or less 12 per cent; however, the PTITC has recently articulated that it is targeting to increase this to around 37 per cent before 2020, at an estimated cost of approximately US $10 billion, with possible increases.

In Libya, mobile phone services have been available since 1997 when the GPTC established the Al-Madar "Orbit" system as an affiliate specializing in mobile communications. At that time it cost US $3,300 per line, which later was reduced gradually to US $710 per line. In September 2004 a new state-owned company, Libyana, started its mobile phone operation, initially covering the three major cities of Tripoli, Beghazi, and Sebha, but aiming at extending its network throughout the country by the end of 2005. With an initial 60,000 lines the Libyana service was based on the design, construction, and consultancy by Chinese firms. Libyans are now able to purchase these new lines for US $478, with costs continuously decreasing.

Many believe that the above-mentioned changes in the laws herald a new beginning in this sector, aimed at encouraging foreign companies to participate in its development, moving away from a state-controlled and operated telecommunications system. But others see the situation differently. Although, undoubtedly, major investment is required to improve the current state of the country's telecommunications sector, in both mobile and land-line networks, it appears that Libya is playing it safe by maintaining a monopoly in telecommunications ownership while utilizing foreign technology and know-how. As the head of Libyana said in 2004, "Foreign mobile network companies can invest millions in establishing their companies here, but the reality is that within a few years they will generate billions in profit, which will be taken abroad. This would be counterproductive to our economy. At least the profits generated by Al-Madar and Libyana will be invested in future projects aimed at developing our telecommunications sector and improving the lives of Libyans" (BBC 2004).

In July 2004 the GPTC offered tenders for installation of the next-generation backbone and switching networks, targeting approximately 3 million lines by 2005. The need for this was because of the high costs and low efficiency of maintaining equipment and facilities originally designed and constructed by Ericsson, including telecommunications switchgear, which has been in the country for over two decades. In September 2004 France's Alcatel and Finland's Nokia were successful in bidding for this contract, worth US $244 million, to develop and construct the Libyan mobile network for 2.5 million new mobile lines within a period of less then 30 months. The companies were required to employ Evolium TM mobile radio access and core network solution to serve GSM/EDGE and 3G users.

In this contract Alcatel will construct facilities for the eastern and southern region of the country, whereas Nokia's coverage will be of the whole area from Tripoli along the region of the western mountains. Nokia, since the second half of 2005, has maintained about 90 per cent of market share for cellular and radio communications equipment.

As we have noted, mobile services are still presently expensive in Libya compared with other Arab neighbouring countries where they can be bought for as little as US $20. But even with high prices of IT and mobile services, demand is on the increase, mainly as a result of the country's population where young people under 25 represent over half of the total population. However, it will be interesting to see if the sector is gradually privatized and deregulated. With the current poor Internet lines and weak mobile services coupled with rapidly increasing demand, the situation will inevitably drive PTITC to conclude new deals seeking better and newer technology to service not only the Libyan population but also the vast number of tourists and foreigners projected to visit and reside in the country as the privatization and liberalization of the Libyan economy proceeds. Although the recent laws give PTITC access to new technology using a competitive commercial policy, this is not the same as privatization, which has been successfully used to upgrade and update the sector in Morocco. So far, for PTITC, finance has not been a problem, but as more lines and more technology demand more capital, can PTITC continue to fund these developments internally?

5.4 The Great Man-Made River Project

In the early 1950s, after the passing of Libya's Mineral Law of 1953, followed by The Petroleum Law No. 25 of 1955, the exploration for new oilfields in the deserts of southern Libya led to the discovery not only of major oil reserves, but also vast quantities of fresh water trapped in underlying strata. The majority of this water was collected between 38,000 and 14,000 years ago, and some reservoirs are 7,000 years old.

These gigantic aquifers are situated in four major underground basins. The Kufra basin, lying in the south-east, near the Egyptian border, covers an area of 350,000 km^2, forming an aquifer layer over 2,000 m deep, with an estimated capacity of 20,000 km^3 in the Libyan sector. The 600 m deep aquifer in the Sirte Basin is estimated to hold over 10,000 km^3 of water, while the 450,000-km^2 Murzuk basin, south of Jabal Fezzan, is estimated to hold 4,800 km^3. Further, water lies in the Hamadah and Jufrah basins, which extend from the Qargaf Arch and Jabal Sawda to the coast.

Traditionally Libyans have depended on rain-renewed coastal aquifers to sustain the small urban and mainly rural population. But owing to demographic changes and pressures since Libyan independence in 1951, these coastal aquifers have become seriously over-depleted, as increasing urbanization and population growth along the Mediterranean Coast placed huge burdens on them.

At the beginning of the 1980s Libya therefore decided to develop the Great Man-Made River Project (GMRP) to provide water to this predominantly coastal and urban population, based on the extraction of these gigantic water reserves. The

GMRP is one of the largest civil engineering projects ever undertaken in the world, involving the abstraction of water from these vast fossil aquifers in the south and south-east areas of the country and its transportation over hundreds of kilometres to the coastal strip, where huge demand for water for the domestic, agricultural, and industrial sectors is growing rapidly.

In October 1983, the Great Man-Made River Authority was created as the Libyan government body responsible for implementing the project. Brown & Root and Price Brothers produced the original project design and the main contractor for the initial phases was Dong Ah, with Enka Construction and Al Nah acting as sub-contractors. The Frankenthal KSB consortium won the pumping station construction and technical support contract and SNC-Lavalin were responsible for the pipe production plant operation and maintenance. Libyan Cement supplied the concrete. Thane-Coat and Harkmel provided pipeline-coating services and Corrintec supplied the cathodic protection system. Thyssen Krupp Fördertechnik provided technical services for the excavation planning and a number of local companies carried out elements of the construction and ancillary work.

The GMRP is one of the most ambitious development projects attempted anywhere in the world, and is considered as one of the greatest water delivery systems in the globe, often described as the "eighth wonder of the world". On account of its massive size it had to be carried out in three phases.

Phases I and II (Total Cost US $12.6 billion)

The first and largest phase, providing 2 million m^3/day along a 1,200 km pipeline from As-Sarir and Tazerbo to Benghazi and Sirte, via the Ajdabiya reservoir, was formally inaugurated in August 1991. This was a massive undertaking, using a quarter of a million sections of concrete pipe, 2.5 million ton of cement, 13 million ton of aggregate, 2 million km of pre-stressed wire, requiring 85 million m^3 of excavation.

The Tazerbo wellfield consists of both production and piezometric observation wells and yields around 1 million m^3/day at a rate of 120L/s per well. Only 98 of the 108 production wells are used, with the others on standby. A collection network conveys the water to a 170,000-m^3-off-line steel header tank. From here, the main conveyance system is routed 256 km to the north, to two similar header tanks at Sarir, where the second Phase I wellfield is located. A further 1 million m^3 is produced here, using 114 of the 126 production wells, at an average flow rate of 102L/s per well. The wells at both Tazerbo and Sarir are about 450 m deep and are equipped with submersible pumps at a depth of 145 m.

From Sarir, two parallel, 4 m diameter pipelines convey the now chlorine-treated water to the 4-million-m^3 Ajdabiya holding reservoir, 380 km to the north. The water flows from this 900 m diameter reservoir through two pipelines, one heading west to Sirte and the other north to Benghazi. Each pipeline discharges into a circular earth embankment end reservoir, with a storage capacity of 6.8 million m^3 at Sirte and 4.7 million m^3 at Benghazi, which have been designed to balance fluctuations in supply and demand. In addition, large reservoirs of 37-million-m^3 capacity in the Sirte area and 76-million-m^3 in Benghazi have been built to act as storage facilities for summer or drought conditions.

Phase II involves the transport of water from well fields at East Jabal Hasouna and North-East Jabal Hasaouna to Tarhouna and Tripoli, and has a design capacity of 2.5 million m3 per day, with more than 500 well fields.

Phase III (Cost US $6 billion)

Phase III falls into two main parts. First, it will ultimately provide the planned expansion of the existing Phase I system, adding an additional 1.68 million m^3/day along with 700 km of new pipeline and new pumping stations to produce a final total capacity of 3.68 million m^3/day. Secondly, it will supply 138,000 m^3/day to Tobruk and the coast from a new wellfield at Al Jaghboub. This will require the construction of a reservoir south of Tobruk and the laying of a further 500 km of pipeline.

The preliminary engineering and design contract ran for 41 months and included geotechnical and topographic surveys. The conceptual design phase featured extensive considerations of pipeline routing and profiling, hydraulics, pumping stations, M&E, control/communications system, reservoirs and other structures, corrosion control, power, operational support, and maintenance provision. The evaluation of tenders for the detailed design took place in the first quarter of 2005.

These last two phases of the project involve the extension of the distribution network together with the construction of a pipeline linking the Ajdabiya reservoir to Tobruk and finally the connection at Sirte of the eastern and western systems into a single network.

When completed, irrigation water from the GMRP will enable about 155,000 ha of land to be cultivated – echoing the government's original prediction that the project would make the desert as green as the country's flag. In terms of water usage, Table 5.10 provides the details of volume and application.

In practical terms, apart from the very real benefits to the Libyan urban municipalities of the country's Mediterranean littoral, there have been major impacts in Libya's agriculture sector. In the following brief section we will show how the benefits of water from the GMRP have resulted in agricultural improvements in two regions, the Benghazi Plain and the Hasawna Mountain/Jifara System.

5.4.1 The GMRP and Water Utilization Authorities

Authorities were created to utilize the water of GMRP in order to prepare technical and economic studies and set programmes and plans for agricultural projects and developments to exploit the water of the GMRP. The total area capable of irrigation by the project is estimated to be about 145,000 ha. These authorities have implemented several projects and complementary utilities according to resources available for financing them. By the end of 2002, the number of farms that have been able to utilize the water resources of the GMRP amounted to approximately 2,250. Below we look in detail, in a regional context,

Table 5.10. Allocation of water from GMRP in the first three phases

Sector	%	Phase-I	Phase-II	Phase-III	Total
Agricultural	66%	1506030	1175660	1427000	4108960
Municipal	32%	410170	1316090	253000	1979260
Industrial	2%	83800	8250	0	92050

Cubic Metres/Day
Source: The Great Man Made River Authority, 2002.

at the very real benefits gained by the Libyan agriculture sector due to the GMRP, at two regions, the Benghazi Plain and the Hasawna Mountain/Jifara System.

Water Utilization Authority for the Benghazi Plain

Projects Executed upto 2002

- Project for the installation internal irrigation networks for small farms in the north-east of Khadraa to irrigate 509 farms.
- Execution of Agricultural Khadra Project for joint investment. Here an area of 1,000 ha was developed and targeted for agricultural investment.
- An area of 250 ha was exploited by the axis irrigation technique. Initial results indicated the potential success of this kind of irrigation system in enhancing the quality of the soil in the areas concerned. Further extensions of this method for new areas are currently being studied.

Projects Under Execution, 2003–2005

- A project for water pumping and distribution in the Khadraa area which has achieved a 91.23 per cent success ratio, with the station currently operational and pumping water.
- The construction of small farms in the north-east of Khadraa. Here project achievement percentage has reached about 86 per cent, with the project now operational.
- Omar Mukhtar Great Reservoir, with total capacity of 24 million m^3. The total percentage achievement for this project has reached about 73.87 per cent.
- Station for water transfer to Omar Mokhtar Great Reservoir. Total and actual achievement percentage of project works have reached 70 per cent. It was expected that project completion will be achieved within the first half of 2005.
- Construction of four irrigation reservoirs. Work is currently being executed along the Igdabia/Benghazi system in the areas of Sluq, Magrun, West Coast, and Igdabia. Total achievement percentage reached so far is 32.68 per cent.

Projects in the Contracting Stage

- A Project for the Design and Execution of Transfer Lines and Pumping Stations for currently established projects, covering the projects of Kattarah Valley and Ghut Sultan and Benghazi Plain.
- A Project for productive farms in the north-east of Khadraa, aimed at extending big farms in Khadraa area through availability of irrigation water through a second transfer system from the Omar Mukhtar Great Reservoir in order to completely irrigate a total project area of 13,700 ha. This project will involve a foreign investor.
- A project for constructing silos for storing grains with a capacity of 20,000 tons.
- The design and execution of an electricity station and feeding towers for the Khadra projects.
- A project for modifying the catchment of the Nghaz Valley. This project aims at protecting the Khadraa agricultural area from floods.

Water Utilization Authority for the Hasawna Mountain/Jifara System

Completed Projects

Abu-Eisha Agricultural Project, 687 Farms:

- A Concrete reservoir with a capacity of 40,000 m^3 of water and an irrigation network has been installed.
- The construction and completion of the road to the Abu-Eisha Project.
- A foreign investment contract for an area of 1,000 ha as a preliminary stage has been signed.

Tarhuna Agricultural Project

- Execution of a closed concrete reservoir with capacity of 33,000 m^3 together with a pumping station.

Pastoral Reservoirs along the System

- Twenty-nine pastoral reservoirs have been installed along the two roads of the system. Municipalities located within the zone of these reservoirs have been contacted to receive and operate these reservoirs.

5.4.2 The GMRP and Libyan Agricultural Diversification

From the above details it is evident that the impact of the GMRP has been considerable on the Libyan agriculture sector, successfully attracting FDI in the targeted agriculture sector, as well as sustaining and creating many thousands of permanent jobs for Libyan nationals.

But the GMRP is not without its critics, mainly because of reasons associated with its long-term unsustainability, that is its usage of depleting unrenewable resources, as well as cost comparisons between desalinized and transferred water in Libya. Because of technology advances, for example, the high costs associated with seawater desalination during the late 1970s and early 1980s are becoming more than four times cheaper than transferred groundwater in the case of the GMRP (Alghariani 2003). This researcher believes that in view of this major shift in water costs, the Libyan authorities must reconsider their position on whether to go ahead with completing the remaining stages of the GMRP, and the implementation of other proposed water transfer projects from the Kufra, Ghadames, and Jagboub areas.

There are also environmental concerns associated with the Phase II component of the GMRP project where the average nitrate concentration exceeds 60 ppm. Mixing this transferred water with desalinated seawater could eliminate the negative health and environmental impacts of such high nitrate concentration. Concerns about the long-term sustainability of the GMRP could also be mitigated if desalinated water was mixed with transferred water, since undoubtedly future development in the North African region will depend on large-scale desalination in the final resort for meeting future water demands.

A more balanced view might be that, in view of the considerable costs already sunk into the GMRP, should the environmental impacts of desalination plants be satisfactorily addressed, the planning of desalination plants in Libya as would introduce a level of diversity advisable and necessary to prevent over-dependence on a single resource such as the GMRP or groundwater extraction. In this way, sustainability of the resource is assured and in addition keeping water supply affordable (Great Man-Made River Authority 2004).

5.5 Overcoming Libya's Infrastructure Deficit Through Public–Private Partnerships

As we stated at the beginning of this chapter, in Libya there is a massive infrastructure deficit which has arisen because of the ageing of the Libyan infrastructure itself and the long period of the sanctions. Both of these factors emphasize the need for a detailed national inventory of infrastructure in Libya, which could be effectively broken down into infrastructure surveys in each Sha'biyat, to provide baseline data on which a national plan for infrastructure rehabilitation and development might be based.

In line with the current practice in several modern countries, this situation also emphasizes the need to develop a National Infrastructure Policy. This is because of the importance of efficient infrastructure to Libya's future productivity, international competitiveness, future tourist potential, and the quality of life of all Libyan citizens. Such a policy should be based on infrastructure surveys conducted not only to develop a databank of all facilities, but also a detailed inventory of their history, expenditure, current condition, and future use or expansion. Such baseline surveys together with a National Infrastructure Policy would undoubtedly identify the areas where urgent rehabilitation of deteriorated infrastructure should be undertaken as a matter of priority.

The need for change in infrastructure policy in Libya is again shown by international trends which demonstrate that, although traditionally, most of the major infrastructure systems in a country, such as railways, highways, water supply, and waste disposal systems have been constructed and maintained by the government, the burden of building and maintaining these is now becoming too heavy as the demands of citizens for more sophisticated facilities becomes insupportable. Because of these trends, it is highly likely that the Libyan government will not be able to cope with the infrastructure management issues of the future. As we will discuss below, it will become absolutely essential to determine and develop new funding sources, such as PPPs, to ensure that infrastructure does not lag behind.

In line with the current privatization and liberalization of the Libyan economy significant opportunities will arise in the near future for the many types of PPPs which have been successful in infrastructural development in many other countries, both developed and developing. As part of their overall economic liberalization policy and the emphasis on a dynamic and profitable tourist sector, Libyan policy makers clearly realize that adequate physical infrastructure development is a key element of a sound investment climate. As a recent observer has noted, "Infrastructure is also important for mobilizing other investment. The poor state of economic infrastructure in many developing countries constrains productive investment" (Roeskau 2005).

At the heart of the PPP approach is the government's desire to bring private money and management to public-service provision. The reasons for involving private capital are abundantly clear. The process provides new money, managerial skill, access to innovative technology and novel approaches to service delivery. Probably most important is that when private organizations invest their own money, they have a strong incentive to closely monitor project management to ensure the best possible overall financial return on their investment.

Typically, in PPPs, the public and private sectors join forces to design, finance, build, manage, or maintain infrastructure projects. Such partnerships can take many forms, depending upon the exact allocation of risks and responsibilities. These include the following.

5.5.1 Service Contracts

The private sector provides a bundle of specific services to a public utility, but the public sector retains overall operational responsibility. Service contracts can in practice take many forms, but two of the most common ones are explained in the following sections.

5.5.2 Management Support

The private operator supplies the public authority with human and technical resources for a fee. It provides technical know-how on all operational and financial aspects of project management remaining within the jurisdiction of the public authority.

5.5.3 Operation and Management (O&M)

The private operator is in charge of daily maintenance of the facilities. The private operator is paid for its services by the public authority according to specific and qualified performance criteria. Unlike management support, the private operator may in some cases take on the responsibility for operating the facilities.

5.5.4 Delegated Management Contracts

In this type of contract the public sector retains overall ownership of the assets, but delegates the responsibility for their operation to a private operator for a definite (often long) period of time. There are two most commonly seen models. First is the lease agreement or Affermage, where the private operator manages the services for a period (often 5–15 years) and is responsible for maintaining and renewing the facilities according the terms of the contract. In this capacity, it takes charge of all personnel and existing assets but is not responsible for financing new facilities. The public authority remains responsible for all new investment and compliance to existing norms, while the private operator invoices the end-users directly. The second type is the concession, where the public authorities fully entrust the private operator with management of the services and all necessary investment for a period of 20 years or more. The private operator invoices the end-users directly, the public authorities retaining strict control over service terms as well as all key decisions related to applicable rates and targets.

5.5.5 Construction Support

In the most wide-ranging form of PPP contracts the private operator is involved in the design and construction phases of new infrastructure and carries at least some of the associated risks. Some of the main forms of construction support are explained in the following sections.

5.5.6 Build-Design-Operate (BDO)

The public authorities entrust the private operator for a fixed period of time with design, construction, and operation of new facilities which remain the property of the public authorities. The private operator assumes the risks linked to design and management of the facility. It is paid a fee by the public authorities and commits to an overall cost for the facility's construction and operation.

5.5.7 Build-Operate-Transfer (BOT)

The private operator designs, finances, and builds infrastructure. While formal ownership of the assets is assigned to the government, the private sector operates the project long enough to service any debt incurred and to earn a suitable return.

5.5.8 Build-Own-Operate (BOO)

In contrast to the BOT case, the private investor retains ownership and control of the project.

5.6 Final Remarks

In view of its ambitious plans for economic diversion we believe that at some point the Libyan government, although presently in a strong financial position with virtually no overseas borrowings, will consider using at least some of the many types of PPPs currently utilized in other developing countries. In an international context, the figures are compelling. As recently reported, "between 1990 and 2003, there were over 2,750 projects with private participation in infrastructure in developing countries, with total public and private investment in these projects amounting to USD 786 billion" (Nepad/OECD Investment Initiative, 2005).

In a related context Libya, in the development of its hydrocarbon sector, has already acquired a formidable body of experience in dealing with foreign companies, as has been demonstrated by the continuous evolution of its EPSAs which have resulted in the very sophisticated EPSA IV contracts recently negotiated.

Combined, these factors will inevitably mean that, at some point in the near future, in an effort to accelerate the development process by expanding and improving infrastructure as well as ameliorating its massive infrastructure deficit, Libya will have to consider PPPs, particularly in the telecommunications, electricity and gas, road and rail transport, and water and sewerage sectors.

However, from an investor's viewpoint, there may still exist concerns relating to Libya's legal, administrative, and regulatory capacities to provide an adequate environment for PPPs, the same concerns which might, for example, block the flow of FDI in general to Libya. The authors believe that in view of the many lessons learned from the international PPP experience over the last 20 years, and the many hybrid forms and guarantees that investors can seek and obtain in structuring new PPPs, as well as Libya's long and varied experience in dealing with foreign oil companies, there will be no shortage of interest in PPP infrastructure investment in Libya should the government decide that it is a realistic option for the country.

6 The Rationale for Libyan Privatization

It Must Be Considered That There Is Nothing More Difficult to Carry Out, Nor More Doubtful of Success, Nor More Dangerous to Handle, Than to Initiate a New Order of Things. (Machiavelli, The Prince)

6.1 Approaches to Privatization

6.1.1 Privatization in Theory

State-Owned Enterprises, despite the vast wave of privatization that has swept the world in the last 20 years, still represent the single largest economic sector in the world economy. The SOEs, collectively, employ more people, command a greater asset base and swallow a greater proportion of global GDP than any single area of private sector activity. They still dominate many national economies and remain central in fulfilling key roles in the provision of essential services from electricity to roads to drinking water.

The way in which governments have sought, over the past 20 years, to reform these SOEs and to seek alternative means of maintaining and improving the services provided by them, against a background of rapidly escalating public sector budgets and resources, is at the heart of the reform process known as "privatization".

It is often forgotten that prior to the wave of privatization undertaken by the Thatcher government in 1979, the UK Labour (Socialist) Government was forced to call in the IMF in the mid-1970s, an admission of the total failure of its macro-economic policies. The ideology underlining the Thatcher government's privatization drive was determined at the same period, when the Centre for Policy Studies, the think tank of progressive UK conservatism, published an influential pamphlet in 1975, summing up the arguments for public sector reform.

Entitled "Why Britain needs a Social Market Economy", its initial salvo stated, "There is now abundant evidence that state enterprises in the UK have not served well either their customers, or their employees, or the taxpayers. For when the state owns, nobody owns; and when nobody owns, nobody cares." During that period opinion polls in the United Kingdom showed that nationalized industries and their militant employee unions were becoming increasingly unpopular. This led the Conservative Government under Thatcher to ride the wave of public discontent and to propose, "The long term aim must be to reduce the preponderance of state ownership and widen the base of ownership in our community. Ownership by the state is not the same as ownership by the people."

In theory, the main driving force for privatization is the promise of greater economic efficiency when an SOE is sold or transferred from bureaucratic managers and administrators to private sector control. The improvements in efficiency which result are largely due to differences in the incentives faced by political appointees and those faced by business managers. The former must make decisions based on a variety of goals including state employment policies and quotas, the "jobs for life" mentality of employees, limited market competition, and, usually last, the financial soundness of the enterprise. Political considerations and interference frequently affect plans related to business expansion or diversification, replacement of outdated equipment, and other key decisions which will impact the profitability of the enterprise.

On the other hand, business managers in private companies are much more focused on the hands-on operation of the enterprise, concerned with cost-cutting, productivity improvement, and the maximization of revenue streams, all aimed at producing, at the end of each financial year, a healthy bottom line. The expectation of privatization is a more efficient enterprise, able to consistently generate profits, at the same time staying competitive by improving product quality and productivity and, if necessary, reducing prices to ensure consumer satisfaction. For in a liberalized market economy, it is not the State but the consumer who is the king.

This is fine in theory. But it should be recognized that there is no guarantee that the anticipated results of privatization will materialize. This is because the size and structure of the market, as well as the regulatory environment within which the newly privatized company operates, are both key factors in determining the success or failure of privatization. If a newly privatized firm has to operate within a tightly regulated environment where it enjoys little ability to make decisions, its production volume and market penetration may see little change. Conversely, if a firm is privatized into a monopolistic market, and is free from government interference, the pressures to maximize profit is likely to result in important cost-saving measures such as employee reduction, leading to increases in unemployment, and significant price increases for consumers. This has been the experience of many consumers in the United Kingdom after the massive privatization exercises of the Thatcher era, when prices for important basic services such as electricity, gas, and rail transport have increased immensely, but, as well as leading to job redundancy and unemployment, the quality of service and customer satisfaction has not necessarily risen. In other words, it is not a foregone conclusion that privatization will result in greater economic efficiency, either to the state or to the consumer.

In macroeconomic terms, the advocates of privatization also claim that it will improve the macroeconomic status of the state, undergoing the privatization exercise, leading to general improvements in the economic outlook which will both positively influence investor confidence within the country, and lead to increased investment. Not only this but in nations where SOEs contribute significantly to budget deficits, a privatization exercise appears to be one of the intuitive solutions to the problem.

In this scenario the proceeds gained from selling off SOEs contribute directly to government revenue, at the same time substantially reducing future government expenditure on operating costs, capital expenditure, and the shoring up of loss-making enterprises. Frequently, politicians see this perceived link between budget deficit reduction and privatization as being very useful in justifying their commitment to economic reforms. But again, this must not be taken for granted, since empirical evidence for this claim is hard to find. In, for example, a study of privatization in Latin America, the authors showed that "it is not reasonable to expect significant short-term fiscal gains from privatisation" (Pindeiro and Schneider 1995). They go on to state that privatization cannot be regarded as a serious tool for deficit reduction, warning that a privatization process which focuses on such a goal can have a detrimental effect on economic efficiency.

Proponents of privatization also claim that it is a solution to government corruption, since SOEs present plenty of opportunities for corrupt officials to line their pockets through rigged contract-bidding processes, over-invoicing of costs, preferential tender awards, and favoured suppliers to the enterprise, in short the world of the ubiquitous brown envelope. In actual fact, there is no reason why such practices cannot take place under private control, since there is only a tacit assumption that proprietors and shareholders of businesses have a greater incentive to demand honesty and transparency from their business managers and employees than citizens have from appointed bureaucrats.

But in the cut-throat world of private business, where executive failure can mean instant job loss, it is naïve to assume that corruption does not exist. Far from it, since depending on the nature of the regulatory framework and the pricing mechanisms for determining the cost of, say, privatized public services, there is enormous scope for corruption, since the rewards are huge. New owners and investors in privatized firms are driven by the profit motive, and immorality and the use of illegal practices in the business world is a cliche. Insider trading, for example, is a recurrent and unstoppable feature in the high profile world of stock trading, as brilliantly portrayed in the 1987 Oliver Stone film "Wall Street". When the equity, or part of the equity, of large monopolistic SOEs is floated as part of the privatization exercise, the scope for corrupt practices such as insider trading and asset undervaluation is correspondingly massive.

Despite these dangers, it is apparent that International Financial Institutions (IFI) such as the World Bank (WB) and the International Monetary Fund (IMF) have been unconditional supporters of privatization as a panacea for all economic illnesses in developing countries. In fact not only have they consistently proposed privatization as a cure, but, in many cases, have made it conditional for renewed lending.

For example, part of the IMF approval for a Stand-By Credit for Indonesia of up to SDR7.338 billion (about US $10.14 billion) at the height of the 1997 meltdown of the Asian Tigers stated as follows.

> Privatisation is another element of the structural reform effort. Responsibility for the management and restructuring of public enterprises has been shifted from line ministries to the Ministry of Finance, and a new Privatization Board established. A clear framework for the management and privatization of government assets is being developed, which will establish explicit criteria for determining whether an enterprise

> should be closed, restructured, or privatized. For enterprises remaining in the public sector, the framework will ensure that these operate efficiently, including through establishing profit and performance targets, which will be made public and reported annually. (IMF, Press Release Number 97/50 5 November 1997)

Not only this but IFIs normally insist that the privatization exercise must take place quickly. As one researcher on privatization in Argentina in the mid-1990s stated,

> Standard WB prescription regarding privatisation was that it had to take place as rapidly as possible in order to prevent the organisation of pressure groups that may be effective in opposing it. Unfortunately the rush to privatise not only undermines the possibility of popular participation in the process, but is also likely to result in terms that are unfavourable to the state and a weak regulatory environment. Greater attention to questions of reform sequencing has exposed some of the flaws in IFI policy prescriptions. (Rodríguez-Boetsch 2005)

6.1.2 Mechanisms for Privatization

The objectives of the government, which can range across a wide spectrum, will have the deciding impact on what forms or mechanisms for privatization are selected for any given industry or programme. They can include reducing public sector spending, improving economic efficiency, depoliticizing key industries, raising investment capital for new services from the private sector, and raising funds from sales proceeds and future taxation revenues from the privatized companies.

A wide range of mechanisms on how to privatize state companies and assets is available to governments. These include forms such as public auctions, tenders, public invitations, capital privatization, stock exchange flotation of part of the equity, and employee or management buyouts. Other more indirect methods include various distribution schemes aimed at privatizing a large bundle of state-owned enterprises in one mass privatization programme. In this case the mechanism is conceived of as a give-away of shares or vouchers to citizens for whom state assets were held in trust by the socialist state. The establishment of a mass giveaway scheme is often related to the usefulness of more traditional methods such as direct sale of shares or assets, perhaps because of capital scarcity, the lack of a stock exchange capable of raising the huge amounts of capital involved for acquisition of SOEs, or the lack of savings to absorb the huge amount of state assets.

Depending on the situation and objectives of the government, there are advantages and disadvantages in all of the methods which we will describe below. Generally, however, there are two necessary steps required before any sale can take place, which apply to practically all of the five privatization methods discussed below. First is fragmentation, which enables pieces of big SOEs to be sold as individual firms, and, second, commercialization, which involves restructuring and possibly corporatization (for a Libyan example, see the authors' proposed privatization of BOMC in Chap. 9). The former is aimed at economic viability to the target firms, increasing the number of potential buyers by reducing the amount needed to acquire a division of the previously countrywide or vertically integrated SOE. The latter includes the transfer of control to a government agency during the process, in many cases the privatization board or office, and the conversion of the entity into shares that can be traded.

Another important decision to be made, whatever the privatization method, is the extent of employee participation in the transaction as buyers of the SOEs shares. There are several possibilities: no participation whatsoever, participation of ownership with non-voting shares, and participation with voting shares or control. Management employee buyouts occur in the extreme cases of participation with control. Experience in several countries shows that this scheme endangers the microeconomic success of the reforms, even though it enhances its political acceptability (Rogozinski 1997). For example, in Russia and the Czech Republic, the allocation of controlling shares to managers and employees preceded mass privatization. This distorted the corporate governance structure in the post-privatization stage and hindered the possibilities of the success of the privatization (Pannier 1996). In other cases, employees are allowed to share the monetary benefits through a giveaway of a portion of the stock without voting rights.

Direct Sales to Strategic Investors

Direct sales to strategic investors means the transfer of ownership and control of SOEs to private investors whose expertise is meant to guarantee a successful performance of the firm in the post-privatization competitive environment. This transfer can be done through either competitive bidding or a privately negotiated deal. Obviously, an open competitive bidding process has several advantages over a privately negotiated sale, contributing greatly to the transparency of the process. It also enhances political acceptability and, if properly designed, maximizes revenues for the government, while at the same time, theoretically at least, assigning the company to the most efficient investor.

In terms of the competitive auctions, the two most important considerations in its design are, first, to ensure the largest number of bidders for the company, and, secondly, to somehow deal with the uncertainty regarding the real value of the assets and the generation of future income, which leads sometimes to what has been labelled the "winner's curse". Both of these factors can be effectively dealt with in the design of the mechanism (Milgrom 1989).

The negotiated sale, also known as the "administrative process", usually takes the form of a case-by-case review of the possible buyers by the privatization agency. This has been called "a beauty contest" in the literature. During this process, the government reviews proposals and meets, perhaps several times, potential buyers in order to determine their favourable characteristics. Its advantages are that it gives the government more flexibility and the possibility of imposing specific requirements considered important during the negotiation, and it is, in technical terms, less complicated than the auction method. This is because the auction mechanism undoubtedly requires a technically sophisticated design leading to considerably more privatization costs. Even though, therefore, the negotiated sale is less expensive, its main drawback is the lack of transparency which might result in a very high political cost.

In the auction process the government can also deal with other important issues such as investment requirements or protection to minorities, but more importantly it maximizes revenue and allocates the assets of the SOE efficiently. Other objectives can be achieved by laying down clear rules and requirements with which the participants must comply. For example, the government can first insist on a pre-selection process in which the bidders must qualify; it may also introduce issues of protection to minorities and explicit restrictions against monopolization of the market among other desirable social goals.

But regardless of the mechanism chosen for the direct sale, this type of transaction has the distinct advantage of allowing the government to sell small firms when a public offering of stock in the market would not be cost-effective, or even where a stock market may not exist. Empirical evidence shows that a country is more likely to use a direct sale for small firms, when the country's per capita income is low, the fiscal situation is poor, and the government is more "socialistic", as measured by the ratio of public expenditure to GDP (Megginson et al. 1998).

One important advantage of the direct sale is that the government can receive higher revenues through competitive bidding, by avoiding the income loss associated with the usually observed underpricing of shares in Initial Public Offering (IPO) to ensure their success, as we will discuss below. A second advantage is that direct sales, even when carried out as an auction, are relatively less expensive than public offerings. Moreover, the government can still attract foreign investors with technological and managerial expertise. However, the main disadvantages of a direct sale are that it fails to develop the local capital market and that it limits the possibility of broad ownership, with the downside in terms of corporate governance because the sale usually occurs through a private placement of common equity that gives control of the SOE to high profile buyers. This leaves little room for the participation of small investors in the decisions of the firm. This type of sale, however, should not hinder political acceptability, especially if carried out through a bidding process.

Public Offerings

A public offering of shares is the sale of the company to the general public in the stock exchange, or any other organized market. Generally the fragmentation of large SOEs and their commercialization or corporatization, as discussed above, are prerequisites, so that the enterprise can be traded in the market. Public offerings are good mechanisms to attract foreign investment, both from institutional and from non-institutional investors, but the main disadvantage is the cost. The government has to take a discount through the initial offering, technically known as underpricing, and the process itself requires marketing and technical assistance that increases the transaction costs. In terms of valuation, market-based methodologies, as opposed to the book value approach, should always be used.

Normally, the sequence of events in a public offering are as follows:

- Choosing the sales agents (brokers and underwriters), lead brokers, and placement syndicate members for the operation.
- Drafting the prospectus which will be made available to the public.
- Selecting shares and the share instrument.
- Implementing the sales campaign.
- Marketing, usually including international campaigns, known as road shows.
- Setting the subscription period and book building.
- Determining share pricing, both retail and institutional, and quotas for domestic and foreign buyers.
- Closing, collection of the revenue, and delivery of shares.

In general the practice of underpricing in the initial offering is an empirically established fact for public offerings in general (Mauer and Senbet 1992), and has been shown to be even of a higher magnitude in privatization sales (Menyah and Paudyal 1996). The most accepted theoretical explanation for this is the fact that the underpricing borne by the issuing company signals confidence in future increases in value.

The advantages of public offerings for privatizing SOEs are that they are transparent, encourage the development of capital markets, and create broad ownership. In certain cases, in industries deemed to be strategic such as hydrocarbons, some governments retain part of the shares without voting rights, so they can signal confidence in future gains by delaying the sale of rest of the stock (Perotti and Guney 1993). Retaining part of the stock can also have two other objectives, which are avoiding the flooding of the market when it is seen that the demand is not as high as required and increasing the government's future revenue by seeking capital gains generated by the sale and future performance of the company. Only, however, in very specific cases is retaining voting shares by the government recommended. This is usually done in the form of "golden share-options" that can be exercised under clearly specified conditions, like the firm not providing specific services or disregarding investment commitments.

In order to maximize sales proceeds, offerings usually take place simultaneously in both the domestic and the foreign markets. The government has to decide the amounts offered in each market and that decision depends on the size and degree of development of the local market. Another aspect to consider is that there may be a legal requirement in terms of local as opposed to foreign ownership. Each subsequent offer in the secondary market will involve some of the steps described above, without the valuation stage, because the company shares would already have a price in the market.

The empirical evidence shows that either pure public offerings or mixed sales are more likely to be chosen the more developed the local capital market and the bigger the companies that will be sold are (Megginson et al. 1998). Mixed sales, as discussed below, involve selling the control of the company in the first stage and carrying out a public offering as a second step.

Mixed Sales

In practice, mixed sales are the most common method used in practice by developing countries. For example, telecommunications companies from Mexico, Perú, and Argentina have been sold through mixed sales (Rogozinski 1998; Merryl Lynch 1998a). A mixed sale involves the direct sale of control to a strategic investor, either through a negotiation or a competitive bidding, accompanied by a public offering as a second stage, with the public offering usually taking place 6 months to 1 year after the transfer of the controlling shares.

This combination of methods has proven successful for mainly two reasons. First, it results in a positive impact on the domestic capital markets and it assures that the control goes to investors with the potential to make the firm profitable under a market environment. Also, the reputation of the group acquiring control in the first stage will have a strong impact on the success of the public offering during the second stage. For the first stage the use of a competitive bidding is recommended.

It is interesting to note the success of telecommunications companies that have been privatized using this scheme, since this is not sheer coincidence. Industries and sectors in need of investment for technological innovation and expansion require the controlling group to have complete decision power for at least a specific period of time. The provisions in terms of quality and investment requirements can also be established in the contract of the direct sale, which increases the public policy options when compared to a pure public offering.

But again, the main disadvantage is cost. There are common costs associated with the first and second stages that make the cost in fact higher than the simple addition of the cost of a pure direct sale and a pure public offering. The mechanism is, however, more expensive than any of them separately. In addition, a well-developed local capital market is required to maximize the benefits of the sale and to create local broad ownership. Finally, the fact that the demand for the control and ownership of the firm has to be big enough to justify the cost makes this method applicable only to very large SOEs.

Mass Privatization Through Voucher Schemes

At the end of the communist era, the distributional problem faced by reformers and their advisors in East and Central Europe was the following. Privatization of the massive amount of productive assets held by the public sector was the most crucial element in the transition from a centralized to a market economy. But if the huge number of state-owned firms were sold by the "case-by-case" method traditionally employed in previous Western privatizations such as the United Kingdom, for example, who could or would buy them? The scarcity of potential buyers was because most citizens in post-communist countries had no funds to purchase shares or firms, and the few who did and were willing to do so were thought to have acquired them illegally. How could they deal with this dilemma?

The proposed solution, invented by Poles, but applied first in Mongolia and Czechoslovakia before spreading widely throughout the countries of the Former Soviet Union (FSU) region, was by using the voucher. Distributed by the reformist governments free or for a small fee, to all citizens or adults, the "voucher" or "coupon" as it was often termed could be exchanged in special auctions either for shares in a firm being privatized or for shares in private investment funds that accumulated personal vouchers in order to put together a diversified portfolio of minority holdings.

It was therefore with substantial technical and financial assistance from IFIs, particularly the World Bank, the European Union, and a number of bilateral donors, that huge technical and administrative obstacles to the implementation of voucher programmes were overcome. The main stages of the process were portfolio analysis, corporatization of the firms, sometimes bundling several firms into one main company, voucher distribution, underpinned by decisions in terms of employee ownership, creation of investment funds, auctioning, and ownership allocation. Between 1991 and 1996, voucher schemes for privatization were applied in 21 of 27 transition countries. In 10 of these – Armenia, Bosnia, Czech Republic, Georgia, Kazakhstan, Kyrgyztan, Lithuania, Moldova, Mongolia, and Russia itself – vouchers were the primary privatization method. Tens of thousands of firms were privatized by this method, with 15,000 in Russia alone.

The main advantage of mass privatization through voucher schemes was that it assured political acceptability by giving ownership to the public. It has also been argued that it constitutes a good way of developing a capital market with a broad base of investors in countries with an incipient entrepreneurial sector. However, there were significant drawbacks. First, it considerably reduced the proceeds to the government. Secondly, it undermined corporate governance in the post-privatization stage by offering advantages to insiders, unions, and former public managers, enabling them to retain control and to easily acquire and accumulate vouchers from small investors (Pannier 1996). Finally it imposed many obstacles against the attraction of foreign investment and the transfer of financial, technical, and managerial expertise.

Mass privatization should be considered only when political acceptability is a major constraint, and in places where the private sector is poorly developed as an entrepreneurial group. Otherwise, the costs clearly offset the benefits and can easily result in a financial, economic, and political failure. Whenever possible, the case-by-case approach consisting of selling each firm in a separate transaction, so that sales benefits are maximized, is a better strategy.

Concessions

In markets characterized by networks such as pipelines (water) or cables (electricity), which in most cases represent a natural monopoly with high sunk costs, the simple sale of the company may not be the best option because there is too much scope for monopolistic fees to be exploited by the providers of the service. Those markets require a regulatory framework. This regulatory mechanism between the government, which must protect consumers' welfare, and the investors, wanting to get the highest possible return from their investment, must be put in place with care, and achieving the right balance is important. In the right circumstances certain industries with natural monopoly conditions may be sold in the standard way, such as telephone and electricity in many countries, as long as the Regulatory Authority functions fairly and is acceptable to all parties.

Other industries, however, are more suitable candidates for privatization of control without transfer of ownership. The most efficient way to carry out those arrangements is by concessions, or the right to build the operating facilities and to provide the goods or services to the public for a certain period of time, usually at least 20 years in view of the huge investment costs involved. The factors that make concessions a better option in certain cases are the existence of large, sunk investments and inherently high uncertainty in demand forecasts.

The most common sector in which concessions have been successfully implemented is construction of infrastructure through "Build-Operate-and-Transfer" schemes , as in the cases of transport (toll-roads, ports, airports, railroads) in Indonesia and Malaysia, and possibly, as we discussed earlier, in Libya itself (Chap. 5), and water distribution in the United Kingdom and Jordan.

Obviously, in the design of the concession contract the issues of concern are the future scope for opportunistic behaviour by the government through expropriation of investments or profits, the re-negotiation of contracts, and the exploitation of its monopoly position by the private sector. Given that one of the relevant factors in this case is the risk involved in the project, a proper distribution of risk is a determinant of success, measured as the existence of a good service, low prices, and no requirement of subsidies from the government by the investors. The cost of the facilities and the service provided has to be borne by either the users or the taxpayers.

Indeed, infrastructure and public services like water distribution and utilities in general were originally private at many periods throughout the modern history of many nations, for example, in Libya's case, the early electricity sector under the Italians and the immediate post-independence period. This cycle from private to public ownership and back again has been called the "privatization–nationalization wheel". In concession contracts, only policy-associated risks should be borne by the government, generally by giving contingent guarantees. All commercial risks should be borne by the private sector. The government thus has the incentive to minimize those risks by establishing as complete a contract as possible and specifying in advance the regulatory regime, if any, that will prevail in the post-privatization stage. The duration of the concession and the conditions under which competition for the transfer of assets will take place must also be clearly determined.

In summary, in sectors with natural monopoly characteristics and high demand uncertainty, where the introduction of competition in the market would be socially inefficient, concession arrangements are the recommended privatization strategy. In spite of the failures observed in several countries using BOT schemes, creative methods that solve the problem of distribution of risk and minimize the room for renegotiation have been proposed and successfully implemented. All of these assume a competitive bidding for the right to provide the service, in a "competition for the market". Table 6.1 illustrates the five main privatization mechanisms, and requirements and advantages/disadvantages of each method.

Table 6.1. Privatization methods

Objectives	Mass privatization	Direct sale through negotiation	Direct sale/ competitive bidding	Public offering	Mixed sale *	Concessions **
Enhance micro efficiency		√ provided delegation and opening	√ provided delegation and opening	√ provided delegation and opening	√ provided delegation and opening	√ provided delegation and opening
Maximize revenue	×	√	√	Under pricing	√ Proper timing	
Constraints:						
Political acceptability	√		√		√	√ Properly designed
Transparency		×	√	√	√	√
Market structure: competitive		√	√	√	√	
Market structure: natural monopoly	×	×		×		√
Development of capital market	Not a constraint	Not a constraint	Not a constraint	√ Considering absorption capacity	√ Considering absorption capacity	Not a constraint
Size: small firms		√	√			
Size: large firms	√			√	√	

*Assumed that the first stage was carried out through competitive bidding.
**Assumed that they are assigned through competitive bidding.
√ = Recommended.
× = Not Recommended.
Source: Adapted from López-Calva, 1998.

6.2 Privatization: International Perspectives

6.2.1 The Latin American Experience

The privatization record of Latin America is remarkable. In the 1990s, Latin America accounted for 55 per cent of total privatization revenues in the developing world (Chong and López-de-Silanes 2003).

In a painstaking analysis of the privatization process in Argentina, another researcher describes the sequence of events which took place after the accession of Carlos Menem to office in July 1989 (Rodríguez-Boetsch 2005). At the time of Menem's accession, maintaining inefficient SOEs accounted for some 15–18 per cent of Argentinean GDP every year (De la Balze 1995). Many were completely dependent on public subsidies. In 1989 alone, the 13 largest SOEs had an aggregate operating deficit of $3.8 billion, and an accumulated external debt of $11 billion (Alexander and Corti 1993). In fact Menem's predecessor, Raúl Alfonsín, had also attempted to reduce the state's holdings, and had launched a major privatization initiative in 1985 (Corrales 1998). However, it was undermined by the Peronist-dominated Senate which effectively blocked all three privatization bills submitted by Alfonsín's government in 1988 (Llanos 2001). Only four SOEs were eventually privatized under Alfonsín, netting the government just $32 million in revenues (Manzetti 1999).

Menem was perhaps more fortunate than his predecessor, for on assuming power his Justicialista Party dominated both houses of parliament. This enabled the rapid enactment of the Law of State Reform in September 1989, which defined the ground rules for private investment in SOEs. With this enabling legislation in place, the Menem administration, under IFI pressure and anxious to establish its reform credentials, began its expediting of the Argentinean privatization process. In the 5 years between 1990 and 1994 the Argentinean "crown jewels" were sold to private investors, or dismantled in their entirety. In this period Argentina privatized some 90 per cent of all SOEs (IMF 1998). The National Telecommunications Enterprise, ENTEL, the airline company, Aerolıneas, the state oil enterprise, YPF (Yacimientos Petrolıferos Fiscales), most state electricity generation and distribution enterprises, state petrochemical firms, steel mills, radio and television channels, the state natural gas company, shipyards, and many others were privatized. As one commentator stated, Menem set out to "privatise everything that (was) privatisable" (Corrales 1998).

As a result, privatization revenues to the Argentinean government shot up from the $32 million under Alfonsin in 1985–1989 to $5.5 billion in 1992 alone. One hundred and seventeen enterprises were privatized in 1990–1994, compared to four in 1983–1989 (Corrales 1998; Manzetti 1999). By 1995, few major enterprises remained in the hands of the state (Triesman 2002).

But by 2001 the results of this rushed privatization process became apparent in Argentina. In a contagious effect brought about by the 1997–1998 Asian meltdown, characteristic of the globalized world in which we live, an outflow of capital from Argentina gradually evolved into a 4-year economic depression, which culminated in a financial panic in November 2001, followed in December by the resignation amidst bloody riots, of Menem's successor, President De la Rue. Soon after, Argentina defaulted on $88 billion in debt, the largest sovereign debt default in history.

As Rodrıguez-Boetsch concluded, a rushed and flawed privatization process, without an adequate regulatory framework and independent regulatory agencies, was responsible for much of the disappointment surrounding this privatization process that served only to concentrate wealth and power, resulting in hardly any benefits to society at large. Contrary to what happened in Argentina, privatization should not result in the complete forfeit of state authority over public services. Governments of developing nations should pursue privatization with extreme caution. "A regulatory and legal framework that limits the activities of privatised companies and grants the state broad powers of intervention ought to be established prior to the transfer of state assets to the private sector. As the case of Argentina shows, swift privatisation for the sake of short-term expediency can carry enormous long-run costs" (Rodrıguez-Boetsch 2005).

6.2.2 Malaysian Privatization Policy and Results

In Malaysia the approach to privatization was, again, different, but ultimately effective, although it entailed many policy reversals. The Malaysian Prime Minister Mahathir Mohamad assumed office in 1981, promoted to Prime Minister after the retirement, due to ill health, of the then Prime Minister Hussein Onn. In the 1982 General Election Mahathir led his coalition Party, the Barisan Nasional, to a convincing victory in which he controlled 132 out of 154 seats in the Malaysian Parliament. But this was a trying period for the Malaysian economy, and by 1983 he had announced his government's intention to embark on a privatization policy, which represented a dramatic turnaround of his own, as well as previous Malaysian government policy.

Throughout the two decades following Malaysian independence from the United Kingdom in 1963, successive Malaysian governments had enhanced and expanded government expenditure on SOEs, albeit on a much magnified scale when compared to the fiscally prudent and conservative British colonial administrations preceding independence. Expenditure on utility providers such as electricity and water was considerable, and under Mahathir's industrialization strategy for heavy industry, massive investments in the form of steel, cement, auto-assembly, and motorcycle plants were made through new industrial SOEs in the late 1970s and early 1980s. These were largely financed by foreign borrowings, usually yen denominated, in line with another of Mahathir's basic strategies, the "look east policy".

However, in 1985, the international recession severely reduced Malaysian export earnings from its major export commodities such as palm oil, rubber, and tin, as well as from its nascent electronics industry. In the September of that year, the major industrial economies agreed to a major international currency realignment, which led to the yen appreciating significantly against the US dollar for a whole decade until mid-1995. The Malaysian currency, the Ringgit, which became increasingly tied to the US dollar after independence, especially after the sterling devaluation of 1967, then depreciated against the US dollar, which resulted in a virtual doubling of the value of the yen in Ringgit terms, which in turn meant a massive increase in the yen-denominated foreign borrowings to finance Malaysian heavy industry and Japanese-oriented industrial diversification. As a consequence, Malaysia experienced negative growth in 1985 for the first time since independence. When the oil price collapsed in early 1986, the Malaysian government was under considerable pressure to respond with policy changes.

This, as we have said earlier, took the form of the announcement of the Malaysian government's own commitment to privatization in 1983. But it should be noted that Malaysia was among the first in the South to voluntarily climb on the privatization bandwagon (Jomo and Tan 1995). This desire, or impetus, to privatize, with its pragmatic acceptance that the existing system does not work, is important for any country which is evolving from a centralized to a free market economy. Thus it was for Malaysia far preferable, as the later Indonesian experience showed, to voluntarily consume the medication for economic reform, that is privatization, in the mid-1980s, as opposed to the Indonesian experience of having it forced down its throat by the IMF in 1997.

Mahathir's convincing victory at the polls in 1982, followed up by another impressive victory for his Barisan Nasional (National Front) coalition in the general election of 1986, in which it won 148 seats or 84 per cent out of the total of 177 seats, put Mahathir in a strong position to drive through his economic reform policy. Already, in 1985, the Economic Planning Unit, the planning and implementation body in the Prime Minister's Department tasked with the structuring of Malaysia's 5-year economic development plans, had announced its "Guidelines for Privatisation", spelling out the official rationale and broad guidelines for Malaysian privatization and as part of an overall strategy to Industrialize Malaysia and diversify its economic base. In February 1991 Mahathir announced his "Vision 2020" as an all-embracing concept to achieve developed country status for Malaysia by 2020, on the basis of a liberal economic programme with a strong emphasis on privatization. In the same month, the government issued its Privatization Master Plan (PMP), including a Privatization Action Plan.

It is useful to note, however, that the Malaysian privatization experience has been significantly different from that of Latin America. This is for a multiplicity of reasons, derived from distinct historical, political, and socio-cultural practices. But in the Malaysian privatization experience, two key features stand out. First, the Malaysian experience of privatization has been more of a public–private sector partnership, with the government frequently retaining a considerable percentage of the equity, unlike, say, the Argentinean approach of a complete and usually irreversible sell-off of state assets. Secondly, there has been no undue haste or pressure in the process.

In this sense what has happened in Malaysia may not be privatization as defined in the strictest sense, when it is generally defined in terms of the sale of 100 per cent, or at least a majority share of a SOE, or its assets, to private shareholders. The term can also refer to the use of private contractors to provide services previously provided by the public sector, for example for sewage or refuse collection or even health services for that matter. In Malaysia, however, such privatizations have not been the norm, and the most prominent case of 100 per cent privatization has been that of the North–South Highway, the main artery of Malaysia now made up of a series of toll-paying superhighways.

In Malaysia, then, the term "privatization" is often understood to include cases where less than half of the assets or shares of SOEs are sold to private shareholders, with the government retaining control through majority ownership. Before 1992, privatization in Malaysia included nine official divestitures by the Economic Planning Unit, and nine sales of relatively small enterprises by UPSAK, the Unit for Monitoring Government Agencies and Enterprises, charged with reforming ailing SOEs. Of the former, there have only been four full divestitures. These were Sports Toto, Padang Terap Sugar Limited, the Security Printing Branch of the Government Printers, and the Malaysian Airline System, which was totally divested only in early 1994. The other five – Kelang Container Terminal (the main component of the main Malaysian seaport, Port Kelang), Airod, Tradewinds (a major palm oil plantation company), the Malaysian International

Shipping Corporation (MISC), and Sarawak Cement Manufacturers – only involved partial divestiture, with the Malaysian government retaining control, even without majority ownership.

The second feature of the Malaysian experience was that privatization, or "partial privatization" as is a more appropriate term for this experience, was affected over an extended period, with no unseemly and ultimately self-destructive crash programme. It took place steadily over much of the 15 years of the late 1980s and 1990s, as opposed to the rushed programme of divestiture over the 5-year period 1990–1994 when virtually 90 per cent of all SOEs in Argentina were sold.

Apart from these two important features of the Malaysian privatization exercise, it has to be said that it was also effected within a systematic framework, after baseline assessments of the state of health of all of the Malaysian SOEs were made in the early 1980s. This entailed a sequence of examinations which, to continue the medical metaphor, led to a diagnosis, which then necessitated a course of treatment, leading to a cure. We will describe this sequence in detail since it demonstrates both the pragmatic approach taken by the Malaysian authorities and its relative transparency, the lack of which, for example, severely compromised the legality and methodology of the Russian privatization experience in the 1990s when Yeltsin bent over backwards to involve the domestic business titans, the "oligarchs", by allowing them to snap up major oil and minerals enterprises at extremely low prices.

Initial surveys showed that at the end of March 1990 there were 1,158 SOEs (78 per cent of them operational), with a total paid-up capital of RM23.9 billion (US $8.84 billion, at the rate of US $1 equal to MR2.7044, Bank Negara Malaysia 1990), as is seen in Table 6.2. Of these companies, 396, or 34 per cent, were 100 per cent government-owned; a further 429, or 37 per cent, majority government-owned; of the remaining 333 representing 30 per cent, the government held minority equity stakes. The total government equity share in the SOE sector at this stage accounted for 70.3 per cent of the total, amounting to RM16.7 billion.

Thereafter, a sectoral analysis of SOEs was done. This is important, since it allowed the government to identify and prioritize companies for privatization in

Table 6.2. Malaysia: state-owned enterprises by paid-up capital

Level	No. of companies	Total capital (RM million)	Govt. equity (RM million)	Govt. equity as % of total capital	Average capital (RM million)
Federal	556	18,521	12,738	68.78	33.3
State	553	5,048	3,829	75.85	9.1
Regional	49	241	170	70.54	4.9
Total	1,158	23,810	16,737	70.29	20.6

Source: Adam and Cavendish, 1995.

line with government policy. If, for example, the promotion of tourism was a key government policy, then SOEs involved in the tourist business in the service sector, however unhealthy their financial condition, warranted special consideration. In such cases it was realistic for the government to consider a cure or partial cure for an SOE involved in this sector, bringing it to a condition that made it saleable, as opposed to a total write-off. Here again the time factor was significant, enabling the government to maximize returns from the privatization exercise, as well as promoting and expanding key sectors in line with general policy.

The survey showed that Malaysia's SOEs in 1988 were broadly spread across all sectors, with finance (12 per cent of all SOEs), services (27 per cent), and manufacturing (28 per cent) dominating in terms of number of enterprises. This is shown in Table 6.3.

Since Malaysia is a Federation with State Legislative bodies holding considerable power, as well as being divided into the main regions of East and West Malaysia separated by the South China Sea, an analysis of the condition of State/Federal/Regional SOEs was done to determine their levels of debt in relation to capital. This is illustrated in Table 6.4.

An analysis of Table 6.4 showed that Federal SOEs tended to have correspondingly larger debt than state or regional SOEs. Interestingly, the level of debt as a share of total capital in 1990 did not vary all that much, with Federal SOEs

Table 6.3. Malaysia: distribution of SOEs by sector

Sector	Federal	State	Regional	Total
Agriculture	5	19	3	27
Construction	8	26	1	35
Extractive	6	27	1	34
Finance	100	33	1	134
Manufacturing	153	155	14	32
Plantation	22	61	12	95
Property	44	53	1	98
Services	162	135	16	313
Logging	0	25	0	25
Transport	56	12	0	68
Others	0	7	0	7
Total	556	553	49	1,155

Source: Adam and Cavendish, 1995.

Table 6.4. Malaysia: state-owned enterprises by source of borrowing

Level	No. of companies	Govt. loans	Foreign loans	Domestic loans	Total loans	Debt/Total capital
Federal	556	21.38%	27.54%	51.08%	100.00%	184.89%
State	553	34.67%	24.28%	41.05%	100.00%	169.53%
Regional	49	41.35%	11.81%	46.05%	100.00%	98.34%
Total	1,158	24.13%	26.81%	49.06%	100.00%	180.73%

Source: Adam and Cavendish, 1995.

slightly less dependent on federal government loans and more dependent on both private domestic and foreign loans. The average debt for each SOE from all sources of federal funds was RM61 million, that for state SOEs was RM15 million, and for regional SOEs less than RM5 million. As might be expected, the federal SOEs also had, on average, much larger exposure in domestic and foreign financial markets (accounting for 51 per cent and 27 per cent of total debt respectively), while the principal debt for state and regional SOEs was from the government. The overall SOE debt–equity ratio of 180 per cent was significantly higher than the average private-sector ratio, estimated to be approximately 100 per cent.

The next step was a detailed analysis of the financial performance of the SOEs over the previous 9-year period in order to establish key performance indicators of the SOEs as a whole and their total weighting as a percentage of GDP. This is shown in Table 6.5.

Table 6.5 provides a broader and more accurate picture of the SOE sector's aggregate financial performance, indicating, in general, both poor operating profits and very poor fixed capital formation. It showed SOE turnover accounted for between 40 and 50 per cent of GDP, and a considerable rise in overall interest costs. Clearly, the Malaysian SOE sector was a net consumer of public resources and, if not for the petroleum sector, the financial burden would have been significantly greater.

Table 6.6 shows that for the 9-year period surveyed, approximately 40–45 per cent of all SOEs were unprofitable throughout the 1980s. Of these, almost half, or 25 per cent, of all SOEs had negative shareholders' funds, a situation which would have been untenable under private ownership.

The relative performance of the Malaysian SOEs was again analysed over time in line with general performance criteria, based on enterprise profitability relative to capitalization. Although it does not unfortunately show the relative size of "sick", "weak", "satisfactory", and "good" companies, Table 6.7 does indicate the existence of a very large number of unprofitable companies drawing on taxpayers' funds in the reviewed period. Even at the height of the public sector boom in the early 1980s, over 40 per cent of all SOEs were either "sick" or "weak". The findings undeniably showed that Malaysian SOEs had been allowed to survive when in a free market they would have been closed down or made bankrupt, with their resources allocated to more profitable activities.

This comprehensive review or baseline survey of the health of Malaysian SOEs in the 1980s enabled the Malaysian government, in the early 1990s, to embark on a privatization programme based on sound economic data. Importantly, the accountability of politicians and ministers for future policy changes could be based on solid facts.

Having determined the extent of the sickness, it was possible for the Malaysian authorities to devise ways of effecting a cure. However, it is again important to stress the gradual process towards privatization which characterized the Malaysian approach. Two years after Mahathir's first announcement in 1983, the Economic Planning Unit (EPU) of the Prime Minister's Department issued its Guidelines on Privatization, which remained the main official document on privatization until early 1991. In February 1991 the government published the PMP document not

Table 6.5. Malaysia: SOE financial performance (RM million and as percentage of GDP)

	1980	1981	1982	1983	1984	1985	1986	1987	1988
Gross turnover	24,172	22,910	22,868	26,013	32,870	34,468	34,076	42,849	51,026
Operating profit	11,378	9,751	8,764	8,022	10,273	10478	9,133	8,738	11,277
Interest charges	536	697	912	1,218	1,673	1,643	2,099	2,820	3,103
Post-tax profit	7,368	5,285	4,465	3,208	5,096	4,731	3,553	3,217	5,096
Dividends	440	496	2,082	2,711	2,504	3,001	3,075	3,014	3,608
Gross fixed capital formation	0	3,612	4,642	5,784	5,407	2,713	2,233	8,093	1,620
Overall balance	6,928	1,177	(2,259)	(5,286)	(2,815)	(983)	(1,754)	(7,890)	(132)
External debt									
Debt to govt. (o/s)	3,218	4,917	5,253	5,247	5,247	4,569	4,589	9,590	8,658
External debt (o/s)	4,483	5,964	7,345	8,672	8,578	10,031	9,744	9,542	9,669
Domestic debt (o/s)	2,560	2,904	3,536	3,317	3,698	4,085	4,623	4,397	4,147
Total debt	10,261	13,785	16,135	17,235	17,523	18,685	18,956	23,529	22,504
SOE performance as percentage of GDP									
Group turnover	45.3	39.8	36.5	37.4	41.3	44.4	47.9	54.5	56.2
Operating profit	21.3	16.9	14.0	11.5	12.9	13.5	12.8	11.1	12.4
Interest charges	1.0	1.2	1.5	1.8	2.1	2.1	2.9	3.6	3.4
Post-Tax profit	13.8	9.2	7.1	4.6	6.4	6.1	5.0	4.1	5.6
Dividends	0.8	0.9	3.3	3.9	3.1	3.9	4.3	3.8	4.0
Gross fixed capital formation	0.0	6.3	7.4	8.3	6.8	3.5	3.1	10.3	1.8
Overall deficit	13.0	2.0	–3.6	–7.6	–3.5	–1.3	–2.5	–10.0	–0.1
External debt									
Debt to govt. (o/s)	6.0	8.5	8.4	7.5	6.6	5.9	6.4	12.2	9.5
External debt (o/s)	8.4	10.4	11.7	12.5	10.8	12.9	13.7	12.1	10.7
Domestic debt (o/s)	4.8	5.0	5.7	4.8	4.6	5.3	6.5	5.6	4.6
Total debt	19.2	23.9	25.8	24.8	22.0	24.1	26.6	29.9	24.8

Source: Adam and Cavendish, 1995; From Permodalan Nasional Berhad Central Information Collection Unit.

Table 6.6. Malaysia: summary of profitable and unprofitable state-owned enterprises (Percentages)

	1980	1981	1982	1983	1984	1985	1986	1987	1988
Profitable*	61	60	54	58	58	52	52	53	60
Unprofitable	39	40	46	42	42	48	48	47	40

*Reporting net operating profit.
Source: CICU Report, February 1990.

Table 6.7. Malaysia: relative performance of state-owned enterprises, 1980–1988

	Sick[1]	Weak[2]	Satisfactory[3]	Good[4]
1980	12.53	26.24	10.88	50.35
1981	13.19	26.74	9.63	50.44
1982	15.25	29.15	9.86	45.74
1983	12.12	30.12	10.04	47.72
1984	14.02	26.98	11.80	47.20
1985	16.79	30.20	11.09	41.92
1986	18.95	29.54	13.31	38.20
1987	19.23	27.43	13.87	39.47
1988	16.67	24.15	14.42	44.76

[1] Companies with negative shareholders' funds.
[2] Loss making companies with shareholders' funds <200% of paid-up capital.
[3] Shareholders' funds <100%, but currently profitable.
[4] Shareholders' funds >100% and profitable.
Source: Adam and Cavendish, 1995.

long after the October 1990 general election, and just before announcing the rest of its post-New Economic Policy for the 1990s. The PMP was one the major policy documents issued in 1991 outlining Malaysian economic development policy for the foreseeable future. Claiming success for its privatization programme thus far, the PMP announced the government's intention to "expand and accelerate further the pace of the privatization process". Therefore, privatization, as a major policy of the Malaysian government, had evolved over a 17-year period, from Mahathir's original announcement of 1883 to the end of the PMP period at the end of the 1990s.

To highlight this gradualist as well as the Malaysian government's subtle and strategic approach to privatization, it is useful to look at one of the earliest major privatization successes, that of Kelang Container Terminal (KCT), the main international seaport in Malaysia. This was no accident, as KCT was carefully chosen as the pioneering entity for privatization to ensure the success, acceptance, and public support for the government's privatization policy. The container terminal was an excellent candidate to become Malaysia's first successful privatized project since it met a number of criteria. First, it was not a politically sensitive organization, such as the railways or a major utility or health provider, which would have impacted large numbers of the Malaysian public. As categorized by a researcher of this key privatization, "the container port terminal was a hard service because it involves limited human interaction or involvement in service delivery and did not impact heavily on vulnerable groups, with privatisation unlikely to cause drastic changes" (Noorul Ainur 2001). Also, the enterprise to be privatized needed to have a track record of profitability to ensure its success with potential buyers (Leeds 1989).

According to Noorul Ainur, from 1980 until 1985, the 6 years immediately prior to its privatization as KCT in 1986, Kelang Port Authority (KPA) made profits and did not suffer losses in any of these years from its operations. However, profits were declining during this period, for example, by 5.8 per cent in 1981 from the previous year, by 16.2 per cent in 1982, before an increase of 23 per cent in 1983, and renewed decline by 0.03 per cent in 1984 and by 21.7 per cent in 1985 (Noorul Ainur 2001).

The partial privatization exercise proceeded smoothly and was effected as follows. In October 1985, KPA incorporated KCT as its wholly owned subsidiary. The KCT was awarded a 21-year licence to operate the KPA container terminal. In March 1986, KPA sold 51 per cent of KCT to Konnas Terminal Kelang Sdn Bhd (KTK), retaining the remaining 49 per cent. The KTK was a joint venture between Malaysian and foreign interests, with Kontena Nasional (KN) owning 80 per cent and P & O Australia Limited (POAL) holding the remaining 20 per cent. For its 51 per cent divestiture of KCT, besides the sale of business and movable assets the Malaysian government received RM111 million in 1986; privatization of the remaining services and assets of KPA was effected in 1992 and 1994, as is seen Table 6.8.

Although certain researchers believed that the Malaysian government's privatization of KCT was like selling a goldmine, and that the government's choice of KCT as the first major privatization was "playing it safe", there was no unfavourable publicity after the privatization of KCT; its choice of KCT as a "showcase privatization" effectively guaranteed the success of subsequent privatization policy. Should a less successful or failed entity have been privatized first, and if problems had subsequently emerged, adverse publicity could easily have derailed the entire privatization programme.

Table 6.8. Malaysia: Kelang Port Authority privatizations – payments received by the Malaysian government

Year	Company	Method	Lease period	Amount received
1986	Kelang Container Terminal	Sale, Lease of Assets	21 years	RM 111 million
1992	Kelang Port Management	Sale, Lease of Assets	21 years	RM 361 million
1994	Kelang Multi Terminal	Sale, Lease of Assets	33 years	RM 110 million
			Total	RM 582 million

Source: Noorul Ainur, 2001; Data provided by Finance Division Kelang Port Authority, 1999.

The authors have chosen to discuss exhaustively both the Argentinean and the Malaysian experiences of privatization, because they believe that a careful examination and comparison of the two experiences demonstrate, at the very least, how not to carry out a privatization exercise. In the Malaysian experience, privatization proceeded slowly and gradually, with policy taking shape in the early 1980s, with the water being tested in the period 1885–1891, before the Malaysian government felt confident enough to embark on a major privatization programme in the 1990s. After initial successes such as TV3 and the KCT divestiture discussed above, the PMP went into effect for the rest of the 1990s. Although in certain respects it may not, on further investigation, have been entirely free of allegations of lack of transparency and corruption and cronyism, as, for example, the privatization in 1990 of Food Industries of Malaysia Bhd (FIMA) and Peremba Bhd as management buyouts to close friends and associates of Malaysian Finance Minister Daim Zainuddin and the Malaysian Prime Minister Mahathir himself, with the former going to Mohd. Razali Mohd. Rahman, and the latter to Hassan Abas (Gomez 1991), we believe that it still possesses many pointers as to how a small- to medium-sized developing country can successfully embark and sustain a privatization exercise.

6.3 Privatization in MENA Countries

The MENA countries in general have been slow to implement privatization, with the first steps towards privatization usually reluctant ones. In fact Morocco was the first Arab country to formally endorse privatization as a policy, and was quickly followed by Tunisia, Jordan, and Egypt. In this connection, it is significant that except for Tunisia, Arab countries that started on the path of privatization did so under some degree of pressure from international financial institutions.

But as a leading Arab researcher has stated in 2002, "the question that should be paramount in the minds of policy makers and citizens in Arab countries is not *whether* to privatise but *how* to privatise State-Owned Enterprises (SOEs) and attract private participation in infrastructure. Arab countries have lagged far behind the rest of the world in terms of privatisation and Private Participation in Infrastructure (PPI), and they cannot afford to ignore the lessons from earlier privatisations" (Shehadi 2002). To endorse his enthusiasm for privatization, he has provided some interesting data on pre-/post-privatization business indicators in developing countries, which is shown in Table 6.9.

In the following sections we will critically examine the very different legislative, practical, and often selective approaches of the privatization experiences of several MENA countries including Egypt, Tunisia, Morocco, Algeria, and Jordan before turning to a detailed analysis of the Libyan case.

Table 6.9. Privatization business indication in developing countries

Variable measured	No. of observations	Mean value before privatizations	Mean value after privatizations	Main change due to privatization	Percentage of firms with performance improvement
Profitability (return on sales)	78	4.9%	11%	6.05%	62.8%
Efficiency (real sales per employee)	56	0.922	1.17	24.79	80.4%
Investment (capital expenditures/ sales)	48	10.52%	23.75%	13.22%	62.5%
Output (real sales, adjusted by CPI)	78	0.969	1.22	25.3	75.6%
Total employment	57	10,672	10,811	139	57.8%
Leverage (debt/total assets)	65	54.95%	49.86%	–2.48%	63.1%
Dividends (dividends/ sales)	67	2.84%	5.28%	2.44%	76.1%

Source: Boubakri and Cosset, 1998.

6.3.1 Tunisia and Egypt: Different Means, Different Ends

In a North African context, the privatization experiences of Tunisia and Egypt, both immediate neighbours of Libya, reveal interesting features. As an economic researcher commented about these two countries, "students of the Middle East and North Africa (MENA) have noted multiple similarities between Egypt and Tunisia in terms of past and present political orientation, economic choices and state-society interaction" (Belev 2001). But as an analysis of the privatization process in these countries reveals, the outcomes of this process in the two countries have been quite different. Again, as the author notes, "in Egypt, on the one hand, the process stalled: in spite of the seemingly favourable environment, little real privatisation work was done. On the other hand, there was serious progress in Tunisia: in spite of the inevitable ups and downs, divestiture added strength to the private sector in the long run."

There are specific reasons to explain why privatization succeeded in Tunisia but has not yet been entirely successful in Egypt. This is not due to a paucity of enabling legislation for privatization in either country for, if anything, Egypt perhaps had too much of this. Rather it was due to the context of the interaction between the central government, which was the major agent of reform, and the relevant state and extra-state actors who were stakeholders in the privatization process. It would appear that the greater the involvement of the central government in the process of devising, adopting, and pushing through the privatization programme, the greater the chance of success. This is because the smaller the role and say of other stakeholders in the privatization process, such as the bureaucracy, public sector managers, labour unions, political parties, and private sector investors, the less chance there is of these groups combining to derail the privatization process. This ability to derail the process was well illustrated in the situation of Argentina, for example, at the time of the Alfonsín administration which, although it had launched a major privatization initiative in 1985, saw this successfully undermined by the Peronist-dominated Senate which effectively blocked all three privatization bills submitted by Alfonsín's government in 1988.

In other words, it is the end (a successful privatization programme) which justifies the means (a restrictive and politically illiberal approach to and control of the privatization process and mechanisms). Paradoxically, as Belev states, "the comparison of the two cases shows that the country which has been more restrictive in the management of the privatisation program (Tunisia) has achieved greater success in pursuing liberal economic goals than the country which has adopted a more liberal approach" (Egypt) (Belev 2001).

From the initial launching of a privatization exercise in any country, the state may assume a more or less activist role. With a liberal privatization strategy, the privatization programme would be the product of a wide-ranging consultation among stakeholders affected in one way or another by the reforms. If the government adopts a more restrictive strategy, then the programme would be the product of decision-making from the top with little input from below. Accordingly the Egyptian government allowed various actors and stakeholders to voice their opinion regarding the urgency and necessity of privatization, the privatization targets themselves, and the methods by which the reform should be carried out. As the debate in Egypt turned out to be very controversial, the government had to be very cautious in moving forward at the same time sustaining the political status quo. Consequently, the launching of the privatization programme was delayed, policies involved serious compromises and the regulatory environment remained vague, incoherent, and often contradictory. Also, at even a more fundamental political level in Egypt there was still much confusion and hesitation among politicians themselves as well as intellectuals – should Egypt move rapidly in the direction of the market economy or was it better to retain as much as possible of the legacy of the Nasserite "socialist" past?

The Tunisian government, on the contrary, from the beginning, limited debate and consultation on the privatization programme. The central government had virtually unlimited discretion in dealing with privatization-related issues; the attention of most of the actors in politics was kept away from public sector reform, and stakeholders were rarely consulted and allowed to have an input in the policy-making process.

In Tunisia, after the benefits of a market economy were perceived and crystallized in the late 1970s and the first half of the 1980s, the country's leadership under Bourghiba already had a clear answer to the question on the necessity of radical reform for the public sector, which had become an unbearable burden for the government to bear. While the government maintained popular support throughout this period, it seized the opportunity to adopt a strategy of depoliticization and greater restrictiveness in the management of the reform process, and deliberately avoided sensitive questions, refusing to justify its actions.

Information on the privatization process flowed only one-way, from the top down, and little feedback was asked for by other stakeholders. Public discussion and debate, as much as it existed, took place within the government's initial public relations campaign, where popular newspapers and magazines published a series of articles by academics on the inefficiency of the public sector, the need for reform and the success stories in foreign countries, such as, for instance, in Thatcher's privatization approach in the United Kingdom.

One way used for depoliticizing potentially disruptive issues was the use of vague or technical terms in public discussions on public sector reform. The word "privatization", for instance, was hardly mentioned, and instead, "participation in public enterprises" and "restructuring" replace it. In this way unnecessary opposition and resistance to the idea of privatization on ideological grounds was avoided. All the IPO of shares of stock of public enterprises were considered as "participations", implying a wider participation in private ownership while the sale of a part or of an entire enterprise to a strategic investor went under the heading of "spin-off" (cession) or "merger" (fusion).

In general the method by which Tunisia reduced the role of the bureaucracy in the process of formulating their privatization programmes was very shrewd. Because the impact of privatization on the bureaucracy is probably greater than on any other sector or stakeholders, since obviously civil servants manage the public sector on behalf of the state, divestiture represents a direct attack on their source of power.

The scope for bureaucratic obstructions, as well as for delays from other stakeholders, is demonstrated by the complex and all-inclusive approach that Egypt took in its legislative and regulative approach to privatization in order to achieve consensus. As the Egyptian government wanted to soften the criticism of its opponents, and obtain the seal of societal approval, it opted for a detailed legislative regulation of most of the issues related to privatization, no matter if this involved of a large number of people, much scope for discussion, a long period of time for implementation, and potentially long delays. This strategy produced a regulatory framework in which the laws outnumbered all the other relevant documents (e.g. Presidential Decrees, Executive directives, etc.). There are at least eight major laws on various aspects of public sector reform: Law No. 159 of 1981 (Companies Law); Law No. 230 of 1989 (Investment Law); Law No. 203 of 1991 (Public Business Sector Law); Law No. 95 of 1992 (Capital Market Law) as well as texts on companies from the Civil Code and the Commercial Code, and texts on exemptions and incentives in Law No. 59 of 1979 and Law No. 143 of 1981 (Fahmy 1994). It would be fair to say that in attempting to create a comprehensive regulatory framework the Egyptian government came up with too much legislation, adopted at different times and under different circumstances and strongly affected by group interests.

This resulted in a complex and confusing regulatory framework which lacked coherence and contained many contradictory provisions. Thus, for instance, in clear contradiction with the logic of the proposed market-oriented reform and the privatization process, the existing constitution, adopted in 1970 and amended in 1980, postulated that Egypt is a "socialist democratic state", and the national economy is regulated by a comprehensive development plan; it states that "the people" control all means of production and allocate the produced surplus with the goal of achieving equity in distribution, and eradicating of unemployment through welfare benefits, minimum wages, and ceilings of income (Fahmy 1994).

The most important law for the process of privatization in the strict sense, however, is Law No. 203 of 1991 on the Public Business Sector. It was meant to remove the obstacles to efficient performance under previous legislation by achieving three objectives. First, by limiting the public sector to strategic activities only. Secondly, by arranging for the sale of non-strategic public sector and joint projects to the private sector and the liquidation of those units which could not be reformed. Thirdly, by separating management and ownership of public sector units in order to free them from the red tape by introducing sound management methods and practices in line with measurements of pure economic efficiency.

Since, also, the existence of well-functioning capital markets such as a money market, financial capital market, and securities market were important conditions for successful privatization and efficient functioning of the private sector, Law No. 95 of 1992 was also adopted "to regulate the issuance and circulation of the stock exchange and the companies operating in the field" (Fahmy 1994).

In Egypt, Decrees and Executive directives also provided regulatory functions in the economic reform process, although they did not play a direct role in privatization. Thus, interest rates were deregulated completely in 1991 and private foreign exchange transactions were legalized. Investment opportunities under the Investment Law No. 230 of 1989 were expanded to all fields besides those in the negative list published in 1991, to include high energy consumptive industries, some assembly industries, military products and related industries, tobacco and its products, investment in the Sinai Peninsula except for oil exploration, and natural gas and mining sources. In 1992 the Corporations Law was amended further by a ministerial decree stipulating minimum requirements for the issued share capital for companies participating in the stock market to strengthen public confidence in their position.

In fact there is only one general executive regulatory text dedicated to divestiture, which is the "General Procedures and Guidelines for the Government's Program or Privatisation, Restructuring and Reward System", issued by the Public Enterprise Office on 14 February 1993. This document – elaborating the principles underlying the need for privatization, such as raising efficiency, opening markets for competition, deregulation, dealing with public debt, reserving special rights for the government if it holds a minority interest in certain cases of strategic importance, equality for all investors, and so on – presented the structure of the agencies involved in the process and defined the scope of the programme. It also included a list of companies which were to become privatized in the next three years (20–25 annually), the methods of divestiture, and the use of the proceeds from the sale. Although the "General

Procedures and Guidelines" initially provided some ground for discussion, they later became almost redundant, especially after it became obvious that the privatization schedule was falling far behind.

From this pastiche of legislation and regulations it is clear that the major drawback of the privatization process in Egypt was its lack of focus through its use of too many laws and regulations, many of whose objectives were different and sometimes contradictory. Many observers note that there is a need for legislation on privatization as such to cover all relevant issues, including provisions for bankruptcy, merger, and arbitration procedures, enacting anti-trust regulations to prevent the transfer of public sector monopolies into private hands, amending the labour law to allow future private owners greater flexibility in recruitment, contract duration, and employment termination. It is because most of these issues are politically sensitive, and defy quick and easy solutions, that a privatization approach such as Egypt's, aimed at wide public participation and consensus, failed to really get off the ground.

In Tunisia, on the other hand, the privatization process moved forward much more efficiently and quickly in a focused manner, after initial setbacks due to the complexity of the initial framework. From the outset the government decided that it did not need to redo the general framework regulating economic activities. Instead, it decided to target the issue of privatization itself and spend less time and effort on obtaining legislative approval for most of the aspects of the reform. The first official document was Law No. 87-47, adopted in August 1987. It created the initial institutional structure of public sector reform: an inter-ministerial commission to choose the enterprises to be privatized; a restructuring/privatization commission to undertake the required analysis and structure the privatization transactions; and a follow-up commission to carry out the transactions.

But this fairly complicated arrangement did not function well enough, and did not produce the desired results, because it turned out to be difficult to coordinate the activities of the multiple bodies involved, while the implementation process was too complicated and time-consuming. As well as this there was no adequate staff support for the three commissions, and their members lacked the necessary specialized knowledge and experience. They were, in any case, often busy with their own full-time jobs, leaving little time for consideration of the complex problems of valuation of firms or seeking prospective buyers. No priorities for divestment were laid down and no overall strategy was developed. As a result, little had been accomplished in the months before the overthrow of the Bourghiba regime (Cowan 1990).

Therefore a new and much simpler approach was taken by the new President Ben Ali in 1989 with Law No. 89-9, which provided for the overall framework for the public sector reform in which the organizational structure of the public sector and the procedures of privatization were streamlined. Thus, Law No. 89-9 abolished two of the former three commissions and kept only one, Commission pour l'Assanissement et la Restructuration des Enterprises Publiques et pour les Participations (CAREPP), which turned into the driving force of privatization. As well as this the law gave a definition of "a public enterprise" in the manufacturing and the service sectors, specified procedures, roles and responsibilities, and transferred managerial responsibility over a number of enterprises to non-governmental shareholders. Total or partial liquidation of non-viable SOEs was allowed; companies which could not be privatized were also to undergo serious restructuring. In August 1994 this law was amended with Law No. 94-102 which redefined the scope of the public sector and allowed privatization of banks and insurance companies. Other relevant legislation was Law No. 94-117, adopted in November 1994, which reorganized the financial markets and created the Tunis Stock Exchange. It should be mentioned that, unlike their Egyptian counterparts, the texts of most of these laws are short, and provide only some basic concepts and determine the bodies participating in the process.

These laws, however, did not explore major issues such as planning, selection, valuation, marketing, and sale and post-sale regulation, thus leaving a lot of space for discretion and placing all of the authority in the hands of the agencies in charge, that is the political appointees, technocrats, and experts identified and designated by the government. Unlike Egypt, in Tunisia the use of consultation mechanisms which could provide opportunities for opposition was extremely limited and a number of important policy issues were handled by acts of the executive, usually adopted with no preliminary discussion and sometimes even with no prior knowledge of most officials directly involved in the implementation of the programme.

The Presidential Decree 87-65 of 12 January 1987, for instance, dealt with issues of administrative reform. Among other things, it elaborated on the functions of the Directorate General of Public Enterprises (DGEP) within the Prime Minister's Department which was supposed to be the major actor in the restructuring and turnaround of the SOEs and in dealing with their impacts, including personnel remuneration, lay-offs, and conflict resolution. It is remarkable that this decree came out before the parliament had even adopted the first privatization law in August 1987, which shows the marginal role accorded to a wider consensus.

Another important executive act was Decree 93-2408 of 29 November 1993, which transferred authority away from the DGEP. In a major shift of responsibility it stipulated that the Ministry of Planning and Regional Development would become the major body in charge of the preparation of public enterprises for divestiture and control over the execution of privatization transactions.

Other important government decisions took the form simply of government circulars signed by the Prime Minister. They came out practically every 6 months and dealt with issues, which in other countries were handled by laws and deliberated by legislators. For example, Circular 33 of 21 June 1989 outlined the procedures for privatization in detail, defined and codified the roles of CAREPP and DGEP. Circular 55 of 11 August 1993 described the field of action of the Ministry of Planning and Regional Development and brought further centralization to the process as it extended control to include all enterprises with direct or indirect public participation. This circular also assigned new responsibilities to the above-mentioned ministry before a document of a higher order, in this case Decree 93-2408, was adopted.

In yet another very important respect the Tunisian approach protected the privatization process from early derailment by opposition groups or stakeholders, such as public sector employees who were worried about their jobs or suspicious of the government's motives. From the very beginning, the Tunisian government decided not to publish the list of candidates for privatization. The CAREPP announced, however, that all SOEs should be sooner or later privatized. By taking this approach it wanted to prevent the management of individual SOEs from developing a complacent attitude once they did not see their companies on the list. Management was thus encouraged to greater efficiency in the expectation that the restructuring secretariat could knock on the door at any time. "CAREPP has clearly streamlined the process of privatisation, at least at the top level of the government. Its restricted membership, access to the highest authority, and limited documentation has made decisions on the form of divestment both rapid and simple" (Cowan 1990). At the same time, public sector employees would not be faced with the uncertainties and psychological impact of seeing their organization as part of a list of companies to be privatized, thus preventing general public opposition.

There was also one very crucial and important matter that the Tunisian government addressed very early on, which prevented much of the corrupt insider privatization which took place in many countries of Eastern Europe and the former Soviet Union, under which the former SOE managers retained their positions by arranging some kind of buyout. In this connection the Tunisian government did its best to clearly delineate responsibilities and avoid conflict of interest in the process of divestiture. The bodies in charge of privatization made it clear that the SOE managers could not be among the primary buyers of divested assets, thus making a serious contribution to the integrity and lack of opportunities for corruption in the process.

As we have seen above, the redundant employees represent a major issue in the process of privatization. In many countries undergoing structural adjustment, governments have had to delay or compromise important reform measures for fear of social and political unrest. Privatization, at least in the short run, definitely represents a threat to labour as the new private owners are likely to undertake lay-offs while restructuring former SOEs. It also threatens the position of those employees who retain their jobs, while the possibilities of wages going down, working conditions deteriorating, and the privatized companies ceasing to be part of the social security system providing not only pensions after retirement but also health insurance, housing, and other perquisites perceived as very real ones. In addition, in countries with developed labour movements union leaders are likely to feel that privatization and the consequent reduction of the labour force would reduce their power and prestige, generally based on wide membership in unions and their capacity to act as spokespersons or figureheads.

This is why any government opting for privatization expects a certain degree of resistance, overt or covert, both from labour union leaders and the rank and file. The restructuring of the public sector in Egypt by itself at the end of the 1980s was expected to result roughly in 380,000 lay-offs and expenses of LE 4,000 per worker for retraining and new job creation, or LE 1.5 billion total, but the phasing out of public sector reform was supposed to attenuate the shock to a bearable level as the necessary lay-offs would not take place all at once (UN ECOSOC 1993). On closer scrutiny another researcher expected this number to be smaller, since privatization would initially touch only non-strategic public enterprises employing roughly 368,000 people with the estimated redundant labour around 30 per cent, or 122,680 people being laid off. In an optimistic scenario this number would be 25 per cent of total employment, that is 122,680, and in a pessimistic scenario, 50 per cent or 184,020 (Cao no date). In this context the researcher concluded that "unemployment caused by redundancy is not as significant as it first seemed" and suggested alternative approaches for the government strategy for privatization, estimating that the costs of retiring workers was between LE 52,556,112 to LE 18,394,068 based on an average pension paid to the retirees of LE 1,428 per year (the average pension in Egypt in 1987/1988) and the cost of retraining younger displaced workers (based on the current annual wages of these displaced workers) to be between LE 576 and LE 1,478 per worker. This resulted in an unweighted average cost of about LE 1,027 per worker or for the entire group between LE 8,685,339 and 16,158,818 (Cao no date).

The situation in the labour market in Tunisia at the time of the launching of the privatization programme was similar. At the beginning of the 1990s Tunisia had a workforce of about 2.5 million. Unemployment was a particularly serious problem amounting officially to 14 per cent of the workforce although some estimates claimed it was much higher than this, around 20 per cent, half of which were people under the age of 25 (Abt Associates 1995). At the end of the 1980s SOEs in Tunisia provided jobs for 156,000 people, or approximately 13 per cent of the total number of employees.

The available data shows, however, that the threat of labour unrest as a result of lay-offs did not prevent the Tunisian government from implementing the privatization programme. By 1989, out of 7,509 employees in the privatized SOEs 3,039 had kept their jobs (40 per cent), 2,102 were transferred to other SOEs (28 per cent), 324 benefited from anticipated retirement (4 per cent), and only 103 were effectively laid off (1.5 per cent). Other available numbers, as of June 1990, show 6,483 laid-off or redirected employees out of 21,206 employed in privatized companies; 46 per cent of the labour force of these companies stayed on, 19 per cent chose early retirement, and 16 per cent left voluntarily after receiving a severance package (Saghir 1993). Towards 1995 most of the redundant labour of the privatized SOEs had more or less been taken care of through transfer to new positions or early retirement. Contrary to the expectations of the pessimists, privatization itself did not produce massive lay-offs and did not boost unemployment.

In fact a number of former SOEs were able to offer new employment opportunities after their privatization due to the inflow of newly invested capital – thus, for instance, Carnelages Tunisiennes and the apparel manufacturer SITEX each added 10 per cent to their workforce, Comptoirs Sfaxiens, 32 per cent, and SHTT, which managed 8 hotels, 38 per cent (Belev 2001). Although the number of new jobs was not great enough to seriously ease the unemployment situation in the country, it showed that privatization as such did not aggravate the overall situation of the labour market.

With respect to the situation of workers made redundant by privatization, the privatization process clearly has a greater chance of success if the government is more actively involved in dealing with redundant labour. Excessive reliance on market mechanisms, and new employers, which might not be fully developed enough at the transition stage of economic reform to take care of the displaced workers is a grave challenge to the privatization process. As a result, both privatization and the policies of economic liberalization would lose rather than gain supporters.

Again, crucial differences existed at the top in the Egyptian and Tunisian approaches which led to the greater success of the latter. The former set up a more liberal regulatory framework and attempted to bring together private and political and public sector stakeholders while providing nominal leadership, paying little attention to the coordination of the efforts of these actors and relying primarily on foreign donors for financial support of the necessary measures. However, in the case of Tunisia it was the government itself which set up the necessary support structures within the state apparatus, and financed and managed the work itself. In Egypt the provision of compensatory schemes has become the responsibility of individual parties all of whom had different preferences, hence, different bias for shifting the efforts in the direction of solving their own problems.

In Tunisia the centralized control over this activity has allowed the government to focus only on the main issue, the provision of relief for displaced workers, and not to attempt to use the limited financial and bureaucratic resources for solving general economic and social problems. As a result, the problem of redundant labour has been more directly addressed in Tunisia than in Egypt and labour issues have tended to be less of an obstacle to divestiture for the Tunisian government.

The body set up to deal with labour redundancy in Egypt was the Social Fund for Development (SFD), "an autonomous institution established in 1991 by presidential decree No. 40 to create job opportunities, decrease the rate of unemployment, minimize the adverse effects of ERSAP (Economic Reform and Structural Adjustment Programme) and protect low-income groups from its effects". It was designed to become the basis for the new social safety net replacing the old social security system which functioned through government agencies and SOEs. The SFD launched a number of programmes, such as a public works programme, a community development programme, an enterprise development programme, an employment and retraining programme targeting specifically those SOEs undergoing restructuring, and an institutional development programme. On first view, the fund appeared to be an institution with a strong bureaucratic organization. The Prime Minister was the Chairman of the Board of Directors and it had an Executive Committee, a Secretariat, and staff headed by a Managing Director. It was not, however, a government agency, and the Prime Minister's leadership was nominal, similar to his leadership of dozens of other bodies and committees.

The SFD was meant to coordinate the efforts of the government, the labour unions, foreign donors, and others in providing relief for the "losers" in the economic transformation process. In setting it up the government hoped to solve the problem of laid-off workers in the course of public sector reform, but placed this task in the context of the broader objective of reforming the entire social security system and creating the backbone of a new social safety net.

It came as no surprise, therefore, that this semi-autonomous agency, whose relationship to the existing public and private structures as well as its own authority was not very clearly defined, could not accomplish its ambitious goals. This was primarily because it did not have the necessary bureaucratic capabilities, while funding for its programmes was provided on an ad-hoc basis mainly by foreign donors with its activities targeting the problem of unemployment in general, and not linked directly to the results of the implementation of the privatization programme. One way of doing this, for example, could have been by committing a fixed percentage of the proceeds from the sale of the SOEs to private investors to retraining and relocating workers through programmes supported by the SFD.

Due to such diverse constraints it took 18 months in the period from 1991 to 1992, just to set up its administration, offices, and facilities, and hire skilled and qualified staff. Developing the programmes themselves, negotiating with donors, and following the different procedures and requirements for receiving financial resources further delayed the implementation of the SFD programmes. But most importantly, there was a sharp divergence between the amount of funds committed for its operation and those actually made available, which was a fundamental flaw.

Similar to Egypt, the government of Tunisia also created an institution for dealing with redundant labour – the "Fund of Rationalization of the Employment in the Public Enterprises" (FREEP), established in 1987. Crucially, however, and unlike its Egyptian counterpart, this institution was not supposed to take on the general problem of unemployment in the country, and solve the entire problem of public sector reform lay-offs. In fact it was expected only to help solve the problem of unemployment in a small segment of the labour market, those laid off by privatizations or "participation in public enterprises" and "restructuring" as it was termed in Tunisia.

The FREEP has had the following responsibilities. First, to provide temporary financial relief to laid-off workers; secondly, to create and manage a database of the personnel at the SOEs and effectively intervene on relocation if necessary; and thirdly, to study the profile, the salary range, and the social perks of redundant labour. These goals were to be achieved through taking care of certain liabilities of the former SOEs, such as accumulated arrears to the social security system, pension funds, and certain third-party liabilities, providing professional expertise and technical assistance in accounting, auditing, management, organizational managerial development, and advisory services on individual privatization transactions. The most important element of the relief that FREEP offered was the compensatory payments for the laid-off employees in case no opportunities for alternative employment could be found.

Up to 1990, laid-off workers received a severance package based on 1 month's salary for each year of work with a cap of 12; in addition, they received a bonus of 30 per cent. Starting in 1991, the severance payment was increased to 2 months' salaries plus one for each year of work with no cap. In certain cases of downsizing the government came up with specific provisions regarding workers' compensation (Saghir 1993). But the superior effectiveness of FREEP was not just its focused and well-defined rules, as opposed to the all-embracing Egyptian approach, but also the effective way in which it provided the necessary financing to take care of all these matters. A part of the resources which would otherwise have been used for supporting excessive labour in the SOEs was committed to FREEP. Periodic allocations were made by the state. For example, up to July 1991 they totalled US $80 million, covering severance packages ($35 million), pension liabilities ($9.8 million), and outstanding debt of SOEs ($35.2 million) (Saghir 1993). Although, as a safety net, the Tunisian government had also negotiated a line of credit with the World Bank to finance a retraining programme for the laid-off employees, it in no way had relied too much on outside donor's contributions.

Finally, unlike the Egyptian SFD, the Tunisian FREEP has been, since its inception, a state institution. The Tunisian government clearly understood the damage that uninvited and unwarranted external interference could do to a domestic situation inadequately understood, as, for example, the Indonesian experience of 1997 and later showed. The government assumed all the responsibility for managing it; it aimed at providing relief only for the workers laid off in the course of privatization and did not attempt to solve larger problems of unemployment or economic restructuring, for which it had no adequate capacity. The fund was set up under the auspices of the Ministry of Economic Development, the body with the major responsibilities and delegated power for the implementation of the privatization programme, and became an effective instrument for separating the general issue of unemployment from the short-term problems generated by privatization, a very crucial distinction.

6.3.2 Privatization in Morocco

Morocco was the first Arab country to formally endorse privatization as a policy, quickly followed by Tunisia, Jordan, and Egypt. It is noteworthy that most of the Arab governments that endorsed privatization early on, such as Egypt, Jordan, and Morocco, did so as part of an IMF-backed package of reforms to consolidate their public finances, bring their budget deficits under control, and address external imbalances, typically, an unsustainable current account deficit. It was not, however, until 1999 that Morocco re-energized its privatization programme. To best summarize the Moroccan privatization methodology, the authors present a series of tables highlighting its most important features and successes.

Regarding the prior reform of the capital market, many governments around the world, including Morocco, have taken measures to reform these in preparation for privatization. Table 6.10 outlines the Moroccan experience.

Table 6.10. Privatization-fuelled reform of the Moroccan capital markets

Year	Measure	Implications
1994	Establishment of securities and exchange rate commission	Capital market regulation: – Disclosure requirements. – Regulation covering mutual funds
1995	Privatisation of the Casablanca Stock Exchange	Reform of the domestic capital market
1995	Legislation allowing for capital mobility	– Free movement of capital across border – Accumulation of foreign investment – Repatriation of capital gains and dividends
1995	Approval of 13 mutual funds	Propelling foreign investment

Source: Fremond, O., Morocco's Case-by-Case Privatisation Program (from Lieberman and Kirkness 1988).

The Legal and Institutional Framework

In many countries, as we have noted, the legal framework surrounding privatization can be either minimal, as in, for example, the United Kingdom, or else excessive, as we noted in the Egyptian case above. In Morocco, the approach is considerably less complex than the Egyptian case, and is provided in summary form in Table 6.11.

Historically, governments have been reluctant to cede regulatory responsibilities to an autonomous or independent authority. But experience has shown that independent regulators are more credible and more effective than regulators who depend on political whims. Morocco has opted for the commission model, and the 1990 law defines the organizations responsible for privatization:

- The Ministry of Privatization: the main institution.
- The Transfer Commission: this is made up of five ministers, and advises on the most appropriate transfer means for each case.
- Valuation Authority: this is an evaluating body composed of seven independent members and sets the bidding price for each company being privatized.
- Privatization Implementation Procedure.

Again, in Morocco there are three predominant mechanisms used for privatization, which are sale through financial markets, bid invitations, and direct disposal of assets, or a combination of all three. Table 6.12 describes the typical sequence of steps for privatization.

Table 6.11. Morocco: the legal framework for privatization

	Political
Public law	Constitutional
System	Constitutional Monarchy Elected Parliament Government Appointed by, and answerable to, the King and parliament.
Judicial	Pattern of Courts (including Commercial Courts)
Economic	
Property rights	Intellectual and Industrial Property Rights Law: Complete regulatory and legislative system
General legislation	1995 Investment Code: improves investment climate and encourages foreign participation in investment Labor Law: decreases firing flexibility Antitrust Law
Privatization enabling legislation	1990 Privatisation Law

Source: Shehadi, 2002.

Table 6.12. Morocco: typical steps for privatization

Steps	Objects	State body
Step 1	Decision to privatise	Ministry of privatisation undertakes relevant feasibility studies
Step 2	Process initiation	Report on sale options submitted to the transfer commission for approval
Step 3	Preparation for the sale	Selection of a private firm to carry out the audit and evaluation for the transfer and prepare further sale options. Companies prepared for privatisation through work with their management, major shareholders, and employees, in addition to the supervisory ministry
Step 4	Finalizing sale condition	Transfer commission receives final audit and evaluation and finalizes conditions for sale: Time for the transfer set after consultation with advisers Price determined for the shares to be sold under each option
Step 5	Advertising campaign	Public announcement of prospects Launch of promotional campaign
Step 6	Bid evaluation	Technical and financial bid evaluation
Step 7	Sale closure	Actual payments or awarded of the tender
Step 8	Announcement of the sale	Press release or press conference

Source: Shehadi, 2002

Table 6.13 illustrates major privatization achievements in Morocco from 1993 to 2001.

The Moroccan Banking Sector – Important Lessons

In the following section we will discuss in detail the milestone privatization of the Banque Marocaine du Commerce Exterieur in Casablanca, which commenced in late 1994. We have chosen this particular case, after analysing major financial reforms in other MENA countries, because we believe that by discussing and analysing this in detail there may be important lessons for Libya's current financial sector reform, in particular the poorly received privatizations of Sahara and Wahda banks there.

At the time of its privatization, Banque Marocaine du Commerce Exterieur (BMCE) was Morocco's second largest bank, with a balance sheet representing 19 per cent of the country's banking credit and 17 per cent of deposits. The bank's 176 branches and 2,778 employees were spread around the country. A minority interest was quoted on the Casablanca stock exchange. The government owned 50.01 per cent of the bank, and its Chairman and Chief Executive Officer was a civil servant. Foreign commercial banks owned 12.55 per cent of the BMCE; the rest (37.44 per cent) was owned by private Moroccan investors. Net profits for 1994 totalled $29.5 million. The privatization took the form of a mixed sale, combining an open tender for 26 per cent of the bank's share capital and management control, a secondary offering on the stock market (targeted at small investors and mutual funds) for 14 per cent, and a private placement with the bank's employees for 3 per cent. The government retained 7 per cent through the Caisse de Depot et de Gestion, a public agency overseeing Morocco's social security system.

Table 6.13. Morocco: major privatization achievements 1993–2001

Enterprise	Year	Sector	Privatization producers	$US	Purchaser
Shell Maroc	1993	Petroleum	Direct sale	46.6 million	Shell Petroleum International
SNEP	1993	Petrochemicals	Direct sale	37.7 million	Group Dimitati
CIM International Bus Company	1993	Transport	Public offering tender	26.8 million	(Private and international investors)
Societe Nationale d'Investissement	1994	Insurance	Public offering	226.6 million	–
Casblanca hotel	1994	Tourism	Direct sale	20 million	Interedec
Total Maroc	1994	Gas distribution	Direct sale	65.8 million	TOTAL OutreMer
Banque Marcaine de Commerce Exterieur (BMCE)	1995	Banking	Public offering employee offer	352.6 million	Nomura International Commerzbank
Societe Anonyme Marocaine de l'Industrie de Raffinage (SAMIR)	1996	Petroleum	Direct sale employee offer Public Offering	275.5 million	Corral Petroleum
Societe Cherifienne de Petroles (SCP)	1997	Oil Refinery	Direct sale employee offer	78.5 million	Corral Petroleum
Lyonnais des Eauxde Casablanca	1997	Water	Concession	–	Foreign and local investors
Societe National de Sidurergie (SONACID)	1997	Steel	Public offering Direct sale Employee offer	138 million	Consortimtium Led by Societe Nationale d'Investissement (SNI)
National Gas	1998	Gas Distribution	Direct Sale	–	Repsol
Second GSM License	1999	Mobile Telecom	Auction	11 billion	Media telecom, consortium including Telefonica, Portugal Telecom, a local bank
Maroc Telecom	2001	Telecoms	Direct sale	2 6 billion	Vivendi

Source: Shehadi, 2002.

The tender started in December 1994 and was due to close at the end of February 1995, with domestic institutional investors showing strong interest in participating in the open tender. Based on this, the Ministry of Privatization launched and closed the secondary share offering before closing the open tender.

Between 16 January and 20 January 1995, the shares were offered to the public at \$38.35 per share. The offering was more than 6.1 times oversubscribed and attracted more than 51,000 subscribers. The closed private placement to the bank's employees offered shares at a 15 per cent discount, while the BMCE also provided loans to help its employees buy these shares. The minimum price for the 26 per cent of shares offered at open tender was the issue price of the public offer.

The terms of reference for the open tender stipulated that the stake was reserved for bidders organized in consortiums of at least four parties. The shares offered for sale were structured in two tranches. Half of the 26 per cent stake, or 13 per cent of the banks share capital, was reserved for Moroccan investors, with two caveats. Banks and investors that owned 20 per cent or more of the capital of a Moroccan bank or that were owned 20 per cent or more by a similar institution were excluded from the tender. In addition, no more than one Moroccan insurance company was allowed in each consortium, and even then only insurance companies that did not own shares in the BMCE prior to the tender were allowed. The remaining 13 per cent of shares were open to domestic and foreign investors. Article 4 of the Terms of Reference stipulated that consortiums should include at least one foreign bank committed to buying at least 5 per cent of the BMCE's share capital, and that the nationality of at least one such bank should not already be represented in the BMCE's share capital (World Bank 1998).

The situation by the end of February 1995 was that two main consortiums were in competition, while both were facing difficulties in finding a foreign commercial bank not already represented in the BMCE's share capital, which was willing to buy a 5 per cent stake. Consequently, the tender period was extended until the end of March 1995, while alternatives were debated to bring the transaction to a close. The end result was that, instead of trying to motivate foreign commercial banks to buy the 5 per cent stake, either for themselves or on behalf of nominee accounts, Morgan Grenfell forged an alliance with one consortium and Citibank with the other, which led to the tender being successfully closed at the end of March 1995. Eventually the winning consortium, led by a Moroccan industrialist allied with Morgan Grenfell. paid a price for the 26 per cent stake at a 47 per cent premium to the price of the secondary offering, which worked out at 19 times anticipated earnings for 1994.

The complex and protracted series of events surrounding BMCE's privatization experience provides some important lessons for countries contemplating mixed sales, basically that privatization officials should not overcomplicate the terms of reference of their tenders. Simplicity is always preferable; it allows the market to speak for itself, and it gives privatization officials some discretion in responding to market signals. It is misguided to assume that transparency will be compromised if privatization officials have some discretion in finalizing privatization transactions. Transparency is safe as long as the rules regarding the selection of the winning bidder are publicly disclosed from the outset and scrupulously observed by government officials. Imposing restrictions on the identity of potential bidders or on the use that they can make of their investment does not enhance the transparency of the selection process. In fact, it may hinder it (World Bank 2002).

Morocco has continued with its successful privatization plans, and in December 2004 the IPO for 15 per cent of Maroc Telecom raised US $1billion (£520 million) for Morocco's government finances, with the offer oversubscribed 18 times and overseas institutional investors getting a 30 per cent slice of the offering. This successful IPO again highlighted the importance of the privatization of the Casablanca Stock Exchange in 1995, as a precursor of the country's successful privatization drive.

6.3.3 The Algerian Case

As early as the late 1980s, the Algerian government launched a series of economic reforms in an attempt to boost growth and diversify the economy away from the hydrocarbon sector, attempting to transform its centralized socialist economy to an open market economy. Restructuring and the privatization of the state-owned industrial sector was seen as the key to the success of this process (African Development Bank/OECD 1993).

However, the privatization process has been characterized by severe social and political problems since 1988, when youth demonstrations were harshly repressed by the government, leading to continuous political upheavals. This serious and long-standing social unrest has been a fertile ground for Islamic fundamentalists. As well as this employee resistance to change and the considerable support given to the main Algerian trade union, the Union Générale des Travailleurs Algériens (UGTA) have meant that the privatization process has been characterized by a start–stop pattern which has made sustained macroeconomic recovery very elusive.

The privatization process emerged as part of an overall reform package caused by a severe economic crisis. As stated in an article, "not later than 1993, Algeria's economy was in the grip of a severe financial crisis that left the authorities with no other alternative than the inevitable rescheduling of the external debt and the undertaking of comprehensive economic reforms" (Aghrout and Hodd 2005). In response to this crisis the Algerian authorities formulated a comprehensive structural adjustment programme that received the support of the IMF in May 1994, through a 1-year Stand-By Arrangement totalling SDR 731.5 million and, from May 1995, through a 3-year arrangement under the Extended Fund Facility totalling SDR 1.1 billion (IMF 1995).

May 1994 witnessed the initial move towards privatization which was the Loi de Finance Complementaire, in which Articles 24–25 authorized the privatization of SOEs, under terms and conditions which allowed for up to 49 per cent of the equity of a public enterprise to be acquired by private persons or legal entities through both the Stock Exchange and the negotiated agreements. These included the partial divestment of entire production units of SOEs, or in other cases, when the management of a SOE could be divested to the private sector. This law also permitted public/private JVs.

Later, additional legislation for privatization was approved in August 1995 in the shape of Ordonnance 95-22, which provided for up to 100 per cent privatization, on a case-by-case basis, of a very wide range of economic activities, such as hotels and the tourist industry, the building and construction industry, the distributive sector, ports and airports, textile manufacturing and agribusiness, some processing industries, roads, and regional small- and medium-sized enterprises. This law also initiated the framework for the Conseil de Privatization tasked with the implementation of Algeria's complete privatization programme. However, its methodology was unwieldy and subject to too much red tape, although the process was simplified in 1997 by Ordonnance 97-12 (World Bank 2000).

Ordonnance 95–22 was consolidated in 1995 by Ordonnance 95-25, Gestion de Capitaux Marchands de l 'Etat. This originally established 11 (which was increased later to 12) sectoral, and 5 regional, public holding companies, with overall responsibility for the management and administration of all the public enterprises falling under the portfolios concerned. These were controlled and directed by the Conseil National des Participations de I 'Etat (CNPE), which comprised of 17 Ministers, headed by the Prime Minister backed up by a technical Secretariat.

Under this legislation, public enterprises and public holding companies, as joint-stock companies, were given the right to dispose of their assets in line with the Algerian Commercial Code, including divesting them following a simple procedure under the stipulations for partial privatization. Public enterprises could therefore sell their assets, even by breaking them into individual units for divestment, to private buyers or contribute them as part of the assets of new JVs with private partners. If approved by CNPE, the public holding companies created were allowed to sell full units or significant equity stakes of public enterprises in their portfolio.

The public holding companies have been instrumental in introducing some accountability in enterprises, where managers had previously acted without much accountability by the State, and in the house cleaning and preparing many enterprises in their portfolios prior to the privatization exercise. This involved the introduction of proper accounting systems and the submission of more reliable financial statements, as well as the regularization of their property titles as well as financial restructuring involving huge debt write-offs by the State and reductions in staff. The holding companies have downsized many large conglomerates as well as liquidating many enterprises on life support systems. This massive liquidation effort resulted in the closure of 935 out of a total of 1,324 local public enterprises, and of 76 out of a total of 411 national public enterprises, with the costs of industrial and financial restructuring massive. In the context of this restructuring, some 320,000 employees were laid off in the period of 1996 and 1998 alone. At the same time, the regional holding companies facilitated the creation of some 1,050 new private enterprises through spin-off or sale of assets to employees and managers, resulting in an estimated 25,000 job creations. Under the partial privatization regime, the holding companies also arranged for three public offerings at the newly created Algiers Stock Exchange, involving 20 per cent of shares each for a pharmaceutical enterprise, a food-processing firm, and a large hotel in Algiers, as well as for eight JVs, six of which originated with the holding companies for chemistry and pharmacy, and mining (World Bank 2000).

The Conseil de Privatization was asked to prepare the total privatization of 88 SOEs with a total of 383 subsidiaries through international competitive bidding. A first batch of 35 subsidiaries was offered for sale late in 1998, followed by a second batch of 26 subsidiaries in February 1999. However, because of major political changes in 1999, the process was not continued, in spite of the fact that 36 tenders submitted, many from international investors, met technical qualifications and exceeded the stipulated minimum price.

Although the Algerian government launched a 3-year Economic Revival and Support Plan (PSRE) in 2001 to encourage economic growth, the poor social and political situation have produced a vicious circle which is pushing standards of living down even further. As authoritative commentators on the Algerian economy stated in 2005, the key reforms now on the agenda are the privatization of the still substantial number of state-owned enterprises, and the re-structuring of the financial sector to include the introduction of international banks (Aghrout and Hodd 2003). But the fact remains that more than 15 years after Algeria started in the long process of market liberalization and privatization, the combination of poor evaluation practices applied for SOEs and the persistent lack of transparency in the privatization process have severely impacted its progress so far. Indeed, out of a total number of 1,280 SOEs slated for privatization, only 111 privatization deals were concluded in 2004.

Much discussion relating to privatization have also surrounded Sonatrach, the Algerian national oil and gas company, when, in the early 2000s, ambitious plans for its partial privatization and deregulation were drawn up by Dr. Chekib Khelil, Algeria's Minister for Energy and Mines, and formerly OPEC President in 2001, aimed at redefining the state's role in the regulation, production, and marketing of oil, effectively opening it up to competition and private investment.

Sonatrach's current deregulation programme is aimed at a complete liberalization of the hydrocarbon sector, by fully commercializing the company and separating its operational procedures and responsibilities from those of its owner, the state, to expose it to full competition. "The only responsibility Sonatrach should have", says Dr. Khelil, "is to make money, create employment and be competitive". Although there has been much controversy and misunderstanding surrounding Sonatrach's deregulation, Chetib has gone on record as saying in March 2005, "Sonatrach will not be privatised – the new legislation envisages the reorganisation of the national energy sector and not its privatisation. The Algerian state has no intention of losing its control over the energy and mineral sectors" (Otman and Karlberg 2005).

6.3.4 Jordan: A Pragmatic Approach

While successive governments in Jordan have promoted a market economy based on individual initiative and the forces of supply and demand, the public sector has continued to play a vital role in strategizing and directing economic policies to serve the national economy, including both subsidies and fixed pricing of goods and services whenever needed. The public sector's role has also extended to the construction, development, and maintenance of the country's infrastructure. It is also in partnership with the private sector in producing major commodities such as cement, phosphate, and potash, and providing utilities and infrastructure such as electricity, communications, public transport, tourist and industrial investments, and others, in situations where the private sector was unable to shoulder the burden of those projects alone, or where there was high risk involved.

However, on account of the increased private sector involvement in the country's economic life, as well as the growing entrepreneurship of many Jordanian businessmen, together with the rapidly increasing economic, social, legislative, and regulatory responsibilities of the government, privatization was seen as a viable option towards the beginning of 1985. It was therefore was part of an overall economic package that the government adopted in this period, as part of an economic adjustment programme emphasising self-reliance in response to the economic crisis afflicting Jordan at that point.

Not only this, but the government required a new approach to the impacts of globalization, including a more competitive environment, the lifting of customs and administrative barriers in regional alignments, capital inflows, all of which were underpinned by the communications and information revolution. This dictated a corresponding policy change by Jordan to open up to the world, through partnership agreements with the European Union and accession to the World Trade Organization. To come to terms with these new global realities the government had to devise a new set of macroeconomic and microeconomic objectives, many of which could only be achieved through privatization.

Privatization in Jordan was therefore dictated by new realities, with policies devised and determined as a result of various surveys and studies of public sector projects and institutions. The findings of these studies showed that many public sector institutions and corporations were grossly inefficient in terms of both administrative and employment policies, at the same time squandering public funds, while the level of service delivery to the public was extremely low. Invariably they had very high levels of indebtedness to the state.

The government of Jordan was thus faced with a situation in which many of its public enterprises had massive accumulated losses, while future development of the economy was hampered by lack of funds for necessary infrastructure development. As an example, cumulative losses in the Transport and Water Sectors alone, by the end of 1998, amounted to more than 20 per cent of GDP.

Objectives of Privatization in Jordan

Based on the findings of these studies of the public sector a list of objectives targeted by the privatization process was drawn up. These were as follows:

- Optimizing project efficiency, productivity, and competitiveness by activating market forces and eliminating economic imbalances and distortions.
- Mobilizing domestic savings and attracting more private domestic Arab and foreign investments by opening up the markets and abolishing state monopolies.
- Stemming the flow of public funds by way of assistance or loans to private projects, in order to alleviate the financial burden of the Treasury.

- Reducing the need to turn to external lending for the purposes of covering the deficit of existing projects or the financing of new projects.
- Deepening the local capital market and directing private savings towards long-term investments.
- Facilitating access to much needed technology and modern management techniques to foster competitiveness in the global markets as well as providing access to new and stable markets.

Progress and Framework of Privatization in Jordan

To regulate the privatization process, the government established a special unit within the Prime Minister's department in July 1996, named the Executive Privatization Unit (EPU), under the supervision of a higher council chaired by the Prime Minister, with its membership comprising of several ministers and heads of the departments involved. The EPU was responsible for the implementation of the privatization process within the framework of the government's overall policy. As such it performed several tasks, including the selection of projects to be privatized, project assessment and valuation, the selection of the appropriate form of privatization, the preparation of offers to interested parties, and the appraisal of offers submitted for privatization.

Given the importance of privatization in Jordan, and with the aim of providing an appropriate legislative framework, the Privatization Law No. 25 of the year 2000 was promulgated. It set out explicit provisions to regulate the privatization process and to enable its implementation, and provided the necessary ground rules for the transparency and clarity of the implementation procedures of privatization operations under mechanisms subject to government control. Some of the most salient features of Law No. 25 are as follows:

- The setting up of a Higher Ministerial Committee for Privatization, chaired by the Prime Minister, with the membership of the Minister of Finance, the Minister of Trade and Industry, the Minister of Planning, the Minister of Justice, the Governor of the Central Bank of Jordan, the Chairman of the Executive Privatization Commission (EPC), the President of the Accounting Board, the relevant minister when any issue related to that ministry or any connected institution is to be discussed, and three experts appointed by the Council of Ministers upon recommendation of the Prime Minister.
- The establishment of the EPC, which is the legal successor to the EPU. One of the most important objectives of the new EPC was to study and follow up on the implementation of restructuring and privatization operations.
- The establishment of the Privatisation Revenue Fund, under the supervision of the Higher Ministerial Committee for Privatization.
- The granting to the government of distinct voting powers through the "Golden Share" concept, enabling it to oppose resolutions of a Company's Board of Directors if the national interest so determines this.

As a result of the Jordanian government's policy, the privatization of government institutions and corporations proceeded steadily. Below we summarize only a small representative sample of the most significant recent privatizations in Jordan.

Public Transport Corporation (PTC)

- The Corporation was split into four units under a concession-type agreement.
- The PTC signed 10-year agreements with three local companies to operate buses on the inner lines of Greater-Amman municipality; 165 new buses were operated to serve customers on these lines.

Jordan Telecommunications Corporation

On 23 January 2000, 40 per cent of Jordan Telecom Company (JTC) shares were sold to the Arab Bank/France Telecom consortium, 1 per cent to the employees' Savings Fund and 8 per cent to the Social Security Corporation. On 15 September 2000, MOBILECOM, a JTC wholly owned cellular-phone company, was set up and started its operations. The government then sold 15 per cent of its share in JTC through an IPO in Jordan, the Arabian Gulf, and Europe, from 9 October to 29 October 2002. And 70 per cent of the offered shares were sold, which represented 10.5 per cent of the Company's capital. Thereafter, the government's ownership represented 41.5 per cent of the capital of JTC.

Water Authority of Jordan

In April 1999 an agreement was signed with Lyonnaise Des Eaux Company to manage the water network in the Greater Amman area. After signing this agreement, Jordan was able to secure a $55 million loan from the World Bank to maintain the water network in the Greater Amman area.

Electricity Sector

The Electricity Power Authority was converted to the National Electricity Power Company, wholly owned by the government, and its activities were separated into three: generation, distribution, and transport. The generation and distribution were privatized, while transport and electrical control activities continue to be owned by the government, with a German consulting company Fitchner hired to assist in company separation. A study on the privatization strategy of the generation and distribution companies was prepared in December 2002. This covered evaluation of companies for privatization; the submission of recommendations on development of the regulatory and legal framework of the electricity power sector, in line with the objectives of attracting domestic and foreign investment; the preparation of technical documents on the companies to be privatized in February 2002; and the selection of an appropriate privatization method, either selling out to a strategic investor or selling out to a financial and technical syndicate, that is a group of financial investors including a technical partner.

Aqaba Port

In 2001 the privatization strategy for Aqaba Port was agreed. This comprised of splitting up the port activities and services into separate units, and the phased privatization of these units. The government kept its ownership of the installations and land along with its supervisory role, while the investment, management, operation, and maintenance were privatized.

Arab Potash Company

This privatization approach consisted of separating the Company's main activities from the supporting ones (transportation, housing and medical services, and others). This allowed for private sector investment and the selection of the best privatization options for the Company's expansionist plans, improving the standard of services provided, and enhancing the Company's efficiency and competitiveness. The government sold 50 per cent of its share in the Arab Potash Company, amounting to 21,622,550 shares on 16 October 2003 to a strategic holder; the Canadian Potash Corporation of Sasketchewan, with government ownership declining to 27 per cent.

The Benefits of Privatization to the Jordanian Economy

Jordan's privatization programme has been so successful that "it has ranks as one, if not the most, successful programmes in the Middle East region... A closer look at how Jordan managed to activate a stagnant privatisation programme and achieve so much in so short a time holds important lessons for governments as well as privatisation practitioners... the honours go to the government and people of Jordan for steadfastly dealing with the overwhelmingly complex issues one-by-one and making the [privatization] programme a grand success" (World Bank 2001).

Privatization proceeds at the end of 2003 reached more than US $1,200 million or 16 per cent of GDP and according to the new Privatization Law, privatization proceeds are to be invested in a separate fund to be used to repay loans owed by the privatized firms to the government, and finance economic and social development projects.

Privatization has yielded direct fiscal benefits for the Government. In the case of PTC, for example, the government no longer has to subsidize up the US $2.1 million of annual losses. In addition, the US $0.8 million in annual franchise fees from the new operators will go directly to the Government's budget. Net profit of Jordan Cement and Fertiliser has increased by 50 per cent in the first year alone, contributing an additional estimated US $3.5 million in tax revenues. Investments of approximately US $500, directly related to privatization, are scheduled for the next 4 years. Most of the investments relate to the Tourism and Telecommunication Sectors. In the Telecommunication Sector alone, it is anticipated there will be close to US $400 million of new investment. In the Power Sector, the IPP is expected to invest a total of US $300 million.

The Water Authority of Jordan transaction enabled Jordan to obtain a US $55 million World Bank investment loan. Furthermore, a new water treatment plant costing US $150 million will be funded, with 50 per cent by the private sector on a BOT basis and the rest through donor grants. Also in the water sector, the 320 km conveyor of fossil water from Disi to Amman, at a cost of US $700 million, will be financed on a BOT basis. These privatization-related investments, totalling more than US $2.1 billion, averaging seven per cent of GDP per year during the next 4 years, have become important factors for the revival of the Jordanian economy.

Jobs are being created due to the new private sector investments and opportunities. Although it is still early to assess the impact of the Programme on employment, preliminary evidence indicates that already more than 6,000 jobs have been created on a net basis relative to a labour force of about one million. As indicated above, according to the strategy, no one has lost their jobs involuntarily, but the Programme may have generated pockets of hidden unemployment. Employees of the old enterprises have either been retained in the new privatized organizations or transferred or absorbed in other agencies, either into vacant positions or merely in pending outplacement opportunities. Nevertheless, the experience clearly shows that opening up sectors such as Telecommunication to private sector competition can produce new jobs quickly.

Consumer benefits are also being seen from the privatization programme. The waiting period for a telephone line has been reduced from years to weeks, and phone rates, though still high according to international standards, have been reduced significantly. The PTC transaction has yielded immediate results. With private investment, buses are more frequent and usage has increased dramatically from 60,000 to 100,000, while the fares have remained the same. On a more qualitative level, the buses are new, clean inside, and less polluting. This has been a boon to the average working person whose commute has been significantly reduced, in some cases from two hours each way every day to under half an hour, and has enabled them to seek employment opportunities in locations which were previously difficult to reach except by car or taxi.

We have looked at the Jordanian experience in some detail, because we believe that its pragmatic and flexible approach was the key to its success. Although there was a strong legal and institutional framework initially put in place, an analysis of the methodologies and approaches to the sale of individual Jordanian SOEs shows that each case was privatized in a different way. For example, the divestiture of the Jordanian Investment Company's varied portfolio was accomplished on a case-to-case basis, with sales of publicly held shares going sometimes to new investors, to employees, or the Social Security Fund, while in the case of the electricity sector, the selection of an appropriate privatization method, either selling out to a strategic investor or selling out to a financial and technical syndicate, that is a group of financial investors including a technical partner, was open to consideration. Again, as we have seen, in the case of the Water Authority of Jordan, a long-term concession was given to the Lyonnaise Des Eaux Company, which in turn enabled the Jordanian government to secure a $55 million World Bank loan to maintain the water network in the Greater Amman area.

6.4 The Libyan Experience

6.4.1 Nationalization and Privatization, Untying the Knot

Since the early 1970s, the Libyan government, in line with its socialist ideology, had embarked on a programme of state-sponsored economic development and control of the economy. Throughout this period the government expanded its role, effectively taking control of the entire Libyan economy. As well as nationalizing the key hydrocarbon industry, the Libyan state established controlling interests in the supply and operation of electricity, water, transportation, communications, the ports, and airports, while public corporations also entered the banking, insurance, and retail markets. The Nasco, a publicly owned import company the operations of which were explained in detail in Chap. 4, was also, in the early 1970s, awarded a monopoly for the import and sale of many basic consumer items.

In the context of its time, the Libyan nationalization programme was not unique. From the 1950s to the mid-1970s, in line with a general anti-colonial backlash in the plethora of newly independent nations which emerged at the end of the Second World War, many foreign-owned resource firms were nationalized, a process which many have argued, had a variety of negative long-term consequences for many developing states. As early as 1952, for example, the Iranians nationalized the Anglo-Persian Oil Company and created the National Iranian Oil Company. Thereafter, a succession of major nationalization programmes took place in countries such as Indonesia, Egypt, Sri Lanka, and Cuba, with shipping, land, mining, and hydrocarbon industries, utilities and airlines as targets.

It has been posited that the legacy of this massive global wave of nationalization resulted in many negative consequences for those countries, such as Libya, which had gone through the privatization cycle. What, in the 30 years since this massive global wave of nationalization, are the perceived negative consequences of nationalization? First, it has been contended, foreign multinationals and in-country foreign JVs could have acted as buffers against export instability; but when these were nationalized, the governments and economies of developing states became directly impacted by international market shocks (Shafer 1995). This was, for example, what occurred to the Libyan economy when the oil price collapsed in 1896, 1993, and 1998 when ambitious development plans had to be put on hold. Secondly, state ownership may have also "softened" the budget constraints of resource exporting governments, producing fiscal laxity (Kornai 1986). Finally, and most obviously, SOEs are generally exceptionally inefficient and overstaffed, with the ability to cover losses "by increasing the next annual budgetary requirements"; often they operated in developing countries under thinly disguised cronyism and paternalism (e.g. the Philippines under Marcos, Indonesia under Suharto).

In the period of more than three decades which have passed since this massive nationalization programme, it has become apparent to all that the nationalized and centralized system of government in Libya has failed to deliver its economic goals. As Colonel Qadhafi himself stated publicly at the General People's Congress in Sirte in January 2000, "…the system is finished. I have to step in today to stop this wheel from spinning in a rut and wasting fuel", accusing

Members of the GPC of deliberately wasting the country's resources, saying, "You're holding onto obsolete methods in order to justify wasting oil."

Following this, in June 2003, he called for the privatization of the oil, banking, public sector companies, and the aviation sector. On 24 November 2003 the new Libyan Prime Minister, Dr. Shukri Ghanem, announced a comprehensive plan for privatizing state-owned factories and companies, stating that the plan would cover "privatisation of mineral industries, especially iron, steel, chemical industries, and factories to assemble trucks and buses, textile, and shoe companies, and state owned farms". He added that the initial number of companies in covered in the privatization plan would be more than 360, while the plan itself was to be applied in three phases until the year 2008, stating that "the Central Bank will sell shares of these companies and factories until a stock market is founded". He stressed that this plan was aimed at "improving the national economic performance and the living standards of individuals through expanding the base of property owners". It is worth noting, however, that this was not the first Libyan effort to expand Libya's entrepreneurial base in the decades succeeding the 1970s.

6.4.2 Early Attempts at Privatization in Libya

As a socialist state defined by Article 6 of the Constitutional Declaration of 1969, the massive nationalization process which took place throughout the 1970s was effected to reduce perceived social inequalities, effectively to return exploitative businesses, whether domestic or foreign, to the Libyan people. The role of the state in this operation was to act as a trustee of these nationalized and publicly owned productive assets, which in fact were ultimately owned by the people. By the mid-1980s, when the new government had consolidated its position and had successfully embarked on and accomplished ambitious education, housing, and health programmes, as was elaborated in Chap. 4, initial efforts were made to accomplish this handover from the state to the workers, the de facto owners of state-directed and state-managed businesses.

The first stage in this process came in 1986 when the People's Congress passed Law No. 1, laying the ground rules for worker's ownership through Syarika Musahima (Participation Companies or Share Holding Companies). Linked to this, the government, in the same Law, established the National Investment Company (NIC), whose main objective was to bring about the ownership of state companies by Libyans. The NIC was to be funded by using the 1.5 per cent of compulsory salary contributions from Libyan employees in the state enterprises under the Law No. 15 of 1981, as well as a sum of not less than 60 LD per annum per employee working in the private sector.

In practice the start of the ownership transformation programme came in 1987 when the General People's Committee issued Resolutions No. 219 and No. 225, followed by Resolutions No. 183 and No. 214 of 1988, regarding the transfer of certain of these factories to private shareholders. But these resolutions proved to be ineffective, a contributing factor being that, in overall economic terms, for the first time since the 1973 oil boom, the Libyan government faced trade balance deficits in the 3 years from 1987 to 1989 which diverted its activities to more pressing matters.

The need for policy change and the extent of the inefficiency of the Public Manufacturing Sector at this period can be gauged from Table 6.14.

In 1989 the General People's Committee issued a new Resolution, No. 427, regarding the creation of machinery for implementing the transformation of state economic units to private ownership. In this law the responsibilities for achieving these aims were assigned to the relevant Cabinet Secretariats (Ministries) and the provincial authorities. Under this system the government would receive payment of the amount of the "tamleek", or cost of privatization, from the financial returns of the units to be privatized. However, as specified in Article 7, the privatization or ownership certificate could only be issued after the new shareholders had together paid one-fifth of the cost of acquiring all the shares in the company. However, the period for subsequent payment of the remainder four-fifths was not specified, only that future available income from the business operations could be used to pay for this.

However, in practice, all of these resolutions were ineffective and were unable to achieve their objectives, which was the transfer of ownership of state enterprises to the employees who worked in them. In the few cases when such

Table 6.14. Libyan public sector, 1988: maximum design capacities and utilization

Factory	Maximum design capacity	Actual capacity	Utilization rate (%)
Flour mill, Al-Marj	60,000 tons	10,780 tons	18.0
Flour mills, Benina	105,000 tons	18,212 tons	17.0
Flour mill, Tobruk	45,000 tons	14,758 tons	32.8
Fodder factory, Benghazi	288,000 tons	154,000 tons	53.8
Fodder factory, Tobruk	192,000 tons	108,000 tons	56.0
Fodder factory, Al-Abiar	56,700 tons	29,346 tons	51.7
Cement factory, Al-Hawari	2,000,000 tons	458,300 tons (1987)	21.0
Cement factory, Al-Fatayeh	1,000,000 tons	293,000 tons (1986)	29.0
Longitudinally welded pipes factory	40,000 units	16,938 units	32.0
Spirally welded pipes factory	75,000 tons	3,336 units	4.0
Spray irrigation pipes factory	6,000,000 M^3	3,140,896 M^3	52.0
Oxygen factory	504,000 M^3	307,756 M^3	61.0
Acetylene factory	120,000 kg	65,378 kg	54.5
Blankets complex, Al-Marj:			
a. Blankets	475,000 blanket	199,216 blankets	41.9
b. Mattresses	500,00 mattresses	96,000 sq.ft	19.3
Modern tannery, Benghazi	–	1,780,000 sq. ft	29.6
Cables factory	6,000,000 sq.ft	2,210 tons	28.0
Hair wire factory	8,000 tons	960 tons	48.0
Dairy factory, Green mountain	200 tons	–	–
Juice factory Beida	–	2,087,736 boxes	34.8
Beverage Factory, Benghazi	6,000,000 boxes	1,321, 660 boxes	16.5

Source: Aleslam, 2002.

transfers took place, "the appropriated foundations (i.e. factories transferred to the ownership and control of the employees) suffered from deterioration in performance and production was similar to if not worse than their modest output when they were part of the public sector" (Aleslam 2002). The same author goes on to provide reasons why this happened, which imply the lack of a support system for these units either before or after transfer from the public sector.

> Perhaps the methods followed in the transfer of ownership were partly responsible for that because these foundations had not been restructured before the appropriation process in such a way that secures good performance afterwards. Furthermore, these foundations continued to work under the umbrella of the public foundations. Add to that the fact that the transfer of ownership was limited only to the people working in the foundations. (Aleslam 2002)

Working under this public umbrella meant that economic success after transfer would always be elusive. The sanctions on Libya at this time also meant that spare parts for machinery for the transferred factories were not only expensive, and the hard currency to acquire them in very short supply, but that technically trained staff to service foreign manufactured machinery were unavailable. On the other hand, it also meant that prices of the manufactured goods in the newly privatized units were still controlled by the Economy Secretariat (Ministry) as was normal in a centralized economy, so that it was difficult if not impossible to manufacture profitably as in a market economy.

By the early 1990s, not only was Libya suffering seriously from the effects of the sanctions, but a drop in oil prices was placing a huge strain on the Libyan state's ability to finance its massive and inefficient public sector. It was in an effort to correct the defects of these earlier resolutions and to try to share the burden of the crippling public sector costs with the private sector that the General People's Congress issued another privatization law, Law No. 9 of September 1992.

Law No. 9 covered privatization issues in Articles 9–15. Article 10, for example, dealt with the transfer of ownership from the public to the private sector, while Articles 11 and 12 provided for credit from state and commercial banks to support newly privatized companies, also permitting relief from income tax. Other provisions contained in Article 5 limited individual percentages of shares in the privatized SOEs.

In 1993 the General People's Committee passed Resolution No. 300, again regarding the privatization policy for state enterprises. This regulation was much more comprehensive than Resolution No. 427 of 1989. It clearly specified the body responsible for the privatization or "tamleek" process, in this case the Central Committee established by the General People's Committee, which consisted of a Secretary (Chairman) and members who were specialists and experts in their respective fields or sectors. However, many observers in Libya believed at the time that the power and autonomy of the Central Committee was extremely limited, with power over key processes such as establishing evaluation committees for the businesses to be privatized still directly under the authority of the General People's Committee.

As well as this, other measures towards economic liberalization or "infitah" were announced by the Libyan government in 1993. These included the liberalization of the wholesale trade and the right to form partnerships for that purpose, provided for in Decree No. 491. Later in 1993 and in 1994 there were provisions approved for legal guarantees covering foreign capital investment, permission for the promotion of tourism through assistance from foreign companies, as well as regulations liberalizing the convertibility of the Libyan Dinar. In fact, taken together, the legal framework for privatization and infitah were extensive and far-reaching (Vanderwalle 1998).

But in actuality very little was achieved throughout the 1990s. Again, an illustration of just how grossly inefficient the majority of manufacturing companies in the Public Sector SOEs were at the end of the 1990s is shown in Table 6.15.

Why had so little been achieved towards privatization in Libya in this earlier phase? The basic reason was that, through its earlier dismantling of a market economy in the 1970s by the nationalization process, which had affected every business and every sector, the Libyan government had abolished the very institutions and entrepreneurial spirit which were necessary to ensure its success. Few people in Libya were willing to trade the uncertain economic future of a full-scale market economy for the steady wages and subsidies which enabled them to enjoy a standard of living envied by their neighbours. At the same time, the main beneficiaries of the public ownership system such as the middle and senior managers, the military, and the technocrats who ran the oil business and derived many benefits from it, as well as the political elite, had little to benefit from a major change in the status quo.

Table 6.15. Libya public sector, 30th September 1999: achieved production as percentages of maximum capacity

Company name	Achieved production as percentage of maximum capacity (%)
Textile national company	60
Furniture public company	60
Trailer national manufacturing company	54
National company for soap and cleaning materials	33
Aman company for tyres and batteries	33
General company for pipes	33
Arab company for manufacturing and bottling	28
National company for foodstuffs	24
General company for paper	20
General company for plastic and artificial sponge	12
Libyan company for tractors	5

Source: Aleslam, 2002.

6.4.3 Recent Privatization Policy in Libya

The General Board of Ownership Transfer (GBOT) ("Tamleek")

As we was noted above, earlier efforts at privatization in the period from the mid-1980s up to the new century did not succeed, due to a variety of factors. In one important respect the Libyan government eventually recognized its failure. This was with regard to one crucial component of the entire privatization process, the setting up of an independent and autonomous privatization board or commission similar, for example, to the EPC established in Article 9 of the Jordanian Privatization Law No. 25/2000. To address this deficiency, the GPC issued Regulation No. 198 in 2000, regarding the establishment of the GBOT as a sovereign and financially independent state body similar to other Secretariats (Ministries) and under the direct supervision of the General People's Committee (the Cabinet).

Powers and Responsibilities of the GBOT

The GBOT reported to the General People's Committee (the Libyan Cabinet) and was delegated with executing the programme of transferring the ownership of Public Companies and Economic Units to the Private Sector. This policy was intended to widen the base of ownership, to expand the domestic economic sector, to develop proficiency efficiency and competitive capability in the production and services sector, and to contribute in general to the economic development process of the nation.

The responsibilities/remit of the GBOT were set forth and elaborated in line with the bylaws for transfer ownership stated by the General Peoples Committee Resolution No. 31 of 2003 (discussed in the next section) and can be summarized as follows:

- To perform preliminary studies relating to the companies and economic units targeted for transfer ownership (privatization), to recommend plans for their transfer and present these to the Secretary of the General People's Committee or the People's Committee of the relevant Sha'abiyat for approval to proceed.
- To determine the most suitable way to effect transfer of ownership for each public company or economic unit in line with their levels of technical capability, and to decide on the necessary procedure to restructure them in preparation for a fast and successful transfer of ownership.
- To list the surplus assets of the company or economical unit targeted for transfer of ownership, estimate their value, and set regulations for action in accordance with existing legislations and to identify the appropriate method or mechanism for each unit to be privatized.
- To evaluate the target company and its assets in a way that reflects its present financial position according to normal financial practices.

- To establish Syarika Musahima (Participation Companies or Share Holding Companies) and Tashrukkiyah (Partnerships) to hold the assets of the target companies and underwrite them.
- To present the findings of the evaluation of the target units ready for ownership transfer before approved by the Secretary of the General People's Committee.
- To follow up on the outcome of transfer of ownership and to arrange for payment for privatization to be made to a special account opened for that purpose.
- To coordinate with all the authorities concerned to effect a transfer of ownership that will would speedily assist in accomplishing the successful implementation of the transfer ownership programme.
- To suggest investment opportunities suitable for foreign investment.

Modus Operandi of GBOT

- The GBOT was to perform its functions through a group of administrative centres and offices which were to undertake a sequence of initial planning studies, follow-ups, execution, and right through to operational phase of the newly privatized company, as well as the preparation of periodic reports.
- It was to rely on a group of permanent committees of experts and specialists in different fields to supervise the process of company selection and analysis, and the follow-up of GBOT business and ownership transfer activities in every Sha'abiyat.
- The evaluation of individual companies or economic units was to be undertaken by a group of local experts/institutions and committees formed for this purpose. Such an evaluation was to be achieved objectively and in line with a company's technical abilities in accordance with the domestic business environment, at the same time opening the door for cooperation with foreign investors if deemed necessary.
- The establishment of Syarika Musahima and Tashrukkiyah was to be accomplished by competent committees formed by the GBOT to arrange for all the legal procedures framework covering the issue of new shares, and to undertake the promotion and marketing of the shares in every possible way, directly or through other parties qualified for the job, together with suitable legal advisors.

Future Activities: Additional Responsibilities of the GBOT

- To ensure that the ambitious timetable for transfer of ownership was executed efficiently and in a timely manner within the time frame laid down.
- To enable the new owners/investors to benefit from different various financing opportunities made available to underwrite share acquisition.
- To prepare a comprehensive publicity programme including symposia, conferences and media advertising.

- To prepare feasibility studies to show how Libya would benefit from the capabilities of foreign investors by enabling them to acquire shares in SOEs.
- To study the employment situation and the impact of the transfer of ownership programme on the employment market, both before and after the different phases of the programme.

6.4.4 Framework and Evolution of Key Legislation

As well as the legislation of 2000 which established the GBOT, the next key piece of legislation which initiated the privatization programme after the appointment of Dr. Shukri Ghanem as Prime Minister in June 2003 was Resolution No. 31 of 2003 issued by the General People's Committee, together with its articles and regulations. This was a very significant piece of legislation which signalled that the Libyan government was preparing to embark on a major privatization exercise, similar to those which had been undertaken much earlier in the 1980s and 1990s by its North African neighbours, Morocco and Tunisia, and, to a lesser extent, Algeria.

Another key piece of privatization legislation was the General People Committee Resolution No. 92 of 2003, amended by Resolution No. 64 of 2004, which, together, established the Higher Committee for Administrating the Programme of Transformation of Property. Its mandate was to create and put in place the underlying strategy regarding the transfer of SOEs to the private sector, to identify and specify the units to be privatized, to approve the evaluations made for individual units, with the flexibility to follow up on all the necessary procedures and the requirements, and to guarantee the success of the privatization process and its targets.

As well as this, Supervisory Committees to monitor the progress of the privatization programme in the each Sha'abiyat were established, in line with the General People's Committee Regulation No. 93 of 2003. These, consisting of members from representative bodies who were experts and specialists in their fields, representatives from the Sha'abiyat, and representatives from the General Producers (Labourers or Workers) Unions. These regional committees were set up to provide linkage with other bodies participating in the privatization process, as well as to supervise the actual transfer of units or companies from the public to the private sectors according to locality.

Combined, Regulation No. 198 in 2000 and Resolutions No. 31, 92, and 93 of 2003 must therefore be seen as the key legislation which placed the Libyan privatization process on a sound legal and administrative footing, and these were reinforced by a series of related resolutions to ensure the success of the privatization programme. These were as follows:

- General People's Committee (GPC) Resolution No. 42 of 2003, regarding the establishment of the Domestic Manufacturers Support Fund (DMSF).
- The GPC Resolution No. 94 of 2003, regarding the transfer of certain general departments in SOEs targeted for privatization to the DMSF.

- The GPC Resolution No. 95 of 2003, regarding the transferring of the debts of SOEs from Commercial Banks to the DMSF.
- The GPC Resolution No. 96 of 2003, regarding the transfer of certain obligations to the DMSF.
- The GPC Resolution No. 98 of 2003, regarding the transfer of debts due to the Social Security Supporting Fund by SOEs to be privatized to the DMSF.
- The GPC Resolution No. 100 of 2003, regarding the transfer of the debts of those SOEs to be privatized due to the Development Bank and Foreign Banks to the DMSF.

By issuing these key regulations the Libyan government, in transferring the accumulated debts of the state enterprises to the DMSF, set the stage for state enterprises to be privatized debt-free.

As well as this, the General People's Committee passed a series of supportive regulations aimed at assisting SOEs targeted for privatization to achieve successful privatization through a package of flexible support mechanisms. These included the following:

- The GPC Resolution No. 97 of 2003, placing production and consumption taxes on certain commodities.
- The GPC Resolution No. 99 of 2003, Article 1 of which stated that state units after privatization were free from income tax, production taxes, customs duties, and charges on operating equipment, spare parts, raw materials, and all ancillary equipment required for operation, for a period of five years starting from the effective date of privatization.

Taken together, this series of resolutions established a comprehensive framework within which the government felt confident in proceeding with its privatization plans. Consequently, the GPC passed Resolution No. 100 of 2004, in which it appointed the GBOT to commence with the privatization process, for the initial transfer of 126 state units to the private sector.

It is in this connection that it is important to note that Law No. 1 of 2004 which amended Law No. 21 of 2001, together with Regulation No. 53 of 2004, regarding the Practice of Economic Activities, which was discussed at length in Chap. 3, were also very significant in setting the scene and redefining a suitable legal and institutional base for privatization. For example, in Section Five of Law No. 1 "Joint-venture Companies", Articles 22–30 defined Joint Venture and Holding companies, permitting nominal shareholdings. This has important implications for future PPPs and FDI, as well as bringing Libya in line with modern company law and foreign investment practices. Section Nine, which discusses "Facilities and Assistances", again deals with the availability of credit from state banks for both share acquisitions and development capital for newly privatized companies, while Section Ten "Financial Paper Markets" effectively prepares the way for a Libyan Stock Exchange through Article 59, which states, "The rules related to the organization of the financial papers market, determination of its competencies and body undertaking the supervision of its works, and other relevant rules, are issued by virtue of a decision to be taken by the Secretariat of the General People's Committee."

Later, GPC Decision No. 52 of March 2005 on the Issuance of Regulation for Privatizing Companies and Economic Units was approved. In this legislation, all the major legislation and GPC decisions relating to the privatization process, as far back as the year 1970, and including but not limited to all the Laws and Decisions, together with their underlying principles as discussed extensively above, were defined, with the main objective of the entire privatization programme unequivocally defined in Article 2. This stated, "privatising companies means to transfer the ownership of the companies from public sector to private sector to give a more important role to the private sector in the economic field". While the first part deals with issues and mechanisms discussed previously, the section headed "Partnership base for Foreign Investment", and Articles 43–63 deal with future privatization issues in relation to foreign acquisition of Libyan SOEs. Again, Article 43 reiterates that foreign investment or management would only be permitted in two situations. The first is if it would to improve the technical, economic and administrative skills of companies and the SOEs which depended for production on local raw materials, or had foreign markets for their products, while the second is for projects or SOEs in which shares to be divested exceed the national market's capacity to absorb.

The means for publicizing the sale of these major Libyan SOEs, such as through the printed media, the Internet, and Libyan foreign embassies, is also dealt with in Article 48, as well as the time frame (60 days) within which offers for these must be made. In Articles 56 and 57 issues relating to the percentage of shares to be sold in such SOEs are covered, and also the concept of private sector management of SOEs without sale. In Article 58 the Libyan authorities bite the bullet, and it is stated for the first time that "If the results of the pre-privatisation study of economic units currently or in the future exhibit obstructions to the privatisation process due to technical, financial or marketing reasons, their sale without their employees either as a whole or in units can be done by auction according to GPC Decision No.8 of 2004 regarding Administrative Contracts."

6.4.5 Implementation of the Privatization Programme

In practice the actual privatization process, in line with Resolution No. 31 of 2003, commenced with the naming of 360 SOEs for privatization in a wide range of sectors, including industrial, agricultural, animal, and marine resources (Table 6.16). It specified that they should be privatized either in full, or as PPPs, over three stages. The first stage comprised 260 companies, to be accomplished in the period from 1 January 2004 to 31 December 2005; the second phase, covering 46 units, was to take place within the period from 1 July 2004 to 30 June 2007; while the third phase encompassing 54 units, which would become PPPs, was scheduled to take place between 1 January 2004 and 30 December 2008.

Table 6.16. Libya: proposed initial 360 state economic units for privatization

Phase	Industrial project	Agriculture projects	Livestock projects	Marine projects	Total
First phase	145	28	71	16	260
Second phase	41	4	0	1	46
Third phase	18	24	11	1	54
Total	204	56	82	18	360

Underlying the privatization process was a series of principles or conditions which had to be met before a company could become a candidate for privatization. These were as follows:

- The unit or company to be privatized had to be free of any prior obligations such as bank loans, outstanding taxes, outstanding social security payments, creditors, or unpaid wages and salaries.
- The new owners had the right to keep what they wanted or needed from moveable assets such as raw materials, stock, spare parts, and machinery and also the right to own the real estate, land, or maintain the leasehold arrangements of the previous public owner.
- The assets of the company to be privatized had to be valued fairly based on both their age and their remaining technical capability.
- A study had to be undertaken to evaluate the labour requirement of the privatized unit to ensure its efficient operation, and the issue of the situation of surplus workers had to be dealt with before privatization could take place.
- Finance for new investment in the privatized company could be raised through public invitation.
- The privatized company was to be free of all taxes and customs duty for a period of 5 years from the date of privatization.
- The government would encourage Libyan banks to support the newly privatized units and arrange for them to provide subsidized loans to these units at the rate of 3 per cent per annum.

In order to secure privatization goals and to achieve greater economic efficiency, employees were encouraged to become owners by means of an attractive and flexible government-assisted scheme:

- Depending on the size and value of each company, factory, or project, shares in the target company should first be offered in whole or in part to the employees, with small units being offered directly to the existing employees and, if they did not take these up, to private investors.
- To acquire their shares in the privatized company, the government made it possible for employees to withdraw and use their accumulated 1.5% salary contributions made compulsory by Law No. 1 of 1986 as payment for these shares.

- Any due wages, salaries, or vacation pay could also be used in kind to acquire shares in the privatized company.

6.4.6 Employees Made Redundant by the Privatization Process

As we have seen earlier in the privatization policies and experience of MENA countries and elsewhere, the thorny question of employees surplus to requirement after the privatization of SOEs was one of the most fundamental issues facing their respective privatization programmes, since without doubt, in the pursuit of efficiency and productivity, a reduction in employee numbers was, initially at least, the norm in post-privatizations. In general the Libyan approach to this crucial issue was guided by the following principles:

- There was to be a separation between employee ownership and the right to work, that is ownership did not guarantee a job in the privatized company. This was based on the right of the new owners to determine labour needs and numbers using criteria based on the efficient operation of the business. Should an existing employee be seen as necessary and productive he/she would be retained, but there was no guarantee of this.
- This meant that no employee had any right to expect favourable treatment; this was because prior to approval of privatization for that particular company, a plan had to be proposed by the new shareholders regarding the selection and numbers of employees in the privatized company. This post-privatization employee plan had to be approved by the GBOT, which would earlier have decided whether a new job in the public sector could be found for an employee made redundant by privatization, failing which the employee would have to take early retirement.

6.4.7 The Legality of Privatization in Libya

In view of the socialist nature of the Libyan state in which everything is theoretically owned by the people, with the state acting simply as custodian, observers both within and without Libya have questioned the legality of privatization, that is does it contravene those articles of the Constitutional Declaration of 1969 such as Articles 6 (Socialism), 7 (Economy), and 8 (Property), as well as the 1977 Declaration on the Establishment of the Authority of the People, where in the preamble it is stated that the Libyan people "declare their adherence to socialism as a means of achieving People's ownership".

It would appear that this has been addressed by Resolution No. 15 of 2001 of the General People Congress, which called for the establishment of a committee to recommend the reconstruction and deregulation of the state enterprises, by offering shares in them by public invitation to the private sector, or as joint partnership investments, or the complete shutdown of very sick state enterprises.

Again, during the 2002 Annual Meetings of the Libyan Basic Congresses, followed up by the passing of the final draft resolutions made by the General

People's Congress as Regulation No. 1 of 2003, Libyan society was urged to improve the performance of SOEs and also to increase the involvement of the private sector in them.

From both of these laws, therefore, it appears that the privatization programme is based on solid legal ground. However, as was discussed in Chap. 3, should the principles enunciated in the Constitutional Declaration of 1969 and the 1977 Declaration on the Establishment of the Authority of the People have been a fundamental part of a unified Libyan constitution, it would not have been possible, or, if possible, not easy to change these and provide a legal basis for privatization.

6.4.8 Details of the Current Status of the Privatization Process in Libyan SOEs Identified for Privatization

The First Group for Privatization

By the the end of 2004 the GBOT had, in line with General People's Committee Regulation No.100 of that year had finalized the details, approved the valuation of the assets, and put the legal framework in place for the privatization of 126 SOEs units in line with General People's Committee Regulation No. 100 of 2004 (Appendix 6.1). It had identified the method of privatization for these companies based on their legal character as either Syarika Musahima or Tashrukkiyah. These were defined using the following guidelines:

- Tashrukkiyah Sanaia (Industry) were for factories or productions units with less than 100 employees with an approved privatization value of less than 500,000 LD.
- Syarika Musahima with special bidding or subscription for units with less than 100 employees and a net asset value (the approved amount for privatization) of not more than 1 million LD.
- Syarika Musahima using public invitation applied to all the companies, factories, and units with more than 150 employees, with a net asset value (i.e. the approved amount for privatization) more than 1 million LD.

Payment for these targeted privatized units was to be effected over a 5-year period through bank loans and the other methods discussed above. The privatization was to be free of taxes, customs duties, and charges on the buildings and lands belonging to the privatized SOE for a 3-year period. Transfer (privatization) of all the units were to be free from any previous claims and the new owners rights to specify the assets required by them.

The Second Group for Privatization

A second group, characterized as medium size, was also identified for privatization, with these units available for privatization through public invitation characterized as medium size, and the method for their privatization was based on an independent accounting and technical evaluation. The most suitable mechanism for their privatization was determined to be through the establishment of Syarika Musahima whose share capital was in line with their privatization values. Their privatization was to be achieved by public invitation from Libyan investors, after specifying the percentage of the shares earmarked for the employees already working in these SOEs. These are detailed in Appendix 6.2.

The Third Group for Privatization

These SOEs were identified for privatization through PPP or JV investments, and are characterized as significantly larger investments than those previously mentioned (Appendices 6.3–6.6), with their output being considered to be of strategic importance to the Libyan economy, and they were characterized as too large and technologically difficult for the Libyan private sector to absorb, not only on account of massive acquisition costs, but also because of further investment required to update them to improve their efficiency. They comprised of 54 economic units, divided into 18 industrial, 24 agricultural, 11 livestock, and 1 marine unit. The GBOT recommended that these SOEs were more suitable for joint investment with international groups, to be arranged through international offerings, after first determining the percentage of shares available for public invitation to Libyan citizens and local investors.

6.4.9 Results of the First Year of Privatization

By the end of 2004, 14 Libyan SOEs had been successfully privatized, as shown in Appendix 6.7. Analysing this appendix enables us to draw two brief conclusions about the early success, or lack of it, in the Libyan privatization process, which will be considerably expanded in the conclusion of this chapter. First, it seems that, with only 14 units successfully privatized at the end of 2004, the process appeared to be inordinately slow. Secondly, the presentation of the data by GBOT was not transparent, especially regarding the total value of the privatizations which gives the total but not individual privatization values, for reasons that are not clear. Such lack of transparency sends out wrong signals both to concerned Libyan citizens currently following the privatization process, as well as to foreign observers who will be interested in future privatization opportunities in Libya.

6.4.10 The Privatization Record, January 2005–August 2006

As stated above, despite a huge amount of legislative change, as well as investigative groundwork, asset evaluations, and legal changes performed by the GBOT, privatization results by the end of 2004 could only be described as disappointing. On 20 June 2005, a major change in the privatization framework was effected when the General People's Committee (Cabinet) transferred the supervision of the GBOT from the direct control of the Prime Minister to the Secretariat (Ministry) of Economy, Trade, and Investment. It is worth noting that this Ministry at the time was headed by Dr. Abdulgader Omar Belkhair, who can be regarded as a protégé of Dr. Ghanem, confirmed later during the major cabinet reshuffle in March 2006 in which the Prime Minister lost his job, with Dr. Abdulgader also losing his portfolio.

In retrospect, the exact motives for this change are difficult to comprehend. It could simply be interpreted as a straightforward delegation of authority, with the Prime Minister confident that, with an apparently comprehensive legislative framework in place to move the privatization process forward, he wished to deal with other pressing issues related to Libya's ambitious economic makeover. More cynical observers might perceive it as the first sign that the privatization programme was running into serious difficulties, with the Prime Minister in effect handing over responsibility for the implementation of the privatization programme to one of his subordinates, to divert future personal attacks on him and his privatization approach. Whatever the actual reasons for this move, it appeared that obstacles in implementing the programme had emerged, probably connected with the valuations of the assets of target companies, in particular the land and buildings owned by them, part of the GBOT's remit, as defined in Resolution No. 31 of 2003.

Despite this, a further piece of privatization legislation, the General People's Committee Resolution No. 107 was issued on 21 June 2005, approving the GBOT's evaluation of a further 21 SOEs (Appendix 6.8) and granting approval for their privatization, confirmed in Article 1. Article Two highlighted that these economic units would be privatized without any financial or other obligations, and provided that the GBOT should follow through all the legal procedures required for their privatization, while Article 3 provided that the employees of these 21 SOEs, to be privatized as Syarika Musahima, would be allowed to apply for 30 per cent of the shares of each company. Payment for these shares was to be effected by 20 per cent immediately on purchase, with the balance payable over 3 years. In this regard, employees' compulsory Social Security payments previously deducted from their salaries under Law No. 1 of 1986 was to be made available to them for payment. Finally, Article 4 specifically mentioned the rights of the new shareholders to benefit from the future sale of land on which these economic units operated and which was owned by them.

But in the year which succeeded the issuing of this resolution, there were signs that the privatization process had run into serious obstacles, because in that period nothing had been concluded regarding the privatization of these 21 SOEs. This was highlighted by the Cabinet's Resolution No. 341 of 13 August 2006, concerning the establishment of a new high level committee to deal with privatization delays and issues, consisting of eight members. The Chairman was the Secretary of the General People's Committee (the Prime Minister), with two members each from the Secretariats of Finance and of Economy, Trade and Investment, and one each from the Secretariat of Manpower, Training and Employment, of Industry, Electricity and Mines, and of Justice.

The remit of this high level committee was to investigate the reasons for the delays of all the previously established committees regarding the evaluation process of the SOEs targeted for privatization. Article 3 of this decision specified that this committee had to complete its investigations and submit its report by 31 December 2006.

This was succeeded by another Resolution of the new Libyan Cabinet, No. 199 on 20 August 2006, in which the supervision and approval for the privatization for these same 21 economic units was transferred to the Secretariat of Industry, Electricity, and Mines, newly established after the Cabinet reshuffle of March 2006. Article 2 of this resolution gave this secretariat full power to supervise the evaluation and auditing process for these SOEs, but this time with the participation and assistance of the Centre of Economic Studies in Benghazi as well as the GBOT. To the authors, the implications of bringing in and specifying a third party for assistance in economic appraisal was that the GBOT, on its own, had not been able to satisfactorily accomplish the process of evaluation, a key part of the privatization process and one, as seen in other countries, open to abuse and financial manipulation.

On the same date, 20 August 2006, a further Resolution related to the privatization programme, No. 200, was issued by the Cabinet. Article 1 approved the privatization of a further 21 SOEs (Appendix 6.9) through the Secretariat of Industry, Electricity and Mines, while Article 2 specifically provided for the complete supervision by this Secretariat of all the preliminaries, including valuation, for their privatization. Specifically, there was no mention of the role of GBOT. Finally, Article 3 cancelled all previous regulations in conflict with this Resolution.

Finally, on the same date, 20 August 2006, a further Resolution related to privatization, No. 201 was issued. Article 1 of this resolution specified that the Secretariat of Industry, Electricity, and Mines was to supervise, with immediate effect, and follow up on all the activities of all SOEs privatized from 2004 up to August, 2006, amounting to 67, with a total value of LD 696,136,174 (Appendix 6.10).

6.4.11 Lessons from Privatization

Before commenting in detail, in the next section, on the Libyan privatization experience up to August 2006, the authors believe that it is worthwhile considering some of the most obvious lessons learned through more than 30 years of global privatization. By understanding these, it is felt that valuable insights can be gained to perhaps understand why the Libyan privatization programme has, if not currently stalled, at the least run into serious obstacles.

The present global wave of privatization which started in the United Kingdom in the 1970s is still ongoing, and it is now generally accepted that the process has been beneficial in terms of improving economic efficiency. As two researchers have stated, "on the whole, privatisation has proven its economic worth. The shift to private ownership generally improves a firm's performance. There are some exceptions, but this finding holds up in most countries, including some that are very poor, and many of the formerly socialist economies in the transition region. Post-privatisation, profitability has generally increased, often substantially, as have output dividends and investment" (Birdsall and Nellis 2002). This view has been reinforced by an intensive literature review covering 65 empirical studies at the firm level, and across firms within and across countries, in which the authors conclude flatly that "privately-owned firms are more efficient and more profitable than otherwise-comparable state-owned firms" (Megginson and Netter, 2001).

As we have observed from our survey of the privatization experience of countries ranging as widely as Argentina, Malaysia, Egypt, Tunisia, Morocco, Jordan, and Libya, there is no "one method fits all". At the same time, considerable experience in privatization has been gained over the previous 25 years in practical terms and methodologies, and it can now be said that a consensus is emerging about the main requirements for the implementation of a successful privatization programme. These lessons can be summarized as follows.

There Is Not a Perfect or "Right" Approach

In a given country, the privatization process must be adapted to the circumstances of the country and the condition of the SOEs to be privatized. Although as we have seen there are a number of generally accepted privatization methods, only careful preparation, timing, and sequencing can guarantee success. The emphasis should be on flexibility and willingness to try new solutions and methods, rather than imposing a rigid set of rules which must deal with all situations.

Privatization Should Be Accompanied by Structural Reforms

Governments can only effectively implement privatization programmes within a framework of related economic reforms, including macroeconomic and currency stabilization, trade liberalization, banking and financial sector reform and development, public sector reform, social security reform, and regulatory reform. If these reforms are delayed, privatization cannot be sustainable and will not achieve its goals of economic restructuring.

High Level Political Support

There must be political will and support at the highest level to ensure privatization's success, and it must receive such support to overcome inertia and resistance from the bureaucracy, as we noted in the Egyptian case, as well as special interests, as for example the unions during the Thatcher period. The implementation should be the responsibility of pragmatic individuals with political clout and no vested interest in the status quo. At the very minimum, the privatization agency should report to a senior minister, if not the Prime Minister or the President.

The Leader of the Privatization Body Is of Crucial Importance

The leadership of the Privatization Body is crucial in ensuring the success of a privatization programme. The ability of the top leader/leaders in this body to access and influence top politicians, economists, and decision-makers is vital in maintaining the political will, support, and sustainability of the privatization process. These leadership skills will, in the long term, nurture and develop the Privatization Body to grow and build within itself the needed technical competencies to better support and keep the privatization process on course.

Pre-privatization Restructuring: Focused and Limited

Pre-privatization restructuring should only concern itself with SOEs' balance sheet assets and debts, as well as organizational changes such as decisions to close or wind up particular SOEs, workforce reductions, and transfers of social services. Major technology changes involving capital investment and equipment purchases should be left to the new owners, not to government officials.

Educating the Public

Informing and educating the public prior to and during privatization is very important. Countries with successful privatization programmes have placed strong emphasis on preparing the ground by educating the public about the needs for privatization. Media campaigns such as newspaper articles and TV programmes and debates can help to overcome initial resistance.

The Timetable Issue

Governments should not announce and try to adhere strictly to an artificially fixed timetable. Although there is always pressure for the privatization to proceed quickly, unrealistic timetables serve little purpose. One useful approach is to sequence several sales according to market conditions. Moreover, governments should bear in mind that not all transactions will be successful, and that it might be necessary to reject all bids and start the bidding process anew or change the method of divestiture.

The First Privatization Transaction Is Crucial

High profile, early successes are essential in capturing the public imagination and securing investor interest, and thus the choice of the first major privatization is crucial. It needs to be completed successfully in order to get the privatization process going, even if these need to be "stage managed" to a certain extent. In the cases of Malaysia and Jordan this helped to allay many of the apprehensions regarding privatization and provided institutional confidence to pursue other major privatizations, while demonstrating the immediate benefits of privatization.

The Role of World-Class Technical Expertise

In designing and implementing a national privatization policy, it is important to use world-class expertise and consultants. This is because, although privatization is a public process, it requires private sector skills. The manner in which businesses or assets are transferred from the public to the private sector is complex, time-consuming, and often resource- and highly labour-intensive.

Developing Institutional Competence and Experience

Government institutions responsible for privatization must gain experience and develop competence with the process. Privatizing state enterprises is difficult, and often requires commercial skills that officials in developing and transition economies do not have. To develop this expertise, a single privatization body should be established to gain experience over time. Spreading the privatization effort over a number of institutions or ministries is a mistake, and will lead to conflicts and undermine the institutional capacity needed in privatization. Moreover, the privatization agency should be adequately funded so that it can hire financial, legal, and other advisers, as required.

Transparency in the Decision-Making Process

Transparency generally includes two aspects. First, ensuring competition in bidding and pricing to get the best deal for the country, and secondly the avoidance of side deals. The consensus approach had both a cost and a benefit. The cost is that progress may seem to be slow with large committees and several approval levels. However, the benefit is that, when progress is achieved, it is more sustainable and on a more solid foundation with support from most of the major constituencies in the country.

Valuation, Transaction Design and Structure

In this, probably the most crucial stage of the privatization exercise, effeciency needs to be balanced with transparency. Valuation of the SOE is of paramount importance because it establishes a market price range for the enterprise. Valuations based on market principles are essential to stifle criticisms that the state is not receiving a fair price and to ensure that there is sufficient investor interest. In Western market economies valuation is based on discounted cash-flow projections of future earnings and comparisons of similar firms' market prices (when sold through trade or negotiated sales) or stock market's offer valuations (if publicly traded). Replacement value and book value are not measures of market value. Book value may understate real value because it is based on historical costs, and replacement value may overstate value because firms are often sold below replacement cost. In addition to the valuation, financial advisers often prepare a sensitivity analysis that models the purchase price under changing conditions prior to the closure of the transaction.

A Privatization Law: Important but Not Essential

Countries with a civil law tradition such as Egypt, Tunisia, Algeria, and Libya have normally approached privatization by preparing a general privatization law.

This law will define the rules and targets of the privatization programme and establish and empower the institutions charged with executing it. But this is not always necessary. For example, Canada and the United Kingdom and countries with a common law tradition have privatized without a privatization law, using specific legislation only where required. Privatization laws can have both advantages and disadvantages. When carefully drafted, they strengthen the state's capacity to carry out structural reforms. They also help make more transparent the transfer of state property to the private sector. Once ratified, however, a law cannot easily be changed. If procedures need to be revised in response to market conditions, an amended law or new regulations may be required. Also, as was noted in the case of Egyptian privatization, the existence of too many and often conflicting laws have made the privatization process both slow and unwieldy.

Privatization and FDI

Privatization of major SOEs should be structured to attract foreign investment. Against this, there exists in certain countries an argument that, in general, foreign investors have no interest or stake in the long-term economic or social well-being of the country in which they are investing. This leads them to behave and treat their investments in a way they would not either consider or be allowed to in their "home" environment. The conduct of Shell in the upstream hydrocarbon industry of Nigeria in the period 1985–2005 is one of the most cited examples of this. But there are compelling arguments, as the privatization experience of the above-mentioned period has demonstrated, to show that returns to governments from any sale or contracting out are likely to be higher due to fully competitive bidding, which should involve all interested parties, foreign and domestic.

International capital markets and/or strategic investors may also be able to absorb greater investment than the domestic market can support. Subsequent tax revenues from the privatized SOE are likely to be higher due to the greater economic efficiency engendered by technology, knowledge, and managerial skills transfer offered by international investor. In this respect the state must assure foreign investors that it will not use its political power, residual shares, or "golden share" in a way that might influence the company's ability to maximize profits and efficiency. Again, management and staff will tend to benefit from foreign ownership. The involvement of direct foreign investment often brings with it the pressure to move towards international standards on pay and conditions. The impact of this trend is both to improve the day-to-day terms and conditions of employees in privatized companies, as well as to open up opportunities for access to new training, and career development models not always accessible in the domestic market.

Privatizing the Monopolies: The Key Role of the Regulator

A natural monopoly has been defined as an industry or service that does not lend itself to competition because of the monopolistic nature of its infrastructure such as pipelines, cables, roads, and so on. In general this definition has usually been applied to electricity, water, and communications networks. The argument against their privatization is that because these industries are naturally monopolistic, they cannot be privatized because of the risk to the public interest of giving private operators unfettered monopoly power over the geographical reach of services as well as prices and tariffs. Apparently, the state is supposed to be better able to defend the public interest, so therefore a state-owned monopoly is acceptable.

In actuality state-owned monopolies across the world have proven themselves unable to invest properly in infrastructure, often offering relatively expensive and inefficient services, and have poor labour relations records. Generally they also have poor customer service records, often combined with little or no incentives for good management and staff.

The key to a successful privatization of a monopoly is a successful regulation policy. This is at the same time a key part of the presentation package to selling privatized monopolies, since no one will buy unless they know the post-sale rules the business will be forced to operate under, as well as a prerequisite to ensure that such monopolies are rendered politically acceptable. Indeed, it has come to be regarded as the single greatest catalyst of privatization, giving governments a means of protecting consumers whilst allowing investors a reasonable return on their investment. Ultimately, regulation is no more than a transitional mechanism until full competition can be introduced but in the more complex industries this period could be many years, even decades in development. Where regulation has not been introduced, significant litigation and significant confusion have often arisen. The independence of the regulator is crucial as he/she is charged with safeguarding both public and investor interests. Choosing the right candidate and even the method of choice can present significant challenges in themselves.

The objective of the regulator should be to encourage efficiency and give investors a chance to earn a reasonable rate of return. Regulators should be as independent as possible from political interference. Capricious or politically driven regulations detract from the value of an enterprise being privatized and, in extreme cases, can make privatization impossible. It is also important not to give the regulator too much power. If the regulator is allowed to influence investment and business priorities then this is bad, because it merely transfers the inefficiencies of the state sector policy-making machine from state-owned SOEs to state-controlled (through regulation) SOEs. In this type of situation it is clear that getting the balance right is the key to success.

Strategic Industries – To Privatize or Not?

In selecting companies for privatization, many countries have drafted a positive list, which covers SOEs that can be privatized, and a negative list, containing SOEs that cannot be privatized, because they are considered to be strategic. A positive list is useful because it has the full power of the law behind it. Companies are committed to privatization within the deadline for the programme, and can be privatized at any time by the institution in charge of executing the transfers. With regard to the negative list, as many countries have learned, private ownership does not necessarily imply a loss of state control. Thus many state enterprises that were once deemed strategic, for example oil and gas companies, telecommunications firms, water, and other utilities, have already been privatized. Many governments have chosen not to have a positive or a negative list, preferring to privatize state enterprises without restriction, as and when market conditions appear favourable, as we have noted in the generally opportunistic and pragmatic approach that Jordan has taken.

Overcoming the Commitment Problem

The commitment problem arises because governments are sometimes tempted to diverge from or reverse economic policies over time, and because institutions are not strong enough to prevent such reversals. Commitment problems increase the perceived risk of expropriation and drive out investment. In post-socialist economies, for example, governments face a particularly severe commitment problem because of the vast influence of state enterprises which were the nexus of a powerful coalition of beneficiaries with privileged access to public resources. In addition, governments in transition economies – as elsewhere – have encountered public hostility towards the sale of a country's "crown jewels" to foreign investors.

In some countries the commitment problem is pronounced by two features of the institutional and legal framework: overlapping jurisdictions and excessive discretionary authority. Many countries have a proliferation of veto-holding agencies, each with the power to obstruct cash sales of state enterprises. For example, privatization powers are often divided between the line ministries responsible for an enterprise and the agencies responsible for the mechanics of the sale and (possibly in another body) the oversight of privatization programmes and sales. There are good reasons for policy makers to prefer discretion to rules if governments are fragmented. Discretion is flexible; rules are not. With discretionary powers, enterprises can be sheltered in friendly ministries or municipalities, offering useful leverage for parties or factions with uncertain political futures. Moreover, discretion is opaque, not subject to the oversight of regulators, courts, and the like. Although good institutions cannot eliminate a large number of veto holders and an inclination towards discretionary policy-making, they can ameliorate them. Autonomy and rationality in institutional design are of particular importance. Autonomy is the extent to which an institution is insulated from outside interference, and thus from the veto power held by politicians or social groups. Rationality is the degree to which institutional procedures are based on uniform rules that must be followed.

The Redundant Employee Issue

It is often argued that public sector reform, particularly where it results in full-scale privatization, will always be to the detriment of state sector employees.

This means that, first, there must be in place a set of general rules covering the rights of employees in all privatized enterprises and institutions. Secondly, transition packages, including compensation based on service as we noted with the Tunisian FREEP, must also be put in place. Share ownership in the privatized SOE on advantageous financial terms is also an incentive in some cases, as are training and placement assistance to help the workers during the transition phase which might mean redundancy for them. However, once governments decide on the need for privatization, they must inevitably proceed and somehow deal with the employment issue. The implicit logic in this seems to be that if the labour issue prevented privatization, the government would need to continue to employ these people anyway, so why not privatize.

In fact experience since the 1980s has often shown that the labour issue has been grossly overstated. This is because privatization has the same liberating effects on former state employees as it does on other aspects of the business and economy in general. Employees can benefit in a number of ways. State sector employment usually entails regimented working conditions and limited flexibility, either in working methods or in pay and rewards systems.

This also applies to career development. Promotion and mobility in the state sector is often limited and predetermined by length of service rather than ability. Training and career development programmes are also focused, when they exist at all, on narrow priorities and do not provide employees with the latest skills needed to function in the modern job market. The private sector, if for nothing more than its own self-interest, has far more motivation to train its employees to the highest standards and using the latest techniques. This is not to suggest that there are not many capable employees in the state sector, only that they often lack the tools to succeed.

Flexibility in working conditions, better pay and conditions, performance-related remuneration which treats people as individuals not faceless groups, and better training to equip employees for a more complicated world – these are the benefits often overlooked when discussing privatization and its impact on state employees.

6.4.12 Privatization in Libya – Quo Vadis?

The current ongoing privatization process in Libya, as we have noted, seems to fulfil the definition of the "privatization wheel", that is an economy originally having its entire retail and private sector arbitrarily shut down and nationalized in the 1970s, now in the process of being restructured for significantly greater private involvement. Underlying this is a frank admission by senior figures in Libya that many of the economic attributes and institutions of the previous 37 years have failed to produce an efficient economic system. In fact, there is growing evidence which suggests that privatization is no longer just an option but an undeniable necessity for Libya, with the burden of a massive public sector continuously expanding.

Although it is still rather early to predict its outcome, since only a little over 3 years have transpired since the appointment in June 2003 of Dr. Shukri Ghanem as Libyan Prime Minister to drive the economic reform process forward, we feel that it might be worth commenting on how the privatization process and its institutional framework have been set up in Libya, and how these relate, in view of the extensive literature and experience of the privatization experience in many countries since the 1980s, to its long-term chances of success.

As discussed earlier Libya, like Jordan and Egypt, has opted for a privatization commission or board, in this case the GBOT. The fact that it reported directly to the Libyan Prime Minister signalled that it has strong support at the very highest levels in Libyan government. But as was noted earlier, on 20 June 2005, a major change in the privatization framework took place when the General People's Committee (Cabinet) Resolution No. 217 transferred the control over the GBOT from the Prime Minister to the Secretariat (Ministry) of Economy, Trade, and Investment. Later, in March 2006, the Prime Minster himself was removed in a major cabinet reshuffle and transferred to become head of the Libyan National Oil Corporation. These frequent changes in the personalities or authorities driving the privatization process cause confusion and delays, and also much conjecture regarding the motives behind them.

These changes also demonstrated that the General People's Congress, as the supreme law-making body in Libya, which in fact appointed Dr. Ghanem in the first place as Prime Minister, has the power to derail the privatization process if, as it proceeds, it begins to upset political figures and alliances. Many key members of the political establishment, who have held positions at the highest political levels in Libya for the period 1975–2005, represent a powerful force. An example of this was the Libyan Prime Minister's backing down in the case of the proposed privatization of the Libyan Marine Company, due to concerns mainly related to labour redundancy debated during the General People's Congress Annual Meeting in Sirte in 2004, when he was taken to task on this issue by the GPC.

Again, if we look in detail, as discussed earlier, at the facility offered to workers to acquire shares in the company to be privatized, the government stated that it was possible for them to withdraw, and use their accumulated 1.5 per cent salary contributions, made compulsory by Law No. 1 since 1986, as payment for such shares. Again, this raises several issues. First, the government only stated it was possible to do this but did not explain the circumstances in which such possibility applied. Secondly, even if this was known, and a worker did have access to and use these accumulated funds to acquire shares in his/her privatized company, why could not another worker who, say, did not want to acquire these shares, simply ask for the cash?

The right of the new owners, whether workers or not, as determined in the reconstruction exercise carried out by the GBOT before offers for privatization, to decide on employment categories and numbers also seems to leave many questions unanswered about crucial issues relating to post-privatization downsizing. For example, the fate of a worker made redundant will be decided by the GBOT who will either allocate him/her to a new job in the public sector or, if unsuccessful, force him/her to take early retirement, which is clearly very unsatisfactory. In this connection the role and function of the Tunisian government agency responsible for dealing with redundancies caused by privatization appears to be much more focused and, from the point of view of the worker concerned, more realistic. The Tunisian "Fund of Rationalization of the Employment in the Public Enterprises" (FREEP) guaranteed, in 1990, that laid-off workers would receive a severance package based on 1 month's salary for each year of work with a cap of 12; in addition, they received a bonus of 30 per cent. Starting in 1991, the severance payment was increased to 2 months' salary plus one for each year of work with no cap.

In other respects, the institutional framework for the privatization process might appear to some observers to be somewhat unwieldy, with, as we have seen, four separate entities involved in the privatization process: the Higher Committee for Administrating the Programme of Transformation of Property, the GBOT itself, the Supervisory Committees of the GBOT in the Sha'abiyat, and the DMSF. While this might mean that a system of checks and balances exists to combat corruption in such areas as asset valuation, there clearly also exists a lot of room for extemporising and delay in any of these entities, thus slowing down the privatization process. As well as this, it appears that the level of representation of the Libyan General Federation of Producers Trade Unions in the various privatization entities would also appear to be very low – surely a serious omission in view of the organization, which ostensibly represents those stakeholders most affected by the privatization exercise.

It would also appear that little has been done in Libya, apart from the press and TV coverage on individual privatized units, towards formulating a comprehensive and coordinated publicity plan to educate the public about the key issues surrounding privatization as well as its benefits, that is a public awareness programme. The global experience since the 1980s has shown that major policy changes such as privatization can often fail because inadequate attention is paid to the communications support necessary to build and maintain public support for such major reforms. Privatization can and does affect millions of consumers, suppliers, investors, and, very importantly, workers. Well-designed and effectively executed communications programmes are essential so that the public and key stakeholders understand the nature of privatization, the benefits it will bring and the alternatives if it does not take place. Without this, the political risks increase and the obstacles to change can quickly become insurmountable.

Again, as we discussed earlier, the announcement of fixed timetables to achieve specific privatization objectives often puts unnecessary strain on a government and its privatization board. Although, in the nature of any policy advocating change, there is always pressure for the privatization process to proceed quickly, unrealistic timetables serve little purpose. One useful approach is to sequence several sales according to market conditions. Moreover, governments should bear in mind that not all transactions will be successful, and that it might be necessary to reject all bids and start the bidding process anew or change the method of divestiture. In this respect, again the Tunisian approach appeared to work. Here the government stated that eventually all SOEs would be privatized, but did not state which ones would be first, or when each one would happen. In taking this approach the "Commission d'Assainissement et de Restructuration des Entreprises à Participation Publique" (CAREPP), the Tunisian privatization authority, gained important benefits. It prevented the management of individual SOEs from developing a complacent attitude once they did not see their companies on the list, encouraging them towards greater efficiency to prevent this happening. At the same time, public sector employees were not faced with the uncertainties and psychological impact of seeing their organization as part of a list of companies to be privatized, thus preventing general public opposition.

If we look at the current status of Libya's privatization programme as of August 2006, data published by the government shows that 67 SOEs have been privatized.

This is very far behind the privatization schedule announced in 2003, where it stated that the first stage of privatization, comprising 260 companies, would be completed in the period from 1 January 2004 to 31 December 2005, while the second stage, covering 46 units, was to take place within the period from 1 July 2004 to 30 June 2007, a period of 3 years of which only 9 months remained at the time of writing (September 2006). As commented on earlier, the formation, through Resolution No. 341 of 13 August 2006, of a new high level committee to deal with privatization delays and issues, clearly demonstrates that the privatization programme has run into serious problems. In our view, however, the establishment of yet another committee to deal with these might only serve to complicate existing affairs, which are complex enough. A more positive approach would be to establish, as soon as possible, a dedicated Libyan Secretariat for Privatization, with strong political backing and the ability to reinvigorate the machinery of the GBOT, to once again drive the process forward. Global experience in the past has shown that a Prime Minister or the head of another Ministry such as Economy, Trade and Investment cannot have the time, together with his/her other responsibilities, to comprehensively and effectively supervise what is a highly complex and often socially contentious process.

In this regard we believe that the Libyan government has failed to understand the true dimensions of the problems associated with a major privatization programme. As stated earlier, privatization is a public sector reform which requires private sector skills. In an earlier section, the global experience since the 1980s has shown that the role of world-class technical expertise in the entire process can never be overestimated. The way in which businesses or assets are transferred from the public to the private sector is an extremely complex, time-consuming and often resource- and highly labour-intensive. For example, at the height of the Russian privatization programme in the mid-1990s one consultancy firm alone had over 800 staff dedicated full time to managing the process on behalf of government (Leary 1999).

In comparative terms, it is useful to look at the Polish experience from 1989 to 1992. In the 3 years, by the end of 1992, small privatization in Poland was almost complete, with the successful privatization of 194,000 units, that is 82 per cent of the units existing in 1989. Most of such units were in retail trade and services; they were allocated to former employees at well below market value, and in many ways were similar in size and employee numbers to the 260 state enterprises which were to be initially privatized in Libya. Small-scale privatization in Poland was relatively non-contentious, and has been judged to have been a great success, in terms of improving the quality and quantity of the services and goods provided, in creating a large number of jobs for those shifting out of the restructured SOEs and privatized firms, and in generally smoothing the path for the return of capitalism (World Bank 2002).

But assuming that Libya can deal successfully with the privatization of its small SOEs, and this seems to be a large assumption at the moment, the fundamental privatization problem in Libya will be the issue of the privatization of medium- and large-sized firms. Methods and experience derived from the OECD and middle-income privatizing countries clearly show how slowly the nationalization process of these actually unfolded. In the United Kingdom, for example, Margaret

Thatcher's enthusiastic and dedicated privatization team had managed to divest about only 20 companies in a 10-year period.

Although the Libyan government has shown its willingness to undertake economic reforms such as currency stabilization, and trade liberalization, and has gone some way towards banking and financial sector reform, we believe that in one important respect its privatization policy cannot succeed until it does what Morocco (Casablanca) and Jordan (Amman) did in 1996 and 1999 respectively, that is to privatize its stock exchange. Although the way forward for this in Libya was paved through Regulation No. 53 of 2004, regarding the Practice of Economic Activities, under Sect. 10, Article 59 which allows for "the organization of the financial papers market, determination of its competencies and body undertaking the supervision of its works, and other relevant rules". It was, however, only in May, 2006, almost 2 years into the privatization programme, that an official announcement regarding the establishment of a Libyan Stock Exchange was made.

It is difficult to imagine, without a fully operational stock exchange, how an effective privatization programme in Libya can be accomplished. The advantages of using public share offerings on stock markets for privatizations of large, profitable, and relatively well-known state enterprises are now well documented in the literature, with the landmark privatization of British Telecom in 1982 as the trendsetter. The success of the privatization experiences of Morocco and Jordan to date are inconceivable without the ability of their stock exchanges both to absorb the size of the offerings, as well as to successfully attract FDI to privatization offerings on their exchanges, such as, for example, Vivendi Universal's acquisition of an operating control of Maroc Telecom in 2001, and the sale of 52 per cent of the capital of Morocco's Union International de Banques to France's Societe Generale in 2002.

As well as guaranteeing value for money for the SOE offered, international privatization sales through the stock market also achieve other desirable economic objectives such as broadening share ownership by allocating a portion of shares to small investors. Not only this but recent economic research has conclusively documented a direct link between capital market development and economic growth (Henry 2000a). It is because of this link that many governments have adopted share issue privatization programmes as a means to jump-start the growth of their capital markets.

Again, research has shown that the market value of privatized firms grew from less than $50 billion in 1983 to almost $2.5 trillion in 1999, that is roughly 10 per cent of the world's aggregate market capitalization, and 21 per cent of the non-US total, while privatized firms are the most valuable companies in seven of the ten largest non-US stock markets, including the four largest, as well as in most developing countries (Megginson 2002). Based on the findings of such empirical evidence, it is difficult to be optimistic about the long-term success of the Libyan privatization programme without the active participation of a stock exchange.

With regard to the domestic banking sector, there is also evidence to suggest that in terms of experience and technology it is ill-prepared to play its role in a major privatization exercise, although several steps towards the economic and legal reform of this sector have already been taken, as early as 1993 in fact, when the establishment of branches of foreign banks in Libya was permitted. There have also been, in late 2004, several media reports that five Libyan domestic banks were to be privatized. These include the Jamariya Bank, the Libyan Arab Foreign Bank, the National Commercial Bank, Al-Sahari Bank, and the Wahda Bank. In this connection the Central Bank of Libya in June 2005 announced that "in order to expand the public shareholding base of Sahara Bank, and to boost private sector investments, it will make a public offering to Libyans of its entire stake in this bank at the price of LD 10 per share".

Since that initial announcement the offer period for shares in Sahara Bank was extended, suggesting a rather lukewarm response from the Libyan public to acquire, on the ground floor, shares in the leading commercial bank in Libya, with 44 branches around Libya, and ranked among the best 25 Arab banks. Eventually in 2006, the government succeeded in attracting interest in only 15 per cent of the offered shares in the bank. Another major domestic bank, the Wahda Bank, is also currently being considered for divestment, again to Libyans only. But again, media reports suggest that this divestiture process might take up to 2 years, after which "the Libyan Central Bank may look at the possibility of foreign institutions entering the local market".

The slow pace and lack of transparency surrounding the privatization of these major and profitable banks is sending very negative signals to the international financial community. In other countries, such as Malaysia and Morocco, the sale of these two banks would be ranked as "showcase privatizations" designed to kick-start public confidence in the privatization process. It seems to suggest that Libya, by not promoting a public awareness campaign surrounding the privatization of these major banks, known to every Libyan, has lost a major opportunity for generating a positive public response to its privatization programme, which could have gone a long way to ensure its success.

This is not to say that Libya lacks conduits through which, if the timing and pricing of Libyan assets was right, could not be used to immediately attract FDI into the privatization of some of Libya's major companies and infrastructure providers. The Arab Banking Corp., which is 27 per cent owned by the Central Bank of Libya, and Lafico, the Libyan Arab Foreign Bank, both have long and successful track records in international finance, with the latter having been involved in many major deals, particularly in Italy, even during the sanctions period. But somehow the synergy which this could bring to Libya's privatization drive has escaped Libya's policy makers, who will have to realize at some point that privatization is not an isolated event, but a process constantly evolving and changing over time, which must embrace every part of the Libyan economy.

To conclude, it appears that securing the ambitious aims of the Libyan privatization programme appears, for the moment at least, to be somewhat elusive. Whether this is due to lack of political will to see the process through, high level conflict in the Libyan government, or a basic lack of human resources to satisfactorily handle the width and depth of the economic, social, and financial sides of privatization is not yet clear at this, admittedly, early stage. Soon after the appointment of the new Libyan Prime Minister, Dr. Al-Baghdadi Ali al-Mahmoudi in March 2006, the series of resolutions dealing with privatization issues, which emerged from the Libyan Cabinet in June 2006 suggests that the government is determined to address, through high level intervention, the problems which are causing delays in implementing the privatization programme. But if the Libyan government fails, this time around, to successfully implement this major policy initiative with the potential to impact all sectors of Libyan society for many years to come, then, like the earlier efforts in the 1980s and 1990s, the present privatization programme will amount to merely a cosmetic exercise.

7 Libya's Investment Potential and Trade Blocs

7.1 The FDI Debate and Libya

Since the 1980s, there has been an explosive growth in FDI, brought about by empirical evidence and growing acceptance of its contributions to economic growth. While in the 1980s FDI was viewed in many developing and even developed countries with suspicion, the consensus now is that foreign-owned companies could be important contributors to innovation, growth, and employment. This has meant that all countries and regions have begun competing for FDI, with virtually every country setting up a Foreign Investment Board. But as a perceptive observer has noted, the FDI picture is not only about maximizing the amount of FDI flow into a country, "Some compare FDI to a beauty contest. But the winners will not necessarily be those countries that attract the most in revenue or number of projects. They will be the countries that are able to derive the most benefits from an FDI policy that is embedded in an overall national development or industrial strategy" (Hamdani 2005).

This is because there is still much controversy on the purported benefits of FDI. A review of the literature on the effects that FDI firms have on the local economy into which they are integrated comes up with both predictable and not so predictable conclusions. According to Lipsey (2002) and Ebersberger and Lööf (2004), a large number of studies report on several empirical similarities arising from FDI corporate investment. First, there is robust evidence that within countries, foreign-owned firms almost always pay higher wages than domestically owned firms. Secondly, foreign-owned firms have higher productivity than local firms. Thirdly, and surprisingly, the literature does not present any strong evidence of positive impacts from FDI firms on innovation activities and output. In this case the empirical information is mixed. Fourthly, and again surprisingly, there is no unambiguous support for the idea that FDI firms will positively affect the growth rate in the local economy (Johansson and Lööf 2005).

These issues about the role of FDI in the globalization process have been elegantly presented in a paper – "how could developing countries harness the positive effects of globalization and FDI? Another dimension has since been added: how can developed countries avoid the 'negative' effects of globalization and FDI?" (Hammerich 2005).

As discussed earlier, the ongoing reform agenda of the Libyan government, aimed at making its investment climate more attractive, has been engineered, especially since 1997, through a wide range of reforms in its regulatory and institutional framework, the streamlining of its bureaucratic procedures, and important reforms of the financial and banking systems. By effecting these changes, the Libyan policy makers believe that substantial FDI into the tourism, manufacturing, agriculture, fishing, and service industries will be attracted to Libya. To see just how far FDI to Libya had deteriorated during the sanctions period, it is instructive to look at Table 7.1. It was only in 2002 that FDI inward flows to Libya began, after a long absence, to increase again from average negative annual figures of US $81 million for the years 1985–1995 and US $133 million for 2001, to positive inflows of US $145, 143, and 131 million respectively for the years 2002–2004 inclusive, basically reflecting the freezing of UN sanctions in 1999 and the lifting of UN and US sanctions in 2004.

As the most recent UNCTAD projections for FDI for the period 2005–2008 demonstrates, the African continent, in global terms, receives relatively little FDI but inflows are expected to increase, with favoured country destinations being the large economies and those well endowed with natural resources (mining, quarrying, and petroleum), particularly South Africa, Egypt, Morocco, Nigeria, and Algeria. Generally, also, FDI is attracted to such industries as tourism, hotels and restaurants, computer/ICT in services, and food and beverages (UNCTAD 2005).

Table 7.1. Libya: FDI overview in regional and global contexts, 1985–2004

FDI flows						As percentage of gross fixed capital formation				
	1985–1995	2001	2002	2003	2004	1985–1995	2001	2002	2003	2004
Libya										
Inward	–81	–133	145	143	131	0.6	–3.7	5.5	4.8	3.9
Outward	1	175	–136	63	62	1.6	4.9	–5.1	2.1	1.9
Algeria										
Inward	67	1198	1085	634	882	0.7	9.6	7.7	4.0	4.5
Outward	13	9	100	14	258	–	–	0.7	–	1.3
Angola										
Inward	208	2148	1872	3505	2048	30.5	85.5	48.1	82.8	42.7
Outward	–	15	29	24	30	–	–	0.8	0.6	0.6
North Africa										
Inward	1341	5458	3872	5262	5270	3.1	11.6	8.0	10.5	9.2
Outward	55	293	22	115	514	1.0	0.7	–	–	1.0
Africa										
Inward	3584	20027	12994	18005	18090	4.0	20.7	13.0	15.0	12.5
Outward	1238	–2557	427	1215	2824	2.2	–2.6	–	1.1	2.4
Developing economies										
Inward	49868	217845	155528	166337	233227	4.6	12.9	9.5	8.8	10.5
Outward	21580	78571	47775	29016	83190	1.9	3.7	2.8	1.6	4.2
World										
Inward	182438	825925	716128	632599	648148	3.8	12.0	10.6	8.3	7.5
Outward	203256	743465	652181	616923	730257	4.3	10.8	9.7	8.2	8.7

Source: UNCTAD, World Investment Report, 2005.

As can be seen from the above table, for the years 2002–2004 inclusive, FDI in Libya represented 5.5, 4.8, and 3.9 per cent respectively of Gross Fixed Capital Formation (GFCF), which covers new investments in land improvements, plant, machinery, and equipment purchases, and the construction of roads, railways, and the like, including commercial and industrial buildings, offices, schools, hospitals, and private residential dwellings. In a Libyan context the potential importance of FDI for capital formation is highlighted by the need to replace large amounts of obsolete capital equipment accumulated during years of SOE ownership of inefficient manufacturing capacity, as well as the rundown production equipment of the hydrocarbon and petrochemical sector, starved of spare parts and new production processes during the sanctions period, all again negatively impacted by an inefficient financial sector. Not only this, but as noted in Chap. 5, the infrastructure deficit in Libya is currently massive and eventually it is believed that the government will have to turn to some types of PPP involving FDI to address this.

To put the Libyan FDI decline into some sort of perspective, it is useful to look at Table 7.2, which shows FDI as a percentage of GFCF in all the North African countries for the period 1970–2004.

From this graph the distance that Libya needs to travel to catch up with its North African neighbours such as Tunisia, Egypt, and Morocco in terms of FDI, measured as a percentage of GFCF, is huge. From a peak of 46.6 per cent in 1970, the nationalization process meant that starting from a decline to 9.5 per cent in 1972 and then –16.2 per cent in 1975 as assets were pulled out of the country, FDI as a percentage of GFCF remained in negative territory until 1983 when it reached scarcely 2.3 per cent. Hovering around 2–3 per cent in the late 1980s and early 1990s, it plunged into negative territory again from 1994 to 1999 as the results of the sanctions began to really impact the Libyan economy. For 2000, after the UN sanctions were frozen in 1999, it reached 3.3 per cent, before plunging to –3.7 per cent again in 2001 and then to 5.5, 4.8, and 3.9 per cent respectively for 2002, 2003, and 2004, as Libya began to be seen again as a respectable destination for FDI. In contrast, neighbouring Tunisia has consistently attracted FDI throughout the period, with peak levels of FDI/GFCF at 13.4, 16, 13.6, 15.4, and 15.3 per cent for the years 1982, 1993, 1998, 2000, and 2002 respectively. Egypt, again, has been in positive territory throughout, with peaks of 25.4 and 15.9 per cent in the years 1979 and 1993 respectively, while its lowest level of 2 per cent in 2003 rose again to 9.9 per cent in 2004.

As for Morocco, the benefits of its privatization programme, including the privatization of the Casablanca Stock Exchange in the mid-1990s began to reap considerable rewards in the late 1990s and early years of the millennium, with FDI's percentage of GFCF peaking at 17.2, 37.4, and 22.5 per cent for the years 1997, 2001, and 2003 respectively. The case of Algeria is however much more complex as negative political factors related to long-standing civil unrest only began to change in the late 1990s and early years of the new century, with the FDI/GFCF ratio peaking at 9.6 per cent in 2001.

Table 7.2. FDI as a percentage of gross fixed capital formation (GFCF) in North African countries, 1970–2004

	1970	1971	1972	1973	1974	1975	1976	1977	1978	1979	1980	1981
Algeria	5.2	0.0	1.8	1.5	8.8	2.0	2.5	1.9	1.1	0.2	2.4	0.1
Egypt	0.1	0.3	0.0	0.1	0.0	0.3	1.7	2.2	4.8	25.4	9.4	10.3
Morocco	3.4	3.5	1.9	0.6	–1.8	0.2	1.4	0.2	0.4	0.2	2.1	1.5
Libya	46.6	8.8	9.5	–9.5	0.2	–16.2	6.3	–9.7	–13.4	–9.4	–11.7	–8.3
Tunisia	5.5	7.1	7.4	9.9	3.9	3.9	8.4	6.0	5.0	2.2	10.2	12.5
	1982	1983	1984	1985	1986	1987	1988	1989	1990	1991	1992	1993
Algeria	–0.3	0.0	0.0	0.0	0.0	0.0	0.1	0.1	0.3	0.7	0.2	0.0
Egypt	3.3	4.2	5.7	7.9	6.7	4.7	4.1	4.7	4.4	3.2	5.8	15.9
Morocco	1.9	1.4	1.6	0.7	0.0	1.6	1.9	3.2	2.7	5.1	6.7	8.0
Libya	–4.2	–3.8	–0.2	2.3	–4.1	–3.1	2.7	3.2	4.0	2.5	2.8	1.2
Tunisia	13.4	8.1	5.8	6.4	4.1	5.3	4.0	4.0	2.9	5.5	9.8	16.0
	1994	1995	1996	1997	1998	1999	2000	2001	2002	2003	2004	–
Algeria	0.0	0.0	2.3	2.4	4.0	4.3	3.7	9.6	7.7	4.0	4.5	–
Egypt	13.2	6.1	5.9	6.3	5.9	5.7	6.7	3.2	4.3	2.0	9.9	–
Morocco	8.8	4.7	4.5	17.2	4.2	10.2	5.3	37.4	5.8	22.5	7.5	–
Libya	–1.6	–3.0	–3.0	–1.9	–4.3	–3.8	3.3	–3.7	5.5	4.8	3.9	–
Tunisia	12 8	7.4	6.2	7.8	13.6	7.0	15.4	9.3	15.3	10.0	9.9	–

Source: UNCTAD, World Investment Report, 2005.

7.2 Lack of Depth in Libya's Financial Sector

One of the undoubted major problems faced by Libya in successfully attracting FDI is the lack of depth of its banking sector and financial markets. Obviously, all of the FDI directed by Merger and Acquisition (M&A) which has since 1990s years revolutionized, for example, the business, construction, and employment sector in Dubai will be denied to Libya because there is no stock exchange. This connectivity between FDI inflows and financial market depth is discussed at length by an Arab researcher who examines the MENA region as an FDI recipient. His view is that "the emerging literature on Foreign Direct Investment (FDI) now stipulates that FDI's positive impact on growth depends on absorptive capacities. Prime among these capacities is financial development." He finds that "Arab FDI will have a favourable effect on growth if interacted with financial variables at a given threshold level of development." In his analysis of these thresholds his findings are that "Libya, Saudi Arabia, Sudan, and Yemen are below the desired threshold, whereas Syria is almost equal to it. All the other countries, however, especially Lebanon, Tunisia, and UAE, are comfortably above it" (Omran and Bobol 2003).

Another way in which maturity of the financial markets is important is in the spillover effect of technology brought by the FDI firms into the local market. In particular, to take advantage of the new knowledge, local firms need to alter everyday activities and, more generally, reorganize their structure, buy new machines, and hire new managers and skilled labour. Although some local firms might be able to finance new requirements with internal financing, the greater the technological-knowledge gap between their current practices and new technologies, the greater the need for external finance. In most cases, such external finance is restricted to domestic banks and financial institutions, and the lack of financial markets which might be used to raise cheaper funding can limit the growth prospects of domestic entrepreneurs.

This is especially true when the arrival of an entirely new technology brings with it the potential to tap not just domestic markets but export markets. A case in point is the emergence of the textile export industry in Bangladesh in the early 1980s, following the establishment of a textile plant by Daewoo in 1979. Of the 130 Bangladeshi workers who were trained in Korea to become familiar with the technology, 115 eventually left to set up their own garment export plants. It is difficult to imagine that all these workers managed to finance factories with their own cash (Alfaro et al. 2004).

Other matters concerning the rate of success for FDI in a given country are related to human capital, that is the extent or level to which the working population of the target country is educated. In the fast-moving world of IT and rapid technological obsolescence, this is becoming an increasingly important factor. A paper stated, "the growing importance of human capital for competitiveness is paralleled by an increased geographical mobility of individuals. It is relatively common now for skilled people to live in several different countries in the course of their working lives" (Birkinshaw 2005). Another researcher using data on US multinational enterprises finds that a country needs to reach a minimum human capital threshold in order to benefit from the technology transfer of US multinationals through FDI, and that most Developing Countries do not meet this threshold (Xu 2000). The World Bank in a recent edition of their global development finance survey also touched on this issue, when it discussed the importance of "absorptive capacities" for the success of FDI. Absorptive capacities here include macroeconomic management (as captured by inflation and trade openness), infrastructure (telephone lines and paved roads), and human capital (share of labour force with secondary education and percentage of population with access to sanitation) (World Bank 2001).

More recent research on FDI flows shows also that sectoral targets are changing. As one researcher has stated,

> manufacturing operations are no longer the main area, but services have become predominant in FDI. Further, globalization is no longer limited to large-scale manufacturing operations, but small and medium-sized enterprises (SMEs) are becoming seriously engaged. SMEs tend to be more tied than large firms to local resources and capabilities, are affected by globalization in other ways, and encounter special risks. However, industrial performance is now less based on economies of scale at plant level but increasingly fuelled by networking capacity and flexibility. (Andersson 2005)

There are clear lessons from this trend for Libyan policy makers. If Libya, on account of its relatively small market size, is unable to successfully attract large-scale manufacturing operations in sunset industries, then its policy could, for example, be tailored to attract smaller SMEs with niche technologies, especially in the Oil and Gas sector, which currently dominates the Libyan economy and which has significant potential for further growth and potential, especially if coupled with stringent laws related to in-country procurement and content.

7.3 The Libyan Foreign Investment Board

One of the watershed pieces of legislation regarding FDI to Libya was the adoption of Law No.5 of 1997, later amended in 2004, concerning the Encouragement of Foreign Capital Investment, which led to the establishment of the Authority for the Encouragement of Foreign Investment (the Libyan Foreign Investment Board). Regarding this, Article 5 of Law No. 5 stipulates, "There shall be established an Authority to be known as the Libyan Foreign Investment Board having its own independent juridical personality, under the jurisdiction of the General People's Committee for Planning, Economy and Commerce. The Authority shall be established by a decision from the General People's Committee upon a proposition by the Secretary stating the Authority's legal domicile, its secretary and members of its Management Committee."

Regarding the remit of the Board, Article 6 stipulates that "The Authority shall work for the encouragement of foreign capital investment and promotion for the investment projects by various means, in particular it shall:

- Study and propose plans to organize foreign investment and supervise foreign investments in the country.
- Receive the applications for foreign capital investments to determine whether they satisfy the legal requirements and the feasibility study for the project and then submit its recommendations to the Secretary accordingly.

- Gather and publish information and conduct economic studies relevant to the potential of investments in the projects that contribute to the economic development of the country.
- Take proper actions to attract foreign capitals and promote the chances of investment through various means.
- Recommend exemptions, facilities or other benefits for the projects that are considered important for the development of the national economy, or recommend the renewal of the exemptions and benefits as provided for in the law for further periods of time. It shall submit its recommendations to the relevant authority.
- Consider without prejudice to the right of the investor to petition and litigate complains, petitions or disputes lodged by the investors resulting from the application of this law.
- Study and review periodically the investment legislations, propose improvement thereof and submit same to the concerned authority.
- Perform any other functions assigned to it by the General People's Committee".

In terms of simplifying the tortuous bureaucratic procedures previously existing in Libya, the Libyan Foreign Investment Board (LFIB) has also established a One-Stop Shop Service located within the LFIB's premises. It provides all services needed by foreign investors including a Customs, Immigration and Passports, Tax, and Labour force office and allows for the following procedures and approvals to be performed:

- Licence and permit procedures.
- Export and import procedures.
- Import of foreign manpower procedures.
- Amendments and changes introduced to the project procedures.
- Ownership and renting of real estate procedures.
- Transfer of dividends procedures.
- Complaint procedures.

7.4 FDI Projects Approved, August 2006

The actual record to date of approved projects by LFIB for the period from 1 January 2000 to the end of August 2006, excluding the Oil and Gas sector, which comes under the direction of the LNOC is given in Table 7.3.

As can be seen, in the review period 130 projects were given approval, after project cancellation for a variety of reasons, including failure to complete legal documen–tation, failure to commence project within the approved time frame, lack of further correspondence by original applicants or their representatives in Libya, or projects cancelled by mutual consent with the LFIB. Total value of approved projects amounted to approximately US $3.86 billion. Share of foreign capital in all projects aggregated to 96 per cent with Libyan national investors holding only 4 per cent, while in three sectors, tourism, agriculture, and marine wealth, Libyans hold no equity. Job creation from approved projects will eventually amount to 12,890, with approximately 83 per cent or 10,654 employees being Libyan nationals.

Table 7.3. FDI projects approved, August 2006

Sector	No.	%	Foreign investor		Local investor MM LD	Total MM LD	Jobs created		
			MM US$	MM LD			Libyan	Foreign	Total
Industry	83	63.86	3075.741	3998.464	146.094	4144.559	7247	876	8123
Services	20	15.38	234.074	304.296	41.437	345.734	1,433	365	1,798
Health	15	11.53	100.497	130.647	22.177	152.824	1202	473	1675
Public facilities and services	6	4.61	250.292	325.380	0.520	325.900	490	54	544
Agriculture	3	2.31	7.950	10.335	0	10.335	106	129	235
Tourism	2	1.54	182.036	236.647	0	236.647	126	319	445
Marine wealth	1	0.77	4.618	6.004	0	6.004	50	20	70
Total	130	100	3,855.212	5011.776	210.229	5,222.006	10,654	2,236	12,890

Source: Libyan Foreign Investment Board, August 2006.

Again it is the industrial sector, with 83 out of 130, which dominated FDI approvals, while the service sector (20) and health (15) also attracted significant investment. As percentages of the total number of projects approved, the industrial sector took 63.86 per cent, with services and health at 15.38 per cent and 11.53 per cent respectively, while tourism secured only 2 projects amounting to 1.54 per cent. It is worth pointing out, however, that these do not include the tourism projects approved by the Tourism Investment and Development Board which, as discussed in the following chapter, amount in total to US $3.07 billion or LD 3.99 billion alone.

In terms of job creation for both Libyan and foreign manpower, again it is the industrial sector which dominated. For foreigners, 876, 365, and 473 jobs, representing 39, 16, and 21 per cent of the total respectively, were created, while for Libyans these figures were 7247, 1433, and 1202, or 68, 13, and 11 respectively.

The extremely high percentage of foreign equity in all of these projects may be attributed to several factors. The first is that Libyans and Libyan entrepreneurs do not have the cash to come up with project equity, or if they do, they are not willing to reveal it because of questions later arising as to how it was acquired, that is corruption. Secondly, that, despite the various funds set up to assist business and entrepreneurial growth in 2006, as well as preliminary reforms in the Libyan banking system as previously discussed, the procedure for fund disbursement or project loans is not very efficient or perhaps non-transparent. Thirdly, that Libyans do not have the same confidence level as foreign investors in the success of these new projects, perhaps a legacy of the 30-year subsidy and jobs-for-life mentality prevalent in most Libyans, especially the older generations.

7.4.1 Status of FDI Project Implementation, August 2006

The current status of project implementation for these 130 projects is shown in Table 7.4. Those operational amounted to 48 or 36.9% of the total projects, with a

Table 7.4. LFIB: project implementation status, August 2006

Project status	No.	%	Foreign investor		Local investor MM LD	Total MM LD	Jobs created		
			MM US$	MM LD			Libyan	Foreign	Total
Establish-ment	35	26.91	3,221.748	4,188.272	53.619	4,241.892	2,988	632	3,620
Construction	47	36.19	310.985	404.280	81.642	485.923	3,266	768	4,034
Operational	48	36.90	322.479	419.223	74.967	494.191	4,400	836	5,236
Total	130	100	3,855.212	5,011.776	210.229	5,222.006	10,654	2,236	12,890

Source: Libyan Foreign Investment Board, August 2006.

value of LD 494.191 million, of which LD 419.223 million (84.83 per cent) came from foreign investment. These projects together created 5,236 new jobs, of which Libyan workers accounted for 4,400 or 84.03 per cent. In terms of sectoral investment they broke down as 28 industrial, 9 services, 7 health, 2 agriculture, one tourism and one marine wealth.

Projects in the construction phase amounted to 47, accounting for 36.19 per cent of the total projects, with a total capital of LD 485.923 million, of which LD 404.280 million (83.19 per cent) was foreign investment, providing 4,043 total job opportunities, of which 3,266 or 80.78 per cent were Libyans. These projects distributed among the sectors as follows: 31 industrial, 6 service, 7 health project, 2 projects for public facilities and services, and one for the tourism sector.

Projects in the establishment phase accounted for 35 projects or 27 per cent of the total. These involved capital investment amounting to approximately LD 4,241, with the foreign contribution amounting to approximately 4,188.272 or 98.73 per cent, eventually providing 3,620 job opportunities, of which Libyans make up 2,988 employees or 82.54 per cent.

7.4.2 Major FDI Source Countries, 2006

In Table 7.5, the value of approved FDI projects by major source country for the period 2000–2006 is detailed. As can be seen, the United Kingdom is by far the largest foreign investor, with a total project value of US $2.13 billion. The United Kingdom's traditional historical interest in the country post Second World Warand in the early period of Libyan independence after 1951, as well as the considerable overseas expertise of UK businessmen and investors, strongly supported by the UK government, go a long way to explain United Kingdom's very high level of interest in a country which they see as having vast and relatively unexploited potential. The United Kingdom's prime ranking is followed by Mauritius, UAE, and Libya's neighbours Algeria and Malta, with the latter's investment largely represented by only one investment, the Corinthia Africa Gate Hotel in Tripoli. Libya's eastern neighbour, Egypt is also a significant investor, with approved FDI at US $94.4 million, which come as no surprise to most Libyans who already see a strong Egyptian presence in many of their SMEs.

Table 7.5. LFIB: Value of approved FDI projects in LD by major source country, 2000–2006

No.	Country	Value (US$)	Value (LD)
1	UK	2,129,229,269	2,767,998,050
2	Mauritius	658,846,154	856,500,000
3	UAE	371,432,281	482,861,965
4	Algeria	200,328,170	260,426,621
5	Malta	143,724,870	186,842,332
6	Tunisia	102,927,898	133,806,270
7	Egypt	94,435,126	122,765,665
8	Italy	71,971,501	93,562,954
9	USA	39,032,760	50,742,588
10	Cyprus	36,593,742	47,571,865
11	Portugal	30,059,551	39,077,416
12	South Korea	15,000,000	19,500,000
13	France	11,504,155	14,955,402
14	Netherlands	11,222,709	14,589,522
15	Jordan	10,677,941	13,881,324
16	Germany	8,215,986	10,680,782
17	Turkey	8,123,037	10,559,947
18	Belarus	7,650,000	9,945,000
19	Qatar	7,094,615	9,223,000
20	Bahrain	6,000,000	7,800,000
21	Greece	5,833,462	7,583,500
22	Spain	5,210,524	6,773,681
23	Morocco	5,063,077	6,582,000
24	Canada	3,896,185	5,065,041
25	China	3,863,400	5,022,420
26	India	3,832,950	4,982,836
27	Saudi Arabia	3,769,230	4,899,999
28	Belgium	3,555,538	4,622,200
29	Palestine	3,135,200	4,075,760
30	Bosnia	2,972,384	3,864,099
31	Bahamas	2,733,077	3,553,000
32	Kuwait	2,287,175	2,973,328
33	Austria	1,717,392	2,232,610
34	Slovakia	484,000	629,200
	Total	4,012,423,359	5,216,150,377

Source: Libyan Foreign Investment Board, October 2006.

Surprisingly, however, investments from Italy and Germany, two countries which have a strong export record to Libya, and which have played a major role in Libya's hydrocarbon sector even during the sanction period through Agip and Total, are not particularly impressive, while the involvement of South Korean companies in the petrochemical and the GMRP explain their relatively high level of FDI. Conspicuous by its lowly ninth ranking is of course the United States, with only US $39 million, due to the enforcement of the US sanctions, lifted only in 2004. However, in the immediate years ahead this figure will increase dramatically as confirmed multi-billion US $ investments from the US

IOCs Occidental and the Oasis Group, comprising ConocoPhillips, Marathon Oil Corp, and Amerada Hess, have already been pledged. These investments were expected to come through US successes in both the EPSA-IV first and second bidding rounds in 2005, and in deals negotiated for the return of these groups in 2005–2006 to their Libyan assets, held in trust for them by the LNOC since 1986 through the Standstill Agreements with the Libyan government.

7.5 FDI and Free Trade Zones in Libya

The concept and usage of free trade zones is one of the major innovations impacting the global economy in recent years. They can be defined as "as a territorial enclave in which foreign firms (in many cases also in cooperation with indigenous companies) benefit from generous incentives and privileges and thereby produce industrial goods mainly for export" (Schweinberger 2003). They are increasingly popular in developing countries, notably in newly industrialized Asian economies such as Malaysia, Singapore, and Indonesia, as well as the Middle East, for example in Dubai. The idea was taken up by Libya with the General People's Committee Resolution No. 20 of 1999, which dealt with the Establishment of the Free Zones Authority. Free Zones in the above resolution are those areas defined by law and allocated "for the exchange of commercial and industrial goods and service rendering free of any customs, taxes and monetary restrictions". Under the above resolution the General Authority for Free Zones was set up, with the power to supervise the Free Zones and carry out measures to develop their commercial, industrial, and service aspects for the benefit of the national economy. The tasks of the Authority include the following:

- The management and development of the Free Zones, and the development of international commercial exchange, transit trade, and export industries.
- The study and development of local or joint Free Zones
- The study of the laws and regulations related to local and foreign investments in the Free Zones.
- The establishment and development of different utilities and structures necessary for the Free Zones.
- The provision of all modern telecommunication and transportation facilities and services needed for proper management of commercial, industrial, and service activities within the Free Zones.
- The allocation, renting, and leasing land and real estate for economical activities in the Free Zones.
- The arrangement of procedures of entry and exit to and from the Free Zones.

7.5.1 The Permitted Fields of Investment and Economic Activities in the Free Zones

- The storage of transit and domestic goods, as well as goods produced within the Free Zones which are intended for export and goods imported for re-export.
- The unpacking, cleaning, mixing, (even with local products), re-packing, and similar operations which significantly change the value of products in the Free Zone and guarantee their manufacture to meet the demand of the market.
- The performance of industrial processes such as assembly, disassembly, or full manufacture.
- The provision of financial, banking, insurance, and other related service required by investors within the Free Zone.

7.5.2 Privileges and Exemptions of the Free Zones

- The free repatriation of invested capital and profits.
- The movement of capital and products between the Free Zone and the foreign countries without being subject to any monetary restrictions or monitoring regulations.
- Income tax exemption for 5 years, extendable by an additional 3 years.
- Profits gained from these activities also enjoy the same exemptions if reinvested.
- Investors can transfer losses suffered during the exemption period to succeeding years.
- Legal guarantees against the nationalization of projects established in the Free Zone and against acquisition or subjecting projects to any similar procedure.
- Ownership of projects can be either in full or partial, and is transferable to another investor.
- The project life can be in line with client's demand.
- Machinery, equipment, and instrumentation needed for projects established in the Free Zone are exempt from customs duties and other similar taxes.
- Equipment and spare parts necessary for the implementation of projects established in the Free Zone are exempt from all customs duties, import taxes, and all similar taxes.
- Goods exported or imported from or to the Free Zone are not subject to time limitation for warehousing.
- Movement of goods between the Free Zone and outside Libya are not subject to customs duties.
- Projects established in the Free Zone are not subject to the normal procedures for trade registry and for the register of importers and exporters.
- Investors are entitled to employ and import foreign labour with specialized technical qualifications required for the establishment or operation of projects in the Free Zone.

7.5.3 Misuratah Free Zone

The first Free Zone Libya to be managed by the General Authority for Free Zones is the Misuratah Free Zone, which occupies an area of 430 ha adjacent to Misuratah port, located 207 km east of Tripoli. Full details of facilities, services, and utilities at this zone are provided in Appendices 7.1–7.5.

As well as Misuratah, other suitable locations as well as border sites are being planned for future free Zones by the Authority. A recent example, approved by the General People's Committee Decision No. 215 of 6 September 2006 regarding the Establishment of a Zone of Particular Nature, situated between Zuwarah and Abu Kammash close to Libya's border with Tunisia, is a case in point, although this massive new undertaking, encompassing tourism, hi-tech industry, and medical and educational projects, would appear to be a highly specialized and unique case.

Clearly, however, the establishment of the Free Zone Authority in 1999 and its interest in expanding Free Trade Zones is another example of Libya's desire to re-integrate into the global community. With the lifting of the sanctions the advantages of such Free Trade Zones in Libya should now be abundantly clear to foreign companies who wish to take advantage of Libya's liberal investment laws and unparalleled geographical location with respect to the other Maghreb countries, Egypt, and Southern Europe, and indeed the whole of the African continent to the south.

7.6 FDI: Important Lessons for Libya

In some ways it is fortunate that Libya, because of the sanctions, is a relative latecomer into the "FDI beauty show". This means that Libyan policy makers have the opportunity to benefit from the mistakes of others as well as understand and capture the recent trends in FDI which we have touched on earlier. We will discuss the most important of these in the following section.

7.6.1 The Underfunding of the LFIB

One obvious lesson is that the LFIB as an institution is grossly underfunded. As recently advised (*OFAK Magazine* October 2004) in an article by Rajab Shiglabu, the Chairman of the LFIB, its total annual budget is only LD 275,000. As the body primarily responsible for attracting global foreign investment into Libya, it is entirely unrealistic for Libyan policy makers to expect this body to compete globally, where, as we have stated, virtually every country in the world has a foreign investment board aggressively bidding for FDI. In this respect Libya would do well to learn from and emulate the Malaysian track record in attracting FDI. The Malaysian Industrial Development Authority (MIDA), the key driver for attracting FDI into Malaysia, has been an aggressive instrument of Malaysian FDI policy since 1967, transforming the country from a commodity-based economy to one in which the manufacturing sector has become the engine of growth. In 2005 the manufacturing sector contributed about a third of the country's GDP, while manufactured goods made up more than 80 per cent of Malaysia's total exports.

Headed by the very aggressive Malaysian Minister of Industrial Trade and Industry, Rafidah Azziz, it has 16 fully staffed overseas offices including 5 in the major US cities, 5 in the major European capitals, and 6 in Australia and the Far East, including Korea, Japan, Taiwan, and the People's Republic of China. Every year it holds foreign road shows. In 2005, for example, 18 Overseas Trade & Investment Missions, each of which lasted around 10 days, were scheduled between February and August, including the United States, the Middle East, ASEAN Countries, China, and Turkey. Because of MIDA's aggressive approach to competing for FDI, multinational corporations from more than 40 countries have invested in over 3,000 major projects in Malaysia.

In the 2005 Malaysian Budget the Ministry of International Trade and Industry was allocated RM 85,699,200 (approximately US $22.6 million), a large percentage of which was utilized by MIDA. Against competition and expenditure of this type, it is inconceivable that the LFIB with an annual budget of LD 275,000 (US $207,000) can compete in the international arena for FDI. As a country with formidable financial resources, it is unacceptable that Libya's policy makers can allow such a situation to exist.

7.6.2 Expedite and Simplify Immigration Formalities for FDI

There have been many horror stories about the difficulties involved in getting a 3-month holiday visa to Libya, not to say a work permit, both of which involve lengthy processes involving significant expense, passport translations, and long delays, all adding up to a very negative view of the country. Libyan policy makers should note that in the modern world, many countries are considerably expediting visa and work permit approval times. In recognition of this trend, for example, as early as August 2000, the German Federal Institute for Employment approved legislation which allowed for up to 20,000 foreigners with a university degree and who are non-residents of the European Union to obtain work permits for a maximum of 5 years. Singapore offers not only a simplified and expedited work authorization process but also a rapid permanent residency and citizenship granting process. In the Middle East, the government of Dubai has lifted all restrictions on the number of foreign nationals hired by any information technology company. Again, many countries now offer work visas for spouses. In Canada, for example, spouses accompanying temporary foreign workers coming to Canada for jobs in certain high-skill occupations in key growth sectors of the economy will be permitted to work in their chosen field. In a competitive world where technology skills and networking ability are in strong demand, why go to Libya to work if there are so many problems?

7.6.3 Accelerate Financial Reform

In our view the acceleration of the liberalization process for the Libyan banking and insurance sectors to allow for foreign ownership and the establishment of the Libyan Stock Exchange are vitally and urgently required. Without fast tracking, the ongoing privatization process as well as the many efforts made to attract FDI cannot be assured to achieve any level of success. The present lack of absorptive capacity of the Libyan financial sector in general, as well as a domestically focused banking sector, means that many FDI opportunities will be lost to Libya, moving instead to other more investment-friendly countries in MENA such as Morocco, Egypt, and Dubai. In Chap. 8 this matter will be discussed in detail.

7.6.4 Publicize Libya's Competitiveness

The series of high level visits to Libya by the Italian, British, and French leaders in the immediate post-sanctions environment in mid-2004 demonstrated how important Libya is perceived to be both as an ally in the fight against terrorism and as a key player in the fight to contain illegal immigration from Africa into Europe. It also showed that Libya's impressive hydrocarbon assets and geographical proximity to Europe are also highly valued by European nations, all of which at some time in the future will face energy crises. In this regard the importance of the lifting of the sanctions cannot be overemphasized. While, for example, the EPSA III bidding round of May 2000 offered 137 blocks during the sanctions period, only 21 agreements covering 50 blocks had been signed by the end of December 2003. However, in the immediate post-sanctions scenario, the EPSA-IV first and second round offerings of January and October 2005, amounting in total to 142 blocks, were all taken up, with a high level of interest in the 41 blocks under offer in the third EPSA-IV bidding offered in August 2006.

After two years from the lifting of the sanctions, Libya still needs to aggressively publicize its many FDI advantages, over and above these geopolitical and hydrocarbon credentials. For example, as we have seen, Law No. 5 of 1997, regarding the encouragement of foreign investment, is, as stated by the Libyan Minister of Finance Mohamed Ali El Huwej himself, "one of the most advantageous of its kind in the world" (*FDI Magazine* February 2005) in terms of tax breaks and repatriation of profits, as well as other key aspects such as duty-free importation of project capital equipment. This needs to be emphasized in a high-powered Libyan government-funded PR and advertising campaign not only via the commercial sections of Libyan embassies throughout the world, but also by a strategic and sustained international media policy. The message needs to percolate down from the level of European leaders and policy makers to all levels of potential investors, all the way from multinationals and SMEs to individual investors who might wish, for example, to open up Turkish, Malaysian, or traditional English restaurants to cater for a predicted tourist boom. Libyan policy makers have perhaps forgotten about how little citizens of other countries really know about their marvellous country, and because of its turbulent international past many foreigners are probably struggling with false stereotypes about the new Libya. There is clearly an important role to be played by the LFIB and other Libyan international agencies in improving the quality of information about prospects for foreign workers and investment moving to Libya for the first time. Libya still needs to do a huge amount of promotion in this regard.

7.6.5 LFIB Needs More Focus

As stated earlier, the Decision of the General People's Committee No. 147 of 2004 listed in considerable detail the fields open to foreign investment, which are extremely wide-ranging. The authors believe that it would be much more productive if LFIB were to identify, promote, and concentrate on specific sectors within this huge range of investment opportunities. In this way these selected sectors could act as powerful drivers for other sectors.

If, for example, LFIB were to concentrate on item one of sector one, "Construction of Airports", the benefits to Libya, if the LFIB were successful in attracting a world-class FDI player in this sector such as the Singapore Airport Authority or the Malaysia Airports Holdings which manages the Kuala Lumpur International Airport, would be gigantic. A new and technologically sophisticated showpiece, Tripoli airport, for example, would in itself act as a magnet for many travellers. State-of-the-art equipment and technology would mean that all of the world's top airlines and all sizes and classes of planes could utilize its systems and facilities, with high levels of safety, security, repair, servicing, and refuelling facilities and equipment guaranteed.

This would mean that the cost of air travel to Tripoli would be reduced, thus ensuring an influx of tourists to Libya as a new and fashionable destination for European and US travellers. As we will discuss extensively in Chap. 8, Libya possesses in abundance all the tourist credentials to attract and maintain many types of tourist activities, ranging from cultural and ecotourism to sunbathing, sailing, scuba diving, and snorkelling on its nearly 2000 km of untouched beaches. In turn this would stimulate the construction of hotels and tourist facilities and lead to huge employment opportunities for Libyans. Not only this but the strategic central location of Libya on the northern border of the African continent makes it the logical location for an international airline hub, able to effectively service a huge volume of travellers from all the countries of the African continent for every destination in Europe or indeed for direct flights to the United States, as well as vice versa.

Similarly, if LFIB were to strategize to secure a major international player in educational excellence to set up a campus in Libya, to provide tertiary education not only to Libyans but also to foreign students, the benefits to Libya would be equally impressive. This is very achievable because Libya already has an impressive record of educational reform upon which to build. Not only is education a recession-free and non-cyclical business, and therefore attractive to investors, but it is also changing rapidly in a global context.

Traditionally, the tertiary education market has operated on a purely national basis, with funding in Libya coming directly from the state, while students selected their university on a local or national level. However, the global education situation has changed significantly over the last 50 years, and the beginnings of a global market for tertiary education are clearly emerging, due to a variety of factors The main one is that the traditional state-funding model can no longer keep up with the costs of and demand for tertiary education, with the salary costs of the educators themselves as well as capital equipment and buildings proving too much for the public sector to bear. This has led to a vast increase in the private sector in tertiary education, and in the United States, for example, private universities have been commonplace for many years. Related to this is the fact that the number of foreign students is growing rapidly. This trend is most noticeable in post-graduate education, and among students from less developed countries such as India and China. According to one estimate, 25 per cent of all US science and engineering graduate students come from abroad (i.e. around 50,000–100,000 people).

International evidence again shows that new tertiary education institutions are transcending traditional boundaries. Universities are now being challenged by new models, such as virtual universities that offer online learning, franchise universities, and corporate universities. For example, according to one estimate, 25 per cent of the 80,000 foreign students at Australian universities are actually in offshore campuses in Malaysia and Singapore. Henley Management College in the United Kingdom has students studying for its MBA degree in over 100 countries via 25 global offices. Taken together, these trends in education are pushing inexorably towards a global market for tertiary education (Birkinshaw 2005).

It is against this background that Libya has the opportunity now to seize the initiative to make the country a centre for educational excellence. Again, as in the case of a new international Tripoli airport, the spin-offs from an international tertiary educational institute are truly enormous. As well as the direct injection of tuition fees, the demands for food, housing, clothes, and transport from foreign students contribute massively to the local economies of cities where large universities are situated. It is estimated, for example, that the two campuses of the University of Aberdeen and Robert Gordon University in the Scottish city of Aberdeen pump in around £1 billion into the local economy and account for many thousands of local jobs. Libya, with its strategic location for African and European students, as well as MENA students who are currently providing huge revenues to UK universities, has truly enormous potential in this sector. Even more importantly it would ensure that Libyans themselves, in a world where knowledge and lifelong learning dominate every industry, would have access to a quality of education on their doorstep, equipping them for the rapid pace of technological change in the key hydrocarbon industry as well as in the emerging telecommunications and IT sectors.

A final sector that LFIB might wish to prioritize is the establishment, possibly in the existing Misuratah Free Zone or a future extension of it, of a complex for industries, service contractors, and equipment related to the oil and gas industry, similar to the Batam Authority Free Trade Zone offshore the island of Singapore, which services the south-east Asian oil and gas industries of Indonesia, Malaysia, Thailand, and Vietnam. The potential for oil- and gas-related service industries in Libya, not only as Libyan hydrocarbon production increases from its current level of around 1.6 to 3 million barrels per day but also as the Libyan gas industry heads for massive expansion, is again enormous. On account of Libya's strategic location, oil sector business from neighbouring North African countries as well as the MENA region could also be targeted. Because of its 50-year history in the hydrocarbon sector, the country itself possesses many Libyan experts in this sector, which would provide a solid base for Libyan entrepreneurs and contractors to build on, perhaps as sole owners or as key employees in this very lucrative business.

To reiterate our point, Libya, on account of its small market size, will probably not be able to attract serious FDI money into the huge range of sectors and industries currently targeted by Libyan legislation, ranging from fish canning and the food industry to the plastics, chemical, and cement industries. An LFIB policy of successfully targeting major key FDI investments in relatively few sectors, as discussed above, together with others identified and prioritized for FDI by the Libyan policy makers, will ensure that these key major FDI investments will in themselves go a long way in driving the diversification of the Libyan economy and securing Libya's modernization goals.

7.7 Libya and Regional Trade and Global Organizations

7.7.1 Libya and the Arab Free Trade Area (AFTA)

When the guiding terms and conditions underlying the foundation of the League of Arab States were being formulated by Egypt, Syria, Lebanon, Iraq, and Transjordan during the Alexandria Protocol of 7 October 1944, "in response to Arab public opinion in all Arab countries," Clause 2 of the Protocol, entitled "Cooperation in Economic, Cultural, Social and Other Matters", stated, "the Arab States represented on the preliminary committee shall closely cooperate in the following matters: economic and financial matters, that is commercial exchange, customs, currency, agriculture, and industry".

In its early years a series of Arab regional bodies were set up under its auspices to encourage cooperation and develop a unified Arab approach to a wide range of issues and problems. Among these were the Arab Postal Union, the Arab Labour Organization, the Arab Telecommunications Union, and perhaps it most recognized offshoot, the Organization of Arab Petroleum Exporting Countries (OAPEC).

Although efforts aimed at bringing about inter-Arab trade integration started decades ago within the League, it was not until 1982 that an agreement between Member States for the facilitation and development of intra-regional trade, Decree 848 of 27/2/1982, Social and Economic Council of the Arab League, was finally put in place. But little progress was made towards the effective creation of an Arab trading bloc. The main drawback of the 1982 agreement was the adoption of a product-by-product approach to trade liberalization, whereby negotiating countries were allowed to pick and choose manufactured items for tariff exemption. In addition, the Agreement did not specify a time frame for the elimination of tariffs and trade barriers. Political barriers and mutual suspicion also worked against efficiency, so nothing major was accomplished in the following 15-year period.

In fact it was not until 1997 that a renewed interest in forming an Arab regional trading entity seriously emerged again. In that year, 18 of the 22 Arab League Member States, including Libya, approved an executive resolution establishing the Arab Free Trade Area (AFTA), which was designed to progressively eliminate import duties and other trade barriers on goods of Arab origin over a 10-year period. By 2008 it was planned that all tariff barriers between these 18 countries would be eliminated.

As might be expected in such a complex undertaking, which in the European Union has spawned a massive bureaucracy at gigantic cost to European taxpayers, as well as a new breed of consultants in this field, serious questions remain about the political will as well as the huge amount of funding required to effectively establish and enforce its objectives. Presently, management of AFTA is through the Council of Ministers of Member States, and through an executive and follow-up permanent body. It has a functioning Secretariat that comes under the Economics Department of the Arab League Secretariat, which is in charge of handling the circulation of papers between the commissions and working subgroups.

An innovation is the call for the private sector, through Chambers of Commerce and Industry in the affected countries, to monitor the implementation of the different stages of the programme. Pursuant to this, the Union of Arab Chambers of Commerce has been requested to submit to the Council of Ministers and its executive body a semi-annual report detailing the difficulties that traders encounter in dealing with the customs administration and any other regulatory agencies of individual member countries. This private sector report aims at enhancing the transparency of AFTA (Economic Research Forum for the Arab Countries, Iran, and Turkey 1998).

There also appear to be very complex rules surrounding individual exceptions to regional tariff elimination, which are intended to enable local industry to carry out the necessary restructuring to improve competitiveness before having to face competition from foreign imports. The member country requesting such exceptions should provide a report showing in full the economic impact on the national economy and the duration for each requested good to be exempted from the tariff reductions.

One of the main difficulties facing its successful implementation is that currently the main markets for both imports and exports for its members are outside the Arab region. Table 7.6 shows this clearly.

Intra-Arab trade in the case of Libya, although it increased slowly from 5.5 per cent in 1993 to 8.8 per cent in 1998, actually declined thereafter to 6.59 per cent in 2003, despite the existence of US and UN sanctions for most of this period, which in theory at least prevented Libya from trading freely in a global context.

This underlies why it is important to find an appropriate balance between regional Arab integration and integration of the Arab region within the many multilateral trading blocks which have emerged as the effects of globalization have made their impact. Clearly the establishment of AFTA is a realistic response to the new challenges of international trade which require a more aggressive approach to regional integration. But the case of Libya itself is even more complex, and it appears it will become even more so; for as well as, since 1963, being a member of the OAU, which in 2001 became the African Union, it has been a member of the UMA since 1989. As well as this, it has been a leading member of the CEN-SAD since 1998, and a member of the COMESA since 2005. It is also currently a potentially active participant and signatory to the Barcelona Process in a post-sanctions scenario, as well as being keen on joining the WTO as part of its international economic rehabilitation.

Table 7.6. MENA countries: Ratio of total inter-Arab trade to total external trade, 1993–2003

Country	1993	1994	1995	1996	1997	1998	1999	2000	2001	2002	2003
Jordan	24.26	26.89	29.03	29.64	31.52	26.86	24.73	25.51	31.13	31.84	33.34
Emirates	7.2	7.2	7.3	6.93	4.85	6.41	7.52	5.44	6.73	6.32	6.8
Bahrain	29.67	26.8	27.54	28.06	29.28	19.86	17.3	15.87	18.42	19.1	22.02
Tunisia	6.69	6.53	7.18	7.56	6.22	5.92	7.08	7.98	7.42	6.84	6.82
Algeria	2.53	3.51	2.78	2.14	2.62	2.3	2.18	1.66	2.87	3.2	2.99
Saudi Arabia	7.31	7.85	8.36	8.86	9.28	8.45	9.21	6.52	7.52	7.61	7.69
Sudan	33.14	28.17	29.87	33.19	34.23	14.87	19.66	13.3	12.02	11.22	27.19
Syria	13.78	14.84	14.95	7.4	8.24	16.4	13.61	12.55	18.66	16.33	21.21
Somalia	39.28	35.03	44.43	38.83	33.59	34.44	33.67	25.15	22.81	26.94	28.08
Iraq	53.16	62.29	65.51	57.53	21.39	8.11	5.9	7.93	11.57	13.28	9.67
Oman	22.56	21.48	20.96	17.63	19.67	24.9	22.3	19.3	20.38	20.51	17.81
Qatar	10.21	10.62	10.19	7.91	7.47	10.06	8.62	8.55	6.85	10.94	8.03
Kuwait	5	6.08	6.1	5.74	5.99	7.16	6.98	6.7	7.21	7.33	6.44
Lebanon	16.39	15.41	10.16	14.86	12.64	12.08	12.34	15.79	14.38	17.04	17.23
Libya	5.55	5.81	6.67	5.66	7.21	8.08	7.62	6.21	7.32	7.62	6.59
Egypt	6.6	6.61	6.09	6.02	6.24	6.91	6.91	8.54	7.74	11.72	12.12
Morocco	10.45	9.17	7.92	8.04	8.68	5.03	4.29	8.91	8.89	8.68	7.16
Mauritania	4.45	2.98	3.01	1.74	6.55	4.09	2.8	3.35	4.01	3.87	4.44
Yemen	20.66	24.23	20.97	11.5	12.2	20.8	19.69	17.03	18.81	22.28	24.44
TOTAL	9.33	9.61	9.54	9.09	8.81	8.88	8.89	7.89	9.07	9.5	9.28

Source: Arab Monetary Fund, 2006.

7.7.2 Libya Trade Potential with the Maghreb Arab Union

From the early 1970s Libya, as the smallest country, population wise, of the Maghrib countries of Algeria, Morocco, and Tunisia, had based its foreign relations on a quest for regional security, as well as its objective of "total Arab unity" categorically stated in Article 1 of the Constitutional Declaration of 1969. Various Libyan initiatives for Arab unity led to the formation, in January 1972, of the Federation of Arab Republics, comprising Libya, Egypt, and Syria, and again, in 1972, Libya concluded an agreement with Egypt to merge the two countries in 1973, but none of these actually materialized. Libyan proposals for union with Tunisia in 1974, Syria in 1980, Chad in 1981, Morocco in 1984, Algeria in 1987, and Sudan in 1990 also proved elusive.

However, new fears of a Fortress Europe across the Mediterranean which "took the form of an enlarging and closing Europe that contained its major suppliers of Mediterranean products within harmonized tariff walls and excluded their competitors" (Aghrout and Sutton 1990) began to impact the thinking and policies of the Maghreb nations. As well as this, the prolonged stalemate in the Western Saharan war by 1981 also required some type of closure. This stimulated the parties involved to attempt to resolve regional antagonisms, concurrently countering the European threat. A series of Moroccon–Algerian Summits in 1987–1988 led to an all Maghreb summit on 17 February 1989, at Marrakech, where the Maghreb Arab Union, better known by its French name and acronym Union du Maghreb Arabe (UMA), was formed during the meeting of the Heads of State of Algeria, Libya, Mauritania, Morocco, and Tunisia. Article 2 of the Union de Maghreb Arab Treaty stated as one of its main objectives, "To work progressively towards the free movement of persons, services, goods and capital" within its constituent borders.

But its progress has not been smooth. In 1994, Libya, then suffering both US (since 1986) and UN (since 1991) sanctions, threatened to leave the UMA unless Member States ceased to comply with the UN sanctions imposed on Libya, and by 1995 Libya refused to assume the chairmanship of the organization, owing to their continuing compliance to the UN sanctions. As well as this major disagreements between Rabat and Algiers over the Western Sahara conflict persisted. It was not until two events occurred in 1999 that there was an interest in its revival. One was the election of the new Algerian President Abdul Aziz Bouteflika, which was favourably received in Rabat and other Arab Maghreb states. The other was the settlement of Libya's Lockerbie issue through the successful intervention of Nelson Mandela. Combined, these events led to a realistic expectation that it could be meaningfully revived again.

However, persistent problems between Algeria and Morocco continued, which led Libya again in 2004 to threaten to leave the Union if these difficulties could not be resolved. Morocco maintains that the Western Sahara is an integral part of its national territory while Algeria, backed by the United Nations, labels the Western Sahara as a territory occupied by Morocco. Throughout this dispute, Algeria's support for an independent Sahrawi Republic in the Western Sahara has never wavered, making reconciliation unlikely. It is symptomatic of the situation that in May 2005 the seventh Summit of the Union, which was to open that month in Tripoli, was postponed indefinitely. With this lack of interest and political will, even its most ardent supporters, such as its Secretary General Lahbib Boulares, must currently feel that it remains an impossible dream, especially after the formation of CEN-SAD in 1998 which can now claim, with only Algeria and Mauretania absent, to actively represent Maghreb interests in Africa.

Clearly, however, the total demise of UMA would mean many lost opportunities for an effective North African trading bloc, especially with Europe, where the synergy of economic relations with over 30 million members of the North African diaspora in most of the major cities of Europe could make it, potentially, a formidable economic bloc.

7.7.3 Libya Trade Potential with CEN-SAD

The Community of Sahel-Saharan States (CEN-SAD) was established on 4 February 1998 at a conference of leaders and Heads of States held in Tripoli. The original signatories were Libya, Burkina Faso, Mali, Niger, Chad, and the Sudan, joined by the Central African Republic and Eritrea during its First Summit Conference in Sirte in Libya in April 1999, and then by Senegal, Djibouti, and Gambia during the N'djamena Summit Conference held in February 2000. Member states as on June 2005 were Libya, Burkina Faso, Mali, Chad, the Sudan, Niger, Eritrea, the Central African Republic, Senegal, Nigeria, Somalia, Togo, Benin, Gambia, Djibouti, Egypt, Morocco, and Tunisia, Guinea Bissau, Cote d'Ivoire, Liberia, Ghana, and Sierra Leone. In economic terms its main objectives are to achieve the following objectives within the CEN-SAD bloc:

- Free movement of persons, capital, and interests of nationals of Member States.
- Right of establishment, ownership, and exercise of economic activity.
- Free trade, movement of goods, commodities, and services originating from the signatory countries.

Libya, as the driving force behind CEN-SAD, meant to position it as an African Regional Economic Community (REC), one of the basic building blocks of African unity and integration, in line with the concept of RECs laid down in the OAU Abuja Treaty for Establishing the African Economic Community of 1991. Originally five RECs were designated, the Southern Africa Development Community (SADC); the Economic Community of Central African States (ECCAS); the Economic Community of West African States (ECOWAS); COMESA; and the Arab Maghreb Union (AMU). It is worth noting that in the long-term time frame of 40 years for achieving its economic objectives envisaged by the Abuja treaty of 1991, the coordination and harmonization of tariff and non-tariff barriers among various RECs with a view to establishing an African Common market is a major goal. Because AMU, as we have seen, was virtually from its foundation a "dead duck" because of internal Algerian–Moroccan tensions over the Western Sahara, the Libyan leader, in frustration, decided to establish and consolidate CEN-SAD as a regional replacement for the AMU, at the same time stamping his authority and patronage over this body as another platform for his African policy. It is worth noting that Tunisia and Morocco are members, while the Libyan leader has been trying to get Algeria to join. Ghana and Sierra Leone joined CEN-SAD during its Seventh Ordinary Session in Burkina Faso in early June 2005. Unsurprisingly the Secretariat of CEN-SAD is located in Libya.

Overlapping membership of some members of CEN-SAD with other RECs such as COMESA and ECOWAS currently represents a peculiar but not insurmountable feature of CEN-SAD in the long run. Full credit must be given to the Libyan government in forging a potentially formidable socio-economic bloc aimed at the eventual establishment of a United States of Africa. The significant presence and acquiescence of key African politicians such as Hosni Mubarak of Egypt and Olusegun Obasanjo of Nigeria to be part of this 400-million bloc means that CEN-SAD must in the future emerge as a very significant economic force in Africa.

Others argue that CEN-SAD and the officially AU-sanctioned NEPAD (New Partnership for Africa's Development) are in competition and on a collision course. But as a recent researcher has stated, "the African Union and NEPAD have taken CEN-SAD at face value, recognizing it as one of the five regional pillars of African integration and an implementing agency of NEPAD" (Sturman 2003). Similarly, the Communiqué of the NEPAD Heads of State and Government Implementation Committee Meeting in Abuja, November 2002, noted that "the RECs, namely CEN-SAD, COMESA, ECCAS, ECOWAS and SADC participated and presented papers on their roles in the implementation of NEPAD...in light of their status as building blocs in the integration of the continent".

7.7.4 Libya Trade Potential with COMESA

The Treaty which established COMESA was ratified in 1994. Currently COMESA comprises of 20 members: Rwanda, Uganda, Djibouti, Zambia, Kenya, Malawi, Swaziland, Mauritius, D R Congo, Egypt, Zimbabwe, Burundi, Ethiopia, Comoros Islands, Eritrea, Madagascar, Seychelles, Sudan, Zimbabwe, and Libya.

Its aims and objectives, as defined in Article 3 of its Treaty of Establishment entitled "Aims and Objectives of the Common Market" are as follows:

- To attain sustainable growth and development of the Member States by promoting a more balanced and harmonious development of its production and marketing structures.
- To promote joint development in all fields of economic activity and the joint adoption of macroeconomic policies and programmes to raise the standard of living of its peoples and to foster closer relations among its Member States.
- To cooperate in the creation of an enabling environment for foreign, cross-border, and domestic investment including the joint promotion of research and adaptation of science and technology for development.
- To cooperate in the promotion of peace, security, and stability among the Member States in order to enhance economic development in the region.

- To cooperate in strengthening the relations between the Common Market and the rest of the world and the adoption of common positions in international fora.
- To contribute towards the establishment, progress, and the realization of the objectives of the African Economic Community.

From its beginnings, COMESA has been primarily focused on economic concerns and in many ways its establishment was a conscious and deliberate plan to deal with the effects of globalization, and in its website it identifies "the last decade of the 1990s as the globalization decade". Recognizing that globalization has many winners and losers, it goes on to state, "The challenge for COMESA is to ensure that, through its regional integration arrangement, domestic growth and competitiveness of small economies are strengthened, powers of domestically entrenched special-interest groups and rent-seekers weakened, and policy stability and credibility enhanced thus making it easier to attract investment."

The COMESA's initial goal of establishing a Free Trade Area (FTA) was achieved on 31 October 2000, when nine member countries – Djibouti, Egypt, Kenya, Madagascar, Malawi, Mauritius, Sudan, Zambia, and Zimbabwe – eliminated all tariffs on products from fellow COMESA countries, while Rwanda and Burundi joined the FTA in 2004, bringing the total number of countries to 11.

Clearly COMESA, with a combined population of its 20 members of 374 million and its immediate neighbours Egypt and Sudan as members, was an organization that Libya could not afford to be left out of, despite concerns of overlapping membership with CEN-SAD. Accordingly in March 2003 Libya submitted an official request to join COMESA at its eighth Heads of State Summit held in Khartoum, the Sudan. At the time of its submission Libya's African Unity Minister Ali Abdel Salam Triki, one of Libya's most senior ministers and a veteran of Libya's African policy-making, said his country supported "any African action that advances the development of the African continent" (Economist Intelligence Unit, Country Profile Libya 2004). On 6 June 2005 Libya was officially admitted as a member, with its admission formally ratified in August 2006.

The rationale for Libya joining this regional grouping can be analysed on at least two several levels. First, in economic terms, it seems that COMESA had achieved, in practice, with its initial FTA of 11 countries in 2004, many of the economic objectives that AFTA and UMA had been unable to achieve over a much longer period. In pragmatic terms, the attractions of membership of a functioning regional FTA also fits in well with the economic reforms and privatization programme which Libya embarked on in 2003. Secondly, as we will discuss later, Libya in the context of its current diplomatic thrust to seek international recognition and respectability, would like to be a member of the WTO. There were obvious attractions in joining COMESA in this regard, since as a regional trading bloc it was already notified to the WTO under its Enabling Clause on 29 June 1995, and was the only African regional trade arrangement in this position, while 16 COMESA members were also members of WTO.

7.7.5 Libya and the African Union: Economic Integration?

Although in its earlier years the relationship between Libya and the OAU could sometimes be described as rocky, especially after 1977 when Libya occupied Northern Chad, Libya's interventions and support for many African governments had by the mid-1990s rehabilitated the Libyan government in African eyes. For example, in the OAU Summit of 1996 in Youande the African countries adopted a resolution calling for the immediate lifting of UN sanctions against Libya. The African leaders further suggested that, should the Security Council fail to remove the sanctions, the OAU countries might find themselves compelled to act on their own to restore normal air links and restore trade with Libya in order to spare the Libyan people further suffering. Subsequently resolutions calling for sanctions against Libya to be lifted were passed at every OAU Summit from 1997 onwards.

In 1999 the OAU summit in Sirte, Libya, called for "the establishment of an African Union, in conformity with the ultimate objectives of the Charter of our Continental Organization and the provisions of the Treaty establishing the African Economic Community" and called for "the shortening of the implementation periods of the Abuja Treaty". The revamping of the OAU into the "African Union", with a new Constitutive Act to strengthen and update the organization's scope and mandate, was in fact scheduled to be launched at another extraordinary summit in Libya in 2001; however, the Lusaka Summit of 2001 decided that South Africa would host the AU inauguration at the ordinary session of July 2002.

At this assembly there were clear signs of dissension between Libya and South Africa. Libya proposed a range of amendments to the Constitutive Act, including a single currency and army for Africa, an AU Chairman with presidential status and greater powers of intervention in Member States, in line with the Libya's proposals for a "United States of Africa". But because of procedural arguments advanced by South Africa, Libya's ambitious plans for a United States of Africa were put on ice (Sturman and Baimu 2003).

Clearly Africa, as demonstrated by Libya's key roles in both CEN-SAD and in the new AU, is now a focal point for Libya's policy makers. But in many ways African Unity is proceeding too slowly from the Libyan standpoint, which has led some observers to claim that "CEN-SAD has long gone beyond being a community of Sahelian states. Its members have adopted ambitious plans, including entering into obligations of a political, security and military nature. To many, CEN-SAD looks like a 'fast track AU' strongly influenced by Libya" (National Intelligence Council 2004).

Undoubtedly since the 1980s Libya's dealings with Africa have often been controversial and invariably costly. However, as Libya embarks on its comprehensive plans for economic reconstruction, it is now time for Libya's African policy to be solidly grounded on economic integration, in effect "cashing in" on the years of political and financial aid given to many African countries. Because of its strategic location, Libya is well suited, as its long history has proven, to be the entrepot between Europe and Africa. A future of closer economic integration based on transnational roads and airlines, as well as gas pipelines connecting Libya to African countries should be seen, in the long term, as desirable economic goals for Libya's policy makers (Otman 2005).

7.7.6 Libya and the Barcelona Process

In November 1995 the European Union signed a far-reaching declaration with the 12 littoral states of the South Mediterranean at the end of a major conference in Barcelona, which set the scene for future relations between the European Union and the Mediterranean partners. This initiated the Barcelona Process for regional cooperation, also known as the Euro-Mediterranean Partnership. The 12 Mediterranean partners of the European Union are Morocco, Algeria, Tunisia, Egypt, Israel, Jordan, the Palestinian Authority, Lebanon, Syria, Turkey, Cyprus, and Malta. Libya currently has observer status at certain meetings although it does not yet have formal diplomatic relations with the European Union. The Barcelona Declaration was adopted at the end of the conference.

One of the main aims of the Euro-Mediterranean Partnership as part of the Barcelona Process was to promote long-term regional stability through economic development and trade liberalization. Economic development was assumed to have positive impacts on the political, social, and security situation by providing more job opportunities in the partner countries, thus easing pressures on immigration into the European Union region and reducing the attractiveness of extremist ideologies. This aspect has assumed even more significance since the Madrid bombings of 2003 and the London bombings of 2005. It was also felt that liberal economic policies would in the long term lead to more liberal democratic institutions in the partner countries, which will have the effect of enhancing cooperation and stability both domestically and internationally.

Libya currently holds observer status but in a post-sanctions era appears now to be under significant pressure to join the process. For example, a recent media report stated about the Libya leader's visit to Belgium that "on 27 February 2004 President Romano Prodi and Muammar Gaddafi had a very warm and friendly meeting, at which Gaddafi stressed that Libya was ready to start working immediately to join the Barcelona Process" (European Union 2005). During his visit to Libya at the end of 2004, the French President Jacques Chirac raised the issue directly with the Libyan leader.

Currently there exist at least two points of view about the advantages to Libya in joining the EMP. At an intellectual level there are many who believe that the partnership stems from a neo-colonialist approach which seeks to transform the southern Mediterranean into a kind of backyard of Europe, as a poor relation to the European Union. In opposition to this, there are those who see it as an opportunity to be seized, since all other historic efforts for Arab economic integration such as UMA and AFTA have patently failed. However, Libya would do well to weigh its options well before it makes any decision about this matter. For example, Libya at present, with a very long Mediterranean coastline, can regulate its fishing industry as it wishes. This is important because as we have noted elsewhere in this book, fishing in Libya is a long-standing tradition which provides economic activity and valuable nutrition to many Libyan coastal communities. In the past conservation has been achieved by using smaller boats in a limited offshore range. The long-term implications of Libya joining the EMP could mean that more northern Mediterranean countries such as Spain, using sophisticated fishing technology and much larger vessels, could have access to

Libyan waters and devastate the Libyan fishing industry, much the same as has happened to many European Union (EU) countries, where the common fisheries rules have destroyed the fishing industry in several European countries.

Again, with regard to hydrocarbon pricing and volumes into Europe, Libya is free to pursue a policy which responds to supply and demand. With the lifting of the UN and US sanctions in 2004, the potential now exists for Libya to become again one of the major African exporters of natural gas to Europe. On February 2002, Libya joined the Gas Exporting Countries Forum (GECF), formed in 2001 to promote cooperation in the world natural gas industry. Potential exists for a large increase in Libyan gas exports to European markets seeking more North Africa gas, taking the advantages of proximity and stability. However, the implications regarding regulation of volume and pricing of Libyan gas, if Libya were to join the EMP, must be seriously considered by the Libyan authorities. This is because "the Circum-Mediterranean Partners will be affected by the liberalization of the European market in energy and by the various pieces of European Law that forbid monopolistic practices, domestic company preferences, and other market distortions. No doubt the status and privileges of their State Oil Companies will come under the microscope as well. The reader will need no reminding that in this respect international treaties take precedence over domestic law" (Otman and Bunter 2005). In this regard, binding rules for access to gas networks came into effect in Europe on 1 July 2006. They guarantee, among other things, Third Party Access to pipelines and also adopt measures for capacity allocation, congestion management, and transparency in setting tariff structures. Any gas entering the European market will be expected to adhere to EU market rules.

From these considerations it is clear that there may be significant economic disadvantages accruing to Libya in joining the EMP. There are now doubts emerging within Europe itself about the effectiveness of the Barcelona Process. As remarked in a paper on the Barcelona Process 10 years after its commencement,

> if the standard of assessment were that the Barcelona process should have been already transforming the region's economic and political trends, then it has not succeeded. The economic performance of the region has stagnated and its relative performance in relation to Central and Eastern Europe and most of Asia has deteriorated. Political reform has also been almost non-existent. Societal trends, for example tendencies in favour of radical Islam, are deeply worrying. (Emerson and Noucheva 2005).

To correct this, the European Union embarked in 2004 on the European Neighbourhood Policy (ENP), which observers see as an attempt to invigorate the Barcelona process. But many doubts already exist in the minds of the North African countries with regard to the whole rationale and motivation of the process from an Arab viewpoint. One fundamental tension appears to be concerning the amount of European funds allocated for the reconstruction of the Former Soviet Union (FSU) countries, compared with what has gone into North Africa. As one high level observer, Mrs. Khalida Toumi, the Algerian Minister of Culture, has ruefully noted,

> the financial rewards for opening up the markets of the South to the products of the North have proved to be negligible in comparison with the large sums allocated for the structural adjustment of the economies of the Eastern European countries. The only option left to us today is to note that some of these countries have since become full members of the European Union, while the income gap between the EU countries and those on the Southern shores of the Mediterranean continues to widen. (Toumi 2005).

7.7.7 Libya and the World Trade Organization

Libya first applied for membership of the WTO in December 2001, shortly after the appointment of Dr. Shukri Ghanem, as Minister of Trade and Economy, but this request was blocked by the United States for political reasons. After the lifting of the UN and US sanctions in 2003 and 2004, Libya again applied on 10 June 2004. The WTO General Council established a working party on 27 July 2004 to formally consider Libya's application, after WTO members agreed to start talks with Libya on its membership bid.

The World Trade Organization itself was created in 1995 at the completion of the "Uruguay Round" of the GATT (General Agreement on Tariffs and Trade) negotiations. It did not replace GATT, but in fact emerged in 1995 as a powerful international agency to enforce it, along with a series of international trade agreements and declarations on a range of issues from agriculture to intellectual property rights. Unlike GATT, however, which was effectively a business contract between nations, the WTO has a legal personality and the power to enforce its rulings.

In effect this means that once a country accepts the terms and conditions attached to its joining the WTO, it has little choice but to agree to later decisions regarding most aspects of its economy and governance. The dangers in this situation are obvious: using WTO mechanisms, any government, acting on behalf of the corporate interests in their own country, can challenge the laws, policies, and programmes of another government. Dispute resolution is effected using a panel of technical experts, meeting behind closed doors, to decide whether the disputed trade practice constitutes a violation of the WTO rules and, if so, seeks to overturn the offending policy or practice. The losing country in a dispute resolution is faced with three choices: change its law to conform to the WTO ruling; face harsh, permanent economic sanctions; or pay permanent compensation to the winning country. On the other hand, there are also clearly advantages; for example, "one benefit of the accession process is that it forces the government to examine all laws, policies, and institutions affecting international trade and investment. It provides the opportunity to integrate trade policy into the country's overall strategy for economic reform" (World Bank 2006, Country Report on Libya).

7.7.8 WTO and Its International Agreements

The major international agreements administered by the WTO include the following.

The General Agreement on Tariffs and Trade (GATT)

Its mandate is to eliminate all remaining tariff and non-tariff barriers to the movement of capital and goods across nation-state borders.

The General Agreement on Trade in Services (GATS)

A multilateral legally binding agreement on trade in services. Negotiations are currently underway to expand the scope of the GATS to cover all services, which could effectively force any WTO member to open its economy to competition from multinational corporations; this includes key public services such as water, transport, and sewage as well as legal, accounting, auditing and bookkeeping, taxation, medical and dental and veterinary services, and so on. As well as this the entire postal, telecommunications, construction, banking, insurance, tourism, and agriculture industries would also be completely open to foreign competitors.

Trade Related Intellectual Property Rights (TRIPS)

This sets enforceable global rules on patents, copyrights, and trademarks which restrict access to pharmaceuticals and permit the patenting of many plant and animal forms, as well as seeds, opening the door to bio-piracy and the modification of bio-diversity.

Trade Related Investment Measures (TRIMS)

This defines what governments can and cannot do in regulating foreign investment.

The Agreement on the Application of Sanitary and Phytosanitary Standards (SPS)

This sets constraints on government policies relating to food safety and animal and plant health, ranging from those governing pesticide use and biological contaminants to policies on food inspection, product labelling, and genetically engineered foods.

The Financial Services Agreement (FSA)

This was established to remove obstacles to the free movement of financial services corporations, including banks and insurance companies.

The Agreement on Agriculture (AOA)

This sets rules on the international food trade and restricts domestic agriculture policy, including protection against dumping, protection for small-scale farmers producing for their domestic market, government support for farmers and sustainable agricultural practices, maintaining emergency food stocks, and ensuring that citizens have an adequate food supply.

The Agreement on Subsidies and Countervailing Measures (ASCM)

This sets limits on what governments may and may not subsidize and contains many loopholes favouring wealthy countries and agribusiness.

The Agreement on Technical Barriers to Trade (TBT)

This was set up to limit national regulations (non-tariff barriers) that interfere with trade, such as eco-labelling regulations.

The Agreement on Government Procurement (AGP)

This sets limits on government purchasing, including "domestic content", whereby public entities are prohibited from discriminating on grounds other than price and performance when purchasing goods and services. This casts a legal shadow over widely used preferential-bidding practices designed to benefit, for example, small businesses or domestic companies.

7.7.9 Objectives of WTO

The objectives of the WTO are to promote competition by discouraging governmental impediments to the free flow of trade across borders through, among other things, the prohibition of trade-distorting governmental measures and the encouragement of reciprocal reduction elimination of import tariffs. In the case of the latter, Libya has already done this when in September 2005 it cut import tariffs on more than 5000 items.

It is difficult to perceive if at this juncture, in their apparent rush to gain international acceptance and respect, the Libyan Authorities are aware of the extent to which they stand, over the long haul, to compromise national sovereignty, as a WTO member, over key matters relating to the currently ongoing economic transition. The divestment of the Sahara Bank in 2005, for example, which limited potential buyers of shares to Libyan nationals and institutions, would contravene The Financial Services Agreement (FSA). Similarly, Libya's generous subsidy system, whether as direct food subsidies, discussed extensively in Chap. 4, or indirectly in the form of domestic fuel prices and electricity tariffs, would go against the WTO's ASCM. Again, many local government tenders at the Sha'abiyat level, which give preferential treatment to Libyans and Libyan firms, go directly against the AGP.

Again Libya is dissimilar to many third-world countries in Africa, Asia, and the Americas which depend on unrestricted access to major US and European markets for their agricultural produce such as rice, fruit, cocoa, vegetable oils, coffee, and so on which make it imperative for them to join WTO. Libya's traditional agricultural exports are presently limited to relatively minor quantities of olive oil and dates to Europe, while its only major export, oil and gas, currently enjoys virtually unrestricted access to world markets. In this regard, many commentators see, in the future, great potential for conflict between OPEC, of which Libya is a member, and the WTO.

Historically, the relationship between these two institutions has in fact been one of mutual distrust if not open hostility. To begin with, the WTO has yet to decide on OPEC's application for observer-ship, arguably a result equivalent to a silent rejection. Secondly, three important OPEC members, Iraq, Iran and Libya, which account for about 22.2 per cent of the world's proven oil reserves and 10.8% of the world's production, still remain totally outside the WTO system. Saudi Arabia, the most influential OPEC member, could not conclude its accession negotiations for many years until its acceptance as a WTO member in December 2005, allegedly because of its leading role in OPEC, as well as other domestic economic issues.

The question of compatibility of membership, that is whether or not one and the same country could satisfy the membership requirements of these two organizations at the same time is therefore difficult to resolve, since the WTO prohibits its members from using export restrictions, whether individually or through a concerted arrangement with others, while OPEC implicitly demands it. At some point in the near future we believe that the crucial importance of oil in the world economy must lead to a showdown on this issue. In this regard many analysts maintain that the two Gulf wars undertaken by the United States were concerned more with the supply of oil than with issues relating to governance or democracy.

In one respect membership of the WTO would, however, appear to be advantageous in the long term to governments serious about embarking on sustainable economic reform. As two German researchers have stated, in joining the WTO and "submitting a wide range of trade-related policies to international scrutiny and by entering into binding commitments on the conduct of these policies, reform-oriented governments in vulnerable economies can make it more likely that their reforms will be successful" (Langhammer and Lücke, 2000). However, if such reform comes at the price of the virtual surrender of sovereignty over key economic and social issues such as education, health, and housing, support for newly privatized firms, the regulation of the telecommunications and transport industries, the operation of the financial and insurance sectors, and finally key issues relating to production volumes and pricing in Libya's key hydrocarbon industry, then the price of WTO membership might be too high to pay for Libya.

7.8 Libya's Future Trade Options: Striking the Right Balance

In the above analysis of Libya's regional and international economic alignments, both actual and potential, it is interesting to note that, despite the debilitating effects of the US and UN sanctions on ordinary Libyans and Libyan entrepreneurs and policy makers, the Libyan government has, in a post-sanctions era, emerged with many options regarding its future international economic realignment.

This is in spite of the fact that, as many would argue, both national and international policies have been idiosyncratic and short-sighted, ignoring long-term costs. Clearly most credit for her present enhanced standing in the international community must go to the Libya's shrewd diplomacy, which has accomplished what the previous Iraqi government could not – an accommodation with the United States in spite of all the odds stacked against the country.

In our detailed analysis of the whys and wherefores of Libya's regional alignments, it is perhaps useful to distinguish, in general terms, between three types of motivation underlying Libyan policy. The first type, in the case of AFTA or UMA, may be described as part of a regional policy directed to promote security and economic ties and build collective identity among members, in these cases either Arab or Maghreb. This is the type of regional policy also demonstrated by, for example, the Association of South East Asian Nations (ASEAN), where distinct geographical and cultural ties drive the economic objectives. Clearly, however compared, with the growing economic success of ASEAN, both of the Arab regional groupings have failed.

Bearing in mind Libya's geographical location as part of the African continent, we can also perceive that perhaps both CEN-SAD and COMESA fall into this category. While, as we have seen, the dramatic rise of CEN-SAD has in some senses led to a north–south political polarization in the AU, with the Libyan-led CEN-SAD competing for domination with the South African–led NEPAD bloc, the gradual economic expansion and pragmatic successes of COMESA show that it is much more focused in seeking the purely economic advantages offered by a regional grouping. Libya clearly could not afford to ignore these impressive successes and this led to her joining this regional grouping in 2005.

The case of Libya and the Barcelona Process is more complex. Excluded as a member by the sanctions, her present "observer status" and the active wooing for her to join in the Process by France and Italy have both come at a time when it seems that this 10-year-old EU initiative has demonstrably failed. There now exist strong suspicions among North African countries about its real motives – the use of North Africa as a security buffer against the rest of Africa, both in terms of immigration as well as long-term economic competition from the African continent, and to secure North Africa's hydrocarbon production and reserves for southern Europe. It was, in fact, fortunate for Libya that the sanctions precluded her from joining this regional grouping, since its concept of a "Mediterranean identity" was clearly spurious when compared with that of an Arab or European identity. This dichotomy is clearly brought out in the European Union's treatment of Turkey; while the FSU countries have been fast-tracked into the European

Union, Turkey's attempts at membership were initially sidelined and subsequently subjected to protracted delays and conditionality.

A second type of regional action might be more simply described as "hedging"; in this situation the country takes part because others do so, but without necessarily possessing, at time of joining, a clear vision of where they want to go. Here the view might be to wait and see. It appears that COMESA falls also into this category, both because CEN-SAD appears to already fulfil many of COMESA's regional objectives, and because the latter's rapid economic success suggests that its future potential might be considerable.

The third type is when belonging to a regional bloc might be perceived as a necessary part of the globalization process. Here regional groupings represent the first step in preparation for global competition. This is part of a widespread perception, actively promoted by the WTO and its two sister organizations, the IMF and the World Bank, that globalization constitutes an ineluctable process which will slowly and surely end in one global market. But Libya would do well to avoid such simplistic thinking, since by doing so she will allow herself, like many Africa, Asian, and South American nations, to become hostage to the dominant IMF/World Bank/WTO ideology which has an agenda not entirely focused on the individual well-being of member countries. Many countries ranging from Indonesia and the Philippines to South Korea to Argentina and Brazil have learned, to their chagrin, that the process is not entirely altruistic.

Are we therefore to assume that the present growing trend towards regionalism, evidenced by the recent expansion of ASEAN and the European Union itself, is a response to the now recognized dangers of globalization as defined by the WTO? The answer must be an unequivocal yes, with many nations now realizing, through bitter experience, the impacts of diminished sovereignty, increasing interference, a ruined agricultural sector, and in certain cases outright humiliation.

The fact is that there are around 148 WTO member countries, but their interests both individually and regionally are very diverse. There cannot be a "one size or policy fits all" approach as the repeated WTO/IMF policy failures have shown. It is now even more imperative that those countries who have similar kinds of interests come together and form trading blocs to benefit the populations living in those countries.

In respect to Libya's application to join the WTO, which gained approval to proceed with the first stage of entry discussions in July 2004, Mrs. Najat Mehdi al-Hajjaji, Libya's Ambassador to the United Nations, stated, "Sometimes developing countries might not get all the benefits they need, but it is something that we cannot stay outside. It is a disadvantage to the country to stay outside of this organization" (Associated Press 27 July 2004).

Normally the approval process will take several years and doubtless a continuous dialogue will emerge surrounding the conditionalities for Libya's joining. As recognized by the Libyan authorities, this will involve major changes in the country's laws and policies, which at this point cannot be precisely determined. More significantly, however, membership of the WTO will consolidate the reform process and in the long term contribute to Libya's successful economic transformation.

8 Economic Reform and Diversification

8.1 Modernizing Libya's Financial Sector

Watershed legislation in Libya such as Law No. 5 for the year 1997 concerning the Encouragement of Foreign Capital Investment, and more recently Banking Laws No. 1 and 2 which will be discussed later in this chapter, have demonstrated the seriousness of Libya's policy makers regarding economic reform and the privatization and deregulation of its centralized economy, the legacy of the nationalization drive of the 1970s. Part of this process is a desire to attract FDI into Libya, with massive amounts of investment required, especially to overhaul the ageing and technologically antiquated hydrocarbon, refining and petrochemical sectors, the infrastructure deficit, as well as revitalizing the tourist, service and, manufacturing industries.

Many studies have shown that the lack of development of local financial institutions and markets can adversely affect an economy's ability to take advantage of the potential benefits of FDI (Borensztein et al. 1998). In simple terms it is clear that poor financial markets may mean that a country will not be in a position to cope with or absorb either short- or long-term capital flows. A study has, based on the empirical data, also shown that "FDI plays an important role in contributing to economic growth. However, the level of development of local financial markets is crucial for these positive effects to be realized" (Alfaro et al. 2004).

Similarly, in an analysis of the roles of different types of financial institutions, Levine and Zervos (1996) have shown that while efficient banks and stock markets provide a variety of different financial services, both stock market liquidity and banking development positively predict growth, capital accumulation, and productivity improvements. In the following sections we will look at the Libyan government's recent record in reforming its financial institutions. Our conclusion is that while the process has already started, Libya still has a long way to ensure that foreign investors, with every country to choose from in a globalized world, would necessarily choose to invest their capital in Libya.

8.2 The Need for Reform of the Banking Sector

Since the demise of the Former Soviet Union, a huge body of literature has emerged about banking reform in transition countries, and a useful way of distinguishing and deciding on reform methodologies is to compare two basic approaches, either new entry or rehabilitation. A prominent economist has defined these as follows:

> The new entry approach entails the spontaneous break up and privatization of existing state banks, the entry of many new banks, and in some cases the liquidation of old banks. The approach is best illustrated by Russia and Estonia where it resulted in a rapid expansion in the number of banks, in Russia for example from 5 in 1989 to 2,500 in 1995. The rehabilitation approach emphasizes the recapitalization of existing state banks together with an extensive programme to develop them institutionally and eventually to privatize them. Break-ups and new entry are relatively limited. This approach is exemplified by Hungary and particularly Poland (Claessens 1995).

In actual fact in the early stages of reform it may not be evident that a consistent financial approach at all is being practised, and the reform process may include aspects of both approaches. In Libya, as usually elsewhere, the situation is even more complicated by the fact that banking reform is not taking place in a vacuum, but is closely related to an overall reform agenda aimed at both the privatization of many inefficient SOEs, as well as a conscious effort by the government to attract FDI into such industries as tourism, manufacturing, and agriculture. This is seen as crucial in order to diversify the economy away from overdependence on revenue from hydrocarbons.

Similarly the extent and tempo of legal and enterprise reform will also have an effect on the reform and evolution of the financial system. Banks rely on the legal system, including procedures for collateral recovery and bankruptcy, to enforce their claims and perform their roles as monitors of firms. In this respect the legal framework in Libya, based on the Commercial Code of 1953, and the Civil Code and Civil Code of Procedure of 1954, which were based on French and Italian Civil Laws, have, despite the revolution, continued to function alongside Islamic legal principles, known as the "Sharia", to provide a fundamental source of commercial law relating to banking.

In this regard another recent key piece of legislation discussed extensively in Chap. 3, the Executive Regulation of the Law No. 21 of 2001, regarding the Practice of Economic Activities, amended by Law No. 1 of 2004, has also attempted to put in place a comprehensive set of legal rules and regulations regarding contract law, covering both Libyan national companies as well as foreigner companies.

8.2.1 The Evolution of the Libyan Banking Sector

It can be said that, generally speaking, the financial sector in Libya has been solidly based in law, and this applies also to the bank nationalization exercise, which took place after the 1969 revolution. Even before this, in 1963 Law No. 4 "Promulgating the Banking Law" was gazetted, and in Chap. 1, entitled "The Central Bank", the National Bank of Libya was replaced by the CBL, and provisions for its establishment and management were laid down. With an authorized capital of one million Libyan pounds it possessed, among other things, the sole right to issue currency, with the responsibility for maintaining monetary stability and the external value of the Libyan currency, as well as for regulating credit. In Law No. 4, as defined in Article 25, "the par value of the Libyan pound is equal to 2.48828 grams of fine gold", and the Libyan currency unit remained tied to sterling until the sterling devaluation of November 1967, when the Libyan pound failed to devalue.

The 92 Articles of the 22 page Law covered a wide range of banking issues, ranging from board composition, management, currency issue, sale and import of gold, its regulatory role as the watchdog mandated to monitor commercial banks and their management and liquidity and reserve ratios, as well as issuing banking licences. For its time it can be said to represent a fairly standard comprehensive piece of legislation in which the role and functions of a Central Bank and monetary authority were transparently defined and set out.

The banking sector, together with all others, changed dramatically when in November 1969 the new Libyan government required that all banks in the country should be Libyan controlled, buying out the 51 per cent control of the commercial banks that had not already converted to Libyan control. In July 1970, the government took 100 per cent control of four of the major banks with foreign minority ownership. In December 1970, the government purchased outright all banks that still had some foreign minority participation and, by merging, reduced the number of commercial banks to five.

The situation up to 1987 was that in addition to the National Commercial Bank, other commercial banks in operation included the Jamahiriya Bank (formerly Barclay's Bank), previously known as the Jumhuriya Bank until 1977, the Al-Sahari Bank (formerly the Banco di Sicilia), the Umma Bank (formerly the Banco di Roma), and the Wahda Bank, formed in 1970 from the merger of five other banks. Since the mid-1990s the Libyan government has been actively encouraging the setting-up of regional or Ahliah banks, and several new banking licences were issued, leading to the situation that by 2005, there were a total of 54 banks in operation, comprising 6 commercial banks, 4 specialized banks subsequently discussed, and 44 regional or Ahliah Banks (Appendices 8.1 and 8.2).

As well as these state-owned commercial banks, the Libyan government owns the National Agricultural Bank, the Industrial and Real Estate Bank of Libya, the Libyan Arab Foreign Bank (LAFB) and the Development Bank. The NAB, a specialized institution, had originally been established in 1957 to assist the agricultural sector by providing interest-free production loans to farmers. As well as this, it made medium-term loans for up to 5 years for machinery and materials and long-term loans for up to 15 years for land reclamation projects, irrigation, and agricultural construction. The NAB purchased produce from farmers at a guaranteed profit and sold the supplies at subsidized prices.

The Industrial and Real Estate Bank of Libya was both a developmental bank, offering industrial credits, and a home finance agency, making loans for home purchases.

In early 1972, the government established the LAFB as a wholly owned subsidiary of the Central Bank, but not subject to the Central Bank's legislation, regulations, or exchange control, and it is the only Libyan bank with offshore status. It engages in financial and banking operations outside the country and acts as the foreign agent for the government and Libyan commercial banks. Its main purposes were to encourage regional development, particularly of countries friendly to Libya, to become active in international financial markets, and to serve as a vehicle for Libyan aid to other countries.

Since its establishment it has expanded its influence and prestige overseas, with now more than 38 subsidiaries in 25 countries, where its international standing is well known and appreciated, being the only Libyan financial institution able to handle foreign accounts during the sanctions period. Reflecting the bank's new strategy of diversifying its channels of investment and a desire to maintain a strong position in regional and international markets, LAFB significantly increased its balance sheet in 2004, growing by 18.1 per cent to $11.2 billion. In pre-tax profit terms the bank increased profits by a factor of 6 in 2004 to reach $51.5 million compared with $8.4 million in 2003, in short showing, in a dramatic way, the immediate effects of the lifting of the sanctions on Libya, with 2004 results producing an Return on Equity (ROE) of 16 per cent.

In 1981 the Development Bank was established under law No. 8 to replace the former Industrial Department of the Industrial and Real Estate Real Estate Bank which then became known as the Savings and Real Estate Bank. (Table 8.1)

Law No. 1 of 1993 for Banking, Currency and Credit effectively replaced the 1963 Law No. 4 discussed earlier, covering and updating its main provisions, and increased the authorized capital of the CBL to LD100 million. In theory the 1993 Banking Law allowed foreign banks to open branches in Libya, with approval from the Central Bank and the Libyan Cabinet, but so far this has been limited to the opening of a representative office of Bahrain-based Arab Banking Corporation in Misuratah in 1996 and later the Maltese-based Bank of Valletta and Egypt's Suez Bank.

In a domestic Libyan context one of the main results of the 1993 Law was the establishment of the Bank of Commerce and Development (BCD) in 1994, with 2,000 private shareholders, the only privately owned commercial bank in the Libyan market, which eventually started operations in 1996. Since then it has grown rapidly, from having one branch in Benghazi to eleven branches throughout Libya. Compared with state-owned banks, the BCD has championed innovations including telephone, PC, drive in, and internet banking services. While the government-owned banks focus on corporate banking and on serving the huge public sector, BCD does not have a government-sourced asset base, and so must compete with a superior service strategy, providing customers with services such as ATMs and credit cards, in essence representing the way forward for modern banking in Libya.

Table 8.1. Libya: specialized banks

Bank name	Branches	Date of establishment	Legislation
Development Bank	23	1981	Law No. 8
Saving and Real Estate Bank	27	1981	Law No. 2
Agriculture Bank	–	Founded in 1955 and re-established in 1970	Law No. 133
Libyan Arab Foreign Bank	–	Established in 1972	Law No. 18

Source: Authors.

8.2.2 Regulating Libya's Banking Sector: Towards a Modern System

In the most comprehensive banking legislation approved for many years, the two Banking Laws Nos 1 and 2 of 2005 have finally attempted to deliver a banking system to Libya corresponding to its international aspirations for economic renewal and globalization. The first deals with the CBL, specifying its powers and operating framework, as well as defining its precise legal relationship to the Libyan government, which in recent years has given much cause for speculation in Libya (Aleslam 2002), while the second sets out to deal effectively with money laundering and its connections with international terrorism as well as domestic corruption in Libya.

With respect to the CBL's relationship with the government, Article 2 of Law No. 1 is very specific, stating

> The Bank shall be under the auspices of the Secretariat of the General People's Congress and shall carry out its duties in pursuit of its objectives as stipulated in this law within the framework of the government's general policy. To this end, the Central Bank of Libya may adopt the principles and procedures it deems appropriate, and it may establish rules and regulations related to its operations and to financial, administrative, or other matters by means of decrees of the board of directors.

Regarding authorized capital, Article 4 states: "The authorized capital of the CBL shall be LD500 million, which may be increased by decree of the secretariat of the General People's Congress upon the recommendation of the Board of Directors, in coordination with the secretariat of the General People's Committee on Finance."

The broad macroeconomic responsibilities of the bank are outlined in Article 5, in line with Libya's changing economic posture. These are to:

- Issue the Libyan currency and maintain its stability within Libya and abroad
- Manage the government's reserves of gold and foreign exchange
- Regulate monetary policy and supervise currency conversion transactions within Libya and abroad
- Regulate credit and banking policy and supervise its implementation within the framework of the government's general policy
- Achieve the goals of economic policy in terms of stabilizing the general level of prices and maintaining the soundness of the banking system
- Manage the liquidity of the national economy
- Regulate and supervise the foreign exchange market
- Provide advice to the government on matters related to the general economic policy

The CBL's functions and relationship with Libyan public administrative units and public entities and enterprises as well as other Libyan government-owned commercial banks are spelled out in Article 9.

The CBL shall provide banking services according to the following rules:

- The Bank shall engage in banking activities relating to public administrative units required to deposit their balances in the CBL, and it shall provide banking services to those units. The Bank shall not pay any interest on the sums and balances deposited in the accounts of public administrative units, and it shall not collect any fee for the banking services that it provides to such units.
- The Bank may accept deposits from, and provide banking services to, public entities and enterprises. The Bank shall collect consideration for the banking services that it provides according to the provisions of this paragraph and the banking services price list issued by decree of the CBL's board of directors.
- The Bank may, with the approval of the Financial Secretariat, assign commercial banks to hold the account balances of several public administrative units and provide banking services to these units based on the limits and terms decreed by the CBL's board of directors.

Clarification is provided for the relationship between the CBL and the Financial Secretariat in Article 11, again previously an area undefined and not transparent:

The bank may provide temporary advances to the public treasury to cover any temporary deficit in general budget revenues based on the terms agreed between the CBL and the Financial Secretariat, which must include the following:

- Such advances must not exceed one-fifth of the total estimated revenues in the general budget.
- Any advance must be repaid at the end of the fiscal year in which it was provided. No advance may be provided to the public treasury in a given fiscal year until after the advances provided to the public treasury during the previous fiscal year have been repaid.

Similarly in Article 17, the banks' subordination to the General People's Congress with respect to the appointment of its most senior officials is clearly set out:

The governor and the deputy governor shall be appointed by decree of the General People's Congress for a period of five years. They may be reappointed. The four members other than the under-secretary general stipulated in Article 14 of this law shall be appointed by decree of the secretariat of the General People's Congress, after consultation with the governor, for a period of three years. They may be reappointed.

Again, Article 24 unequivocally defines its ongoing accountability to the General People's Congress:

Immediately after the end of the last day of each month, the CBL shall prepare and publish a statement of its assets and liabilities at the close of its operations on that day or at the close of the immediately preceding business day if the last day of the month is a holiday. It shall send a copy of this statement to the secretariat of the General People's Congress and the secretariat of the General People's Committee. The statement shall also be published in the Register of Procedures.

Turning to the important area of exchange rates in the rapidly changing role of Libya in the international arena, as the reform, diversification, and privatization processes of the Libyan economy proceed, Article 32 provides that:

> The Bank, in coordination with the General People's Committee, shall set and shall be responsible for managing, the exchange rate of the Libyan Dinar against foreign currencies according to domestic and international financial and economic developments so as to achieve the interests of the national economy.

Again, to emphasize Libya's very recent realignment with the United States and Europe, Article 56, Part II, Sect. 2, states, "The Central Bank of Libya shall establish the rules needed to counter money laundering operations and the financing of terrorism."

It is in Chap. 2 of the Law, covering The Establishment and Supervision of Commercial Banks, that the full extent of the liberalization of the Libyan banking system can be observed, with regard to the ease of establishment of both Libyan domestic and foreign banks, covered in Articles 65, 66, and 67 quoted in full below:

Article 65

I. Any company that ordinarily accepts deposits in current demand accounts or time deposits, grants loans and credit facilities, and engages in other such banking activities according to the provisions of paragraph (II) of this article shall be considered a commercial bank.

   A specialized bank whose main purpose is to finance and grant credit for specific activities, and whose basic activities do not include the acceptance of demand deposits, shall not be considered a commercial bank. Special banks may be permitted to engage in some commercial banking activities for the beneficiaries thereof by decree of the board of directors of the Central Bank of Libya.

II. The following shall be considered activities in which a commercial bank engages:
   - The cashing of checks made out to and by customers.
   - Services relating to documentary credits, documents for collection, and letters of credit.
   - Issuance and management of instruments of payment including monetary drawings, financial transfers, payment and credit cards, traveller's checks, etc.
   - Sale and purchase transactions involving monetary market instruments and capital market instruments to the credit of the bank or its customers.
   - The purchase and sale of debt, without or without the right of recourse.
   - Lease financing operations.
   - Foreign exchange transactions in spot and forward exchange markets.
   - The management, coverage, distribution, and transaction of banknote issues.
   - The provision of investment and other services for investment portfolios, and the provision of investment trustee services, including the management and investment of funds for a third party.
   - Management and safekeeping of securities and valuables.

- Provision of trustee or financial investor services.
- Any other banking activities approved by the Central Bank of Libya.

Article 66

I. Each commercial or specialized bank must obtain a license to engage in banking activities before commencing such activities. The board of directors of the Central Bank of Libya shall issue this license. This license shall replace the license stipulated in the Commercial Law. The following shall be observed before the license is granted:
   - The founding committee shall submit a request to the Central Bank of Libya with the attached documents stipulated by the committee.
   - Capital shares shall not be offered for subscription until after the Central Bank of Libya's preliminary approval has been obtained.
   - The granting of a license should not entail a violation of any provision of this law, other laws, and regulations.
   - The commercial name adopted by the bank shall not be identical or similar to the name of any other bank or other establishment to the degree of causing confusion.

II. It shall be prohibited for any establishment not licensed to engage in banking activities under this law to use the word "bank" and synonyms thereof or any expression similar thereto in any language, whether in its designation, commercial address, or advertising.

Article 67

I. Commercial banks must assume the form of a Libyan joint-stock company with paid-up capital of at least LD10 million divided into shares. The value of share shall not exceed LD10. The shares may be held by natural persons and public and private legal entities according to the rules and conditions stipulated in a decree issued by of the board of directors of the Central Bank of Libya, subject to the stock ownership limits established under legislation in effect. Each bank should fulfil its subscribed capital during a period not exceeding five years from granting its license. However, granting such a license to commercial banks to carry out their activities should not avert the Central Bank from discharging its power to assess their ownership structure.

II. Banks in existence upon this law's entry into force must render their situations consistent with the provisions of this law within three years of this law's entry into force. The board of directors of the Central Bank of Libya may extend this period by another three-year period.

III. The Central Bank of Libya may permit the establishment of banks with foreign capital. It may also permit foreign banks to hold shares in domestic banks and to open branches or representation offices in Libya according to the terms and conditions established by the Board of Directors of the Central Bank of Libya, provided the head office of the foreign bank branch has a specific nationality, the foreign bank is subject to the supervision of the monetary authority in the country where the head office is located, and the capital allocated for the branch's activity in Libya is at least $50 million.

However regarding mergers and privatizations, Article 87 clearly demonstrates the watchdog status of the Central Bank: "No bank may merge with another bank without the approval of the board of directors of the Central Bank of Libya. The governor shall stipulate in a decree the procedures that must be followed in this case."

Article 91 deals with the importance of individual bank failures and the security of depositors funds held in such banks, establishing a "Depositors' Funds Guarantee Fund":

I. A fund designated the "Depositors' Funds Guarantee Fund" shall be established to insure deposits in banks operating in Libya. It shall be a legal entity and shall have independent financial liability. Its members shall include all banks in operation that accept deposits. The fund shall be subject to the supervision of the CBL. The fund's head office shall be in the city of Tripoli.

Article 97 deals with important issues relating to conflict of laws and transparency, as well as resolving key issues related to e-commerce, bringing Libya in line with international banking practices and mitigating many concerns of potential investors in Libya:

- The provisions of the Civil and Commercial Codes shall apply to banks to the extent that these provisions do not conflict with the provisions of this law.
- Electronic documents and signatures executed in the framework of banking transactions and other transactions related thereto shall be honoured and shall have a determinative effect in substantiating the data contained therein.
- Computer output pertaining to banking transactions shall be regarded, as stipulated in the previous paragraph, as equivalent to the legal books stipulated in the Commercial Code and laws that complement it. Banks must retain, for the period established in the law, miniature copies of books, records, statements, documents, correspondence, cables, notices, and other documents relating to its activities on hard, floppy, or compact disks or other current data or information storage devices instead of the originals. These copies shall have the determinative effect of the original for evidentiary purposes.

Finally the pre-eminence and importance of this groundbreaking new banking legislation is confirmed in Article 120, which states:

> Law No 1 of 1993 regarding Banking, Currency and Credit is hereby repealed and so are any other provisions that may contradict the provisions of this law. Any other regulations and decrees that are not in conflict with the provisions of this Law shall remain in effect until are repealed by a new regulations and decrees issued pursuant thereto.

8.2.3 Financial Governance and Legislative/Executive Tensions

In this brief survey of the early and recent reform of Libyan banking law, we have demonstrated how the Libyan government, realizing the fundamental role of the banking sector as one of the main pillars for the development of the private sector in any market-oriented economy, has shown serious intent in promoting its reformist strategy. To ensure this it has not only strengthened and broadened the role of the Libyan Central Bank, but also has introduced a new paradigm in transparency, as well as making a major effort to realign Libya with international financial institutions and practices, at the same time opening the door for the establishment of foreign banks in Libya. These, when operational, will be instrumental in providing conduits for the significant volume of FDI targeted by Libya's policy makers not only to modernize and expand the Libyan hydrocarbon sector, but also to privatize many key industries now on life-support systems, as well as diversifying the economy away from overdependence on oil into tourism, manufacturing, real estate, and agriculture.

But there is still a long way to go towards banking reform, and clearly before any new banking licences are issued many generic problems covering the entire banking sector need to be addressed. Again, to quote the 2006 IMF Country Report on Libya "A more efficient, market-oriented and sound banking system is also needed if Libya is to succeed in reforming its economy. This will require (i) enhancing banking supervision; (ii) restructuring the banking system; (iii) modernizing the domestic payment system; and (iv) revising the legal and regulatory frameworks" (IMF 2006).

However in certain other ways Banking Law No. 1, although recapitalizing and bringing the CBL with global norms in the banking industry is still a fundamentally flawed piece of legislation. This is because, as we have noted earlier, Article 2 specifically states that "the CBL shall be under the auspices of the Secretariat of the General People's Congress". However as we have seen in Chaps. 1 and 3, the GPC as the supreme legislative body meets only once or twice a year, for periods of less than two weeks. This means that macroeconomic changes and fine tuning cannot be implemented on an ongoing and perhaps urgent basis, by the Libyan Prime Minister in Cabinet, since this can only be approved by the CBL whose authority emanates from the GPC. Because of this there are inherent tensions in this relationship, placing great pressures on the General People's Committee, or Libyan Cabinet, in its coordination of the economic reform efforts.

8.2.4 Privatization of Domestic Banks

In this connection the Libyan government's plans to sell two large state-owned banks to private investors, the Al-Sahari Bank and the Al-Wahda Bank, have, since an announcement in early 2005, raised much media speculation.

The Al-Sahari Bank is a Libyan Stock Company, formerly the Banco di Sicilia, established in July 1964. In 1966 Banco di Sicilia sold 51 per cent of its capital to the Libyan private sector, 29 per cent to the Bank of America and kept 20 per cent of its capital and it became a national bank, Al-Sahari Bank. Later, the bank was re-organized and the shares of the Italian and American banks were nationalized, with the Libyan Central Bank owning 70 per cent of the share capital and the private sector holding 30 per cent equity. The financial position of the bank (Fig. 8.1) shows that the value of assets of the bank has more than doubled during a period of 10 years between 1994 and 2003, from LD808 million in 1994 to LD1,716 million in 2003.

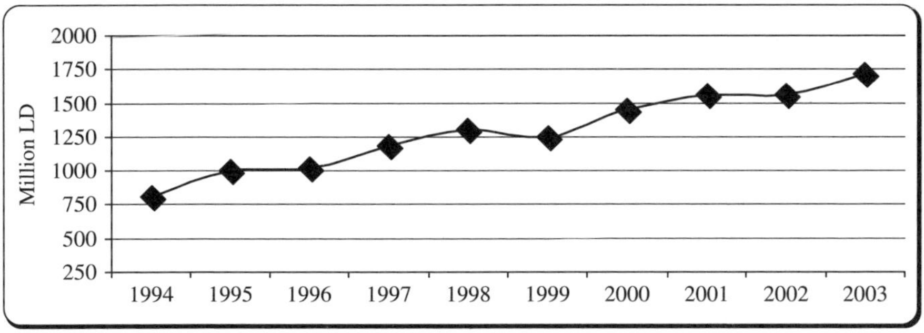

Source: Al-Sahari Bank, Annual Reports 2000, 2002, 2003

Fig. 8.1. Al-Sahari Bank: total financial position between 1994 and 2003

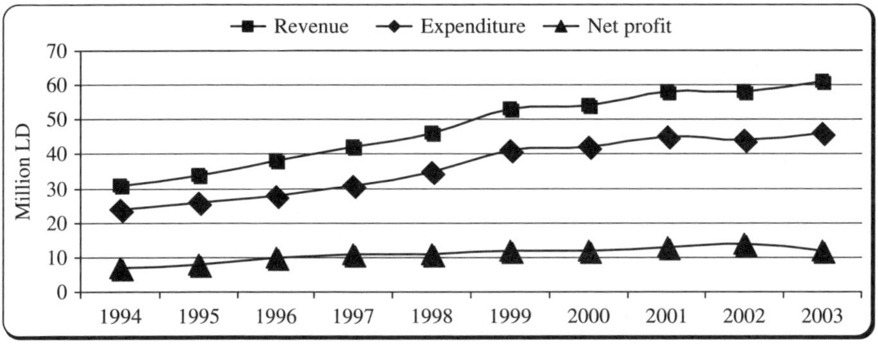

Source: Al-Sahari Bank, Annual Reports, 2000, 2002, 2003

Fig. 8.2. Al-Sahari Bank: revenues, expenditure, and net profit, 1994–2003

As regards revenues, expenditure and net profits, revenues more than doubled during the same period (1994–2003), and so did expenditure (Fig. 8.2). However profits, due to high expenditure, were only a fraction of the total revenues, ranging between LD7.8 million in 1994 and LD14.147 million in 2003.

In a public offering in mid-June 2005 the Libyan Central Bank made available 50 per cent of its stake in the Al-Sahari Bank at LD10 per share. However, by 2006, it became clear that the divestment of the Al-Sahari bank had not been successful, with only 15 per cent of its shares taken up by the Libyan public and institutions. The gradualist approach to banking reform is also highlighted by an announcement at the end of June 2005 by the CBL Governor, Ahmed al-Menissi, that the Benghazi-based Wahda Bank was also being assessed for privatization (Libya Focus 2005). Although, as we have seen, the new banking law allows foreign banks to operate in Libya, it seems that the CBL strategy is to privatize and strengthen selected local banks first before opening up the banking sector to foreign participation.

8.2.5 The Libyan Dinar's International Exchange Rate

Operating as a Central Bank or monetary board, the Libyan Central Bank is tasked with a wide range of responsibilities and powers, among which are to "issue the Libyan currency and maintain its stability within Libya and abroad" and to "regulate and supervise the foreign exchange market." As a general policy the bank has followed a policy of pegging the LD, either to the US dollar or to the IMF's SDR. In historical terms this has led to the LD being overvalued in international terms. Since the early 1970s until fairly recently, all businesses in the country were state controlled, and were essentially operated without the need to make profits in a conventional sense, but only to supply a range of goods and services to the Libyan people at controlled prices. In these circumstances this overvaluation of the LD did not have a major impact on Libya's general economic situation, and in any case there were no significant external demand factors, which could cause wild market fluctuations in the value of the LD.

However, in the current situation where the Libyan policy makers have embarked on an economic reform agenda, where one of the main objectives is the successful attraction of FDI into Libya, the value of the LD assumes much more significance. This is because exchange rate movements have long been considered to be a crucial factor for FDI, although in the literature, explanations of the role that the exchange rate plays in FDI decisions have varied widely. One interpretation is that multinational firms consider investing in a foreign country if it perceives the currency of that country to be undervalued, so that the initial investment outlay is lower than if the currency is overvalued. A related explanation for a negative relationship between FDI and currency valuation is that the firm may attempt to offset the changing demand for their exports due to exchange rate movements. For instance, if a company builds a manufacturing plant in a foreign country, it can reduce exposure to possible depreciation of that country's currency by incurring production costs in that country that offset the reduced revenues in that country's currency.

On the other hand, some researchers hypothesize that multinational firms are more likely to invest in a country when its currency is stronger. This occurs if a weak currency is associated with higher exchange rate risk, which in turn affects the expected profits from that country. This line of reasoning also implies a negative relationship between foreign exchange volatility and FDI flows. Empirical findings on the relationship between exchange rate movements and FDI are however mixed. Edwards (1990) identified a positive relationship between a country's currency value and its FDI inflows, while Blonigen and Feenstra (1996) reported a negative relationship. However Blonigen (1997) and Goldberg (1993) showed that the exchange rate has a major effect on FDI. While Crowley and Lee (2003) found evidence supporting a negative effect of exchange rate volatility on FDI in some countries, Goldberg (1993) and Campa and Goldberg (1995) found the effect to be largely insignificant.

But clearly the CBL's perception was that an overvalued LD would have a negative impact on FDI. In a major move towards a market-driven economy, the Libyan Central Bank devalued the LD by 51 per cent at the beginning of 2002. Until June 2003 a dual exchange rate system still existed in Libya, in which individual or private companies requiring foreign currency used the "commercial rate" while an "official rate" was set for transactions involving state firms. In that month, however, again as part of its efforts to reform the economy and attract FDI, the CBL unified its LD exchange rate.

As seen by the IMF, the effects of these reforms appear to be positive: "In view of the existing price rigidities, it is difficult to assess the appropriate exchange rate level for Libya. The authorities indicated, however, that the exchange rate market is functioning smoothly and no parallel market for the Libyan currency has developed since the unification of the exchange rate in 2002." Again, to quote the IMF 2006 Country Report, "the absence of pressures on the exchange rate following the implementation of current account convertibility and the increased liberalization of external trade are indications that the current exchange rate of the LD is broadly appropriate" (IMF 2006). However, the IMF also deems it necessary to propose that "by the end of the first reform phase (2008), as structural and macroeconomic reforms progress and the non-oil economy starts to develop, the authorities could consider the desirability and feasibility of switching to a more flexible exchange rate regime that would give them more room of manoeuvre to respond to sharp changes in oil prices" (IMF 2006).

Changes in LD's value against the US dollar and sterling are shown in the following Fig. 8.3, for the period 1966–2005.

8.3 Liberalizing of the Libyan Insurance Market

In any country, the main economic functions of the insurance sector are to cover financial risks associated with health, longevity, property, and trade and commerce, at the same time mobilizing long-term savings. In Libya, however, as discussed in Chap. 4, the "cradle to the grave" state social security philosophy adopted by the revolutionary government after 1969 has meant that, for an average Libyan citizen, concerns about health and accidents covered in some countries by private insurance, such as injury at work, sickness, pensions, redundancy and even the cost of burial, are all catered for by the comprehensive social security safety net provided by the state. Free healthcare and comprehensive education up to the university level also mean that many types of life insurance or annuity policies used in western countries to plan for the financing of higher education of children, or for retirement, are also deemed to be unnecessary.

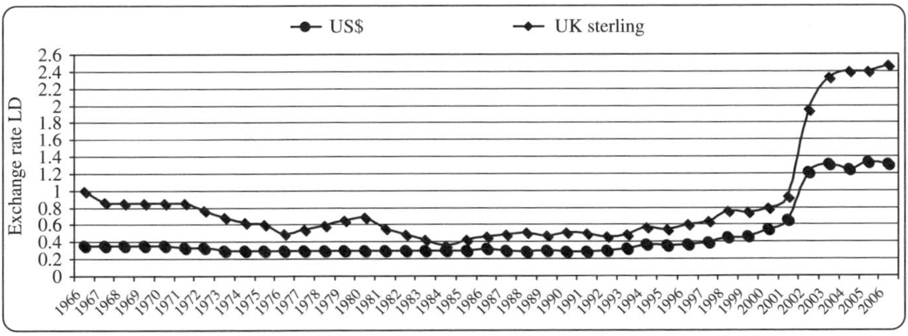

Fig. 8.3. Libya: US dollar and Sterling/LD exchange rate, 1966–2006

There may also be concerns in cultural and religious terms about insurance in the western sense, and for generations, many Muslims around the world have grown with a mind set that insurance, particularly life insurance, is "haram" (forbidden) because it contravenes Islamic Sharia tenets. Life insurance as sold in conventional way was declared unacceptable in 1903 by some prominent Islamic scholars in the Arab countries. However, as the Malaysian insurance experience demonstrated in the 1990s, the development of the Islamic "Takaful" insurance system became acceptable to Muslims in that country after, in 1985, the Grand Counsel (Majma al-Fiqh) of Islamic scholars in Makkah, Saudi Arabia, approved the "Takaful" system as an alternative form of insurance written in compliance with Islamic Sharia.

In the early years of independence, most commercial insurance activities in Libya were carried on by foreign companies. Law No. 7 of 1959 was the first piece of legislation, which attempted to regulate the Libyan insurance industry. In 1970, in line with the nationalization policy of the new government, Law No. 31 of 1970 was the first law that dealt with the insurance industry as such. Under it, the Ministry of Economy was named as the sole government body responsible for the issuance of valid licences for conducting insurance businesses, as well as supervising the formation of new insurance companies. After this a series of insurance-related laws were enacted, starting with law No. 156 of 1970, which led to Decree No. 14 of 1971, which permitted the government to take over all foreign companies operating in the Libyan insurance market, and finally Law No. 80 of 1971 which effectively nationalized all insurance companies operating in Libya.

In 1971 Decree No. 52 of the Ministry of Economy limited all insurance activities in the country to two companies, the Al-Muktar Insurance Company and the Libya Insurance Company. This was followed in 1981 by a legislation, which provided for the merging of these two companies into one, the Libyan Insurance Company, and later the capital of the renamed Libyan National Insurance Company was increased from LD2 to LD30 million. Since then this company has expanded its branch coverage to virtually every corner of Libya, and it writes wide-ranging insurance business including motor insurance, family protection, life insurance, fire, burglary, marine cargo and hull and aviation as well as domestic transport.

A certain amount of deregulation in the insurance market commenced in 1999, when a new company, a public/private sector JV named the United Insurance Company was established. Since its establishment in 1999 the company has made considerable progress, expanding its branch network to seven in 2003, being Tripoli, Benghazi, Misuratah, Al Zawia, Sebha, Al Khums, and Ra's Ajdir on the Tunisian border. Its business volume and profitability has also expanded in the same period, as illustrated in Table 8.2.

Table 8.2. Libya: United Insurance Company – financial indicators, 1999–2003

[in Libyan dinar]

	1999	2000	2001	2002	2003
Revenue	765,565	3,727,252	5,820,792	6,523,391	8,100,342
Expenses	296,998	427,054	1,008,457	1,430,011	1,049,276
Profit before tax	468,568	3,300,198	4,812,334	5,093,380	7,051,067
Net profit	166,314	1,168,951	1,567,620	1,653,052	2,340,515

Source: Libya, United Insurance Company, 2005.

Approvals for two more private sector insurance companies, Rabta Insurance Services Company and Al-Hussein Insurance Company, were given in 2000, but so far neither of these companies appears to be operational.

In broad terms, there are strong links between an efficient capital market and the insurance industry. As one commentator has noted, talking about the Indian experience of the demonopolization of the insurance industry which commenced with the passing of the Insurance Regulatory and Development Authority (IRDA) Act of 1999,

> life insurance, funded pension systems and (to a lesser extent) non-life insurance, will accumulate huge amounts of capital over time which can be invested productively in the economy. In developed countries (re)insurers often own more than 25 per cent of the capital markets. The mutual dependence of insurance and capital markets can play a powerful role in channelling funds and investment expertise to support the development of the Indian economy (Sinha 2005).

This landmark Indian law, which permitted domestic private-sector companies to enter both life and non-life insurance business, as well as allowing foreign companies to participate in the insurance business, albeit with a ceiling on shareholdings of 26 per cent, has also had a dramatic effect on both the growth and the competitiveness of the Indian insurance market, creating a much wider range of innovative and competitive products and distributive channels.

Similarly in Jordan the Insurance Supervision Act No. (33) of 1999 was passed at the request of the WTO, as a piece of legislation aimed at bringing Jordan's insurance industry in line with major structural changes relating to privatization and diversification being implemented in the country, as we have touched on earlier in Chap. 6. This has led to a situation where, for example, Jordan together with Algeria and Qatar recorded the highest insurance premium growth in the Arab world, where in 2004 the 88 leading Arab insurance companies wrote premiums worth \$3.86 billion, up from \$2.62 billion in 2003, an increase of 126 per cent (Muhanna Rating Services 2005).

As stated earlier the insurance sector has a crucial role to play in developing the private sector and modernizing the financial and securities market. However to enable it to effectively perform these economic and financial roles, it must operate within a framework of forward looking and stable regulation that enables insurance companies to innovate and be more efficient, and create a competitive market with relatively free entry and exit. In Libya, clearly the government with its early nationalization and virtual state monopolization of the sector since 1971 has done the opposite of this. By imposing strict controls on new entries into the sector, prohibiting ownership by private domestic investors and foreign companies, fixing premiums and necessitating prior approval of tariff changes and new products, the government has virtually strangled the insurance business at its birth.

In the light of this we believe that, in line with its overall reformist strategy, at some point, in the not too distant future, the Libyan authorities must seriously consider innovative and modern legislation relating to the deregulation of the insurance industry, allowing part or total privatization of existing insurance companies, as well as the entry of foreign players. New investors will see such a move as a sine qua non before they decide to park large amounts of capital in the Libyan economy.

8.4 Urgent Priority for a Libyan Stock Market

In the last 15 years many Arab countries have embarked on economic diversification, including the creation of stock markets and their liberalization and privatization. Their aims have been varied – to provide greater financial depth to their economies, making available a source of finance to nascent indigenous firms for expansion and diversification, to provide absorptive capacity for the privatization or deregulation of many state-run telecommunications or basic infrastructure providing SOEs, or to improve corporate governance for an evolving private sector. As remarked in a paper on the emergence of Arab stock markets, "changing the output and technology mix of their industries will need stock markets to better allocate their investments to new industries, because stock markets provide a better way of checking that new firms are well run when there are divergences of opinion on how they should be run" (Bolbol and Omran 2003).

Presently in the Arab world, there are stock markets in Algeria, Egypt, Jordan, Lebanon, Morocco, Sudan, and Tunisia, Abu Dhabi, Bahrain, Dubai, Kuwait, Qatar, Oman, and Saudi Arabia. Of these it is generally recognized that five countries dominate Arab stock markets, possessing the largest and the most active markets – Egypt, Jordan, Morocco, Saudi Arabia, and Tunisia – while four Arab countries have yet to physically establish stock markets – Libya, Iraq, Syria, and Yemen.

However in Libya, the enabling legislation for this is already in place, Law No. 1 of 2004, which amended Law No. 21 of 2001, together with Regulation No. 53 of 2004, regarding the Practice of Economic Activities. In the latter, Sect. 10: Financial Paper Markets, Article 59 states: "The rules related to the organization of the financial papers market, determination of its competencies and body undertaking the supervision of its works, and other relevant rules, are issued by virtue of a decision to be taken by the Secretariat of the General People's Committee." This was followed up by Resolution No. 134 of 3 June 2006, which paved the way for the establishment of a Libyan Stock Market, in the form of a Syarika Musahima, with a capital of LD20 million divided into 2 million shares of 10LD each, under the auspices of the Secretary of Economy, Trade and Investment. Its headquarters, under Article 2 of Resolution, will be in Tripoli, but the main branch will be in Benghazi.

As we have discussed extensively in Chap. 6 on privatization in Libya, it is a moot point whether a major privatization programme in any country can take place successfully without a stock exchange. This is shown, as discussed in the introduction to this section, in an extensive body of empirical evidence demonstrating a strong causal relationship between stock markets and stock market liquidity, and economic growth. For example, Levine and Zervos (1996), using a dataset for 47 countries from 1976 to 1993, found that stock market liquidity, measured in various ways, is "a robust predictor of real per capita gross domestic product growth, physical capital growth and productivity growth."

In our view it is therefore of crucial importance that the establishment of a Libyan Stock Market is treated as a matter of priority by the Libyan authorities. If not, there is a danger that many legal reforms for the banking and commerce sectors recently approved and in process, the formation of the GBOT and the

Libyan privatization initiative itself, the devaluation of the LD and tariff liberalization, will all fail in their efforts to reform and modernize the Libyan economy. Libyan policy makers themselves might ponder why the recent legislative and privatization blitz have so far yielded so little dividends in terms of foreign investment into Libya. Undoubtedly, one answer is that it is still very early in the reformist process to expect tangible long-term results. But until a Libyan Stock Exchange is fully operational, it is difficult to envisage the flow of FDI into Libya on the scale visualized and planned by the Libyan policy makers.

8.5 Libya's Major Contribution Towards Combating Global Money Laundering

Law No. 2 of 2005, "Combating Money Laundering" is the second major piece of legislation, passed at the same time as Law No. 1 reforming the CBL, which is targeted, again, to bring Libya in line with other banking and corporate jurisdictions, signalling its return to the international community. Its main provisions are clearly directed against international terrorism as well as speculative funds derived from drugs and other illegal sources, and can be interpreted as the first major salvo against corruption and illegal possession of funds, in Libya and abroad, by Libyan nationals, the amount of which does not correspond to an individual's normal sources of income, for example, a salary or legitimate bank account. These sources are defined in Article 2, Money laundering:

1. Anyone who perpetrates any of the following acts shall be considered to have committed a crime of money laundering:
   - Possessing, owning, using, exploiting, disposing of in any manner, transferring, transporting, depositing, or concealing illegal property in order to disguise its unlawful source.
   - Disguising the true nature of illegal property, concealing its location, method of disposal or movement, rights related to it, or its ownership or possession.
   - Participating in the above acts in any manner whatsoever.
2. Property shall be considered illegal if it was obtained from a crime, including the crimes described in the International Agreement to Combat Organized Crime and the Protocol attached thereto, the International Agreement to Combat Corruption, or other international agreements to which Libya is a party.

In such a situation the punishment is severe and set to fit the crime, as stipulated in Article 4, Punishments for Money Laundering:

> Without prejudice to the punishments imposed by the Penal Code or any other law for crimes that are the source of the illegal property, a crime of money laundering as described in Paragraph 1 of Article 2 above shall be punishable by imprisonment and a fine equal to the value of the illegal property, which shall be confiscated. If the malefactor participated in the crime from which the property was obtained [the

> predicate offence], whether as a perpetrator or accomplice, he shall be subject to the more severe penalty, both elements of which shall be increased in severity by one-third. If the malefactor was aware that the property was obtained from a crime with a more severe penalty but did not participate in the crime, the punishment corresponding to the crime shall be imposed on him.

In Article 9 the formation and powers of a Financial Information Unit are defined, again bringing Libya into line and direct communication and cooperation with foreign judiciaries and international practices:

- The Central Bank shall establish a unit called the Financial Information Unit to combat money laundering activities. Reports on suspicious transactions shall be sent to the Unit from all concerned financial, commercial, and economic establishments, and information on these transactions may be submitted by any person or entity. This Unit may exchange information and reports on cases suspected of being linked to money laundering activities with its counterparts in other countries, in accordance with the international agreements to which Libya is a party or with the principle of reciprocity.
- All banks operating in Libya shall establish a subsidiary unit called the Subsidiary Unit for Information on Combating Money Laundering, which shall be responsible for monitoring all activities and transactions carried out by the bank or financial institution or by those who deal with them, when such activities or transactions are suspected of being linked to money laundering activities or activities involving the deposit or transfer of funds whose source is unknown.
- This subsidiary unit shall be responsible for reporting information or data related to these activities to the Financial Information Unit of the CBL described in Paragraph 1 of this article.
- The Governor shall issue a decree regulating the Financial Information Unit of the CBL and the subsidiary units in banks, defining their duties, responsibilities, and work procedures.

Article 10 defines the Role of the Financial Information Unit:

- The Unit described in Paragraph 1 of the preceding article, after reviewing the case referred to or reported to it, shall inform the Governor concerning the information and reports in its possession, so that the necessary measures may be taken.
- If the office of the public prosecutor receives a direct report concerning cases of money laundering, it shall take the necessary measures and shall inform the Financial Information Unit of the CBL concerning the contents of the report.

Article 11 demonstrates how seriously Libya regards money laundering and its links to corruption, setting up a high-powered supervisory National Committee for Combating Money Laundering:

In accordance with this law, a committee shall be established called the National Committee for Combating Money Laundering, which shall be chaired by the Governor of the Central Bank of Libya or his deputy and shall include at least one member from the following:

- Central Bank of Libya
- Secretariat of the General People's Committee for Financial and Technical Supervision
- Secretariat of the General People's Committee for Justice
- Secretariat of the General People's Committee for Public Security
- Secretariat of the General People's Committee for Finance
- Secretariat of the General People's Committee for Economy and Trade
- Secretariat of the General People's Committee for Foreign Liaison and International Cooperation
- Customs Authority
- Tax Authority

The delegates shall be nominated by their respective entities after consultation with the Chairman of the Committee. The board of directors of the CBL shall issue a decree establishing the composition of the Committee and the remuneration of its members.

Finally, again emphasizing Libya's international realignment, Article 15 outlines Judicial cooperation with other countries in combating money laundering:

- The prosecutor general may, at the request of a judicial entity in another country, order to pursue the property obtained from a crime of money laundering or the means used in such crime to be tracked, frozen, or impounded, if the incident fits the description of such a crime in accordance with the provisions of this law and the country in question has signed an agreement with Libya for judicial cooperation, or based on the principle of reciprocity.
- The validity of a judicial order issued in another country by the competent court or judicial authority calling for the seizure of property, proceeds, or means linked to a crime of money laundering or a related crime shall be recognized, if the incident fits the description of such a crime in accordance with the provisions of this law and the country in question has signed an agreement with Libya for judicial cooperation, or based on the principle of reciprocity.

8.6 The Libyan Tourist Sector, 2006

In global terms, the tourism and leisure industry has emerged as one of the fastest growing contributors to many economies, whether mature or emerging. Social and demographic trends, not only in Western countries but also in S.E. Asia and the Middle East, point to wealthier populations, shorter working hours, affordable air travel, and obsessions with a healthy outdoor lifestyle as drivers for the tourist boom. In the new millennium, the growth of the international tourism industry is projected to be very significant. According to the World Tourism Organization, the number of international tourists will increase from 698 million to 1.6 billion by 2020, tourist expenditure will more than triple in the same period from the 2005 figure of US $682 billion to US $2 trillion, and international tourism receipts represented approximately 6 per cent of worldwide exports of goods and services (WTO 2006).

Libya's immediate neighbours, Egypt and Tunisia, and another Maghreb tourist destination, Morocco, underwent major expansion in tourism investment, hotel capacity, and tourism arrivals in the 1990s and early 2000s, which complemented their programmes of privatization and financial reform undertaken to reduce massive public sector expenditure and overstaffing, and attract FDI. It is useful to look at Table 8.3, which provide details of the volume of visitors generated by this sector in these and other MENA countries as shown in the most recently available WTO statistics. As can be seen, international tourist arrivals and receipts have continued to rise for the period 2000–2004 virtually across the board, with Yemen, Syria, Qatar, and Jordan registering the highest average annual growth for the 2000–2004 period. In a Libyan context, Appendix 8.3 also provides an illustration of the trends of tourist arrivals and receipts for the period 1999–2003.

As can be seen from Appendix 8.3, visitors from categories 2.1 and 2.6, primarily African and neighbouring country visitors such as Sudanese, Tunisian, and Egyptian amounted to 96, 96, 95, 94, and 94 per cent of total visitors, respectively, for the period 1999–2003. These visitors were either daily trans-border visitors or economic immigrants. However it is the figures for category 2.3, Visitors from Europe, which are interesting. Although they do not demonstrate a steady progress, they have shown, after the lifting of the UN sanctions in 1999, a rise of 27 per cent from 33,000 in 1999 to 42,000 million in 2003, demonstrating the growing interest in Libya as a tourist destination by Europeans.

Table 8.3. MENA: International arrivals by country destination, 2004

Country	International tourist arrival (1000)						Market share in the region (%)			Average annual growth (%)	
	1990	1995	2000	2002	2003	2004*	1990	2000	2004	90/00	00/04
Bahrain	1376	1396	2420	3167	2955	3514	13.7	9.6	9.7	5.8	9.8
Egypt	2411	2871	5116	4906	5746	7795	24.0	20.3	21.5	7.8	11.1
Iraq	748	61	78	–	–	–	7.4	0.3	–	–20.2	–
Jordan	572	1075	1580	2384	2353	2853	5.7	6.3	7.9	10.7	15.9
Kuwait	15	72	78	96	94	91	0.1	0.3	0.3	17.9	3.9
Lebanon	–	450	742	956	1016	1278		2.9	3.5		14.6
Libya	96	56	174	135	142	149	1.0	0.7	0.4	6.1	–3.8
Oman	149	279	571	817	–	–	1.5	2.3	–	14.4	–
Palestine	–	–	330	40	40	–	–	1.3	–		–
Qatar	136	309	378	587	557	732	1.4	1.5	2.0	10.8	18.0
Saudi Arabia	2209	3325	6585	7512	7332	8580	22.0	26.1	23.7	11.5	6.8
Syria	562	815	1416	2870	2788	3032	5.6	5.6	8.4	9.7	21.0
UAE	973	2315	3907	5445	5871	–	9.7	15.5	–	14.9	–
Yemen	52	61	73	98	155	274	0.5	0.3	0.8	3.5	39.2
Algeria	1137	520	866	988	1166	1234	7.5	3.1	3.7	–2.7	9.3
Morocco	4024	2602	4278	4453	4761	5477	26.5	15.2	16.4	0.6	6.4
Sudan	33	29	38	52	52	61	0.2	0.1	0.2	1.4	12.6
Tunisia	3204	4120	5058	5064	5114	5998	21.1	17.9	17.9	4.7	4.4

Source: World Tourism Organization, 2006.

Again, category 6.1, tourist expenditure in Libya, has risen from US $27 million to US $79 million, an almost three-fold increase over the reported period. Category 9.1, number of hotel rooms, is also useful to consider. Despite a rising trend in tourist arrivals from Europe, there has not been a corresponding rise in the number of hotel rooms, which at 11,815 in 2000 rose to only 12,405 in 2001 and has stayed at the same number for the rest of the reporting period. Not only this, but also in terms of quality, there is still only one five-star hotel, the 300-room Tripoli Corinthia Gateway to Africa. Recently, the Libyan Minister for Tourism, in an interview with a major US tour operator, stated that Libya planned to have 100,000 hotel rooms by 2010, but clearly this looks like an unachievable target, although as will be noted later from the data supplied by the Libyan Ministry of Tourism in 2006, confirmed FDI tourist investments as at the end of 2005 will add 13,440 beds, implemented over the next few years.

8.6.1 Tourism and Economic Development

From the standpoint of the host country, tourism represents a key sector for economic development, not only for the physical inflow of the tourist dollar but also for direct job creation in hotels and service companies, as well as in ancillary industries such as souvenir, handicraft, food, and garment manufacture. In, for example, a recent comprehensive study of the economic value of the Egyptian tourist industry, the authors reached important conclusions in support of their thesis concerning the powerful role and multiplier effect that tourism has as a catalyst for economic development. They concluded that for Egypt the impact of "foreign tourists spending" on GDP far exceeds the commonly held figure of around 1 per cent. In fact, with respect to value added and output, foreign tourists' spending is 2–3 times that share, and the direct impact of foreign tourists' spending on total output in 1999 was $3.6 billion dollars (4.4 per cent of GDP). Adding indirect effects, the total contribution to output reached $ 9.6 billion (11.6 per cent of GDP).

As for employment, foreign tourists' spending directly supported 1.2 million jobs in various economic sectors. The total number of jobs directly and indirectly associated with foreign tourists' spending is 2.7 million. The study also estimates tax revenue from foreign tourists' spending at over LE3.6 billion, which corresponds to 5.1 per cent of total direct and indirect taxes. The study therefore concludes that "tourism's ability to contribute positively to Egypt's economic goals earns that activity a higher rank on Egypt's policy priority list" (Tohamy and Swinscoe 2000).

For many years, because of the US and UN sanctions, Libya has been terra incognita to many westerners. At the same time, a growing number of informed travellers and writers have privately celebrated the historical and breathtaking wealth of Libya and the Libyan landscape. As one writer has commented "for so long maligned by a myopic western media as a pariah at odds with the world, Libya surprises almost everyone who sets foot in the country" (Ham 2002).

8.6.2 Restructuring Libya's Tourist Policies

Although tourism has not, until comparatively recently, been regarded as an important economic activity, Libyan policy makers themselves now recognize Libya's tourist potential, not only from their awareness of the obvious success of the tourist industries in neighbouring Egypt, Tunisia, Morocco, and Malta, but also from the point of view of economic diversification. This is why tourism as an investment sector was prioritized in Libya together with other key sectors for economic diversification in Article 8 of Libya's landmark Law No. 5 "Concerning the Encouragement of Foreign Capital Investment".

The year 2004 also witnessed the passing of Law No. 7 "Regarding Tourism", which is a piece of legislation which sets out to deal comprehensively with the future development of the Libyan tourist industry, and which has been discussed extensively earlier in this book in Chap. 3. All in all Law No. 7 represents a major government initiative to comprehensively regulate and provide for the orderly development of the Libyan tourist industry. This Law has been followed up by the General People's Committee Resolution No. 180 of 1 November 2005, regarding the establishment of the Tourist Development Board, replacing the Libyan General Board for Tourism (GBT), which was originally established in 1989. Resolution No. 180 gives the new Board much wider powers than its predecessor, tasking it with the drawing up of a comprehensive national tourist development plan, and providing it with a budget for building infrastructure such as roads, electricity and water supplies for tourist sites, as well as the ability to identify and alienate sites specially for tourism from either already built up or undeveloped state or private sector-owned sites and locations.

8.6.3 Libya's Tourist Credentials

One of the major paradoxes of history, as an Arab researcher has noted, is that "with the exception of a few enclaves, the Arab region remains highly marginalized from the global tourism economy. This fact stands in stark contrast to the vast historical, cultural, and natural resources the region offers for tourism development and which could certainly attract far more robust flows of tourists from across the Arab world as well as from outside it. As the birthplace of ancient civilizations and world religions the region possesses one of densest collections of archaeological monuments" (Hazbun 2004).

In Libya's case, there can be no doubt about its tourist credentials. Apart from its 1,970 km of unsullied Mediterranean beaches, the country presently contains five World Heritage Sites, added to the World Heritage List between 1982 and 1986. The first is Tadrart Acacus, which is situated in the mountainous region near Libya's south-west border, east of the city of Ghat; the second is Cyrene, not yet even fully excavated and located in the Gebel Akhdar region, containing some remarkable relics from the Greco-Roman period; the third is Leptis Magna, known locally as Lebdah, located on the coast 120 km east of Tripoli, which is one of the most extensive archaeological sites in the Mediterranean, measuring in total 2.5×1.5 km; the fourth is Sabratha, located on the coast 60 km east of Tripoli, a city which formed a maritime trading triangle with Leptis and Oea between North Africa and the rest of the Mediterranean from Phoenician times until the decline of the Roman Empire; Ghadames is the fifth Libyan World Heritage Site, known as "the pearl of the desert", and stands in an oasis. It is one of the oldest pre-Saharan cities and an outstanding example of a traditional settlement.

Undoubtedly the five World Heritage Sites and other cultural locations will act in Libya as powerful catalysts for the future targeted growth of the tourist sector. But clearly Libya, with its proximity to Europe, is now ripe for tourist expansion in a wide number and variety of tourist segments. These include heritage and nature-based tourism as discussed extensively earlier, business travel and conferencing, beach, scuba diving and sports-oriented leisure activities, as well as family-oriented vacations.

In a North African regional context, there are clear messages to Libya regarding its direction of tourist development from its neighbouring countries. In Tunisia, Egypt, Morocco, Jordan, and also Syria, government-directed efforts have encouraged private investment in the sector while privatizing many state-owned hotel assets. The Mediterranean coasts of Morocco and Tunisia have encouraged beach-type tourism developments so popular with northern Europeans. Egypt, with a long history of antiquities-oriented tourism, has successfully developed leisure tourism in a number of Red Sea resorts. Tourism promoters across the region have also developed nature-oriented tourism projects such as exploring the Tunisian and Algerian desert, Jordanian geological formations and wildlife, and underwater exploration of the Red Sea. Across these states, tourism revenues amount to 3–8 per cent of their gross domestic product, and may account for up to 10 per cent of domestic employment, while the indirect impact of tourism spending is certainly much greater.

8.6.4 Libya and Ecotourism

The North African countries have used different strategies to develop their tourist potential. As we have seen, Egypt, building on a historical base, has made tourism a key sector in its development, although open tourism may deliver results not always desired by the government or locals. Often, in fact, an open tourism policy can clash with the aspirations of locals, frequently ignoring their needs and rights, despite providing increased employment opportunities for them. As one observer has noted, talking about Sharm El-Sheikh and Hurghada, "in the Sinai there are increasing signs that mass tourism is having a detrimental effect on the culture of the local nomadic Bedouins. Tourism development has triggered rivalries and resentment between Bedouin tribesmen and immigrants from Egypt's Nile Valley, who monopolise jobs in Sinai's vigorous tourism sector" (Al Ahram 2003).

Tunisia targets essentially middle-income tourists with fairly tight budgets, who flock to the island of Djerba, seeking the very desirable combination of sun, sand, and sea, and who may not be particularly interested in the culture or ecosystems in which they are staying. Morocco, on the other hand, is considered to be a fairly expensive tourist destination, aiming for the top end of the market, focusing on wealthier tourists with larger disposable income.

It is therefore important that the Libyan policy makers, with their keenness to attract tourism and encourage Libyan entrepreneurs into the tourism sector, strike the right balance between mass tourism and cultural and ecotourism. Libya, off the beaten track for more than 20 years because of the sanctions, is definitely considered as a new and desirable destination, all the more so because of its proximity to Europe. Ecotourism certainly represents one of the best options for Libyan planners to target and develop, defined as "environmentally responsible travel and visitation to natural areas, in order to enjoy and appreciate nature (and any accompanying cultural features, both past and present) that promote conservation, have a low visitor impact and provide for beneficially active socio-economic involvement of local peoples" (IUCN 1996).

The advantages of ecotourism are many, especially in relation to nature conservation and its benefits to local people. As well as providing a revenue source, locals will soon begin to view their habitat as a valuable resource not to be destroyed or exploited. Instead of building new roads, for example, as is typical in conventional tourist resorts and complexes, ecotourism uses existing trails and infrastructure, preserving them and making them a sustainable economic resource.

Not only this, but ecotourists are, in general, more responsible and aware of the importance of local customs and threatened wilderness areas. In travelling through the Libyan Sahara, for instance, they look for new environmental experiences and education, and they wish to experience local customs, foods and products, and, on moral grounds, they would wish to support the local economy.

In view of the superb natural resources with which Libya is plentifully endowed, ecotourism must be placed high on the list of the Libyan tourist sector planners. Although Libya is conventionally seen as possessing mainly 1970 km of beautiful Mediterranean Coast, and the vast interior arid desert area of the Sahara; these in fact represent only two of its most important natural assets. As has been well observed, Libya is part of an

> arid and semi-arid region, where the greatest diversity and abundance of life is concentrated in particular ecosystems. Among these are the freshwater wetlands, the mountains and woodlands, and coastal habitats such as coral reefs, mangroves, seagrass beds, saltmarshes, and mudflats. Most of these sites are relatively small in area, but they are of enormous importance to the region's biological productivity and ecological integrity. They are the main refugia or sites of endemism and reliction, and serve as vital wintering and stepping-stone sites for migratory birds (Llewelyn 1982).

In this regard it is not in fact generally known that Libya has extensive national parks and protected areas. For example, in two of the most highly regarded travel guides for the eco traveller, Footprint's "Libya Handbook" (2000) and Lonely Planet's Libya (2002), there is virtually no mention of these. However, it is believed that if managed effectively and more widely advertised, these parks and protected areas could contribute substantially to Libya's tourist attractions as well as providing valuable income to Libyans who could become guides and supply food and accommodation to tourists visiting them.

With such a wealth of reserves and unique ecosystems, Libya possesses ecotourism resources sufficient to make it a major ecotourist destination, without necessarily spending vast sums on the types of conventional tourist resorts that litter the Mediterranean coastlines of Tunisia, Egypt, Greece Spain, and Italy. But undoubtedly the management of many protected areas in Libya currently falls below acceptable international standards. In order to protect these unique ecosystems and valuable resources, it is to be hoped that the Libyan authorities, in a post-sanctions era, will seize the opportunity to embark on a series of initiatives, which recognizes the unique ecotourist potential of the country, as well as its importance for future generations of Libyans.

In order to achieve this, it is time for Libyan policy makers to ensure that Libyans are educated in sustainable ecology in internationally available academic and hands-on training programmes, and the structuring of a national ecotourism plan might be considered as a matter of urgency. A Libyan national ecotourism plan could, for example, establish the following guidelines and procedures:

- establish planning procedures for ecotourism developments;
- establish application procedures for ecotourism development;
- expand and improve management of a nationwide system of ecotourism areas;
- elaborate development and management plans for ecotourism areas;
- implement guidelines for ecotourism;
- establish a series of pilot ecotourism projects;
- establish additional ecotourism products at chosen sites such as Karabouli and Kouf National Parks;
- establish and promote a consistent marketing strategy;
- identify and promote further fiscal measures to encourage ecotourism.

As well as this, proposals to strengthen institutions and build capacity under the national ecotourism plan might:

- establish a Human Resources Development Plan;
- ensure local community participation in ecotourism;
- investigate the feasibility of an accreditation scheme for ecotourism;
- establish training and promote certification for ecotourism guides;
- upgrade standards of tourist literature.

With such a plan in place and a review and strengthening of Libyan protected area legislation, the successful long-term management of these very important protected areas and the involvement of Libyans as both managers as well as service providers to these key ecotourism resources will bring immense dividends for present and future generations of Libyans, without necessarily "breaking the bank".

8.6.5 Recent Tourist Investment

With completely new and comprehensive tourist legislation, attractive investment laws in place and a government determined to diversify the Libyan economy, it seems clear that, together with its cultural and natural endowments, the tourism industry in Libya undoubtedly has a bright future. As discussed in Chap. 3, Law No. 5 of 1997 Concerning Encouragement of Foreign Capital Investment, and its subsequent amendments, has created an extremely favourable investment climate for FDI, and the tourist sector is now emerging as one of the main beneficiaries of this. Table 8.4, derived from the data from Libya's Tourism and Investment Board, highlights some of the major investors by nationality, amount of investment, new facilities, and job creation up to end 2005.

The year 2006 has also witnessed a stream of tourist sector investment delegations visiting Libya, from Canada, the United States, Italy, France, Switzerland, and neighbouring Tunisia, many of which will undoubtedly lead to further FDI in this sector. One major tourist investment announced in September 2006 was the Andalus Tourist Center, a JV between the Libyan Economic and Social Development Fund and the Swiss PERCO Holding Company, involving the construction of a five-star tourist hotel with 600 rooms, in addition to various hotel flats on a 4 ha site, costing 200 million euros and providing around about 1,000 job opportunities for Libyans. Another major tourist project, the Tileel Resort in Subratha City, was announced in the same month, comprising a hotel with 80 luxurious suites, 1,600 rooms, and several conference halls and restaurants on a 82.2 ha site. The resort will also include villas, sports facilities, tennis courts, cafes and restaurants, a golf course, and a marina. The sheer scale and rapidity of new FDI in the Libyan tourist sector will mean not only a massive boost to Libyan direct employment opportunities, but also fuel vigorous activity in the Libyan construction sector for many years ahead.

Table 8.4. Tourism sector: total foreign direct investment committed, 2005

Project	Investor nationality	Investment commitment (USDMM)	Employment commitment	Proposed no. of beds	Remarks
Green City Tourist Complex (Al-Krawa)	UK	1,605	6,325	3,520	Construction approval issued
Al-Ghazaia Hotel	UK	253	1,600	493	
Al-Nagaza Tourist Complex	Italy	223	1,700	1,328	
Al-Nakhel Tourist Village	Malta	117	276	1,509	
Falfool Tourist City	Switzerland	80	1,000	960	
Farwa Tourist Hotel	Italy	505	760	3,710	Construction approval under discussion
Al-Bahr Towers Hotel	Pakistan	152	1,000	960	
Ganima Tourist Resort	UK	123	1,800	960	
Sed Roos Tourist and Entertainment Complex	Tunisia	9	160	N/A	
Total		3,067	14,621	13,440	

Source: Libyan Ministry of Tourism: Tourism Investment and Development Board, 2006.

8.6.6 Creating a Libyan Tourist Identity

As we have seen, while several states such as Egypt, Tunisia, Morocco, and more recently the United Arab Emirates have been successful in promoting tourism development, tourism flows to these locations and the rest of the region have long been hampered by regional political instability, negative external perceptions of the region, and patterns of development, which fail to exploit the full potential of tourism as a catalyst for sustainable economic development.

Libya, recently emerging from 20 years of isolation, clearly has a long way to go to develop a successful tourist industry, but we have no doubt that this will come in time. In this respect it might be instructive to review how others have succeeded in this sector. In a recent thought-provoking paper analysing the meteoric rise of Dubai, the author states of the Dubai rulers, the Maktoum family, that

> in the space of four decades, they have managed to shift the city's economic focus from fishing and gold trading to tourism, mass communications, shipping, and finance. Unlike many of its regional peers which have developed unstable regimes and stagnant, oil-dependent economies, Dubai has diversified its economy to become a politically stable centre for commerce and tourism (DeNicola 2005).

Later in this thoughtful analysis, the author quotes Sheik Mohammed Rashid, the Dubai ruler as reportedly saying that "he would like people to have heard of it", thus stressing his desire for Dubai to become a globally recognized brand.

This recognition of the importance of brand names in today's globalized world clearly lies at the heart of Dubai's impressive success in stamping the Dubai name globally as a centre for tourism, shopping, world-class sporting events, and a quality lifestyle. In the tourist sector, a similar approach has been taken by the Malaysia Tourism Promotion Board, or Tourism Malaysia, with its simple but effective logo of "Malaysia, Truly Asia", while Brazil has opted for "If travelling is your passion, Brazil is your destination". The Muslim Sultanate of Brunei's Tourism Division labels the sultanate as "A Kingdom of Unexpected Treasures".

To give Libya a unique and separate identity as a tourist destination, consultants and PR specialists must come up with an angle or concept that can encapsulate Libya's inimitable mix of cultural, geographical, Mediterranean lifestyle, and ecotourist attractions, distinct from its North African neighbours. But in view of more than 20 years of negative media reporting as well as its poor security and unknown quality image, this is not going to be an easy task.

But obviously as an alcohol-free country, where credit cards are not widely accepted, the Libyan government at some point will have to determine at precisely what level it is targeting its tourist business. Without doubt, tourism has been perceived as a positive agent of change for many countries because of its impacts on job creation, income generation, and infrastructure benefits to local communities. While such positive benefits justify tourism expansion and lead to greater economic diversification, the Libyan policy makers must also consider its long-term impacts on key cultural and environmental issues.

8.7 Libyan Agriculture Sector

8.7.1 The Rise and Fall of the Sector

From a historical perspective, Libya was in Roman times the breadbasket of the empire, in which such cities as Leptis Magna and Sabratha had grown immensely rich, flourishing on the livestock and cereal trade to Rome and other parts of the empire. Early settled agriculture had relied on a complex system of rain-derived run-off irrigation, as well as a holistic and seasonal approach to grazing and planting, based on the systems and practices in existence since time immemorial. Consequently large numbers of the population had always been pastoralists or farmers. In the early twentieth century the Italians under the "Fourth Shore" policy had tried to develop their Libyan colony as an economically viable satellite state, built on state-financed agriculture, for which they spent on a massive scale, which at times crippled the home country. In fact, before the discovery of oil in the 1950s, "farming was still the main hope of the country's future" (Wright 1969).

But as another early post-independence author commented on Libya:

> the stickiness of the agriculture problem is readily demonstrable. In the first ten years of independence, public expenditure on agriculture and irrigation had increased almost ten times. Despite this tangible evidence of the significance of agriculture in public considerations, the agriculture sector, by official evidence in 1963, remained largely subsistence agriculture clearly beset by the innumerable adversities which typify the worst of underdeveloped situations (Farley 1971) .

The main reason for this is of course the arid and semi-arid climate experienced by much of the country. Apart from the Mediterranean coastal strip, which has dry summers and relatively wet winters, and the Jabal Natusah and Jabal Akhdar highlands where a plateau climate prevails with higher rainfall and humidity and low winter temperatures, with snow on the hills, the rest of the country, stretching southwards into the Sahel, experiences pre-desert and desert climatic conditions.

In annual terms, rainfall is extremely low, with about 93 per cent of the land surface receiving less than 100 mm/year. The highest rainfall occurs in the northern Tripoli region around the Jabal Nafusah and Jifarah Plain, together with the northern Benghazi region and Jabal al Akhdar. In fact these are the only two areas in Libya where the average annual rainfall exceeds the minimum value of 250–300 mm considered basic to sustain rainfed agriculture. Although rainfall occurs during the winter months, it is very variable both from place to place and year to year.

After the 1969 revolution, food security became one of the moral imperatives for the Libyan government. Huge efforts and significant sums were expended to achieve this elusive goal in the 1970s and 1980s, by developing irrigated agriculture based on local aquifers, while in the 1980s and 1990s the Great ManMade River Project (GMRP) attempted to create optimum conditions for the rehabilitation and development of the coastal agriculture through water transport from the south to the north, as well as adding large new irrigated agricultural areas. However, food security and food self-sufficiency are not the same thing, and it is unlikely that the latter can ever be achieved in Libya.

Figures 8.4 and 8.5 below comprehensively illustrate government expenditure on agriculture both in absolute terms and as a percentage of the total development budgets for the period 1962–2004.

Starting from a base expenditure of LP1.2 million in 1962, by 1969 expenditure on agriculture had reached only LP13.2 million. Thereafter it increased exponentially, by 20 times in 1977 to LD263.7 million, almost doubling again to its peak of LD489.9 million in 1980, as the government made an all out effort to achieve food security. Throughout the 1980s annual expenditure on agriculture averaged LD245.51 million, while for the 1990s this figure halved to 104.41 as oil prices plummeted and the difficulties faced by this sector became more intractable. By 2004 agricultural expenditure had risen to LD263 million.

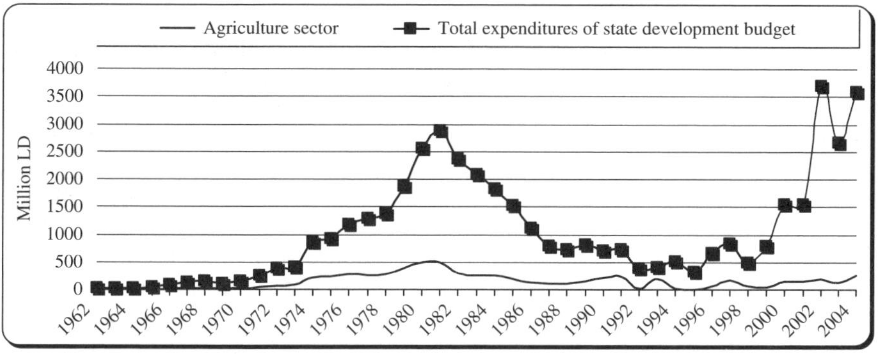

Sources: 1962–2000 Libyan Ministry of Planning; 2000–2003 Central Bank of Libya: 2004, IMF, 2006

Fig. 8.4. Agriculture expenditure Compared with total state total development expenditure in the development budget, 1962–2004

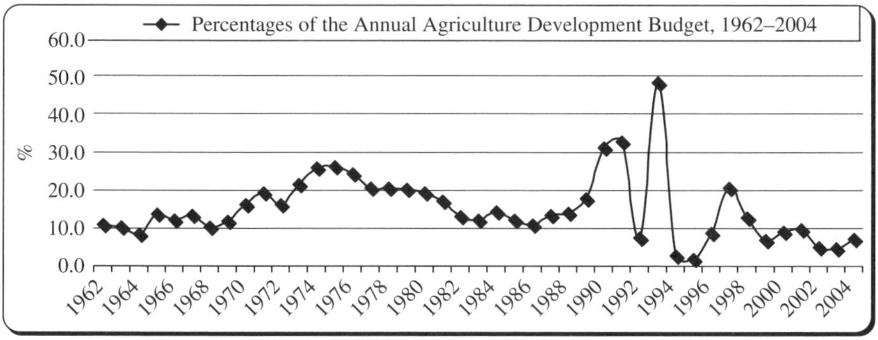

Sources: 1962–2000 Libyan Ministry of Planning; 2000–2003 Central Bank of Libya: 2004, IMF, 2006

Fig. 8.5. Agriculture expenditure as a percentage of the development budget, 1962–2004

In terms of annual expenditure on agriculture as a percentage of the development expenditure, it averaged 11.4 per cent during the period 1962–1969 inclusive, averaging around. Throughout the 1970s, its share of government annual expenditure stood at an average of 21 per cent, while this annual figure fell to an average of 14.3 per cent in the 1980s, rising again to an average of 17.2 per cent throughout the 1990s. In the first 4 years of the millennium, it had stabilized at around 7.1 per cent, taking up only 4.6 per cent in 2003, although increasing again to 7.3 per cent in 2004.

8.7.2 Reasons Underlying the Declining Agriculture Labour Force

These figures are also reflected in Table 8.5, which shows, among other factors, that while at the end of 1981, there had been 234,000 agricultural workers or 25 per cent of the labour force, by 2002 this had decreased to 101,000 or around only 5 per cent of the labour force. It also shows the progressive urbanization of Libya, which has gone from having a rural population of 31 per cent at the end of 1981 to only 12 per cent in 2002, a demographic trend that is in fact increasing. It is also clearly demonstrated that while the massive government expenditure aimed at increasing agriculture's irrigated land base had successfully almost doubled it from 223,000 ha in 1981 to 435,000 ha in 1991, there had in fact been very slight increases in this total area in the period up to 2002. Again, the fight against climate and aridity could not significantly increase the total arable land area, which at 2,080,000 ha in 1981 had only increased marginally to 2,150,000 ha by 2002.

Table 8.5. Population and agriculture labour force, 1979–2002

Indicators	Unit	1979–1981	1989–1991	1999	2000	2001	2002
Population and agricultural labour force	1000	3047	4305	5136	5237	530	5445
Population							
Population annual growth	Per cent	4.6	2.1	2.0	1.9	1.9	1.9
Rural/total	Per cent	31	18	13	12	12	12
Population density	Inh/km^2	2	2	3	3	3	3
Agricultural labour force	1000	234	143	110	108	104	101
Agricultural labour force/ total labour force	Per cent	25	11	6	6	6	5
land use							
Total land	1000 hA	175954	175954	175954	175954	175954	175954
Arable land+ permanents crops	1000 hA	2080	2150	2150	2150	2150	2150
Arable land	1000 hA	1754	1815	1815	1815	1815	1815
Imigated land	1000 hA	223	435	470	470	470	470

Source: FAO, 2004.

Agriculture contributes to about 9 per cent of GDP and provides employment to about 5 per cent of the total economically active population. While 25 per cent of the total economically active population are women, in the agricultural sector they account for 67 per cent of the labour force.

8.7.3 Libya as a Food Importer

As shown in the Appendix 8.4, Libya imports a large percentage of its domestic food requirements, illustrating that any hope of agricultural food self-sufficiency must remain an illusion for Libya. For example, of a total of 2,427,659 MT of cereals including wheat, barley, maize, and millet, 2,213,159 MT or over 91 per cent was imported, while virtually 100 per cent or 311,398 MT of sugar was imported. On the other hand in terms of fresh vegetables, meat, fish, eggs, and milk, Libya had high levels of domestic production, even exporting certain items such as dates and olives.

8.7.4 Future Trends in Agriculture

As noted, agricultural production in Libya is severely constrained by natural factors such as moisture stress due to low and highly variable rainfall, temperature extremes, short cropping seasons, and poor and shallow soils. Underlying these physical and climatic constraints, Libya like the rest of the North African region is characterized by high population growth, expected to more than double by 2025. Many years of effort and massive investment have, in terms of agricultural production, achieved comparatively little. At the national level, it seems that the earlier confusion of food self-sufficiency with food security, where a large amount of limited resources (land, labour, and capital) were earmarked in the 1980s and 1990s for food production, has now been addressed.

In fact currently in Libya many now question whether the high unit production costs in agriculture, based on costly irrigation and water transfer, can remain justified in a situation where the only source of water is non-renewable shallow or deep aquifers and where the economic returns from other sectors such as the oil industry give easy and in comparative terms, relatively cheap access to the international food market.

As a priority sector for economic diversification as identified in the 1997 Law No. 5 for the Encouragement of Foreign Investment, agriculture clearly has a future in Libya as demand for all food products is set to rise in line with strong demographic increases. But global climate change will mean that North Africa in general is predicted to become warmer and drier with a consequent reduction in conventional crop productivity. As well as this, the trend towards desertification will continue. Also, despite the success of the GMRP, water scarcity is predicted to worsen markedly over the next 25 years. As one water expert has stated.

> Depending on the assumptions made on water productivity in agriculture, the total water requirement to support the basic food self-sufficiency and to meet the domestic water demand of the 12 million Libyans in the year 2025 is estimated to be ranging

> between 10.5 and 16.4 km^3/year, compared to the 4.3 km^3/year at present. When the GMRP will be fully operational, the total amount of water available for all uses, assuming that the present groundwater production equipment will be maintained until 2025, will be in the order of 6.5 km^3/year and will thus hardly cover 50% of the total water requirement (FAO 2005).

What then is the way ahead for Libyan agriculture? In general terms to increase agricultural output using conventional growing systems, there are two options: increase land area used for agriculture or increase output per hectare. Because of all of the above physical constraints as well as the trends in climate change, it will be difficult and expensive to achieve the former.

However the latter option, by using biotechnology to develop new wheat and barley hybrids, as well as developing new irrigation techniques, is one of the options. As stated in a recent report,

> There is real potential for the second option, that of increasing the productivity of crops. For example, in 1991, Syria, the breadbasket of the ancient world, became self-sufficient in wheat for the first time since the 1950s. Since 1989, production has virtually doubled to 3.6 million MT per annum, due to new technology, increasing national income by an estimated $414 million annually. This was achieved mainly by increasing productivity; yield, 0.6 MT per hectare in the 1950s and early 1960s and 1.5 MT per hectare in the late 1980s, climbed to 2.6 MT per hectare by 1993. Egypt has also had real success. Egyptian wheat production is 125 per cent higher today than it was in the early 1980s. It has risen from 2 million MT to 4.5 million MT per annum. Average wheat yields grew from 3.6 MT per hectare to 5.4 MT per hectare between 1981–1983 and 1990–1993, growing at a rate of 4.7 per cent per annum. This dramatic improvement resulted from a combination of new wheat technology, effective technology transfer, and a series of bold reforms by the Government of Egypt to get the market moving (CGIAR 1997).

As Libya opens up in the post-sanctions era, it is inevitable that agribusiness entrepreneurs will have access to a wide range of biotechnology inventions in food and agriculture, particularly genetic engineering, which has become the focus of a global war of rhetoric (Stone 2002). While supporters see genetic engineering as essential in solving food insecurity and malnutrition in developing countries and accuse opponents of "crimes against humanity" for delaying the regulatory approval of potentially life-saving innovations (Potrykus 2003), opponents claim that genetic engineering will engender environmental catastrophe, worsen poverty and hunger, and lead to a corporate takeover of traditional agriculture and the global food supply.

Biotechnological research on the crops that currently provide the bulk of Libya's food supply such as wheat and barley and also crops such as sorghum, pearl millet, pigeon pea, chickpea, and groundnut that are largely neglected in conventional or biotechnology research programmes should also prove to be conducive to assist farmers and entrepreneurs to meet Libya's growing needs. Traits of particular interest for biotechnological adaptation include resistance to production stresses such as drought, salinity, disease and pests, as well as nutritional enhancement.

Libyan entrepreneurs must also investigate the potential of hydroponic agricultural systems for growing crops such as tomatoes, peppers, and chillies, which it currently imports in large quantities. For example, in the province of Almeria, a semi-arid area along the Mediterranean Coast of Spain, hydroponic growing methods have changed the way farmers operate, transforming the poorest province of Spain into one of the ten most affluent. Hydroponic greenhouses currently cover over 30,000 ha (more than 74,000 acres) of land in this province, and produced over 2,700,000 MT of lettuce, cucumbers, watermelons, beans, squash, peppers, and tomatoes.

The horticulture and floriculture sectors are also areas where Libyan entrepreneurs can invest in future years, as tried and tested European technology on Libya's doorstep now becomes widely available. But clearly, again, some sort of general integrated approach or initiative will be required from Libya's General Authority of Agricultural, Animal and Marine Wealth to pass on modern agricultural techniques and management practices, which have revolutionized modern agriculture in Europe and elsewhere over the past 20 years. As well as this, inputs for Libyan farmers and potential agribusiness entrepreneurs in pot harvest techniques and in building an export-oriented agribusiness sector will also be necessary.

8.8 Potential in the Fishing Industry

The potential of the fishing industry in Libya has again been recognized by the government, and it is listed in Law No. 5 of 1997 as a sector for which many advantageous investment incentives apply. Libya, with a coastline of 1,970 km along the Mediterranean and a continental shelf area of 50,000 km2, in fact possesses significant potential for upgrading its fishing industry, as long as fishing stocks can be managed scientifically, and the government has the vessels and equipment to patrol its territorial waters effectively.

8.8.1 Legislation and Decisions Relating to the Fishing Industry

As can be seen below, there has been a series of legislation since 1989 regulating the fishing industry, dealing with licensing issues and procedures, permitted fishing zones and months of fishing, and permitted fishing techniques and equipment.

- Law No. 14 of 1989 is the basic legislation concerning the regulation of the use and conservation of marine wealth. It deals with the type of equipment, both local and imported, allowed for marine fishing, the sizes of fish/species and other marine organisms allowed to be taken, and issues related to the supervision and control of the industry regarding safety issues.
- Secretariat of Marine Wealth (SMW) Decision No. 71 of 1990, which elaborates provisions of Law 14 and the procedures governing its application

- SMW Decision No. 80 of 1991, which provides technical explanations and specifications for the implementation of Law No. 14.
- SMW Decision No. 95 of 1993, which prohibits the use of monofilament nets and No. 11 hooks for fishing.
- SMW Decision No. 97 of 1993, which relates to prohibitions on trawling in specific areas during the July and August spawning period for certain species. This decision has been replaced by the General People's Committee Decision No. 271 of 2004 which defines those areas in which trawl fishing is banned. In brief, this decision prohibits trawlers from fishing in the defined areas during the months of May, June, July, and specifies the areas within which the trawlers are permitted to fish other than these areas.
- SMW Decision No. 98 of 1993 regarding the staff of fishery administrations in the municipalities and regions authorizing them to act as legal officers.
- Law No. 15 of 2001, which replaced Law No. 7 of 1982, concerning environmental protection. In this Law, Chap. 3, which contains 21 articles, comprehensively covers marine fisheries and marine wealth conservation, identifying the means and procedures necessary for the protection of fish stock, as well as the banning of dumping oils and other pollutants from vessels into the sea and the discharge of land-based sewage and industrial water into the marine environment. It also prohibits the use of explosives, radioactive, and other poisonous substances for fishing, and bans dredging for sponges. It also provides for the delineation of sea reservations for the preservation of threatened marine organisms.
- General People's Committee Decision No. 37 of 2005, which declares a protected fishing zone along the Libyan coastline, prohibiting all methods of fishing in the declared permitted zones without advance permission to be issued by an official authority to be determined by the GPC.

8.8.2 Key Indicators Related to Fishing Industry

Table 8.6 below illustrates key indicators of the fishing sector for the year 2003.

Table 8.6. Employment and economic value of the fishing sector

Estimated employment (2003)	
Primary sector	11 500 Full-time and part-time fishermen
Secondary sector	3 500 (landing site services, marketing, administration, canneries)
Gross value of fisheries output (2003, est.)	US $100 million
Trade (2003)	
Value of imports	US $40 628 000
Value of exports	US $10 476 000

Source: COPEMED, 2005.

8.8.3 Structure and Characteristics of the Fishing Industry

Marine Fishery

The marine fishery sector in Libya comprises four major activities: artisanal coastal fishing, lampara (purse seine) fishing, coastal trawling, and tuna fishing. Sponge fishing, which flourished in the 1950s and 1960s and which declined because of industrial and effluent pollution, is now a minor but recently expanding area of production. Most of the catch is taken by artisanal boats working with nets such as Ghezula tat-Tisqif/Ghezula tal Mitlaq (trammel nets and gillnets) or hooks (longlines and handlines), and by the lampara fleet fishing for pelagic fish. Species caught with this type of gear include chub mackerel (*Scomber japonicus*), Mediterranean horse mackerel (*Trachurus mediterraneus*), bogue (*Boops boops*), and allis shad (*Alosa alosa*).

There were a total of 1,866 active artisanal fishing boats counted during the national landing site survey conducted in the year 2000, of which 1300 were smaller than 10 m overall length and 566 more than 10 m LOA. Approximately two-thirds of the smaller crafts were motorized, usually with outboard engines in the 10–35 hp range. The larger units are decked vessels and are fitted with inboard engines. These vessels were based at 135 beaches, anchorages, and harbour landing sites along the coastline, with heavier concentrations along the western coastline of Libya towards the border with Tunisia. Seventy-six landing sites are permanent, that is, operating throughout the year, and 59 are seasonal (Lamboeuf 2000).

The lampara or purse seine fleet is made up of around 135 motorized vessels ranging up to 18 m in length. The term "lampara" is used because fishermen use strong lights to attract fish, which are then caught by purse seining, with the dimensions of a typical net being between 400 and 450 m long and about 105 m wide, with a mesh size of 23 mm knot to knot. During the active fishing season, mainly in the summer months, each unit teams up with one or two smaller lamp boats, known as "dhgaissa", which are non-motorized and are towed along on nightly trips to and from the fishing grounds. Lampara fishing is concentrated along the western section of the coastline, between Misuratah and the Tunisian border.

Tuna fishing is carried out mainly using an industrial fishing fleet of nine longliners and six purse seiners, and tonnaras, which use sets of nets that extend 3–5 km out from the coast. Bluefin tuna (*Thunnus Thynnus*) and little tuna (*E. alletteratus*) constitute the important components of the total pelagic fishing activities in Libya, and form part of the Libyan traditional catch of this highly migratory species along the western Libyan waters during late spring and early summer (El-Tawil and Gashti 1998). It is believed that these fish and other related species migrate every year as a pelagic fish from the Atlantic to the Mediterranean through the Straits of Gibraltar (Tawil 1999; El-Kebir et al. 2001). Tonnara fishing was more common in the past with as many as 18 stations reportedly in operation before the Second World War. Five stations now remain, only two of which were active during the 2003 season (May–July). These are located at Zreq and Dzirah, 200 km east of Tripoli.

The industrial fishing fleet, excluding the tuna fishing fleet, is made up of 123 units, which are steel and wood stern trawlers, with lengths varying from 13 to 33 m LOA, and engine power ranging from 165 to 950 hp. These industrial trawlers are mostly owned privately, either by individuals or in partnerships.

As stated earlier, sponge harvesting was a major economic activity during the 1950s and 1960s, especially along the eastern part of the coast between Benghazi and Tubruk. After a period of drastic decline owing to disease outbreaks in the beds due to oil and effluent-related pollution and the withdrawal of labour from the fishery to more lucrative jobs in the oilfield, sponge harvesting is slowly beginning to pick up again.

Total production of fish and fishery products from Libyan waters was reported to be 50,000 MT in 2000, with an estimated value of US $100 million. This production consisted of around 21,000 MT of small pelagic fish such as sardine, mackerel, horse mackerel, and bogue, 2,000 MT of bluefin tuna, and about 24,000 MT of mixed demersal species, mainly red mullet, breams, groupers, amberjack, common dentex, triggerfish, common pandora, octopus, cuttlefish, squid, shark, as well as 3,000 MT of other types of fish (FAO 2005).

Appendix 8.5 shows the location of main landing sites in Libya, that is harbours that contain more than 15 fishing units, together with an estimated quantity of fish landed in metric tons, based on a sampling survey carried out in 2004.

Twenty-four marine fishery cooperatives, known locally as "Jamaias", have been established at major fishing centres along the coast, with the aim of providing supplies of essential gear and spare parts to the artisanal sector. Membership of these local "Jamaias" is open to all fishermen who have valid boat licences issued by the fishery authorities.

As noted above, the central authority between 1988 and 2000 for the fisheries sector was the SMW, which was a powerful administration with a solid legal and administrative basis that grouped all the administration and technical functions required to manage and develop the fishing industry. During this period, the initiatives of the SMW, backed by significant financial and legislative input from the state, led to a rapid development of the marine fishing sector. To demonstrate this, the Libyan catch grew from approximately 6,000 MT in 1988 to around 50,000 MT in 2000. However in 2000, as a result of the Libyan government decentralization policy, the SMW was dissolved and most of its functions, such as fleet management, enforcement of regulations, management of port structures, etc. were transferred to local regional authorities, the Sha'abiyat.

Inland Fisheries

In comparative terms, the production of inland fisheries in Libya can be said to be negligible. Free stocking of carp and tilapia has been carried out in the past at the reservoir areas of Wadi Kaam in the Al Khums/Zliten area and Wadi Mjinine close to Tripoli, and more recently carp have been stocked in Abou Dzira Lake near Benghazi. However results thus far do not indicate much potential for commercial production.

Aquaculture Developments

There have been several attempts at inland freshwater aquaculture at different sites on a pilot basis over the past two decades, although production remains minimal.

Projects to raise tilapia and other species using farmers' small irrigation water reservoirs ranging in size from 50 to 200 m^3 have been initiated at certain agriculture projects in the desert some 650 km south of Tripoli in the mid-1990s. Around 150 farmers were given free fingerlings and feed plus a regular technical follow-up by experts for two years, and these projects succeeded in realizing their socio-economic goals in encouraging the production and consumption of fish in these fairly remote areas. Currently the total number of farmers raising tilapia in their own reservoirs has increased to around 250, and production has correspondingly increased to 200–250 tonnes per year according to field visit reports.

A good deal of emphasis has been put on promoting mariculture since 1990. Pilot/trial stations have been established at Ain Kaam, near Al Khums, Ain Ziana, near Benghazi, and Ain El Ghazala, near Tobruk. Work at Ain Kaam has involved brackish water cage culture of mullet and red tilapia. The lagoon at Ain Ghazala has been used for cage culture of sea bass, sea bream, mullet, and eels, and some cultivation of mussels has also been carried out on a trial basis. A major new hatchery and grow-out pond and cage culture of sea bass and sea bream complex is now under construction at Farwa Lagoon, near the Tunisian border. There have also been some attempts by the private sector to establish cage and pond farming in the last few years but the level of expansion and production is still well below the expected planned target of around 400 tonnes annually, mainly due to technical and financial constraints. However this is clearly an area with considerable potential and a huge amount of tried and tested technology from Europe and the United States is now available to Libyan entrepreneurs wishing to invest in this potentially lucrative business.

8.8.4 Fisheries Research

Fisheries research is under the responsibility of the Marine Biology Research Centre (MBRC) located on the coast at Tajora, near Tripoli.

Currently the main MBRC activities are:

- Bottom and acoustic survey along the Libyan coast
- Bluefin tuna population dynamics study
- Exotic fish study
- Studies on the development of fishing methods and gear
- Study of seaweed
- A study monitoring of heavy metals and hydrocarbons in the Libyan coastal area
- Studies on the impact of the discharge of untreated sewage on the marine environment

In view of the stringent provisions of Law No. 15 of 2001 concerning environmental protection, it is crucial that the Libyan government has the political will to enforce the provisions of this law to ensure a sustainable fishing industry, especially in view of the vast amount of sewage disgorging into the Mediterranean from Libya's rapidly growing urban population in the Mediterranean coastal strip. Although there are major sewage treatment plants for Libya's main cities, with, for example, the Tripoli plant designed to handle 247,000 MT of raw sewage per day, the fact is that the pumping stations in these plants frequently break down, while in Tripoi and Benghazi, as examples of the major conurbations, 30 and 13 outlets for rain and sewage water, respectively, disgorge directly into the sea (National Report on the Environment 2002).

8.8.5 COPEMED Project, 1996–2004

The COPEMED area covers the Western and Central sub-regions of the Mediterranean, comprising Morocco, Algeria, Tunisia, Libya, Malta, Italy, France, and Spain Timeline. This comprises a series of research programs on artisanal fisheries, gear selectivity, socio-economic indicators, tuna and swordfish, dolphin, and the use of Geographic Information Systems (GIS) in fishery research and development.

The project covered the following activities in Libya:

- Bluefin tuna population dynamics research
- Landing Sites Survey
- Socio-economic Indicators Study
- The development of national staff skills through training activities and the support travel of key Libyan experts to attend regional meeting and workshops
- Supplying the MBRC at Tajora with laboratory equipment and PCs.

A second phase of the COPEMED project has been officially approved with fundings from the Spanish Agencia Española de Cooperación Internacional (AECI) and two new donors, the DG Fisheries of the European Commission and the Spanish Secretaría General de Pesca, for a minimum period of 3 years (2005–2008).

8.8.6 Enhancing Catch Utilization

In Libya, all marine and inland catches are sold and consumed fresh in large urban market areas, except for a small part of the pelagic catch which is canned for the domestic market or sold to be made into fishmeal during the summer peak production period. As far as commercialization is concerned, facilities for receiving, handling, and distributing fish have improved considerably, especially over the past few years after the privatization of the marketing chain. Most major landing and marketing centres are now served by ice plants and cold/chill storage facilities.

There are currently seven fish canning plants belonging to state companies, which can process tuna and small pelagic species, with a daily raw material capacity of 85 tonnes of tuna, 51 tonnes of small pelagic, and 130 tonnes of fishmeal, established during 1980s. None of these plants seem to operate in a satisfactory condition due to problems relating to raw material supply as well as lack of spare parts and poor state of equipment maintenance. Most if not all of these facilities are candidates for privatization under Libya's current privatization initiative.

In terms of fish exports, the industry reports very small quantities. Around 2,000 MT of bluefin tuna are exported annually to international markets, mainly Japan, and minor quantities of high-value fish are exported to Tunisia. Here again exists tremendous potential for Libyan entrepreneurs who, with post-harvest technology and sophisticated automated filleting and packing plants now available after the sanctions, can benefit commercially from this high-value global industry.

8.8.7 Current and Future Status of the Fishing Industry

Although the government through the SMW has devoted significant resources for improving the harvest and post-harvest sectors, particularly in the provision of landing sites, harbour development, processing plants, and associated infrastructure, the Libyan fishing industry still performs well below its real potential. The fisheries sector provides employment for only a small fraction, around 1 per cent, of the total national labour force.

There have been several studies carried out, with French and other foreign assistance, aimed at examining the current status of Libyan fish stocks. For the western part of Libya, between the Tunisian border and Misuratah, scientific examinations were carried out in 1993–1994 under the LIBFISH project. It was concluded that the demersal stocks are nearing full exploitation and that there should be no increase in fishing effort. For the central and eastern part of Libya, from Misuratah to the Egyptian border, a scientific cruise was organized in August 2003 by the Libyan MBRC, in collaboration with a Greek research institute. It was concluded that the demersal stocks were healthy and that there was significant potential for further exploitation.

In particular, there are good prospects for exploiting the presence of large quantities of bluefin tuna in Libyan waters. Again, with national planning objectives calling for further diversification of the economy, particularly in food production, there is undoubtedly in future a substantial role for Libya's marine fishery, mariculture, and aquculture sectors of the fishing industry. In 2001, the average per capita consumption of fresh fish in Libya was slightly over 7 kg. This compares to the average global consumption of fish, which has increased from about 9 kg per person per year in the early 1960s to 16 kg in 1997 (www.oceanatlas.org). In general, in line with demographic and consumer trends, the demand for domestically produced quality fish is bound to grow. Undoubtedly this trend could be considerably encouraged by upgrading product quality and improving marketing. Again, demand for fishmeal is also likely to show a steady increase in response to continuing pressure to expand the production of local animal feed plants to serve the poultry industry.

From virtually all angles the fishing sector in Libya appears to have a bright future, and the Libyan marine fishery and fish stocks, unlike many other parts of the world, have a present capability, if developed sustainably and prudently, to contribute significantly to Libya's economic diversification and food requirements for many years in the future.

9 The Libyan Energy and Mining Sector

9.1 The Libyan Electricity Sector

9.1.1 The Electricity Sector: The Early Stages

Before the discovery of oil and the major changes which this brought about in Libya economic status, electrical power was very poorly developed, the service undependable, and the unit cost of supply very high. Even in 1965, Libya's total installed capacity for electrical energy amounted to only 70,000 KW. As Table 9.1 shows, this was less than one-third of the installed capacity of Tunisia, also one of the most backward nations in the world at that time. Total energy production in Libya in 1965 stood at 157 million KiloWatt Hours (KWH), while annual use was estimated at 101 KWH per capita. Between 1950 and 1965, capacity utilization stood at only 29 per cent, and the average annual increase in production in these years amounted to the low figure of 11 per cent.

Much earlier, in fact, the inefficiency of Libya's electrical power had predated Libya's independence. When Libya became independent, power in Tripolitania was provided privately by an Italian company. The company ran plants in seven towns, with the Tripoli Power Plant being the most important. This plant, built in 1930, was, by 1952, old, inefficient, and defective. Despite the fact that the high generating costs per KWH were covered by an even higher user rate, the plant was so inefficient that the government had to repeatedly subsidize its annual deficit. Even then, the plant failed to meet power surges at peak seasons and periods. The position of the other Libyan generating plants was not much different. In fact, in Cyrenaica there was, by 1951, an additional problem of repairing damage caused by war. Financing adequate power provision was simply beyond the domestic fiscal capacity of Libya in 1951.

In 1958, at the time of the visit of the World Bank Mission, the supply of electrical power had been, since 1956, under public control, with Tripoli power station still the most important. The total power generated in all Libya amounted, however, to not more than 67 million KWH, with Tripoli power station selling 42 KWH of this total. Of the power sold by Tripoli power station in 1958, only 17 per cent was for industrial use, while 39 per cent was sold for agricultural and pumping purposes, and 44 per cent for lighting and domestic power. All the basic problems such as the inability to meet demand, load shedding, complex tariff structures, excessively high costs to industrial users, the need for heavy subsidization to cover operating losses, and difficulties even in forecasting the demand for electrical power, continued to characterize the Libyan

Table 9.1. Selected MENA countries, comparison of installed capacity, and production of electrical energy, 1960–1965

Country	Installed capacity. 000 of (KW)		Energy production (million KWH)		(KWH per capita)	Capacity utilization, 1960–1965	Average annual increase in production, 1960–1965
	Total	Hydro	Total	Hydro			
Libya	70	–	157	–	101	29	11
Tunisia	213	28	494	42	113	28	9
UAR*	1335	351	5106	1670	185	37	16
Algeria	500	228	1096	400	94	11	4

* United Arab Republic: Egypt and Syria.

Source: UN, World Economic Survey, 1967, New York.

electricity sector. Poor service was a feature of all the 35 publicly owned power stations outside the major cities of Tripoli and Benghazi. By any measurement of commercial standards, the overall management of the electrical power sector was extremely poor.

However, there were some encouraging indications of development observable if we compare 1954 with 1963. The installed capacity of electricity-generating plants under the Electricity Corporation of Tripolitania increased by fourfold from 10,600 KW in 1954 to 42,356 KW in 1963. The production of electricity throughout Libya more than doubled, increasing from 40,405,226 KWH in 1954 to 82,130,206 KWH in 1963 (Doxiadis Associates 1964).

Despite these indicators, the supply of electrical energy was neither able to keep up with the demand of commercial and industrial expansion, nor was the electricity being supplied at rates any less costly than before. During 1955–1964, the power stations in Benghazi, for instance, continued to be overburdened and were subjected to frequent breakdowns and black outs. In order to tackle this problem, in 1963, the government of Libya allocated 8,562,000 Libyan pounds out of the total public works development allocation of 38,662,000 pounds to the development of electricity supplies.

The situation of Libya with regard to other MENA countries in the early period is summed up in Table 9.1.

9.1.2 The Electricity Sector: 1970–1980

As oil revenues increased and the socio-economic development budget of the new government after 1969 accelerated, total installed generating capacity grew sixfold and the power actually generated grew threefold between 1970 and 1979. At the same time, there was a more than threefold increase in the per capita consumption of electrical energy, from 335 KWH per head of population in 1970 to around 1050 KWH per head in 1977.

The growth of the electricity-generating capacity was accompanied by the extension of a grid system of high tension transmission lines throughout the country. More than 1000 km of extra high voltage lines (i.e. 220 kV) were installed between 1970 and 1977 to connect the towns of Misuratah, Ejeilat,

Tripoli, Abu Argoub, and the towns of Tubruk, Derna, Benghazi, Agdabia, and Zuweitina. Also, high tension lines (600 kV.) increased from 150 km in 1970 to 1965 km by 1977, with over 600 km of these covering the Sebha area, along Wadi-Shatti, Wadi Ajal, Wadi Murzuq, and another 200 km covering Benghazi and the Jebel Akhdar areas. Moreover, a number of transmission line projects were also build in the late 1970s. One of these covered the Jebel Gharbi area with 220 kV. lines, spanning the towns from Zuwara to Misuratah with 66 kV. extensions leading from these. Another 220 kV. line was extended from Zuweitina to El Brega, together with a further extension of a 66 kV. line to Jebel Akhdar and Benghazi. Through these important increases in electrical energy supply, power was gradually made available to every Libyan citizen, even those residing in the remotest villages and oases of the interior desert regions.

Simultaneously, another major activity of this sector was the development of desalination plants in line with increasing generating capacity. Thus, while 16 main generating stations were established along the coastal belt, 10 of these were for both electrical generation and sea water desalination. The most important of these were the steam power-generating and desalination plants, located in Western Tripoli, with a generating capacity of 325 MW, another was located in North Benghazi with a total generating capacity of 180 MW, while third was in Tobruk with 127 MW total capacity.

By 1980, after more progress in power distribution, the total generating capacity of these stations was 2240 MW and the total water desalination capacity had raised from 166,000 m³ in 1997 to 206,000 m³ in that year, as shown in Table 9.2.

Table 9.2. Libya: development of electricity sector, 1970–1980

Description	Measure-ment unit	1970	1976	1977	1980 (Projected)
Total installed capacity:		248	1173	1500	2240
Steam	MW	60	541	766	1506
Gas	MW	98	496	601	601
Diesel	MW	90	136	133	133
Generated electricity from:		675	2380	2900	4900
– Steam power stations	GWH		1260	1955	3640
– Gas turbine power stations	GWH		910	750	995
– Diesel power stations	GWH		210	195	265
Productive capacity of desalination plants:			82,500	166,000	206,000
– Steam	M³/Day	–	46,500	103,700	143,700
– Gas	M³/Day	–	36,000	63,000	63,000
Electricity standards:					
Installed capacity	0,123	0,464	0,542	0,718	0,718
General capacity	335	896	1,049	1,570	1,570
Connection and transmission network:					
– Very high tension networks 220 kV.	Km	–	–	1,035	1435
– High tension networks 60 kV.	Km	150	–	965	1565

Source: Libya: Secretariat of Planning, 1978.

9.1.3 The Electricity Sector, 1981–Present

Presently GECOL (the General Electricity Company of Libya) is the electric utility in Libya solely responsible for the generation, transportation, and distribution of electrical power to the entire country. Figures 9.1 and 9.2 and Table 9.3 together provide an overview of the current status of the electricity sector in Libya.

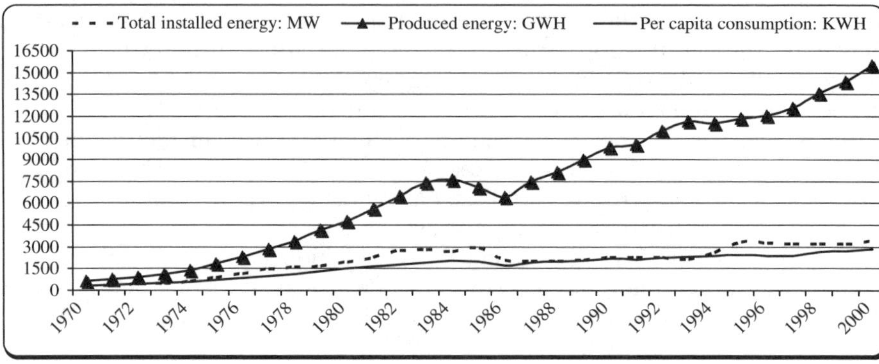

Source: Libyan General Planning Council, 2001.

Fig. 9.1. Libya: total installed and produced electrical energy, 1970–2000

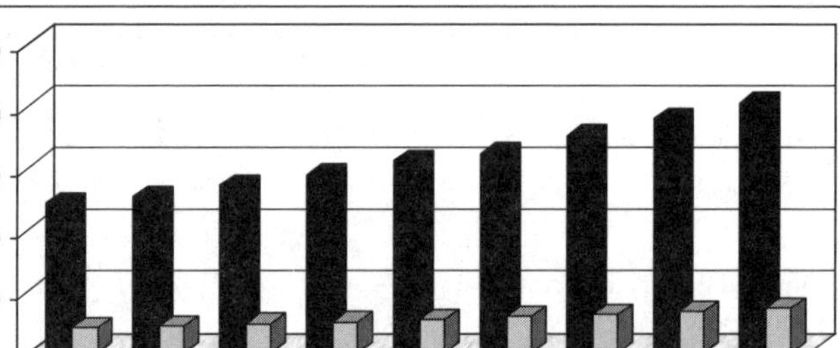

	1996	1997	1998	1999	2000	2001	2002	2003	2004
■ Produced power (GWH)	12086	12620	13528	14407	15496	16111	17531	18943	20202
□ Peak load (MW)	1977	2140	2360	2448	2630	2934	3081	3341	3612

Source: GECOL, 2005.

Fig. 9.2. Libya: produced power (GWH) and peak load (MW), 1996–2004

Table 9.3. Status of the Libyan electricity sector, 2004

	Value and unit
Peak demand	3,612 MW
Installed generation capacity	4,700 GW
Generated energy	20,202 GW h
220 KV transmission system	13,000 km
66 & 33 KV Sub-transmission system	21,000 km
11 KV Distribution system	38,000 km
Customers	1,200,000
Per capita consumption	2,770
Urban & rural electrification rate	>99%
Desalination installed capacity	260,000 M^3/day

Source: GECOL, 2005.

9.1.4 Electricity Sector Reform: Corporatization, Deregulation, and Privatization

GECOL's future plans are based on the expansion of the country's network of power stations, which presently are situated in the country's largest consumer regions of Tripoli, Benghazi, and Sebha respectively. Following rapid expansion in capacity in the 1990s with the establishment of two 725-MW plants at Zueitina and Zuwarah, GECOL plans to develop another 800-MW plant at Zuwarah, with another proposal for a plant of approximately 1400 MW to be situated between the major cities of Tripoli and Benghazi, as well as a combined power and desalination complex of 1200 MW at Sirte.

The transfer to new gas conversion technology is crucial in order to meet future demands as well as to mitigate costs, as well as being more environmentally friendly, and GECOL proposes to implement this in two phases, the initial phase from 2002 to 2006 and the second phase from 2006 to 2012. During the initial phase from 2002–2006, funding will be 100 per cent Libyan government's, but it is possible that for the period 2006–2012 external funding will be required, perhaps using some form of PPP. Libyan electricity demand is growing rapidly, estimated at around 7 per cent p.a. based on the existing customer base and demographic trends, but this does not account for the inevitable upsurge in demand expected through Libya's current diversification programme, such as the massive expansion of the tourist sector. To meet the demand, GECOL intends to double its capacity, which was 2650 MW in 2001, to approximately 5000 MW by 2010 and then double this again, by 2020, to 10,000 MW. Investment costs required to achieve this, including new power stations, the installation and upgrading of existing grids, distribution networks and control centres, are estimated at approximately US $6 billion by 2010 and US $10 billion in total by 2020.

These major investment requirements raise the question of how GECOL can possibly fund such a massive expansion, especially since it is losing money, primarily because of the extremely low and heavily subsidized tariffs charged to Libyan consumers as part of the overall social welfare programme. Although GECOL's policy of substituting gas for oil in power generation will mitigate GECOL's future losses, its operating deficit will continue to increase.

It is for these reasons that the Libyan government must now initiate plans for the corporatization, deregulation and eventual privatization, or at least partial divestment, of GECOL, enabling the company to operate in a purely commercial way. The company's future operations should be based on paying prices to the Libyan government for its feedstock, whether oil or gas, and charging prices to its consumers, whether commercial or industrial, based on international parity energy prices. By doing so, the government will, as in the BOMC case discussed extensively later in this chapter, be relieved from paying huge annual subsidies to prop up a sick commercial entity and realize the true value of Libya's increasingly valuable hydrocarbon resources. At the same time, Libyan consumers will realize that electricity, although a vital component of everyday life, comes at a cost much higher than the existing levels, and one which is set to increase.

To achieve these objectives, the electricity industry, run by an SOE fully controlled by the Libyan government, needs first to be internally restructured. The first phase of this restructuring could be achieved by corporatizing GECOL, that is by separating it completely from the Ministry of Energy and setting up a new company to operate it, based on a comprehensive valuation and asset review. At this point its assets would still be owned by the government, but its management would be market-responsive and market-driven, and responsible for meeting corporate commercial targets. Through the corporatization process the management would enter into a dialogue with the government to agree on new tariff levels as well as the cost of energy such as fuel oil or gas to the new company, which, when agreed, would be the basic building blocks for its future corporate strategy.

Determining and agreeing with the Libyan government on self-financing targets in a progressive manner, over an agreed time frame, say for example, of 40 per cent self-financing by 2008, 60 per cent by 2010, 80 per cent by 2012, and 100 per cent by 2014, would also be a key part of this initial corporatization exercise. Additionally, the retraining and reorientation of key personnel through exposure to the business environment would be necessary, through seminars and awareness programmes in modern management concepts such as total quality management and business process reengineering.

Once the objectives of GECOL's corporatization exercise had been successfully achieved, with the new company self-operating and self-funding, and profitability guidelines based on a realistic return on government assets, the Libyan government might wish to consider deregulation, at which point the framework and timeframe for this could be discussed. Deregulation, by introducing competition, would mean that the corporatized GECOL would have to fight for profits in a competitive environment and therefore become more efficient, since it would no longer have the advantages of being a monopoly.

Once the deregulation framework had been devised and implemented by the Libyan government, its options would then be either to hold on to an efficiently operating GECOL or divest and privatize it. At this point, the deregulated market would be opened up to competition, whether for Libyan companies interested in competing with GECOL as electricity generators or distributors or for foreign companies with expertise and successful track records in this field.

Should it be interested in divesting or privatizing GECOL, the government should probably do this through "unbundling", that is by spinning off the generation, transmission, and distribution sectors separately. However, our view is that rather than total privatization of this sector, the government should hold on to at least 50 per cent of these debundled entities, in view of their future potential for profit. The other 50 per cent could be floated on the new Libyan stock exchange, discussed earlier in Chap. 8, or by private placement, or by any other privatization methods appropriate for the utility sector.

It is interesting to note that the mass privatization of utilities in Africa and South America has come about in the previous 20 years mainly because of external pressures and conditionalities from international institutions such as the World Bank or the IMF. Clearly Libya is not in this position and should consider its utility privatization options very carefully. It is noteworthy that public sector electricity companies continue to exist in many countries in Europe, presently including the state-owned companies of France (EdF), Ireland (ESB), Italy (ENEL), Norway (Statkraft), Sweden (Vattenfall), and Finland (Fortum/IVO, although only 50 per cent state-owned).

9.2 The Marketing and Consumption of Petroleum Products

9.2.1 The Private Sector: 1951–1971

In a best seller which is regarded by many as the definitive history of the oil industry, the author stated "hydrocarbon man shows little inclination to give up his cars, his suburban home, and what he takes to be not only the conveniences but the essentials of his way of life" (Yergin 1991). In fact the relentless increase in the demand for oil affects the hydrocarbon man not only in his domestic setting but also in all productive sectors such as agriculture, industry, transportation, distribution, and marketing.

In Libya, as in other countries, we can note a steady increase in the use of oil over the past half century since its discovery there, with data showing that sales of fuel and other oil products over this period increased many times. The discovery and widespread availability of oil brought significant changes to the traditional Libyan way of life, leading both to higher expectations as well as to a steady increase in the overall quality of life for Libyans.

In the early years sales of fuel oil and related products were very limited. For the year 1951 total sales of fuel and other oil products reached about 67 million litres, comprising eight varieties of oil products, valued at about LD1.4 million. Gas oil constituted more than one-third of this quantity while aircraft fuel accounted for about 28.4 per cent, while regular gasoline constituted about 13 per cent and the remaining 5 varieties about 25 per cent. The years 1952 and 1953 witnessed moderate increases in overall sales with annual increases of approximately 15.5 per cent pushing totals up to 77 million and 89 million litres, respectively. The year 1954 was a record year for expansion in the consumption of oil products, amounting to a 114 per cent increase with total sales of the petroleum products rising to 191 million litres valued at LD3.5 million.

These early increases were undoubtedly due to the steady post-independence rise in economic growth and expansion in public expenditure, which resulted in the creation of new employment opportunities and the growth of public utilities. As well as this, the establishment of foreign military air bases contributed significantly to the increase in the consumption of oil products – for example, sales of aircraft fuel during 1954 also recorded a 121 per cent rise compared with the preceding year.

Throughout the 1950s this upward trend in sales of fuel oils continued except for the years 1955 and 1959, which recorded a drop in sales amounting to 2 and 7.5 per cent, respectively. The growth in sales of fuel oils during the three years 1956, 1957, and 1958 was about 13, 38.5, and 17.1 per cent, respectively, with total quantities sold during these years amounting to 212, 293, and 344 million litres, respectively. In 1956 there was addition of a new variety of gasoline (premium gasoline) to the existing eight varieties of fuel oils, after which the relative market share of premium gasoline increased steadily in comparison with ordinary gasoline.

The substantial increase in the activities of oil companies operating in Libya, and the beginning of oil exports during the 1960s, also resulted in a general rise in disposable income, which led to the comparatively large-scale ownership of private cars. These factors together contributed to a huge increase in the volume of consumption of fuel oils. Throughout the 1960s the rate of increase in sales of fuel oils ranged between 3 and 39 per cent, reaching a total of about 1.2 billion litres during 1969, with a total value of about LD25 million. Because of a temporary decline in the economic activities during the transitional period following the Libyan Revolution, and the evacuation of foreign military bases, fuel oil sales in Libya suffered slight decreases of about 2.7 and 7.5 per cent during 1970 and 1971, respectively. Another factor that contributed to the decline in fuel oil sales in this period was the government's request to oil companies operating in the country to limit their expenditure, particularly in respect of transport services, which had a great influence on the amounts of fuel consumed. However, by the 4th quarter of 1971, statistics again indicated an improvement in the volumes of the principal items of consumption, bringing these in line with their previous growth rates.

In the early 1970s a large proportion (about one-third) of local consumption was met by the El Brega Refinery, which began production during 1971 with a productive capacity of about 9,500 barrels per day, with refined products amounting to a total of about 2.8 million barrels during 1971. El Brega Refinery also succeeded in meeting local market needs for heavy oils, producing 1.2 million barrels during 1971 against a local demand of approximately 1.1 million barrels. Overall, locally refined products of both premium and regular gasoline constituted about one-third of local consumption (556,000 barrels of the former and 1.8 million barrels of the latter), while local production of kerosene amounted to about 335,000 barrels in 1970, against 521 thousand barrels in 1971, generally sufficient to meet local market requirements for heavy oils. In this period of the early 1970s a new plant, the Al-Zawia Refinery, was also constructed which, together with El Brega, covered more than the local demand.

With regard to domestic retail prices of oil products in Libya, these were reduced across the board from 1 May 1967, following the agreement between the government and the Esso Company at the beginning of the operation of the El Brega Refinery. Table 9.4 shows consumption and total value in LD from 1951 to 1971.

Table 9.4. Libya: consumption of fuel and fuel oils, 1951–1971

[in thousand litres]

Year	Premium gasoline	Regular gasoline	Kerosene	Diesel oil	Heavy oil	Turbine oils	Lubricant	Liquid gas	Aircraft fuel	Others	Total	Rate of increase	Value LD000
1951	–	8621	4745	22633	7808	2403	1405	–	19018	438	67071	–	1383
1952	–	13747	5198	25169	8563	3879	1875	–	17719	1188	77338	15.3	1691
1953	–	19475	7196	27760	8288	3696	1992	–	19598	1427	89432	15.6	1832
1954	–	25361	8054	35242	7156	69300	1863	–	43317	939	191227	11.38	3500
1955	–	29068	8267	36695	7384	79715	2211	–	23896	290	187526	2.0	3671
1956	4641	32625	7514	42172	4839	72465	2614	–	41556	3396	211822	13.2	4006
1957	11941	33096	12782	60642	7824	102821	2656	–	55949	11033	293744	38.5	5420
1958	17658	34480	13564	65928	2203	161381	2488	–	44095	2353	344150	17.1	5900
1959	15044	43767	14995	89199	4176	104418	4084	–	38936	3754	318373	7.5	6031
1960	18908	50337	17577	123811	4723	39422	6141	3619	38392	9354	312284	2.0	7291
1961	22922	46772	20826	143542	7909	40889	6403	4088	23086	32749	349186	11.8	8116
1962	28547	48962	25293	158175	30738	42654	7416	4533	20741	12517	379576	8.7	9171
1963	33445	52220	27265	181905	37521	43933	8446	5347	21709	9797	421588	11.0	10533
1964	42989	60887	34873	206921	48060	51362	9070	6609	23920	7429	492120	16.7	12022
1965	48974	70001	42814	220569	61469	52298	9825	8474	22748	17297	555369	2.5	12470
1966	65012	78744	46274	271273	69308	56264	10444	10070	16327	22897	646613	16.4	14052
1967	81522	77969	52299	316326	70505	53971	12866	11842	13521	104992	795813	23.1	16795
1968	116517	86666	68884	428012	93845	71024	17855	14034	15991	192201	1104229	38.7	22071
1969	147666	81838	88430	489602	103050	81307	17534	17211	16310	157827	1200775	8.7	25005
1970	186190	78513	107429	481192	133910	74436	12104	19173	17756	57602	1169305	2.7	24756
1971	208016	76347	80814	371024	182213	48421	14285	15035	6628	77943	1080726	7.5	26518

Source: Central Bank of Libya.

Table 9.5. Libya: consumption of fuel and fuel oils, 1972–1984

[in thousand litres]

Year	Premium gasoline	Regular gasoline	Kerosene	Diesel oil	Heavy oil	Aircraft fuel + turbine Oils	Lubricant	Liquid gas	Others	Total
1972	264713	76524	94976	521344	175883	62748	21404	21226	79933	1318751
1973	329759	76138	97200	670077	239166	145147	26738	27056	98428	1709709
1974	430928	69573	126396	695632	284178	110006	28889	33446	107481	1886529
1975	542736	66611	121268	1229346	355080	213726	39366	34101	171429	2773663
1976	623172	63467	119399	1331129	571422	236819	39783	49055	85673	3119919
1977	832857		122899	1141876	777426	253957	36018	55122	93137	3313292
1978	899916		138742	1538047	767314	226486	42803	63448	173468	3850224
1979	919651		360519	1589192	939521	289853	43308	62236	158060	4362340
1980	1090251		161081	1507641	1261804	382074	51689	61692	103953	4620185
1981	1214223		158292	2344111	1527376	314928	224313	97171	196748	6077162
1982	1220024		95904	2508637	1889416	481158	65894	90212	0	6351245
1983	1274790		583723	2462335	1865364	3394	61203	85385	69003	6405197
1984	1274331		545086	2251798	1263581	2315	59847	128755	313895	5839608

Source: Libyan Central Bank and Libyan National Oil Corporation (LNOC), 2004.

Table 9.6. Libya: consumption of fuel and fuel oils, 1985–2004

[in thousand litres]

Year	Gasoline	Kerosene	Aircraft fuel	Fuel oil	Gas oil	LPG	Others	Total
1985	959.3	0	408.9	1750.1	1565.8	130.7	154.8	4969.6
1986	988.6	63.4	420.1	1536.5	1410.9	139	88	4646.5
1987	991	55.3	326.4	1900.4	1532.5	126.4	148	5080
1988	1033.1	59.7	293.2	2181.6	1810.7	147.5	0	5525.8
1989	1158	53	274	2386	1775	154	205	6005
1990	1263	56	273	2532	1684	163	0	5971
1991	1379	74.8	263.9	2428.9	1699.2	176.3	135.7	6157.8
1992	1496	74.4	152.9	2289.6	1998.8	188.9	123.8	6324.4
1993	1525	84.4	84.9	2149.2	1986.4	199.3	119.3	6148.5
1994	1546.9	81.3	74.2	2151.2	2061.4	205.5	106.6	6227.1
1996	1521.1	156.9	0	1621.9	2576.6	224.8	75.3	6176.6
1997	1580.4	151.2	0	1641.8	2799.2	233.9	0	6406.5
1998	1646.2	162.1	0	1673.7	2888.6	245	0	6615.6
1999	1701	208	0	1805.8	2882.9	247.5	0	6845.2
2000	1818.7	297	0	2084.8	2875.8	262.2	0	7338.5
2001	1747.4	295	0	1808.5	2493.1	235.5	0	6579.5
2002	2016.6	324.6	0	2373.2	3073.1	267	0	8054.5
2003	2146.3	391.7	0	2548.8	3428.8	271.5	0	8787.1
2004	2256.6	533.3	0	2472.8	3783.1	280.8	0	9326.6

Throughout the 1980s and 1990s, as Libyan oil and gas production increased and infrastructure such as long distance roads were constructed linking all the major cities in Libya, as well as connecting the country's road arteries with neighbouring Egypt, Tunisia, Chad, and Algeria, the demand for fuel continued unabated, as can be seen from Tables 9.5 and 9.6.

As can be noted from Tables 9.5 and 9.6, although the effects of the US and UN sanctions against Libya on fuel consumption began to be initially experienced, they did not have a major impact on sales of the various grades of fuel, which, in a domestic context, continued to rise steadily, apart from the demand for aircraft fuel, which with effect from 1995 literally froze as Libyan Airways stopped operations and foreign airlines ceased their flights to Libya.

In Fig. 9.3, we show, in percentage, the sources of supply of fuel and other downstream products to BOMC, both domestic and abroad.

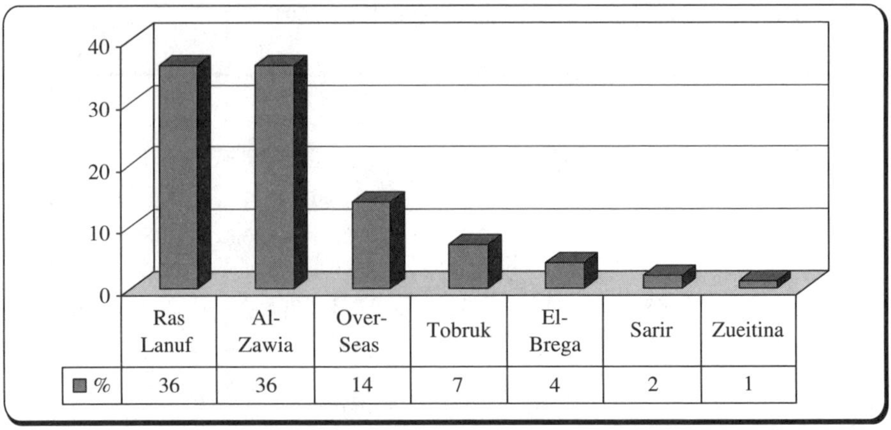

Fig. 9.3. Supply of downstream products to BOMC by Libyan and overseas refineries, 2005

9.2.2 Nationalization and the Establishment of Brega Oil Marketing Company (BOMC)

The commencement of host government participation or nationalization of the downstream Libyan oil industry began on 4 July 1970, with the passing of Revolutionary Law No. 69. This law restricted the import, selling, and distribution of oil products to the Libyan National Oil Corporation (LNOC), while the ownership of the facilities of foreign oil marketing companies was transferred to the government. The companies concerned were the Asseil Company S.A., (owned 50:50 by Agip and Libyan private shareholders), Shell Libya Ltd, Esso Standard Libya S.A. (Marketing Division), Petrolibya S.A., and Esso Standard Middle East (Libya Branch). According to Law No. 69 LNOC took over all the rights and obligations of these companies and their installations together with all their activities and operations in the country. In this nationalization process, the Libyan government undertook to treat these companies fairly, and it recognized the importance of paying them compensation, to be estimated by a committee presided over by a Counsellor of the Courts of Appeal in the Ministry of Justice (Otman and Bunter 2005).

These moves were seen by the new government as essential steps, deemed logical even by the oil companies themselves. It was ironic that a country, which at that time was one of the largest oil-producing countries in the world, should depend on foreign companies for the distribution of oil products domestically, for not only did these products represent the daily needs of the Libyan people, but also they were fundamental to the successful operation of the government, public establishments, and agencies. Most importantly, they were required by the Libyan armed forces to guarantee national security.

Thereafter oil distribution sector remained under the direct control of LNOC until it was deemed essential to merge all nationalized marketing companies into one company to avoid duplication. This led to Law No. 74 of October 1971, which merged all the existing oil distribution companies and assets under BOMC. In the wake of the above law nationalizing the downstream sector, it was only a matter of time before a wave of nationalization hit most of the oil companies operating in the country. Many of them were only too aware of their poor record in the previous decade, when they had taken full advantage of a weak Libyan government with regard to deliberate obfuscation in their fiscal and marketing reporting to the government with regard to computation of tax obligations and issues related to posted prices (Otman and Bunter 2005).

Under the new law, BOMC was the only company in Libya approved to undertake the transportation, distribution, and marketing of all oil products both within Libya and abroad. It provided BOMC to take the form of a joint-stock company with a limit of 25 years on its operations, which could be extended. The BOMC began with a capital of six million LD divided into 600,000 shares, each of 10LD owned by the LNOC, fully paid up.

Later, in 1976, the Libyan government passed a new Law, No. 46 regarding the marketing and distribution activities of petroleum products, permitting BOMC to exclusively own all petroleum distribution stations and centre. This was reinforced by the General People's Committee in 1980, which authorized BOMC to manage and run all these downstream activities directly using its own employees, with the salaries of its employees the same as other state enterprises. In the event, however, BOMC's hurried implementation of this policy, without actually studying and evaluating the situation and circumstances of the company and without establishing new internal rules and guidelines to manage its activities and manpower, led to many problems that have continued to impact the company in the long term. These involved, for example, employing special workers or contractors to manage its petroleum stations, while in most cases these workers were poorly qualified and lacked experience in the management of public sector establishments.

In this period many station managers failed to submit their annual financial reports which, in many cases, led to their being taken to court. Moreover, although all downstream petroleum marketing activities in the country fell under BOMC's supervision, there were no firm rules or regulations in place, which led to many abuses of the system. Even when the Libyan government from the mid-1980s permitted the Libyan private and individual sectors to practise a wide range of economic activities, the petroleum downstream marketing and distribution sector was not included in these. In 1990 the General People's Committee passed Resolution No. 1225 permitting the establishment of public "tashrukiyyas" or self-managed cooperatives operated and managed by the employees themselves, which enabled them to take over the sales of petroleum products through stations and centres.

But both cases, whether direct marketing by the company or through the tashrukiyyas, still suffered from low efficiency, mainly for two reasons. First, partners in these tashrukiyyas never felt that these stations belonged to them, since BOMC still owned the station and its assets, and the partners had never paid for their participation or had shares in these stations. Secondly, the management system of the tashrukiyyas was not entirely professional. The quality of service was poor, products were usually sold above BOMC's recommended prices, and there were many financial irregularities in their operations.

On the other hand, the few private tashrukiyyas or stations established at this time by individuals or groups of people using their own capital, whose operation and management were not directly owned and controlled by BOMC, were much more successful and profitable than those belonging to BOMC.

9.2.3 Subsequent Development of BOMC

As we have noted, under Article 2 of Law No.74 that established BOMC, it was clearly stated that the transportation, distribution, and marketing of oil were solely under the control of BOMC within Libya. This led, in its early days, to many problems, most of which have continued to affect BOMC up to the present. The following analysis, figures and tables provided by the authors are based on extensive data and information supplied by LNOC and BOMC.

Transportation Activities

Immediately after the nationalization of the above-mentioned foreign distribution companies, the new BOMC management faced crucial difficulties in the transportation sector, where former operating companies had used private contractors to transport petroleum products throughout Libya. Their aim had been to achieve this at as low cost as possible, without, unless absolutely necessary, building a dedicated infrastructure to achieve this. Because of this, when BOMC took over, it was faced with enormous transportation and distribution problems.

In its early days BOMC was forced to handle the transportation issue through short-period contracts with individuals and private associations under the direct supervision of BOMC. This situation remained until the 1980s when the company began to establish its own transportation wing, by importing large number of tankers, at the same time creating ancillary facilities such as repair workshops and a separate division for importing spare parts for their fleet maintenance. However, in taking this step, the company created even more difficulties for itself, because of the extra financial burden imposed on it. One of the main outcomes of this was the dramatic increase in the number of employees. While the number of employees in BOMC in 1971 was 904 Libyan nationals, in 11 years to 1982 this had increased to 8379, an increase of approximately 926 per cent. By 1992 this had increased to 10,365, an increase of 1146.6 per cent over 1971. Although this number was reduced in 1992 when the company established the tashrukiyya system, when approximately 2122 company employees were transferred to these new economic bodies (Figs. 9.4 and 9.5), the total number of manpower stood at 8243, of which 6774 employees or approximately 88 per cent were permanent, while 1469 or about 18 per cent were temporary.

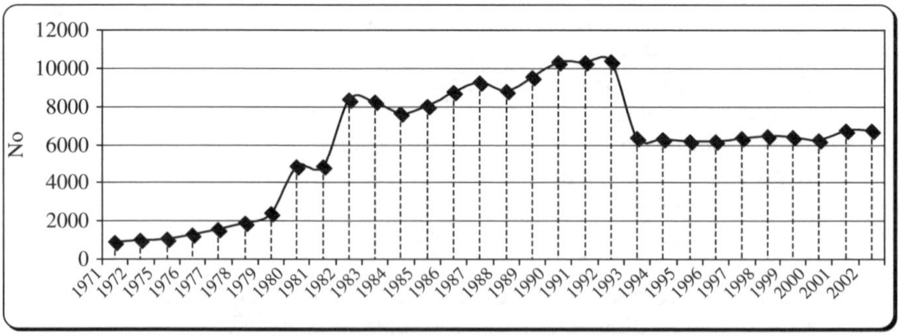

Fig. 9.4. BOMC: permanent employees, 1971–2002

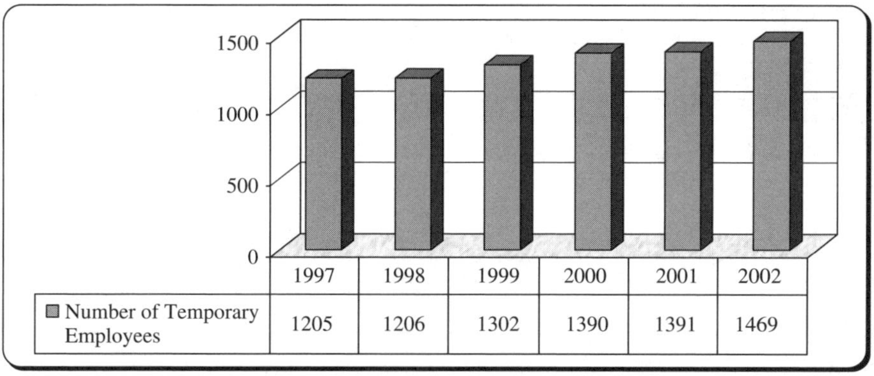

Fig. 9.5. BOMC: temporary employees, 1997–2002

At the same time, for reasons best known to itself, BOMC, instead of creating its own independent transport section for the transportation and distribution of specialized products, decided to contract out these services to private concerns. These included liquefied gas cylinders as well as supply of fuels to the power-generating stations, and an independent section would have been logical since BOMC had its workshops and spare parts depots in place. The huge financial burden placed on the company by these conflicting and poorly devised transport policies is shown in Fig. 9.6. This highlights that, amazingly, for the period from 1983 to 2001 the company's expenditure on transportation activities averaged 30 per cent of the company's total operating budget.

Figure 9.7 illustrates the breakdown between company and private sector transport costs for the period from 1983 to 2001.

If we examine, in some detail, the year 2000, we note from Fig. 9.8 that out of a total tonnage of 3,831,010 MT transported, the company's transport division handled 2,121,580 MT or approximately 55 per cent, while private transport carried 1,709,430 MT or about 45 per cent (Fig. 9.8). For the same year, total transportation costs amounted to approximately LD36,216,000 of

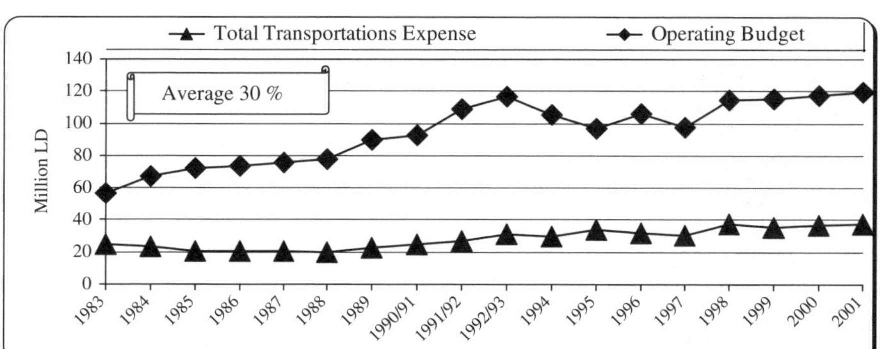

Fig. 9.6. Libya: BOMC, expenditure from 1983 to 2001

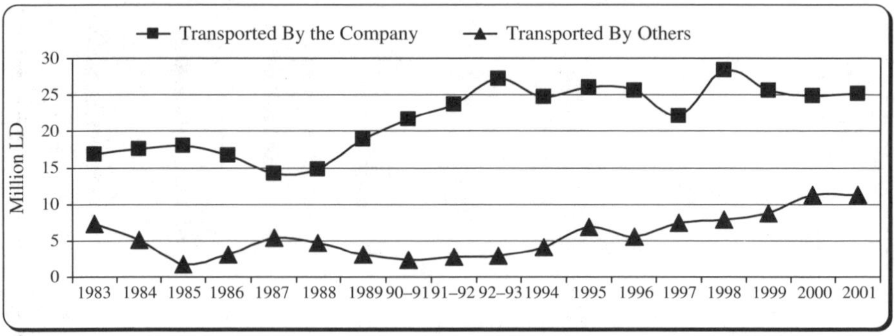

Fig. 9.7. Breakdown in company/contactor transport costs, 1983–2001

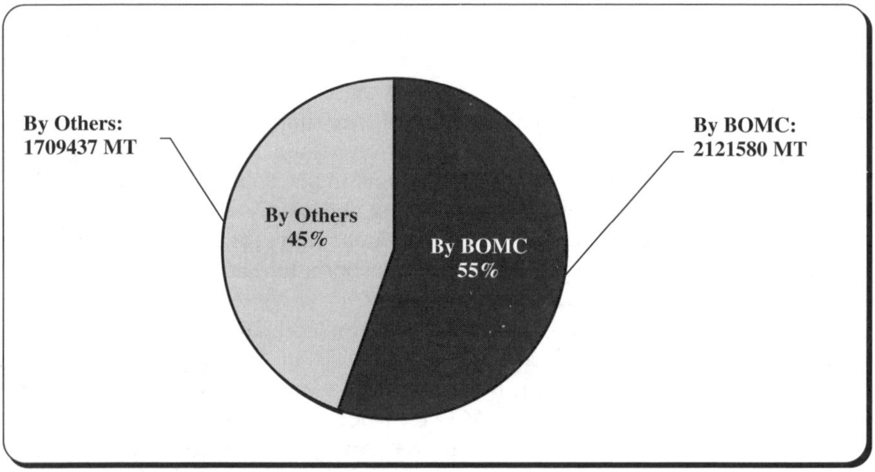

Fig. 9.8. Percentage of BOMC/private transport, 2000

which 69 per cent or LD24,940,000 was allocated to BOMC's own transport sector (BOMC 2003), while approximately LD11,276,000 or 31 per cent was for private sector transport (Fig. 9.9). This clearly demonstrates the efficiency and lower unit cost per MT of private transportation compared to BOMC's own transport division. While BOMC's average transport costs averaged LD11.76 LD/MT, the unit cost for private contractors was only LD6.60/MT, that is BOMC's own transport was 78 per cent /MT more expensive than private transport. Putting this in another way, if the company had relied exclusively on private transport in 2000, its total transport bill would have been LD25,284,666 instead of LD36,216,000, that is a massive saving of more than LD10 million or 30 per cent of its total transport costs (LNOC 2004). If we extrapolate these figures for the previous 10 years, say, we are clearly talking about massive savings. The question remains – why did no one in BOMC do anything throughout this period to correct the situation?

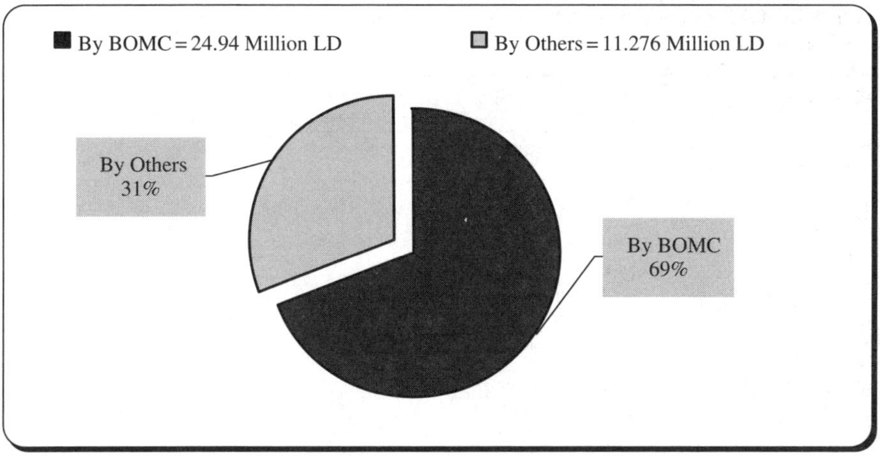

Fig. 9.9. BOMC: allocation of transport expenditure, 2000

BOMC: Development of Filling Stations and Storage Capacity

Undoubtedly one of the company's major achievements was the construction of infrastructure for local marketing activities in terms of storage and retail distribution centres. The total area capacity of the company's petrol stations increased considerably from 20,000 m^2 in 1970 to approximately 70,000 m^2 in 1995. In 1975 the company's total storage capacity was 0.168 million MT, which by 2002 had increased to approximately 1.5 million MT. Figure 9.10 illustrates the development in storage capacity from 1975 to 2002.

Details of the expansion of retail petrol stations and centres by region and by numbers are shown in Table 9.7 and Fig. 9.11.

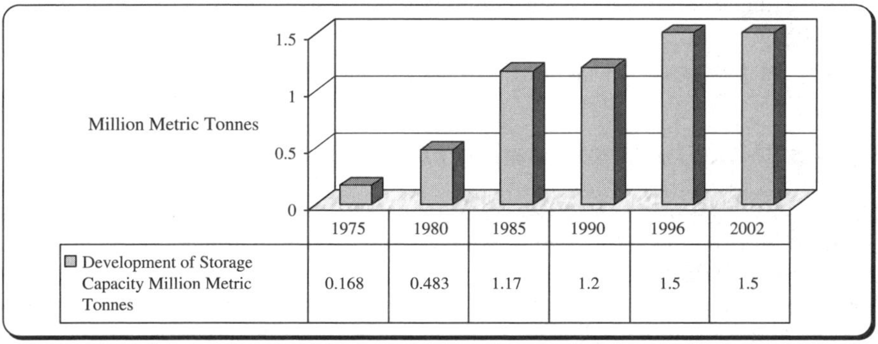

Fig. 9.10. BOMC: development of storage capacity, 1975–2002

Table 9.7. BOMC: distributions of stations and gas centres by region, 2003

Region	No. of stations	Region	No. of centres
Tripoli	65	Tripoli	7
Al-Gebel Al-Grbe	47	Al-Zawia	6
Al-Zawia	43	Al-Khums	10
South Region	36	Misuratah	1
Benghazi	32	South Region	3
Al-Khums	25	Al-Gebel Al-Grbe	2
Ejdabia	20	Eastern Region	7
Sirte	19		
Misuratah	18		
Bedia	15		
Derna	14		
Al-Merj	13		
Tobruk	11		
Total	358	Total	36

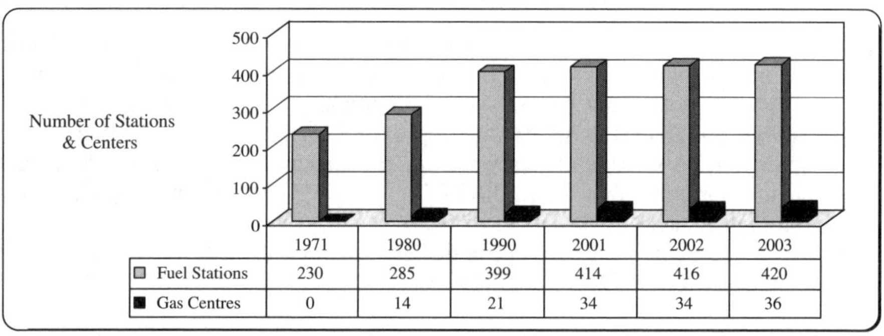

Note: The number of station belonging to BOMC are 358; the remainder are owned by the private sector.

Fig. 9.11. BOMC: Development of fuel stations and gas centres, 1971–2003

9.2.4 BOMC: The Deteriorating Financial Picture

Undoubtedly BOMC has witnessed rapid expansion since its early days, as can be clearly seen from the above tables, which demonstrate the growth of the company and its geographically diverse infrastructure for domestic marketing and distribution of petroleum products in line with the dramatic growth in Libyan domestic demand and consumption. Undoubtedly, however, the company has been facing a tough time financially for the since 1980s due to several decisions taken by the government, which placed a heavy burden on the company.

First, the transferring of employees from the distribution stations to the company resulted in a large increase in the company's manpower. Secondly, the transfer of the government's steel drum factories to BOMC also resulted in increasing the burden of the company. Thirdly, the large number of tashrukiyyas established in the early 1990s, which could not meet their loan obligations to the company as well as their social security and tax payments, has amounted to a huge burden to BOMC. Added to this are substantial delays caused by the tashrukiyyas in settling accounts, which badly affected BOMC's cash flow. In fact, since 1998 it has been costing BOMC between LD7 and LD8 million annually to support these sick and ailing tashrukiyyas.

These factors together have added up to a vast financial burden on the BOMC's annual budget, as can be seen from Figs. 9.12 and 9.13. While the company's annual budget in 1971 was LD5 million, it had increased to LD90 million in 1990 and to LD140 million by 2002.

Since its establishment by far, the largest part of the budget allocation has been for salaries, which have averaged approximately 48 per cent. Although salary payments decreased from LD60 million in 1992 to approximately LD39 million in the following year, this was attributable to the transferring of manpower under the tashrukiyya system early in 1993. However, this trend was reversed with effect from 1999 onwards, demonstrating that the BOMC's objectives of reducing its high salary burden by introducing the tashrukiyya system in the early 1990s was not a success (BOMC 2003).

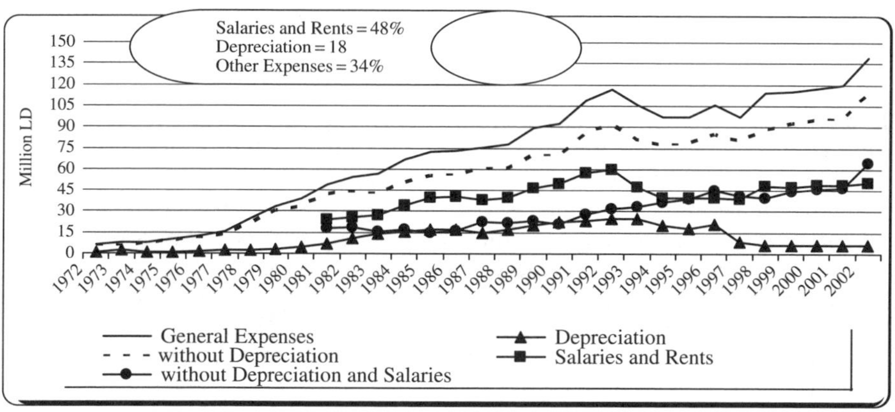

Fig. 9.12. BOMC: total annual budgets, 1972–2002

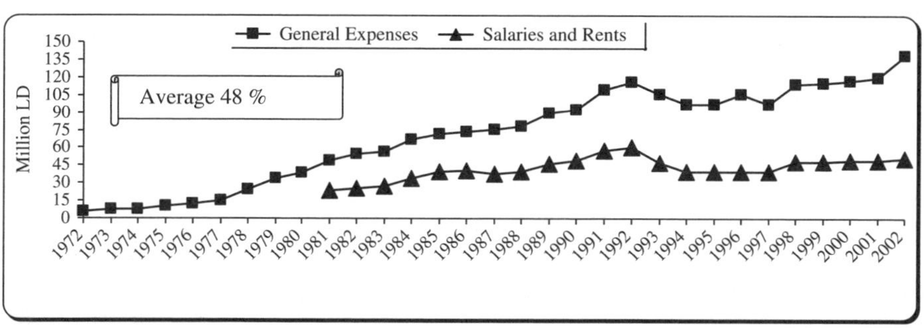

Fig. 9.13. BOMC: share of salaries and rents in total annual budgets, 1972–2002

Apart from the BOMC itself there are currently also 58 privately owned stations operating in Libya, accounting for approximately 15 per cent of the total number of stations in the country (Fig. 9.11). According to domestic market observers these private sector stations are operated much more efficiently than those belonging to the company.

9.2.5 BOMC: The Privatization Option

It is abundantly clear, in view of BOMC's inefficiency and massive accumulated losses and in line with the present Libyan policy of diversifying and privatizing the economy, that BOMC is a prime candidate for privatization. In fact, in view of its massive size and many market functions, we believe that if this is not done, then as well as continuing to act as a drain on state funds, its inefficient and outdated management style will in fact severely hamper Libyan privatization plans and prevent efforts to attract FDI to the country.

Broadly speaking BOMC is involved in four main areas of activity. These are:

- Transportation
- Distribution
- Storage complexes, freight consolidation centres, and pipelines
- Real Estate

It is obvious of course that any proposal to privatize BOMC is a sensitive issue, especially on account of the large number of Libyan national employees on its payroll who would be personally affected by such a move. Clearly any privatization programme for BOMC must be based on logical solutions taking into consideration a variety of social, economic, and strategic factors. From a purely economic viewpoint it is understandable that the Libyan government, by privatizing BOMC, might desire some sort of financial return for the massive capital it has invested in the company's development since the early 1970s.

But this is surely not the overriding factor. The key factor is that BOMC continues to act as a drain on the government, requiring considerable annual capital injections just to keep it functioning. Surely this is unacceptable when the company has a monopoly in a sector, which is one of the most profitable and lucrative sectors in most countries. In fact the advantageous situation of BOMC should mean that if it were efficiently and professionally operated, it should be a major contributor to government funds. But the issue does not stop here. If Libya is serious about economic diversification into manufacturing and tourism, it is clear that this sector needs to be much more efficient.

In the manufacturing sector, for example, fuel as well as power are required and any foreign company needs to know that a given quantity of fuel, whether diesel or gasoline, is continuously available at a special bulk discount price to make its manufactured products competitive. At the moment it is very difficult, if not impossible, for any foreign company to sign this type of long-term contract with BOMC.

Again, as the tourist sector opens up, there will be massive increases in demand for fuel for cultural and ecotourism, with a huge increase in the use of four wheel drive vehicles, buses, and trucks, as well as increased aviation fuel demands. This will together, especially in view of Libya's vast size, mean huge increases in fuel consumption. This means not only more demand for fuel itself, but also for fuel stations, whose coverage of Libya at the moment is very limited. It also means that the facilities at stations need to be significantly upgraded in line with European and US expectations of quality and service. This growth situation will in fact mean, if handled properly, significantly more employment as well as business opportunities for Libyans in the future.

One strategy for BOMC's privatization would be for the LNOC to consider splitting BOMC into four main activities of transportation, distribution, storage (including complexes, freight consolidation centres, and pipelines), and real estate holdings, and consider these for separate privatization along the following lines.

Transportation

As discussed at length earlier, we believe that the company's decision in the early 1980s to handle its own transportation activities was a mistaken one, and was done without a proper feasibility study. Not only did this prevent the Libyan private transportation sector from investment and growth, but it placed a huge financial burden on BOMC (LNOC 2004), which had to provide vehicle servicing, maintenance and spare parts, as well as maintaining salaries for the large number of employees. As can be seen from Table 9.8, for example, the number of unserviceable vehicles in the BOMC fleet is simply unacceptable from an efficiency and management viewpoint.

For the 7-year period 1997–2003, on an average, approximately 45 and 34 per cent of BOMC's tanker and trucks have been non-operational, figures which would be totally unacceptable in any privately run organization.

This, as well as our previous private versus BOMC transport cost analysis, has clearly demonstrated that BOMC has failed disastrously in its efforts to run an efficient transport sector, both in terms of costs and even to operate a basic and professional vehicle maintenance programme.

Table 9.8. BOMC transport fleet, 1997–2003

Items	1997	1998	1999	2000	2001	2002	2003
Number of operational tankers	273	345	228	212	200	200	278
Percentage of operational tankers	37%	79%	56%	52%	51%	51%	57%
Number of non-operational tankers	468	94	178	196	193	194	211
Percentage of non-operational tankers	63%	21%	44%	48%	49%	49%	43%
Total number of tankers	741	439	406	408	393	394	489
Number of operational trucks	372	369	269	263	259	255	279
Percentage of operational trucks	56%	84%	66%	63%	64%	63%	65%
Number of non-operational trucks	296	71	138	154	145	152	149
Percentage of non-operational trucks	44%	16%	34%	37%	36%	37%	35%
Total number of trucks	668	440	407	417	404	407	428

Many case studies on the privatization of state-owned transport fleets in the countries of the FSU done in the 1990s showed that the best model of privatization of tankers and lorries was by selling or leasing individual units to their drivers or driving teams. In a Libyan context, for this strategy to succeed it would be important that these teams should have access to funding for these acquisitions from Libyan banks, a scenario that was discussed in Chap. 6. In this privatized sector, the newly privatized individual transport units would then contract directly with LNOC refineries such as Al Zawia or Ras Lanuf for their transport requirements.

However, under the existing Libyan legislation, a final step would need to be taken to ensure that the fuel transport sector, and indeed the transport sector in general, is completely deregulated, to bring about real competition in this sector leading to significant benefits to the Libyan economy as a whole. Table 9.9 provides an overview of various models in the transport sector.

In Libya the model is currently No. 1. In some countries, Model 2 has also been utilized, but it is felt that there currently exists no Libyan company which might be capable or willing to undertake the total private management of BOMC's entire transport fleet, complete with workshop and backup facilities required for efficient fleet maintenance. Ideally in a Libyan context, if the government's privatization and diversification plans continue to their logical conclusion, it would mean that Model 3, in which an independent industry regulator would ensure that there existed a free and competitive transport sector with easy entry for Libyan entrepreneurs, would emerge.

Distribution

Currently there are 416 fuel distribution stations located in the entire Libyan region, of which 358 belong to BOMC and 58 operate as private tashrukiyyas. As well as this, there are 36 main gas distribution centres. The present inefficiency of those stations operating under the public tashrukiyya system introduced in 1992 and their total dependence on BOMC subsidies and support, as well as their inability to invest in new equipment and services, means that drastic steps are now required to improve this sector. This is not only because of shortage of facilities and increased domestic demand, but also, as we have seen, to prepare Libya for anticipated expansion of the domestic manufacturing and tourist sectors, among others.

The government needs to look very seriously about how to improve if not completely overhaul downstream distribution, and again privatization could be the answer. As noted, the 58 privately owned tashrukiyyas in this sector are well run and profitable, so opening it up for private investment would mean that there will be no shortage of interested parties prepared to commit the time, money, and management expertise to make their investments work for them. In addition,

Table 9.9. Models in the transport sector

	Ownership	Operation	Regulation
1. Nationalized	Public	Public	Public
2. Commercialization	Public	Private	Public/independent
3 Privatization	Private	Private	Independent

Tamoil Africa, a subsidiary of the Libyan-owned multinational Tamoil group with more than 2000 state of the art petrol stations in Italy, France, Holland and Spain, could also take part in providing the country with modern facilities, perhaps through a negotiated privatization of BOMC's service stations to Tamoil.

Another alternative would be for individual stations to be offered to private investors, who would buy their fuel products directly from LNOC using strict commercial practices. In this scenario, the sector would have at the same time to be opened up completely, so that individual private Libyan investors could apply to LNOC to open new fuel stations wherever they felt there was a marketing opportunity, with regulations in place to ensure that no application could reasonably be refused if it met, for example, health, safety, and financial criteria. With such deregulation of this sector many new job opportunities would be created, competition would flourish, and Libya, with its huge geographical extent, could prepare to cater effectively for the vast influx of tourists and investors presently planned for by its policy makers.

In our view the recently established Libyan government-owned Speedy-road Service Company, which has already build two complete service complexes in the Zawiya and Benghazi regions, which include petrol stations, restaurants, service facilities, and shops may not be the answer to Libya's future demands for an efficient fuel distribution system. If not handled professionally and efficiently by LNOC, this new organization might also finish up as a case of history repeating itself, with future requirements for government subsidies, at the same time denying the entry of private Libyan entrepreneurs into this lucrative market.

Storages Complexes, Freight Consolidation Centres, and Pipelines

The BOMC currently owns a combined total of 18 storages complexes, and freight consolidation centres distributed around the main Libyan cities ports and airport (Table 9.10). The company has also constructed huge facilities at main Libyan airports such as Tripoli International Airport, Tripoli Matage Airport, and Sebha, Benina, Tobruk, Labraq, Sirte, and Ghat Airports. As well as this, the company has built since 1971 an extensive network of pipelines totalling 592 km to transport petroleum products to their own storage complexes and to industrial areas, factories, and ports such as the Misuratah Iron and Steel Complex and GECOL's electricity-generating plants.

Because of the technological and safety requirements for such storage complexes and pipelines, as well as their large size and complexity, the potential for privatizing these, at least to Libyan companies, could prove to be limited. In the case of the dedicated facilities provided by BOMC for oil refineries, however, the situation could be resolved easily by LNOC, which, as the owner of the refineries concerned as well as of BOMC, could simply arrange for an asset transfer of these facilities, with employees being transferred in the same exercise.

Table 9.10. BOMC: dedicated storage facilities, 2005

No.	Storages complexes and freight consolidation centres at ports/airports	The company or refinery
1	Al-Zawia	Al-Zawia Company
2	Janzur	Al-Zawia Company
3	Al-Fatah	Al-Zawia Company
4	Al-Hanee	Al-Zawia Company
5	Tripoli Airport	Al-Zawia Company
6	Sidee Gaber	Al-Zawia Company
7	Freight consolidation facilities at Sha'ap	Al-Zawia Company
8	Freight consolidation facilities at Zuwarah	Al-Zawia Company
9	Sebha	Ras Lanuf Company
10	Musrata	Ras Lanuf Company
11	Freight consolidation facilities at Misuratah	Ras Lanuf Company
12	Ras Al-Mangar	Al-Gulf Company Benghazi
13	Freight consolidation facilities at Ras Al-Mangar	Al-Gulf Company Benghazi
14	Tubruk	Al-Gulf Company Tubruk Refinery
15	Tubruk Gas	Al-Gulf Company Tubruk Refinery
16	Freight consolidation facilities at Tubruk	Al-Gulf Company Tubruk Refinery
17	Al-Sarir	Al-Gulf Company Al-Sarir Refinery
18	El Brega	Sirte Oil Company

Another possible solution might be for BOMC to negotiate the sale or lease of its Libyan airport facilities, again to an efficient operator such as Tamoil Africa or to a private Libyan company, to produce a good return from its previous massive investments in these facilities and infrastructure. With regard to the pipelines (Appendix 9.1), these could be a part of an internal LNOC asset transfer, or alternately, they could be bought or leased by interested parties.

Real Estate

Apart from these main storage facilities and pipelines, BOMC has over the past 30 years accumulated a massive portfolio of administrative buildings, depots, workshops, and other facilities in all the major Libyan cities. There is a huge potential for the sale or redevelopment of these major assets into residential or commercial complexes for rental to local or FDI companies as Libya heads for economic diversification and goes down the privatization route. In such a situation their sale or privatization to a Libyan group or groups of property developers could realize huge revenue for BOMC, enabling it to repay some of the massive accumulated debt, which it currently owes to LNOC.

Alternately if, for example, BOMC wished to achieve long-term returns from these key strategically situated assets, located literally in every corner of Libya, then the possibility of a JV or PPP with a Libyan or foreign partner for long-term redevelopment and leasing of these assets could be explored, with the new BOMC JV. Company assumes the role of a property-holding company with an excellent source of long-term income.

9.2.6 BOMC, Fuel Subsidies, and Debt Collection

The above proposed privatization model for BOMC might deal with some, but not all of BOMC's financial problems. This is because two very important issues, which have also historically impacted BOMC's ability to operate efficiently and profitably, have yet to be addressed. These issues are, of course, first, the very high levels of fuel subsidies provided by the Libyan government through LNOC/BOMC to key state bodies in the Libyan public sector; and secondly, the very high level and duration of indebtedness of such public sector companies to BOMC. These are illustrated by Tables 9.11–9.13.

Table 9.11. BOMC: total of fuel subsidies according to sectors, 1995–2000

[in million LD]

Sectors		1995	1996	1997	1998	1999	2000
Defence	Direct	5.05	5.44	5.21	5.28	4.92	5.16
Sector	Indirect	1.41	2.54	2.28	1.16	2.98	7.50
Electricity	Direct	125.27	125.75	138.70	147.41	208.25	149.6
Company	Indirect	74.59	107.00	103.15	56.21	125.44	174.48
Stations	Direct	0.00	0.00	0.00	0.00	0.00	0.00
	Indirect	17.03	25.07	24.39	18.80	27.57	37.35
Industry	Direct	1.11	1.08	1.01	2.63	2.57	1.41
	Indirect	6.71	8.37	7.20	5.02	9.16	11.39
Ferries	Direct	2.95	2.43	2.38	4.50	4.90	2.43
supply	Indirect	0	0.398	0.156	0.00	0.40	1.20
Secretariats	Direct	0.22	0.235	0.24	0.085	0.17	0.243
	Indirect	0.11	0.11	0.11	0.056	0.031	0.473
Civil	Direct	0	0	0.00	0.00	0.00	0.00
aviation	Indirect	0.14	0.88	0.60	0.00	1.77	13.78
Total	Direct	134.62	135.00	147.56	159.92	220.83	158.89
	Indirect	100.01	144.40	137.92	81.25	167.37	246.19

Table 9.12. BOMC: total of fuel subsidies according to products, 1995–2000

[in million LD]

Products		1995	1996	1997	1998	1999	2000
Gasoline	Direct	2.99	3.17	3.10	2.49	2.85	3.53
	Indirect	0.00	0.00	0.00	0.00	0.71	3.29
Kerosene	Direct	0.52	0.52	0.44	0.54	0.60	0.59
	Indirect	0.89	2.22	1.57	0.55	3.45	21.47
Diesel fuel	Direct	124.51	125.48	138.12	151.07	152.20	146.80
	Indirect	37.19	73.51	71.41	30.54	85.28	113.36
LPG	Direct	0.00	0.00	0.00	0.00	0.00	0.00
	Indirect	15.83	17.38	18.06	18.93	19.12	20.13
Heavy fuel	Direct	6.60	5.76	5.89	5.81	65.17	7.96
oil	Indirect	46.08	51.27	46.88	31.22	58.79	87.93
Total	Direct	134.63	134.95	147.56	159.92	220.83	158.89
	Indirect	100.01	144.40	137.92	81.25	167.37	246.19

Table 9.13. BOMC: cost of indirect subsidies, 1995–2000

[prices in LD]

Items	1995			1996			1997		
	DP	IP	D	DP	IP	D	DP	IP	D
LPG	14.9	30.7	–15.8	16.4	33.8	–17.4	17.0	35.1	–18.1
Gasoline	240.363	91.897	148.465	236.77	110.587	126.183	248.89	121.026	127.865
Kerosene	10.150	15.694	–5.544	10.258	21.116	–10.858	13.659	23.387	–9.728
Diesel Fuel	77.909	36.690	41.218	768.182	15.033	–73.518	82.761	154.191	–71.429
Heavy fuel oil	18.264	64.150	–45.888	15.689	66.951	–51.261	15.988	62.810	–46.822

Items	1998			1999			2000		
	DP	IP	D	DP	IP	D	DP	IP	D
LPG	17.827	36.762	–18.934	18.009	37.135	–19.126	18.958	39.093	–20.134
Gasoline	257.425	96.604	160.820	268.014	148.812	119.202	286.097	283.223	2.874
Kerosene	10.599	6.815	3.783	13.068	14.567	–1.498	17.526	39.000	–21.473
Diesel fuel	90.506	117.812	–27.305	91.460	176.743	–85.283	88.878	202.240	–113.361
Heavy fuel oil	16.630	47.601	–30.971	17.776	76.561	–58.784	20.228	108.164	–87.936

Note: DP, Domestic Prices; IP, International Prices; D, Different = (DP – IP).

In respect of the above tables, direct subsidies mean subsidies over and above the indirect subsidies, which represent the difference between international prices and Libyan domestic prices, in effect a subsidy within a subsidy or a special subsidy to Libyan public sector companies. As can be seen from Tables 9.14 and 9.15, the largest subsidy as a percentage of total subsidies goes to the electricity sector, which has received around 93 per cent of all subsidies to the Libyan public sector companies, or an average of LD252.33 million per year or a total of LD1.514 billion for this 6-year period. This leads us to ask important

Table 9.14. Percentage of direct subsidies to all sectors, 1995–2000

Sector	1995	1996	1997	1998	1999	2000
Electricity (%)	93.0	93.2	94.0	92.2	94.2	94.2
Defense (%)	3.8	4.0	3.5	3.3	2.3	3
Ferries supply (%)	2.2	1.8	1.6	2.8	2.2	1.5
Industry (%)	0.8	0.8	0.7	1.6	1.2	0.9
Secretariats (%)	0.2	0.2	0.2	0.1	0.1	0.2

Table 9.15. Percentage of the indirect subsidies to all sectors, 1995–2000

Sector	1995	1996	1997	1998	1999	2000
Electricity (%)	74.7	74.2	74.9	69.3	75.0	70.9
Stations (%)	17.1	17.4	17.7	23.2	16.5	15.2
Industry (%)	6.7	5.7	5.2	6.1	5.5	4.6
Defense (%)	1.4	1.7	1.6	1.4	1.8	3.0
Civil aviation (%)	0.1	0.6	0.4	0.0	1.1	5.6
Ferries supply (%)	0.0	0.3	0.1	0.0	0.2	0.5
Secretariats (%)	0.0	0.0	0.0	0.0	0.0	0.2

questions about the operations of GECOL, the Libyan public electricity-generating corporation discussed earlier. For example, could it continue to operate effectively without these massive subsidies? Could the cost of these subsidies, if they were withdrawn completely by the Libyan government, be passed directly on to the Libyan consumer, whether domestic, industrial, or commercial? What implications would such a withdrawal of subsidies, presumably followed by substantial increase in energy prices, have for Libya's industrial diversification programme as well as for its ability to attract foreign investors, who perhaps perceive the low cost of energy as a major incentive to base activities there? These questions and many others currently surround the fuel subsidy debate in Libya.

As well as the thorny question of fuel subsidies, BOMC also faces an unenviable situation regarding the non-payment of its bills by other state sectors for products supplied by the company. As illustrated by Fig. 9.14, GECOL is, in this regard, presently the biggest offender. For example, up until 31 December 2001, GECOL's overdue bills to BOMC amounted to approximately LD850 million. Figure 9.14 shows the significant amount of public sector payments due to BOMC for the two years 2002 and 2003, which amounted to LD489.340 million of which GECOL accounted for 67.6 per cent.

Undoubtedly these and many other problems would have to be addressed and solved before any privatization exercise for BOMC could be contemplated. At the same time there exist many methods and financial arrangements which could effectively deal with this situation, structured to give BOMC's debtors sufficient time, say 2–3 years, to repay outstandings completely. Viewed critically, the lamentable financial state that BOMC currently finds itself in acutely demonstrates the dangers of public sector ownership and management. If no proper rules and guidelines are in place in state-owned bodies and for financial arrangements between them, prudent financial management is impossible.

Regarding the issue of fuel subsidies in general, these are extremely high in Libya, reflecting the historical status of Libya as a major petroleum producer. Domestic fuel retail prices showing this for the period 1996–-2004, and after the fuel increases of 2005, are illustrated in Tables 9.16 and 9.17.

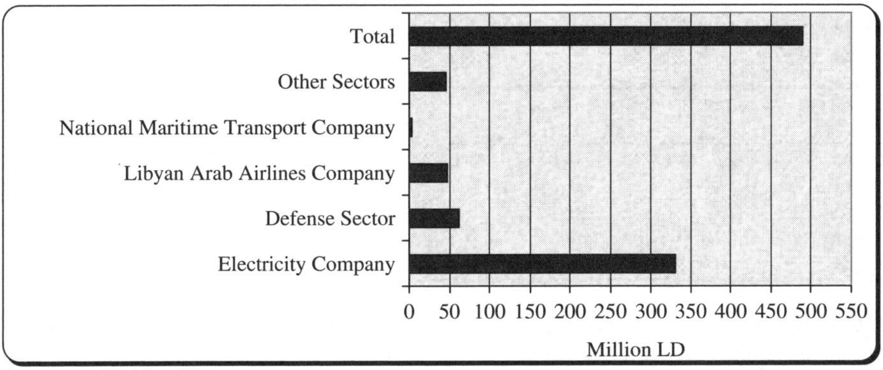

Source: BOMC, 2004.

Fig. 9.14. BOMC: state sectors debts for the year 2002–2003

Table 9.16. Domestic retail prices of petroleum products, 1996–2004

[in dirhams per litre]

Petroleum product	1996	1997	1998	1999	2000	2001	2002	2003	2004
Premium gasoline (98 Octan Premium)	140	140	140	140	140	150	150	150	150
Premium gasoline (94 Octan Premium)	105	105	105	105	105	115	115	115	115
Kerosene	60	60	60	60	60	70	70	70	70
Gas oil	110	110	110	110	110	120	120	120	120
Fuel oil (dinar per ton)	12	12	12	12	12	27.60	27.60	27.60	27.60
LPG (per 15-kilo cylinder)	1250	1250	1250	1250	1250	1250	1250	1250	1250

Source: Central Bank of Libya, 2005.

Table 9.17. The New Libyan fuel pricing, 2005

[price in Libyan dirhams]

Petroleum product	Retail consumption	To BOMC, end storage	State sector	To GECOL	Military uses
LPG (per 15-kilo cylinder)	1500	1350	1500	1500	1500
Premium gasoline (L)	150	147.5	147.5	147.5	115.5
Fuel diesel (L)	140	137.9	77.9	58	58
Kerosene (housing use) (L)	80	77.9	57.9	–	–
Heavy fuel oil (L)	Increasing the price by 50 dirhams to the selling price of one kilogram to the consumer from all types of oils and lubricants				

Source: Secretariat of General People's Committee (Prime Minister Department), April 2005.

Table 9.18. North African countries: fuel pump prices, 1999

Country	Super gasoline (US $ per liter)	Diesel (US $ per liter)
Libya	0.22	0.17
Algeria	0.31	0.16
Morocco	0.79	0.47
Egypt	0.29	0.12
Tunisia	0.60	0.33

Comparing prices at the pump in Libya with other North African countries shows how major the price differences are, as shown in Table 9.18.

The perceived advantages and disadvantages of domestic fuel subsidies are matters for the Libyan government and its policy makers to decide on. But doubtless, one of the main adverse effects of subsidies is market distortion, where the price of a commodity does not reflect its actual cost. This, in the long term, jeopardizes the national economy, as has been undisputedly shown by the recent structural changes attempted by the Indonesian government at the behest of the IMF. The damaging effects of fuel subsidies are also currently being experienced in Malaysia, where they have rocketed, in terms of taxes forgone, from Malaysian Ringgit (MR) 190.8 million in 1993 to MR2.6 billion 1999, and are estimated to cost the Malaysian government MR7.9 billion (US $2.09 billion) in 2005 (Malaysian Economic Planning Unit 2005).

Fuel subsidies also undoubtedly lead to excessive fuel consumption and wastage, and to such practices as illicit trade and smuggling to neighbouring countries like Egypt and Tunisia, where fuel prices are significantly higher. Also, the huge cost of subsidies in Libya are in effect "opportunity costs", which prevent the Libyan government from allocating more funds to other sectors in national development to benefit the population at large. For example, savings from subsidies could be used to build more schools, universities, hospitals and public facilities, as well as upgrading Libya's infrastructure.

In line with the Libyan government's current efforts to realign itself internationally, policy makers need to look at the fuel subsidy issue in much more detail. Undoubtedly, Libya has enough petroleum to last for many years ahead. But the day will come when this finite resource will dry up. It would be far better, for example, to have a plan or policy in place whereby fuel subsidies might be gradually phased out over a period of, say, 5 years, so that consumers, public bodies such as GECOL, as well as foreign investors can plan for the future. This is far better than the Indonesian situation where the issue of fuel subsidies effectively led to the fall of the Suharto government in 2001 and if not handled sensitively could also lead to the present Indonesian government's fall.

9.3 The Libyan Mining Sector

Libya's non-hydrocarbon mineral and mineral-based commodity production includes ammonia, cement, clay, dolomite, gypsum, limestone, lime, salt, silica sand, steel, stone, sulphur, and urea. Tables 9.19 and 9.20 provide details for the years 2000–2004, including the data on Libyan cement and steel production for the year 2004.

Table 9.19. Libya: production of mineral commodities, 2001–2004

[in thousand metric tones]

Commodity/Year	2000	2001	2002	2003	2004
Cement, hydraulic	3,000	3,000	3,300	3,300	3,500
Gypsum	175	150	150	150	175
Iron and steel, metal:					
Direct-reduced iron	1,500	1,090	1,170	1,340	1,580
Lime	270	250	250	250	250
Nitrogen:					
N content of ammonia	552	495	533	577	577
N content of urea	407	365	400	425	425

Source: Mobbs, 2005.

Table 9.20. Libya: structure of the mineral industry in 2004

[thousand metric tonnes, annual production]

Commodity	Major operating companies	Location	Capacity
Cement:	Libyan Cement Co. (Government)	Benghazi	1,500
Do	Arab Union Contracting Co.	Zliten	11,200
Do	Arab Cement Co. (Government)	Homs 2, Lebda	1,000
Do	do.	Souk el Khamis, Tripoli	1,000
Do	do.	Zliten	1,000
Do	Libyan Cement Co. (Government)	El Fataih, Derna	1,000
Do	do.	El Hawari	400
Do	Arab Cement Co. (Government)	Homs 1, El Margueb	300
Iron and steel:			
Iron:			
Hot briquetted iron	Libyan Iron and Steel Co. (Government)	Misurata	650
Sponge iron	do.	do.	1,100
Steel:			
Crude	do.	do.	1,250
Rolled:			
Bar and rod	do.	do.	800
Cold-rolled srip	do.	do.	140
Hot-rolled strip	do.	do.	580

Source: Mobbs, 2005.

Because of the application of the UN and US embargoes on Libya, only recently lifted, its mining sector, apart from hydrocarbon mining, has been virtually neglected apart from the development and extraction of mineral deposits for its major cement plants. Currently the country is keen to attract foreign investment and expertise in this industry which it feels has been underdeveloped and underexploited because of the traditional emphasis on the hydrocarbon sector.

9.3.1 Establishment of Libyan Mining Company (LMC)

Presently non-hydrocarbon mining throughout Libya is vested in the Libyan Mining Company, which was established by a decision from the General People's Committee No. 151 of the year 1996, as a public corporation with a distinct legal personality and independent financial obligations.

Its initial capital was LD10,000,000 comprising 100,000 shares of LD1000 each. Its original shareholders were:

- Libyan Iron and Steel Company
- General Company for Chemical Industries
- The International Company for Investment and Trade

- National Company for Soap and Detergents
- The Development Bank
- Arabic Cement Company
- Qasr Ben Ghesheer Al-Ahly Bank
- Assamaka Company for Paint Manufacture

9.3.2 Objectives of the Libyan Mining Company

- The development of the national economy through profiting and investing in the natural resources and mineral ores in Libya
- Diversifying the national income by developing technology in the mining industry
- Ensuring the commercial development of naturally occurring ore sites and available natural resources
- Offering employment opportunities and building national technology in one of the most important economic fields in the Great Jamahiriya
- Meeting the needs of the industrial companies, domestic and foreign, in locally available mineral ores
- Attract foreign capital for JV investment in mining and ore processing
- Create opportunities for cooperation and integration between the Great Jamahiriya and the African Nations in the field of mineral resource investment in the African Continent
- Extracting and processing local mineral resources
- Preparation of technical and economic feasibility studies in the field of mining
- Exploitation and marketing mining products

9.3.3 Mining Opportunities Initially Targeted by the LMC

- Extracting and processing gypsum deposits in Bir El-Ghanam and As Sidra
- Exploitation of pure silica sand in Edri
- Exploitation and processing kaolin deposits in Sebha
- The exploitation of decorative stones

9.3.4 Libyan Mining – A Sleeping Giant

As stated, the historical emphasis on the hydrocarbon sector, as well as Libya's vast extent and its negative media portrayal because of the sanctions, has effectively turned the Libyan mineral industry into a sleeping giant. For example, as well as the above minerals discussed in detail, the presence of several high-grade metamorphic belts in the country also suggest potential for gold, iron ore, and base metals in Libya. As can be seen from our brief account above, the Libyan

Mining Corporation exists as a separate vehicle in Libya for mineral extraction and processing, and currently welcomes foreign investment and participation. In view, again, of Libya's strategic location in the context of the Mediterranean and African markets, we believe that Libya offers significant potential in the mineral sector for companies holding the technology and marketing expertise to exploit such potential.

10 Libyan Environmental Law and Issues

10.1 Future Environmental Challenges

It is apparent that major environmental and sustainability issues are fundamentally associated with the petroleum industry, a polluter by nature, in Libya. In a legal context it is also crucial for the role and importance of the judiciary in the enforcement of environmental legislation to be appreciated in most of the Arab countries, including Libya, where its key role has not perhaps yet been fully understood from the point of view of long-term environmental protection (Al-Awadhi 1996, 2002).

In future years Libya will face serious environmental challenges, not necessarily those associated with the oil industry, such as gas flaring, marine and groundwater pollution, but including declining per capita water resources and the loss of arable land. For example, water is in short supply with the situation deteriorating. Countries of the MENA region are home to 5 per cent of the world population but have less than 1 per cent of the world's renewable fresh water. The region's per capita supply stands at only one-third of its 1960 level, with water availability anticipated to be cut by 50 per cent over the next 30 years. Managing water as an economic resource and looking into the regional dimension of the water challenge are crucial for human welfare and economic growth and stability in the region (World Bank 2004). As Libya industrializes and diversifies in line with the current economic policy, pollution-related health problems particularly in urban and industrial areas such as Benghazi and Misuratah are bound to increase, with causes related to open municipal waste dumps and the use of leaded gasoline in vehicles and fossil fuels for power generation.

The North African region in general is also threatened by the loss of arable land and increased coastal degradation, which are caused principally by unsustainable agricultural practices and unmanaged competition for land and marine resources. In the MENA countries as a whole, permanent cropland, currently less than 6 per cent of the total land area and less than 1 per cent in Libya, is shrinking due to serious land degradation and recurrent droughts (UNDP 2004). Together it is clear that combined with weak environmental institutions and legal frameworks, environmental and sustainability problems can only become greater if not addressed comprehensively, as for example within the series of EU policy initiatives such as the Water Framework Directive.

10.2 Libyan Environmental Legislation

In Libya, since 1958, there have been a series of Laws and Decrees concerning environmental protection, which have dealt with the treatment of effects and risks of environmental pollution, with, in theory, the imposition of severe penalties on violation of the provisions of such laws. In this respect Libya can be said, on paper at least, to be a leading country in this field among the developing countries. In the following section we provide a list of the main environmental laws:

- The Libyan Maritime Law, issued on 28 November 1958. This law includes 335 articles, the most important of which are issues related to collisions at sea (Articles 236–247), in particular, with regard to law applicable in the event of a collision between two ships or more, and compensation for damage to the vessels and the objects and persons abroad (Articles 237–240), defining the difference between accidental or phenomenal collision, collision arising from the fault of a ship, collision arising from mutual error, and collision arising from the fault of a pilot.
- Law No. 81 of 1971 regarding seaports. This Law includes 155 articles, covering rules concerned with vessels, loading and unloading of explosives and dangerous material, and rules covering for oil loading and unloading, together with the penalties applicable on the violation of its provisions with regard to the set of obligations and prohibition stipulated by this law.
- Law No. 8 of 1973 with respect to the prevention of oil pollution to sea waters. This law includes a set of rules and provisions for its application, derived from the 1954 London Convention, which is considered an integral part of this law. The provisions of this law are limited to oil pollution sources, excluding other sources.
- Health Law No. 106 of 1973 and its Executive Regulations, which elaborates in detail all aspects of the environment and environmental protection. The preamble deals with the problems associated with water and its protection from pollution, outlining the pertinent risks and the necessary procedures and measures to manage water pollution. It lists the types of water sources, and how to treat them and take samples, and relevant standards. It also covers controls for the circulation of foods and the necessary health provisions for locally manufactured or imported foodstuff and dairy products, as well as health standards associated with meat, fish and poultry and bird shops, and how to transport and handle such food products. In Chap. 5, it elaborates the regulations, starting from Article 109, relating to environmental safety in public baths and laundries, toilets, control of mosques, and the filling up and drying of pools and swamps. It also covers health provisions and the necessary environmental requirements for construction and buildings, as well as the drainage of waste water, preventive health, and the treatment of diseases common to man and animals, dealing also with the necessary measures to control epidemic diseases. Addressed also in detail is the subject of the disposal of wastes, together with a wealth of related provisions as well as punishments for the violations of these provisions.

- Law No. 25 of 1976, amending certain provisions of the Maritime Law mentioned in the above paragraph. Here the second paragraph in Article 119 stipulates that a pilot shall be responsible for keeping an oil log for the prevention of water pollution, as per the provisions made in this regard.

10.3 The Role of the Law No. 7 of 1982

Law No. 7 of 1982 with regard to environmental safety and its accompanying Executive Regulations, issued by the Resolution of the General People Committee No. 386 of 1998 can be considered to be Libya's most important law on environmental protection, defining clearly and unequivocally most environmental terms, meanings, and situations. Together it comprises 45 Articles, with Chap. 1 dealing with general provisions, and Article 1 providing concise definitions as follows:

- "Environment" is defined as the surrounding in which man and all organisms live, including air, soil, and food.
- "Environment Safety" is defined as the control of all environmental factors affecting, directly or indirectly, the physical, psychological, and social safety of man.
- "Environmental Pollution" which is defined as the occurrence giving rise to risks to human health or environmental safety, as a result of pollution of air, seawater, water sources or soil, imbalances to living organism, including noise, vibration and bad odours, or any other pollutants resulting from the activities of a natural or corporate person.
- "Air Effects" which cover vehicle exhausts, radiation, dust volatile compounds, micromolecules, and biocides.
- "Spillage", being oil spilling, leakage, or mixing for whatsoever reason.
- "Oil" defined as crude oil, fuel oil, heavy diesel oil, lubrication oil, and other oil by-products.
- "Oil Waste", that is oil exhaust of all types, forms and properties.
- "Oil Mixture", being any type of mixture with an oil content.
- "Centre" – by which is meant the Technical Centre for Environmental Protection, established in accordance with Article 7 of the law, and which is substituted by the General Environment Authority.

The objectives of the law are explained in Article 2, which explains that the law is aimed at the protection of the milieu in which man and all living organisms exist. Article 3 stipulates that all individuals, organizations, corporations, companies and public departments must make every effort to contribute to pollution control and observance of the relevant instructions. Article 6 provides that public authorities must take into account the ways and means necessary to maintain environmental balance when planning for urban development. Article 7 deals with the establishment of the Technical Centre for Environmental Protection, which has been superseded by the Environmental General Authority, the powers of which shall be discussed in a later section. In Chap. 2, from Articles 11 to 18, the protection of air and the atmosphere is dealt with, while Chap. 3 deals with the protection of the sea and marine wealth laying down the rules and provisions to achieve this, essentially filling gaps in Law No. 8 of 1973. It includes many prohibitions, whether in respect of fishing boats, tankers, or other vessels on waste disposal into the sea, with many provisions preventing both corporate bodies and individuals from disposing wastes and poisonous substances on to Libyan territorial beaches and waters. In view of the crucial importance of this comprehensive piece of legislation, which is currently in force and in practice, we shall detail its important provisions.

10.3.1 Substantive Provisions

The law lists many important provisions in regard to the prevention of pollution of sea by oil, stating:

- It is prohibited to spill oil or oil mixture, discharge of heavy or light oil, or ballasts in ports and territorial waters. These prohibitions apply to waters to tankers and vessels of all nationalities in Libyan waters (Article 23).
- Every Libyan National pilot must keep oil logs (Article 25).
- All the captains of the vessels carrying the Libyan flag; Libyan Arab Airlines pilots and personnel must immediately report accidents which cause or may cause water pollution by oils or burned fuel, in addition to creating a floating cover of oil or fuel on the sea (Article 26).
- All the captains of the vessels, immediately on arrival at Libyan ports, must submit to the port authorities a report of every oil or oil mixture spill in Libyan territorial waters (Article 27).

10.3.2 Exclusions not Covered in Previous Legislation

In Article 24 the Law stipulates a number of exclusions to the previous provisions:

- Oil or oil spillage from a tanker or a vessel in order to secure the vessel's safety or for life-saving purposes.
- Oil or oil mixture leakage due to defects or unavoidable leakage, provided that all the necessary measures should have been taken to prevent or reduce the occurrence of such defect.
- If oil erupts in the process of its extraction and the only possible way to dispose of such eruption is to spill it in the sea, this is allowed provided that all necessary measures for its prevention or reduction have been taken.
- Military and paramilitary vessels.

10.3.3 Organizational Provisions

The law defines certain provisions with an organizational nature, including:

- The competent parties should define the areas equipped to receive oil wastes, from vessels visiting the port, as well as laying down the necessary arrangements for the disposal of these wastes (Article 28).
- The competent parties managing crude oil loading harbours must equip these ports with the appropriate facilities for the reception and treatment of wastes, oil mixtures, and ballasts to be disposed of (Article 30).
- The competent parties in Libya must undertake to inform the State in writing on violations of the provisions of this law and other conventions signed by Libya wherever these might occur, along with ensuring that the notices stipulated in such conventions are made generally known, and must send documents, reports, and summaries to the parties defined by the pollution control agreement. This competent party is concerned, also, with receiving reports from foreign authorities on violations made by Libyan vessels (Article 33).

The protection of water sources is dealt with in Chap. 4, starting from Article 40 in which water sources are defined as the water used, or may or possibly be used for drinking purposes, household purposes, or in agriculture, industry, recreation, as sources of certain chemical elements or substances, for health use, or others, whether the source of such water is "surface, underground, desalinated water, rain, flood or the like". Thereafter the uses of these waters, its provision, distribution, purification, treatment and quality control, safety, and how to dispose of any residues that may distort water sources are covered.

The protection of foodstuff is defined in Chap. 5 starting from Article 51, 52, and 53, which define the methods for foodstuff circulation and the standards for laboratory analysis, in addition to how to use sterility and preservation methods in food stuff storage rooms and grain silos. It also prohibits the sale, display, consumption, import, or distribution of foodstuff and agricultural products unsuitable for human consumption, and also provides for the release and display for sale of imported food products in the event of a confirmed epidemic or disease in the supplying country, which might be sparked by the consumption of such food, whether for humans or animals.

Environmental safety is dealt with in Chap. 6, with Article 54 stipulating that all public authorities must develop necessary programmes to provide services in a healthy environment to Libyan citizens.

Chapter 7 addresses protection from common diseases. Article 55 stipulates that the concerned parties must take the necessary precautions to protect domestic animals from epidemic and infectious diseases in order to prevent such diseases from infecting human beings.

Soil and plant protection is covered by Chap. 8 with Article 56 stipulating that all concerned parties must use land in a rational manner, in accordance with local conditions, in order to improve the soil and increase plant life and prevent soil hardening. The next series of Articles define plant protection methods and stipulate that the concerned parties defined by the current legislation must establish public parks and green areas for various sizes of population settlements, both rural and urban, and must determine the ratio of green belts and areas to the overall area of the city and village plans, in order to preserve the beauty of nature and the people's health, as well as providing recreational facilities. Also, these articles stipulate that that all forests within or around cities and villages should be public parks, and operated by rules and standards to ensure their proper use.

Provisional provisions are dealt with in Chap. 10, where Article 62 refers to executive law regulation which must include, along with the issues defined by this law, the following:

- Allocation of powers and obligations defined by this law between the different sectors.
- Detailed powers of the different sectors for the realization of the provisions of this law.

In Chap. 11, from Article 65 to 74, penalties for the violation of the provisions of the law, without prejudice to the penalties defined in the Penal Code, laws covering economic crime and other relevant laws, are stipulated, ranging from imprisonment, fines, and confiscation in certain cases.

10.4 Resolution of the General People's Committee No. 263 of 1999 Establishing the Environment General Authority

In this landmark piece of Libyan environmental legislation, the Technical Centre for Environmental Protection was substituted with the Environment General Authority (EGA), and gave powers to EGA under 16 main headings, the most important among them being the registration of all chemical substances that may cause environmental pollution, including pesticide use for the public health, agricultural, and veterinary purposes, as defined by a resolution of the People's Committee of Authority. The EGA also has the power to provide opinions and approvals on the environmental effects and impacts of particular development projects, prior to the execution of such projects, to be followed up by environmental plans and agreements covering such projects in the future. In this context the Authority issued Decision No. 43 of 2000 regarding the organizational structure of the Authority.

10.5 Legislation Covering Water Resources

In view of its crucial importance in relation to the environment and environmental issues, we provide below relevant sections of Law No. 3 of 1982 regarding the regulation and utilization of water resources. This law defines the principles and controls that govern its preservation, protection, and utilization. A series of provisions define the following:

- Each and every person shall undertake to preserve the water.
- The people are the owners of water sources.
- Libya is divided into water zones, and the Secretariat of Agricultural Reform and Land Reclamation is assigned with the control and management of water, as well as the issuing of licences for water drilling and utilization.
- The usage of collective irrigation systems and the formation of executive committees to manage them.
- The guarantees to all the right to drink, together with their livestock, from springs and valleys, also that they may drink from private establishments, with prior permission and at a set price.
- The prohibitions on discharging solid and fluid waste into water resources.
- No person or party shall dig or utilize water wells without a licence.
- The prioritization of water utilization licences are as follows:
  - Human usage and animal drinking
  - Agricultural purposes
  - Industrial and mining purposes

- Areas in which water digging or drilling or utilization is prohibited.
- The issuance of licences for more than one user for a single well.
- That holders of licences to utilize water shall not use it in such a way as to injure others, and shall be obligated to remove the source of injury.
- The General People Committee shall issue resolution in respect of:
  - Issuance of the executive regulation of this law.
  - Dividing Libya into water zones.
  - Subjecting water zones to restricted distribution or absolute prohibition system.

- Those persons or parties who shall bear the costs of water sources preservation and development, and sets licence fees.

In addition to the above-mentioned legislation, the following laws have also been passed in respect of Environmental Protection in Libya:

- Law No. 2 of 1992, on protection from ionized radiation.
- Law No. 3 of 1982, on the regulation of water usage.
- Law No. 5 of 1982, on the protection of pastures and forests, amended by Law No. 14 of 1992.
- Law No. 11 of 1984, on traffic on public roads.
- Law No. 13 of 1984, on public cleaning.
- Law No. 14 of 1989, on the regulation of marine wealth utilization.
- Law No. 8 of 1996 in regard to the establishment of the General Water and Sewage Water Company.
- Law No. 15 of 1989, on the protection of animals and tress.
- Law No. 15 of 1992, on the protection of agricultural land together with its amendments.

All these laws make special provisions and stipulations for environmental protection, defining principles, rules, and controls for its protection. In these laws deterrent penalties are set for violators, in accordance with the magnitude and type of violation.

10.6 Environmental Impact Assessment in Libya

In its simplest sense Environmental Impact Assessment (EIA) can be defined as a technique used for identifying the environmental effects of development projects (European Environment Agency 2005). A more comprehensive and iterative definition is "a decision-making process, and a document that provides a systematic, reproducible, and interdisciplinary evaluation of the potential effects of a proposed action and its practical alternatives on the physical, biological, cultural, and socio-economic attributes of a particular geographical area" (US Environmental Protection Agency 1998).

EIA was formally introduced in the United States through the National Environmental Policy Act (NEPA) of 1969. After the UN Conference on the Human Environment in Stockholm in 1972, there was widespread concern about the human impacts on the environment. This led, in the last quarter of the twentieth century, to the rapid spread of EIA regulations to many other countries, both industrialized and developing (Vanclay and Bronstein 1995). Today, EIAs are used in more than 100 countries, and required by all development banks and most international aid agencies (UN Economic Commission for Africa 2005). For example, EIA requirements were first introduced by the World Bank in 1989 through its Operational Directive 4.01 on Environmental Assessment, now Operational Policy 4.01 (Freestone 1996).

Libya's marginalization by the US and UN sanctions from 1986–2004, which is in fact precisely the period when the global spread of the use of EIAs accelerated, as well as the fact that Libya had no major borrowings from the World Bank, IMF, or other international funding bodies throughout the same period, explains, to a large extent, why the necessity for conducting EIAs has not yet become part of the Libyan policy making or planning framework, making it one of the few countries in the world in this situation. In a North African context, for example, the timing for the approval of country's legislation requiring EIAs is closely related to the conditionalities surrounding loans by international lenders such as the IMF or the World bank to the countries concerned, as is shown in Table 10.1.

In fact, as a party to the Convention on Biological Diversity, which Libya ratified on 12 July, 2001, Libya is in fact bound to introduce legislation for project EIA, by Article 14 of the text of the Convention detailed as follows:

- Introduce appropriate procedures requiring EIA of its proposed projects that are likely to have significant adverse effects on biological diversity with a view to avoiding or minimizing such effects and, where appropriate, allow for public participation in such procedures.

Table 10.1. North African countries, EIA legislation

	Sudan	Egypt	Algeria	Morocco	Tunisia
Enabling legislation	In draft	Yes, 1994	Yes, 1983	In draft	Yes, 1988
Specific legislation/ regulations	No	Yes, 1995	Yes, 1990	In draft	Yes, 1991
General and specific guidelines		Yes, 1995	Yes, 1990	Draft law	Yes
Formal provisions for public participation	No	Yes (through guidelines)	Yes (Decree of 1990)	Draft law & EIA decree	No
Main administrative body/bodies	Higher council for Environment and Natural Resources, 1992	Egyptian Environmental Affairs Agency, 1994	Ministry of Land & Environment and the General Directorate of the Environment (DGE)	Department of the Environment	National Environmental Protection Agency, 1988

Source: METAP, 2003.

- Introduce appropriate arrangements to ensure that the environmental consequences of its programmes and policies that are likely to have significant adverse impacts on biological diversity are duly taken into account.
- Promote, on the basis of reciprocity, notification, exchange of information, and consultation on activities under their jurisdiction or control which are likely to significantly affect adversely the biological diversity of other States or areas beyond the limits of national jurisdiction, by encouraging the conclusion of bilateral, regional, or multilateral arrangements, as appropriate.
- In the case of imminent or grave danger or damage, originating under its jurisdiction or control, to biological diversity within the area under jurisdiction of other States or in areas beyond the limits of national jurisdiction, notify immediately the potentially affected States of such danger or damage, as well as initiate action to prevent or minimize such danger or damage; and
- Promote national arrangements for emergency responses to activities or events, whether caused naturally or otherwise, which present a grave and imminent danger to biological diversity and encourage international cooperation to supplement such national efforts and, where appropriate and agreed by the United States or regional economic integration organizations concerned, to establish joint contingency plans.

Undoubtedly as Libya positions itself for entry into the global economic mainstream after the lifting of the US sanctions, it will become increasingly important, indeed absolutely necessary, for Libya to legislate for compulsory

EIA requirement for specific investment activities and projects, as her policy makers strive to attract FDI into the tourism, manufacturing, and hydrocarbon sectors. Currently, for example, the Libyan National Oil Corporation's signing of two Exploration and Production Agreement (EPSA IV) rounds for 25 years in January and November 2005 covering 165,959 km^2 onshore and 82,163 km^2 offshore, respectively, has major implications for potential environmental impacts. The potential for environmental degradation and pollution in Libya is enormous, as oil and gas producers, both Libyan and foreign, will inevitably inflict environmental damage on many onshore localities as well as Libya's offshore region, a vast area with considerable potential for the infant fishing industry, as was noted in Chap. 8.

In fact, this trend in environmental destruction in Libya by the International Oil Companies started much earlier. As remarked in a paper on the archaeologically unique Messak Settafet Plateau, part of the UNESCO-designated Tadrar Acacus (a World Heritage Site in south-west Libya), this area, although already protected by the Antiquities Law of Libya, is a "unique complex of cultural heritage in need of a more appropriate institutional status, in order to face the sudden growth of oil exploration. Development by oil companies, though an unavoidable activity for the economic welfare of Libya, may pose major threats for the preservation of the entire historical and prehistorical landscapes". The paper, which discusses at length the seismic and exploration activities carried out from 1992 to 1997 by a British-independent oil company, LASMO Grand Maghreb Ltd, concludes "most of the damage already done to the Messak is irreversible. In particular, the roads and the seismic lines (started in the 1980s) have definitively altered the landscape" (Anag et al. 2002).

It appears that the negative publicity generated from Lasmo's environmental destruction has led, more recently, the oil companies in the Murzuq Basin to conduct EIAs on a voluntary basis. For example, "Total", which is a partner in a number of blocks in the Murzuq basin, including a 12 per cent interest in Block NC115, which contains the El Sharara oilfield currently producing nearly 200,000 barrels per day, has in consultation with the Energy and Environment Department of the Libyan National Oil Company (LNOC) completed an EIA, in January 2002, aimed at predicting the potential impact of its seismic operations, and formulating recommendations for mitigating these impacts.

For the oil industry it is increasingly apparent that dedicated EIA legislation must be put into reality by the Libyan government to forestall future repetitions of the Lasmo debacle. Presently, as well as Law No. 3 of 1994, which forbids the establishment of mining or industrial camps or buildings at a distance less than 500 m from an immovable antiquity without the approval of the Libyan Antiquities Department, existing legislation with regard to onshore environmental impact is still only provided for in the 1955 Petroleum Law No. 25, which in Article 9, "Concessions", states:

> (12) The concession shall not confer upon the concession holder the right to do any work within the precincts of cemeteries, places used for religious worship and places of antiquity as defined in the antiquity discovered by the concession holder shall be subject to the law from time to time in force.

> (13) No drilling or any dangerous operations shall be conducted within 50 m of any public works or permanent buildings without the previous consent of the director, and subject to such conditions as he may impose.

Again, in Clause 12, "Ancillary Rights", it states:

> For the purpose of its operations under this concession the Company shall have the following rights in the concession area:
>
> (a) With the approval of the Director, to drill for water and impound surface waters and to establish systems for the supply of water for its operations and for consumption by its employees;
> (b) With the approval of the Director, to carry away and use in Libya, materials such as gravel, sand, lime, gypsum, stone, and clay which shall be free of charge in the case of such materials taken from lands other than private lands;
> (c) To erect, set up, maintain and operate houses, fences, engines, machinery, furnaces, buildings, pipelines, storage tanks, compressor stations, pumping stations, processing plant, field road and all other constructions, installations and works required in furtherance of its activities. The Company may likewise for such purposes, erect, set up, maintain, and operate all other communications and transportation systems facilities but shall not do so, other than for temporary purposes, unless drawing of locations of their sites have been submitted to and approved by the Director.

However, conspicuous by its absence is any legislation or conditions related to the prevention or mitigation of the massive environmental impacts that such major projects as pipelines and processing plants invariably cause.

In Clause 19, "Plugging of Boreholes and Wells", it states:

> The Company shall, in accordance with good oil field practices, provide an adequate system for the disposal of its water and waste oil, and shall securely plug all boreholes and wells made by it before they are abandoned.

Whatever such good oilfield practices are, and who determines them, and how they may be legally enforced, are of course moot points.

Although it might be unsurprising that such clauses as the above might exist in a piece of legislation drafted in the early 1950s when environmental concerns were low, if not non-existent on the development agenda of most countries, a perusal of the existing 2004 Libyan Exploration Production Sharing Agreements (EPSA IV) also demonstrates that there is a scant mention of environmental restrictions and no requirement for EIAs to be conducted before work plans are approved in project blocks or production areas. In a standard existing EPSA IV agreement, for example, the following paragraph would appear to be the only section covering potential environmental issues and problems:

> Obligations of Operator: Operator shall conduct the petroleum operations diligently and continuously governed in accordance with the applicable laws and provisions of the Petroleum Law and all other applicable laws and regulations of the GSPLAJ, in particular laws and regulations concerning the protection of health, safety and the environment.

Elsewhere in the current EPSA IV agreement, issues related to project abandonment are covered. Abandonment means "those activities, including but not limited to; the plugging and abandonment of wells, the decommissioning and removal of all plants and activities and the restoration of sites used for Petroleum operations hereunder to a standard required under the laws and regulations of GSPLAJ and in accordance with Good Oilfield Practices." Apart from the obvious fact that the phrase "good oilfield practice" is weak and legally unenforceable, the existing lax Libyan environmental regime does not inspire much confidence. Elsewhere in the standard EPSA IV agreements, however, the LNOC has now included a section covering the costs of abandonment for both the exploration and appraisal, as well as for the development and exploitation, stages of these 25-year EPSA agreements. Article 26, "Abandonment", states:

> 26.1 All costs, expenses and liabilities for Abandonment related to Exploration Operations and Appraisal Operations shall be considered Exploration and Appraisal Expenditures.
>
> 26.2 Each party shall bear and finance 50 per cent of the costs, expenses and liabilities for abandonment which may be occurred as a result of Development and Exploitation operations.

Later provisions of this section provide a formula for how abandonment costs are to be calculated and annual abandonment provisions are to be determined. However, the overall impression is that the complex long-term environmental issues and problems associated with project abandonment have not been fully understood or addressed by the LNOC. An example of this is Sect. 26.2 that states:

> If production terminates within the term of this Agreement (i.e. 25 years) or both parties decide to abandon a field before the end of the term of this agreement, Operator shall proceed with the abandonment operations and make cash Calls to the First party to cover the abandonment costs. Any un-abandoned fixed assets shall be left in a safe condition.

The last sentence in this clause should surely cause alarm bells to ring for Libyan policy makers.

In fact the issue of abandonment costs, especially for offshore oil and gas structures, has become a major global issue after the costs for the decommissioning of Maureen, a Conoco Phillips platform that cost £150 million to break up in a Norwegian fiord in 2002, was more than twice the original £60 million budget, and in fact 25 per cent of the original construction cost. This frequently happens since when a new field development is planned, the cost of abandonment looks insignificant when examined using the normal discounted cash flow methods. But towards the end of the field life, it becomes a real cost that is by no means small.

Because of the long-term environmental issues related to abandonment, and not only in an offshore context, the Norwegian experience is worth looking at. Under the Norwegian Petroleum Act, the licensees are required to submit a cessation plan 2–5 years before expiration of a production licence or a licence for installation and operation, or the use of an installation ceases. Cessation plans consist of a disposal section and an impact assessment section. Based on the plan, the authorities then make decisions regarding disposal (Norwegian Petroleum Directorate 2005).

Under the present circumstances, the lack of Libyan environmental legislation, such as statutory requirements for oil and gas project commencement and the abandonment of EIAs will seriously affect the country in terms of long-term sustainability and health and safety issues related to its people, environment, and ecology. A near neighbour of Libya, Nigeria, decided to tackle these issues head on after Shell's lamentable record of soil and water pollution in the Niger Delta became too intolerable, leading to the death of many Nigerians due to environmental pollution of water sources. In 1991 the Department of Petroleum Resources (DPR), an arm of the Ministry of Petroleum Resources, while recognizing the national importance of the oil and gas industry sector to the Nigerian economy, but also recognizing the serious environmental impacts caused by it, issued its Environmental Guidelines and Standards (EGAS) specifically for the oil and gas sector. This is a 300-page document, which sets out comprehensive standards and guidelines for the implementation and management of hydrocarbon projects with proper consideration for the environment. As well as this, the Nigerian Government's Decree 86 of 1992 made EIA mandatory for both public and private sectors for all development projects.

While we have discoursed at length on the need for EIAs for Libya's hydrocarbon sector, the message is also clear for other key sectors targeted by Libyan policy makers for diversification. For example Libya's next door neighbour Egypt established the legal basis for EIA by Law No. 4 of 1994, the Law on Protection of the Environment, consequently implemented through its Executive Regulations, issued by Prime Ministerial Decree No. 338 of 1995, coming into full force in 1998. By June 1997, the importance of environmental issues led to the creation of Egypt's first full-time Minister of State for Environmental Affairs. Recognizing that different sectors have different environmental impacts, Egypt's Environmental Affairs Agency has issued a set of separate EIA guidelines covering the Oil and Gas Sector, Cement Manufacturing Plants, Pharmaceutical Plants, Land Reclamation Projects, Urban Development Projects, Development of Ports, Harbours and Marinas, Municipal Waste Water Treatment Works, and Industrial Estates Developments (Egyptian Environmental Affairs Agency 2005).

Of particular concern to Egyptian policy makers is the Egyptian coastline, comprising more than 3,000 km along the Mediterranean and the Red Sea, the source of major tourist revenue for the Egyptian government, representing its third largest revenue after oil and gas and bringing in more than US $6 billion annually.

Because of this, as early as 1996 the Egyptian Integrated Coastal Zone Management (ICZM) strategy was formulated. This strategy was the basis of a national programme of short- and long-term actions to enhance coastal zone management, including the Red Sea and Mediterranean cities and tourist resorts, and dealt with important environmental issues related to sustainability such as shore protection, coastal land use planning, coastal and marine water quality management, and the preservation of coastal and marine resources, habitats and historical sites. Later, in 2000, Usaid/Egyptian Tourist Development Agency embarked on the Red Sea Sustainable Tourism Initiative (RSSTI). As part of this project, a series of "Best Practice Environmental Practices" were proposed, to be applied during the planning, construction, and operation of Egypt's coastal tourist projects. These were:

- Environmental/energy assessments conducted to identify opportunities for environmental improvement
- Environmental Management Systems (EMS) developed with properties along the Red Sea Coast
- An environmental management plan framework for an Integrated Development Center (IDC)
- Best Practices for alternative tourism development, including mountain I desert activities, health spa facilities, and Ecolodges in Egypt
- Best Practices for infrastructure development, including construction site preparation and development and innovative water I wastewater systems
- International environmental certification programs for Red Sea Coast properties will be reviewed with support for creation of an Egyptian environmental tourism recognition program.

10.7 Libya and Integrated Coastal Zone Management

We have briefly discussed above the Egyptian experience in developing its tourist sector and the country's approach to sustainable environmental management of the country's coastal resources, because there may be many important lessons to be learned from it by the Libyan policy–makers. In 1949 the French historian Ferdinand Braudel published a landmark study on the Mediterranean world in the second half of the sixteenth century. In this monumental work, Braudel was concerned with the Mediterranean in its broadest geographical and historical contexts, ranging backwards to the great civilizations of Iraq, Egypt, Greece, and Rome and forward to today's Mediterranean world (Braudel 1949). Libya has always been a crucial part of this world, as the magnificent World Heritage Sites of Cyrene, Sabratha, and Leptis Magna demonstrate. The country has a very long shoreline of almost 2000 km along the Mediterranean coast, and Libyan history and commerce have been, ever since sea-going vessels were able to navigate its waters, inextricably tied up with cultural, political, and socio-economic developments occurring in all countries bordering this sea.

It is for these reasons that proper management of this exquisite coastline, which is one of its main natural infrastructures, is of vital importance to Libya. Its coastal zone is rich in a huge variety of natural, commercial, recreational, ecological, industrial, historical, and aesthetic resources, which make it presently and potentially of incalculable value to the present and future generations of Libyans. It is of huge importance that this incomparable asset is managed with a view to its preservation and sustainable use for future generations of Libyans.

UNEP's "One Planet, Many People" has stated this point very succinctly:

> Land adjacent to the ocean is a tremendously valuable resource. Coastal zones are economically, politically, and socially critical to many nations. They are hubs of commerce and home to many major corporations and transportation networks. Coastal landscapes offer fertile soils, flat land for urban development, and sheltered, deep-water bays for harbours and ports. Coasts are used by millions of people annu-

> ally for recreation and they support a growing tourist trade. Although coastal zones account for only 20 per cent of the world's land area, a majority of the world's human population inhabit them. Half of the world's population, some 3,000 million people, lives within 200 km of a coast (UNEP 2005).

The first report published by the Libyan Environmental General Authority states bluntly that present environmental conditions on the Libyan coast are unacceptable for the following reasons (Environmental General Authority, Libya 2002):

- High population density in the coastal regions
- Concentration of oil and commercial ports in the coastal strip
- The presence of major industrial plants, especially oil refineries, steel and iron factories, cement factories, and yarn and textile factories
- The existence of many sewage and industrial waste sites along the coastline

The report goes on to conclude in Chap. 5 "Coastal Area Management" that these factors together have resulted in "the contamination of most beaches in coastal cities with sewage water. For instance, in Tripoli, there are 30 outlets for rain and sewage water directly discharging into the sea. In Benghazi, there are 13 outlets, and all or a part of sewage water is directly discharged into sea for many reasons, including breakdown of pumping stations or incomplete sewage systems and treatment plants". Since sewage, both treated and untreated, is normally discharged to, or just below, the intertidal zone via these pipelines, it becomes mainly a coastal problem. The composition of sewage varies considerably, but major effects reported in the scientific literature result in increased nutrient and suspended solid loading and human health problems associated with coliform bacteria on these recreational beaches, both of which obviously have serious implications for both Libyans and the large projected number of tourists using these facilities.

As well as the impact of sewage and industrial waste on the Libyan coastal zone, the petroleum industry, discussed earlier in the context of the destruction of Libya's cultural heritage and desert ecosystems, is also impacting the Libyan coastline. Again, as the EGA report states as follows:

> Libya is a petroleum exporting country. Oil ports extend along the Libyan coast, through which more than a million barrels per day is exported. Therefore oil hydrocarbons constitute a main source for coastal pollution, from oil substances discharged from oil refineries, oil from drilling and production platforms, and oil substances from human activities discharged to sea by sewage pipes or outlets. (EGA 2002)

The report then concludes, "the growth of agricultural, industrial, commercial and recreational activities augmented pollution problems" and stated that "most Libyan coastal regions are undergoing degradation and damage. This is clearly manifested in the overuse of drinking and irrigation water, the result being seawater encroachment to groundwater, increasing their salinity, and the degraded conditions of many beaches."

The report in fact discusses a wide range of environmental problems in Libya, some discussed earlier and some that will be touched later in this section, and is also concerned about the fact that environmental education and information has "not reached the required degree of progress. This is due to absence of programmes aimed at raising environmental perception in all social layers" (EGA Report 2002, p. 129). In the same section, it also touches a very significant feature of Libyan legislation and its enforcement: overlapping powers between the concerned parties, leading to little or no non-enforcement of environmental laws and legislation.

In comparison with neighbouring countries, and in view of the desire of Libya's policy makers to diversify the Libyan economy with the tourist sector being one of the main sectors targeted for growth, it is clear that the current state of affairs with regard to coastal management is sadly lacking in both policy and direction, with the only real piece of solid legislation regarding the construction of tourist facilities being the Coastline Demarcation Law, which bans construction of buildings at less than 100 m from the sea. This is a potentially dangerous situation in view of the priceless heritage of the Libyan coastline. Using the Egyptian experience discussed earlier and elsewhere in this book, this is undoubtedly the right time for the Libyan authorities to seize the initiative and strategize an Integrated Libya Coastal Zone Management Policy to ensure, among other things, the successful implementation of its ambitious tourist policy, as well as to protect and sustain Libyan coastal resources and aesthetics.

In view of the importance of these issues and the current rate of coastal degradation, one effective way of dealing with the problem might be to establish a Libyan Coastal Zone Management Authority, with an overall planning, approval, and implementation function, with the power to overrule or at least coordinate the approval of all types of coastal developments in the existing Libyan Sha'biyat having coastal areas. In the context of the existing pyramidal structure of direct government in the Libyan political system as discussed in Chap. 1, this might, however, present many practical problems. But the necessity for such an authority is clear and urgent. Again, in this regard, Libyan policy makers might elect to look at the US experience, which led to the approval of the US Coastal Zone Management Act of 1972 and the establishment of the US Coastal Zone Management Program (CZMP). The Act was in fact based on a US Congressional report (No. 302), which almost parallels the following existing Libyan situation:

(a) There is a national interest in the effective management, beneficial use, protection, and development of the coastal zone.
(b) The coastal zone is rich in a variety of natural, commercial, recreational, ecological, industrial, and aesthetic resources of immediate and potential value to the present and future well-being of the nation.
(c) The increasing and competing demands upon the lands and waters of our coastal zone occasioned by population growth and economic development, including requirements for industry, commerce, residential development, recreation, extraction of mineral resources and fossil fuels, transportation and navigation, waste disposal, and harvesting of fish, shellfish, and other living marine resources, have resulted in the loss of living marine resources, wildlife, nutrient-rich areas, permanent and adverse changes to ecological systems, decreasing open space for public use, and shoreline erosion.

(d) The habitat areas of the coastal zone, and the fish, shellfish, other living marine resources, and wildlife therein, are ecologically fragile and consequently extremely vulnerable to destruction by man's alterations.
(e) Important ecological, cultural, historic, and aesthetic values in the coastal zone, which are essential to the well-being of all citizens, are being irretrievably damaged or lost.
(f) New and expanding demands for food, energy, minerals, defence needs, recreation, waste disposal, transportation, and industrial activities in the Great Lakes, territorial sea, exclusive economic zone, and Outer Continental Shelf are placing stress on these areas and are creating the need for resolution of serious conflicts among important and competing uses and values in coastal and ocean waters.
(g) Special natural and scenic characteristics are being damaged by ill-planned development that threatens these values.
(h) In the light of competing demands and the urgent need to protect and to give high priority to natural systems in the coastal zone, present state and local institutional arrangements for planning and regulating land and water uses in such areas are inadequate.
(i) The key to more effective protection and use of the land and water resources of the coastal zone is to encourage the states to exercise their full authority over the lands and waters in the coastal zone by assisting the states, in cooperation with Federal and local governments and other vitally affected interests, in developing land and water use programs for the coastal zone, including unified policies, criteria, standards, methods, and processes for dealing with land and water use decisions of more than local significance.
(j) The national objective of attaining a greater degree of energy self-sufficiency would be advanced by providing Federal financial assistance to meet state and local needs resulting from new or expanded energy activity in or affecting the coastal zone.
(k) Land uses in the coastal zone, and the uses of adjacent lands that drain into the coastal zone, may significantly affect the quality of coastal waters and habitats, and efforts to control coastal water pollution from land use activities must be improved.
(l) Because global warming may result in a substantial sea level rise with serious adverse effects in the coastal zone, coastal states must anticipate and plan for such an occurrence.
(m) Because of their proximity to and reliance upon the ocean and its resources, the coastal states have substantial and significant interests in the protection, management, and development of the resources of the exclusive economic zone that can only be served by the active participation of coastal states in all Federal programs affecting such resources and, wherever appropriate, by the development of state ocean resource plans as part of their federally approved coastal zone management programs.

Such a piece of comprehensive and visionary legislation has ensured that in the United States, the 95,376 national shoreline miles (153493 km) representing 99.9

per cent of the country's coastline, and interests in the United States offshore exclusive economic zone, continue to be successfully and sustainably managed by the CZMP.

10.8 The Environment and Desertification in Libya

The definition of desertification currently employed by the United Nations was adopted at the United Nations Conference on Environment and Development in Brazil in 1992 (UNCED 1992). This defines desertification as "land degradation in arid, semi-arid, and dry sub-humid areas resulting from various factors, including both climatic variations and human activities."

But even a casual perusal of the literature on desertification shows that authors have widely different ideas of which land degradation processes are desertification processes. Some writers believe that wind erosion is the sole desertification process. Others think that it is rangeland deterioration. Still others contend that water erosion is the only important process. To add to the confusion, respected researchers such as Mainguet and many Swedish scientists believe that all true desertification is irreversible land degradation (Mainguet et al. 1991). For this group, desertification is the spread of desert-like conditions. Whatever the definition, broad or narrow, clearly, as a recent researcher has stated, an "understanding of 'desertification', the ecological deterioration of arid lands into semi-deserts and deserts, is critical for the future well-being of the fifth of the world's population who inhabit drylands today" (Barker 2002).

Issues related to desertification in a North African context have been addressed by the Arab Centre for the Studies of Arid Zones and Dry Lands (ACSAD), which was established in Damascus, Syria, in 1968 within the framework of the Arab League. Its primary objective was to unify Arab efforts aimed at developing scientific agricultural research into arid and semi-arid areas and to make use of modern agricultural techniques in order to increase agricultural production (ACSAD 2005).

In 1972 the Libyan Revolutionary council established a law to establish the Agricultural Development Council aimed at increasing the cultivated areas in the country both by land reclamation and desertification control. Since its creation, these issues have continued to dominate the Libyan agriculture sector, and as we have seen elsewhere in this book the Libyan government in the 1970s spent vast amounts on irrigation projects, culminating in the Great Manmade River Project (GMRP), which has currently increased the country's irrigated areas by over 155,000 ha.

Traditionally, in Libya, the arid and semi-arid regions, which characterize much of the country, were used for farming and pasturage. But again population pressure and a long series of so-called agricultural reforms that were set into motion during the period of Italian colonization, when the use of large-scale agricultural estate methods were practised, led to overgrazing, over-cultivation, vegetation and forest clearance, and soil salinization. This is because such cultivable arid and semi-arid regions were adjacent to or surrounded by desert or semi-desert ecological regions and therefore very fragile.

At the same time rapid population growth in Libya's coastal belt has intensified land use and changes in traditional land use patterns, and led to environmental degradation such as soil exhaustion, accelerated water resource depletion and chemical pollution of soil and water. Again, this has come about because, while the growing of food crops and the rearing of animals was traditionally done in a natural way, greater market demands provided a strong stimulus to increase the productivity of the existing farms and orchards by using fertilizers and pesticides. While the utilization of these chemicals undoubtedly, in the short term at least, increased yield, environmental pollution and soil exhaustion were a side effect. As the 2002 EGA report states: "This is what is happening in the Jamahariya, and Jefara plain in particular, where sea water encroached into groundwater layers leading to soil salinity and rendering it unsuitable for agriculture" (EGA 2002).

Libya has attempted to reverse the negative environmental effects of desertification by using a variety of techniques. Traditionally the planting of "Dis" *(Imperata cylindrica)* was most commonly used for this purpose. As an early paper on this method described it, "small, flexible and penetrable obstacles considerably hamper the shifting of sand but do not completely prevent it". They enable trees to gain a foothold in the square or oval patches of *dis*, averaging 4 × 5 m, and can fix sands for young forests. The topography is altered as little as possible (Messines 1952). In 1971 Libya also introduced the so-called "Libyan Method" of sand dune fixation, which involved the high-pressure spraying of petroleum to limit sand dune movement, which led to Libya being recognized during the 1960s and 1970s as a world pioneer in the field of combating desertification.

10.9 Water Desalinization and Its Environmental Impacts

In Libya the use of desalinization plants is an important source of potable water along the Mediterranean coast where, as we have seen, the impacts of salt water intrusion and the lowering of water tables have had severe negative impacts on the supply of drinking water for the rapidly growing Libyan urban population.

As stated in the EGA 2002 report, "according to available data, total design capacity of the desalinization units executed in Libya during the last 30 years has exceeded 230 million M^3 per year, produced by about 400 desalinization plants which makes Libya a leading country in North Africa and the Mediterranean basin in the use of desalinated water". Of this total, thermal plants amount to 60 per cent while the balance is made up of mostly of reverse osmosis with electro membrane separation plants taking up around 10 per cent.

The massive use of desalinization plants produce significant environment impacts, characterized by their effluent to the environment, the air, the nearby land, and to the seas. Desalination is dependent on energy and usually uses fossil energy. All types of air pollution associated with energy production, namely emission of NO_x, SO_2, volatile compounds, particulate, and CO_2, by using electricity produced by a dedicated power station as is normally the Libyan case, although GECOL, the Libyan National Electricity Company, is moving rapidly to gas as an energy source for these plants.

Again, the effluents of desalination plants contain relatively highly concentrated water, which depends on the water recovery from the feed brine. In the case of seawater desalination, rejected brine is twice the concentration of the original seawater. The concentrate also contains chemicals used in the pre-treatment of the feed water. The latter may contain low concentrations of anti-scalants, surfactants, and acid. Although in small-scale production the tidal motion of the ocean can usually disperse such pollutants, large-scale water production as in Libya has caused significant impacts on marine life as well as in local water tables.

10.10 Libya's Declining Air Quality

Declining air quality, especially in the main urban centres of Libya as well as in the dense industrial petrochemical plant and refinery areas of El Brega, Zuetina, and Misuratah, is also a significant environmental concern in Libya. The localities of urban centres continues to be one of the most serious local environmental problems in Northern Africa and a continuing threat to human health. The three principal anthropogenic causes of declining air quality are energy generation, emissions from vehicles, and industrial production, all of which have increased in the past 30 years.

Since much of Libya's industrial base was developed in the 1970s, the equipment of most plants and industries is old and highly polluting. The situation is further complicated by the dominance of the public sector in industry, which provides little incentive for adopting more efficient and cleaner industrial technologies. Few enterprises have air emission controls, and a lack of maintenance and spare parts often impairs the performance of the existing systems (World Bank 1995).

Although it is difficult to acquire meaningful data, there is no doubt that the main Libyan cities of Tripoli and Benghazi and those areas close to refineries, petrochemical plants, and oil-fired power plants using high sulphur fuel far exceed the levels of sulphur dioxide of the World Health Organization (WHO) standard (World Bank 1995).

Atmospheric concentrations of lead and particulates in Northern African cities often exceed WHO guidelines by a multiple of two, with cement and steel industries, both present in a large scale in Libya, producing as much as 50 per cent of the total particulate emissions (World Bank 1995). Again the massive use of motor vehicles and increases in vehicle ownership in Libya also contribute to massive carbon monoxide emissions. Although Libya was fully lead-free by 2003, particulate emissions from poorly maintained public sector diesel-fuelled buses and trucks are five to seven times higher than those from similar but well maintained vehicles (World Bank 1995).

As a result of this, city dwellers, particularly those in congested metropolitan centres, are on a daily basis exposed to a variety of toxic and carcinogenic compounds including heavy metals and PAHs, which contribute to the incidence of respiratory diseases such as asthma, bronchitis, and emphysema.

During the sanctions period Libya undoubtedly suffered from no or poor access to mainstream industrial smokestack scrubbing technology and many other clean environment-enhancing technologies for controlling and monitoring noxious emissions. This has lead to a situation in which the EGA (2002) report has stated "Present environmental conditions, resulting from oil refining…is unacceptable for health or environment. Serious efforts should be made to provide constant monitoring, measurement and control equipment, and to use clean energy in such industries" (EGA 2002 Report, p. 101).

In the current situation, it is incumbent on the Libyan authorities to introduce clean air legislation based, as in Europe, on the "polluter pays" principle, although in view of the fact that most polluters owned by the public sector may lead to difficulty in its enforcement. At the same time, the move towards the use of cleaner natural gas is one encouraging feature of the Libyan energy generation scene. Similarly the use of solar power equipment, now readily available from European and US manufacturers, is an area worthy of serious investigation in view of its vast potential in the country.

10.11 Solid Waste Management

Law No. 13 of 1984, "For Public Cleaning", and its Executive Regulations and Provisions is the legislation that covers collection of waste and issues related to solid waste management in Libya. In its eight chapters it deals with the responsibility of the authorities for waste collection, its methods, times, and personnel and their clothing, as well as the cleaning of public squares, markets, and buildings.

Chapter 8, "On Waste Disposal", defines the technical and health conditions for the dumpsites for household waste. It defines the conditions for site selection and their suitability for excavation and refilling, and limits their selection only for high-density settlements of 50,000 or more, to be located well away from such settlements. It also provides for the transformation of biological waste into organic fertilizers and addresses issues relating to recycling, while under this law burning of waste is prohibited.

However, the law fails to address a multiplicity of issues related to the disposal of poisonous, toxic, or hospital waste, and also fails to define the conditions under which the storage of poisons such as pesticides and herbicides may be undertaken.

It is vitally important, therefore, that in view of the major health and environmental risks faced by Libyans on a day-to-day basis as a result of this outdated legislation, the Libyan authorities come up with a national Solid Waste Management Strategy to bring the country into the twentieth century. Iran faces problems very similar to Libya in relation to solid and hazardous waste disposal, but it has recently turned to the World Bank for assistance through the latter's Environmental Management Support Project (EMSP), which represents the first phase of a long-term effort by the Iranian government to improve environmental management in the country. Its main objective is to enhance the capacity of the Iranian Department of Environment (DOE) and other related agencies to plan, monitor, and enforce environmental regulations.

In fact, again turning to the EGA 2002 Report, there is a clear recognition by the Libyan Environmental General Agency of these very real problems in relation to solid waste disposal, and it has proposed a "General Programme for Strategy Planning" for solid waste. But again it recognizes lack of proper legislation, environmental awareness, conflict of national, and Sha'abiyat laws, as well as inter departmental and Ministerial problems and finally, the acute shortage of trained technical specialists as severe obstacles, which need to be overcome. It is therefore likely that unless the Libyan government seeks external help to address these crucial health and environmental issues, the problem will only increase in line with urbanization and industrial diversification, and could in fact lead to strong impediments to FDI in, for example, the tourist sector.

10.12 Environmental and Sustainability Issues – Need for New Legislation

Although there exists in Libya a body of law to deal with the environment, environmental health, and pollution issues, it is apparent that for many reasons, some related to administrative and legal impasses, these existing environmental laws are not being applied rigorously, although without having access to actual court proceedings and decisions it is difficult to determine how poor the enforcement of existing environmental legislation really is. In the MENA countries in general we have noted a disposition towards weak environmental institutions and legal frameworks, preventing many countries such as Kuwait, for example, from adequately addressing important environmental challenges. It will only be when there is a realization of the crucial link between environmental protection and Libya's future environmental and economic sustainability so that the key roles of the EGA and the Libyan judiciary can be properly understood and maximized.

Again, owing to a severe shortage of baseline data, it is difficult to discuss with precision what actually needs to be done to bring Libya in line with twentieth-century environmental legislation as well as environmental best practices, which are key features in virtually every modern nation or developing nation that aspire to modernity. One very serious gap in Libyan environmental legislation is the absence of any requirement for conducting the EIAs for development projects of any type, a gap which was filled by its neighbouring countries of Egypt, Tunisia, and Algeria in the years 1994, 1988, and 1883, respectively, and other developing nations such as Malaysia in 1987.

As we have seen the lax environmental regime surrounding Libya's hydrocarbon industry, a natural polluter, has already led to many problems, problems which were dealt with comprehensively, for example, in 1991, by Nigeria's Department of Petroleum Resources (DPR) when it issued its 300-page Environmental Guidelines and Standards (EGAS) specifically for the oil and gas sector. As Libya accelerates oil exploration and production, environmental impacts, both onshore and offshore will intensify, leading to ecosystem degradation as well as negative health impacts on many Libyans. Similarly a poor record in monitoring and controlling air pollution has meant that many Libyans will fall victim to carcinogenic diseases brought about by this silent killer, especially in the congested urban centres in which most Libyans now live.

Water contamination of Libya's groundwater brought about by intensive agriculture and overgrazing is another major problem, while Libya's priceless Mediterranean coastline and its unique cultural heritage is also under threat, unless an integrated coastal management policy, which can cut across the regional interests of individual coastal Sha'abiyat and major industrial polluters such as the refinery, steel, and petrochemical industries, is put in place quickly. Again this has major implications for the ambitions of Libyan policy makers who wish to significantly enhance its tourist sector; again valuable lessons can be learned from the holistic approach to these problems which neighbouring Egypt has brought to its Mediterranean and Red Sea coastline. In this connection Egypt's visionary underwater archaeology and coastal management plan for the city of Alexandria, which it labels as the greatest emporium in the inhabited world, could also provide valuable insights for future knowledge and development of Sabratha, one of the finest archaeological sites in the Mediterranean world, into an absolutely unique tourist destination.

Clearly, however, the multitude and magnitude of environmental problems should make it clear to Libyan policy makers that a major overhaul of the country's environmental legislation is urgently required to address the main issues discussed in this section and many more again. Investors in Libya, Libyans themselves, and future generations of Libyans will together call the Libyan government to account if it fails to deal with these urgent environmental problems now, in order to make the sustainable development of Libya a reality. At the very least, an Environmental Master Plan needs to be drawn up, based on a baseline study of data connected with the main terrestrial, atmospheric, and marine problems. Based on its findings, comprehensive environmental legislation must be drawn up, covering every development sector, with substantial powers allocated to the Libyan Ministry of the Environment and the Libyan Environment General Agency. Finally for good order's sake, we append Appendices 10.1 and 10.2 covering environmentally related International Agreements and Conventions affecting Libya.

11 The Forces Shaping Libya's Future

11.1 Demographic Pressures and Unemployment Issues

As discussed at length in Chap. 4, demographic pressures are fundamentally changing the face of Libyan society. The North African region has one of the most rapid population growth rates of the world, with population more than doubling in the last 30 years, and Libya has the fastest growing population in this region. Between 1954, the time of the first national census, and 2005, population increased from slightly over one million to around six million, although a large part of the increase has been due to open immigration policies towards Arabs and Africans. Again, Infant Mortality Rate (IMR) per 1000 live births has fallen over the same period from 300 to 24.4, while at the same time life expectancy has risen from 42.4 years to 76.5 years. The Libyan population structure exhibits a youthful picture where almost one-third of the total population is less than 15 years old. Again, as noted, this comparatively young structure of the population leads to many problems and pressures on the education, health, and other public services, increasing the dependency ratio although such pressure will decrease as the cycle continues, with dependents becoming providers.

Libya's population growth, with the country's population predicted at 7.740 million in 2020 based on a projected growth rate of 2.3 per cent between 2000 and 2010 and 1.8 per cent between 2010 and 2020, will also put tremendous pressures on the country's infrastructure requirements, badly rundown for the previous 30 years, as well as on water resources and arable land, housing, healthcare, and education.

In respect of future employment, there will be four main effects of these trends increasingly felt in Libya in the years ahead. The first, in line with other MENA countries, is the potentially high rate of unemployment, especially among the young and educated, which has emerged in the late 1990s and early 2000s. At 13.2 per cent in 2005, the Middle East and North Africa remained the region with the highest unemployment rate in the world (ILO 2006). Unemployment rates in North Africa range between 12 per cent of the labour force in Egypt and 28 per cent in Algeria, considered to be one of the seven world economies that have unemployment rates in excess of 20 per cent (Zohry 2005).

It is difficult to get reliable data on unemployment rates in Libya. As stated elsewhere in the book, the poor quality of economic data collection and presentation is currently a major problem for the Libyan authorities as they attempt to realign Libya internationally. Until an internationally recognized standard and comparative statistical database is established, it will prove impossible for the Libyan authorities to successfully monitor either domestic progress, for example, in areas such as unemployment and immigration as discussed previously, or to make international comparisons regarding overall progress in the economic transition.

The World Bank currently estimates Libyan unemployment at around 25 per cent (World Bank 2006 Country Report on Libya), while other sources claim it could be as high as 30 per cent. The problem is compounded by Libya's liberal immigration policies, discussed in Chap. 4, which mean that there may be a million or more "phantom Libyans" in the country, casually employed but not officially recognized.

In the transitional phase, the effects on unemployment of the current privatization programme discussed extensively in Chap. 6, where many companies will be privatized or liquidated, will be increasingly felt. The creation of enough new jobs for these redundant workers, as well as Libya's rapidly growing labour force, will become a major social problem faced by the Libyan policy makers. This is because to absorb these, as well as new labour market entrants, significantly faster growth will be required than at present, particularly in the non-oil sector. The labour force, which is currently estimated at around 1.8 million workers, is expected to grow at 3.3 per cent per year over the medium term. But as one authoritative source states,

> using rather favourable assumptions about employment elasticity of growth (assuming an elasticity of 0.75) it is estimated that the productive non-oil sectors will need to grow at least at 4.5 per cent per year to absorb new entrants to the labor market and to avoid an increase in the unemployment rate. Much higher growth, of about 6.5 per cent, would be needed to reduce the unemployment rate, currently estimated at around 25 per cent, by half in a 10-year period (World Bank 2006).

Because of the inefficiency of both a failing and globally isolated Libyan industrial sector, and an overblown Libyan public sector, the economy cannot successfully absorb the increasing numbers of relatively well-educated students exiting from secondary and tertiary education. Issues of education quality also arise – as described in Chap. 4, the move away from an English curriculum in the 1980s has also meant that many of these young people are not only unemployed but also unemployable, especially by foreign companies, due to both poor foreign language skills and limitations in grasping global issues, due to the inward-looking nature of the Libyan society during the sanction period. High job expectations are also a factor, because in the past everyone expected a job in the state sector as soon as they left school or university.

A second source of demographic pressure will be the increasing role of females at all levels in the Libyan society. Many foreign observers, among them Tunisian women, who have long been considered as the most liberated women in North Africa, are impressed by the freedom afforded to Libyan women in comparison to many other Arab countries. In Libya women can drive, dress attractively, and are increasingly employed, as we have seen, in a variety of occupations and professions (Obeidi 1999). Although perhaps by western standards, their clothing is somewhat conservative, they have never been required to wear the veil. Should economic transformation proceed smoothly, privatization and economic development will undoubtedly mean that female labour force participation rates should rise. This will also put pressure on the job market.

Thirdly, the continuing trend in migration from rural to urban areas will increase employment pressures and, potentially, unemployment rates in the cities, although the present emphasis on developing and restructuring the agricultural sector, especially in view of the benefits of the GMRP, might partially halt the rural/urban drift. This again will place additional burdens on Libya's urban infrastructure and services such as health, education, and housing, as well as increasing urban unemployment, which is steadily rising, with the proportion of the young and educated unemployed increasing significantly.

Fourthly, inward migration and problems associated with illegal immigration are also matters that will, in future, cause concern, and must be understood and tackled by Libya's policy-makers. Libya, as a major oil-producing and exporting state has traditionally attracted migrants from neighbouring Arab countries such as Egypt and Tunisia. This is exacerbated by the present open entry policy for immigrants from Libya's southern neighbours in Africa, which, as was discussed earlier, is putting enormous pressure on Libya's social services, as well as contributing to unemployment of Libyans and internal social tensions.

Historically, Libya, on account of oil revenues, has been able to ride these demographic pressures and provide an enviable standard of living for her people compared with all of her immediate neighbours, and indeed the MENA region as a whole. But increasingly higher expectations and levels of awareness among the Libyan population, and the future dominance of IT, FDI, and the influence of regional Arab and international media will mean that Libya's policy makers must plan carefully to ensure that these demographic trends are incorporated into a future development plan specially structured to cater for them.

11.2 The New Economic Realities

The sweeping economic changes currently impacting the Libyan economy and society mean that the country is now embarking on a new kind of laissez-faire economic development, radically different from the centrally planned and government owned economic control engineered in the early 1970s and later. In this new era, genuine economic diversification, based on free competition and market forces, is targeted to take up the unemployment slack, as Libya develops its highly promising tourist sector and re-engages in trade both regionally and internationally. Because of its highly favourable location at the crossroads of the Mediterranean and the African continent, it is safe to say that there will be no shortage of FDI in Libya, as economic and fiscal reforms move forward. Currently, for example, there is a waiting list of 1,400 international companies wishing to base themselves in the Misuratah Free Trade Zone (Otman, Private Interview 2005). Again, as we earlier discussed, the LNOC's runaway successes in the two hotly contested exploration and production sharing agreement (EPSA IV) bidding rounds of 2005 will also favourably impact the Libyan economy, with direct economic linkages to Libyan employment, housing, hotel, transportation, and service sectors.

Undoubtedly in future the quality of education will be a major force in determining the success of Libya's ambitious transformation plans. The last 20 years have witnessed a revolution in technology, brought about by a lowering in prices of both computer hardware and software, effectively revolutionizing every industrial process and commercial sector, including international trade instruments, banking and finance. The countries that stress lifelong learning and a knowledge-based society, such as, for example, Singapore, are the ones that will survive and expand in this new world where IT skills and knowledge of technological processes count for more than the traditional inputs of land, labour, and capital as determinants of economic success.

Linked to this it must be re-emphasized that the Libyan government must move back quickly to an acceptance and recognition of the international importance of the English language. Until the mid-1980s English was still a part of the school curriculum in Libya; yet in a change of policy in 1980, to reduce the preponderance of foreign teachers in Libya, the government enacted the "New Educational Structure". The school curriculum was restructured in favour of technical subjects and, in the humanities, Arabic language and Koranic education were particularly emphasized at the expense of English. For Libya this has proved to be a fundamental mistake, which has set the country back by two generations in terms of educational quality. We advocate a policy change in Libya similar to that undertaken by the Malaysian Prime Minister Dr. Mahathir Mohamed when, in the 1990s, in a complete reversal of the Malaysian government's language policy, he re-emphasized the use of the English language in the school curriculum, leading to its gradual reintroduction as the medium of instruction, first, in 1996, in tertiary education and in the sciences, and subsequently, since 2002, from the beginning of schooling, and in the sciences and maths.

FDI will also, in the future, have a noticeable impact on tertiary education in Libya, as International Oil Companies (IOCs), multinational companies, and foreign SMEs will provide attractive employment opportunities to highly skilled graduates in science, engineering, IT, and business and commerce. This will provide strong incentives for students to complete tertiary education, while in general the demand for skilled labour will increase exponentially, placing further demands on the Libyan government. It is therefore clear that however commendable Libyan educational achievements have been over the past 30 years, Libya should now address what is now known as "borderless education". This modern concept of education dictates that the Libyan authorities should actively encourage foreign universities to have branch campuses in Libya, as discussed at length in Chap. 4.

This will allow Libyan students, around 5,000 of whom are currently studying abroad (Libyan Ministry of Higher Education 2005), to get an internationally recognized educational qualification at home, saving the country's valuable foreign exchange. The authors believe that there will never be a better time for Libya to formulate strategies for attracting international experts and talents in the linguistic, scientific, and technological fields to live and teach in Libya.

It is also important that Libya, in view of its vast and as yet untapped tourist potential and the government's recent announcements regarding massive expansion and diversification of the tourist sector, should start thinking about how to guarantee tertiary education and qualifications for Libyans who wish to make a career in the hotel, tourist, and hospitality industry. Again, valuable foreign exchange could be saved if such a branch campus were set up in Libya, at the same time providing significant career and employment potential for the large number of Libyans under 25 currently unemployed. Similarly, as environmental issues begin to progressively impact legislation and policies globally, Libya needs to ensure that its younger generation does not miss out on the vast opportunities in this field, again by looking at cooperation with international educational institutions recognized in this field.

It is also important for Libya's planners to recognize that in developed countries, it is the services and not the manufacturing sector that currently predominate, accounting for over two-thirds of GDP, while in most developing countries it accounts for less than half. While, as we have seen, entry into Libya for FDI into the manufacturing sector has largely been liberalized through legislation since 1997, the same cannot be said for many service sectors. But the new economic realities of globalization mean that the economic liberalization, deregulation, and privatization are bound to open up more services to FDI. This means that Libyan policymakers must, in the future, realize that industrial FDI, while certainly important, constitutes only a relatively small share of the total and that policy need to focus more on firms offering services. In fact, with Libya's tremendous potential in the hydrocarbon, tourist, and education sectors, as we have discussed at length, as well as its strategic geographical position as a service hub between Europe and Africa, the potential for growth in Libya in the service sector is, although presently untapped, virtually unlimited.

Perhaps it is an old African proverb which encapsulates, in principle, the way forward for Libya's economic policy makers in the new economic environment of FDI and globalization: "Every morning, when the lions wake up, they know they have to run faster than the slowest gazelle not to go hungry in the evening. And every morning, when the gazelles get up, they know they have to run faster than the fastest lion to survive" (Sauvant 2005). The moral of this proverb should be clear to the Libyan Foreign Investment Board – in an increasingly competitive world, FDI will gravitate to the country that offers the best all round investment package.

11.3 e-Government and e-Inclusion

The UN Global E-Government Readiness Report is an annual review, which assesses and benchmarks the public sector e-government initiatives of the UN Member States according to a weighted average composite index of e-readiness. It is based, among other factors, on website assessment, telecommunication infrastructure and human resource endowment. In the latest report, 2005, Libya, as well as 10 other countries including, for example, the Democratic People's Republic of Korea (i.e. North Korea), Haiti, Kiribati, and Liberia, does not even appear on the list of nations offering a public government portal, although certain Libyan government-owned institutions such as the Central Bank of Libya, the Libyan Foreign Investment Board, and the Libyan National Oil Corporation do have individual websites.

In this report, Egypt, Tunisia, Algeria, Morocco, Sudan, and Mauretania are ranked 99, 121, 123, 138, 150, and 164, respectively, out of 179 UN states. It is regrettable that, in spite of its recent economic reform policy and privatization drive, including, as we have seen earlier, significant legal reforms in its financial business and tourist sectors, Libya does not appear at all on the UN e-Government rankings, since this sends out very negative signals to the international community. Libya's immediate neighbour, Egypt, for example, has a government website in both Arabic and English (http://www.egypt.gov.eg) with a wide variety of information related to more than 700 services, ranging from paying utility bills, traffic fines, requesting a birth certificate or ID card, to paying taxes as well as reporting missing items or filing tourism complaints. This Egyptian government website also provides links to Egypt's FDI portal (http://www.investment.gov.eg) as well as to an extremely useful information portal (http://www.idsc.gov.eg), which provides a wide range of data and information on the country.

In many ways the lack of a comprehensive Libyan government website highlights the inability of Libyan policy makers, who are demonstrably keen to attract investment to Libya, to really understand the criteria on which FDI investment decisions are based, and demonstrates that the government has to radically change from an outward looking to a global perspective in order to redefine Libya's future image and position in the modern world. If not, the significant amount of legislative enactments for trade and economic liberalization since 1997 will not yield the anticipated results.

Not only this, but the Libyan government, through lack of an online portal, has missed an excellent opportunity to enhance awareness among ordinary Libyan citizens about its privatization and other new economic policies, providing them with easier access and inclusion, and allowing them, as stakeholders in Libya's future success, to participate actively in decision making. Of course it may be argued that Libya's unique political system, as we discussed extensively in Chap. 1, was designed precisely to ensure such social and political inclusion. But the point here is that if Libya wishes to successfully develop the opportunities and abilities of her citizens as participants in the digital revolution, which is in effect more significant, in terms of the rate of change, than the industrial revolution of the nineteenth century, the country needs to use enabling technology such as ICT to catapult it into the modern world. This does not mean that ICT will necessarily be used to challenge the government, but that it will in fact improve and expedite the realization of the government's economic and social goals. For example, there is an ongoing and sustained debate in Libya about many crucial issues that will, in the future, seriously impact the everyday lives of ordinary Libyan citizens. A good example is the present domestic debate on food and fuel subsidies and the "subsidy mentality" in general, which appears to be a factor in de-motivating many Libyans from achieving success independently in new entrepreneurial fields. An interactive Libyan government website could attempt to gauge the feelings of Libyan citizens about such issues, at the same time assisting policy makers in devising and structuring future development plans. Feedback on such current issues as the impact of charter flight tourism on Libya or issues related to Libya's bloated and inefficient civil service would in fact assist the government in determining policies, which would be broadly accepted by all Libyan citizens.

In other areas, most crucially education, the power of ICT can also massively reduce government expenditure as well as expediting delivery of results. A good example of its tremendous power occurred in 2003 in Mexico, where an upgrading educational course was beamed via satellite and the Internet to over 1800 teachers nationwide, to even the remotest settlements (World Telecommunication Development Report 2003).

An interesting finding of the UN Global E-Government Readiness Report 2005 was its observation that "E-government appears to have a strong relation with income per capita. Resource availability appears to be a critical factor inhibiting e-government initiatives in many countries. Part of the reason for the high e-readiness in most of the developed economies is past investment in, and development of, infrastructure". However, in the Libyan case, this linkage clearly does not apply, since the country has the highest per capita income in Africa. What is missing is that the government has failed to integrate its vision, and long-term planning, as part of the innovative potential of using the considerable advantages of e-Government.

In this connection it is, however, worth noting that on 12 December 2005, Libya and UNESCO signed an agreement that set up a National Plan for Information and Communication Technologies (NICT) that will provide all higher education institutions in Libya with Internet facilities including digital libraries, educational sites, and facilities for distance learning. As stated earlier, by promoting the use of English in schools nationally, the government will ensure that scientific and technology websites are also accessible to Libyan students and researchers.

A very recent development has shown that the General People's Committee, or Libyan Cabinet, has finally realized the crucial importance of having a well-designed, continuously updated, and interactive government portal. On 14 July 2006, the GPC website (www.gpc.gov.ly) was launched in Arabic, which has up to date and detailed information on all GPC Resolutions and also explains details of the legislative process and machinery, with linkages to all the ministries, government bodies, and main organizations in Libya. Eventually this website will also be available in English. This is most definitely one of the major recent achievements of the Libyan government, which sends the right signals to international web-surfers, investors, and governments that Libya, despite the technological, medical, and educational setbacks incurred during the UN/US sanctions period, is a country, which is serious about international reintegration and social progress and determined to change into a digital society. This also has important implications for the perceptions of western investors and their governments about transparency, inclusion, and the quality of governance in Libya.

11.4 Transparency and Corruption

The practice or concept of corruption has existed since the beginnings of organized government. In general terms it is defined as the abuse of public office for private gain, and its implications in those societies in which it is practised can be severe. As stated in an influential publication, "Corruption doesn't just line the pockets of political and business elites; it leaves ordinary people without essential services, such as life-saving medicines, and deprives them of access to sanitation and housing. In short, corruption costs lives" (Transparency International, 2005).

Much of this book has been concerned with the Libyan government's recent efforts at economic reform. The crucial importance of addressing issues related to corruption and transparency in Libya is of course directly related to the very fundamentals of the economic reform process. This is because corruption has a series of socio-economic impacts, which directly impede economic development. These can be described as follows:

(a) Corruption raises transaction costs and uncertainty in the economy.
(b) It skews the policy-making process and results in inefficient and irrational outcomes.
(c) It is regressive in that it lays a larger burden on small and medium enterprises who need to set aside a larger share of their time and income to deal with it.
(d) It undermines state legitimacy and the rule of law.
(e) It leads to wider income disparities because those with influence gain more advantages and those without lose out. (Salem 2003)

Reform programmes such as those which Libya is currently undergoing have in fact been characteristic of policies implemented in a wide range of countries in Africa, South America, and Asia in the last quarter of the past century, often with inputs and conditionality on the reform process required by the IMF or the WTO. As Francis Fukuyama, a prominent writer on state building and governance has commented on this process,

> The so-called first generation reforms – getting macroeconomic policy under control, reducing tariffs, privatisation, deregulation, and so on – were relatively straightforward, because they concerned policies that were at least nominally under the control of governments. But second-generation reforms that focus on strengthening those very state institutions are much more difficult to implement. While a handful of technocrats might be able to "fix" monetary policy or a dysfunctional central banking system, there is no comparable group of specialists who can reform a legal system or clean up a corrupt police force. Such institutions, which are critical for the functioning of a market economy, are large, complex, and deeply steeped in the local traditions and culture of the societies in which they operate. They are, moreover, at the core of the country's political system and can potentially threaten the interests of wealthy and powerful elites (Transparency International 2005).

What is the relevance of Fukuyama's statements on "second-generation reforms" with regard to the present Libyan situation regarding corruption and governance? In, for example, the 2005 Corruption Perception Index (CPI), Transparency International gave Libya a rating of 2.5 out of a possible 10, placing the country in 117th place in the world list of 158 countries, tied with Afghanistan, Bolivia, Ecuador, Guatemala, Guyana, Philippines, Nepal, and Uganda. The CPI rank relates to perceptions of the degree of corruption as seen by business people and country analysts, and ranges between 10 (highly clean) and 0 (highly corrupt). In a shortened version of the ranking table, we show the ranking of 42 countries in the index in Table 11.1.

Table 11. 1. Corruption perceptions index 2005, selected countries

Country rank	Country	2005 CPI score	Surveys used	Standard deviation	High-low range	Confidence range
1	Iceland	9.7	8	0.2	9.3–9.8	9.5–9.7
8	Norway	8.9	9	0.6	7.9–9.5	8.5–9.1
9	Australia	8.8	13	0.8	6.7–9.5	8.4–9.1
11	UK	8.6	11	0.5	7.7–9.3	8.3–8.8
15	Hong Kong	8.3	12	1.1	5.5–9.4	7.7–8.7
17	USA	7.6	12	1.0	5.3–8.5	7.0–8.0
28	Israel	6.3	10	1.2	4.2–8.5	5.7–6.9
28	Oman	6.3	5	1.5	4.2–8.0	5.2–7.3
30	UAE	6.2	6	1.4	4.5–8.2	5.3–7.1
32	Botswana	5.9	8	1.4	4.4–8.1	5.1–6.7
32	Qatar	5.9	5	0.6	5.5–6.9	5.6–6.4
36	Bahrain	5.8	6	0.7	4.7–6.9	5.3–6.3
37	Jordan	5.7	10	1.0	3.4–6.9	5.1–6.1
39	Malaysia	5.1	14	1.2	3.4–8.0	4.6–5.6
40	Italy	5.0	9	0.8	4.1–6.2	4.6–5.4
43	Tunisia	4.9	7	1.1	3.7–6.9	4.4–5.6
55	Colombia	4.0	9	0.8	2.7–5.6	3.6–4.4
59	Cuba	3.8	4	1.6	1.7–5.5	2.3–4.7
70	Egypt	3.4	9	0.8	2.3–5.1	3.0–3.9
70	Saudi Arabia	3.4	5	1.0	2.0–4.5	2.7–4.1
70	Syria	3.4	5	1.1	2.2–5.1	2.8–4.2
78	Morocco	3.2	8	0.7	2.2–4.1	2.8–3.6
83	Lebanon	3.1	4	0.4	2.7–3.5	2.7–3.3
88	Iran	2.9	5	0.8	1.7–3.5	2.3–3.3
97	Algeria	2.8	7	0.7	2.0–4.2	2.5–3.3
107	Palestine	2.6	3	0.5	2.1–3.1	2.1–2.8
107	Zambia	2.6	7	0.5	2.1–3.4	2.3–2.9
107	Zimbabwe	2.6	7	0.8	1.4–3.6	2.1–3.0
117	Guatemala	2.5	7	0.6	1.7–3.5	2.1–2.8
117	Libya	2.5	4	0.7	1.8–3.4	2.0–3.0
117	Nepal	2.5	4	0.7	1.7–3.4	1.9–3.0
117	Philippines	2.5	13	0.6	1.5–3.5	2.3–2.8
117	Uganda	2.5	8	0.5	2.0–3.5	2.2–2.8
126	Russia	2.4	12	0.3	1.9–3.0	2.3–2.6
137	Indonesia	2.2	13	0.4	1.7–3.3	2.1–2.5
137	Iraq	2.2	4	1.0	1.4–3.6	1.5–2.9
144	Kenya	2.1	8	0.5	1.4–3.0	1.8–2.4
144	Pakistan	2.1	7	0.7	1.3–3.4	1.7–2.6
144	Sudan	2.1	5	0.2	1.7–2.3	1.9–2.2
144	Tajikistan	2.1	5	0.4	1.7–2.7	1.9–2.4
152	Nigeria	1.9	9	0.3	1.4–2.2	1.7–2.0
158	Chad	1.7	6	0.6	1.0–2.7	1.3–2.1

Source: Transparency International, 2005.

In discussing any country's ranking, it is important to understand what each heading means. "Surveys used" refers to the number of surveys that assessed a country's performance, and at least three surveys were required for a country to be included in the CPI. "Standard deviation" indicates differences in the values of the sources. Values below 0.5 indicate agreement, values between 0.5 and 0.9 indicate some agreement, while values equal or larger than 1 indicate disagreement. "High–low range" provides the highest and the lowest values of the different sources. "90 per cent Confidence Range" provides a range of possible values of the CPI score. This reflects how a country's score may vary, depending on the measurement precision; with 5 per cent probability the score is above this range and with another 5 per cent it is below. However, particularly when only few sources (n) are available, an unbiased estimate of the mean coverage probability is lower than the nominal value of 90 per cent. It is 65.3 per cent for n=3, 73.6 per cent for n=4, 78.4 per cent for n=5, 80.2 per cent for n=6, and 81.8 per cent for n=7.

Looking at Table 11.1 we note that the country perceived to be the least corrupt in the world is Iceland and the most corrupt is Chad, while Oman, United Arab Emirates, Qatar and Jordan ranked at 28, 30, 32, and 37, respectively, are ranked ahead of Italy. In the case of Libya, we note that it is equally ranked 117th, that the ranking was based on four surveys, that with a standard deviation of 0.7 there was some agreement in the ranking, that the highest and the lowest values were 1.8 and 3.4, respectively, and with four surveys the probability of the survey being unbiased stands at 78.4 per cent. In short, this represents the opinion or perception of the four organizations that completed the survey for Libya, that is the Economist Intelligence Unit, Information International, Merchant International Group 2005, and the World Markets Research Centre 2005.

There can be no doubt, however, that the CPI has become an influential survey, which can influence the decisions of potential investors and perceptions about target countries and destinations for FDI. According to its recent research, if country were to improve its score in the CPI by 1 point out of 10, foreign direct investment would increase by 15 per cent (Transparency International 2005).

In the case of Libya it would be foolhardy to agree or disagree with the CPI score since the country has only recently emerged from many years of sanctions, and access to real data on, for example, the number or success rate of prosecutions brought against corruptors is hard to come by. One high-profile case that reached the international media was that of the country's Finance Minister, Ujayli Abdelsalam al-Burayni who in 2001 was jailed for 1 year, together with 47 other government and bank officials, in connection with the embezzlement of 600 million LD from the Jamahiriya Bank. There has also been much media speculation in the Libyan press itself about corruption at high levels in the Sha'abiyat regarding the granting of high-value infrastructure contracts, but in the absence of concrete data it is difficult to be precise. On the other hand, in the recent two EPSA IV rounds, the extremes to which the Libyan government went to ensure complete transparency were commendable. For both these competitive tenders, the bids were opened publicly in front of all bidders in the Al Mahari Hotel in Tripoli, and the winning bidders for each block were announced on the spot.

Clearly, however, in terms of the definition for good governance as understood by western observers, there is much that is lacking or misunderstood among western observers of Libya's current economic and political system. In terms, for example, of the Annual Index for Economic Freedom drawn up by the Heritage Foundation, Libya is listed as seventh equal out of a total of 18 MENA countries in terms of Government Intervention with a score of 4 out of 5, where the higher the score on a factor, the greater the level of government interference in the economy and the less economic freedom a country enjoys. The overall score for Libya in MENA countries is last with a high score of 4.4 (Table 11.2).

In certain respects it is difficult not to take exception with at least some of the scores applied to specific categories of Libya's ranking. For example, for a score of 5 or "very high" as applied to Libya for "Banking and Finance" the financial sector must exhibit "financial institutions in chaos; banks operate on primitive basis; most credit controlled by government and goes only to state-owned enterprises; corruption widespread". This is very wide of the mark; as we have shown in an earlier chapter, the Central Bank of Libya, closely advised by the IMF, maintains a strong overall regulatory control over the banking system, while banks such as the Development and Commercial Bank offer credit cards, ATMs, and computer banking, and the Libyan Arab Foreign Bank (LAFB) has an overseas network of over 35 subsidiaries or partnerships in 20 countries and is regarded as one of the top banks in the Arab world.

Similarly, to say that in Libya "wages and prices of goods and services are almost completely controlled by the government" as a criteria for a score of 5 in the "Wages/Prices" category is very misleading. While it is true that wages in an admittedly overblown bureaucracy and many Libyan State Owned Enterprises are defined and controlled by Law No. 15 of 1981, wage levels in the private sector, for example in foreign oil and gas service companies employing Libyans, follow supply and demand; again, to say that prices of goods and services are almost completely controlled by the government is simply untrue; while the prices of

Table 11.2. MENA countries: index for economic freedom

GIR	Country	Year	OS	Trade	FB	GI	MP	FI	BF	WP	PR	R	IM
1	Israel	2005	2.36	2.0	4.1	2.5	1.0	2.0	3.0	2.0	2.0	3.0	2.0
1	Tunisia	2005	3.14	5.0	3.9	2.5	1.0	4.0	4.0	2.0	3.0	3.0	3.0
1	Morocco	2005	3.18	5.0	3.8	2.5	1.0	2.0	4.0	3.0	4.0	3.0	3.5
4	Jordan	2005	2.79	4.0	3.9	3.0	1.0	2.0	2.0	3.0	3.0	3.0	3.0
4	Lebanon	2005	3.05	3.0	2.5	3.0	1.0	4.0	2.0	3.0	4.0	4.0	4.0
4	Egypt	2005	3.38	4.0	4.3	3.0	2.0	3.0	4.0	3.0	3.0	4.0	3.5
7	UAE	2005	2.68	2.0	1.3	4.0	1.0	3.0	4.0	3.0	3.0	3.0	2.5
7	Algeria	2005	3.49	5.0	3.9	4.0	1.0	3.0	4.0	3.0	4.0	3.0	4.0
7	Yemen	2005	3.70	4.0	4.0	4.0	3.0	3.0	4.0	3.0	4.0	4.0	4.0
7	Libya	2005	4.40	5.0	5.0	4.0	1.0	5.0	5.0	5.0	5.0	5.0	4.0
11	Bahrain	2005	2.10	3.0	2.0	4.5	1.0	2.0	1.0	2.0	1.0	2.0	2.5
11	Kuwait	2005	2.76	2.0	1.6	4.5	1.0	4.0	3.0	3.0	3.0	3.0	2.5
11	Oman	2005	2.81	3.0	1.6	4.5	1.0	3.0	3.0	4.0	3.0	3.0	2.0
11	Saudi Arabia	2005	2.99	4.0	1.4	4.5	1.0	4.0	4.0	2.0	3.0	3.0	3.0
11	Qatar	2005	3.10	3.0	2.0	4.5	2.0	4.0	3.0	3.0	3.0	4.0	2.5
11	Syria	2005	3.90	5.0	4.0	4.5	1.0	4.0	5.0	4.0	4.0	4.0	3.5
17	Iran	2005	4.16	2.0	3.6	5.0	4.0	4.0	5.0	4.0	5.0	5.0	4.0
18	Iraq	2005	–	–	–	–	–	–	–	–	–	–	–

Source: Heritage Foundation Annual Index for Economic Freedom, 2005.

Note: GIR, Government Intervention Rank; OS, Overall Score; FB, Fiscal Burden; GI, Government Intervention; MP, Monetary Policy; FI, Foreign Investment; BF, Banking Finance; WP, Wages Prices; PR, Property Rights; R, Regulation; IM, Informal Market.

basic foodstuffs such as rice, flour, pasta, and oil are subsidized by the government, a wide range of consumer goods at highly competitive prices, at least since the lifting of the UN sanctions in 1999, gives the average Libyan the same freedom of choice as his counterpart in any European country.

Again the criteria for Factor 8, "Property Rights", which applies a score of 5 for Libya, could not be more misleading. To get a score of 5 for this we note "private property outlawed or not protected; almost all property belongs to the state; country in such chaos (for example, because of ongoing war) that property protection is non-existent; judiciary so corrupt that property is not effectively protected; expropriation frequent". But as we discussed exhaustively in Chap. 4 of this book, one of the main objectives of the revolution of 1969 was to ensure that every Libyan citizen owned a house. Towards this goal massive investments in housing projects in all the main cities and indeed throughout Libya from the 1970s onwards has meant that Libya probably has the highest percentage of private home ownership in the world, approached only by, say, Norway in a European context. Each home or property owner possesses a *Shahaddat Mylkia Akaria* or Certificate of Housing or Land Ownership, registered in their individual name in a nation-wide land registry, with the right to sell it whenever they wish.

It cannot be denied, however, that there are many highly important issues related to corruption and transparency in Libya. But it is becoming gradually clear, in the post-sanctions situation, that Libyans and the Libyan government are aware of the seriousness of these issues and their potential negative impact on the economic transformation of the country. Several obvious examples show its willingness to address transparency and corruption issues related to international concerns about its reporting and benchmarking systems.

The first was the Libyan government's acceptance, in 21 June 2003 of its obligations of Article VIII, Sects. 2, 3, and 4 of the IMF Articles of Agreement. "By accepting the obligations of Article VIII, Libya gives confidence to the international community that it will pursue economic policies that will make restrictions on the making of payments and transfers for current international transactions unnecessary, and will contribute to a multilateral payments system free of restrictions. This enables the IMF to hold bilateral discussions with members, usually every year. A staff team visits the country, collects economic and financial information, and discusses with officials the country's economic developments and policies. On return to headquarters, the staff prepares a report, which forms the basis for discussion by the Executive Board. At the conclusion of the discussion, the Managing Director, as Chairman of the Board, summarizes the views of Executive Directors, and this summary is transmitted to the country's authorities (IMF 2003)".

This in turn led to Article IV consultations with Libya, which resulted in IMF reports published in October 2003, in March 2005, and in April 2006. The importance of this move is highly significant, sending direct signals to the international community that Libya wishes to return to an international system of financial accountability, which is then, through the IMF website, made available in the public domain. These reports have been openly critical of the Libyan government's current system of collecting and reporting data, in many ways the key to identifying corruption at senior levels in the Libyan government. This issue was addressed in very frank terms by IMF's 2004 Article IV Consultation with Libya, published in March 2005, when the report stated in Appendix 3:

> Libya's database suffers from shortcomings that seriously affect the capacity of staff to conduct effective surveillance. Among these are: (i) weaknesses in the conceptual and compilation procedures underpinning the collection of statistics in the various sectors; (ii) deficiencies in data quality, coverage, periodicity, and timeliness; (iii) lack of consistency of data across sectors; and (iv) with the exception of monetary and balance of payments data, lack of a data reporting system to the Fund in order to update MCD's (i.e. the IMF's Middle East and Central Asia Department) operational data base between missions. The above issues are compounded by specific institutional weaknesses affecting data quality and timeliness, in particular the lack of inter-agency cooperation, the proliferation of agencies with unclear and often overlapping responsibilities, and the continuous reshuffling of responsibilities among agencies. Participation in the Fund's General Data Dissemination System (GDDS) would help to address these problems (IMF 2005).

This was followed up by the IMF in its 2006 Country Report No. 06/137 where it announced the Libyan authorities' commitment to strengthen the Libyan statistical system, seen as a basic condition for compiling official statistics in line with international standards. Hopefully this will lead, as discussed above, to Libya's participation in the IMF's GDDS, presently used in over 80 countries, which will provide a comprehensive approach and a vision to build official statistics, spelling out international best practices in statistics and data collection (IMF April 2006).

A second example was Libya's application, on 10 June 2004, to join the World Trade Organization followed by the establishment by WTO on 27 July 2004 of a working party to formally consider Libya's application, after WTO members agreed to start talks with Libya on its membership bid. As discussed in detail in Chap. 7, the implications for Libya in accepting the conditionalities attached to membership will, in the long term, have far-reaching implications for Libya's legal, banking and economic system, which will go to the very heart of those issues related to transparency and corruption in Libyan life.

A third example, this time relating to Libya's key hydrocarbon sector, is the complete transparency surrounding the new Libyan Exploration and Production EPSA IV Round One and Two public bidding procedures and results in January and October 2005. It can be said that this is unique in MENA context, where closed room negotiations are the order of the day, leading to many accusations of corruption and the squandering of state resources, as well as preventing the international bidders from competing on a level playing field due to political favouritism. In the actual implementation of the first and second public rounds of EPSA IV, the Libyan National Oil Corporation arranged and implemented the programme and scheduled in a way that was very close to its stated timetable, in a highly transparent and professional manner.

Bid opening was conducted in a public place, usually in a hotel, in the presence of the bidders and their legal representatives on the bid opening date. The winners of individual blocks were determined on the spot by publicly opening each bid for each area on offer, almost like an auction sale, with the winner selected on the basis of the lowest Second Party Allocation (SPA) of cost recovery offered by each bidder.

Political and institutional corruption in an internal context is also now being seriously addressed. One of the most obvious moves against corruption was the passing of Law No. 2 of 2005, "Combating Money Laundering". It can be interpreted as one of the first major salvoes against corruption and illegal possession of funds, in Libya and abroad, by Libyan nationals, where the amount of such funds does not correspond to an individual's normal sources of income, for example a salary or legitimate bank account, defined comprehensively in Article 2 of the law.

Again, in a broad ranging speech on the 20 August 2006, the son of the Libyan leader, Saif al-Islam Al Gaddafi, addressing the First Forum of the National Organization of Libyan Youth, addressed a series of issues related to the lack of a free press in Libya, the infrastructure deficit, subsidies, and corruption. One particular example of corruption was in the health service, where he states

> In the past, the doctors used to rob the equipment of the university hospitals or the central hospitals to put it in their own clinics. While they worked in the central hospitals and took salaries from them, they made their own clinics which they operated in the evenings and robbed the equipment and took the customers from the central hospital.

Linked directly with issues of corruption and transparency, it is valid to speculate whether the current reform agenda and economic liberalization process will have an impact on Libya's unique system of direct democracy, bringing about changes, which will lead to "good governance" as defined by many western intellectuals and commentators. Put in another way, as Libya opens itself up to FDI, will the forces of globalization collide with Libya's present system of government?

The first point to consider is that it was the application of the sanctions in themselves, applied by external forces, which have led to Libya's economic and academic marginalization for the past two decades. It is conceivable that if there had been a free flow into Libya of international investment, knowledge and technology, as well modern perceptions about governance and economics throughout the sanctions period, accompanied by the inevitable changes in society and expectations brought about by these factors, they themselves might have led to changes in the views of Libyan citizens as well as Libya's policy makers, and possibly the Libyan political system.

It was in fact the frank admission of Col. Qadhafi himself, at the General People's Congress in January 2000, which in fact kick-started the economic reformation process, with he himself appealing again in 2003 for a massive privatization programme, to include the highly inefficient public sector, as well as the oil sector itself. This was an acceptance that an overstaffed centralized bureaucracy had forgotten the rest of Libya, concentrating expenditure and development in Tripoli and Benghazi, largely neglecting the rest of the vast country. After his appeal, changes in the system led to the creation of 32 decentralized Sha'abiyat, subsequently reduced to 20, with significant regional power and political autonomy, and the ability to decide on development expenditure and collection of taxes. But again, in this connection, the present vague definitions of the relative powers of the Sha'abiyat (Provincial Governments) in relation to the Libyan Executive (The General People's Committee) have also led to increasing levels of corruption at both provincial and senior government levels.

Many international commentators also argue that there is no free press in Libya; at the same time, many foreign observers fail to realize that Arab language newspapers at the Sha'abiyat level such as, to mention a minor example, the *Ajdabia Weekly Newspaper* routinely criticize the government and its expenditure and policies, while the previous Libyan Prime Minster was regularly, on Libyan National TV, subject to harsh criticism, as well as through his own website, where his privatization policies, among other matters, were routinely questioned and attacked.

Undoubtedly, in many ways the media is the key to dealing with corruption issues in Libya and elsewhere, and the increasing importance of Arab TV sattelite stations such as Al Jazeera in defining public opinion "on the street", which are available to all Libyans with computers, TV, and the Internet, cannot be ignored. Through these, the Libyan public is being made increasingly aware of the direct effects of corruption on their individual lives, and attacks on corruption and corruptors continues to be a central theme of almost every contemporary Libyan discussion on politics and development.

In this regard, three General People's Committee Resolutions of 1 October 2006 are particularly important. The first Resolution, No. 394, is related to the establishment of regulations concerning taxation declarations of Libyan citizens, requiring them to provide a tax declaration of their annual income and assets, as well as those they support. This resolution provides that every citizen should have a tax file with a special number, and requires the taxation department to provide declaration forms at all its offices and branches all over Libya.

The second Resolution, No. 395, provides for the formation of a committee to verify such declarations, to be chaired by the Chief of the Supreme Court. The committee will assume the task of reviewing tax declarations of those selected for the General People's Congress, those occupying leadership positions in all sectors, and those heading major institutions, public companies, and medical and educational institutions. The resolution obliges the above-mentioned categories to submit declarations of their annual income and assets, including real estate, farms, animal wealth, and other economic activities.

The third Resolution, No. 396, provides for the setting up of committees in all public sectors to review financial advantages such as cars, fixed, and mobile telephones enjoyed by those occupying leadership positions.

In issuing all of these resolutions, the Libyan Cabinet appealed to all citizens to produce such information in the spirit of complete transparency. It seems that finally, with this key legislation, the Libyan authorities are seriously coming to terms with corruption in high places.

11.5 A Proliferation of Funds, 2005–2006

One noticeable development in Libya since the crude oil price started rocketing in early 2005 has been a series of development funds set up by the government. These, in addition to the Oil Reserve Fund (ORF), originally established in 1995, were set up to cushion government expenditure from vagaries in the international crude oil price, and to shield the budget from political pressure to spend when oil revenue increases significantly. In practice, it receives all oil revenues above a reference oil price, which was US $22 in 2004, while in 2005 it increased to US $26.

In a study on petroleum in Libya and economic diversification (Otman and Karlberg 2005), the authors pointed to a range of literature on the economic phenomenon, labeled variously as the "Dutch Disease", the "Resource Curse", or the "Paradox of Plenty", in which many nations favoured with rich natural resources have been tempted to spend the revenues in an unproductive and unsustainable manner. They showed its incidence in countries ranging from the Netherlands, Venezuela, Saudi Arabia, and Nigeria.

In attempts to avoid mistakes of the past, several countries have set up Non-renewable resource Funds (NRFs), often known as oil stabilization funds. The aim of such funds is to separate the extraction of petroleum from the use of revenues derived from it. By retaining a certain percentage of revenues when the cash flow from the extraction of non-renewable resources is high, because of high prices and levels of production, these countries have attempted to deal with two policy challenges. First, to protect the domestic economy from the negative impact of sharp and unpredictable variations in the oil price and revenues. Secondly, to preserve part of the country's wealth and to distribute it between the present and future generations.

11.5.1 The National Development Fund

In April 2003, in a conference entitled "Petroleum and the Libyan Economy" at Attahady University in the city of Sirte, the Libyan leader proposed that the government should set up a fund to save and preserve a high proportion of income from the petroleum sector, and use it for future investment, perhaps in other development sectors, on behalf of future generations of Libyans. The Libyan Government went ahead with this proposal and created the country's petroleum fund, known as the National Investment Portfolio or National Development Fund. In principle, at least, the fund is similar to Norway's State Petroleum Fund (SPF), Chile's Copper Stabilization Fund (CSF), Oman's State General Reserve Fund (SGRF), and Kuwait's Reserve Fund for Future Generations (RFFG).

This fund, through the General People's Committee Resolution No. 6 of 2005 "On Establishing the National Investment Portfolio", was duly set up with an initial capital of US $10 billion, utilizing reserve funds held by the Central Bank of Libya. In this connection it is worth noting that Libya, on a smaller scale, already has considerable expertise in this type of investment through Social Security Law No. 13 of 1980, which established the Social Security Fund with the status of "a public juridical person, and an autonomous budget, distinct from the State General budget as well as independent accounts".

Looking in detail at the provisions of the 13 Articles on two pages, which make up the legal guidelines for the composition of fund members, its management, objectives, and auditing, there are several critical comments which we feel need to be made in view of the crucial importance of this fund for Libya and future generations of Libyans, relating primarily to issues of management, governance, transparency, and accountability.

Regarding the management guidelines and strategy for the fund, these are contained in Article 3, which states:

> The fund is to invest based on policies and technical standards approved by the Libyan Investment Council, taking the following into consideration:
> - It should focus on investments of a commercial nature.
> - It should focus on investment in fields which give large returns
> - It should be protected against known or expected risks.
> - Investments should be liquid to a greater or lesser extent.

Our general comments here are that the investment objectives are far too vague, and in certain cases, misleading. For example, the second item above states that the fund should focus its investments in fields that give large returns, but as every economist knows, large returns mean large risks, and it is the job of the Administration Committee to minimize risks by investing in areas as risk free as possible, as well as spreading these risks across a wide range of investments.

In fact, as in the Norwegian Petroleum Fund, a strong case may exist for placing the fund's assets abroad, since investment in domestic non-governmental financial assets could overheat or cause imbalance to the domestic economy. It is important that specific operational asset management guidelines are laid down to allocate the fund's resources. Again, for example, the Norwegian Petroleum Fund is currently invested in financial instruments outside Norway, where 60 per cent of the portfolio is allocated to fixed income instruments and 40 per cent to equities. The fund is also very well diversified. The equity portfolio has a geographical split of 50 per cent in Europe and 50 per cent in America and Asia/Oceania. For the fixed income portfolio, 55 per cent is invested in Europe, 35 per cent in America, and 10 per cent in Asia/Oceania. Within the regions, the portfolio is distributed between countries according to market capitalization weighting (Norges Bank Investment Management, 2005).

Article 4 states that the fund "is allowed to finance public projects with the portfolio funds as loans if decided by GPC, providing that the decision is based on the interest rate, the payback period and the finance method".

From the economic point of view we believe that in the management of the Libyan Development Fund, it will be crucially important to avoid "moral hazard" type problems, in particular with the public sector. When public entities know that the central government is in a financial position to bail them out, the classical problem of "moral hazard" arises. Because in the past in Libya, substantial petroleum wealth has weakened financial discipline in state enterprises, as we have seen in detail in our earlier case study of El Brega Oil Marketing Company in Chap. 9, where the management assumed that the central government would always provide support, no matter how inefficient the enterprise was. These "moral hazard" problems associated with Libya's "from the cradle to the grave" welfare system, may also interfere with the proper administration of the fund.

Regarding the management of the fund, Article 6 states: "The Portfolio Fund shall to be managed by an Administration Committee established by a decision of the Secretary of General Peoples Committee, based on advice from those members of the Libyan Investment Council specializing in financial, economic and management sectors."

With respect to the composition of the Administration Committee, the authors believe that it is commendable that the fund's management has been separated from the management of the Central Bank of Libya, and in fact should be as far as possible non-political and free from political interference. We believe that it is also desirable for the fund's Administration Committee to contain knowledgeable members from professions that deal with economic and investment issues on a regular basis, such as, for example, a Senior Economist from the Economic Research Centre at Garyounis University, or a senior practising company auditor, or senior managers from LAFICO or LAFB. Ideally, third party external financial experts should also be involved, as is done through the Norwegian Petroleum Fund's Annual Performance Evaluation Report, undertaken by independent international consultants on behalf of the Norwegian Ministry of Finance for the Fund's annual operations (Mercer Investment Consulting 2006).

Regarding the auditing of the fund, Article 11 states that "The fund accounts shall be subject to auditing by the Financial and Technical Control Secretariat, or any independent body assigned to make such an audit as agreed between the Financial and Technical Control Secretariat and the Portfolio Administration Committee, according to regulations of Law No. 11 for the year 1425 (1995) on reorganizing the Financial and Technical Control Secretariat".

Initially it should be noted that there appears to be no stipulation for annual accounts, surely a major omission. Secondly, by limiting the auditing of the fund to government-controlled and nominated organizations, we note that the fund is not subject to independent audit or to an objective third party evaluation of the fund's investment performance. In fact not only should there be at least an annual audit, but frequent disclosure and reporting of the principles governing the fund, its inflows and outflows, and the allocation and return on assets should be made on a regular basis. Ideally, in the digital society of which Libya hopes to become a member, the Fund's accounts should be completely transparent and made available to any Libyan citizen to see through a web portal specially designed for the Fund and its operations.

We believe that the Libyan government in setting up the National Development Fund has given Libya the opportunity to turn petroleum wealth into long-term gains and advantages for future generations of Libyans. Positive results from the future management of the fund will depend on Libya's ability to learn from the mistakes of other resource abundant nations, and a well-structured and effective fund investment strategy, which is free from political interference, and independently audited.

11.5.2 Libya Africa Investment Fund

As was stated in Chap. 2, a major shift in Libya's foreign policy took place in the 1990s, with its focus moving away from the Arab heartland towards Africa. In 1998 the Libyan leader declared that the Libyan state-owned radio "Voice of the Arab World" was to be renamed "Voice of Africa". During this shift there was a pronounced impetus towards Libya's involvement, indeed attempted leadership, in African groupings such as the AU, Cen-Sad, and Comesa. The Libyan leader's role in resolving disputes between African nations, as the "Elder Statesman" of Africa, as for example in the ongoing dispute between Chad and Sudan over

Darfur in 2005–2006 through mediation and dialogue, was primarily aimed at regional stability, but undoubtedly Libya's vision of a United Africa also underscored these initiatives.

In many ways the economic counterpart of this geopolitical shift in Libya's external relations was the establishment of the Libya Africa Investment Fund (LAIF) through Resolution No. 15 of 6 February 2002. Article 3 of this decision permitted the LAIF to invest in a wide variety of economic sectors, including tourism (hotels, camps, valliges, etc.), the financial sector, agriculture projects, oil and gas exploration and exploitation, mining, transportation, trade (export and import), communication services, and industrial projects and manufacturing.

The ambitious scale of the fund is illustrated by Article 9, which provided it with seed capital of US $5 billion to be drawn from Libyan capital reserves, and which instructed the Ministry of Finance to transfer this amount to the fund. In Article 12 the new fund was given authority to manage the affairs of the African Investment Company, Tamoil Africa (African Oil Investment Company), as well as all Libyan shareholdings in the African Bank for Development and Trade. Article 13 provided for the Chairman of the fund to submit annual accounts, as well as annual activities and progress report, to the Libyan Council of Investment.

11.5.3 Economic and Social Development Fund

Soon after the establishment of the LAIF, the General People Committee's Resolution No. 18 of 14 February 2006 established the Economic and Social Development Fund (ESDF) as a financially independent body directed by the Libyan Cabinet.

Article 2 defined the activities of this fund in three main areas. First, it was to participate in dealing with the effects of the natural disasters occurring both within and outside Libya. Secondly, it was to participate in settling all the external legal obligations of Libya such as, for example, the final payment of the Lockerbie Settlement. Finally, and most importantly, it was to participate and assist in financing domestic projects for economic and social development.

Article 3 defined the future sources of income to the ESDF as follows:

1. Any bonuses derived from agreements signed with the IOCs for hydrocarbon exploration and exploitation in Libya
2. Any unfrozen Libyan assets held abroad in foreign institutions as a result of the lifting of the US sanctions in 2004
3. Any funds allocated from fees generated by Administrative Contracts
4. Income generated from the fund's own services and investments
5. Any income from ESDF deposits held in Libyan domestic banks
6. Any funds allocated from the Post and Communications services
7. Any charitable donations or gifts that the Management Committee agrees to accept from Libyan businessmen

Article 4 provided that the fund was to be administered by a committee appointed by the General People Committee (Cabinet), while Article 6 stated that the fund's capital was to be held in independent accounts in Libyan banks. Article 10 provided that the auditing of the fund would be in line with applicable Libyan laws and procedures.

In relation to the ESDF, a new GPC Decision, No. 210 of 5 September 2006, was approved, allocating US $4 billion to the fund, and directing its Management Committee to invest this amount in the form of shares for the benefit of families deprived of wealth through illegal appropriation of their property, mainly during the early phases of the revolutionary period.

11.5.4 Libyan Investment Corporation

A further, and in many ways the most significant fund, the Libyan Investment Corporation, was established through Resolution No. 205 of 2006 dated on 28 August to be located in Tripoli. Article 3 of this Resolution specified that the initial capital of the LIC was to be US $250 million, divided into 250,000 shares, with each share valued at US $100.

Article 4 highlighted the aims of the LIC, which were to invest the capital allocated to the LIC by the GPC (Libyan Cabinet), in order to generate more revenues to the government. Its underlying aim was to diversify the sources of national income away from overdependence on hydrocarbons, and support the treasury by limiting the effects of oil price fluctuations on a periodic basis.

Article 5 of this Resolution empowered the LIC to manage and invest funds originating from:

1. The Oil Reserve Fund
2. The National Development Fund
3. LAIF
4. ESDF
5. Libyan Financial Investment Company
6. Tamoil
7. Any financial surplus realized from the implementation of the annual general budget
8. Any other finance allocated by the GPC (Cabinet)

Article 6 of this Resolution placed the management and direction of the Libyan Company of Foreign Investment directly under the control of the LAIF, effectively removing the former from the control of the Secretariat of Finance. In Article 7, the LIC was granted the authority to invest its capital in all economically productive sectors, and the corporation was given the right to buy shares in worldwide institutions and projects in all sectors.

Most importantly, Article 20 cancelled Resolution No. 65 of 2003 regarding the establishment of Libyan Investment Council, and directed that all its employees would be reassigned to the new LIC. Significantly, it also cancelled Resolution No. 6 of 2005 regarding the establishment of The National Development Fund, the shortcomings of which were discussed extensively in Sect. 1.1.

The motives of the Libyan government behind the proliferation of funds discussed above, which have emerged since the rapid increase in oil prices in early 2005, are undoubtedly based on a genuine desire to stimulate and diversify the Libyan economy, to open up new opportunities for Libyan businesses and entrepreneurs, both at home and abroad. In the long term, their rationale is to prepare for the time when hydrocarbon production alone can no longer guarantee Libya's prosperity. The arrival of this time may be closer than many in Libya appreciate as discussed later in this chapter.

But their rapid proliferation and off-budget nature would appear to limit the comprehensiveness and transparency of the Libyan fiscal system, although at least extra budgetary expenditure from the original stabilization fund, the Oil Reserve Fund, has been abolished "as a first step towards improving transparency in and consolidation of public finances" (IMF 2006). In the same report the IMF has recommended, in a special appendix, the formation of a Stabilization and Savings Fund (SSF) for Libya to replace the ORF and to "achieve long-term fiscal sustainability and for intergenerational equity" with two main objectives, the first to reduce the impact of volatile revenue on public finances and the economy, and the second to save part of the oil revenue for future generations. But clearly the recent establishment and the massive scale of the initial funding and sources of income for the LAIF, the ECDF, and most importantly the Libyan Investment Corporation, all of which operate as extra budget entities reporting to the Libyan Cabinet, would appear to run contrary to the overall objectives of the IMF's proposed SSF.

Undoubtedly these funds have an important role to play in Libya's economic transition, especially in the context of financing Libyan entrepreneurs and kick-starting economic diversification away from the country's excessive reliance on hydrocarbon revenues. There is also a case for the LIC to invest heavily not only abroad, but in Libya itself in the mushrooming tourist industry, as well as in PPSs with foreign partners in addressing Libya's massive infrastructure deficit, as discussed extensively in Chap. 5. Similarly there is a strong case for its role in the massive expansion needed in the housing sector, now seriously pressurized both by demographic factors and the flood of foreigners into Libya as the economic transition builds up speed.

Clearly, also the LAIF, if managed prudently, has excellent potential to redress Libya's economic and diplomatic balance in Africa, where Libyan foreign policy over many years has aided a large number of African countries, earning the country a lot of friends and supporters, and providing Libya with easy access to huge investment opportunities as this vast continent continues to develop. Similarly, the expertise of both the LNOC and Tamoil Africa Holdings Limited (TAHL) is already tapping into significant hydrocarbon-related investments in Africa, such as TAHL's development of a network of service stations in Burkina Faso, Chad, Mali, Niger, and Eritrea, together with the accompanying logistics and facilities.

But unless and until there is greater transparency regarding the sources of funding, investments, annual performance and returns, and accountability, many observers will continue to question the operational efficiency and risk-aversion capabilities of these recently established funds. In this regard the transparency and legal architecture surrounding the establishment, operations, reporting functions, and third-party evaluation of the annual performance of the Norwegian Petroleum Fund, renamed the Government Pension Fund on 1 Janury 2006, are matters worthy of consideration by the Libyan policy makers.

11.6 Non-sustainability in the Oil and Gas Industry

Since the beginning of Libya's oil industry in the late 1950s, the Libyan government has consistently failed to decouple the Libyan economy from an almost total dependence on revenue from oil and gas exports, with potentially disastrous results for future generations of Libyans.

In Libya today, 50 years after its enactment in 1955, the Libyan Petroleum Law No. 25 is still the basic legislation, which covers investment in the petroleum sector, including the current EPSA IV rounds. No new oil concessions have been granted in the past five decades, and the majority of the original concessions in fact ended in 2005, their maximum duration being 50 years.

For several years now, the Libyan government has been drafting a new Petroleum Law. The long delay in its enactment has caused a certain amount of consternation, but one of the main barriers to it from becoming law was in fact the existence of the sanctions. These, in theory at least, have prevented the Libyan government from conducting consultation processes with many countries/potential investors, including the United States.

Another reason for delays in the enactment of the new law is perhaps a growing awareness in the highest government and industry circles in Libya that such an important piece of legislation, which can impact Libya's prosperity and economic performance for many years to come, needs to be drafted and structured in a very comprehensive way, especially in view of the vast changes in global investment trends and fiscal terms in the oil industry, as well as the new geopolitics of the post-Soviet era and the global emergence of the CIS oil and gas producers.

In our view there are certain crucial issues that need to be addressed in the new Petroleum Law. If these are handled well, this will in itself ensure that the law and its enforcement will emerge as a powerful driver towards Libyan industrial diversification. If handled poorly, investment will still come to Libya, but Libyan economic expansion and diversification will be jeopardized.

Although Libya has been exporting LNG since 1971, and it was in fact the second country in the world after Algeria in 1964 to become an LNG exporter, in legal terms an anomalous situation exists in that, mainly for reasons associated with the geography of Libya and early hydrocarbon technology, there is no provision in the original Petroleum Law No. 25 for independent gas developments. In spite of this the Libyan government has attempted to develop a gas fiscal policy to respond to lifting the sanctions in 2004, and sought to boost production capacity to increase both exports and domestic utilization. For example, LNOC outlined a formal framework incorporating clauses for gas in the EPSA IV licensing round. These were announced as part of the modified EPSA III that had already existed for oil exploration and production. This restriction on gas development in previous EPSAs had in the past been cited as a deterrent for IOCs wishing to participate in Libya's gas future. However, the new EPSA IV terms were much more encouraging for gas than those previously available.

The authors believe, however, that this is not the answer to addressing Libya's future role as a major global gas supplier, as well as dealing with complex pricing and capacity issues relating to the use of gas as feedstock for Libya's rapidly rising domestic and industrial consumption, which will be a key factor in Libya's future industrial diversification. Libya has to develop and propose attractive new and separate fiscal terms for gas projects, for it is clear that the gas sector is poised to move rapidly forward with both foreign and domestic demands set to rise.

In our view the key to achieving Libya's ambitious long-term objectives in gas extraction, processing, and export is that any uncertainty relating to potential new gas developments needs to be resolved by having a comprehensive section covering gas in the new Petroleum Law. It should provide for the reinstatement of the Gas Projects Administration or a similar entity, detached from LNOC and having a separate fiscal and investment regime, with full control and authority in relation to gas exploration, development, production, distribution, and marketing.

This is in fact the situation in other major gas producers such as Malaysia (e.g. Malaysia LNG Tiga Sdn.Bhd. is a JV between Petronas, Nippon Oil (Netherlands) B.V., Shell Gas B.V., the Sarawak State Government and Occidental LNG (Malaysia)) and Qatar (Qatar Industrial Gases Company is a JV between Qatar Petroleum, Qatar Nitrogen, and the France-based Air Liquide Middle East), where the law permits the structuring of joint ventures with the government, often in combination with major foreign gas buyers/consumers, in view of the complexity and long-term planning and financing of gas projects. It is only by doing this that the real potential of the Libyan gas sector can be unlocked, placing Libya in a position to compete against current gas mega-developments being planned and initiated in Kuwait, Saudi Arabia, Algeria, and the CIS nations. Last but not least, the synergy and downstream manufacturing capability supplied by a well-regulated and efficient gas sector will also serve to drive the industrial and diversification processes in Libya.

With regard to Libya's key petroleum sector, the most recent estimates, based on the data from OPEC, BP, and the LNOC itself, put Libya's proven oil reserves at 39.12 billion barrels, a level achieved from the commencement of the industry in the 1950s until the present time. They have then estimated that Libya's total extraction from the commencement of oil production in 1961 up to the end of 2005 is 24.5 billon barrels, leaving remaining proven reserves currently at 14.62 billion barrels. We emphasize that these are proven reserves that do not include yet-to-find oil, which, as industry experts have estimated, could amount to 2.5 billion barrels (Hallet 2002).

Based on these figures, it is believed that the Libyan government's present insistence on doubling production from the existing levels of around 1.5 million–3 million bbl/day in as short a period as possible is a policy that needs to be reconsidered very carefully. The authors point out, for example, that it was the Libyan government itself in the early 1970s, which was concerned about linking reserves with production, insisting on sustainable and conservatively managed production levels. At this time it blamed and in fact penalized international oil companies for production excesses, but currently its policy appears to ignore or forget the crucial reserves/production ratio. The authors propose that from a policy aspect any increase in production should be linked to a compensatory increase in reserves.

If, for example, the Libyan Government went ahead with its plans to increase production to 3 million bbl/day, this would mean that Libya's remaining proven reserves as at January 2006 will last only for the next 13 years. If on the other hand current output is maintained at a constant 1.6 million bbl/day, proven reserves will last approximately for the next 25 years. These are sobering figures for Libya's policy makers.

Not only this but if, under the present EPSA IV fiscal terms, LNOC has to turn to the state exchequer to finance the major new JV investments to attain this level of 3 million bbl/day, the question arises "what will remain for diversification and development of other key sectors, for example infrastructure, tourism, agriculture, manufacturing, and transportation, where investment is also crucial, not to mention the massive investments required to upgrade the petroleum and gas downstream sectors, severely rundown during the sanctions period ?"

We also feel that the Libyan government should also carefully review and considerably tighten up contract terms with regard to in-country procurement of personnel, goods, and services. In terms of production cost per barrel of oil in Libya, but depending on a variety of factors, we can say that roughly 50 per cent of this production cost is made up of Operating expenditure (Opex) as opposed to Capital expenditure (Capex). In annual terms this means that, at production rate of 1.6 million bbl/day at an average Libyan production cost of US $5/bbl, there is an annual OPEX expenditure of approximately $2.7 billion in Libya. As Libya's planned production rises to 2 million and then to 3 million bbl/day, these figures rise to $3.6 and $5.4 billion, respectively.

In current fiscal regimes worldwide, there is a varying legal requirement for Opex to be expended within the operating country. Under the existing Iranian buy-back contract, for example, the NIOC stipulates that 50 per cent of Opex must be sourced within Iran, be it composed of goods, manpower, or services. In the early 1960s, when Norway had no indigenous oil industry, there was no possibility of IOCs procuring oilfield-related goods and services in Norway, apart from non-technical supplies such as, say, food or shipping; but by 1972, the Norwegian Ministry of Industry had established the Goods and Services Office, which acted as a watchdog to control the oil companies' contracting and procurement activities: prior to tender invitations, the operator had to announce the tender schedule and companies to be invited. The Ministry's role was to ensure that qualified Norwegian companies were included on the bidders list.

The strong emphasis placed on the Norwegian content made it a crucial factor for all bidders; it was a key criteria when evaluating companies competing for new acreage. The Ministry's policy was to be transparent in its enforcement of the procurement policy. Moreover, with an observer present in all licensed groups, the Ministry secured insight into all the operators' contracting activities. A high level of cooperation between the authorities and the operators, together with the contracting and supply industry, was essential in developing the high local content in Norway, which at times came to exceed 70 per cent. Under the Norwegian licence terms for the IOCs, it was mandatory to transfer skills and competence to the Norwegian companies. Initially personnel from Statoil, Norsk, Hydro and Saga would participate in the oil majors' training courses, receiving on-the-job training in their overseas operations. The majors were forced to recruit young Norwegian engineers for overseas training for a significant period, before they returned home to "Norwegianize" their organizations (Noreng 2004).

Today it is evident that the transfer of technology and the cooperation in research and development in Norway has been a resounding success in terms of petroleum policy. By forcing oil companies to transfer competence and to cooperate in the development of new technology, Norway has assumed the role of a leader in international petroleum development.

By providing insights into the laws of other petroleum-producing nations, we can learn valuable lessons for Libya. The new Petroleum Law is the perfect opportunity for the Libyan government to get really serious about in-country procurement. Traditionally Libya has imported most equipment, key personnel, components, and spare parts for its petroleum industry, since this provides short-term solutions – by awarding a contract to a foreign firm, the problem can be solved. For Libya to diversify and truly benefit from its oil and gas industry, it is time for this "quick-fix" mentality to go. In future, in-country procurement legislation must ensure that there is no leakage. Although difficult at first, such an approach will eventually mean that Libya can develop a genuine oil supply and services industry, which will, in the long term, serve markets in neighbouring oil-producing countries. If the IOCs state that it cannot be done in Libya, listing the usual reasons of lack of infrastructure, qualified personnel, communications, etc. then of course they can invest their funds elsewhere in a wide variety of global hydrocarbon regions and situations.

In Libya the petroleum industry operates on government-owned land. It extracts depleting resources from under the ground and under the sea. In blunt terms, it is the responsibility of any government to ensure that this process is compensated for by building other assets to secure income for the people in the future. As with other global fiscal regimes, the new Petroleum Law must address important issues relating to safety and environmental protection in a petroleum industry, which is by nature a polluter. This is not only for the benefit of the present Libyan population, but for future generations. In Europe and the United States, new PSC's stipulate very demanding terms for field abandonment; expenditure on this phase can make up a large percentage of a project cost. In a Libyan context, the new Petroleum Law presents a perfect opportunity for these important new environmental concerns to be written into any new contracts. As we noted in Chap. 10, issues such as water and air pollution, waste disposal, biodiversity, desertification, and environmental awareness and training are all areas that the new legislation should address. This will ensure that Libya's valuable resources are safeguarded for future generations. Additionally, in the developed nations, the environment is big business, with environmental consultancies and companies involved in, for example, water purification and waste disposal technology and other green businesses being some of the fastest growing companies in their economies. A strong environmental policy will in itself be a powerful driver of diversification and sustainability in the Libyan oil industry in particular and economy in general.

12 Assessing Libya's Post-sanctions Initiatives

12.1 The Journey Towards Economic Transformation

Since as early as 1997, with the introduction of Law No. 5 of 1997, Libya's leaders have embarked on a journey of economic transformation, which will have far-reaching effects both on Libyans themselves and in defining Libya's place in the modern world. In successive chapters of this work we have examined Libyan history, trends in social policy, Libya's infrastructure deficit, the privatization and economic diversification initiatives, and the country's efforts to attract FDI. Now the authors would like to critically assess the progress, to date, of these recent attempts to reshape the Libyan economy and with it, the face of Libyan society.

Credit must be given to the Libyan leadership for the country's undoubted achievements in the social sphere, where health, housing, education, and a social security system were installed in the three decades, providing an enviable quality of life to all Libyans, and as has been noted, through a generous immigration policy, to many other immigrants from its Arab and African neighbours. But there are clear signs that higher expectations and demographic pressures are increasing the already onerous financial burden of providing a cradle to the grave welfare system, and of maintaining an inefficient and grossly overstaffed public sector, which are simply becoming too great to bear. Fortunately, since early 2005, the rising trend in the international crude oil price has temporarily provided relief, but the long-term dangers of relying too heavily on a non-sustainable commodity are only too apparent.

As discussed, particularly from 2003 onwards, the government has pursued a series of inter-related policies aimed at both lightening this burden and diversifying the economy away from overdependence on hydrocarbons. However, apart from the hydrocarbon sector itself, which represents a unique and historically distinct Libyan investment sector, total FDI in Libya in both the tourist and the non-tourist sectors amounted, at end-August 2006, to only approximately US $6.9 billion, a mere trickle when compared to global FDI, projected to reach US $1 trillion in 2006 (Economist Intelligence Unit September, 2006). Although it is still early in the transformation process to judge, this appears to suggest that the reform programme is failing to deliver expected results.

In some important respects there have been significant failures to integrate many parts of the reform package into a comprehensive and unified whole, which means that often reform initiatives are out of step with each other. Fiscal and budgetary matters are also complicated by the often conflicting roles of the Central Bank of Libya, the Ministry of Finance, and the major development funds established during the 2005–2006 period. While the intention to effect economic reform is undoubtedly present, implementing it has proved elusive and often confusing.

One prime example of this is the serious failure to overhaul the Libyan banking system as the crucial preliminary step to attract FDI, and to assist Libyan entrepreneurs in embarking on new projects or in resuscitating firms identified for privatization, which are basically on life-support systems. As discussed earrlier, the failure of the government to divest 50 per cent of the Al-Sahari Bank to Libyans in 2005–2006, ending up with only 15 per cent being divested, is a clear signal that public confidence in the system is extremely low. One of the primary malaises of the banking system is the massive quantity of non-performing loans on the books of Libyan government-owned banks (i.e. 90 per cent of the banking sector) accumulated over the years to public enterprise. In conventional banking terms, most of these banks would be classified as technically insolvent without temporary periodic transfusions from the government. Although, undoubtedly, the 2005 Banking Law No. 1 was approved to address these deficiencies, it should have been initiated much earlier in the reform cycle, both to inspire confidence and improve efficiency.

In other respects, the banking system, particularly in the publicly owned banks discussed in Chap. 8, is incredibly old fashioned, with no modern banking innovations such as cash machines, online banking or even, apart from a few cases, the issuance of credit cards. Similarly, the use of financial instruments such as corporate or mortgage bonds is non-existent, and the use of mutual funds is almost negligible. In this respect "financial deepening", defined as "the overall expansion in financial transactions as a result of the broadening of the products and terms offered by financial institutions, and of the diversification of the financial infrastructure" (Alami 2005), has yet to emerge in Libya.

Again, even for a Libyan, not to say a foreigner, to get a bank mortgage to purchase a house in Libya is impossible, while loan approval and disbursement is non-transparent. These are all important factors directly affecting the success rate of attracting FDI to Libya, since as discussed earlier in Chaps. 3 and 7, such lack of depth in financial markets is a strong disincentive to large FDI investments. Again, the potential of the insurance industry for both adding depth to the financial system and driving economic diversification does not appear to be grasped by the Libyan authorities, with total premium accounting for less than 1 per cent of GDP (World Bank 2006).

Similarly, the failure of the Libyan authorities to create a stock exchange or equity market as a precursor to its crucial privatization programme is yet another case of poor sequencing. By establishing private stock exchanges before embarking on privatization, both Morocco and Jordan were able to give the process a kick-start, attracting a significant amount of foreign capital and achieving better value for privatized units to their respective governments. Although this issue has now been addressed, as discussed earlier, its actual establishment and operations must be fast-tracked to give the privatization programme at least some chance of success.

With regard to the privatization programme itself, it appears now to have run into serious difficulties, as discussed in some detail in Chap. 6. Had the Libyan authorities really done their homework, there would have known clear lessons concerning the do's and don'ts underlying a successful privatization exercise, which were listed in Sect. 6.1. It may be that without an efficient banking system and a Libyan stock exchange, as discussed above, it was doomed to failure in any case, but there were a series of errors made in its preparation and early implementation. One lesson learned from as early as the Thatcher years in the UK was that without powerful and sustained political support at the highest levels, the privatization process, because it affects so many people and so many different stakeholders, can be easily derailed. The changes made in 2005, which moved the responsibility for directing the affairs of the GBOT from the Libyan PM to the Ministry of Economy, Trade and Investment, and the subsequent removal of the architect of the programme, Dr. Shukri Ghanem in March 2006, as head of the Libyan Cabinet, suggested that this high-level support was wavering.

Similarly, setting schedules and naming firms for privatization far in advance tends to be a self-destructive process. It puts significant pressure on the implementors of the programme, who may be tempted to cut corners to meet schedules or alert vested intersets or obstructing parties to prepare plans to undermine it. Privatization is not a one-off component of an economic transformation initiative, but a continuous process, basically without end. Because it involves so many issues, financial, human, economic, and political, it cannot and should not be rushed, as the disastrously flawed Menem privatization programme in Argentina adequately demonstrated.

Again, as touched on in Chap. 6, one of the main issues, that of employees made redundant by privatization, appears not to have been either seriously or comprehensively handled by the Libyan authorities. The provision of safety nets, either in the form of compensation based on the years of employment or as a lump sum to enable the redundant employee to establish a new business or at least survive reasonably well until a new opportunity came along, has not been seriously contemplated or put in place. Similarly, career repositioning programmes or new and updated vocational training programmes, to bring, in particular, young redundant employees up to the speed to satisfy the needs of foreign employers, have not yet been designed. This is understandable in a country where funds are in short supply, but in present day Libya, this is emphatically not the case.

So, too, the failure to arrange an initial "showcase" privatization in Libya, as was undertaken in Malaysia by Dr. Mahatir Mohammed in 1986 with the Kelang Container Terminal, was also a missed opportunity by the Libyan policy makers. Had, for example, a subsidiary of the LNOC such as the BOMC, as discussed in Chap. 9, with its vast landholdings and potentially profitable service outlets all over Libya, been privatized at a price well below its real market value, this could have changed public perceptions about the success of the process in general. It is still difficult, the authors believe, to predict the success or otherwise of Libya's privatization programme at this early stage. Many initial lessons have been learned, but it is believed that without the creation of a dedicated Ministry of Privatization, with strong political backing, the privatization process cannot succeed.

In addressing Libya's infrastructure deficit, comprehensively discussed in Chap. 5, the present economic transformation programme, if handled inclusively, also has the potential to achieve two key objectives. If infrastructure and economic transformation were formally linked through a National Infrastructure Redevelopment Plan, resulting from an infrastructure baseline study, substantial benefits would be achieved for both domestic and inward investment. As an example, Libya's tourism industry would be a direct beneficiary from improved road and rail infrastructure, while domestic industry, with, say European or US manufacturers using Libya as a manufacturing, assembly, or distribution point for the rest of Africa, would also benefit immensely from this.

At the same time, the growth of those sectors participating directly in the upgrading of the existing infrastructure such as construction, cement, building materials, and quarrying, would also enhance the diversification process. The improvements in the existing infrastructure, such as internal and transnational highways, housing, hospitals, airports, schools, and universities, and the provision of new infrastructure would have significant direct and indirect benefits to the Libyan economy. These would also make substantial contributions towards reducing unemployment, particularly among the under 25 year olds, a growing concern to the Libyan authorities, which has potentially destabilizing effects owing to the guaranteed jobs-for-life mentality of many Libyans.

In this connection the Libyan government itself or Libyan private companies have the potential, through the wide range and structure of PPPs which have emerged globally in the previous 20 years, to tap into technology and expertise to bring Libya's infrastructure completely up to the scratch. One beneficiary of such an approach could be the proposed national railway project discussed in Chap. 5, a 4,800 km trans-African rail network designed to link Tunisia and Egypt with a southern spur linking the Libyan cities of Sirte and Sebha. In the long term, it could extend further south into Chad and Niger. Although sidelined for many years, this project, estimated to cost US $9 billion, has now again been given national priority by Dr. Al-Baghdadi Ali al-Mahmoudi, the Libyan Prime Minister.

Another major issue that is presently blocking Libya's journey towards economic transformation is the subsidy system, discussed by the authors in Chaps. 4 and 9, relating to food and energy subsidies, whether made directly to the public as food or petroleum and natural gas products or indirectly to Libyan utilities such as GECOL in the form of subsidized heavy fuel and natural gas, enabling the provision of heavily subsidized electricity prices to Libyan industry and domestic consumers. At the Sha'abiyat level water is also completely subsidized and provided free to all Libyans.

As discussed at length in Chap. 4, there is no doubt that the food subsidy programme is both wasteful and wide open to abuse, particularly by foreign nationals entering Libya either as immigrants or traders, as well as being an expensive exercise for the government, amounting to LD 838.8 million in 2005 (NASCO 2006). Furthermore there is a strong evidence that Libyans themselves no longer wish it, preferring instead that an annual cash equivalent should be provided, either directly or through the wage system. In particular, the explicit subsidy programme has inculcated a dependence mentality, which Libya, if it is to make its way towards developed status, needs to shake off.

However, dealing with the petroleum product and electricity subsidies is a much more complex and politically contentious issue, as has been shown in many other countries such as Indonesia, for example, where it led directly to the fall of the Suharto administration in 2001. In Chap. 9 the authors proposed that the government should start seriously thinking about the future of GECOL, the state electricity provider, which is a major loss-maker without the ability to internally finance its own future expansion. The future efficiency of GECOL is absolutely crucial if Libya is to successfully attract FDI and turn out new products and services competitively.

To address these major fuel and energy subsidy issues, which possess in themselves the potential to undermine Libya's economic transformation plans, the authors believe that planning studies should now be undertaken aimed at the corporatization and eventual privatization, or at least partial divestment, of GECOL, enabling the company to operate in a purely commercial way in a deregulated market in the long term. Future operations should be determined by paying prices to the Libyan government for oil or natural gas, and charging electricity rates to its consumers, whether commercial or industrial, based on the international parity energy prices. In doing so, the government will stop paying huge annual subsidies to prop up a sick commercial entity, while the true commercial value of Libya's increasingly valuable hydrocarbon resources will be realized. Concurrently, Libyan consumers will realize that electricity, although a vital component of everyday life, comes at a cost much higher than the existing levels, and one that is set to increase.

In addition to the above, there are many practical issues related to the reform process, which need to be tackled. Among these are the difficult and time-wasting procedures for company formation, both for foreigners and Libyans themselves, the inefficient tax collection system, which is depriving the Libyan government of massive revenue, and the lack of a professionally operated statistical system to monitor the success of the reform process and justify, to the Libyan population, the need for unpopular policies. In total, there are many obstacles ahead on the road to economic liberalization, but lessons learned in 3 years since 2003 should be well taken. In particular, the very severe human resource constraints present at every level in Libyan organizations must be dealt with urgently, through a variety of development and training programmes linked fundamentally to the concept of a 30-year development plan discussed later in this chapter.

12.2 Appraising Libya's International Realignment

Libya's present rehabilitation and enhanced international status has not emerged overnight, but has been achieved as a result of a sustained diplomatic campaign by Tripoli, which started certainly as early as the early 1990s, during the Clinton administration. In 1993, for example, in an interview in Tripoli with the Rev. Jesse Jackson, the Libyan leader stated the following in reply to Jackson's question "What message would you like to send to President Clinton and to America tonight?"

> First of all, I think, to restore relations and normalize relations, and to exchange economic interests between the two countries; and the return of the American oil companies to Libya and the trade and investing in Libya and Libyan money in America. I think it is better than the sanctions and the escalation, the threats, the enmity. My

> advice to my Democratic friends in America this day is to look at the positive things instead of the negative things, and we open a new chapter (Jackson 1993).

The crippling effects of the sanctions on the Libyan people and Libya's crucial hydrocarbon sector undoubtedly played a major role in bringing about changes in Tripoli's international perspectives. As a Libyan researcher phrased it in 2003, "The impacts of the UN–US Sanctions on Libyan petroleum industry are quite visible; they imposed unaccountable damage and tragedy on a developing country whose citizens depended primarily on the export of oil to generate the means for their livelihood" (Otman 2003). As well as this, Col. Qadhafi himself, targeted within Libya in the 1980s and 1990s by Islamic militant organizations such as the Libyan Islamic Fighting Group and cognizant of events in neighbouring Algeria, was keenly aware, well before the 11 September 2001 Al-Qaeda attacks, of international Islamic terrorist networks and their potentially devastating impacts. This led to a serious re-evaluation of Libya's international alignments, and using the classical political adage "the enemy of my enemy is my friend", it became logical, even necessary, for Libya to reconstruct its foreign policy. Also, the world had changed immensely during the final two decades of the twentieth century, and Libya's policy makers were becoming increasingly aware that, in an era of globalization, the country had become marginalized and out of step with major advances in technology, as well as international trends in education, economic thinking, and business practices.

Libya's readmission into the global mainstream began in earnest in 1999, when Libya met a key UN Security Council demand by surrendering suspects in the Lockerbie Pan Am bombing to an international court, a move which led directly to the suspension of UN sanctions against Libya in April 1999. In the aftermath of the 11 September 2001 Twin Tower inferno, Col Qadhafi himself announced in a speech "we have been terrorized by what happened in America and we express our condolences to the American people who suffered from this unexpected catastrophe".

Libya's contributions were not, however, limited to words. As stated by the Libyan leader's son Saif al-Islam , "Being Arab, Libya has been far more adept than the West at infiltrating the fanatical groups that have been behind so much recent violence. The activities in our own country of cells linked organizationally and ideologically to extremism give us a shared interest with the West in stopping them" (al-Islam 2003). In the immediate aftermath of 11 September 2001, the Libyan government actively cooperated with international agencies in the war against terrorism (Anderson 2003).

Although Libya's publicly announced renunciation of WMD in 19 December 2003 caught much of the world's media by surprise, it was, in fact, the final chapter of a sustained diplomatic dialogue by Libya to rehabilitate the country and its international image. It is therefore clear that Libya's policy makers have successfully achieved a major diplomatic coup in reinstating the country to the international community; despite this, because of its negative international media portrayal, Libya's recent and rapid rapprochement has evidently staggered many observers.

Undoubtedly, however, in September 2006, Libya's international realignment and readmission to the international community of nations is a diplomatic and political reality, with western and media perceptions of the country rapidly changing, with most nations now having a diplomatic presence in Tripoli, or in the process of arranging for this. Libya's recent application to join the WTO, its wooing by the leaders of the EMP, and its key involvement in a variety of African regional groupings such as the AU, Cen-Sad, and Comesa, as discussed at length in Chaps. 2 and 8, together mean that Libya has many options in place. In the future, its international repositioning will mean that its ability to affect external events, particularly on the African continent, is much more significant than the small population of the country would suggest.

Undoubtedly it was the lifting of the US sanctions that was the major watershed in Libya's recent history. Signalling, as this did, that the United States was once again willing to extend the hand of friendship to Libya, it has made all things possible with regard to Libya's reform and modernization. The new US–Libyan rapprochement once again underscores the notion that politics is the art of the possible, while much speculation still surrounds the reasons for the rapidity of US–Libyan reconciliation. From the Libyan side, it was undoubtedly the culmination of a series of initiatives which, as was discussed, started as early as the Clinton administration. For the United States, it has been linked, among other factors, to the oil business and the stalled Middle East foreign policy of the Bush administration, anxious to score an important success in the Arab world.

Many international analysts look no further than oil – by providing access to Libya's valuable hydrocarbon assets to US companies, the lifting of the sanctions was a key policy decision linked to US future energy shortages. To support this view, they cite the oucome of the first EPSA IV bidding round, in which US companies won 11 of the 15 areas on offer, with Occidental either alone or as part of a bidding consortium getting 9 of these. This led to accusations that US companies had received favourable treatment, perhaps part of the horse trading surrounding the lifting of the sanctions. But the transparency of the bidding process, with bid opening conducted in public in the presence of the legal representatives of the bidders, precluded this. The facts were that Occidental's aggressive bidding strategy in offering the lowest percentage allocations for cost recovery, as well as the highest signature bonuses, placed them in the winning position in most areas offered.

Others hold that access to Libyan oil was a vital necessity for the United States because of the looming long-term shortages of oil supply, which holds only 2.5 per cent of the world-proven oil reserves. Traditionally the Middle East, and particularly Saudi Arabia, has provided a large share of total US gross petroleum imports. Middle East supplies to the United States amounted to 20.4 per cent in 2003, and are projected to increase to almost 30 per cent in 2025. For strategic reasons, to reduce vulnerability from overdependence on a single supplier, the United States imports oil from multiple sources including Canada, Mexico, Latin America, Africa, and the Middle East. This diversity of supplies means that in the mid-2000s, the United States is less vulnerable to disruption of oil supplies from one source (Bahgat 2006). So, the argument goes; by adding Libya as another supplier, the United States's long-term vulnerability would be lessened. In theory this sounds plausible, but the facts demonstrate that most Libyan oil ends up in Europe, not the United States, due to both traditional market patterns and geographical proximity.

The explanation underlying Libya's re-acceptance by the United States probably lies elsewhere, and is closely linked with the war against terrorism, the principal tenet of US foreign policy since 11 September 2001. By realigning Libya as an ally, the Bush administration was able to secure not only valuable Libyan intelligence on the activities of terrorist groups, as mentioned earlier, but also the crucial support and understanding of the Libyan leadership, particularly in Africa.

A prime example of this relates to the present situation in Somalia, where the anti-government Islamic Courts Council (ICC) is now in control of Mogadishu and most of South and Central Somalia. Readers may recollect that after the fall of the US-backed Siad Barre dictatorship in 1991, the Bush administration, in November 1992, sent 30,000 US troops to Somalia, ostensibly as a humanitarian mission to assist in the distribution of relief supplies. But as subsequent events highlighted, the US intervention can only be described as a military debacle, with the country pulling out its troops in March 1994, while UN forces were withdrawn a year later. Subsequently a viable Somali policy seemed to disappear from the US foreign agenda.

This is where the advantages of the US–Libyan rapprochement can be seen for the present Bush administration. In fact, on 9 September 2006, Somalia's senior opposition Islamic leaders, Sheikh Hassan Dahir Aweys and Sheikh Sharif Ahmed, flew to Tripoli in a special plane sent by Libya for the occasion of the 7th anniversary celebrations of the creation of the African Union, a Libyan initiative of 1999. The abilities of the Libyan leadership to broker talks and resolve African regional issues before they can flare into major international conflicts may in fact be one of the main pay-offs for the United States in bringing Libya into the international fold. Because of the stature and high regard in which Col. Gadhafi is held by most African countries, including President Obasanjo of Nigeria and President Mubarak of Egypt, the two most populous African nations, the United States has secured a valuable ally in Africa, where traditionally its foreign policy and influence, when compared to France and the UK, have been weak. It is also highly probable that the Libyan leader, with his intimate knowledge of the Arab world, will also prove, in the end, to be a useful ally for the United States in resolving Palestine/Israeli standoff. Despite the rhetoric of the past, Libya's stance towards Israel appears to be softening.

12.3 Consolidating Libya's Repositioning – The Need for a 30-Year Plan

In the early 1950s, Libya's first comprehensive economic plan emerged from the recommendations of the United Nations Mission to Libya, in conjunction with the associated meeting of Experts on the Libyan Financial, Monetary and Development Problems (Farley 1971). Their joint recommendations focused on the need for an initial 6-year plan, with heavy emphasis on training, education, and agricultural research, as well as on public works and utilities, the latter primarily to address the repair of the extensive damage inflicted on the country, which was one of the main theatres of the Second World War. It was determined that the initial 6-year plan would be followed by four subsequent 6-year plans, bringing the country forward to 1981.

As we have seen, the massive social reconstruction that succeeded the change of government in 1969, combined with the country's new oil wealth, led to a radical shift in the scale and pace of development in Libya. However, this too was accomplished within the framework of a series of development plans, which covered the periods 1970–1972, 1973–1975, 1976–1980, 1981–1985, and 1986–1989. Thereafter, however, as a result of the increasing impacts of the UN and US sanctions, and the falling trend in the international crude oil price experienced for much of the 1990s, the use of long-term planning appeared to have fallen out of favour with Libya's policy makers. Annual budgets, known as development and transformation budgets, dealt with allocations and expenditure on sectoral development on a year-to-year basis. It can be said that in the period from 1990 to 2000, apart from the huge ongoing investment of the Great Manmade River Project, long-term planning for the country's social and infrastructure needs, in tune with demographic trends and rising consumer demands and expectations, was largely neglected.

The major shift towards decentralization, implemented by the creation of 32 Sha'abiyat with significant local autonomy in 2000, also meant that the coordination and integration of national planning was further compromised. This in fact was the unenviable situation faced by the new Libyan Cabinet in 2003, necessitating a complete overhaul of a stagnant and inward-looking Libyan economy, and the restructuring and repositioning of the country to face the challenges of an increasingly globalized world.

As discussed in considerable detail, there have been major economic initiatives undertaken by the Libyan government regarding, among other things, the progressive privatization of state-owned bodies, the liberalization of the financial and banking sector, the lifting of a wide range of import tariffs, as well as the devaluation of the Libyan Dinar. From October 2005, the Libyan Cabinet has been discussing and debating the structure of a short-term economic plan for the period 2006–2010, but so far neither the outline nor the details of such a document has been made available to the Libyan public.

In many ways Libya has been extremely fortunate in the immediate post-sanctions period from early 2004 onwards. First, the overwhelming response by the IOCs to the two EPSA IV rounds offered by LNOC in January and October 2005 exceeded even the government's expectations and has began to reinvigorate the country's failing oil sector, completely run down during the sanctions period. Secondly, the rising trend in the international crude oil price, which peaked at US \$70/bbl in the second half of 2005 and averaged over US \$50/bbl for most of 2005, has meant that revenue to the Libyan government increased massively in 2005. This has placed the country in a very favourable financial position, one that it needs to capitalize on by positioning the country on sound long-term economic fundamentals. This is because, in the past, Libya has been lulled into the trap of equating periods of high oil prices with long-term prosperity, the fatal flaw in Libya's planning process. The present period represents a very real opportunity for Libya's policy makers to plan and invest for sustained economic growth, based on economic liberalization and diversification away from its past overdependence on oil.

In Libya's improving geopolitical landscape of the post-sanctions era, there are significant advantages in its new international status. In the past, the country, marginalized and threatened by the United States in particular, has spent massively on weaponry and the development of a WMD programme, mainly for defensive reasons. It is highly probable, therefore, that future defence expenditure will be considerably reduced. This in turn will free up significant capital that can be used more constructively for the much-needed infrastructure development and maintenance, for example, as well as its housing sector that, as we have noted, is now unable not only to keep up with the domestic demographic demands, but also must now prepare for the huge anticipated demand for accommodation by expatriates as its oil and tourist sectors expand.

The present 2006–2010 development plan will most probably concentrate on successfully seeing through the first phase of the country's privatization and economic diversification plans. It will also involve civil service and public sector reform, as well as the revamping of Libya's housing and infrastructure sectors, in line with its ambitious plans for tourism as well as major oil sector expansion. Its favourable financial position could also be used to deal aggressively with its state-owned banking sector, effectively overhauling and recapitalizing it in preparation for future privatization and preparing it for the arrival of foreign banks and international competition in its insurance and equity markets.

The authors believe in this highly favourable financial and diplomatic environment that Libya's policy makers must now conceptualize and carefully structure a 30-year plan, along the lines of, for example, Malaysia's plan in 1991 as a key part of Dr. Mahathir Mohamad's far-sighted and highly regarded economic restructuring programme entitled "Vision 2020". This plan was structured for "Malaysia to achieve an industrialized and a fully developed nation status by sustaining growth at 7 per cent per annum and initiating structural changes in the economy as well as within the manufacturing sectors" (Prime Minister's Department, Malaysia 2005). Since then Malaysia's long-term planning style and methodology has been highly effective, followed by African nations such as Ghana, Uganda, and Malawi.

This approach to long-term planning breaks the plan down into separate components. The first is the 30-year Long Term Planning Horizon or Vision 2020 (1991–2020) itself. Within this framework, there are successive 10-year perspective plans, the first 10-year Outline Perspective Plan (OPP1), 1991–2000; the second 10-year Outline Perspective Plan (OPP2), 2001–2010; and the third 10-year Third Outline Perspective Plan (OPP3), 2011–2020. Medium-term planning is accomplished through six 5-year development plans, each of which has a mid-term review, while short-term planning is effected through the annual budgets.

As previously discussed, in Libya in the period up to 1989, 5-year plans were a consistent feature of Libyan economic planning, but fell out of favour thereafter. However, we believe that it is now the appropriate time for their use again, within the framework of a 30-year plan. Fundamentally the plan will be driven by demographic forces, but must incorporate many of the vital issues discussed at length in this book. Among these are the privatization, public sector reform, globalization and economic diversification processes, and fundamental issues related to education, regional and international trade alignments, institutional capacity building as part of the domestic decentralization process, and the development of Libya's human capital in the digital age.

The 30-year plan must incorporate a long-term component of sustainable human development, within the framework of a series of National Human Development Reports, produced and reviewed at the end of each 5-year plan. This plan should be produced in line with international benchmarking and standards, to ensure that Libyans are completely in touch with the current trends in human resource development.

Again, as discussed extensively in Chap. 10, environmental legislation and enforcement are currently weak and completely outdated in Libya. The 30-year plan should be firmly grounded on concepts of sustainable environment management and development, and the planning process must also be firmly anchored in these concepts. This is particularly applicable to the hydrocarbon sector, which is a natural polluter. In this way, future generations of Libyans will not have to live in a country whose soil, air, and water resources, as well as their natural environment and ecology have been irreversibly degraded. The UNDP's present initiative in working with the Libyan Environment General Authority (EGA), to provide technical assistance for an environment national capacity self-assessment funded by the Global Environment Facility (GEF), should be regarded only as a foundation for comprehensive legislation on environmental protection, based on the sustainable development. This also has important implications for the success of Libya's potentially lucrative tourist industry.

The decentralization programme that began in 2000, which devolved central power to initially 32 Sha'abiyat and subsequently, in February 2006, to 20, was primarily undertaken to reduce development imbalances in the country away from the Tripoli–Benghazi–Misuratah concentration, for equitable nationwide development, as well as to enhance the role of local people in the decision-making process. In fact this is not the first major decentralization initiative undertaken by the government. In 1993 a similar programme was started but ground to an early halt, mainly because of the effects of the sanctions and the downward trend in global crude oil prices. Unfortunately the actual administrative, financial, and managerial abilities of personnel at the Sha'abiyat level is sadly lacking, and this fact should be a wake up call to Libya's policy makers. Decentralization alone is not a magical formula for regional development – it is vitally important that a capacity-building exercise at the regional levels is undertaken or the decentralization process will backfire.

The central government needs to ensure that financial and human resources are mobilized and allocated to the Sha'abiyat to support the decentralization process, involving human resource development, IT, and e-Government, as well as in developing regional plans for job creation, building on the assets of individual regions. For example, the idea of building a new state-of-the-art satellite airport in Sebha to act as a hub for African air traffic could provide a massive injection into its economy. It is also of the utmost importance for individual Sha'abiyat to understand how to generate their own resources through taxation or regional development initiatives, involving specific types of PPPs (Public–Private Partnerships) for, say, highway extensions or improvements or the provision of water or sewerage services.

The data, planning, policies, and budget allocation process for each individual Sha'abiyat need to be incorporated into each national 5-year plan to avoid project duplication and unnecessary expenditure. The establishment of a National Infrastructure Databank will ensure that this does not happen, while a balanced long-term development of all Sha'abiyat should be targeted. A databank that incorporates gross domestic product at Sha'abiyat level as well as cooperation with Libya's neighbours in the development of its extensive border administrative regions should be planned in the long term, since these areas, by definition, provide tremendous potential for economic development.

It is also important that Libya's planners integrate its long-term regional and global trading alignments into the 30-year plan. Will the country direct its future development towards Africa, through such regional groupings as CEN-SAD, COMESA, or the AU itself, in which case highways, railways, airports, gas pipelines, and other infrastructure need to be planned to turn this into a reality? Or should the country integrate economically into a greater Europe, taking advantage of its excellent relations with Malta, Spain, Italy, Greece, and Turkey, and reintegrating into this major economic bloc, for which planning priorities will have to structured accordingly?

If the decisions of Libya's policy makers emerging from these and other related questions are not implemented forcefully in a long-term visionary approach, then a very favourable window of opportunity will be missed. What is certain is that, at some future point, the hydrocarbon resources will run out, and if economic transformation is not effectively achieved, Libya will be destined to remain an economic backwater.

Appendices

Appendix 1.1. Macroeconomic statistics: data on fiscal operations, 2000–2005

	2000	2001	2002	2003	2004	2005
Total revenue	8,075	7,814	12,572	16,336	23,272	37,433
Hydrocarbon	5,557	5,286	9,872	14,228	20,141	34,763
Non-hydrocarbon	2,518	2,528	2,700	2,108	3,131	2,671
Budgetary revenue	4,729	5,802	9,417	11,332	13,755	19,845
Hydrocarbon budget allocation	2,427	3,568	7,323	9,645	10,916	17,425
Non-hydrocarbon tax revenue	2,061	2,056	1,150	725	1,617	1,542
From tax administration	475	524	771	340	1,015	1,025
Taxes on international trade	1,586	1,531	379	385	602	517
Non-tax revenue	241	179	944	962	1,222	877
Extra-budgetary revenue	3,346	2,012	3,155	5,004	9,517	17,588
Oil revenue fund	3,130	1,719	2,549	4,583	9,225	17,337
GMR revenue	216	294	606	421	292	251
Total expenditure and net lending	5,528	8,038	10,063	13,396	17,332	21,102
Total expenditure	5,528	8,038	10,063	13,396	17,231	18,319
Current expenditure	3,721	6,226	6,724	10,564	10,298	8,420
Administrative budget	3,044	3,537	4,183	4,228	5,611	5,075
Expenditure on goods and services	2,801	3,236	3,684	3,499	4,780	6,022
Wages and salaries[a]	1,999	2,297	2,546	2,812	3,577	4,455
Other purchases of goods and services	802	863	1,139	688	1,202	1,567
Interest payments	0	75	0	0	66	0
Subsidies and other current transfer	243	301	499	728	832	1,050
Food subsidies	130	140	431	480	–	–
Other current transfers	113	161	67	248	–	–
Extra-budgetary current expenditure	677	2,689	2,541	6,336	4,686	1,348
Oil reserve fund[b]	121	2,193	1,966	5,636	3,792	368
Defence	556	496	575	700	894	981
Capital expenditure	1,807	1,813	3,339	2,832	6,933	9,899
Development budget	1,541	1,539	2,936	2,204	6,135	9,073

Appendix 1.1. (cont.)

	2000	2001	2002	2003	2004	2005
Extra-budgetary capital expenditure	266	274	403	628	798	826
Lending minus repayments	–	–	–	–	102	2,788
Errors and omission	0	–447	1,229	–1,333	–961	–357
Overall balance	2,547	223	1,280	4,273	6,901	16,683
Overall balance, excluding oil reserves found revenue	–583	–1,495	–1,269	–310	–2,324	–654
Non-hydrocarbon balance	–3,010	–5,063	–8,592	–9,955	– 13,240	–18,079
Domestic financing[c]	–2,547	–223	–1,280	–4,273	–6,901	–16,683
Banking system	–3,275	–213	–1,134	–4,204	–6,654	–16,191
Non-bank financing	728	–10	–147	–66	–247	–492
					In percent of GDP	
Total revenue	45.7	43.1	51.4	54.4	59.1	73.0
Oil revenue:	31.5	29.1	40.4	47.4	51.2	67.8
of which ORF	17.7	9.5	10.4	15.3	23.4	33.8
Non-oil revenue	14.2	13.9	11.0	7.0	8.0	5.2
Tax revenue	12.9	12.9	7.2	3.8	4.8	3.5
Non-tax revenue	1.4	1.0	3.9	3.2	3.1	1.7
Total expenditure and net lending	31.3	44.3	41.2	44.6	44.0	41.2
Total expenditure	31.3	44.3	41.2	44.6	43.8	35.7
Current	21.1	34.3	27.5	35.2	26.2	16.4
Budgetary	17.2	19.5	17.1	14.1	14.3	13.8
Extra-budgetary	3.8	14.8	10.4	21.1	11.9	2.6
Capital	10.2	10.0	13.7	9.4	17.6	19.3
Budgetary	8.7	8.5	12.0	7.3	15.6	17.7
Total net lending	–	–	–	–	0.3	5.4
Overall balance	14.4	1.2	5.2	14.2	17.5	32.6
Overall balance (excluding oil reserve fund revenue)	–3.3	–8.2	–5.2	14.2	17.5	32.6
Non-hydrocarbon balance	–17.0	–27.9	–35.1	–33.1	–33.6	–35.3
Memorandum Items					In million of Libyan Dinars	
Gross domestic dept (million of Libyan dinars)	7,644	7,644	7,644	7,644	25	25
Nominal GDP	17,668	18,148	24,449	30,036	39,361	51,244
Non-hydrocarbon GDP	10,857	11,419	11,622	11,199	12,050	11,520

Sources: Libyan Secretariat of Finance and IMF.

[a] Net of income taxes and includes the contributions to the Social Security Found.

[b] ORF expenditure for 2003 and 2004 includes payments for the Lockerbie settlement of LD 1,388 million and 2,095 million respectively.

[c] Includes current and capital expenditures. Data for 2004 do not include the government's debt buy-back operation.

Appendix 1.2. Macroeconomic statistics: summary of real sector statistics, 2000–2005

	2000	2001	2002	2003	2004	2005
			In million LD			
Nominal GDP at factor costs	17,775	18,592	25,246	31,968	41,950	56,165
Nominal hydrocarbon GDP	7,081	7,297	13,326	19,565	28,142	40,773
Nominal non-hydrocarbon GDP	10,695	11,295	11,920	12,403	13,808	15,391
Real GDP at factor cost	13,934	14,563	15,038	16,412	17,165	17,773
Real hydrocarbon GDP	4,256	4,228	4,213	5,345	5,644	5,724
Real non-hydrocarbon GDP	9,678	10,335	10,825	11,066	11,521	12,049
			Annual percentage change			
Nominal GDP at Factor Costs	26.3	4.6	35.8	26.6	31.2	33.9
Nominal Hydrocarbon GDP	77.2	3.1	82.6	46.8	43.8	44.9
Nominal non-hydrocarbon GDP	6.1	5.6	5.5	4.1	11.3	11.5
Real GDP at factor cost	1.1	4.5	3.3	9.1	4.6	3.5
Real hydrocarbon GDP	–2.7	–0.7	–0.4	26.9	5.6	1.4
Real non-hydrocarbon GDP	3.0	6.8	4.7	2.2	4.1	4.6
GDP deflator	24.9	0.1	31.5	16.0	25.5	29.3
Hydrocarbon deflator	82.2	3.7	83.3	15.7	36.2	42.9
Non-hydrocarbon deflator	3.1	–1.1	0.8	1.8	6.9	6.6
CPI index (1995 = 100)	111.3	101.4	91.4	89.5	87.6	89.8
Inflation rate	–2.9	–8.8	–9.9	–2.1	–2.2	2.5

Source: Libyan Authorities and IMF, 2006.

Appendix 1.3. Macroeconomic statistics: sectoral distribution of GDP at current prices, 2000–2005

	2000	2001	2002	2003	2004	2005
			In million LD			
GDP at factor cost	17,775	18,592	25,246	31,968	41,950	56,165
Non-oil sector	10,695	11,295	11,920	12,403	13,808	15,391
Agriculture, fishing, and foresty	1,438	1,392	1,349	1,376	1,440	1,527
Oil production	7,081	7,297	13,326	19,565	28,142	40,773
Mining	294	307	387	360	418	450
Manufacturing	890	878	813	765	761	794
Electricity, gas, and water	270	285	294	303	334	379
Construction	1,014	1,063	1,342	1,249	1,450	1,614
Trade, hotels, and restaurants	1,686	1,882	2,090	2,205	2,418	2,846
Transportation, communication, and storage	1,214	1,299	1,429	1,516	1,641	1,932
Financing, insurance, and business services	357	377	415	440	477	551
Housing	476	499	515	534	592	646
Total public services	2,666	2,901	2,859	3,205	3,800	4,129
Public services (expected education and health)	1,238	1,301	1,282	1,437	1,704	1,852
Education services	922	1,035	1,020	1,143	1,355	1,473
Health services	506	566	558	625	741	805
Other services	392	411	428	451	477	524

Appendix 1.3. (cont.)

	2000	2001	2002	2003	2004	2005
	In percentage of total					
GDP at factor cost	100.0	100.0	100.0	100.0	100.0	100.0
Non-oil sector	60.2	60.8	47.2	38.3	32.9	27.4
Agriculture, fishing, and forestry	8.1	7.5	5.3	4.3	3.4	2.7
Oil production	39.8	39.2	52.8	61.2	67.1	72.6
Mining	1.7	1.6	1.5	1.1	1.0	0.8
Manufacturing	5.0	4.7	3.2	2.4	1.8	1.4
Electricity, gas, and water	1.5	1.5	1.2	0.9	0.8	0.7
Construction	5.7	5.7	5.3	3.9	3.5	2.9
Trade, hotels, and restaurants	9.5	10.1	8.3	6.9	5.8	5.1
Transportation, communication, and storage	6.8	7.0	5.7	4.7	3.9	3.4
Financing, insurance, and business services	2.0	2.0	1.6	1.4	1.1	1.0
Housing	2.7	2.7	2.0	1.7	1.4	1.2
Total public services	15.0	15.6	11.3	10.0	9.1	7.4
Public services (expected education and health)	7.0	7.0	5.1	4.5	4.1	3.3
Education services	5.2	5.6	4.0	3.6	3.2	2.6
Health services	2.8	3.0	2.2	2.0	1.8	1.4
Other services	2.2	2.2	1.7	1.4	1.1	0.9

Source: Secretariat of Planning and IMF, 2006.

Appendix 1.4. Macroeconomic Statistics: gross fixed capital formation by economic sector, 2000–2005

	2000	2001	2002	2003	2004	2005
	In million LD					
GDP	13,934	14,563	15,038	16,412	17,165	17,773
Non-oil sector	9,678	10,335	10,825	11,066	11,521	12,049
Agriculture, fishing, and forestry	1,274	1,322	15,038	1,384	1,411	1,447
Oil production	4,256	4,228	4,213	5,345	5,644	5,724
Mining	252	263	316	294	309	324
Manufacturing	778	746	727	691	680	692
Electricity, gas, and water	300	316	326	336	353	374
Construction	796	940	1,130	1,051	1,104	1,159
Trade, hotels, and restaurants	1,544	1,698	1,774	1,863	1,975	2,113
Transportation, communication, and storage	1,178	1,290	1,419	1,490	1,565	1,674
Financing, insurance, and business services	228	322	354	374	394	414
Housing	472	493	508	525	545	567
Total public services	2,506	2,579	2,542	2,657	2,763	2,846
Other services	351	368	372	401	421	438

Appendix 1.4. (cont.)

	2000	2001	2002	2003	2004	2005
	In percentage of total					
GDP	100.0	100.0	100.0	100.0	100.0	100.0
Non-oil sector	69.5	71.0	72.0	67.4	67.1	67.8
Agriculture, fishing, and forestry	9.1	9.1	9.0	8.4	8.2	8.1
Oil production	30.5	29.0	28.0	32.6	32.9	32.2
Mining	1.8	1.8	2.1	1.8	1.8	1.8
Manufacturing	5.6	5.1	4.8	4.2	4.0	3.9
Electricity, gas, and water	2.2	2.2	2.2	2.0	2.1	2.1
Construction	5.7	6.5	7.5	6.4	6.4	6.5
Trade, hotels, and restaurants	11.1	11.7	11.8	11.4	11.5	11.9
Transportation, communication, and storage	8.5	8.9	9.4	9.1	9.1	9.4
Financing, insurance, and business services	1.6	2.2	2.4	2.3	2.3	2.3
Housing	3.4	3.4	3.4	3.2	3.2	3.2
Total public services	18.0	17.7	16.9	16.2	16.2	16.0
Other services	2.5	2.5	2.5	2.4	2.5	2.5
	Annual changes (%)					
GDP	1.1	4.5	3.3	9.1	4.6	3.5
Non-oil sector	3.0	6.8	4.7	2.2	4.1	4.6
Agriculture, fishing, and foresty	3.0	3.7	2.6	2.0	2.0	2.5
Oil production	–2.7	–0.7	–0.4	26.9	5.6	1.4
Mining	–2.7	4.4	20.2	–0.7	5.0	5.0
Manufacturing	5.9	–4.1	–2.5	–5.0	–1.5	1.8
Electricity, gas, and water	7.9	5.4	3.2	3.2	5.0	6.0
Construction	10.3	18.1	20.2	–7.0	5.0	5.0
Trade, hotels, and restaurants	–0.4	9.9	4.5	5.0	6.0	7.0
Transportation, communication, and storage	1.0	9.5	10.0	5.0	5.0	7.0
Financing, insurance, and business services	–23.1	41.5	10.0	5.5	5.5	5.0
Housing	3.2	4.6	.0	3.4	3.8	4.0
Total public services	3.5	2.9	–1.4	4.5	4.0	3.0
Other services	3.6	4.6	1.3	7.8	5.0	4.0

Source: Secretariat of Planning (2006).

Appendix 1.5. Macroeconomic statistics: central government development expenditure, 2000–2005

	2000	2001	2002	2003	2004
	In million of LD				
Total development budgetary expenditure	1,541	1,539	3,702	2,050	3,581
Goods producing sectors:	313	305	553	710	865
Agriculture, marine and livestock wealth[a]	163	150	184	124	263
Industry and energy	150	156	369	586	603
Economic services sectors	432	482	688	293	681
Housing and public utilities	234	293	454	195	388
Communication and transportation[b]	198	190	234	98	293
Social services sector:	451	410	1,272	679	988
Education, establishment and youth and scientific research	324	216	739	316	603
Health and social security	107	136	406	326	249
Justice	10	43	72	31	91
Information and culture and tourism	9	15	55	5	45
Others sectors	345	341	1,189	368	1,046
Economy and trade	6	6	3	3	14
Planning and finance	241	12	106	48	83
Foreign affairs	0	0	0	10	50
Regional development	98	104	177	144	183
Great man made river	0	0	365	161	154
Human development	0	0	169	0	0
Working groups and executive staff emergency reserve	0	7	0	0	0
Payoff the previous liabilities	0	188	316	0	366
Others[c]	0	25	23	3	196

Source: High Planning Council.
[a] for 2000 and 2001, includes GMR.
[b] including railway sector expenditure from 1998 onwards.
[c] in 2004, includes expenditure of development projects.

Appendix 1.6. Central government administrative expenditure, 2000–2005

	2000	2001	2002	2003	2004	2005
Expenditure of central secretariats[a]	In million of LD					
General people's congress	51	49	43	44	47	48
General people's committee	184	218	222	204	190	178
Justice and public security	335	202	219	244	284	313
Education and specific research[b]	0	170	175	196	0	0
Finance	158	133	42	41	47	53
Information and culture	36	0	0	0	0	0
Foreign affairs	61	68	178	175	233	240
Planning, economy and trade	0	1	1	1	5	6
Tourism	0	0	0	0	4	5
Miscellaneous and contingencies	0	0	129	119	180	227

Appendix 1.6. (cont.)

	2000	2001	2002	2003	2004	2005
Transfer to public institutions	112	85	67	58	72	172
Public department	110	255	60	60	60	60
Investment expenditure	0	100	100	0	0	0
Subsidies	130	301	499	480	832	1,050
Allocations to the regions	1,978	2,198	2,042	2,140	2,687	2,665
Others	0	0	501	297	336	0
Total administrative expenditures	3,153	3,779	4,278	4,058	4,977	5,017
Allocations to the regions (in per cent of total)	63	58	53	53	54	53

Source: Libyan Secretariat of Finance.

[a] In 1998 many of the responsibilities and functions of government were transferred to the regional institutions.

[b] Expenditures for 2004 and 2005 are recorded in allocation to the regions.

Appendix 1.7. Monetary survey, 2000 – 2005[a]

	2000	2001	2002	2003	2004	2005
			In million of LD			
Net foreign assets	7,774	9,976	19,123	27,123	34,237	56,423
Central Bank	7,296	9,410	18,440	26,573	33,066	54,448
Foreign assets	7,296	9,414	18,444	26,578	33,073	54,460
Foreign liabilities	0	4	4	5	7	12
Deposit money banks	479	566	683	550	1,171	1,976
Foreign assets	529	623	778	794	1,312	2,047
Foreign liabilities	50	57	94	244	141	72
Net domestic assets	2,780	1,745	–6,119	–13,071	–18,893	–36,684
Domestic credit	6,611	7,092	6,899	3,486	–11,253	–26,998
Net claims on government	887	616	–555	–4,820	–19,465	–35,902
Central Bank claims	7,288	7,151	7,010	7,012	828	828
Governments' deposits with Central Bank	7,566	7,765	8,587	12,964	19,519	35,893
Commercial Banks' claims	1,766	1,811	1,811	1,811	373	373
Government' deposits with Commercial Bank	600	582	788	678	1,147	1,210
Claims on the economy	5,724	6,477	7,453	8,305	8,212	8,903
Central Bank	269	339	884	1,300	1,499	2,522
Deposit money banks	5,456	137	6,569	7,005	6,712	6,382
Claims on non-financial public enterprise	1,300	1,831	2,838	3,784	3,477	4,278
Claims on private sector	4,276	4,492	4,438	4,298	4,452	4,573
Claims on specialized banking institutions	50	78	82	77	67	45
Claims on non-blank financial institution	98	76	96	146	215	7
Other items	–3,831	–5,347	–13,018	–16,557	–7,640	–9,686
Broad money	10,555	11,721	13,004	14,052	15,344	19,739
Money	7,433	7,704	8,705	9,029	10,537	13,968
Currency in circulation	2,699	2,560	2,614	2,764	2,613	3,311

Appendix 1.7. (cont.)

	2000	2001	2002	2003	2004	2005
Demand deposits (other than government)	4,734	5,144	6,092	6,266	7,924	10,657
Quasi-money	3,122	4,018	4,299	5,023	4,807	5,771
Of which: restricted deposits	939	1,479	2,138	2,494	2,208	2,703
Memorandum items: net claims on the government excluding social security found	1,269	1,479	–77	–4,284	18,938	–35,129
	Annual rate of change in percent					
Broad money	5.1	11.1	10.9	8.1	9.2	28.6
Money	3.7	3.6	13.0	3.7	16.7	32.6
Quasi money	8.4	28.7	7.0	16.8	–4.3	20.1
Net claims on government	–78.4	–30.6	–190.1	769.0	303.9	84.4
Claims on non-financial public enterprises	–65.3	40.8	55.0	33.3	–8.1	23.0
	Change in percent of beginning of the period money stock					
Net foreign assets	58.1	20.9	78.0	61.5	50.6	144.6
Domestic credit	–50.3	4.6	–1.7	–26.2	–104.9	–102.6
Net Claims on government	–32.1	–2.6	–10.0	–32.8	–104.2	–107.1
Claims on the economy	–18.2	7.1	8.3	6.6	–0.7	4.5
Claims on non-financial public enterprise	–24.4	5.0	8.6	7.3	–2.2	5.2
Claims on private sector	6.4	2.0	0.5	–1.1	1.1	0.8
	As percent of GDP					
Domestic credit	37.4	39.1	28.2	11.6	–28.6	–52.7
Net claims on the government	5.0	3.4	–2.3	–16.0	–49.5	–70.1
Broad money	59.7	64.6	53.2	46.8	39.0	38.5
Nominal GDP (in million LD)	17,668	18.148	24,449	30,361	39.361	51,244

Source: Central Bank of Libya, Reports, 2000–2005.
[a] starting in 2000, data include the regional banks.

Appendix 1.8. Balance of payments, 2000–2005

	2000	2001	2002	2003	2004	Prel 2005
1 – Current account	7,763	4,145	566	5,036	7,303	15,985
A – Goods & services	8,533	5,217	1,127	6,170	10,355	17,758
I – Goods	9,251	6,067	2,309	7,325	11,832	19,234
Exports (fob)	13,380	10,892	9,717	14,525	20,600	30,110
Hydrocarbon sector[a]	12,929	10,472	9,534	14,037	19,723	29,210
Other exports	450	420	184	489	877	900
Imports (fob)	–4,129	–4,825	–7,408	–7,200	–8,768	–10,875
of which: Oil sector	–666	–752	–626	–950	1,271	–1,378
II – Services (net)	–718	–850	–1,137	–1,155	–1,477	–1,476
Debit	890	1,033	1,539	1,597	1,914	1,970
Credit	172	183	402	442	437	494

Appendix 1.8. (cont.)

	2000	2001	2002	2003	2004	Prel 2005
Freight and insurance for imports	–187	–263	–343	–540	–658	–816
Travel	–515	–494	–628	–352	–368	–381
Transportation	–145	–169	–83	–104	–85	–68
Government services (others)	–161	–209	–190	43	45	47
Private Services (others)	–83	–79	–100	–202	–134	–70
Of which: hydrocarbon sector	–58	–49	–23	–23	–33	–48
B – Income	–180	–240	265	540	–543	–870
Direct investment income[b]	–850	–747	–585	–845	–1,634	–2,551
Other investment income	670	507	850	1,385	1,091	1,681
Government sector	420	414	740	1,263	966	1,549
Private sector	250	93	110	122	125	132
C– current transfers	–590	–832	–872	–1,673	–2,509	–903
General government[c]	0	0	0	–1,174	–1,741	–115
Private sector	–590	–832	–872	–499	–768	–788
Oil sector	–123	–127	–105	–156	–210	–259
Other sectors (workers transfers abroad)	–467	–705	–767	–343	–558	–259
2 – Capital and financial account	–149	–976	89	–167	–1,023	–2,349
Direct investment	43	–308	281	79	–643	–1,503
Abroad	–98	–175	136	–63	–1,000	–1,909
In Libya	141	–133	145	142	–312	406
Portfolio investment	–706	–1,358	72	–607	–187	–448
Other investment	514	690	–264	361	–193	–399
3 – Errors and omissions and other capital	–1,115	–1,831	–341	–1,748	–134	0
4 – Overall balance	6,499	1,338	314	3,122	6,146	13,636
5 – Reserve item	–6,499	–1,338	–314	–3,122	–6,146	13,636
Official exchange rate, LD/US $ (pa)	0.51	0.61	1.27	1.28	1.30	1.31
Official exchange rate, LD/US $ (eop)	0.54	0.65	1.21	1.30	1.24	1.36
Gross official reserves (in billion of US $)	13.1	14.1	15.0	19.5	25.6	39.3
Gross official reserves, in months of next year's imports of GNFS	26.7	19.0	20.5	21.9	23.9	31.5
Current account balance (in percent of GDP)	22.5	12.3	2.9	21.5	24.2	40.8
Overall balance of payments (in percent of GDP)	18.8	4.5	1.6	13.3	20.4	34.8
Nominal GDP (in billions of US $, pa)	34.5	30.0	19.2	23.4	30.2	39.2

Sources: Central Bank of Libya & IMF Report, 2006.

[a] Includes foreign partners' oil share.

[b] Includes partner's profit remittances from oil investment.

[c] For 2003 and 2004, includes payments for Lockerbie Settlement of $1,076 million and $1,624 million, respectively.

Appendix 4.1. Number of employees in all sectors (000s), 1962–2000

Year	1962	1963	1964	1965	1966	1967	1968	1969	1970	1971	1972	1973	1974	1975	1976	1977	1978	1979	1980	1981
Sector-1	13.5	13.8	14.2	17.2	20	24	28.4	33	35.4	38	40.9	45.8	51.5	58	64.5	69.9	73.9	81	91	98.2
Sector-2	5	5.3	5.6	7.2	9	11.5	14.2	18.6	19.3	20.1	21	23.5	26.5	30.5	33	35.7	38.4	41	45.8	50
Sector-3	32.4	32.4	32.4	33	34	35.9	38	41	49	59.5	69.5	90.4	121.6	152.6	167.8	171.4	164.3	168.8	173	244.5
Sector-4	145.7	145.5	145.3	142.5	140	135.3	130.5	125	126	127	127.7	129	131.4	133.4	141.2	144.9	147.9	150.1	153.4	162.4
Sector-5	27.4	27.7	28	28.2	28.4	28.6	28.8	29.1	30.3	32.5	35.7	39.3	44.0	48.5	52	52.3	47.5	45	42.9	45.4
Sector-6	3.4	3.6	3.9	4.3	4.7	5.0	5.4	5.8	5.9	6.0	6.1	6.5	7.0	7.7	8.1	8.5	9.1	9.4	9.6	10.3
Sector-7	22.4	23.0	23.5	25	27	29	31	33.4	34.9	38.4	41.7	45.0	48.8	53.4	57.9	63.1	67.5	69.4	71.7	78.6
Sector-8	19.9	20.0	20.1	20.3	20.7	21.0	21.4	21.9	22.4	22.9	23.5	25.5	27.8	30.9	32.4	33.9	36.2	38.0	46.5	44.6
Sector-9	49.1	49.6	50.1	50.7	51.3	52.0	52.8	53.9	55.4	57.3	59.4	63.9	68.1	71.1	74.7	76.8	75.4	70.1	65	65.8
Sector-10	13.4	15.8	18.4	20.1	22.0	25.0	29.2	33.5	34.5	35.9	39.6	43.6	51.2	58.7	63.7	66.8	65.1	63.4	59.5	82.8
Sector-11	23.8	23.8	23.8	23.7	23.1	22.0	20.8	19.4	20.4	21.4	22.9	25.9	29.3	32.9	37.4	41.5	47.4	52.8	58.0	64.0

Year	1982	1983	1984	1985	1986	1987	1988	1989	1990	1991	1992	1993	1994	1995	1996	1997	1998	1999	2000
Sector-1	105.1	109	117	120	125	139.2	139.2	148.2	157.9	158.5	167.4	170.6	171.9	177.5	183	182.4	185.2	191.6	198.2
Sector-2	57.5	60	48.1	52	54	56.8	56.8	59.1	56	56.4	67.5	71.1	71.8	73.9	76	77.3	81.2	83.6	86.1
Sector-3	317.4	371.3	179	152	149.7	149.2	148.1	156.3	157.1	137.1	123	150.2	160.6	165.8	171	181.7	194.2	207.9	222.0
Sector-4	167.5	173	185.5	177	178.5	180	186.9	191.6	188.9	189.6	195.7	201.2	206	212.7	219.5	219.2	225.1	232	239.1
Sector-5	53.5	55.5	47.0	46.0	46.0	46.0	52.5	52.8	53.7	58.7	61.3	65.4	68.2	70.6	73.0	61.4	64.1	66.7	69.5
Sector-6	11.3	11.9	13.0	13.5	13.5	13.5	14.9	15.0	15.8	16.0	16.7	19.0	20.0	21.0	22.0	25.4	27.4	30.1	33.0
Sector-7	87.8	92.0	70.0	72.0	74.0	76.0	77.1	78.5	82.3	83.2	86.7	95.5	97.3	100.6	104.0	115.6	121.8	132.2	143.4
Sector-8	47.5	50.2	43.5	44.5	45.0	45.5	50.2	52.2	53.9	55.6	57.6	59.8	62.3	64.3	66.5	68.4	87.2	90.3	93.4
Sector-9	63.7	61.0	101.0	100.0	100.0	100.0	100.0	101.2	101.4	99.4	103.7	105.3	105.8	109.0	112.5	111.1	113.3	116.1	118.9
Sector-10	98.7	115.1	51.0	42.2	42.0	51.6	51.6	48.3	52.2	56.9	59.0	63.0	64.6	66.3	68.0	64.8	67.4	69.6	71.8
Sector-11	73.7	80.5	72.0	75.0	77.0	79.0	85.5	92.2	99.4	101.1	105.4	112.6	120.5	124.5	128.5	147.8	156.8	163.7	169.6

Note: Sector-1 = Education; Sector-2 = Health; Sector-3 = Construction; Sector-4 = Agriculture, forestry, and fishing; Sector-5 = Wholesale and retail trade, and restaurants and hotels; Sector-6 = Funds, insurance, and business services; Sector-7 = Transport, storing, and communications; Sector-8 = Energy, mining, quarrying, and water; Sector-9 = Public administration services; Sector-10 = Other services; Sector-11 = Transformation manufacturing.
Sources: 1962–2000, Libyan General Council of Planning, 2001.

Appendix 6.1. The first group for privatization

No	Name of the SOE	Method of privatization*	Sha'abiat
1	Automatic Bakery	Syarika Musahima	
2	Tripoli Textile Factory	Syarika Musahima	
3	Fellaa Central Repair Workshop	Syarika Musahima	
4	Fellaa Fridge, Gargor Region	Syarika Musahima	
5	Air-Conditioning Complex	Syarika Musahima	
6	Hathba Incubation Laboratory	Syarika Musahima	Tripoli
7	Truck Bodybuilding Complex	Syarika Musahima	
8	Aluminum Complex	Syarika Musahima	
9	Sawani Metal Works Complex	Syarika Musahima	
10	Centre for Footwear Distribution	Tashrukkiyah	
11	Candle and Chalk Factory	Tashrukkiyah	
12	Al Gharbia Centre for Tyre Distribution	Tashrukkiyah	
13	Tripoli Gas Factory	Tashrukkiyah	
14	Tajora Dyeing and Tanning Unit	Syarika Musahima	Tajora and Alnohee Alarbaa
15	Bin Gasher Footwear Factory	Syarika Musahima	
16	Perfume and Fragrance Factory	Syarika Musahima	
17	Welding Rod Unit	Tashrukkiyah	
18	Suk El-Khamis Chicken Station	Tashrukkiyah	
19	Tajora Chicken Station	Tashrukkiyah	
20	Industrial Covering Factory	Tashrukkiyah	
21	Turhona Condiment Factory	Syarika Musahima	
22	Turkey Complex/Kuea Region	Tashrukkiyah	Turhona and Misllatah Region
23	Turhona Chicken Station	Tashrukkiyah	
24	Misllatah Chicken Station	Tashrukkiyah	
25	Benghazi Factory for Electrical Machineries	Syarika Musahima	
26	Al Sharkia Distribution Office and Tyre Retreading Unit	Syarika Musahima	
27	Central Repair Workshop	Syarika Musahima	
28	Complex for Industrial Metal	Syarika Musahima	
29	Fish Canning Factory	Syarika Musahima	Benghazi
30	Benghazi Footwear Factory	Syarika Musahima	
31	Aroba Factory for Liquid Soap	Syarika Musahima	
32	Benghazi Bicycle Factory	Syarika Musahima	
33	Benghazi Gas Factory	Syarika Musahima	

Appendix 6.1. (cont.)

No	Name of the SOE	Method of privatization*	Sha'abiat
34	Al-Merj Chicken Station	Tashrukkiyah	Al-merj
35	Al-Merj Shoe Factory	Tashrukkiyah	
36	El-Wosta Distribution Centre for Tyres	Syarika Musahima	
37	Misuratah Pneumatic Factory	Syarika Musahima	
38	Misuratah Metal Works Complex	Tashrukkiyah	Misuratah
39	Misuratah Condiment Factory	Tashrukkiyah	
40	Pesticide Factory	Syarika Musahima	
41	Khums Date Syrup Factory	Syarika Musahima	
42	Marine Aquaculture Farm	Syarika Musahima	
43	Khums Textile Factory	Tashrukkiyah	
44	Freshwater Fish Hatchery	Tashrukkiyah	
45	Khums Footwear Factory	Tashrukkiyah	
46	Zlitan Chicken Station	Tashrukkiyah	
47	Khums Wooden Boat Factory	Tashrukkiyah	Almirqueb
48	Zlitan Footwear Factory	Tashrukkiyah	
49	Khums Chicken Station	Tashrukkiyah	
50	Khums Aluminium Factory	Tashrukkiyah	
51	Khums Factory for Liquid Soap	Tashrukkiyah	
52	Fish Hatchery and Rearing farm at Ana Kama Region	Tashrukkiyah	
53	Intensive Chicken Meat Farm	Tashrukkiyah	Baniwaled
54	Intensive Chicken Egg Farm	Tashrukkiyah	
55	Baniwaled Footwear Factory	Tashrukkiyah	
56	Derna Detergent Factory	Tashrukkiyah	
57	Derna Footwear Factory	Tashrukkiyah	Derna
58	Sosa Leather Clothes Factory	Tashrukkiyah	
59	Bap Al-Zuton Chicken Station	Tashrukkiyah	
60	Al-Beida Footwear Factory	Tashrukkiyah	Aljabel Alakhder
61	Ein Al-Gazala Aquaculture Project	Tashrukkiyah	
62	Tobruk Fishing Boat Factory	Tashrukkiyah	
63	Tobruk Centre for Footwear Distribution	Tashrukkiyah	Al Bitnan
64	Tobruk Footwear Factory	Tashrukkiyah	
65	Algobba Chicken Station	Tashrukkiyah	
66	Umm Al Razam Chicken Station	Tashrukkiyah	Algobba
67	Sirte Footwear Factory	Syarika Musahima	

Appendix 6.1. (cont.)

No	Name of the SOE	Method of privatization*	Sha'abiat
68	Sirte Aluminium Factory	Tashrukkiyah	
69	Al-Hammam Chicken Station	Tashrukkiyah	Sirte
70	Bin Juwad Chicken Station	Tashrukkiyah	
71	Gialo Chicken Station	Tashrukkiyah	
72	Gidahiyah Chicken Station	Tashrukkiyah	
73	Kalij Attahadee Wooden Boat Factory	Tashrukkiyah	
74	Aljofra Detergent Factory	Tashrukkiyah	Aljofra
75	Al-Zawia Footwear Factory	Syarika Musahima	Al-Zawia
76	Al-Zawia Chicken Station	Tashrukkiyah	
77	Alnnikat Alghames Factory for Creams and Purees	Syarika Musahima	
78	Zuwarah Air-Conditioning Complex	Tashrukkiyah	
79	Al Nagma Al-Beida Fishing Boat	Tashrukkiyah	
80	Al-Shafak Fishing Boat	Tashrukkiyah	
81	Zarka Alyamama Fishing Boat	Tashrukkiyah	
82	Al-Nasam Fishing Boat	Tashrukkiyah	Alnnikat Alghames
83	Zuwarah Factory of Masbah Bases	Tashrukkiyah	
84	Al Jamil Chicken Station	Tashrukkiyah	
85	Sidi Saeed Factory for Detergent	Tashrukkiyah	
86	Al-Ujaylat Chicken Factory	Tashrukkiyah	
87	Ragdaleen Footwear Factory	Tashrukkiyah	
88	Mellitah Chicken Factory	Tashrukkiyah	
89	Surman Chicken Station	Tashrukkiyah	Surman & Sabratha
90	Sabratha Fish Canning Factory	Tashrukkiyah	
91	Sebha Tomato Paste Factory	Syarika Musahima	
92	Sebha Office for Distribution of Tyres	Syarika Musahima	
93	Sebha Automatic Bakery	Tashrukkiyah	
94	Sebha Centre Chicken Station	Tashrukkiyah	Sebha
95	Sebha Gas Factory	Tashrukkiyah	
96	Sebha Footwear Factory	Tashrukkiyah	
97	Murzuq Chicken Station	Tashrukkiyah	Murzuq
98	Alshate Chicken Station	Tashrukkiyah	Wadi-Alshate
99	Al-Dissa Chicken Station	Tashrukkiyah	Wadi-Alhaya
100	Obarie Chicken Station	Tashrukkiyah	

Appendix 6.1. (cont.)

No	Name of the SOE	Method of privatization*	Sha'abiat
101	Janzur Fish Canning Factory	Syarika Musahima	
102	Zahra Chicken Station	Tashrukkiyah	
103	Mansoura Condiment Factory	Tashrukkiyah	
104	Vegetable and Fruit Factory	Tashrukkiyah	Aljfara
105	Khansa Laboratory for Chicken	Tashrukkiyah	
106	Children's Food Factory	Tashrukkiyah	
107	Al -Hashaan Chicken Station	Tashrukkiyah	
108	Bir Al-Ganam Chicken Stations	Tashrukkiyah	
109	Tin Can Factory	Tashrukkiyah	
110	Sanitary, Plumbing, and Housing Equipment	Syarika Musahima	
111	Ghryan Wall Tile Factory	Tashrukkiyah	
112	Ghryan Aluminum Factory	Tashrukkiyah	
113	Abu-Shiba Chicken Station	Tashrukkiyah	Ghryan
114	Mizda Chicken Station	Tashrukkiyah	
115	Zarat Chicken Station	Tashrukkiyah	
116	Ghryan Footwear Factory	Tashrukkiyah	
117	Yfren Aluminum Factory	Tashrukkiyah	
118	Al-Reana Footwear Factory	Tashrukkiyah	Yfren
119	Rajban Refrigerator Factory	Tashrukkiyah	
120	Ghadames Footwear Factory	Tashrukkiyah	
121	Derj Chicken Station	Tashrukkiyah	
122	Derj Fruit Factory	Tashrukkiyah	Ghadames
123	Jado Chicken Station	Tashrukkiyah	
124	Ejdabia Chicken Station	Tashrukkiyah	Ejdabia
125	Ejdabia Footwear Factory	Tashrukkiyah	
126	Badar Chicken Station	Tashrukkiyah	Nalut

Source: GBOT, 2005.

Appendix 6.2. The second group for privatization

	Name of the economic unit	Privatization values (Tamleek) (LD)	No of shares	Share value (LD)	No of shares applied for	Percentage of shares applied for
1	National Company of Beverages	21,650,000	433,000	50	433000	100 %
2	Misuratah Biscuit and Cake Factory	337,050	11,235	30	11235	100 %
3	Zliten Biscuit and Cake Factory	495,000	16,500	30	16500	100%
4	Arab Company for Manufacturing and Bottling	25,300,000	506,000	50	506000	100%
5	Misuratah Textile Factory	7,500,000	250,000	30	93627	37.5%
6	Misuratah Footwear Complex	8,100,000	270,000	30	29,464	11%
7	Ban-Walid Complex for Cotton Manufacturing	19,100,000	382,000	50	48593	12.72%
8	Misuratah Furniture Factory	6,1389,000	204,630	30	9149	4.5%
9	Clothes Factory	3,609,000	120,300	30	21654	18%
10	Benghazi Furniture Factory	6,795,300	226,510	30	–	–
11	Derna Furniture Factory	6,954,300	231,810	30	–	–

Source: GBOT, 2005.

Appendix 6.3. The third group for privatization: industrial projects

Project	Location
Libyan Iron and Steel Company – LISCO	Misuratah
Arabian Cement Company:	
– Zliten Cement Plant	Zliten
– LABDAH Cement Plant	Labdah
– Marghab Cement Company	Khums
– Souk Al Khamis Cement Plant	Souk Al Khamis
– Baked Bricks and Concrete Beams Plant	Sawani
– Paper Bags Plant	Misuratah
– Gypsum Plant Project	Bir Al-Ganam
Libyan Cement Company	
– Al Hawari Cement Plant	Benghazi
– Benghazi Cement Plant	Benghazi
– El-Fataiah Cement Plant	Algobba
General National Company for Flour Mills and Fodder	
– Mode Macaroni Plant	Tripoli
– Tripoli Macaroni Plant	Tripoli
– United Mills Plant	Tripoli
– Gorji Macaroni Factory	Tripoli
– Sawani Crops Mill	Tripoli
– Ain Zara Semolina Mill	Tripoli
– South Tripoli Crops Mill	Tripoli
– Zliten Crops Mill	Zliten
Surman Crops Mill	Surman & Sabratha
General Company for Chemical Products	Abu Kammash
General Electronics Company	
– Tajora Electronic Complex	Tajora
– Circuit and Microscopes Plant	Tajora
– Garyounis Television Complex	Tajora
Computer Plant	Tajora
General Tobacco Company	Tripoli
General Wires and Electrical Product Company	Benghazi
General Pipe Company	Benghazi
General Company for Sanitary Pipes	
– Asbestos Tubes Plant	Janzur
– Plastic Tubes Plant	Janzur

Appendix 6.3. (cont.)

Project	Location
– Poly Ethylene Tubes Plant	Janzur
– Tube Supplementaries Plant	Janzur
National Textile Company	Janzur
Libyan Mining Company	Tajora
Company Engineering Industries	
– Ghryan Industrial Complex	Ghryan
– Gas Cylinders Plant	Ghryan
– Metal Artifact Plant	Tajora
– Electrical Towers Plant	Tajora
– Street Lights and Galvanic Unit Plant	Tajora
Amman Tire & Battery Company	
– Tire Plant	Tajora
– Liquid Battery Plant	Tajora
Water Heater Factory	Tajora
Janzur Textile Complex	Janzur
Wool Industries Complex	Baniwaled
Qarabuli Complex for Plastics	Qarabuli
Soap Powder Plant	Misruatah
Soap Powder Plant	Benghazi
Al Aziziya Glass Complex	Al Aziziya
Benghazi Tannery	Benghazi

Appendix 6.4. The third group for privatization: agricultural projects

Agriculture projects	Location
Al Kofra Agriculure Project	Al Kofra
Maknosa Agriculture Project	Fezzan
Wadi Parjoj Agriculture Project	Fezzan
El Sarir Agriculture Project	Fezzan
Irwan Agriculture Project	–
Aryl Agriculture Project	–
100 Thousand Hectare Wheat Project	–
Krarat Alkatf Project	Baniwaled
Elood Agriculture Project	Aljofra
Elgoarsha Project for Green Fodder Production	Benghazi
Elhadba Project for Green Fodder Production	Tripoli
Janzur Project for Green Fodder Production	Aljfara
Misuratah Project for Green Fodder Production	Misuratah
Nafeth & Zarar Project (Grasslands)	–
Saso Grasslands and Weels Projects	–
Al Jadeeda Arboretum for Fruit Trees	–
Al Jadeeda Arboretum for Forest Trees	–
Al Washka Grassland Project	Sirte
Wadi Binkabir Project	Sirte
South Zliten Grassland Project	–
Saso Grassland Project	–
Azomi Date Palm Farm	–
Forest Trees Arboretum	–
Fruit Arboretum	Al-Zawia
Fruit Arboretum	Algobba
Tamimi Date Palm Arboretum	Algobba
Surman Forest Trees Arboretum and Saniat Elfar Farm	Surman & Sabratha
Nena Agriculture Project	Aljofra
Temisa Agriculture Project	Murzuq
Mountain Foot Cultivation Project	Benghazi
South Aljabel Alkhader Project	Aljabel Alkhader
Elfej Valley Project	Benghazi

Source: GBOT, 2005

Appendix 6.5. The third group for privatization livestock projects

Project	Location
Libyan Livestock and Chicken Libyan Company	
Hera Livestock and Chicken Complex	Ghryan Mountain Foot
Twesha Livestock and Chicken Complex	Qasr Bin Gashir
Tarhona Livestock Centre	Fam Elaga / Qarabuli / Elquea
Livestock and Chicken Complex	Tawurgha
Got Sultan Livestock and Chicken Complex	AlAbyar
Alagoria Livestock and Chicken Complex	Alagoria
Benghazi Chicken Complex	Benghazi
Benghazi Livestock Centre	Benghazi
Centre for Chicken Rearing	Turhona and Misllatah
Ejdabia Livestock Centre	Ejdabia
Wadi Jaref Chicken Project	Sirte
Elassa Camel Research Centre	Alnikat Alghames
Aljofra Livestock Centre	Aljofra
El Desa Livestock Centre	Wadi Alhaya

Source: GBOT, 2005.

Appendix 6.6. The third group for privatization: open projects

Project	Location
Janzur Fish Canning Plant	Aljfara
Canning Plant	–
Al Ribbat Al Tareeghy Fish	–
Subrata Fish Canning Plant	Surman & Sabratha
Zliten Fish Canning Plant	Al Marj
Zliten Refrigerator Complex	Al Marj
Khums Fish Canning Plant	Al Marj
Khums Refrigerator Complex	Al Marj
Ain Elziana Hydroculture Project	Benghazi
Ain Kaam Hydroculture Project	Kaam
Ain Alkazala Hydroculture Project	Tubruq
Open Sea Farm Project	Al Khums
Fresh Water Fish Cultivation Centre	Al Khums
Faroa Hydroculture Complex	Faroa

Source: GBOT, 2005.

Appendix 6.7. Libyan privatizations achieved in 2004

	Name of the economic unit	No. of workers	New owners	No. of shareholders	Sector	Total value of privatization
1	National Company of Beverages	803	Abu-Atnee participation company of beverages	1182	Industry	NA
2	Zliten Biscuit and Cakes Factory	130	Zliten participation company for food manufacturing	93	Industry	NA
3	Misuratah Biscuit and Cake Factory	75	Al-Ta'aon participation company for food manufacturing	37	Industry	NA
4	Al-Shafak Fishing Boat	35: permanent + seasonal	Tashrukkiyah: Al-Shafak for fishing, marketing, and transporting fish products	13	Marine wealth	NA
5	Al-Nasam Fishing Boat	37: permanent + seasonal	Tashrukkiyah: Al-Nasam for fishing	13	Marine wealth	NA
6	Al Nagma Al-Beida Fishing Boat	36: permanent + seasonal	Tashrukkiyah: Al Nagma Al-Beida for fishing & marketing	13	Marine wealth	NA
7	Zarka Alyamama Fishing Boat	33: permanent + seasonal	Tashrukkiyah: Zarka Alyamama for fishing, marketing, and transporting of fish products	13	Marine wealth	NA
8	Tin Can Factory	91	Tashrukkiyah: Al-Mamora for tin cans	91	Industry	NA
9	Khums Aluminum Factory	40	Tashrukkiyah: mediterranean sea for metals	6	Industry	NA
10	Tomato Paste Factory at Sebha	7	Al-Sharara Al Ulaa participation company for food manufacturing	5	Industry	NA
11	Fruit Factory at Derj	8	Tashrukkiyah: Derj for food manufacturing	8	Industry	NA
12	Derj Chicken Station	5	Tashrukkiyah: Derj for chickens	5	Animal wealth	NA
13	Wadi-Alshate Chicken Station	14	Tashrukkiyah: Wadi-Alshate for chickens	14	Animal wealth	NA
14	Welding Rod Factory	10	Tashrukkiyah: Halal Libya for welding rod manufacturing	3	Industry	NA
Total		1324		1496		28504019

Source: GBOT, 2005.

Appendix 6.8. State companies approved for privatization under Resolution No.107 of 21/6/2005

No.	City	Economic Unit	Ownership transfer form	Privatization value (LD) (Tamleek)	Date of start registration	No. of employees	Operation status
1	Tripoli	Alhoria Plastic and Sponges Factory	Syarika Musahima	2,567,866	15/12/2005	79	Continues
2	Tripoli	Baian Alsaha Sponges Factory	Syarika Musahima	1,902,962	1/1/2006	101	Continues
3	Tripoli	Okba Milk Factory	Syarika Musahima	12,616,238	15/12/2005	197	Continues
4	Tripoli	Altaharor Cleaning Factory	Syarika Musahima	3,945,301	15/12/2005	332	Joint-operation
5	Tripoli	Alamal Refrigerator and Ovens Factory	Syarika Musahima	901,813	15/12/2005	85	Continues
6	Tripoli	Gacool Soap Powder Factory	Syarika Musahima	6,401,382	Postponed	317	Liquidated
7	Tripoli		Tashrukkiyah	637,718	24/9/2005	25	Liquidated
8	Almirqueb	Khums Refrigerator Comples	Tashrukkiyah	578,666	Postponed	13	Under Investment Pact
9	Almirqueb	Khums Milk Factory	Syarika Musahima	7,033,123	15/12/2005	84	Continues
10	Almirqueb	Khums Fish Canning Plant	Syarika Musahima	4,675,039	Postponed	8	Under Investment Pact
11	Aljabel Alakhder	Albeida Plastic and Sponges Factory	Syarika Musahima	1,101,771	15/12/2005	24	Low-operation
12	Al-Zawia	Surman Plastic Factory	Syarika Musahima	7,010,115	15/12/2005	99	Low-operation
13	Al-Zawia	Al-Zawia Oven Factory	Syarika Musahima	1,975,165	15/12/2005	23	Liquidated
14	Aljfara	Al-Sawani Plastics and Sponges Factory	Syarika Musahima	7,525,552	24/12/2005	261	Continues
15	Aljfara	Carton Boxes Factory	Syarika Musahima	2,904,566	1/1/2006	121	Low-operation
16	Aljfara	Janzur Gas Factory	Syarika Musahima	5,837,448	15/12/2005	102	Continues
17	Aljfara	Janzur Soap Factory	Syarika Musahima	3,272,513	20/12/2005	187	Low-operation
18	Aljfara	Janzur Milk Factory	Syarika Musahima	651,794	20/12/2005	35	Continues
19	Aljfara	Mnbaa Bin Ghashir Factory	Syarika Musahima	12,826,838	5/1/2006	182	Continues
20	Misuratah	Misuratah Freezer Factory	Syarika Musahima	1,699,818	1/1/2006	55	Liquidated
21	Misuratah	Misuratah Plastic and Sponges Factory	Syarika Musahima	1,596,937	15/12/2005	20	Liquidated

Appendix 6.9. SOEs to be privatized through decision No. 200, 20 August 2006

No.	Economic unit	City	Ownership transfer form
1	Arab Beverage Company For Manufacturing and Bottling	Tripoli	Syarika Musahima
2	Al-Johara Company for Manufacturing Electrical Machineries	Tripoli	Syarika Musahima
3	Alwehda Plastic and Artificial Sponge Factory	Tripoli	Syarika Musahima
4	Tripoli Furniture Company (School Furniture Factory)	Tripoli	Syarika Musahima
5	Aljfara Milk Factory + 7 October Milk Factory	Aljfara	Syarika Musahima
6	Medical Cotton Factory	Aljfara	Syarika Musahima
7	Khums Fish Canning Factory	Almirqueb	Syarika Musahima
8	Al-Matost Company of Marine Services	Almirqueb	Syarika Musahima
9	Paper Industry Complex	Misuratah	Syarika Musahima
10	Misuratah Foodstuffs Company	Misuratah	Syarika Musahima
11	Benghazi Milk Company	Benghazi	Syarika Musahima
12	Public Company for Textiles and Clothes	Benghazi	Syarika Musahima
13	Benghazi Dyeing and Tanning Unit	Benghazi	Syarika Musahima
14	National Company for Foodstuffs Industry	Benghazi	Syarika Musahima
15	Alhowari Cream Freezers	Benghazi	Tashrukkiyah
16	Alkewefia Cream Freezers	Benghazi	Tashrukkiyah
17	Aljabel Alakher Fruit Factory	Aljabel Alakher	Syarika Musahima
18	Al Beida Furniture Factory	Aljabel Alakher	Syarika Musahima
19	Al-Rabat Al-Tarhakee Fish Canning Factory	Alnokat Alkams	Syarika Musahima
20	Almaarefa Copybook Factory	Al-Zawia	Tashrukkiyah
21	Infants Requirements Factory	Al-Zawia	Syarika Musahima

Appendix 6.10. List of privatized companies, from 2004 to August 2006

No.	Economic unit	City	Ownership transfer form	Privatization value (LD) (Tamleek)	No of shareholders	Current status (privatization/Tamleek)
1	Zliten Biscuit and Cakes Factory	Almirqueb	Syarika Musahima	490,00	93	Privatized to the producers
2	Zliten Biscuits and Sweets Factory	Misuratah	Syarika Musahima	337,062	37	Privatized to the producers
3	Al-Shafak Fishing Boat	Alnokat Alkams	Tashrukkiyah	980,456	13	Privatized to the producers
4	Al-Nasam Fishing Boat	Alnokat Alkams	Tashrukkiyah	947,767	13	Privatized to the producers
5	Al-Nagma Al-Beida Fishing Boat	Alnokat Alkams	Tashrukkiyah	1,004,973	13	Privatized to the producers
6	Zarka Alyamama Fishing Boat	Alnokat Alkams	Tashrukkiyah	923,250	13	Privatized to the producers
7	Tin Can Factory	Aljfara	Tashrukkiyah	1,933,582	91	Privatized to the producers
8	Khums Aluminium Factory	Almirqueb	Tashrukkiyah	127,638	6	Privatized to the producers
9	Fruit Factory at Derj	Ghadames	Tashrukkiyah	107,357	8	Privatized to the producers
10	Chicken Factory at Derj	Ghadames	Tashrukkiyah	235,886	5	Privatized to the producers
11	Obarie Chicken Factory	Wadi-Alhaya	Tashrukkiyah	7,503,292	306	Privatized to the producers
12	Welding Rod Factory	Tajora	Tashrukkiyah	19,952	3	Privatized to the producers
13	Derna Furniture Factory	Derna	Syarika Musahima	3,846,693	214	Privatized to the producers
14	Derna Clothes Factory	Derna	Syarika Musahima	1,434,406	209	Privatized to the producers
15	Children Food Factory	Aljfara	Tashrukkiyah	307,274	53	Privatized to the producers
16	Fruits And Vegetables Factory	Aljfara	Tashrukkiyah	2,561,452	97	Privatized to the producers
17	Murzuq Chicken Factory	Murzuq	Tashrukkiyah	449,567	4	Privatized to the producers
18	Aljofra Detergent Factory	Aljofra	Tashrukkiyah	197,146	4	Privatized to the producers
19	Tripoli Gas Factory	Tripoli	Tashrukkiyah	695,729	36	Privatized to the producers
20	Tripoli Aluminium Factory	Tripoli	Syarika Musahima	378,753	101	Privatized to the producers
21	Candle and Chalk Factory	Tripoli	Tashrukkiyah	209,212	44	Privatized to the producers
22	Perfume and Fragrance Factory	Tripoli	Syarika Musahima	501,993	40	Privatized to the producers
23	Misllatah Chicken Factory	Almirqueb	Tashrukkiyah	502,255	11	Privatized to the producers
24	Zahra Chicken Factory	Aljfara	Tashrukkiyah	1,328,957	42	Privatized to the producers
25	Ghryan Aluminum Factory	Ghryan	Tashrukkiyah	48,669	8	Privatized to the producers
26	Misuratah Condiment Factory	Misuratah	Tashrukkiyah	487,051	8	Privatized to the producers
27	Khums Tires Services Centre	Almirqueb	Tashrukkiyah	394,599	5	Privatized to the producers
28	Minerals Industry Complex	Misuratah	Syarika Musahima	13,692,690	952	Privatized to the producers
29	Trucks Bodybuilding Complex	Tripoli	Syarika Musahima	289,306	122	Privatized to the producers
30	Sabratha Fish Canning Factory	Alnokat Alkams	Tashrukkiyah	342,425	36	Privatized to the producers
31	Electrical Equipment Factory	Benghazi	Syarika Musahima	3,816,640	57	Privatized to the producers
32	Khums Date Syrup and Jam Fruit Factory	Almirqueb	Tashrukkiyah	1,322,864	69	Privatized to the producers
33	Mansoura Condiment Factory	Aljfara	Tashrukkiyah	908,101	58	Privatized to the producers

Appendix 6.10. (cont.)

No.	Economic unit	City	Ownership transfer form	Privatization value (LD) (Tamleek)	No of shareholders	Current status (privatization/Tamleek)
34	Almerj Chicken Station	Amerj	Tashrukkiyah	279,143	5	Privatized to the producers
35	Khums Textile Factory	Almirqueb	Tashrukkiyah	30,212	4	Privatized to the producers
36	Benghazi Fish Caning Factory	Benghazi	Syarika Musahima	121,802	114	Privatized to the producers
37	Ein Al-Gazala Aquaculture Project	Al Bitnan	Syarika Musahima	217,721	14	Privatized to the producers
38	Tobruk Fishing Boat Factory	Al Bitnan	Tashrukkiyah	199,723	20	Privatized to the producers
39	Derna Detergent Factory	Derna	Tashrukkiyah	364,975	8	Privatized to the producers
40	Sebha Footwear Factory	Sebha	Syarika Musahima	272,454	17	Privatized to the producers
41	Derna Footwear Factory	Derna	Tashrukkiyah	125,544	6	Privatized to the producers
42	Yfren Aluminum Factory	Yfren	Tashrukkiyah	24,724	5	Privatized to the producers
43	Khums Factory for Liquid Soap	Almirqueb	Syarika Musahima	1,411,198	14	Privatized to the producers
44	Complex for Industrial Metal	Benghazi	Syarika Musahima	1,216,760	30	Privatized to the producers
45	Benghazi Gas Factory	Benghazi	Syarika Musahima	13,786,611	606	Privatized to the producers
46	Central Repair Workshop	Benghazi	Syarika Musahima	2,399,411	40	Privatized to the producers
47	Benghazi Furniture Factory	Benghazi	Syarika Musahima	4,513,870	205	Privatized to the producers
48	Musrata Air Pressing Factory	Misuratah	Syarika Musahima	1,042,461	15	Privatized to the producers
49	Bin Gasher Foodwear Factory	Aljfara	Syarika Musahima	529,526	50	Privatized to the producers
50	Benghazi Bicycle Factory	Benghazi	Syarika Musahima	686,908	59	Privatized to the producers
51	Janzur Fish Caning Factory	Aljfara	Syarika Musahima	804,812	16	Privatized to the producers
52	Tripoli Air-Condition Complex	Tripoli	Syarika Musahima	489,114	33	Privatized to the producers
53	Tripoli Textile Factory	Tripoli	Syarika Musahima	442,061	14	Privatized to the producers
54	Arabian Cement Factory	Almirqueb	Syarika Musahima	600,000,000	61639	Privatized to the producers, individuals, and public bodies
55	National Company of Beverages	Benghazi	Syarika Musahima	21,650,000	1182	Privatized to the producers, individuals, and public bodies
56	Sebha Tomato Paste Factory	Sebha	Syarika Musahima	251,462	5	Privatized to the producers, individuals, and public bodies
57	Automatic Bakery	Tripoli	Syarika Musahima	649,155	81	Privatized to the producers, individuals, and public bodies

Appendix 6.10. (cont.)

No.	Economic unit	City	Ownership transfer form	Privatization value (LD) (Tamleek)	No of shareholders	Current status (privatization/Tamleek)
58	Sawani Metal Works Complex	Tripoli	Syarika Musahima	169,568	82	Privatized to the producers, individuals, and public bodies
59	Fellaah Fridge, Gargor Region	Tripoli	Syarika Musahima	375,584	13	Privatized to the producers, individuals, and public bodies
60	Misuratah Textile Factory	Misuratah	Syarika Musahima	3,165,134	633	Privatized to the producers, individuals, and public bodies
61	Al Gharbia Centre for Tyre Distribution	Tripoli	Syarika Musahima	851,008	141	Privatized to the producers, individuals, and public bodies
62	Misuratah Furniture Factory	Misuratah	Syarika Musahima	2,820,302	614	Privatized to the producers, individuals, and public bodies
63	Bani-Walid Complex for Cotton Manufacturing	Ban-Walid	Syarika Musahima	16,458,368	448	Privatized to the producers, individuals, and public bodies
64	Misuratah Footwear Industrial Complex	Misuratah	Syarika Musahima	3,505,974	244	Privatized to the producers, individuals, and public bodies
65	Tobruk Footwear Factory	Al Bitnan	Syarika Musahima	61,939	11	Privatized to the producers, individuals, and public bodies
66	Al -Zawia Footwear Factory	Al -Zawia	Syarika Musahima	164,075	10	Privatized to the producers, individuals, and public bodies
67	Tajora Dyeing and Tanning Unit	Tripoli	Syarika Musahima	222,849	13	Privatized to the producers, individuals, and public bodies
	Total	–	–	696,136,174	67,412	–

Source: GBOT, 2006.

Appendix 7.1. Misuratah Free Zone: Misuratah port data.

The Free Zone utilizes Misuratah port, which has the following characteristics:

- Depth 11 m.
- Area 300 ha.
- Total berth's length 4440 m.
- Capacity 6 million tons/year.
- Open storage terminals 290 ha, of which 30 ha concrete paved and 60 ha asphalt paved.
- Covered warehouses 67,500 m^2.
- Grain silos with a capacity of 40,000 tons.

Appendix 7.2. Misuratah Free Zone: Misuratah steel complex

Close to the Free Zone is the Steel Complex, which is the biggest integrated industrial complex in Libya, occupying an area of 1200 ha. The annual output of the complex is about 1,324,000 tons of steel, produced by direct reduction of iron ore using local natural gas.

The primary steel end products of the complex are as follows:

- Bars and wires.
- Light and medium sections.
- Hot-rolled rolls and sheets.
- Cold-rolled rolls and sheets.

Appendix 7.3. Misuratah Free Zone: Services available to investors

The following services, facilities, and utilities are available:

- Land plots of different sizes in line with investor's demand.
- Modern offices and covered warehouses at reasonable costs.
- Energy (oil, gas, electricity) at low rates.
- Potable water, sewage utilities, and other services at competitive costs.
- Modern and versatile financial and banking services.
- Modern telecommunications services.
- Marine transport services to different international ports,
- Road transport services to African countries and to neighbouring Arab countries.
- Health insurance services to investors and employees working in projects established in the Free Zone.
- Complete insurance services.
- Legal and other consulting services.

Appendix 7.4. Misuratah Free Zone: statistics on Misuratah Free Zone

Distances between Misuratah Free Zone and the main cities of Libya (km)

No.	City	Distance	No.	City	Distance
1	Tobruk	1264	11	El Brega	568
2	Imsaad	1427	12	Ben Juwad	420
3	Aljaghbub	1218	13	Sirte	239
4	Derna	1126	14	Tripoli	207
5	Al Beida	1025	15	Zuwarah	322
6	Al-merj	924	16	Ras Ajdir	381
7	Benghazi	826	17	Hun	425
8	Al Kufra	1524	18	Sebha	787
9	Al-Awynat	1881	19	Murzuq	935
10	Ejdabia	664	20	Ghadames	813

Distances between Misuratah Free Zone and the borders of neighbouring countries (km)

No.	To borders of	Distance
1	Tunisia	381
2	Egypt	1427
3	Algeria	890
4	Sudan	1864
5	Niger	1332
6	Chad	1960

Misuratah Free Zone has a total area of 430 ha, divided into zones and areas connected by roads as follows:

No.	Zone	Area (m^2)
1	Zone 1	900,000
2	Zone 2	500,000
3	Zone 3	700,000
4	Open storage zone A	540,000
5	Open storage zone B	300,000
6	Exhibition area	80,000
7	Administration area	80,000
8	Recreation area	260,000
9	Greenbelt	220,000
10	Accommodation area	200,000
11	Office/camp area	130,000
12	Roads and railways	390,000
	Total	4,300,000

Appendix 7.5. Misuratah Free Zone: details of Misuratah Free Zone Component areas

Zone 1

The area of this zone is about 90 ha. It allows construction of 120,000 m^2 of covered plants and warehouses.

Zone 2

This zone is located in the northern part of the Free Zone behind the administration and exhibition areas. Its total area is approximately 50 ha and it is allocated for electronic and light industries. It is connected to Zone 1 by a dedicated road.

Zone 3

This coastal zone is suitable for industries which need to be close to the sea, and is suitable for heavy industry, with a total area of about 10 ha.

Open Storage Zone A

The total area of this zone is about 54 ha, and is used for container handling, storage and re-distribution activities. In the future it can be used as loading and unloading area because of its proximity to the railway line and the port.

Open Storage Zone B

This zone is located south of the railway alignment. The total area of this zone is about 30 ha. Large areas of this zone are allocated for car parking and storage of raw materials. It can be used for loading and unloading of railway cars.

Exhibition and office area

The proposed location for the exhibition centre is located at the northern gate of the Free Zone, and it is complete with car parking lots. Office facilities are also available for use as headquarters of foreign companies and their branches, as well as for high quality accommodation. The total area is about 8 ha, and it allows for construction of over 30,000 m^2 of covered space.

Administration area

The 8-ha administration area is located in the centre of the Free Zone and contains administrative, customs, and security buildings.

Recreation area

The recreation area includes sports, facilities, parks, and green areas. It is located adjacent to the employees' accommodation area and is situated on about 26 ha of land. This area can be expanded into the neighbouring area towards the sea in case of necessity for other sports activities.

Greenbelt

This area of 22 ha is located between Zones 1 and 2 and improves the overall environment of the Free Zone.

Accommodation area

An area of 20 ha close to the recreational area is allocated for accommodation of employees.

Office/camp area

A 13-ha area close to the accommodation area is allocated for various uses such as offices company camps.

Roads and railways

Roads and railways occupy an area of about 39 ha of the land area. There are also large areas east of the Steel Complex available to the General Authority for Free Zones for future expansion.

Appendix 8.1. Libya: number of branches and agencies of commercial banks with municipalities, 2000

Cities	National Commercial Bank	Jamahiriya	Ummah	Wahda	Al-Sahari	Trade & development	Total
Tripoli	15	22	18	16	11	2	84
Benghazi	5	7	3	14	8	2	39
Sebha	7	7	5	1	4	–	24
Zawia	5	6	7	7	6	–	31
Sirte	7	11	9	12	4	2	45
Jebel Akhdar	14	6	1	10	5	1	37
Jebe Algerbee Region	5	7	7	9	1	–	29
Total	58	66	50	69	39	7	289

Appendix 8.2. Libya, Regional or Ahliah Banks

Name of the Ahliah (Regional) Bank	Date of opening	Name of the Ahliah (Regional) Bank	Date of opening
Tripoli	11 October 1997	Janzur	14 September 1998
Ghryan	7 September 1997	Misuratah	7 December 1996
Tajora	3 July 1999	Tobruk	28 March 1998
Surman	19 August 1997	Qaminis	20 September 1998
Alnnikat Alghames	18 May 1997	Al Beida	10 August 1997
Khums	17 January 1997	Albanees	30 October 1997
Sahl Al-Jafara	24 September 1997	Murzuq	26 August 1997
Tawurgah	6 September 1997	Sirte	28 April 1997
Al-Ujaylat	7 May 1997	Soflgeen	7 July 1997
Derna	10 March 1997	Wadi Alhaya	28June 1998
Sebha	23 May 1997	Wadi Alshate	13 November 1997
Qasr Bin Gashir	26 March 1997	Al-Merj	26 August 1997
Ghadames	7 January 1997	Algobba	22 September 1997
Sabratha	2 April 1997	Jado	31 March 1998
Kufra	30 October 1997	Ras Algazal	23 August 1998
Zlitan	16 August 1997	Aljfara	22 March 1998
Nalut	26 November 1998	Haee El-Andales	16 November 1998
Suq Al Jam'ah (Tripoli)	18 May 1997	Yfren	27 November 1997
Misllatah	10 July 1997	Ejdabia	15 March 1998
Benghazi	19 March 1997	Shahat	27 November 1997
Turhona	24 January 1997	Mizda	16 December 1997
Alabiar – Alagoria	22 December 1997	Ghat	1 October 2000

Appendix 8.3. Libya: inbound foreign visitors, 1999–2003

Inbound tourism	1999	2000	2001	2002	2003
Arrivals (in 000s)					
1.1 Visitors	965	963	953	858	958
1.2 Tourists (overnight visitors)	178	174	169	135	142
1.3 Same-day visitors	787	789	784	723	816
1.4 Cruise passengers	–	–	–	–	–
Arrivals by region: (in 000s)					
2.1 Africa	531	533	515	439	458
2.2 America	–	1	1	2	2
2.3 Europe	33	34	40	36	42

Appendix 8.3. (cont.)

Inbound tourism	1999	2000	2001	2002	2003
2.4 East Asia and the Pacific	3	2	6	7	7
2.5 South Asia	1	1	4	4	4
2.6 Middle East	396	392	388	370	445
Arrivals by means of transport (in 000s)					
3.1 Air	–	–	343	309	342
3.2 Rail	–	–	–	–	–
3.3 Road	926	925	590	531	591
3.4 Sea	39	38	20	18	19
Arrivals by purpose of visit (in 000s)					
4.1 Leisure, recreation, and holidays	43	41	49	47	45
4.2 Business and professional	51	50	58	38	40
4.3 Other	84	83	62	50	57
Accommodation: (in 000s)					
5.1 Overnight stays in hotels and similar establishments	320	582	571	453	477
5.2 Guests in hotels and similar establishments	–	–	–	–	–
5.3 Overnight stay in all types of accommodation establishments	339	–	–	–	–
5.4 Average length of stay of non-resident tourists in all accommodation establishments (by nights)	7	7	7	7	7
Tourism expenditure in the country (in US $ Million)					
6.1 Tourism expenditure in the country	39	–	–	–	–
6.2 Travel (in US $ Million)	27	97	94	75	79
6.3 Passenger transport	12	–	–	–	–
Domestic tourism accommodation: (in 000s)					
7.1 Overnight stays in hotels and similar establishments	–	–	–	–	–
7.2 Guests in hotels and similar establishments	–	–	–	–	–
7.3 Overnight stays in all types of accommodation establishments	969	971	970	972	968
7.4 Average length of stay of resident tourists in all accommodation establishments (by nights)	–	–	–	–	–
Outbound tourism					
8.1 Departures	–	–	–	–	–
8.2 Tourism expenditure in other countries (in US $ Million)	574	–	–	–	–
8.3 Travel	402	–	–	–	–
8.4 Passenger transport (in US $ Million)	172	–	–	–	–
Tourism industry: hotels and similar establishments (in units)					
9.1 Number of rooms	–	11,815	12,405	12,405	12,405
9.2 Number of beds–places	–	19,969	20,967	20,967	20,967
9.3 Occupancy rate (per cent)	53%	54%	53%	42%	45%
9.4 Average length of stay (by nights)	–	–	–	–	–
Related indicators: share of the tourism expenditures (%)					
10.1 Gross domestic product (GDP) (%)	0.1	–	–	–	–
10.2 Exports of goods (%)	0.5	–	–	–	–
10.3 Exports of service (%)	66.1	–	–	–	–

Source: World Tourism Organisation, 2004.

Appendix 8.4. Libyan food production/Imports, 2002

Items	Domestic production (metric tons)	Imports (metric tons)	Total
Cereals total	214500	2213159	2427659
Wheat	125000	1649916	1774916
Rice (milled equivalent)	–	125012	125012
Barley	80000	205381	285381
Maize	2000	212340	214340
Rye	–		
Oats	–	2763	2763
Millet	7500	319	7819
Sorghum	–	5	5
Cereals, Other	–	17424	17424
Starchy roots	195000	8707	203707
Cassava	–		
Potatoes	195000	8707	203707
Sugar crops total			311398
Sugar cane			0
Sugar beet			0
Sugar & sweeteners	750	155398	156148
Sugar, non-centrifugal			0
Sugar (raw equivalent)		140598	140598
Sweeteners, other		14652	14652
Honey	750	148	0
Treenuts	31000	720	31720
Oilcrops total	168900	5892	174792
Soya beans		17	17
Groundnuts (shelled Eq)	18900	135	19035
Sunflower seed		17	17
Rape and mustard seed		1	1
Cottonseed		0	0
Coconuts, incl. copra		366	366
Sesame seed		317	317
Palmkernels		25	25
Olives	150000	4988	154988
Oilcrops, other	0	26	26
Vegetable oils	7750	70858	78608
Soyabean oil		10100	10100
Groundnut oil		0	0
Sunflowerseed oil		8000	8000
Rape and mustard oil		38	38
Cottonseed oil		0	0

Appendix 8.4. (cont.)

Items	Domestic production (metric tons)	Imports (metric tons)	Total
Palmkernel oil		200	200
Palm oil		5068	5068
Coconut oil		222	222
Sesame seed oil		11	11
Olive oil	7750	15300	23050
Rice bran oil			
Maize germ oil		30400	30400
Oilcrop oil, other	0	1519	1519
Vegetables total	821000	459879	1280879
Tomatoes	160000	456784	616784
Onions	180000	485	180485
Vegetables, other	481000	2610	483610
Fruits – excluding wine	324500	41849	366349
Oranges, mandarins	53000	1906	54906
Lemons, limes	14500	49	14549
Grape fruit	0	248	248
Citrus, other		2527	
Bananas	0	485	2527
Plantains			
Apples	5000	11272	16272
Pineapples		856	856
Dates	140000	197	140197
Grapes	40000	1233	41233
Fruits, other	72000	23076	95076
Stimulants			13345
Coffee		1208	1208
Cocoa beans		1953	1953
Tea		10184	10184
Spices		1844	1844
Pepper		63	63
Pimento		1138	1138
Cloves		6	6
Spices, other		637	637
Meat	141950	13782	155732
Bovine meat	6300	1254	7554
Mutton & goat meat	33350	12198	45548

Appendix 8.4. (cont.)

Items	Domestic production (metric tons)	Imports (metric tons)	Total
Pig meat		40	40
Poultry meat	98800	290	99090
Meat, other	3500	0	3500
Offals, edible	5961	6	5967
Animal fats	1006	3825	4831
Butter, ghee		997	997
Cream		589	589
Fats, animals, raw	1006	2239	3245
Fish, body oil		0	0
Fish, liver oil			
Milk – excluding butter	211408	174132	385540
Eggs	60000	3743	63743
Fish, seafood	33339	9822	43161
Freshwater fish	100	119	219
Demersal fish	14500	259	14759
Pelagic fish	15189	7545	22734
Marine fish, other	3550	1832	5382
Crustaceans		40	40
Pulses, Total	20100	4522	24622
Beans	1000	878	1878
Peas	5700	206	5906
Pulses, other	13400	3438	16838

Source: FAO, 2004.

Appendix 8.5. Libya: main marine fishery landing sites, 2004

Port Name	Latitude	Longitude	Fleet No., atrisanal	Fleet No., industries	Landing pelagic	Landing demrsal	Total landing
Farwah	33.04:736 N	11.44:152 E	128	0	28	700	728
Zuwarah	32.55:275 N	12.07:194 E	130	36	7200	2920	10120
Zuwagahah	32.48:820 N	12.27:702 E	68	0	4080	320	4400
Marsa Sabrataha	32.48:298 N	12.27:273 E	20	0	0	140	140
Ras El Wassif	32.48:129 N	12.31:380 E	45	0	0	315	315
Marsa Sidi Zeid	32.47:702 N	12.34:452 E	21	0	0	140	140
Marsa Dila	32.47:576 N	12.44:877 E	39	0	0	258	258
Sidi Blal	32.47:576 N	12.57:308 E	50	0	2228	83	2311
Gasriah	32.52:540 N	13.06:900 E	59	0	0	236	236
Bab El Bahar	32.54:052 N	13.10:629 E	79	42	1882	2921	4803
Enadi El Bahari	32.54:597 N	13.14:084 E	220	0	1615	1489	3104
El Magtah	32.63:739 N	13.22:547 E	24	0	0	146	146
Ras Laman	32.47:580 N	13.44:831 E	24	0	0	100	100
Mina & Marsa Al Khums	32.40:687 N	14.14:672 E	49	10	943	966	1909
Zliten	32.29:951 N	14.34:295 E	83	0	1650	257	1907
Zreg	32.26:250 N	14.54:153 E	27	0	0	155	155
Dzairah	32.25:172 N	15.00:330 E	24	0	0	108	108
Mina Qasr Ahmed	32.22:455 N	15.13:043 E	115	12	680	2000	2680
Sirt	31.112:695 N	16.35:017 E	30	0	0	298	298
Harawa	31.05:034 N	17.17:618 E	34	0	0	338	338
Marsa Laweija	30.54:633 N	17.52:006 E	18	0	0	99	99
Mina Ras Lanuf	30.30:251 N	18.34:181 E	23	8	116	800	916
Mina Bengazi	32.05:227 N	20.02:895 E	173	11	165	2300	2465
Susah	32.54:212 N	21.57:853 E	31	0	0	171	171
Derna	32.45:631 N	22.39:203 E	31	0	0	229	229
Tubruk	32.04:716 N	23.58:444 E	23	4	0	520	520
Total			1453	123	20587	18009	38596

Source: COPEMED, 2005.
Note: This table does not include tuna fleet (15 units), which are harboured in Tripoli commercial port.

Appendix 9.1. El Brega oil marketing company: pipelines

S.No.	Name of line and location	Line start	Line end	Diameter (in.)	Length (km)	Construction date	Operation date	Pumping radio (m^3/H)	Kind of product
1	Al-Zawia Storehouse (W3)	Al-Zawia	Al Fatah	16	55	1982	1992	330	White products
2	Al-Zawia Storehouse	Al-Zawia	Al Fatah	10	55	1974	1975	250	White products
3	Al-Zawia Storehouse	Al-Zawia	Janzur	8	34	1974	1975	100	Heavy oil/oil
4	Al-Zawia Storehouse (W2)	Al-Zawia	Watiah	16	89.8	1982	1982	400	Jet fuel
5	Al-Zawia Storehouse (W1)	Al-Zawia	Jamil	16	64.7	1982	1982	400	Jet fuel
6	Jamil Storehouse	Jamil	Watiah	16	44.65	1982	1982	400	Jet fuel
7	Line between (W1) and (W2)	Line (W1)	Line (W2)	16	5.6	1982	1982	400	Jet fuel
8	Jamil Storehouse	Jamil	Zuwarah Port	16	8.2	1982	1982	400	Jet fuel
9	Al Fatah Storehouse	Al Fatah	South Tripoli	6	6	1976	1976	100	Oil
10	Al Fatah Storehouse	Al Fatah	Tripoli Airport	10	13.5	1983	1984	100	Jet fuel
11	Al-Hanee Storehouse	Al-Hanee	Sha'ab Port	6	4.6	1983	1984	100	Liquid gas
12	Al-Hanee Storehouse	Al-Hanee	Sha'ab Port	4	4.6	1983	1984	–	Return line
13	Ben Gaber Storehouse	Ben Gaber	Sha'ab Port	12	3	1971	1982	250	Heavy oil
14	Ben Gaber Storehouse	Ben Gaber	Sha'ab Port	8	3	1962	1982	400	Oil
15	Naser Storehouse	Naser	Misuratah Port	12	3.725	1984	1988	500	Benzene (two kinds)
16	Naser Storehouse	Naser	Misuratah Port	12	3.725	1984	1988	500	Oil
17	Naser Storehouse	Naser	Misuratah Port	18	5.7	1984	1988	600	Heavy oil
18	Naser Storehouse	Naser	Misuratah Port	8	3.725	1984	1988	100	Liquid gas
19	Musrata Port	Musrata Port	Iron & Steal	18	7.5	1984	1988	600	Heavy oil
20	Naser Storehouse	Naser	Misuratah Gas	12	13	1984	1986	270	Oil
21	Naser Storehouse	Naser	Air Academy	8	21	1984	Ceased	Ceased	Jet fuel
22	28 March Storehouse	Platform	Heavy Oil S.	14	0.5	–	–	–	Heavy oil
23	28 March Storehouse	Platform	28 March Storehouse	10	24	–	–	–	White products
24	28 March Storehouse	Platform	28 March Storehouse	10	24	–	–	–	White products
25	28 March Storehouse	Al Misfat (Refinery)	28 March Storehouse	10	2	–	–	–	White products
26	Al Sarir Storehouse	Al Misfat (Refinery)	Sarir Storehouse	8	90	–	–	–	White products
27	Al Sarir Storehouse	Al Sarir	Electricity Plant	8	1.5	–	–	–	White products

Appendix 10.1. Conventions concerned with the environment signed by Libya and effective date

Name of convention and agreement	Date of signature	Effective date
Agreement of the establishment of a general council for fisheries in the Mediterranean, in its modified form from Rome, 1949	6 December 1949	20 February 1955: effective date for Libya as signatory was 14 May 1963
International agreement on plant protection, Rome, 1951	6 December 1951	3 April 1952: effective date for Libya as signatory was 9 July 1970
International agreement on the prevention of sea pollution, in its amendment from 1969	12 May 1954: signed by Libya on 18 February 1972	26 July 1958: the amendment was approved on 19 July 1976.
Treaties on the prohibition of nuclear weapons in the air, outer space, and under water surface, Moscow, 1963	5 August 1963	10 October 1963:effective date for Libya as a signatory was 15 July 1968
Agreement on the principles regulating states activities in outer space exploration and use, including the moon and other celestial bodies, 1967	27 January 1967	10 October 1967: effective date for Libya as signatory was 3 July 1968
Agreement on the protection of world cultural and natural heritage, Paris, 1972	23 November 1997	17 December 1975: effective date for Libya as a signatory was 13 January 1997.
Agreement on the prevention of sea pollution from the disposal of wasters and other substances, and its amendment from 1972	29 December 1972	30 August 1975: effective date for Libya 22 December 1976.
London agreement on the protection of human life in seas, 1974.	Signed by Libya on 2 of July 1981	Came in effect in Libya on 2 October 1981
Agreement on the protection of the Mediterranean Sea from pollution , Barcelona, 1976: the appendix protocols are in four stages	Ratification date 16 February 1976: signed by Libya on 31 January 1977	12 February 1978: effective date for Libya 2 March 1979
A– Protocol on the protection of the Mediterranean Sea from waste disposed by vessels and air craft, Barcelona, 1976	16 February 1976: signed by Libya on 31 January 1977	12 February 1978: effective date for Libya 2 March 1979
B– Cooperation protocol on the control of Mediterranean Sea pollution by the oil and other harmful substance in emergency cases, Barcelona, 1976	16 February 1976: signed by Libya on 31 January 1977	12 February 1978: effective date for Libya 2 March 1979
C– Protocol on the protection of the Mediterranean Sea from land sources pollution, Athens, 1980	17 May 1980: signed by Libya on 17 May 1981	17 June 1983: effective date for Libya 5 July 1989
D– Protocol on areas enjoying particular protection in Mediterranean Sea, Geneva, 1980	Signed by Libya on 5 July 1989	Effective date for Libya 5 July 1989
Vienna agreement on the protection of the ozonosphere, 1985	22 March 1985: signed by Libya on 9 October 1990	22 September 1988: effective date for Libya, n.a
Montreal protocol on ozonosphere deletion substance–Montreal	Signed by Libya on 9 October 1989	1 January 1989: effective date for Libya, n.a
Agreement on the provision of assistance in the event of nuclear accident or radiation emergency , Vienna, 1986	26 September 1986: signed by Libya on 28 July 1990	26 February 1987: effective date for Libya, n.a

Appendix 10.2. International conventions not signed or ratified by Libya

Name of convention and agreement	Libya legal status
Protocol on prohibition of transportation and moving poisonous and dangerous substances across the Mediterranean Sea – A2mer, 1976	Not signed or ratified
Protocol on the utilization of the continental shelf, sea bottom, and sub-soil, Madrid, 1994.	Not signed or ratified
Protocol concerning areas enjoying special protection and biodiversity in the Mediterranean Sea , Barcelona, 1955	Not ratified
UN agreement (law and sea) marine law, Montengo Bay, 1982	Not signed or ratified
International agreement on the protection of biodiversity, Rio de Janeiro, 1992	Not ratified
Bazel agreement in the control of dangerous waste and their disposal across borders, 1989	Not signed or ratified
Agreements on the protection of immigrant wide animals, Bonn, 1979	Not signed or ratified
Agreement on whale protection in the Black Sea, Mediterranean Sea, and ports of the Atlantic Ocean, Monaco, 1969	Not signed or ratified
Rotterdam agreement on the application of Prior-approval procedures for certain dangerous chemicals and pesticide circulated in international trade, 1990	Not signed or ratified
Agreement on the regulation of trade in threatened species, Washington, 1973	Not signed or ratified
Agreement to the agreement of the protection of the mediterranean sea from pollution, Barcelona 1995, 10 June 1995	Not ratified
Amendment to the protocol on the protection of the Mediterranean Sea from Land pollution Sources – Sera cosa 1996	Not signed or ratified
Amendment to the protocol on the prevention of Mediterranean Sea Pollution from the disposal of vessels and aircraft wastes, Barcelona, 1995	Signed on 10 June 1995 not ratified

References

Abt Associates (1995) *Privatization in Tunisia. A Review of the Experience to Date*. Private Enterprise Promotion Project, Government of Tunisia/USAID

ACSAD The Arab Center for the Studies of Arid Zones and Dry Lands (2005) http://www.acsad.org/

Adam CS and Cavendish W (1995) *Privatizing Malaysia: Rents, Rhetoric, Realities*, in KS Jomo (Ed.), Westview Press Boulder, CA

African Development Bank/OECD (1993) African Economic Outlook, Algeria, http://www.oecd.org/dataoecd/3/54/2497129.pdf

African Union: http://www.africa-union.org/

Africasia (1970)

Aghrout A and Hodd M (2005) *Algeria's Economy: Mutations, Performances and Challenges*, Development, International Business, Strategy & the Environment Research Group Research Papers No. 1 Westminster Business School, London

Aghrout A and Sutton K (1990) Regional Economic Union in the Maghreb, *Journal of Modern African Studies*, 28:1

Al Ahram (2003)

Alami R (2005) Changing Financial Structures in the Arab World: Some Implications for Oil and Gas Oxford Institute for Energy Studies F 10

Al-Awadhi B (1996) Legal Foundation for Kuwait's Environmental Claims, *Journal of Gulf and Arabian Peninsula Studies*, Kuwait

Al-Awadhi B (2002) Environmental Legislations and Its Impact on the Protection of the Environment, Arab Center for Education Research of The Gulf Countries, April

Aleslam S (2002) *Libya and the XXI Century*, Editar Spa, Italy

Alexander M and Corti C (1993) Argentina's Privatization Program: Experience, Issues, and Lessons. CFS Discussion Paper 103. World Bank, Confinancing and Financial Advisory Services Department, Washington, D.C.

Alfaro L, Areendam C, Kalemli-Ozca S and Sayak S (2004), FDI and Economic Growth: The Role of Local Financial Markets, *Journal of International Economics*, 64

Alghariani SA (2003) Water Transfer Versus Desalination in North Africa: Sustainability and Cost Comparison, Occasional Paper 49, SOAS Water Issues Study Group School of Oriental and African Studies (SOAS)/King's College London University of London, March

Al Haqiqa, Tripoli, 15 July (1971)

Al Hayat, Beruit, January (1969)

Al Qadhafi M (2002) *The White Book, A Vision for Peace in the Middle East*, Tripoli

Al-Sahari Bank, Libya, Annual Reports (2000, 2002, 2003)

Anag G, Cremaschi M, Lernia S and Liverani M (2002) Environment, Archaeology, and Oil: The Messak Settafet Rescue Operation (Libyan Sahara), *African Archaeological Review* 19(2)

Anderson, L (2003) in an interview, 22 December Libyan Expert: Qaddafi, Desperate to End Libya's Isolation, Sends a 'Gift' to President Bush, Council on Foreign Relations http://www.cfr.org/publication/6617/libyan_expert.html?breadcrumb=%2Fbios%2F317%2Flisa_anderson

Andersson T (2005) "Coping Skills" in *Strategic Views on Foreign Direct Investment* ISA in cooperation with UNCTAD and WAIPA
Arnold G (1996) *The Maverick State: Gaddafi and the New World Order*, Cassell, New York
Associated Press, 27 July, 2004, Mrs. Najat Mehdi al-Hajjaji, Libyan Ambassador to UN
Atlantic Council (2001)
Bacon KH (1996) United States Department of Defense News Briefing Tuesday, 23 April, http://www.dod.mil/transcripts/1996/t042396_tbrfg-42.html
Bahgat G (2006) The United States and the Middle East: Interdependence not Independence, *OPEC Review*, 30
Balfour Declaration (1917) http://www.yale.edu/lawweb/avalon/mideast/balfour.htm
Barisan Nasional (National Front) Malaysia http://www.bn.org.my
Barker G (2002) A Tale of Two Deserts: Contrasting Desertification Histories on Rome's Desert Frontiers, *World Archaeology*, 33
Barth H (1857) Reisen und Entdeckungen in Nord und Central Afrika, Ghota, Perthes
BBC News, 5 February, 2001
Belev (2001) Privatization in Egypt and Tunisia: Liberal Outcomes And/Or Liberal Policies? *Mediterranean Politics*, 6:2
Birdsall N and Nellis J (2002) Winners and Losers: Assessing the distributional impact of privatization, *The Center for Global Development*, Working Paper Number 6
Birkinshaw J (2005) Brains Matter *in Strategic Views on Foreign Direct Investment.* ISA in cooperation with UNCTAD and WAIPA
Black I and Morris B (1991) Israel's Secret Wars: A History of Israel's Intelligence Services, Grove Weidenfeld, New York
Blackwell S (2003) Saving the King: Anglo-American Strategy and British Counter-subversion Operations in Libya 1953–59, *Middle Eastern Studies*, 39:1
Blonigen BA (1997) Firm-specific Assets and the Link Between Exchange Rates and Foreign Direct Investment, *American Economic Review*, 87:3
Blonigen BA and Feenstra RC (1996) Protectionist Threats and Foreign Direct Investment, NBER Working Papers 5475, National Bureau of Economic Research, Inc
Blundy D and Lycett A (1987) *Qaddafi and the Libyan Revolution*, Boston: Little, Brown
Bolbol A and Omran M (2003) Foreign Direct Investment, Financial Development, and Economic Growth: Evidence from Arab Countries, *Review of Middle East Economics and Finance*, 1:3
Bolton J, Under Secretary of State, Testimony before House International Relations Committee, 4 June (2003)
Borensztein E, De-Gregorio J, Lee JW (1998) How Does Foreign Direct Investment Affect Economic Growth? *Journal of International Economics*, 45
Boubakri N and Cosset J (1998) The Operating and Financial Performance of Newly Privatized Firms: Evidence from Developing Countries, *Journal of Finance*, 53
Braudel F (1997) La Méditerranée et le monde méditerranéen à l'époque de Philippe II, Paris: Armand Colin (© 1949)
Brega Oil Marketing Company (BOMC) (2003)
Brega Oil Marketing Company (BOMC) (2004)
Brusentsev V (2006) Evolution of Female Labor Force Participation in the United States: 1967 to 2003, *International Advances in Economic Research*
Bush Public Papers (1993)
Campa JM and Goldberg LS (1995) Investment in Manufacturing, Exchange-Rates and External Exposure, *Journal of International Economics*, 38
Cao A (no date) Privatization of SOEs in Egypt: Labour Issues and Prospects for Development, *Applied Research Series Feasibility Studies*, International Privatization Group, Price Waterhouse
CEDAW UN Convention on the Elimination of all Forms of Discrimination Against Women http://www.un.org/womenwatch/daw/cedaw/

CEN-SAD, http://www.cen-sad.org/
Central Bank of Libya, Reports (2000–2003)
Centre for Policy Studies (1975) "Why Britain needs a Social Market Economy", London
Central Bank of Libya Annual Reports www.cbl-ly.com/
CGIAR (1997) http://www.worldbank.org/html/cgiar/publications/annreps/1997ar.pdf
Chang WN and Radulescu DM (2004) Do Corporate Tax Concessions Really Matter for the Success of Free Economic Zones? *Economics of Planning*, 37 Springer, Netherlands
Chong A and López-de-Silanes F (2003) The Truth about Privatization in Latin America, Inter-American Development Bank. Research Dept
Christides V (2000) Byzantine Libya and the March of the Arabs towards the West of North Africa, London, British Archaeological Reports International Series 851, 20
CIA (2003) Director of Central Intelligence Reports to Congress, 2002 and 2003
Claessens S (1995) The Emergence of Equity Investment in Developing Countries: Overview. *The World Bank Economic Review*, 9:1, 1–18
Claessens S (1996) Banking reform in transition countries, Policy Research Working Paper Series 1642, The World Bank
Claussen M, Kubatzki C, Brovkin V, Ganopolski A, Hoelzmann P and Pachur H-J (1999) Simulation of an abrupt change in Saharan vegetation in the mid-Holocene *Geophyical Research Letters* 26:14
COMESA (Common Market of Eastern and Southern Africa) http://www.comesa.int
Committee on International Relations, US House of Representatives: http://wwwc.house.gov/international_relations/108/wel092204.html
Cooley J (1982) *Libyan Sandstorm*, Holt, Rinehart & Winston, New York
COPEMED (2005) http://www.faocopemed.org/en/index.htm
Corrales J (1998) Coalitions and Corporate Choices in Argentina, 1976–1994: The Recent Private Sector Support of Privatization, *Studies in Comparative International Development*, 32, 4
Corrales J and Cisneros I, Corporatism, Trade Liberalization and Sectoral Responses: The Case of Venezuela, 1989–1999, World Development
Cowan LG (1990) *Privatization in the Developing World* Greenwood Press: New York, Westport, CT, London
Crowley P and Lee J (2003) Exchange Rate Volatility and Foreign Investment: International Evidence, *International Trade Journal*, 13
Crumley C (1996) The Historical Ecology of Global Climate Change, *Cultural Knowledge and Changing Landscapes*, Santa Fe
Crump RL (1974) *Diary of a Desert Rat*, Pan Books, London
Davis BL (1990) *Qaddafi, Terrorism, and the Origins of the US Attack on Libya*, Praeger, New York
Davis DK (2004) Wastes of the Maghreb: Desertification Narratives in French Colonial Environmental History of North Africa, *Cultural Geographies*, 11
De Candole EVA (1990) *The Life and Times of King Idris of Libya*, Mohamed ben Ghalbon, Manchester
Deeb M (1989) Inter-Maghribi Relations since 1969: A Study of the Modalities of Unions and Mergers, *Middle East Journal*, 43:1
Deeb M (1991) *Libya's Foreign Policy in North Africa*, Westview Press, Boulder, CO
De Felice R (1985) *Jews in an Arab land: Libya, 1835–1970*, Trans. Judith Roumani, J. University of Texas Press, Austin
De la Balze FAM (1995) *Remaking the Argentine Economy*, Council on Foreign Relations Press, New York
DeNicola C (2005) *Dubai's Political and Economic Development: An Oasis in the Desert?* Thesis, Political Science Dept., Williams College, United States

Dioxides Associates (1964) Transport in Libya: A General Survey and Study of the means of Communications Athens, 2 Vols
Douglas K (1966) *Alamein to Zem Zem*, Penguin Modern Classics, Harmondsworth, Middlesex
Earth Trends (2003) earthtrends.wri.org
Eban A (1977) *Abba Eban: An Autobiography*, Random House, New York
Ebersberger B and Lööf (2004) Multinational Enterprises, Spillovers, Innovation and Productivity, Working Paper Series in Economics and Institutions of Innovation 22, Royal Institute of Technology, CESIS – Centre of Excellence for Science and Innovation Studies
Economic Research Forum for the Arab Countries, Iran and Turkey (1998)
Economist Intelligence Unit, Country Profile Libya (2004)
Edwards S (1990) *Capital Flows, Foreign Direct Investment, and Debt-Equity Swaps in Developing Countries*, Working Paper Series, National Bureau of Economic Research, Cambridge, MA
Egyptian Environmental Affairs Agency (EEAA) (2005) http://www.eeaa.gov.eg/
El-Kebir NK, Rodriguez-Cabello C and Tawil MYO (2001) *Age Estimation of Bluefin Tuna (thunnus thynnus, l.) Caught by Traps in Libyan Waters Based on Spine Reading*, COPEMED Scientific Documents SCRS/01/135
El-Shahat M (1978) *Libya Begins the Era of the Jamahiriya,* Rome
El-Tawil and Gashtî (1998) An Overview of Tuna Catches in Methodology-Biology and Statistics scrs/98/92
Emerson M and Noucheva G (2005) *From Barcelona Process to Neighbourhood Policy: Assessments and Open Issues* Centre for European Policy Studies, Brussels
Environmental General Authority, Libya (2002) The First National Report on the Environment, Tripoli
European Commission (2005) Technical Mission to Libya on Illegal Immigration 27 November–6 December (2004)
European Environment Agency (EEA) (2005) www.eea.eu.int
European Union (2005) http://europa.eu.int/comm/external_relations/lybia/news/ip04_279.htm
EU-Water Framework Directive, http://www.wfd-info.org/Laws/index.htm
Fahmy M (1994) Background Paper: Legal and Judicial Framework, presented at the Conference on Private Sector Development in Egypt: Investing in the Future, Cairo, 9–10 October
FAO (2004) http://www.fao.org/es/ess/compendium_2004/pdf/ESS_LIB.pdf
FAO (2005) OECD-FAO Agricultural Outlook: 2005–2014, http://www.oecd.org/document/5/0,2340,en_2649_37401_35015941_1_1_1_37401,00.html
Farley R (1971) *Planning for Development in Libya: The Exceptional Economy in the Developing World*, Praeger, New York
Farsoun SK and Zacharia CE (1997) *Palestine and the Palestinians*, Westview P ress, Boulder, CO
Financial Times, 9 March, 2004, The Iraq War did not Force Gadaffi's Hand
Foreign Direct Investment Magazine, February (2005)
Foreign Office, FO 371/131793, JT 1091/1, No. 160, Ogden to Lloyd 14 July 1958; JT 1091/3/G, No. 196, Lloyd to Ogden, 15 July 1958; Minute by Hooper, 15 July 1958; JT 1091/3/G, 'Libya', Minute by Watson, 15 July 1958
Freedom House (2005) Libya Country Report, http://www.freedomhouse.org
Freestone D (1996) Legal Dimensions of Environmental Management, *Environmental Matters*, 38–39
Fulford M (1989) To East and West: The Mediterranean Trade of Cyrenaica and Tripolitania in Antiquity, *Libyan Studies*, 20
General Electric Company of Libya, Annual Report (2005)

General People's Congress Resolution No.3-2000, March (2000) *The Official Gazette*, 6: 29.4
General Secretariat of the General People's Congress of Libya (1973) Qadhafi's Historic Speech at Zuwara, Tripoli, 15 April (Translation from Arabic)
Goldberg L (1993) Exchange-rates and Investment in US Industry, *Review of Economics and Statistics*, 75
Gomez ET (1991) *Money Politics in the Barisan Nasional*, Forum Publications, Kuala Lumpur
Government of Malaysia (2005) Prime Minister's Department
Government of Tunisia (2004) Census
Graziosi P (1969) The Pre-History of South-Western Libya, In Kanes, William H (Ed.) *The Geology, Archaeology, and Pre-History of the South-Western Fezzan Libya*, Petroleum Exploration Society of Libya, Tripoli
Habiby R (1979) R. Mu'ammar Qadhafi's New Islamic Scientific Socialist Society, *Middle East Review*, Summer
Haley E (1984) *Qaddafi and the United States since (1969)*, Praeger, New York
Hallet D (2002) *Petroleum Geology of Libya*, Elsevier
Ham A (2002) *Lonely Planet: Libya*, Lonely Planet Publications
Hamdani K (2005) Going for the Crown in Strategic Views on Foreign Direct Investment ISA in cooperation with UNCTAD and WAIPA
Hammerich K (2005) WAIPA World Investment Conference 9 –10 March (2005), Geneva, Switzerland
Hansard, House of Commons Debate, The United Kingdom Parliament, 19 January (2005)
Haynes DEL (1965) *An Archaeological and Historical Guide to the Pre-Islamic Antiquities of Tripolitania*, Antiquities, Museums and Archives of Tripoli, Libya
Hazbun W (2004) Globalization, Reterritorialization and the Political Economy of Tourism Development in the Middle East, *Geopolitics*, 9:2
HDR (2005) http://hdr.undp.org/reports/global/2005/
Healey D (1989) *The Time of My Life*, Penguin, London
Heikal M (1975) *The Road to Ramadan*, New York University, New York
Henry PB (2000a) Stock Market Liberalization, Economic Reform, and Emerging Market Equity Prices, *Journal of Finance*, 55:2
Henry PB (2000b) Do Stock Market Liberalizations Cause Investment Booms? *Journal of Financial Economics*, 58:1–2
Heritage Foundation, Annual Index for Economic Freedom (2005) http://www.heritage.org
Herrmann DG (1989) The Paralysis of Italian Strategy in the Italian–Turkish War, 1911–1912, *The English Historical Review*, 104: 411
Holt PM, Lambton AKS and Lewis B (Eds.) (1997) *The Cambridge History of Islam Volume 1*, Cambridge University Press, Cambridge
Hume LJ (1980) Preparations for Civil War in Tripoli in the 1820s : Ali Karamanli, Hassuna D'Ghies and Jeremy Bentham, *Journal of African History*, 21, 311–322
Ibrahimi AT (1988) Le Traité de fraternité et de concorde ou le Maghreb en movement, *Revue Algérienne de Droit International*, 9:1
ICOMOS (1981) Cyrene World Heritage Site
ICOMOS (1985) Sabratha World Heritage Site
IMF, 10 April (2006) The Socialist People's Libyan Arab Jamahiriya: Selected Issue–Medium-Term Economic Reform Strategy, and Statistical Appendix Series: Country Report No. 06/137
IMF, Press Release No. 95/31 May 22 (1995) "IMF Approves Credit under Extended Fund Facility for Algeria"
IMF, Press Release Number 97/50, 5 November (1997)
IMF (1998) 27:17
IMF Country Report Libya No. 05/83 (2005)

IMF Article IV Consultation, Libya (2004)
International Bank for Reconstruction and Development (1960) *The Economic Development of Libya*, The John Hopkins Press, Baltimore
International Court of Justice, The Hague (1993) Verbatim Record, Concerning Territorial Dispute: Libyan Arab Jamahiriya
International Monetary Fund, Public Information Notice (PIN) No. 03/125, 23 October, 2003 IMF Concludes 2003 Article IV Consultation with the Socialist People's Libyan Arab Jamahiriya http://www.imf.org/external/np/sec/pn/2003/pn03125.htm
IMF (2005) Socialist People's Libyan Arab Jamahiriya 2004 Article IV Consultation-Staff Report; Staff Statement; and Public Information Notice on the Executive Board Discussion
Inter-Parliamentary Union (2005) *Women in National Parliaments*, http://www.ipu.org/wmn-e/world.htm
Iran: Department of Environment, http://wbln0018.worldbank .org/mna/mena.nsf
Italian–Libyan Archaeological Mission in the Acacus and Messak – Università degli Studi di Roma "La Sapienza" Via Palestro 63, 00185 Rome – Italy http://www.acacus.it/eng/index.htm
IUCN (1996) *Tourism, Ecotourism, and Protected Areas: The State of Nature-Based Tourism Around the World and Guidelines for Its Development*, Cambridge
Jackson J, 26 June (1993) Interview with Col. Mu`ammar al Qadhafi, http://www.geocities.com/Athens/8744/mqjj.htm
Johansson B and Lööf H (2005) FDI Inflows to Sweden: Consequences for Innovation and Renewal The Royal Institute of Technology, Centre of Excellence for Science and Innovation Studies, Sweden, http://www.infra.kth.se/cesis/documents/WP36.pdf
Jomo KS and Tan WS (1995) Privatization and Renationalization in Malaysia: A Survey, http://unpan1.un.org/intradoc/groups/public/documents/un/unpan021546.pdf
Katzman K (2003) *U.S.–Libyan Relations: An Analytic Compendium of US Policies, Laws & Regulations*, The Atlantic Council, August 2003
Keenan J (2002) Tourism, Development and Conservation: A Saharan perspective Saharan Studies Programme University of East Anglia, UK
Khadduri M (1963) *Modern Libya: A Study in Political Development*, Johns Hopkins Press, Baltimore
Kingdom of Libya, Ministry of Planning and Development (1963)
Kingdom of Libya, Public School Study for Tripoli (1965)
Klieman A (1990) *Israel and the World After Forty Years*, Pergamon-Brassey's McLean, VA
Koechler H (2003) Statement on the agreement between the United States, the United Kingdom and the Libyan Jamahiriya on the remaining issues relating to the fulfilment of all Security Council resolutions resulting from the bombing of Pan Am 103 over Lockerbie, http://i-p-o.org/Koechler-Lockerbie-statement-Aug2003.htm
Kornai J (1986) Contradictions and Dilemmas Cambridge, MA: The MIT Press
Kubbah AQ, *Libya Its Oil System and Economic System*, The Arab Petro-Economic Research Centre, Baghdad
Langhammer R and Luecke, M (2000) *WTO Accession Issues*, Kiel Institute of World Economics, Germany
Lavauden L (1927) Les Forets du Sahara, *Revue des Eaux et Forets*, 65
Lamb H, Eichner U and Switsur V (1989) An 18,000-year Record of Vegetation, Lake-Level and Climate Change from Tigalmamine, Middle Atlas, Morocco, *Journal of Biogeography*, 16
Lamboeuf M (2000) Artisanal Fisheries in Libya – Census of Fishing Vessels and Inventory of Artisanal Fishery Metiers (2000) – COPEMED http://www.faocopemed.org/en/activ/research/artfsh.htm
Lemarchand R (Ed.) (1988) *The Green and the Black: Qadhafi's Policies in Africa,* Indiana University Press, Bloomington, Indiana

Leverett F Middle Eastern Affairs National Security Council (2002–2003)
Lewis B (1968) *The Kemalist Republic, in The Emergence of Modern Turkey*, Oxford University Press
Lhote H (1958) *A la découverte des fresques du Tassili*, Arthaud, Paris
Library of Congress Document (1970) The Libyan Revolution in the Words of Its Leaders, *Middle East Journal*, 24, http://lcweb2.loc.gov/frd/cs/libya/ly_bibl.html
Libya (1977) Declaration of the Establishment of the Authority of the People
Libya: Authority for Information and Documentation (2005)
Libya: First (1976–80) and Second (1981-1985) Development Plans, Tripoli
Libya Focus (2005)
Libya, General Board of Ownership Transfer (GBOT) (2005)
Libya, General Board of Ownership Transfer (GBOT) (2006)
Libya, General Council of Planning (2001)
Libya, General Planning Council (2005)
Libya, High Planning Council (2006)
Libya, Ministry of Planning (1962–2000)
Libya, The Great Man Made River Authority (2002) http://www.gmmra.org/
Libya, United Insurance Company (2005)
Libya: Ministry of Planning and Development, Transport in Libya (1964) A general Survey and Study of the Means of Communications, Preliminary Report, Doxiadis Associates, Consultants on Development and Ekistics (2 vols) Athens
Libya: Ministry of Planning, Economics and Trade (1996) Achievements of the National Economy for 27 Years
Libya: National Supply Corporation (NASCO) (2006) www.nasco.ly.com
Libya, Railway Executive Board (2005)
Libya Saving and Real Estate Investment Bank (2005)
Libya, Secretariat of Finance (2006)
Libya: Secretariat of Planning (1978) *Economic and Social Achievements in the Socialist People's Libyan Arab Jamhariya*,Tripoli
Libya, Secretariat of Planning (2006)
Libyan Central Bank and Libyan National Oil Corporation (LNOC) (2005)
Libyan Constitutional Declaration (1969)
Libyan Civil Aviation Authority (2004)
Libyan Information and Documentation Authority (2005)
Libyan Higher Committee for Statistics and Census (2006)
Libyan Mining Company, Tripoli (2005)
Libyan Ministry of Higher Education (2005)
Libyan National Authority for Information and Documentation, Economic and Social Survey 2002–2003
Libyan National Oil Corporation (2004)
Libyan National Oil Corporation (LNOC) (2005) Downstream Department, Tripoli
Libyan Secretariat of Planning (1978) Economic and Social Achievements, 1970–1977
Lieberman IW and Kirkness CD (1998) Overview of Privatization and Emerging Equity Markets, In IW Lieberman and CD Kirkness (Eds.) *Privatization and Emerging Equity Markets*, The World Bank/Flemmings, Washington, DC
Levine R and Zervos S (1996) Stock Market Development And Long-Run Growth, The World Bank Policy Research Working Paper Series 1582
Levis M (1993) The Long-Run Performance of Initial Offerings: The UK experience, 1980–1988, *Financial Management*, 22:1
Lhote H (1959) *The Search for the Tassili Frescoes*, Hutchinson, London
Lippman TW (2000) *Madeleine Albright and the New American Diplomacy*, Westview Press, Boulder, CO
Lipsey RE (2002) Home and host country effects of FDI, NBER Working Paper 9293

Literacy Trust (2005) www.literacytrust.org.uk

Liverani M, Cremaschi M and di Lernia S (2000) The "Archaeological Park" of the Tadrart Acacus and Messak Settafet (south-western Fezzan, Libya). A Preliminary Project, *Sahara*, 12

Llanos M (2001) Understanding Presidential Power in Argentina: A Study of the Policy of Privatisation in the 1990s, *Journal of Latin American Studies*

Llewelyn O (1982) Desert Reclamation and Conservation in Islamic Law, *The Muslim Scientist*, 11:9

López-Calva LF, On Privatization Methods Development Discussion Paper No. 665 Harvard Institute for International Development Harvard University

Louis WR (1984) *The British Empire in the Middle East, 1945–1951: Arab Nationalism, The United States and Post-War Imperialism*, Oxford University Press. Oxford and New York

Lutz W, Yousif HM and Goujon A (1996) Future Population and Education Trends in the Countries of North Africa RR-96-11. Laxenburg, Austria: IIASA

Maghreb Digest (1965)

Mainguet M (1991) *Desertification: Natural Background and Human Mismanagement*, Springer-Verlag, Berlin

Malaysian Economic Planning Unit (2005)

Manzetti L (1999) *Privatization South American Style*, Oxford University Press, New York

Mauer DC and Senbet WL (1992) The Effect of the Secondary Market on the Pricing of Initial Public Offerings: Theory and Evidence, *Journal of Financial and Quantitative Analysis*, 27, 55–79

Mediterranean Environmental Technical Assistance Program (METAP) (2003)

Megginson WL (2000) The Long-Run Return to Investors in Share Issue Privatization, *Financial Management*

Megginson WL, Nash RJ, Netter J and Poulsen A (1998) *The Choice of Privatization Method: An Empirical Analysis*, mimeo, Department of Finance, Terry College of Business, The University of Georgia, Athens, GA

Megginson WL and Netter JM (2001) From State to Market: A Survey of Empirical Studies on Privatization, *Journal of Economic Literature*, 39

Meliani H (1985) Le Traité de fraternité et de concorde de (1983), ou un nouveau droit de la coopération maghrébine *Annuaire de l'Afrique du Nord*, CNRS, Paris

Menyah K and Paudyal K (1996) Share Issue Privatisations: The UK Experience, In Levis, M (Ed.), *Empirical Issues in Raising Capital*, Elsevier, Amsterdam

Mercer Investment Consulting (2006) Norwegian Government Petroleum Fund. Annual Performance Evaluation Report (2005) http://www.regjeringen.no

Merryll Lynch (1998a) *The Privatization Process: Role of Equity Capital Markets*, Presentation for the Harvard Institute for International Development, New York

Merryll Lynch (1998b) *The Privatization Process*, Presentation for the Harvard Institute for International Development, New York

Messines J (1952) La fixation et le reboisement des sables en Tripolitanie (The Fixing and the Afforestation of Sands in Tripolitanie, Libya). Food and Agriculture Organization of the United Nations (FAO), Rome, Unasylva 6:2

METAP (2005) Mediterranean Environmental Technical Assistance Program Partnership for an Improved Environment http://lnweb18.worldbank.org/mna/mena.nsf/0/8fc955045c197a038525694a004ebe77?OpenDocument

Middle East Intelligence Bulletin, June, 2000

Milgrom P (1989) Auctions and Bidding, A Primer, *Journal of Economic Perspectives*, 3

Mirza S and Haider M (2003) The State of Infrastructure in Canada: Implications for Infrastructure, *Planning and Policy*, Montreal, Canada

Mobbs P (2005) The Mineral Industry of Libya http://minerals.usgs.gov/minerals/pubs/country/2004/lymyb04.pdf

Muhanna Rating Services (2005)

National Intelligence Council (2004)

Nelson HD (Ed.) (1979) *Libya: A Country Study*, American University, Washington DC

NEPAD, www.nepad.org

NEPAD/OECD Investment Initiative (2005)

Neumann RE (1999) Speech for Middle East Institute, November 30 (1999) Office of International Information Programs, US Department of State

Newsweek, 20 July (1981)

New York Times, 6 April, 1974

Nigeria: Department of Petroleum Resources (DPR) (1991) Environmental Guidelines and Standards for the Petroleum Industry in Nigeria

Norges Bank Investment Management (2005) Management of the Government Petroleum Fund, Report for the second quarter of 2005 http://www.norges-bank.no/english/petroleum_fund/reports

Noorul Ainur (2001) Data provided by Finance Division, Kelang Port Authority (1999)

Noreng Ø (2004) The Predicament of the Gulf Rentier State, In Daniel Heradstveit and Helge Hveem (Eds.) Oil in the Gulf: Obstacles to Democracy and Development. Ashgate, Aldershot

Norwegian Directorate of Immigration (2004)

OAPEC Organisation of Arab Petroleum Exporting Countries http://www.oapecorg.org/

Obeidi A (1999) Changing Attitudes to the Role of Women in Libyan Society, *Journal of Economic Research*, 10: 1.2. The Economic Research Centre, Benghazi, Libya

Obeidi A (2001) Political Culture in Libya, Curzon Press, Surrey

Omran M and Bolbol A (2003) Foreign Direct Investment, Financial Development, and Economic Growth: Evidence from Arab Countries, Review of Middle East Economics and Finance, 1(3)

OPEC Annual Statistical Bulletins (2001–2005) http://www.opec.org/

Otman WA (2003) Economic and Technical Evaluation of the Libyan Petroleum Industry, MSc Dissertation, University of Aberdeen, UK

Otman WA (2004) Libyan Petroleum Law: Its Impact on Oil & Gas Development In Libya – Economic and Policy Aspects, *Oil, Gas & Energy Law Intelligence*, 2:2

Otman WA (2005) “Libyan Gas Industry” in *Hydrocarbon Reserves: Abundance or Scarcity*, Joint Seminar arranged by the Organisation of Arab Petroleum Exporting Countries, French Petroleum Institute Joint Seminar, 28 June, Paris, France

Otman WA December 2005, Private Interview with Misuratah Governor

Otman WA and Bunter M (2005) The Libyan Petroleum Industry in the Twenty First Century: The Uprtream, Midstream and Downstream Handbook, OGEL/MARIS

Otman WA and Karlberg EJ (2005) Libya: Petroleum Industry & the Economic Diversification, OGEL, 3:3

Pannier D (1996) Corporate Governance of Public Enterprises in Transitional Economies, World Bank Technical Paper no. 323

Perotti EC and Guney SE (1993) The structure of privatization plans, *Financial Management*, 22;1

Pindeiro AC and Schneider BR (1995) The fiscal impact of privatization in Latin America, *Journal of Development Studies*, 31:5

Potrykus I (2003) From “golden” to “nutritionally optimized” rice – and from a scientific concept to the farmer. Presentation delivered at the conference “In the Wake of the Double Helix: from the Green Revolution to the Gene Revolution”, Bologna, Italy, 27–31 May

Public Records Office, London, FO 371/119729, JT11170/1, “Libya”, Minute by Watson, 7 December (1956)

Qanwus S et al. (1999) Libya al-Thawraf Thalathwn Amman: Revolutionary Libya in Thirty Years: Political–Economic–Social Transformational 1969–1999, Misrata: A-Dar al-Jamahiriya lil-Nashir
Rafael G (1981) Three Decades of Israeli Foreign Policy,Stein & Day, New York
Raviv D and Melman Y (1990) Every Spy a Prince: The Complete History of Israel's Intelligence Community, Houghton Mifflin, Boston
Reagan R (1986) Libyan Sanctions, Department of State Bulletin 86:36–39, March
Red Sea Sustainable Tourism Initiative (RSSTI) (2005) http://www.rssti.org/links/Mar_2000/sustainble.html
Reynolds J (1976) Libyan studies; select papers of the late R.G. Goodchild, Paul Elek, London
Ritchie JC (1984) Analyse pollinique de se´diments holoce`nes supe´rieurs des hauts plateaux du Maghreb oriental, Pollen et Spores 26
Robiquet P (Ed.) (1897) Discours et Opinions de Jules Ferry, Paris: Armand Colin & Cie
Rodger G (1944) *Desert Journey*, The Cresset Press, London
Rodríguez-Boetsch L (2005) Public service privatisation and crisis in Argentina *Development in Practice*, 15:3–4
Rognon P (1987) Late quaternary climatic reconstruction for Desert "wastes" of the Maghreb, *Palaeogeography, Palaeoclimatology, Palaeoecology*, 58
Rogozinski J (1998) High Price for Change: Privatization in Mexico, Inter-American Development Bank
Roeskau M, Synergies between Private Investment and Foreign Aid: A Practitioner's Point of View, World Bank (2005) siteresources.worldbank.org/intamsterdam/resources/michaelroeskau.pdf
Ross ML (2001) Does Oil Hinder Democracy? World Politics, 53
Saghir J (1993) Privatization in Tunisia, CFS Discussion Paper Series, The World Bank
Salem P (2003) The Impact of Corruption on Human Development in the Arab World: A Concept Paper, The Lebanese Transparency Association, The Fares Foundation
Sauvant KP (2005) UNCTAD, Global and Regional FDI Trends
Scheffler T (2003) 'Fertile Crescent', 'Orient', 'MiddleEast': The Changing Mental Maps of Southwest Asia European Review of History – Revue Europeaenne d'Histoire, 10;2
Scottish Sunday Times, October 23 (2005)
Segrѐ Claudio G (1975) Fourth Shore: The Italian Colonization of Libya (Studies in Imperialism Series), University of Chicago Press, Chicago
Shafer DM (1995) Winners and Losers: How Sectors Shape the Development Prospects of States. Sub-Saharan Africa. Africa Economic Policy, Discussion Paper, Cornell University Press, Ithaca, NY
Shaw BD (2003) A Peculiar Island: Maghrib and Mediterranean, *Mediterranean Historical Review*, 18:2
Shehadi K (2002) Lessons in Privatisation: Considerations for Arab States Sub Regional Resource Facility UNDP, New York
Shenon P (1996) *New York Times*, 20 December
Sicker M (1987) *The Making of a Pariah State: The Adventurist Politics of Muammar Qaddafi*, Praeger, New York
Sinha T (2005) An Analysis of the Evolution of Insurance in India, CRIS Discussion Paper Series, University of Nottingham
Sirte Declaration (1999) Fourth Extraordinary Session of the Assembly of Heads of State and Government, 8–9 September Sirte, Libya EAHG/Draft/Decl. (IV) Rev.1
Social Fund for Development (SFD) (1994) Annual Report, Cairo
St. John RB (1998) *Historical Dictionary of Libya*, Scarecrow Press, Lanham, MD
St. John RB (2002) *Libya and the United States: Two Centuries of Strife*, University of Pennsylvania Press, Pennsylvania

St. John RB (2003) Libya and the United States: Elements of a Performance-Based Roadmap, *Middle East Policy*, X:3

Sturman K (2003) The Rise of Libya as a Regional Player, *African Security Review*, 12;2

Standard Oil Company, undated

Stone GD (2002) Both Sides Now: Fallacies in the Genetic Modification Wars, Implications for Developing Countries, and Anthropological Perspectives. *Current Anthropology*, 43:4

Stone O (Director) (1987) *Wall Street*, 20th Century Fox Film Co. Ltd

Sturman K and Baimu E (2003) Amendment to the African Union's Right to Intervene. A Shift from Human Security to Regime Security? African Security Review, 12:2

Sudan Tribune, 11 May (2005)

Takeyh R (2001) Qadhafi's Libya and the Prospect of Islamic Succession, *Middle East Policy*, February

Tarablus al Gharb, 29 July (1956)

Tawil MYO (1999) Libyan National Report ICCAT, *SCRS/ 99/121*

The Great Man Made River Water Utilisation Authority, Tripoli, Libya (2005) http://www.gmmra.org/infrastructure.htm

The Great Man-Made River Authority (2005) Tripoli, Libya http://www.gmmra.org

The Norwegian Petroleum Directorate (2005) http://www.npd.no

The National Centre for Policy Analysis (2005) http://www.nepa.org/

The Scotsman, 1 November (2005)

Tohamy S and Swinscoe A (2000) The Economic Impact of Tourism in Egypt, ECES Working Paper 40

Toumi K (2005) *Culture Lies at the Heart of the Mediterranean Construction in Ten Years after the Barcelona Process: Assessment and Perspectives*, EC

Transparency International, Global Corruption Report (2005) http://www.transparency.org/publications/gcr

Treisman D (2002) *Cardoso, Menem, and Machiavelli: Political Tactics and Privatization in Latin America*, Department of Political Science, University of California, Los Angeles

Tremlett G (1993) *Gadaffi: The Desert Mystic*, Carroll and Graf, New York

Tripoli Chamber of Commerce, *Ofuk Magazine*, November, 2004 (Author's Translation)

Tyler PE (2004) American and British Weapons Experts Return to Libya, *New York Times*, 20 January

Transparency International Corruption Perceptions Index (2005) http://ww1.transparency.org/cpi/2005/cpi2005_infocus.html

Tunisie, Institut National de la Statistique (2005) http://www.ins.nat.tn/

UNCED United Nations Conference on Environment and Development (1992) http://www.ciesin.org/datasets/unced/unced.html

UNCTAD (2005) Global Investment Prospects Assessment (GIPA)

UNCTAD (2005) Gross Fixed Capital Formation, by Host Region and Economy, 1970–2004 http://www.unctad.org/

UNDP Arab Human Development Reports, Years 2002, 2003, 2004

UNDP (2005) http://hdr.undp.org/reports/global/2005/

UNEP (2005) One Planet Many People: Atlas of Our Changing Environment, United Nations Conference on Environment and Development http://www.ciesin.org/datasets/unced/unced.html

United Nations Economic and Social Council (UN ECOSOC) (1993) Structural Adjustment and Reform Policies in Egypt: Economic and Social Implications. Economic and Social Commission for Western Asia E/ESCWA/SED/1993/14

United Nations Environment Programme (UNEP) (2005) One Planet Many People http://www.na.unep.net/OnePlanet

UNESCO, EFA Global Monitoring Report (2005)

UN Economic Commission for Africa (UNECA/ECA), Sustainable Development Division (2005) Review of the application of environmental impact assessment in selected African countries http://www.uneca.org/eca_programmes/sdd/documents/EIA_book_final_sm.pdf
UN Global E-Government Readiness Report (2005)
Union du Maghreb Arabe http://www.maghrebarabe.org/
United Nations Security Council, Resolution 748
United Nations Security Council, Resolution 1192, 27 August 1998
United Nations World Economic Survey (1967) New York
UN Resolution 883, November (1993) http//www.i-p-o.org/security_council_resolution_883.htm
US Bureau of the Census, September, 2005
US Coastal Zone Management Act Of 1972 http://coastalmanagement.noaa.gov/czm/czm_act.html
US Congress (2004) President George W. Bush's Address before a Joint Session of the Congress on the State of the Union, 20 January
US Department of State, Foreign Relations of the United States (1945) Washington, DC: US Government Printing Office (1967), Vol. 18, p. 273
US Environmental Protection Agency (1998) The National Environmental Policy Act (1969), http://www.epa.gov
US Presidential Documents, 1993, 1994, 1996, 1998, 2001
US Presidential Public Papers (1992)
US Senate, Committee on Foreign Relations, Staff of the Committee and the Department 1955–57, Vol. 18
US Senate, Subcommittee on US Security Agreements and Commitments Abroad, Morocco and Libya, Hearings, 20 July 1970, p. 2002
Vanclay F and Bronstein DA (Eds.) (1995) *Environmental and Social Impact Assessment*, John Wiley & Sons, Chichester UK
Vanderwalle D (1998) *Libya Since Independence, Oil and State-Building*,Cornell, Ithaca
Verne H (1869) La France en Algerie Paris: Douniol, 1869
Welch D and Fremond O (1998) The Case-by-Case Approach to Privatization: Techniques and Examples, World Bank Technical Papers, No. 403, The World Bank, Washington, DC
White House, 19 December (2003) *Weapons of Mass Destruction*
WHO (2004) Selected Indicators, Norway, http://www.who.int/countries/nor/en/
WHO (2004) Selected Indicators, Libya, http://www.who.int/countries/lby/en/
World Bank (1995) Sustainable Development Environmental Management
World Bank (2000) Project Appraisal Document on a Proposed Learning and Innovation Loan in the Amount of US$5 million Equivalent to the Republic of Algeria for Privatization Assistance Private and Financial Sector Development Department Middle East and North Africa Regional Office
World Bank (2001) Global Development Finance: Building Coalitions for Effective Development Finance
World Bank (2002) Technical Paper No. 403
World Bank (2004) Middle East and North Africa Region Strategy Paper http://lnweb18.worldbank.org/mna/mena.nsf
World Bank, Report No. 30295-LY, July 2006, Socialist People's Libyan Arab Jamahiriya, Country Economic Report http://siteresources.worldbank.org/INTLIBYA/Resources/libyacountryeconomicreport.pdf
World Bank World Development Indicators (2005) http://devdata.worldbank.org/wdi2005
World Development Report 1998/1999
World Population Data Sheet (1998)
World Telecommunication Development Report (2003)
World Tourism Organization (WTO) (2006) http://www.world-tourism.org/

Wright C (1981) Libya and the West: Headlong into Confrontation, International Affairs, Winter, 1981–82

Wright J (1969) Libya (Nations of the Modern World Series) New York, Praeger

Xu Bin (2000) Multinational Enterprises, Technology Diffusion, and Host Country Productivity Growth, *Journal of Development Economics*, 62

Yediot Ahronot, December (2003)

Yergin D (1991) *The Prize*, Simon and Schuster, New York

Zartman W, The Ups and Downs of Maghrib Unity, In Hudson, MC (Ed.) (1999) *Middle East Dilemma*, Tauris & Co. Ltd

Zohry A (2005) 'Migration Without Borders: North Africa as a Reserve of Cheap Labour for Europe'. UNESCO Discussion Paper. http://portal.unesco.org/shs/en/ev.php-URL_ID=7181&URL_DO=DO_TOPIC&URL_SECTION=201.html

Zoubir YH (2000) Algerian–Moroccan Relations and Their Impact on Maghribi Integration, *Journal of North African Studies*, 5/3

List of Tables

List of Figures

List of Appendices